Mike Meyers' Computer Skills

Introduction to PC Hardware and Troubleshooting

Michael Meyers

McGraw-Hill/Osborne

New York   Chicago   San Francisco
Lisbon   London   Madrid   Mexico City   Milan
New Delhi   San Juan   Seoul   Singapore   Sydney   Toronto

The McGraw·Hill Companies

McGraw-Hill/Osborne
2100 Powell Street, 10th Floor
Emeryville, California 94608
U.S.A.

To arrange bulk purchase discounts for sales promotions, premiums, or fund-raisers, please contact **McGraw-Hill/**Osborne at the above address. For information on translations or book distributors outside the U.S.A., please see the International Contact Information page immediately following the index of this book.

Introduction to PC Hardware and Troubleshooting

  234567890 QPD QPD 019876543

ISBN 0-07-222632-3

This book was composed with Corel VENTURA™ Publisher.

Publisher
  BRANDON A. NORDIN

Vice President & Associate Publisher
  SCOTT ROGERS

Acquisitions Editor
  CHRISTOPHER C. JOHNSON

Project Editor
  LAURA STONE

Acquisitions Coordinator
  ATHENA HONORE

Peer Reviewers
  MOH DAOUD, ERIC S. ECKLUND,
  JANE HOLCOMBE, FARBOD KARIMI,
  BILL LIU, JAMES MILLARD,
  LISA RATTO, BOHDAN STRYK

Copy Editor
  JUDY ZIAJKA

Proofreader
  KAREN MEAD

Indexer
  RICHARD SHROUT

Computer Designers
  CARIE ABREW, TABITHA M. CAGAN

Illustrators
  DAVID BIGGS, MELINDA LYTLE,
  MICHAEL MUELLER, LYSSA WALD

Series Design
  JOHN WALKER, PETER F. HANCIK

Series Cover Design
  GREG SCOTT

About the Author

Michael Meyers is the industry's leading authority on A+ and Network+ certification. He is the president and cofounder of Total Seminars, LLC, a provider of PC and network repair seminars, books, videos, and courseware for thousands of organizations throughout the world. Mike has been involved in the computer and network repair industry since 1977 as a technician, instructor, author, consultant, and speaker. Author of several popular PC books and A+ and Network+ courseware, Mike is also the series editor for both the highly successful Mike Meyers' Certification Passport series and the new Mike Meyers' Computer Skills series, both published by McGraw-Hill/Osborne. Mike holds multiple industry certifications and considers the moniker *computer nerd* a compliment.

About the Contributors

No person is an island, so I must give heartfelt thanks to my accomplished wordsmiths for their mighty contributions to this book.

Scott Jernigan wields a mighty red pen as Editor in Chief for Total Seminars. With a Master of Arts degree in Medieval History, Scott feels as much at home in the musty archives of London as he does in the warm CRT glow of Total Seminars' Houston headquarters. After fleeing a purely academic life, Scott dove headfirst into IT as an instructor, editor, and writer. Scott has edited and contributed to more than a dozen books on computer hardware, operating systems, networking, and certification. He has taught all over the United States, including stints at the United Nations in New York and the FBI Academy in Quantico. Practicing what he preaches, Scott is an A+ and Network+ certified technician.

David Biggs does double duty at Total Seminars, as a writer and a graphics guy. His work puts his BA in English Composition/Computer Science/Education from UNT to constant use. David has spent the last few years collecting hobbies, ranging from studying 500-year-old Italian fencing texts to web design to constructing historical musical instruments. Given David's wide range of interests, the phrase, "Hey! Let's get David to do that!" is not uncommon at Total Seminars.

About the Peer Reviewers

This book was greatly influenced by the dedicated group of teachers and subject-matter experts who reviewed this book and whose suggestions made it so much better. To them we give our heartfelt thanks.

Moh Daoud (A+, MCSE, CNE, CCNA/CNP) is an instructor at Las Positas Community College in Livermore, California. His passions are avionics, computers, and networks, and he speaks and he can converse in French, Spanish, German, North African Berber, and some Arabic. He owes his success to his parents who believed in education and gave him a quarter for each word he could spell correctly.

Eric S. Ecklund (BS, MBA) is an instructor in the Management and Computer Applications Department of Cambria-Rowe Business College. Eric earned a BS degree and Pennsylvania education certificate from the University of Pittsburgh and an MBA degree from Seton College.

Jane Holcombe (A+, Network+, MCSE, MCT, CTT+, CNA) is a pioneer in the field of PC support training. Since 1984, she has been an independent trainer, consultant, and course content author, creating and presenting courses on PC operating systems. She also coauthored a set of networking courses for the consulting staff of a large network vendor. In the early 1990s, she worked with both Novell and Microsoft server operating systems, finally focusing on the Microsoft operating system and achieving her MCSE certification for Windows NT 3.*x*, Windows NT 4.0, and Windows 2000. Jane coauthored *Survey of Operating Systems* (McGraw-Hill/Osborne, 2002) with Charles Holcombe.

Farbod Karimi (BA, MA, A+, Network+, CIW) is a computer consultant and an instructor specializing in computer networking and web administration at Heald College in San Francisco. Mr. Karimi is a graduate of the University of Ottawa, Canada and San Francisco State University.

Bill Liu (BA, MA, Ed.D) is the Dean of Telecommunications Management and Business Information Systems at DeVry University's Fremont, California campus. He received his Bachelor of Arts from Tamkang University in Taiwan, received a Master of Science degree from Western Kentucky University, and was awarded a Doctorate of Education from the University of Louisville.

James Millard (A+, CCAI, CCNA, MCP) is an instructor of information systems at Craven Community College in New Bern, North Carolina. Mr. Millard recently retired from the United States Marine Corps as a Chief Warrant Officer 4 after nearly 24 years of service, during which he earned numerous personal awards and served in Operations Desert Shield and Desert Storm. Mr. Millard earned a Bachelor of Science in Information Systems Management from Park University, and is pursuing a master's degree in Digital Communications at East Carolina University.

Lisa Ratto (BA, AAS) is an instructor at Heald College in Concord, California, where she has been teaching both first- and fourth-quarter students for two years. She graduated from Cal State Hayward with a Bachelor of Arts in Sociology. Ms. Ratto then attended Heald College, where she received an A.A.S in Computer Technology and an A.A.S in Networking Technology with an emphasis in Cisco Systems.

Bohdan Stryk (BA, BSEE, MBA) is a Senior Professor of Computer Information Systems at DeVry University. He has a BA in Physics and Math from Hunter College of the City University of New York, a BSEE in Computers and Circuits from the University of New Mexico, and an MBA in Finance & Investments and Computers from Baruch College of the City University of New York. He also has a consulting company that specializes in client-side (Swing) and server-side (JSP) Java applications. In addition, his consulting company is an Intel Product Dealer (IPD) that builds PCs, servers, and networks from components.

■ Acknowledgments

Of course, first billing has got to go to my Acquisitions Editor, Chris Johnson. His vision and leadership were the keys to making this book and this series take place. Simply listing all that he achieved would completely pack the entire book, so let me just say, "Thanks Chris!" even though that is in no way enough.

Scott Jernigan has been my right hand for over five years now. Although his official title is Editor in Chief, his real title should be more like, *The Guy We Turn To When the Heat Is On!* I don't think there's a book I've written that hasn't been improved tremendously by Scott's guiding hand at every level, from writing, editing, creating graphics, or dueling in Half Life.

David Biggs has used his many years in the computing business to good use with my company. Not only is he by far the best graphic artist in the company, he's also proved himself to be a crackerjack writer and a real asset when things get crazy. Trust me, you'll be seeing a lot more of this guy in the future!

Oh my gosh! Where do I go next? So many people have helped in so many ways! Let's start with the folks at Total Seminars—my in-house staff.

First thanks go to Cary Dier, *editor extraordinaire*. It was Cary who acted as the first line of editing (the toughest job of all), as well as wielding the conductor's baton to make sure everything happened with some semblance of order and timing, and pinch-hitting for just about everyone involved in the process. Thanks for going above and beyond to get the job done.

Cindy Archer came in at the tough times and helped keep things moving when we got overwhelmed, while at the same time holding down her own workload of projects.

Our intern and token Gen Y team member, Jeremy Conn, handled all those tedious yet critical jobs (like repeatedly renumbering all the graphics because I can never make up my mind!) with efficiency and good humor.

Roger Conrad, a senior instructor at Total Seminars, lent a practiced hand at shooting and editing pictures, and building and testing machines.

On the Osborne side there are a bunch of folks who've performed with equal heroism.

Athena Honore, the Acquisitions Coordinator, has worked with me on a number of projects, and she once again did a great job. Thanks Athena!

Laura Stone's real title is Project Editor, but I call her *The E-mailer*. Laura kept a steady stream of corrections and updates flowing into our otherwise empty inboxes. Just as Cary held the bat…er, baton over us at Total Seminars, Laura held the big baton over the whole show. Just out of curiosity, Laura—is there anything you *can't* do?

Jill Batistick's developmental editing still haunts me. A developmental editor's job is to rip, tear, squish, and stretch a textbook to make it do what it is supposed to do: teach. I think of Jill as this book's personal trainer—she ran the book through many a long, hard workout, but it sure is a lot nicer to look at as a result of her labors.

Judy Ziajka is one lean, mean, editing machine. Her eagle eye caught stuff that normal folks would never see. But I guess that's what makes her such a great Copy Editor. Thanks, Judy!

Roger Conrad, David Welling, Jeremy Conn, and Lyssa Wald produced some gorgeous graphics. Thanks, guys!

■ *I dedicate this book to all the Texas drummers, burners, spinners, and to all my fellow nubbins. We are winning!*

About This Book

■ Important Technology Skills

Information technology (IT) offers many career paths, leading to occupations in such fields as PC repair, network administration, telecommunications, Web development, graphic design, and desktop support. To become competent in any IT field, however, you need certain basic computer skills. The Mike Meyers' Computer Skills series builds a foundation for success in the IT field by introducing you to fundamental technology concepts and giving you essential computer skills.

Step-by-Step *exercises put concepts into practice.*

Notes, Tips, and Warnings *create a road map for success.*

Cross-Check *questions develop reasoning skills: ask, compare, contrast, and explain.*

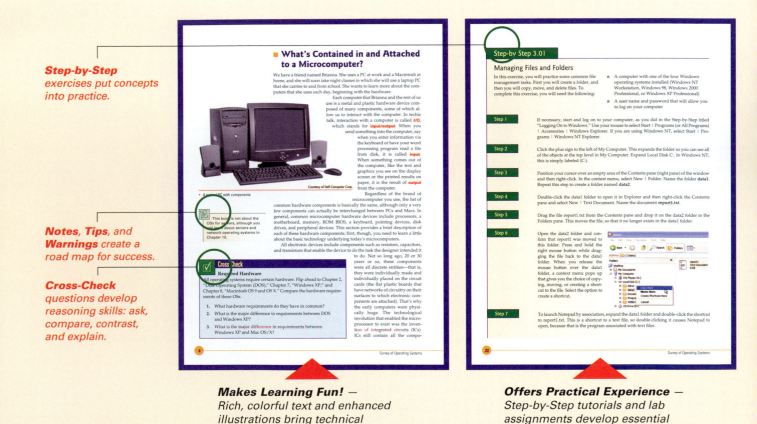

Makes Learning Fun! — *Rich, colorful text and enhanced illustrations bring technical subjects to life.*

Offers Practical Experience — *Step-by-Step tutorials and lab assignments develop essential hands-on skills and put concepts in real-world contexts.*

Proven Learning Method Keeps You on Track

The Mike Meyers' Computer Skills series is structured to give you a practical working knowledge of baseline IT skills and technologies. The series' active learning methodology guides you beyond mere recall and, through thought-provoking activities, labs, and sidebars, helps you develop critical thinking, diagnostic, and communication skills.

■ Effective Learning Tools

This colorful, pedagogically rich book is designed to make learning easy and enjoyable and to help you develop the skills and critical thinking abilities that will enable you to adapt to different job situations and troubleshoot problems.

Mike Meyers' proven ability to explain concepts in a clear, direct, even humorous way makes these books interesting, motivational, and fun.

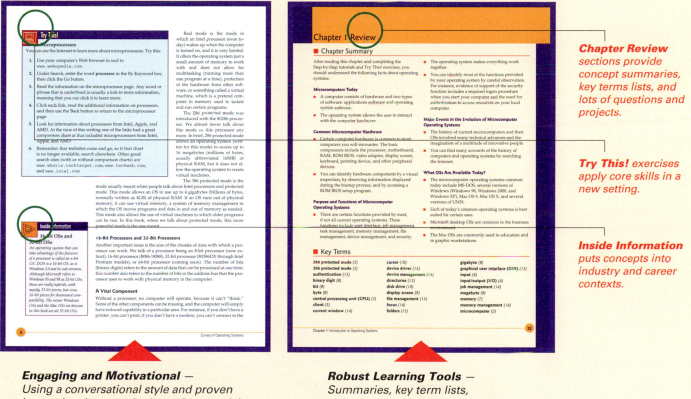

Chapter Review *sections provide concept summaries, key terms lists, and lots of questions and projects.*

Try This! *exercises apply core skills in a new setting.*

Inside Information *puts concepts into industry and career contexts.*

Engaging and Motivational —
Using a conversational style and proven instructional approach, the authors explain technical concepts in a clear, interesting way using real-world examples.

Robust Learning Tools —
Summaries, key term lists, quizzes, essay questions, and lab projects help you practice skills and measure progress.

Each chapter includes:

- **Learning Objectives** that set measurable goals for chapter-by-chapter progress

- **Four-Color Illustrations** that give you a clear picture of the technologies

- **Step-by-Step Tutorials** that teach you to perform essential tasks and procedures hands-on

- **Try This!**, **Cross-Check**, and **Inside Information** sidebars that encourage you to practice and apply concepts in real-world settings

- **Notes**, **Tips**, and **Warnings** that guide you through difficult areas

- **Chapter Summaries** and **Key Terms Lists** that provide you with an easy way to review important concepts and vocabulary

- **Challenging End-of-Chapter Tests** that include vocabulary-building exercises, multiple-choice questions, essay questions, and on-the-job lab projects

CONTENTS

Preface xii
Introduction xiii

Chapter 1
◼ Your PC Revealed 1

Big Iron, Cryptic Code, and IBM 1
    It Takes Two to Tango: Hardware
      and Software 1
    A Short History of Computers 1
    Mainframes 2
    Minicomputers 3
    Microcomputers 4
    Enter the Personal Computer 5
Safeguarding Your PC 5
    Don't Let PCs Scare You 6
    Respecting Power 7
    Electrostatic Discharge (ESD) 7
Identifying the Major Components of a PC 10
    System Unit 12
    Monitor 13
    Keyboard 14
    Mouse Devices 14
    Handling PC Connections 16
Identifying the Internal Components of a PC . . . 17
    Opening a System Unit 20
    Handling Expansion Cards 21
Chapter 1 Review 23

Chapter 2
◼ CPUs 28

The Function of the CPU 29
    What Is a CPU? 29
    Where Are the Programs? 29
    Putting It All Together 30
Identifying the Right CPU for
  Any Motherboard 31
    CPU Manufacturers 31
    Processor Models 32
    CPU Speeds 32
    Processor Packages 33
    Five Ways to Identify a CPU 35
    Identifying the Type of CPU in Your PC 37
    Motherboards 38
Installing and Upgrading CPUs 41
    Installing a CPU 42

Select and Install the Proper Heat Sink
  and Fan Assembly 47
    Heat Sinks 47
    Fans 48
    Installing a Fan and Heat Sink Assembly 49
Chapter 2 Review 52

Chapter 3
◼ RAM 56

What Does RAM Do? 57
    RAM Sticks 58
    Accessing RAM 58
    A Bit o' Binary 58
Types of RAM Technologies 59
    FPM RAM 60
    EDO RAM 61
    SDRAM 62
    DDR SDRAM 63
    RDRAM 63
RAM Packages 63
    SIMMs 64
    DIMMs 67
    SO DIMM 68
    RIMMs 69
Adding and Upgrading RAM 71
    Why Add RAM? 71
    Checking Your System Resources 72
    Upgrading RAM 74
    Removing and Installing SIMMs 76
    Removing and Installing DIMMs and RIMMs . . 77
Chapter 3 Review 80

Chapter 4
◼ Motherboards and BIOS 84

Common Motherboard Features 85
    Your Personal Tour of the Motherboard 86
Types of Motherboards 94
    AT Motherboards 94
    Baby AT 94
    ATX Motherboards 95
    microATX 96
    FlexATX 96
    Proprietary Motherboards 97
    Removing a Motherboard from a PC Case . . . 97
Installing a Motherboard 100
    Installing a New Motherboard 100

The System BIOS 102
   Why Do We Need BIOS in the First Place? . . . 102
   Every Device Needs BIOS 104
   Changeable System Devices 104
   Flashing the BIOS 105
Chapter 4 Review 106

Chapter 5
■ Expansion Bus 110

Expansion Buses 111
   Why Expansion Buses Exist 111
   The Next Step Involves a Clock 112
   Device Drivers 114
   System Resources 114
   Checking Device Drivers 118
Internal Buses 121
   8-Bit ISA 121
   16-Bit ISA 121
   MCA 122
   EISA 123
   VESA Local Bus 124
   PCI 125
   AGP 126
   AMR/CNR 128
   Mini PCI 128
   Checking the Expansion Bus 129
Installing a Plug and Play Expansion Card 130
   Picking the Right Card 130
   Picking the Right Bus 130
   Getting the Correct Drivers 130
   Removing the Old Drivers 131
   Installing a Plug and Play Card 132
   Installing a Driver for a New Expansion Card . . 134
   Installation Problems 137
External Expansion Buses: USB and FireWire . . . 138
   USB 138
   FireWire 141
   FireWire or USB? 141
   PC Card 141
Chapter 5 Review 143

Chapter 6
■ Power Supplies and Cases 148

Case Form and Function 149
   External Size 149
   Drive Bays 151
   Back Plates 153
   Screws and Stand-offs 154
   Case Form Factors 154
   Connections 155
Power Supply 155
   Wattage 157
   Connectors 158
   Power Switches 160
   Power Supply Fans 162

   Removing a Power Supply 163
   Installing a New Power Supply 166
Cooling 167
   Power Supply Fan 167
   Heat Sinks and Fans 168
   Case Fans 168
   Installing a Case Fan 169
   Airflow 170
Chapter 6 Review 172

Chapter 7
■ Removable Media 176

Identifying, Installing, and Troubleshooting
  Floppy Drives 177
   How Floppy Drives Work 177
   The History of Floppy Disks 178
   Floppy Drive Cables 179
   Installing a Floppy Drive 180
   Care and Feeding of Your Floppies 181
   Bootable Floppy Disks 183
   Formatting Nonbootable Floppy Disks 184
Identifying and Installing Zip Drives
  and SuperDisk Drives 186
   Booting to a Floppy, Zip, or SuperDrive Disk . . 188
Modern Tape Drive Technologies 189
   Tape Drive Options 189
Tape Backup Strategies 191
   Backup Programs 192
   Working with Attributes 194
Chapter 7 Review 196

Chapter 8
■ Hard Drives 200

How Hard Drives Store Data 201
   Geometry 201
   Partitions and File Systems 203
   Identifying Your File System 206
Installing a Hard Drive 208
   EIDE Versus SCSI 208
   Hard Drive Terminology 209
   EIDE Cables 210
   Master/Slave 210
   ATA Speed Ratings 211
   BIOS Limitations 212
   Physically Installing a Hard Drive 214
   Adding a Second Drive 215
Configuring a Hard Drive 216
   Partitioning 216
   Formatting 220
   Third-Party Tools 223
   Working with Partitions Using the
     Disk Management Utility 225
Hard Drive Maintenance and Troubleshooting . . 227
   Hard Drive Maintenance 227
   ScanDisk 227

Defragmentation 229
Disk Cleanup 231
Troubleshooting 233
Chapter 8 Review 236

Chapter 9
■ CD Media 240

Understanding CD Media Technologies 241
CD Data Storage 241
CD-ROM 241
Speeds and What They Mean 243
Lots of Standards 244
CD-R and CD-RW 244
DVD 247
Installing CD Media Drives 248
Physical Installation 249
Driver Installation 250
Application Installation 252
Installing a CD-ROM Drive 252
Using CD Media 255
Audio Files Versus Audio Tracks 255
Autoplay 255
Burning CDs 257
CD Media Troubleshooting 259
Drive Problems 259
Disc Problems 260
Breaking Your CD-ROM Drive 262
Chapter 9 Review 263

Chapter 10
■ SCSI 268

Major SCSI Components 269
SCSI Chains and Host Adapters 269
Working with SCSI Chains 274
The Different Flavors of SCSI 275
SCSI-1 275
SCSI-2 276
SCSI-3 278
Mixing Flavors 279
Installing SCSI Devices 279
Buying a Host Adapter 279
SCSI Cables 281
Termination and SCSI IDs 281
Installation and Host Adapter Settings . . . 282
Drivers 285
EIDE and SCSI 286
Installing SCSI Devices 286
Basic SCSI Troubleshooting 287
Chapter 10 Review 288

Chapter 11
■ Video 292

Selecting the Right Monitor 293

CRTs 293
Installing and Configuring a CRT 296
LCDs 297
Selecting the Right Video Card 299
Inside the Display Adapter 299
Expansion Bus Interfaces 302
Video Card Ports 303
Multiple Video Cards for Multiple Monitors . . 304
Installing and Configuring Video Software . . . 304
Drivers 304
Using the Display Applet 305
Working with Drivers 306
Updating Video Drivers the Right Way 308
DirectX 310
Testing DirectX on Your System 311
Maintenance and Troubleshooting 312
Caring for Your Monitor 312
Troubleshooting Monitor Problems 312
Troubleshooting LCD Monitors 313
Video Card Problems 314
Troubleshooting Configuration Errors 314
Chapter 11 Review 316

Chapter 12
■ Input Devices 320

Installing a Keyboard 321
Keyboard Ergonomics 321
Making Connections 322
Installing a Keyboard 324
Installing and Configuring a Mouse 325
Ah, the Choices! 325
Mouse Connections 328
Installing a Mouse 328
Identifying Less Common Input Devices 329
Game Ports 330
Microphones 332
Still and Video Cameras 332
Tablets 332
Touch Screens 333
Installing and Configuring a Game Controller . . 333
Maintaining and Troubleshooting Input Devices . . 335
Cleaning 335
Dirty or Broken Devices 336
Driver Issues 336
Chapter 12 Review 337

Chapter 13
■ Sound 340

How Sound Works in a PC 341
Sound-Capture Basics 341
Recorded Sound Formats 342
Playing Sounds 342
MIDI 343
Other File Formats 343
Video 344

Applications 344
Streaming Media 344
Purchasing the Right Sound Card 345
Processor Capabilities 345
Speaker Support 345
Recording Quality 346
Jacks 347
Extra Features 348
Speakers 348
Installing a Sound Card in a Windows System . . . 351
Physical Installation 351
Physically Installing a Sound Card 352
Installing Drivers 354
Installing Sound Programs 355
Installing Applications 357
Troubleshooting Sound 357
Hardware Problems 357
Configuration Problems 358
Application Problems 359
Chapter 13 Review 360

Chapter 14
Printers 364
Identifying Current Printer Technologies 365
Dot Matrix Printers 365
Inkjet Printers 365
Laser Printers 367
Buying a Printer 367
The Real PPM! 369
Installing a Printer on a Windows PC 370
Port Options 370
Unpacking and Assembly 371
Drivers 371
Configuration 376
Installing a Printer 378
Performing Basic Printer Maintenance 379
Consumables 379
Laser Printer Maintenance 380
Inkjet Printer Maintenance 381
Maintaining an Inkjet Printer 382
Recognizing and Fixing Basic
   Printing Problems 383
Tools 383
No-Print Problems 383
Paper Problems 384
Bad-Print Problems 384
Exploring Printer Errors 385
Chapter 14 Review 386

Chapter 15
Networks 390
How Networks Work 391
Dial-Up Networks 391
Local Area Networks 392
Installing and Configuring a Dial-Up Network . . 394
Modem Technology 394
Installing a PCI Modem 396
Setting Up Software 398
Installing and Configuring a Local
   Area Network 400
Topology 401
Ensuring Compatibility: Ethernet 402
Fiber-Optic Networks 404
Wireless Networks 404
LAN Hardware Connections 405
Installing and Cabling a Hub 407
Ensuring Communication:
      Software Protocols 407
Making the Connection with TCP/IP 408
Sharing Resources and Accessing
      Shared Resources 409
Troubleshooting Basic Network Problems 412
Dial-Up Networking Problems 412
LAN Problems 412
Chapter 15 Review 415

Appendix
About A+ Certification 420
What's Certification? 420
A+ Certification 420
Preparing for the A+ Certification Exam 421
1.0 Installation, Configuration,
      and Upgrading 421
2.0 Diagnosis and Troubleshooting 421
3.0 Preventive Maintenance 422
4.0 Motherboards, Processors, and Memory . . 422
5.0 Printers 422
6.0 Basic Networking 422

Glossary 423

Index 433

PREFACE

This book, like the other books in this series, is designed for exactly one function: to give you a broad introduction and overview of various aspects of the information technologies (IT) world. If you're new to computers, then welcome! This book is for you. If you're trying to decide where you want to go within the big world of IT, then again welcome—this book will help you sort out the many options and figure out where your interests may or may not lie. Do you want to become a Microsoft Windows expert? Do you want to get into troubleshooting and repair of PCs? What about becoming a network administrator? These books will help you understand the many aspects of IT and the many jobs within the IT world that are available.

So how will this book help you understand what IT is all about? Well, let's start by exploring the text in front of you right now. Like all of the books in this series, it is written in a very relaxed, conversational style that's a pleasure to read. We've tossed the staid, boring technical writing style out the window and instead write as though we're speaking directly to you—because as far as we're concerned, we are. In this and the other books in this series, we aren't afraid of the occasional contraction, nor do we worry about staying in third person. We've pretty much dumped all those other dry, pedantic rules that most technical writing embraces. I've suffered reading those books, and I swore when it came time to put together this series that we were going to break that mold—and we have! With over a million copies now in print using this series' conversational style, we think a lot of folks agree with what we're doing.

Keep your finger on this page and leaf through this book for a moment. Isn't it beautiful? Sure, there are plenty of exercises and questions for you to use to practice your skills, but let the left side of your brain take a nap and let the right side appreciate just how attractive a book this is. The four-color printing and all of the colorful elements give the book what I describe very scientifically as a *happy feeling*—akin to walking the aisle at a grocery store.

Last—and this is very important—you'll never find yourself lost in any of these books. You'll never get blindsided by a term that hasn't been defined earlier. You won't find yourself reading one topic and suddenly finding yourself grinding gears as new, totally unrelated topics smack you in the face. Every topic leads from simple to complex, from broad to detailed, and from old to new, building concept upon concept while you read, making the book hard to put down. This is what I call *flow*, and it's the most important aspect of these books.

So enjoy your reading. If you have any questions, feel free to contact me at michaelm@totalsem.com.

Mike Meyers
Series Editor

INTRODUCTION

■ What Will You Learn?

In this book, you'll learn about the hardware that makes up a personal computer. You'll learn the basics of how the CPU, RAM, motherboard, expansion buses, power supply, and system case create a platform for useful activity. You'll learn how the many different storage technologies work and how best to use them. You'll learn about computer input and output, including basics like mice, keyboards, CRT monitors, and printers, as well as modern technologies such as SCSI, flat panels, and game controllers. You'll learn at least some basics about how to fix all of this technology when things break. Finally, you'll look beyond your individual box to the wider world of computer networking. This book is organized into fifteen chapters:

- Chapter 1, *Your PC Revealed*, sets the stage for your exploration of the personal computer. The goal of this chapter is to get you to the point that you can recognize equipment, name it properly, and discuss the basics of what these components do.

- Chapter 2, *CPUs*, introduces you to the CPU in detail. This chapter teaches you the basics of how CPUs function, which different makes and models are available, and how to upgrade and install both the CPU itself and its key partners in processing glory, the heat sink and cooling fan. Understanding, selecting, installing, and upgrading CPUs are essential skills for all PC technicians.

- Chapter 3, *RAM*, focuses on this critical system component. This chapter teaches you how RAM functions in a PC; how to identify different RAM technologies and RAM packages, past and present; and how to install RAM in a PC.

- Chapter 4, *Motherboards and BIOS*, introduces the component that binds the whole system together. It explains how motherboards work to unite all of the different system components into one harmonious system. It covers the different types of motherboards, the various parts of a motherboard, the procedure for installing a motherboard, and a critical tool called the System Setup utility that you use to configure special programming code called the BIOS, which is used by devices that connect to the motherboard.

- Chapter 5, *Expansion Bus*, explains why expansion buses exist and the basics of how they work. Topics include the different types of expansion slots used on motherboards, procedures for installing an expansion card in an expansion slot, the chipsets that support expansion buses, and two popular modern external expansion buses: USB and FireWire.

- Chapter 6, *Power Supplies and Cases*, covers these two critical parts of the PC. CPUs, memory, motherboards—all of these live in the computer case. When you get a case, you almost always get a power supply, too, which you need to know how to replace if it fails. This chapter teaches you what you need to know to make informed choices about computer cases and power supplies, and how to remove a bad power supply and install a replacement. Among the topics covered are the different parts of a case and the purpose of each, which motherboards are compatible with which computer cases, and the different types of power connectors.

- Chapter 7, *Removable Media*, teaches you about the many types of removable media available for the PC, beginning with the oldest and most common type, the floppy disk and its associated drive. The chapter also covers the popular Iomega Zip drive and the LS-120 SuperDisk. Finally, it discusses different tape backup devices and strategies to help protect your valuable data.

- Chapter 8, *Hard Drives*, is all about this incredibly complex and totally critical component of your PC. This chapter lets you look inside a hard drive to see how it works. You learn how to install a hard drive in a typical system, how to keep your hard drive running at top efficiency, and how to fix some of the more common hard drive problems you're likely to encounter.

- Chapter 9, *CD Media*, teaches you about the CD-ROM and all of the other offshoot CD media technologies. Originally designed more than 20 years ago as a replacement for vinyl records, the CD reigns today in the computer world as the primary method of long-term storage for sound, video, and data. This chapter teaches you how to install a CD-ROM drive, how to use and maintain CD media drives and discs, and how to perform basic troubleshooting procedures on them.

- Chapter 10, *SCSI*, explains this widely used standard for connecting devices to PCs, especially storage devices such as hard drives and CD-ROM drives. This chapter discusses how SCSI works, compares and contrasts the various types of SCSI standards, and takes you through the process of installing and troubleshooting SCSI devices.

- Chapter 11, *Video*, leads you through the selection and setup of the three layers of a computer's video system: the monitor, the display adapter, and the software, including the operating system and applications. It teaches you how each individual component works and all about installation and configuration. Finally, it helps you master the art of troubleshooting the video system of a personal computer.

- Chapter 12, *Input Devices*, teaches you about both the most common and less common input devices, including a bit about their history, the more popular options available, and what the differences between the options mean to you, the user and future tech. This chapter covers the various connectivity options and why one option might be better than another. It walks you through the configuration of some standard devices, shows you how to modify settings for a custom fit, and teaches you some maintenance Dos and Don'ts.

- Chapter 13, *Sound*, focuses on an integral component of the modern computing experience. Setting up and optimizing sound for the personal computer has become an integral skill for all computer techs. This chapter teaches you how sound works in a PC, how to select the right sound card and install it in your Windows PC, and how to perform some basic sound card troubleshooting procedures.

- Chapter 14, *Printers*, guides you through the key challenges that today's printers present for the conscientious computer user. It teaches you about the current printer technologies, including inkjet and laser printers, so you can pick the right printer for your needs. It shows you how to install a printer, perform the always critical printer maintenance chores, and deal with the most common printer problems you're likely to encounter.

- Chapter 15, *Networks*, finishes your introduction to computer hardware by reaching beyond the solitary box. Much of what makes modern computers so powerful is their ability to connect to other computers to share files and resources. This chapter explains what comprises a network and what makes networks tick. It teaches you about some of the most common hardware used to create small networks and how the various hardware components interact. You also learn how to install a modem and network card, set up a basic network, and troubleshoot basic network problems. Every PC tech worth knowing knows the basics of networking.

■ You Will Learn to...

We don't want to simply give you an encyclopedia of information because we don't want you to feel like you're standing in front of an information fire hose! Rather, we're going to present just the key points about PC hardware and guide you in your own exploration of the specifics of the technology. This book is designed to teach you skills that you need to be successful on the job.

Walk and Talk Like a Pro

Each chapter starts with a list of learning objectives followed by lucid explanations of each topic, supported by real-world, on-the-job scenarios and a liberal use of graphics and tables. To give you hands-on experience and to help you *walk the walk*, each chapter contains detailed Step-by-Step tutorials and short Try This! exercises that enable you to practice the concepts. To help you *talk the talk*, each chapter contains definitions of computer terms, summarized in a Key Terms list and compiled into a Glossary at the end of the book. Be ready for a Key Term Quiz at the end of each chapter!

Troubleshoot Like a Pro

Although there is a ton of good information in this book, one book simply can't give you everything you need to know about PC hardware and troubleshooting. So in addition to providing a solid introduction to hardware, we also give you the tools that will help you help yourself, which is a valuable asset when you're on the job. For example, we show you how to use important software tools such as ScanDisk, Defrag, and Device Manager to find and fix hard drive problems, and we teach you the right way to maintain key pieces of hardware such as printers, mice, and disk drives so you can stop problems before they occur.

Think Like a Pro

We've also included Inside Information sidebars, which provide insight into the real-world experiences of a computer tech, and Cross-Checks that help you solidify your understanding of key concepts and technologies. Notes and Tips are sprinkled throughout the chapters, and Warnings help prevent mishaps (or an emotional meltdown). At the end of each chapter, a Key Term Quiz, Multiple-Choice Quiz, and Essay Quiz help you measure what you've learned and hone your ability to present information on paper. The Lab Projects challenge you to independently complete tasks related to what you've just learned.

■ Resources for Teachers

Teachers are our heroes to whom we give our thanks and for whom we have created a powerful collection of time-saving teaching tools that are available on CD-ROM, including:

- An Instructor's Manual that maps to the organization of the textbook
- ExamView® Pro testbank software that generates a wide array of paper or network-based tests and features automatic grading
- Hundreds of questions, written by experienced IT instructors
- A wide variety of question types and difficulty levels, allowing teachers to customize each test to maximize student progress
- Engaging PowerPoint® slides on the lecture topics

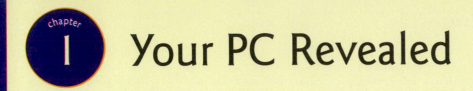

Your PC Revealed

"I think that a machine could be designed to do this."

—ALAN TURING WHILE LOOKING AT A LOGARITHM TABLE IN THE 1930S

In this chapter, you will learn how to:

- **Explain the historical development of the PC, and the relationship between hardware and software**
- **Describe and execute the proper procedures for handling PC components**
- **Identify and describe the functions of the major PC components**
- **Identify and describe the functions of the internal components of a PC**

When people describe the personal computer, one of the first words they usually utter is *beige*. Evocative? Enticing? Hardly, but underneath the drab exterior of the personal computer hides a heart of gleaming silver, gold, and red-lacquered electronics. Welcome to the playground of the PC technician!

Chapter 1 sets the stage for your exploration of the personal computer. To help you understand how the PC became the dominant technology it is today, I'll start with a short history and a brief explanation of how the two defining pieces of a computer—software and hardware—work together. You'll then tour the major parts of the PC, to learn how they interconnect. You'll also learn how to handle a PC and observe some of the extra equipment that comes with most PCs. At that point, you'll grab that screwdriver and open up your PC to learn about the many internal components.

This chapter does not go into much detail on individual parts—that's the job of later chapters. The goal of this chapter is to get you to the point where you can recognize equipment, name it properly, and discuss the basics of what these components do. Look at this chapter as a mechanic walking you around a car with the hood up, showing you the different parts of the car and explaining to you what they do, helping you recognize them, and giving you their proper names.

■ Big Iron, Cryptic Code, and IBM

Before we dive headlong into the history of the PC, I want to make certain you understand a key concept in computers, namely the relationship between hardware and software. After all, as the saying goes, it takes two to tango, and the computer provides a perfect example.

It Takes Two to Tango: Hardware and Software

Everything in your computer fits into one of two categories: hardware or software. Anything on your computer that you can touch is hardware. So everything that we will cover in this chapter—monitors, system units, CPUs, hard drives, motherboards, and so on—is hardware. However, hardware alone cannot handle all of the PC's complex activities—it needs the help of software. Software is the technical word for computer programs, the sets of instructions that tell the hardware how to do things. Computer programs are often compared to cooking recipes. The recipe tells you how to use the tools to manipulate the ingredients, and if all goes well, you produce something edible. In the same way, software instructs the hardware as it manipulates data to produce the desired result, whether that's a memo, a digital picture, or an e-mail message. Figure 1.1 shows a sample of program code.

A Short History of Computers

The PC is so common in modern society that it seems hard to imagine a world without them, but in fact, the PC is a relative newcomer. Just a few decades back, the small, sleek, incredibly powerful devices we take for granted were consigned to the realm of science fiction. Not only did PCs not exist, but it wasn't clear to most people why anybody would ever *want* to own a computer. But as it has always been with humans and technology, so it is with computers: new inventions created to solve old problems give rise to new problems, which give rise to more new inventions to solve the new problems, which cause more new problems, and so on. Each new advance in computing technology spurs the next one. What follows is a short history of that progression, to help you understand how computers advanced

```
//==============================================================================
//method processnumbers is where processes the numbers inputed by the user
//==============================================================================
public void processnumbers() {

    // the program enters this "if" block when an operator is pressed for the
    // first time
    if ( firstpress ) {

        if ( equals ) {
            num1 = answer;   //answer is stored in num1 if user enters equal operator
            equals = false;  // equals is set to false to allow additional input
        } // end if
        else
            num1 = double.valueof( input ).doublevalue();  // converts a string number to double

            oldoper = oper;          // store current operator to oldoper

        // if operator is square root, calculation and output is done immediately
        if ( oper == sqrt ) {
            answer = calculate( oldoper, num1, 0.0 );
            showanswer( double.tostring( answer ));
            morenums = true;
        }
        firstpress = false;      // no longer the first operator
    } // end if
```

• **Figure 1.1**   Sample of program code

from a specialized niche technology at the end of World War II to become a dominant presence in twenty-first century society.

Mainframes

The 1940s ushered in the Age of Modern Computers, with the mammoth **mainframe** computers. The first mainframes were number-crunching machines that took up whole buildings and cost huge sums of money. These complex, cutting-edge technological marvels needed a veritable army of highly skilled people to operate them, but the speed with which they could calculate made them incredibly useful for math-intensive jobs like analyzing scientific data (the first big mainframes were developed for atomic energy research) and calculating ranges for artillery fire.

Their prohibitive cost made mainframes by necessity *centralized* systems—you went to the computer; the computer didn't come to you. If you wanted to do some computing, in other words, you had to bike or walk or drive to its climate-controlled home, almost always called the *computing center,* where you would spend lots of time preparing the machine and processing your data. Later-generation mainframes featured the convenience of remote terminals, so you could at least sit in a different room with a cup of coffee while you worked. The last generations even supported multiple simultaneous users (trust me, it was a *big* deal), but all of the processing work was still done in one central location.

The earliest mainframes had to be controlled using cumbersome binary *machine language;* later models used somewhat abbreviated but still cryptic sets of instructions called *assembly language,* which still involved writing painstakingly detailed step-by-step directions for the computer to follow. By the early 1960s, more human-friendly languages like FORTRAN and COBOL were in common use. These so-called *high-level* languages employed English words and standard math formulas in place of cryptic codes, speeding the development of computer programs for a variety of business tasks. Today, only specialized systems programmers work directly with assembly language. Most programmers work with modern high-level languages like Visual Basic, Java, and C++.

Even though this section talks about mainframes in the past tense, be aware that there are many mainframes still running all over the world.

The Ferranti Orion

• Mainframe computers were so large that they filled up entire rooms.

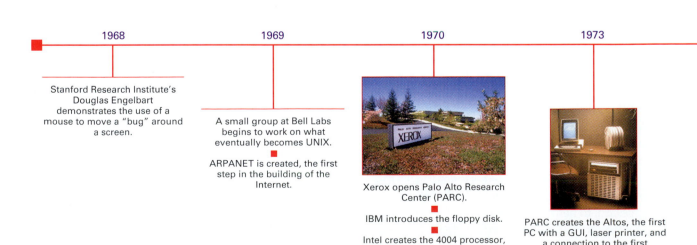

1968
Stanford Research Institute's Douglas Engelbart demonstrates the use of a mouse to move a "bug" around a screen.

1969
A small group at Bell Labs begins to work on what eventually becomes UNIX.

ARPANET is created, the first step in the building of the Internet.

1970
Xerox opens Palo Alto Research Center (PARC).

IBM introduces the floppy disk.

Intel creates the 4004 processor, leading the way to the birth of the PC.

1973
PARC creates the Altos, the first PC with a GUI, laser printer, and a connection to the first Ethernet network.

The high cost and complexity of operating a mainframe computer limited the types of work it could reasonably be used to accomplish. Mainframe computers were a big, expensive solution intended to solve big, expensive problems. To borrow an analogy, it didn't make sense to use an elephant gun to shoot a flea. By the mid-1960s, mainframes were being used routinely by large businesses for calculation-heavy tasks like payroll and accounting. Then in the late 1960s, people began to use a new class of computers for smaller, more personal tasks like writing memos. This new class of computers, called the minicomputer, was smaller, cheaper, and simpler to use than mainframes, offering a new solution that could be applied to a new range of problems.

Minicomputers

Minicomputers enabled multiple simultaneous users to access an expanded range of applications, and did so at a substantially reduced size, complexity, and price compared to mainframe computers. Although still not small—they were much closer in size to a Mini car than to a minicam—closet-sized minicomputers were nevertheless a marked improvement over the building- or room-sized mainframes they replaced.

• DEC VAX minicomputer

The minicomputer's more modest price meant that instead of a single monster mainframe housed in a central computing center, buyers could invest in several minicomputers and locate them in smaller, geographically dispersed computing centers. A university campus that used to have a single mainframe might now have five or six minicomputers distributed across the campus, each capable of handling hundreds of simultaneous users.

The single most important result of the substantially lower price of minicomputers compared to mainframes, was that it spurred buyers to expand beyond heavy-duty number crunching. The development of the minicomputer made possible the first broad development of software for use by individuals, such as text processing programs, spreadsheet utilities, and relatively user-friendly database tools.

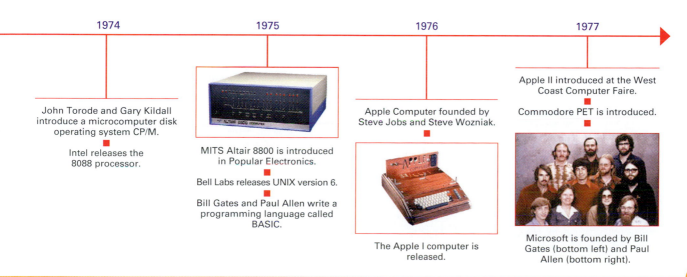

1974 — John Torode and Gary Kildall introduce a microcomputer disk operating system CP/M.

Intel releases the 8088 processor.

1975 — MITS Altair 8800 is introduced in Popular Electronics.

Bell Labs releases UNIX version 6.

Bill Gates and Paul Allen write a programming language called BASIC.

1976 — Apple Computer founded by Steve Jobs and Steve Wozniak.

The Apple I computer is released.

1977 — Apple II introduced at the West Coast Computer Faire.

Commodore PET is introduced.

Microsoft is founded by Bill Gates (bottom left) and Paul Allen (bottom right).

Microcomputers

In the mid-1970s, a number of manufacturers began to realize the dream of fitting the parts that make up an entire computer into a single box that could fit on a desktop. Thus was born the microcomputer. Microcomputers were designed for use by one person at a time, but could run many different types of applications, just like minicomputers. And they were cheaper yet, by far. Famous microcomputers developed the in the late 1970s and early 1980s included the Tandy TRS-80, the Commodore 64, and the first commercially successful portable personal computer, the Osborne 1.

Fitting a computer in a box wasn't actually the most noteworthy aspect of the microcomputers. The truly revolutionary development related to microcomputers concerned their software, not their hardware. First, programmers developed operating systems that could run on multiple brands of microcomputers. This led naturally and rapidly to the development of specific applications that could run on more than one brand of computer. Before this, software was unique to each particular brand of computer. This move from individualized to standardized software was an important factor in the incredibly rapid expansion of the role of computers.

While the world was for the first time enjoying the ability to share applications across different brands of computers, the hardware was still not interchangeable. Microcomputer makers developed their own proprietary hardware and didn't allow third parties to use their designs. This changed with the introduction of the IBM PC.

• An early microcomputer: the Commodore 64

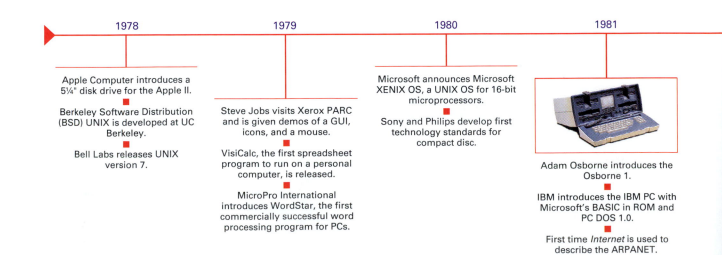

1978	1979	1980	1981
Apple Computer introduces a 5¼" disk drive for the Apple II.	Steve Jobs visits Xerox PARC and is given demos of a GUI, icons, and a mouse.	Microsoft announces Microsoft XENIX OS, a UNIX OS for 16-bit microprocessors.	Adam Osborne introduces the Osborne 1.
Berkeley Software Distribution (BSD) UNIX is developed at UC Berkeley.	VisiCalc, the first spreadsheet program to run on a personal computer, is released.	Sony and Philips develop first technology standards for compact disc.	IBM introduces the IBM PC with Microsoft's BASIC in ROM and PC DOS 1.0.
Bell Labs releases UNIX version 7.	MicroPro International introduces WordStar, the first commercially successful word processing program for PCs.		First time *Internet* is used to describe the ARPANET.

Enter the Personal Computer

Most computer folks put the beginning of the era of the **personal computer** at around 1981, when IBM announced the new IBM PC. The term *PC* is, in fact, a registered trademark of the IBM Corporation, and only the original IBM PC may legally use that name. Technically, all other computers designed for individuals should be called microcomputers. But just as the term *Band-Aid* (a registered trademark of Johnson & Johnson) is commonly used to refer to any brand of adhesive bandage, PC is the standard term for all types of microcomputers.

Once IBM invented the original IBM PC, the company did a very clever thing. It publicly released the specifications for most of the technical innards of the system, enabling other manufacturers to make their own brands of PCs based on IBM technology. This also allowed companies to make components for PCs that were interchangeable with similar parts in just about every other PC. Companies that made their own computers based on the IBM PC technology were known, and still are known, as *clone* PC makers.

IBM's tremendous success, combined with the success of the IBM clone makers, virtually eliminated every other type of microcomputer within just a few years. Only one non-IBM type of microcomputer still exists today in any reasonable quantity: Apple's Macintosh systems, called Macs for short. Introduced in 1984, the user-friendly Macintosh could be operated using a mouse to interact with screen icons instead of a keyboard to type instructions.

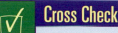

• The original IBM PC

■ Safeguarding Your PC

The prospect of interacting directly with the innards of a PC seems to divide most people into two camps. The *computerphiles* want to dive right in and start pulling parts out of their PCs without regard to the potential for damage. The *computerphobes,* by contrast, are afraid to cause any damage and as a

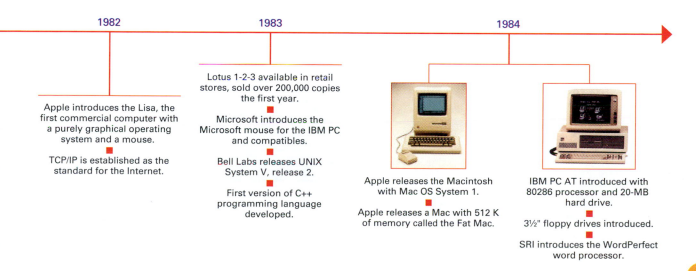

1982

Apple introduces the Lisa, the first commercial computer with a purely graphical operating system and a mouse.

TCP/IP is established as the standard for the Internet.

1983

Lotus 1-2-3 available in retail stores, sold over 200,000 copies the first year.

Microsoft introduces the Microsoft mouse for the IBM PC and compatibles.

Bell Labs releases UNIX System V, release 2.

First version of C++ programming language developed.

1984

Apple releases the Macintosh with Mac OS System 1.

Apple releases a Mac with 512 K of memory called the Fat Mac.

IBM PC AT introduced with 80286 processor and 20-MB hard drive.

3½" floppy drives introduced.

SRI introduces the WordPerfect word processor.

result don't want to touch anything in their computers. This section addresses both computerphiles and computerphobes.

Improperly handling PC hardware can ruin your day, possibly your week, possibly more. It is easy for a careless or ignorant tech to destroy expensive computer components—sometimes just a touch will toast some tiny but important bit of electronics. Even worse, you could hurt yourself by getting a nasty shock or slicing a finger on sharp metal. So before you crack open the case and start touching things inside your computer, it is important to learn proper procedures for handling PC components. That way no parts—yours or the PC's—get zapped.

Don't Let PCs Scare You

Most technicians, novice or experienced, will at some point face an unfamiliar situation with the PC and back away, often saying, "But I don't know how to do that!" Such fear is natural—none of us want to break something or appear incompetent—but it must be overcome if you want to gain skill and knowledge. Plus, people who make this statement miss an important fact: they've probably done something that's similar enough to enable them to figure out the new situation.

I drive a Ford F250 pickup truck. Have you ever driven a Ford F250 pickup truck? For the sake of argument, let's say your answer is no. Do you think that you can start the windshield wipers on my truck? Of course you can. The reason you can run the windshield wipers on my truck is that you understand the *concept* of automobile windshield wipers, and you have experience with running the windshield wipers on your own car. That experience gives you the confidence to believe that, with a bit of careful experimentation, you could successfully start my windshield wipers.

As you poke around looking for the wiper controls, you are all the time evaluating what might happen if you turn the wrong knob. Experience tells you that most of the time the answer will be "not much," especially if the engine is off, and that gives you the confidence to try things and see what happens. Most people new to computers tend to be extremely cautious about trying anything unless they are positive they know what it will do. Computer tech work, however, is often a matter of diagnostic poking around: "If I do this, what happens?" followed by, "Hmm, okay, that was

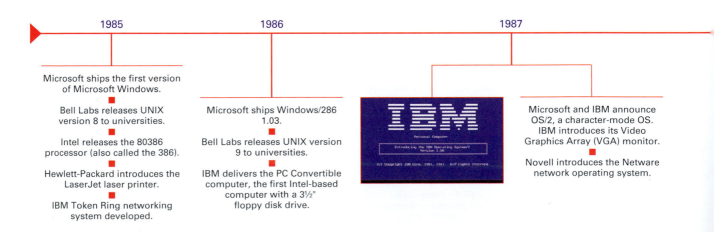

1985

Microsoft ships the first version of Microsoft Windows.

Bell Labs releases UNIX version 8 to universities.

Intel releases the 80386 processor (also called the 386).

Hewlett-Packard introduces the LaserJet laser printer.

IBM Token Ring networking system developed.

1986

Microsoft ships Windows/286 1.03.

Bell Labs releases UNIX version 9 to universities.

IBM delivers the PC Convertible computer, the first Intel-based computer with a 3½" floppy disk drive.

1987

Microsoft and IBM announce OS/2, a character-mode OS. IBM introduces its Video Graphics Array (VGA) monitor.

Novell introduces the Netware network operating system.

interesting—how about if I do *this*?" So, be prepared to poke around, and if you start to feel intimidated, just remember the windshield wipers!

You will find it extremely handy to have a real PC in front of you as you read this chapter. If that isn't possible, I would suggest some window-shopping at your local computer retailer. Being able to look at real examples of the hardware you're reading about helps you see the overall similarities as well as the individual differences in hardware from one system to the next.

Respecting Power

The single most important thing to remember before handling your PC is always to turn off the PC and *unplug it* from its electrical power source. Despite how things seem sometimes, you as a human are more important than the PC. It is a very difficult for a PC to hurt you if it is unplugged. Simply turning off a PC is not enough to protect you.

Electrostatic Discharge (ESD)

Ever pulled a shirt out of the clothes dryer only to find it decorated with several of your socks? As if by magic, they cling tightly to the shirt and crackle loudly when you peel them away. It's not magic, of course, but a bit of simple science. Rubbing against each other in the dryer, the shirt and socks transfer electrons between them, building up opposite electrical charges. This causes them to cling to each other like a pair of magnets. The crackle you hear when you forcibly separate them is the built-up static electricity being released.

Static electricity is electricity that has stopped moving. Simplifying a bit, all electricity wants to move toward the ground, using the quickest and easiest route available. Human bodies conduct electricity, and so do metal computer cases. When static electricity starts moving again, bad things happen. This is why touching a metal doorknob after you cross a carpet in your stocking feet can result in a very noticeable shock: the static electrical charge you have built up by rubbing your feet on the carpet finds an escape route through the doorknob into the ground. Zap! This phenomenon is called **electrostatic discharge (ESD)**.

Know now that if something I show you in this book could truly damage you or the computer, I will very clearly warn you about it. As long as you heed these warnings, you should feel free to relax, have fun, and by all means poke around!

Some system units have a special on/off switch on the back next to the connection for the power plug. Assuming that the built-in power supply is working properly, you should be able to work on the unit safely once that switch has been set to *off;* however, that begs the question of whether you want to trust your safety to whoever inspected your built-in power supply. Bet wrong and you could be in for a nasty shock. Personally, I play it safe and always unplug.

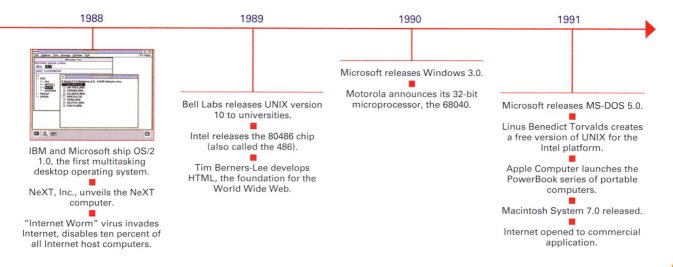

1988

IBM and Microsoft ship OS/2 1.0, the first multitasking desktop operating system.

NeXT, Inc., unveils the NeXT computer.

"Internet Worm" virus invades Internet, disables ten percent of all Internet host computers.

1989

Bell Labs releases UNIX version 10 to universities.

Intel releases the 80486 chip (also called the 486).

Tim Berners-Lee develops HTML, the foundation for the World Wide Web.

1990

Microsoft releases Windows 3.0.

Motorola announces its 32-bit microprocessor, the 68040.

1991

Microsoft releases MS-DOS 5.0.

Linus Benedict Torvalds creates a free version of UNIX for the Intel platform.

Apple Computer launches the PowerBook series of portable computers.

Macintosh System 7.0 released.

Internet opened to commercial application.

Why worry about such a common occurrence? Because ESD is far and away the *number-one destroyer* of PC components. The sort of ESD you encounter in your house may be little more than an annoyance to you, but it can and will completely destroy the delicate electronic components inside your computer! Happily for you and your computer, you can avoid ESD by using proper component handling procedures. The goal is to avoid turning you and your computer into you and the doorknob.

One way to protect your computer is to use a very simple and inexpensive tool called an **antistatic wrist strap**. Antistatic wrist straps work by keeping you from building up an electrical charge that you could then discharge into your computer when you touch it. The computer is grounded by its power supply when it's plugged in. When it's not plugged in, you should place it on an antistatic mat.

Most people don't even notice electrical shocks smaller than 3,000 volts, but some computer components can be destroyed by shocks as small as 30 volts. Walking across a carpet can generate anywhere from 1,500 to 30,000 volts of static electricity, depending on the rug, your footwear, and the humidity of the air. Just by picking up a common plastic bag, you can easily generate over 1,000 volts, and often much more. These examples should make it clear that antistatic protection is a critical part of any good PC tech's toolkit.

Now, as much as I would love to live the fantasy that every tech will always have an antistatic wrist strap handy, I'm also practical enough to know that many times you will leave home without one. If you do not have an antistatic wrist strap with you, there is a trick you can use to minimize the danger of ESD. As you work on a computer, make a point of touching the metal frame or power supply box of the system unit *before* you touch any other part (Figure 1.2). Touch it again every time you move around, pick something up,

- Wrist straps have an alligator clip that you can connect to any handy bare metal spot on the system unit.

Try This!

Antistatic Protection Devices

In some circumstances, wearing an antistatic wrist strap could get in the way or otherwise stop a perfectly good tech from doing his or her job. Manufacturers have developed some alternatives to the wrist strap, so try this:

1. Take a field trip to a local computer or electronics store.

2. Check out their selection of antistatic devices

3. Report what options you can find for protecting your equipment from ESD. Weigh the pros and cons and decide what you would use in different situations.

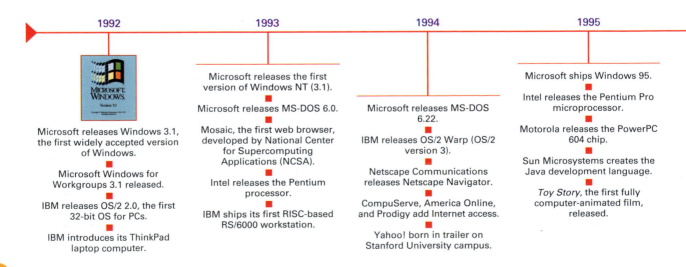

1992	1993	1994	1995
Microsoft releases Windows 3.1, the first widely accepted version of Windows.	Microsoft releases the first version of Windows NT (3.1).	Microsoft releases MS-DOS 6.22.	Microsoft ships Windows 95.
Microsoft Windows for Workgroups 3.1 released.	Microsoft releases MS-DOS 6.0.	IBM releases OS/2 Warp (OS/2 version 3).	Intel releases the Pentium Pro microprocessor.
IBM releases OS/2 2.0, the first 32-bit OS for PCs.	Mosaic, the first web browser, developed by National Center for Supercomputing Applications (NCSA).	Netscape Communications releases Netscape Navigator.	Motorola releases the PowerPC 604 chip.
IBM introduces its ThinkPad laptop computer.	Intel releases the Pentium processor.	CompuServe, America Online, and Prodigy add Internet access.	Sun Microsystems creates the Java development language.
	IBM ships its first RISC-based RS/6000 workstation.	Yahoo! born in trailer on Stanford University campus.	*Toy Story*, the first fully computer-animated film, released.

Introduction to PC Hardware and Troubleshooting

or touch something else, or at least every couple of minutes no matter what you're doing. This will at least work to equalize the amount of static electricity stored up and waiting to move in you and in the PC. If you and it have the same electrical charge, there's no incentive for electricity to move between you. No ESD, no damage, and everybody's happy!

With the system unplugged and a wrist strap on your arm, you've pretty well eliminated most of the electrical hazards of working with a PC. Some of the internal components of the system unit, however, are so sensitive that you must take extra precautions when handling them. Later you will learn how to handle every single component in a PC, but for the moment all you need is a general understanding of how to handle electronic computer parts. Here's a good general rule: If it looks like electronics, try not to touch it any more than absolutely necessary.

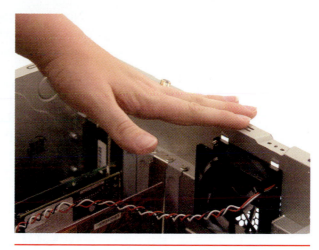

● **Figure 1.2** Touching the PC

Figure 1.3 shows someone handling an electronic component. We call this component RAM. You'll learn about RAM later, but for the moment don't worry about the component and instead look at the way the person is handling it. Notice how his fingers are all over the sensitive electronic chips? This is a bad thing. Your fingers are not only a conduit for electricity; they are also likely to be contaminated with dirt and skin oil. Try to hold components by the edges, as you would a fragile old photograph.

● **Figure 1.3** Improper handling of component

● **Figure 1.4** Proper handling of component

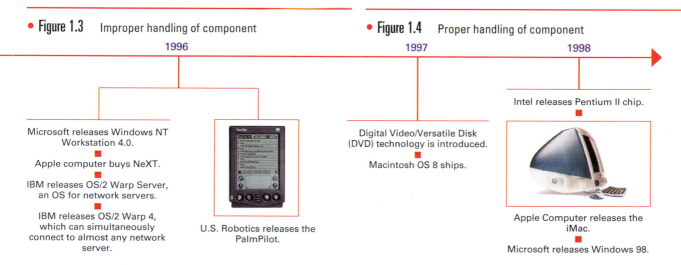

1996

Microsoft releases Windows NT Workstation 4.0.
■
Apple computer buys NeXT.
■
IBM releases OS/2 Warp Server, an OS for network servers.
■
IBM releases OS/2 Warp 4, which can simultaneously connect to almost any network server.

U.S. Robotics releases the PalmPilot.

1997

Digital Video/Versatile Disk (DVD) technology is introduced.
■
Macintosh OS 8 ships.

1998

Intel releases Pentium II chip.
■

Apple Computer releases the iMac.
■
Microsoft releases Windows 98.

Now look Figure 1.4. Notice how he is touching the component only where there are no electronics or electrical contacts. This is the proper way to do it—every time, all the time!

Following these few simple ESD procedures should enable you to open your system unit safely and inspect the internal components of your PC. Keep in mind that there is always a degree of risk when you open a system unit. Never open the system unit unless you're prepared to accept responsibility for causing a part to fail. Before you crack the case, however, you should become familiar with the major components that make up a modern PC.

■ Identifying the Major Components of a PC

The first step in understanding PC hardware is learning the correct names for the major parts of the PC. Figure 1.5 shows a standard PC setup. You should be able to identify and describe all the major components:

- The **system unit** is the box that contains the essence of the computer. In the system unit, you will find the computer's brain, its short- and long-term memory, and the wiring that links all the pieces together. Peripheral devices attach to it using special connectors, usually on the back of the box.

- The **keyboard** is the typewriter component of a PC. It enables you to enter letters, numbers, and special characters into the computer.

- The **mouse** is a primary input device on a modern computer. It enables you to interact with images on the monitor screen by controlling an on-screen icon called a cursor.

- The **monitor** is the computer's primary output device. Over the years, monitors have progressed from small, black screens with crudely formed glowing green or orange characters to large, flat-panel screens that display photographic-quality images in over 4 billion colors.

- **Speakers** provide the audio output for your system. The first PC speaker systems often consisted of two rather cheap speakers, but today's computer sound systems may have up to six speakers, including a subwoofer.

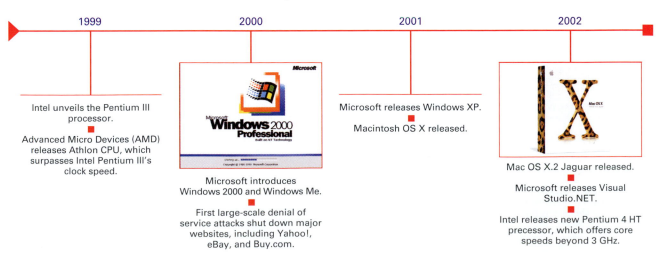

| 1999 | 2000 | 2001 | 2002 |

Intel unveils the Pentium III processor.

Advanced Micro Devices (AMD) releases Athlon CPU, which surpasses Intel Pentium III's clock speed.

Microsoft introduces Windows 2000 and Windows Me.

First large-scale denial of service attacks shut down major websites, including Yahoo!, eBay, and Buy.com.

Microsoft releases Windows XP.

Macintosh OS X released.

Mac OS X.2 Jaguar released.

Microsoft releases Visual Studio.NET.

Intel releases new Pentium 4 HT precessor, which offers core speeds beyond 3 GHz.

Speaker   Monitor   System unit   Speaker

Keyboard   Mouse

• **Figure 1.5**   The basic components of a PC system

Pretty much everything attached to the system unit is known generically as a **peripheral device**. Peripheral devices perform what are called **input/output (I/O)** functions for the system unit. That is, they move information into and out of the computer. A keyboard is a good example of an input device because it enables a user to enter data into the computer. A monitor (the computer's TV-like screen) is an example of an output device. The computer communicates with us through its output on the monitor screen.

Almost every PC consists of a system unit, keyboard, monitor, mouse, and speakers. However, many other peripherals are also quite common on a typical PC. Figure 1.6 shows my personal system, which, as you can see, has quite a few additional peripherals:

- **Cameras** are quite popular on many systems today.
- With a **microphone**, you can input sounds into your computer.
- **Joysticks** are primarily used for computer games.
- **Scanners** convert paper documents and photographs into electronic files.
- **Speakers** bring you sound. See the subwoofer system?
- You still need a **printer** to create paper output.
- A **Zip drive** is one way to store or transfer files that are too large for a floppy disk.

Let's take a closer look at the system unit, monitor, keyboard, and mouse. Pay attention to how the three peripherals connect to the system unit.

> Don't think for a minute that these are the only possible peripherals. The list of things you can add onto your PC is virtually endless!

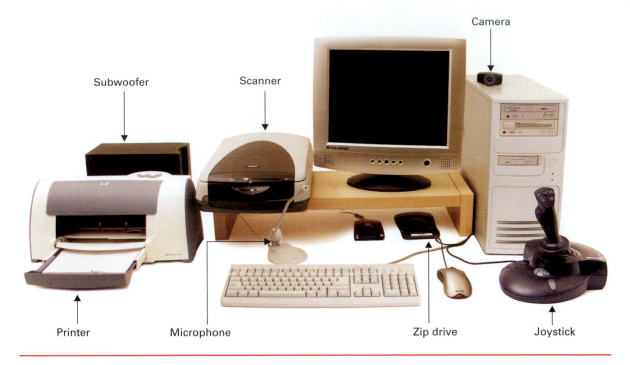

Subwoofer   Scanner   Camera

Printer   Microphone   Zip drive   Joystick

• **Figure 1.6**   Mike's PC—with lots of peripherals

System Unit

The **system unit** is far and away the most complicated part of a PC. It houses the actual computing power of the system, provides the connections to all the peripherals, and holds the disk drives where you insert removable storage media such as CDs and floppy disks.

The Back of the System Unit

Let's start by taking a close look at the back of the system unit, shown in Figure 1.7. Notice the many connection points. The generic term for these connection points is **ports**. The back of this system has a place to plug in the power cord; a vent for the cooling fan; special ports where you can plug in a monitor, keyboard, mouse, speakers, communications devices, and a joystick; plus a parallel port for a printer, a serial port (used by some older peripherals), and USB ports (used by many newer devices).

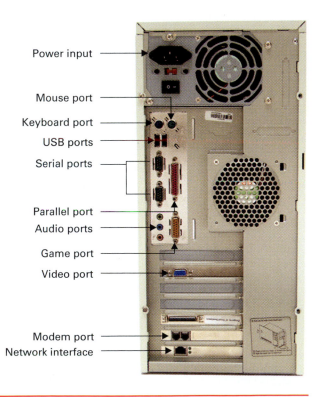

Power input

Mouse port

Keyboard port

USB ports

Serial ports

Parallel port

Audio ports

Game port

Video port

Modem port

Network interface

• **Figure 1.7**   System unit from the back

- ■ **Power input**   The power input is where you plug in the PC's electrical power cord.

- ■ **Keyboard port**   This special dedicated port is just for the keyboard.

- ■ **Mouse port**   This dedicated port is just for the mouse.

- **USB ports**   Universal Serial Bus (USB) ports are general-purpose connectors found on newer PCs. The more unusual the peripheral, the more likely it will use a USB port.

- **Serial port**   This 9-pin connector is one of the oldest and most universal ports found in the back of a PC. Before the introduction of USB in the mid 1990s, serial ports were heavily used.

- **Parallel port**   Virtually as old as the serial port, the 25-pin parallel port has been updated a number of times over the years. Despite the growing prominence of USB, parallel ports remain a popular means for connecting printers.

- **Video port**   This unique three-row, 15-pin connector is where the monitor connects to the system unit.

- **Audio ports**   These are used to connect speakers, microphones, and other audio devices.

- **Game port**   Also known as a joystick port, this 15-pin connector can be used both for joysticks and for MIDI musical devices.

- **Modem port**   This looks like a telephone jack, and for a good reason—that's what it is. Modems enable your computer to communicate with other computers via a telephone line. Notice that there are two connectors. One is an IN jack, which you use to plug your computer into the wall jack, and the other is an OUT jack, which you can use to plug in a telephone.

- **Network interface**   The network interface is normally called just that, and not a port. It is sometimes referred to as an Ethernet connector. It connects your PC to other PCs in a Local Area Network.

I generally refer to the piece that inserts into a port as a *plug,* but you will also hear this called a connector.

Monitor

Monitors come in one of two types: the older cathode ray tube (CRT) type or the more modern liquid crystal display (LCD) variety. CRT monitors have a picture tube like a TV, so they have a big front-to-back footprint. By contrast, LCD monitors are quite thin, but the technology is still new and thus much more expensive. Both kinds of monitors have roughly the same types of controls and connections:

- The on/off switch—often a button—turns the monitor on and off.

- Screen adjustment controls, which vary widely in how they operate from one monitor to another, can be used to adjust many features of the display, including its size and position on the screen; its shape characteristics; and its clarity, brightness, and color tones.

Figure 1.8 shows the front of a typical monitor. Figure 1.9 shows the back of a CRT-type monitor. Although an LCD-type monitor uses a totally different display technology, CRTs and LCDs share the same types of connections. Both have a power connection, where you plug in the power cord that provides electricity to the monitor, and a special video connection on the back of the system unit for the video cable that transmits the video signal from the system to the display screen.

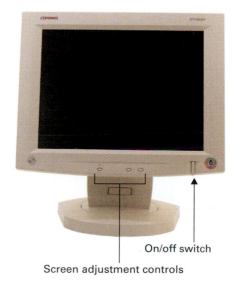

On/off switch

Screen adjustment controls

● **Figure 1.8**   Front view of a modern computer monitor

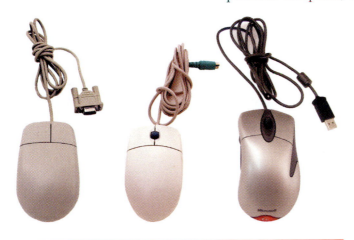

• **Figure 1.9** Back view of a CRT monitor

Power connection   Video cable

• **Figure 1.10** Two keyboards with different connectors

Keyboard

Figure 1.10 shows two types of keyboards. The keyboard at the top of the figure uses a round connector called a PS/2 connector. The keyboard at the bottom uses a USB connector. Systems with both PS/2 and USB ports can use either of these keyboards; however, no system is designed to use two keyboards at the same time.

Mouse Devices

Can you imagine a PC without a mouse? Well, for the first 10 years of the personal computer, until about 1990, computer mice were the exception rather than the rule. Until Windows became a standard feature of PCs, there was little you could do with a mouse on a PC (Apple computers had graphical interfaces from the beginning, so they have always used mice). Instead, you used the keyboard to type instructions to the computer. Even today, Windows still enables users to operate most of its features using keystrokes rather than mouse clicks. Figure 1.11 shows three mice, each with a different type of connector.

The first and still the most common way that computer mice detect motion is with a small roller ball set into the bottom of the mouse. These ball-type mice work best when used with a special mouse pad to provide good traction for the ball. A standard mouse has two buttons on top that are used to interact with elements on the screen. At one point, somebody had the bright idea of inverting the operation of a standard

• **Figure 1.11** Three mice: on the left is the oldest mouse, which uses a serial connector; the center mouse uses a PS/2 connector; and the mouse on the right uses a USB connector.

mouse; instead of positioning the ball on the bottom of the device so that you must push the mouse around on a pad to turn the ball, the ball was positioned on the top of the mouse, so that you must turn it with your thumb or fingers. This type of mouse is called a *trackball* mouse. Another spin (pardon the pun) on the traditional ball mouse is the *optical* mouse, which uses light sensors instead of a mechanical ball to detect the mouse's motion. You still push around an optical mouse, but it doesn't require a mouse pad. Figure 1.12 shows all three types of mouse devices.

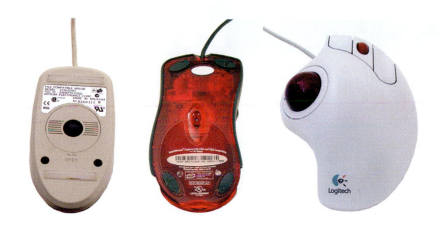

• **Figure 1.12** Three more mice: the one on the left is the bottom of a ball mouse; the center rodent is an optical mouse; and the fellow on the right is a trackball.

Try This!

Research Keyboards

A PC tech needs to be familiar with a variety of keyboards. Try this:

1. Launch your Internet browser and surf to a search engine, such as www.google.com.

2. Do an Internet search on the words **computer keyboard** to see how many different shapes, sizes, and layouts of keyboards you can find.

3. Compare a standard 101-key keyboard with an ergonomic split or natural keyboard. Locate the numeric keypad and special control keys (INSERT, DELETE, HOME, END, PAGE UP, PAGE DOWN, arrow keys, and function keys) that are found on all PC keyboards. Notice which keyboards have PS/2 and which have USB connectors.

Because of the need to get specific pins lined up with specific holes in the connectors, all plugs and ports for peripherals are designed to restrict their insertion to a single orientation. Because of this, *always* recheck what you're doing if a connection resists your efforts to plug something into it. Chances are the connector needs to be oriented differently.

Cross Check

Check Out Your Peripheral Devices

If you have access to a PC, compare the mouse, keyboard, and monitor on that system with those shown in this chapter. Then answer these questions.

1. What type of mouse does your system have: ball-type, trackball, or optical?

2. What type of connector does it use to attach to the system unit: serial, PS/2, or USB?

3. Is the monitor on your system an LCD or CRT monitor?

4. Is your keyboard a standard type, an ergonomic type, or something different?

5. Is the keyboard connector PS/2 or USB?

Handling PC Connections

Troubleshooting PCs almost always involves plugging and unplugging various peripherals from the system unit. This step-by-step exercise is designed to help you feel comfortable handling the various types of connections on the back of a system unit. If you have trouble with a connection, try plugging and unplugging it several times to get the feel of it. Look carefully at the plug on the end of the cable and the connector on the back of the case. Notice any design features, such as the shape or color of the plug and connector, that may have been added to help you connect them properly. Notice which one is *male* (has pins sticking out of it) and which one is *female* (has holes for inserting the pins). It is standard to refer to many computer connectors as either male or female, and some types come in both flavors, so it matters which one you're looking at. Okay, take a deep breath and let's begin!

To complete this excercise, you will need the following:

- A computer with standard peripherals attached, including a mouse, keyboard, and monitor

| Step 1 | Before you do anything else, you must shut down your system. Make sure to do this using the proper shutdown procedure for your operating system. |

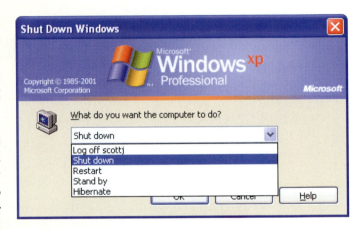

Disconnect your system's power cord from the wall socket, power strip, or other electrical power source. Do the same thing with your monitor's power cord and the power cords for any other devices attached to your system, such as printers or external drives.

Step 2 Unplug the other end of the power cord from the back of the system unit. Take a close look at the plug. Notice that its irregular shape ensures that it can be inserted in only one orientation. Plug the power cord back into the system unit *only*—do *not* plug the cord back into the wall socket!

Step 3 Now find your mouse connection. Unplug the mouse and inspect the plug. What type is it? If it's a PS/2 plug, observe the orientation of the pins. Note that the mouse plug, too, must be properly oriented to plug in successfully. Now plug the mouse back into the mouse port. Unplug it again and then *very* gently try to plug the mouse into the port incorrectly. It won't go, of course, and that's a good thing.

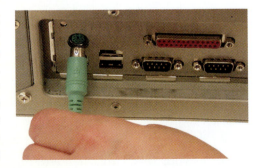

Step 4

Now find your keyboard connection. On many systems, both the keyboard and mouse are PS/2 ports, often right next to each other. This arrangement makes it quite easy to insert the mouse plug accidentally into the keyboard port, and the keyboard plug into the mouse port. Happily, doing this will not do any damage, although neither device will work. If you boot a system after reconnecting these devices and they don't work, check the plugs. If you got them reversed, simply turn off the system and switch them.

Step 5

Finally, locate the video connection, where your monitor cable connects to the system box, and unplug it. Some of these plugs are held in by thumbscrews on either side of the plug. If yours is this type, you must unscrew both thumbscrews before you can unplug it. Usually these screws are designed to remain attached to the plug, so don't try to remove them entirely. When you think the screws are disengaged, pull gently on the plug to remove it. The video connector may take slightly more force to remove than the mouse and keyboard plugs did, but still not a lot. If it resists strongly, check to see whether one of the screws is still engaged.

Step 6

Take a look at the plug once you've removed it. Is it male or female? How many rows of holes does it have? *Only* monitor plugs have this exact arrangement. Okay, now you get to reattach the connector to the system box. Don't forget to screw in the thumbscrews.

Step 7

Recheck everything to verify that all of the connections are in place. Now plug the power cord back into the socket and boot the computer. If you didn't get the main power cord reinserted correctly, the computer will sit there like a giant paperweight. If you got that but messed up on the monitor power cord, the system unit will make noises, but the monitor's power light will stay off and you won't see anything. If you switched the keyboard and mouse ports, neither peripheral will respond. If you didn't quite get one of those plugs in all the way, then one or both of them won't respond. If this happens, don't worry about it—even experienced PC techs mess these things up periodically. It just means you get a chance to do your first real troubleshooting. If you did everything right the first time, high-five somebody!

■ Identifying the Internal Components of a PC

Now that you've learned about ESD and familiarized yourself with the major components of a PC, it's time to learn about the parts most people never see. Your first look inside a PC system can be a bit scary. In this case, however, a little fear is not a bad thing. The average PC costs enough to make it one of the more expensive appliances in most homes, and an expensive business machine as well. So if cracking the case on a PC to poke around inside seems like a big deal, good—it *will* be a big deal if you destroy somebody's precious system, and no tech should get so cocky that he or she forgets to be careful!

⚠️ Pay attention to the instructions about how to handle the components properly. The inside parts of the PC are much more sensitive and more easily damaged than the outside parts. Other than watching for sharp metal edges, you needn't worry that any of the components in the box will hurt *you*, but you can hurt them. That said, as long as you follow the instructions, you are free to muck around happily inside the box.

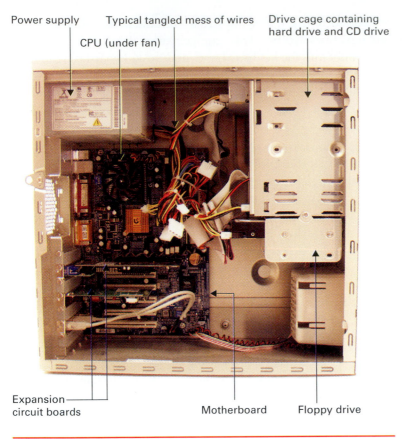

Power supply   Typical tangled mess of wires   Drive cage containing hard drive and CD drive

CPU (under fan)

Expansion circuit boards   Motherboard   Floppy drive

● **Figure 1.13**   Opened system unit

Before you open a real case, you should have a good idea of what's inside. Figure 1.13 shows a typical system unit opened to make the internal components visible.

- The **central processing unit (CPU)**, also called the microprocessor, is the brain of the computer, the place where all the work gets done. Two companies currently control almost the entire PC CPU market: Intel and AMD. The CPU is usually easy to locate because it's covered by a large fan.

- **Random Access Memory (RAM)** is, in effect, the CPU's short-term memory. Just like facts stored in your short-term memory, data stored in RAM can be accessed very quickly, but it disappears when the power is turned off. For long- term storage, your computer uses the hard drive. The CPU uses RAM to store information relevant to whatever it is currently doing, so what's actually in RAM is constantly changing. RAM comes packaged on small, flat cards commonly referred to as *sticks* of memory. They connect to the motherboard by snapping into specially designed slots. Computer memory is measured in megabytes (MB) for most PCs, or gigabytes (GB) for high-end systems.

- The **motherboard** is the big printed circuit board that covers most of the bottom of the system unit. The motherboard's main job is to provide an area where all of the internal components of the PC can connect. All motherboards have connections for the CPU, RAM, and storage drives, as well as a variety of general- purpose expansion slots.

- **Expansion slots** enable you to expand the capabilities of your system by adding extra components. Any device that snaps into an expansion slot is known generically as an expansion card. Many expansion cards are designed with a long, thin metal plate on one end that shows through a matching hole in the back of the case. The plate contains connectors for devices that use that card. For example, the sound card and network card in Figure 1.13 have external connections.

- The **hard drive** is your PC's primary storage area. It's like the computer's long-term memory; data stored there remains available for later use, unlike data in RAM, which disappears when you power off the computer; however, the hard drive can't be accessed as quickly as RAM. The computer uses the hard drive to store all of the software that it uses and all of the documents and pictures and other data that you create and save on the PC. Modern hard drive storage is measured in GB.

Inside Information

Warranties

Most new PC systems have one- to three-year warranties, and all PC makers look for reasons to avoid doing warranty work, so before you crack open a new PC, make sure that doing so won't void the warranty!

- Compact disc–read-only memory drives, or **CD-ROM drives**, are designed to read CDs. All modern computers come with some version of a CD-ROM drive. Basic CD-ROM discs can only be read from—you cannot write any data onto a CD-ROM disc. Compact disc–recordable (CD-R) discs allow you to write data to them, but only one time. Newer PC models usually include compact disc–rewriteable (CD-RW) drives that enable you to read and write repeatedly to special CD-RW discs, just like a floppy drive.

- **Floppy drives** read floppy disks. The disks are known simply as *floppies*. Floppies were the first kind of storage used by PCs, even before hard drives. Compared to more modern storage media, floppy disks hold only a very small amount of information, but they can hold a good number of documents or pictures, and they are cheap, small, and easy to buy. Their continued usefulness, combined with PC manufacturers' fear of eliminating backward compatibility, means that most PCs still come with a floppy drive.

- Also known as a *graphics adapter*, the **video card** acts as the interface between the computer and the monitor. It takes a lot of computing power to generate the complex visual displays on the average computer screen, so most video cards come with their own on-board CPUs. Thanks to the explosion of video games in recent years, the power of the CPUs on high-end graphics adapters rivals that of the system CPUs of just a few years ago.

- The computer **power supply** is misnamed. It doesn't actually *supply* power to the computer; that's the power company's job. A computer power supply *converts* standard household A/C current into the D/C current needed by the PC. Note the many cables coming out of the power supply to provide power to the various internal components.

- **Sound cards** provide the sound input and output for your PC. The earliest PC sound cards often consisted of nothing more than a stereo output and a stereo input. Modern PC sound cards often come with surround-sound capabilities, digital inputs, and most recently, support for DVDs. Many PCs have the sound built into the motherboard.

- To access a Local Area Network (LAN) like the ones connecting many office computers, most PCs require a special expansion card called a **Network Interface Card (NIC)** that snaps into one of the PC's expansion slots. Many newer motherboards have this capability built in.

- Before network cards and broadband access, there were **modems** and phone lines. For many people, a modem and phone line are still their primary tools for accessing the Internet. Modems come in two flavors: external and internal. The earliest modems were all external devices that you plugged into a serial port on the back of the case. Modern modems tend to be the internal type, which are expansion cards that snap into standard expansion slots on the motherboard.

- RAM stick

Opening a System Unit

Now that you're familiar with the outside of the computer and you know how to protect it against ESD, it's time to look inside. Inside is where the most interesting things live, but first you have to figure out how to get at them. Unlike many parts of a PC, the case itself has never been standardized. There are as many different case designs as there are people designing them. All this diversity means that opening a case you've never seen before is always an adventure.

To view the inside of the case, you will need to remove at least one of the metal panels that form the cover of the system unit. Some cases are designed with a single U-shaped cover over the top and sides.

Others allow you to remove just one side. Older cases tend to be fastened with standard, small Phillips screws, whereas newer ones are more likely to feature larger, easier-to-turn thumbscrews. You should expect to have to examine a new case with some care to figure out its secrets. Let's step through the process of opening an unfamiliar case.

To complete this excercise, you will need the following:

- A PC
- A Phillips screwdriver
- Preferably, an antistatic wrist strap

| **Step 1** | Inspect the outside of the case and initially look for two things: a removable panel and screws on the case edge in the back. From the perspective of the back of the case, check the right side cover. If that side seems to be a separate, removable panel and you see two or three screws along the case edge in the back, you're in luck. Remove the screws and place them in a safe spot—a cup will do in a pinch—so that you can find and reinsert them later. |

| **Step 2** | If your system unit is enclosed in a single piece of metal that covers both sides and the top, you'll need to remove all of the screws along the edges of the case back. This single piece design is common in older PCs. |

| **Step 3** | If you don't see any screws along the back of the system unit, you may have a case that requires you to remove the front faceplate before you can expose the insides. These types of cases usually feature an obvious release latch at the bottom of the faceplate; however, they often require a fairly sizable amount of force before they pop off the front. A word of caution: Be *very sure* you are working on this sort of case before pulling too hard on a front faceplate. If there are any screws along the back, the case is probably not this kind, and you'll just be breaking somebody's pretty case. |

Once the faceplate is off, check for screws on the left side edge when looking at the front of the case. Remove them and set them aside for safekeeping.

Note that you might have a one-piece cover that requires you to remove screws on all three sides, just like in step 2.

Step 4

Higher-quality cases often offer much easier access. Some have a handle on the door with a latch to enable easy access into the system unit. If you're lucky enough to have one of these, simply pull the latch to free the side panel.

Step 5

Once you've removed the screws or discovered the magic secret latch or lever, remove the cover from the system unit. On cases with a removable panel, just remove the one panel; otherwise, take off the entire cover.

One of these methods will enable you to access the internals of the system unit. The only thing to watch out for with case cover removal is potential damage to your fingers from sharp metal inside the system unit. Be careful and go slowly, and you should be fine.

Step-by-Step 1.3

Handling Expansion Cards

Now that you have opened the case on your PC, your next tech job is to remove and reinsert an expansion card. Remember to ground yourself and to proceed slowly and carefully—with your brain in gear at all times!

To complete this excercise, you will need the following:

- A PC running Windows 9x/2000/XP
- A Phillips screwdriver
- A straight-slot screwdriver
- An antistatic mat and wrist strap
- A three-prong parts retriever

Step 1

First you must prepare to work inside the case. Shut down your system and unplug the power cable from the wall outlet. Set the system unit on an antistatic mat. Open the case, putting any screws in a safe place, and attach yourself to the case with the antistatic wrist strap.

Step 2

Using a straight-slot screwdriver or your fingers, disconnect the video plug from the video port on the back of the system unit. Now look inside the case and locate the screw at the top of the metal plate that secures the video card to the case. Use your

Phillips screwdriver to remove the screw, being careful not to drop the screw into the system unit.

If you do drop it, and we all do sooner or later, use the three-prong parts retriever (the little grabber tool that comes in a standard computer toolkit) to retrieve the screw, taking care not to touch the motherboard itself if at all possible.

Step 3

Grasp the card on the top edge, front and back, being careful not to touch components on the card. Using a very gentle front-to-back rocking motion, carefully remove the video card from the expansion slot.

Step 4

After removing the video card, inspect (without touching!) the connectors that snap into the expansion slot. Also observe the expansion slot from which you removed the video card—can you see how it is it different from the other expansion slots? On modern systems, the expansion slot for the video card is unique. On older systems, it is the same as some or all of the other slots.

Step 5

After you've looked all you want, it's time to insert the card into its expansion slot. This procedure is simply the removal procedure in reverse: Take the card by the edge and the metal plate and then gently lower the card into the expansion slot, trying to make sure that it stays at right angles to the case surfaces. Push down gently but firmly, keeping an eye on the orientation of the metal plate with respect to the back of the case. Remember to keep your fingers away from any electronics. Once you think you have the card in the slot, give the top edge of the card a few gentle pushes directly downward to make sure. Reinsert the securing screw and then reattach the video plug to the video port.

Step 6

As a final test of your tech work, boot the system to be sure that you properly inserted the video card. Save yourself some time by doing this *before* you close up the case! If a video card is not properly installed, almost all PCs make a beeping sound and refuse to boot. Particularly if you were just working with the video card, you should check to see if it's seated incorrectly or perhaps was jiggled loose when you plugged things back in. When you know it works, resecure the cover on the system unit.

Chapter 1 Review

■ Chapter Summary

After reading this chapter and completing the Step-by-Step tutorials and Try This! exercises, you should understand the following facts about the major PC components:

Explain the historical development of the PC, and the relationship between hardware and software

- Everything in your computer fits into one of two categories: hardware and software. Anything on your computer that you can touch—monitors, system units, CPUs, hard drives, motherboards, and so on—is hardware.

- Software is the technical term for computer programs. Computer programs are sets of instructions that tell the hardware how to do things. They are often compared to cooking recipes. The software instructs the hardware as it manipulates data to produce the desired result.

- A microcomputer is a computer that fits into a single box that can sit on a desktop and is designed to be used by only one person at a time. Like their immediate predecessors, the closet-sized minicomputers, and unlike their more distant ancestors, the room-sized mainframes, microcomputers can run many different types of software applications.

- PC is short for personal computer. The personal computer era began around 1981, when IBM announced the new IBM PC. Although the term *PC* is a registered trademark of the IBM Corporation, it is commonly used to refer to all types of microcomputers.

- IBM publicly released the specifications for its IBM PC, enabling clone PC manufacturers to make their own brands of PCs based on IBM technology.

Describe and execute the proper procedures for handling PC components

- Electrostatic discharge (ESD) is far and away the number one destroyer of PC components. You can avoid ESD by following proper component handling procedures.

- When working on your PC, be sure to turn off the PC and unplug it from your electrical power source.

- If possible, use an antistatic wrist strap when working inside a PC. If you do not have an antistatic wrist strap, touch the metal frame or power supply box of the system unit.

Identify and describe the functions of the major PC components

- Almost every PC consists of a system unit, keyboard, monitor, mouse, and speakers. The system unit of a PC is the rectangular, usually beige-colored box containing the CPU, memory, storage, and wiring that links all the pieces together. Peripheral devices attach to it using special connectors on the back of the box.

- Peripheral devices perform I/O functions for the system unit. That is, they move information into and out of the computer. A keyboard is a good example of an input device. A monitor is an example of an output device. Speakers provide the audio output for your system.

- The generic term for the connection points on the back of the system unit is *ports.* Universal Serial Bus (USB) ports are general-purpose connectors found on newer PCs.

- The 9-pin serial port is one of the oldest and most universal ports found on the back of a PC.

- Virtually as old as the serial port, the 25-pin parallel port remains a popular option for connecting printers.

- The unique three-row, 15-pin video port is where the monitor connects to the system unit.

Identify and describe the functions of the internal components of a PC

- The central processing unit (CPU), also called the microprocessor, is the brain of the computer, the place where all the work gets done. Two companies currently control almost the entire PC CPU market: Intel and AMD. The CPU is usually covered by a large fan.

- Random Access Memory, or RAM, is, in effect, the CPU's short-term memory. Data stored in RAM can be accessed very quickly, but it disappears when the power is turned off. The CPU uses RAM

- to store information relevant to whatever it's currently doing. Computer memory is measured in megabytes (MB) or gigabytes (GB).

- The motherboard is the big printed circuit board that covers most of the bottom of your system unit. The motherboard's main job is to provide an area where all of the internal components of the PC can connect.

- Expansion slots enable you to expand the capabilities of your system by adding components. Any device that snaps into an expansion slot is known generically as a card.

- The hard drive is your PC's primary storage area. Data stored on the hard drive remains available for later use, unlike data in RAM. Modern hard drive storage is measured in GB.

- CD-ROM drives are designed to read CD-ROM discs, but cannot write data onto a CD-ROM disc. CD-R discs can be written on, but only once. Newer PC models usually include CD-RW drives that enable you to read and write repeatedly to special CD-RW discs.

- Floppy drives read floppy disks, known simply as floppies.

- Also known as a graphics adapter, the video card acts as the interface between the computer and the monitor.

- The computer power supply doesn't actually *supply* power to the computer; it *converts* standard household A/C current into the D/C current needed by the PC.

- Sound cards provide the sound input and output for your PC. Many inexpensive PCs have the sound built into the motherboard.

- To access a Local Area Network (LAN) like the ones connecting many office computers, most PCs require a special expansion card called a Network Interface Card, or NIC, that snaps into one of the PC's expansion slots. Some newer motherboards now come with this capability built in.

- Modems enable PCs to access the Internet using a telephone line. The earliest modems were all external devices that you plugged into a serial port on the back of the case. Modern modems tend to be the internal type, which are expansion cards that snap into standard expansion slots on the motherboard.

■ Key Terms

antistatic wrist strap *(8)*	**keyboard** *(10)*	**personal computer (PC)** *(5)*
CD-ROM drive *(19)*	**mainframe** *(2)*	**port** *(12)*
central processing unit (CPU) *(18)*	**modem** *(19)*	**power supply** *(19)*
electrostatic discharge (ESD) *(7)*	**monitor** *(10)*	**Random Access Memory (RAM)** *(18)*
expansion slots *(18)*	**motherboard** *(18)*	
floppy drive *(19)*	**mouse** *(10)*	**sound card** *(19)*
hard drive *(18)*	**Network Interface Card (NIC)** *(19)*	**system unit** *(12)*
input/output (I/O) *(11)*	**peripheral device** *(11)*	**video card** *(19)*

■ Key Terms Quiz

Use terms from the Key Terms list to complete the following sentences. Not all terms will be used.

1. The _____ is your PC's primary long-term storage area.

2. A good way to prevent _____ is to use an antistatic wrist strap.

3. A computer's video card and modem snap into _____ on the motherboard.

4. The _____ is the computer's primary output device.

5. Peripheral devices perform _____ functions for the system unit.

6. The primary input device besides a keyboard is a _____.

7. A _____ enables a computer to connect to a LAN.

8. The primary job of the _____ is to convert AC current from the wall socket to DC current the PC can use.

9. Many PCs have a separate _____ to enable the system to play music, but a lot of modern PCs have this capability built into the _____.

10. The _____ acts as the interface between the computer and the monitor.

Multiple-Choice Quiz

1. What is the generic term for any connector on the back of a PC's system unit?

    a. Socket

    b. Port

    c. System

    d. Power

2. The term *personal computer* is a registered trademark of what company?

    a. Dell

    b. Microsoft

    c. Apple

    d. IBM

3. Which of the following devices will *not* connect to a port on the back of a typical system unit?

    a. Mouse

    b. Keyboard

    c. Hard drive

    d. Monitor

4. Which of the following is *not* a type of port normally associated with a mouse?

    a. USB

    b. Parallel

    c. Serial

    d. PS/2

5. A serial port has a ___-pin connection.

    a. 9

    b. 15

    c. 20

    d. 36

6. Walking across the carpet can generate up to 30,000 volts of static electricity in your body. People cannot feel ESD below _____ volts; computer equipment can be destroyed with a discharge of as little as _____ volts.

    a. 1000, 200

    b. 2000, 100

    c. 3000, 30

    d. 10,000, 10

7. Mary's boss asked her to open a system unit to add more RAM. She examined the back of the case, but could find no visible screws. What could be the problem?

    a. All cases open from the back; therefore, she needs to look again.

    b. The screws might be hiding under the front faceplate of the system unit.

    c. It's a push-pull locking case that requires a push downward on the top of the system unit followed by a pull to the back.

    d. It's a factory-sealed case typical of those manufactured by Dell, Gateway, and Hewlett-Packard.

8. How many pins does a video connector have?

    a. 9 pins in two rows

    b. 15 pins in two rows

    c. 15 pins in three rows

    d. 25 pins in three rows

9. Joe dropped by his mother's place to fix her ailing computer. She needs it up and running right away to pay a bill. As he picked up a screwdriver to remove the cover from the system unit, however, he realized that he'd forgotten his antistatic wrist strap at home. What should he do?

    a. Proceed as planned. Modern PCs are at little or no risk from ESD. The wrist strap is therefore irrelevant.

    b. Proceed as planned, but be careful to ground himself on the power supply or other bare metal spot on the system unit frame frequently while working inside the system unit.

    c. Stop. Go home and pick up his antistatic wrist strap and return. His mother and her bank will understand.

    d. Stop. Return home and call another technician. You should *never* work on your mom's PC.

10. Jenny's monitor just died. She took the opportunity to replace it with a sleek new monitor. When she turned the PC on, however, the system unit made noise, but the LED on the monitor stayed off and nothing appeared on the screen. What most likely happened?

    a. She forgot to plug in the power cord for the monitor.

    b. She forgot to plug in the data cable for the monitor.

    c. The new monitor is dead.

    d. The system unit is dead.

11. How many times can you write to a CD-R?

    a. Once

    b. Twice

    c. Ten times

    d. Unlimited times

12. Jenny the intrepid tech decided to replace the video card on her system. Being careful to avoid ESD, she removed the old card and inserted the new card. When she powered up the PC, however, the system unit beeped several times, but the computer did not boot. What's most likely the problem?

    a. The video card must be bad.

    b. The video card did not get seated properly.

    c. The monitor must be dead.

    d. There's no problem. All modern video cards cause the system to fail on first try after installation.

13. Marcus purchased a new sound card for his system. His friend Jenny cautioned him to hold the card only along the edge, but Bill said he should hold the card by the gold parts on the bottom so he wouldn't mess up the chips on the card. Who's right?

    a. Only Jenny is correct.

    b. Only Bill is correct.

    c. Both Jenny and Bill are correct.

    d. Neither Jenny nor Bill is correct.

14. Solea removed the cover from a PC system unit and carefully attached the alligator clip for her antistatic wrist strap to the frame inside. She then placed the wristband snugly on her right wrist. What did she forget to do?

    a. Activate the power band.

    b. Plug in the PC.

    c. Power up the PC.

    d. Nothing. She did things just right.

15. John bought a new mouse, but got quite a surprise when he removed it from the box. Instead of the small, round connector on the end like his old mouse, this one had a thin, flat rectangular connector. What's the deal?

    a. The mouse plugs into the serial port.

    b. The mouse plugs into the PS/2 port.

    c. The mouse plugs in the parallel port.

    d. The mouse plugs into the USB port.

■ Essay Quiz

1. You are contributing to an article for your school's online help area. Your part of the job is to write (a) a paragraph explaining the differences between RAM and hard drive storage; (b) a paragraph explaining the differences among ball-type mice, trackballs, and optical mice; and (c) a paragraph explaining the differences among CD-ROM discs, CD-R discs, and CD-RW discs as they are used in PCs.

2. Reread the truck windshield wipers analogy that explains why this book doesn't need to cover every detail of how different computers are designed. Think of your own analogy to make this point and write a paragraph about it.

3. Write a brief essay about why ESD is dangerous to a computer and what you should do to prevent it when you are working on a PC. Include at least three examples of specific actions you should take.

4. What would be your ideal set of peripherals? Write a short essay explaining your choices.

5. Standard beige boxes are boring, but can they be improved on? Write a brief essay describing how you would design your ideal system unit. Feel free to get creative, but think carefully about what you change because you must justify any design modifications.

Lab Projects

• Lab Project 1.1

Your school has received funding and plans to buy new PCs for the tech lab. The lab instructor wants to make certain that she gets the cases that are the easiest to open. You are asked to open several cases on the list of systems that the school might buy and then make a recommendation on a particular case model.

You will need the following:

- Several different cases
- A Phillips screwdriver
- A notepad and pen for taking notes on each case

Then do the following:

1. Open each case, noting how each opens and any difficulties you encounter.
2. Present an argument advocating a particular case after you finish your testing.

• Lab Project 1.2

In the spirit of "practice makes perfect," remove and reinsert a sound card. Make certain to run the PC after you reinstall the card to determine whether the card works. Also, be very careful to follow the proper procedures to avoid electric shock to you or ESD to components.

You will need the following:

- A PC with a sound card installed
- A Phillips screwdriver
- An antistatic wrist strap

Then do the following:

1. Turn on the PC and run a sound file of some type to make sure the sound card works.
2. Turn off the PC and open the system unit.
3. Determine the location of the sound card and remove it.
4. Reinstall the sound card, but leave the cover off the system unit.
5. Start the PC and check the sound. If it works, put the cover back on the case. If it doesn't, you need to run through the installation procedure again.

CPUs

*"Brain and Brain!
What is Brain?"*

—ALIEN FROM ORIGINAL *STAR TREK*
SERIES, EPISODE "SPOCK'S BRAIN"

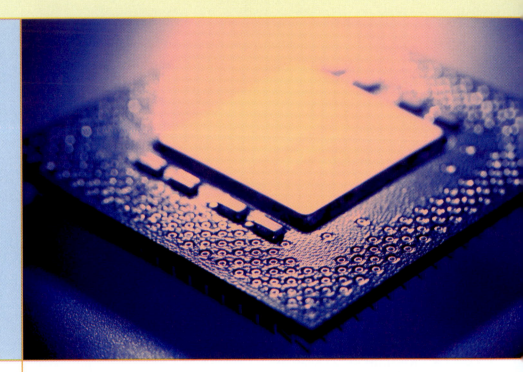

In this chapter, you will learn how to:

- ■ **Describe the function of the central processing unit (CPU)**
- ■ **Identify the right CPU for any motherboard**
- ■ **Install and upgrade a CPU**
- ■ **Select and install the correct heat sink and cooling fan assembly**

I recently asked a friend of mine what she knew about the computer *CPU*, to which she responded, quite logically I thought, "the *central processing unit...* the brains of the computer." When pressed for details, though, she thought for a moment and then, in a moment of triumph for Intel Corporation's marketing department, blurted "Intel Inside!" excitedly, but then she shook her head, unable to provide any more details.

Intel is one of the two major processor makers, by the way, with Advanced Microdevices (AMD) its chief competitor.

This chapter introduces you to the CPU in detail. You'll learn the functions of the CPU first and then discover the many different models manufactured today. The third and fourth sections of the chapter teach you how to upgrade and install a CPU and the ever-important heat sink and cooling fan, respectively.

Understanding, selecting, installing, and upgrading CPUs are essential skills for all PC technicians. Let's explore the CPU.

■ The Function of the CPU

My friend's description of the CPU as the brain of the computer is a good starting place for understanding this vital component, but we need to take that definition one step further and more clearly define the *function* of a CPU. It is critical to appreciate that there are a number of different CPUs on the market today. CPUs vary tremendously in capabilities, making your choice of CPU a challenge if you don't appreciate what the CPU does inside your PC. Understanding the function of a CPU enables you to become an informed consumer and a better PC tech.

What Is a CPU?

A CPU is an electronic device that accepts input and performs hundreds of different types of functions on that input. These may be as simple as basic arithmetic functions, such as adding 2 + 2, or they may be something vastly more complex, such as "Take this value and send it to the video card so it can display a color on the screen." The collection of all of the functions that a CPU can perform is called the CPU's **instruction set**. Commands sent to the CPU to tell the CPU to do something are called programs.

• A typical CPU: an AMD Athlon XP

Where Are the Programs?

Without programs—the commands that tell the CPU what you want to do—the CPU is useless. For the CPU to work, the computer must have a way to grab programs and send them to the CPU so the CPU can do whatever you want it to do. So where are the programs?

When your computer is turned off, all of the programs are stored on your hard drive. In theory, you could build a computer that sends data from the hard drive directly to the CPU, but there's a problem with that idea: the hard drive is too slow.

Your CPU can process many millions, even billions, of commands every second. Hard drives simply can't give the data to the CPU at a fast enough speed. To compensate for this problem, commands do not go directly to the CPU, but rather are stored in RAM. Chapter 1 described *RAM* as the *short-term memory* of the computer, and that's not a bad way to look at it. Programs are loaded into RAM from the hard drive, and then the very fast RAM gives the CPU access to the programs. When a program is loaded into RAM and fed into the CPU to do whatever it does, we say the program is *running*.

The flow of data among the hard drive, RAM, and CPU is not a one-way process. Your CPU will generate the

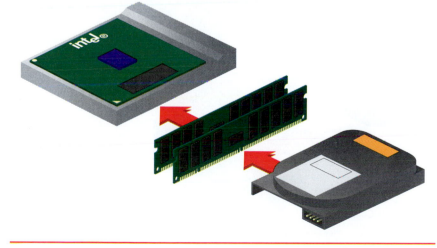

• Hard drive to RAM to CPU

results of programs—some sort of data—and that data must be stored somewhere. Initially, the data is sent to RAM, but if you want that data to continue to exist after you turn the computer off, you must save it to the hard drive. In general, it's safe to say that programs flow into the CPU, and data flows out. So RAM temporarily stores both programs and data.

Programs and data are not the only things flowing in and out between the CPU and RAM. The CPU also has the ability to determine whether an input device such as your keyboard or mouse has been used. If you move the mouse or press a key on the keyboard, the CPU will know that this has happened and act upon it, telling a letter to appear on a screen or moving the mouse pointer across your screen. This also means that the CPU can tell devices such as your monitor or sound card to produce output (for example, to display a letter on the screen or play a sound).

If RAM is so great, then why not just put the program in RAM and dispense with hard drives? First, hard drives can store hundreds of times more information than can RAM. Second, RAM is volatile—it loses all of its information the moment you turn off the computer. Third, you never run all of the programs on your computer at the same time. The only time you load a program into RAM is when you want to run it, so why waste RAM just to hold a program you're not currently running?

Based on what you've read here, isn't it a safe bet that everything in your computer is connected to everything else in some fashion? It's certainly the case that the RAM and the CPU don't communicate by telepathy. Let's take a moment to see how all the parts of the PC connect to the CPU.

Putting It All Together

In Chapter 1, you saw that the CPU, RAM, and other parts of the PC are all attached to the motherboard. The motherboard is filled with tiny wires called *traces*, the connections between the different components on your motherboard. But where do all those traces go?

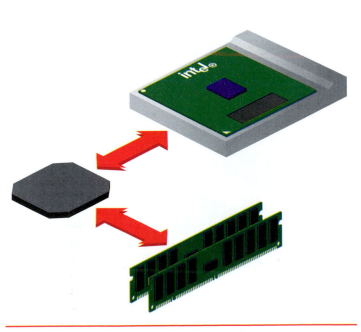

Let's start by looking at the connection between the CPU and RAM. Your CPU (assuming it was made in the past 10 years) has 64 special wires that come out of the CPU and run to a special helper chip called the **Northbridge**. The Northbridge in turn connects to your RAM.

It is important that you appreciate that these connections aren't one wire but many wires. Any time multiple wires are used to connect two or more devices, we call those wires a *bus*. The bus that interconnects the CPU, Northbridge, and RAM is called the **frontside bus**.

The frontside bus consists of two parts. One part, called the *data bus*, carries all of the data and programs that move between the CPU and RAM via the Northbridge. The other part of the frontside bus is called the *address bus*. The CPU uses the address bus to tell the Northbridge the location in RAM of the data it wants next. The address bus will usually have 32 or 36 wires.

• CPU, Northbridge, and RAM

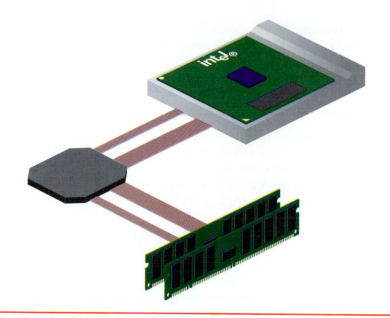

Depending on whom you ask, the Northbridge is also referred to as the *memory controller hub* or the *system controller chip*.

• Address bus and data bus connecting to the CPU and Northbridge

The Northbridge also acts as the connector to the rest of the devices on your PC, although it may have intermediary support chips to help it connect the many parts of your PC to the CPU. These buses that run from the Northbridge to the other devices in your computer are discussed in detail in Chapter 5. The function of the CPU is closely intertwined with the functions of the RAM, Northbridge, and other devices in the CPU.

Armed with this newfound knowledge of the CPU, let's turn to the more practical and see how to identify the different types of CPU.

■ Identifying the Right CPU for Any Motherboard

The one constant with CPUs is change. Especially in the past decade, chip manufacturers have produced a dizzying array of increasingly powerful new chips in a variety of designs. So many different chips have been produced in such a short period of time that you can tell a lot about the relative age and power of a PC just by knowing what CPU it uses. So what do you look for to identify a CPU? Four key facts tell the story: the manufacturer, the model, the speed, and the package.

CPU Manufacturers

Currently, two companies compete virtually alone in the CPU business: Intel Corporation and Advanced Micro Devices (AMD). Each company produces CPUs that run Microsoft's Windows operating system and applications designed for it quite nicely. The processors from both companies therefore offer no stark choices for consumers as either will do the job in the PC. Technicians need to know substantially more, of course, because the CPUs

Inside Information

The Difference Between Intel and AMD Processors

Intel and AMD processors—especially at the high end—differ fairly dramatically in the way that they process information. The details of these differences fall outside the scope of this book as they matter more to programmers and high-end users than to techs. I happen to love this kind of detail, so if you're curious about the competing architecture of CPUs, check out the Tech Files at my web site, www.totalsem.com.

are not interchangeable in systems. An Intel processor will not work with a motherboard designed for an AMD processor, in other words.

Processor Models

Intel and AMD currently offer several models of CPUs for consumers and businesses, plus variations within those models. Different models are targeted at different groups of buyers, such as consumers focused on low price, enthusiasts focused on high performance, and businesses focused on power and reliability. What's a quick way to tell one model from another? Luckily, both AMD and Intel are very proud of their CPUs and label them nicely.

• Manufacturer name and model on an AMD Duron processor

• Manufacturer name and model on an Intel Pentium 3 processor

CPU Speeds

Have you ever seen the movie *Ben Hur* starring Charlton Heston? There's a scene in the galley of a ship powered by slaves (including Ben Hur) rowing in unison. Remember the guy at the front of the boat with the drum, the row master? What was he there for? That's right: to keep all of the rowers synchronized—he set the beat to which the rowers were to row. CPUs are somewhat like the galley slaves in *Ben Hur*, and a special chip on every motherboard, called the **clock chip**, is like the guy at the front of the boat.

The clock chip is a crystal that oscillates at a certain frequency when electricity is applied to it, providing the *system speed*. Each click of the clock is measured in millions or billions of cycles per second. One cycle per second is a **hertz (Hz)**, one million cycles per second is a **megahertz (MHz)**, and one billion cycles per second is a **gigahertz (GHz)**.

The system speed provides the default rhythm for the system, meaning that data and commands flow on the clicks of the clock. Almost everything runs at some factor or multiple of the system speed. A sound card, for example, can send or receive data at 33 MHz, a number one-third or one-fourth the speed of a typical system. The frontside bus that governs the flow of data from the CPU to RAM and vice versa, on the other hand, in many systems runs at twice or even four times the speed of the system clock.

For all you Gen X and Y folks out there who've never seen *Ben Hur*, do yourself a favor. Put this book down right now and go rent a copy. It's epic cinema like they don't make any more and a fine, timeless story.

Introduction to PC Hardware and Troubleshooting

● **Figure 2.1** Speed marked on a CPU

Because the CPU does the vast majority of the work in a PC, processor manufacturers have worked very hard over the years to crank up the internal processing speeds of CPUs. A modern CPU runs at many, many times the speed of the system crystal, but always on a multiple. The original Pentium 4, for example, ran internally at 1.3 GHz on a 100 MHz system clock, a multiple of 13. All CPUs have a maximum speed, and that speed is marked (usually fairly clearly) on the CPU itself, as shown in Figure 2.1.

To achieve speed gains over time, CPU manufacturers generally do three things. First, they simply get better at producing a specific model of CPU, and that refinement pays off in speed gains. Second, manufacturers reduce the physical size of a CPU, which enables them to reduce the amount of voltage needed to run the CPU, which in turn reduces the heat produced by the processor. Then the manufacturer can crank up the core speed of the processor without fear of overheating, and you can run your games at super speeds. Everybody's happy!

> Manufacturers crank up the speeds on models over time and then phase out the earlier, slower models. The Intel Celeron initially ran at 266 MHz, for example, but as of this writing, you can't find a new processor that runs slower than 1.2 GHz.

Processor Packages

The CPU **package** is the form factor of the chip: its shape, size, and external features. CPUs come in a wide assortment of packages. Why so many different looks? There are a number of reasons. First, as CPUs became faster and smarter, they used more pins to link them to the motherboard. A CPU with more pins is almost always more modern than one with fewer. Second, newer, more advanced CPUs tend to run hotter than older ones. For the first 10 years of the PC, CPUs did not even have cooling fans, but as manufacturers added more and more transistors to each chip, heat began to become a serious problem. In addition to adding metal heat sinks and chip-top fans, CPU makers got creative, producing CPUs with some really strange packages, the most famous being the slot-type **single-edge cartridge (SEC)** introduced in the mid-1990s. The illustration shows a popular CPU that used this package: the Intel Pentium II. SEC-style CPUs are on the wane.

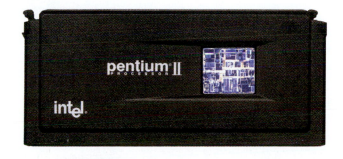

● Intel Pentium II SEC package

Don't assume just because two CPUs are of the same make and model that they share the same package type. Figure 2.2 shows two Pentium 4 chips. Note the different packages. Both packages are variations of what is generically referred to as a **pin grid array (PGA)** because of the tiny golden wires sticking out the underside of the CPU. Almost all current CPUs from both Intel and AMD come in some form of PGA package.

Each of these different CPU packages has a name, as do the different types of sockets used for each. The names of modern sockets usually reflect the number of pins in the corresponding packages. For example, the two P4s in the figure are examples of a 423-pin package (on the right) and a 478-pin package (on the left). The sockets that accept those chips are called 423 sockets and 478 sockets, respectively.

Intel processors will not work in sockets or slots designed for AMD processors, and the reverse is true as well. You should be able to determine the likely model of processor—including the manufacturer—by glancing at a motherboard. Table 2.1 compares recent models of Intel and AMD CPUs by their speed ranges and packages. Note that both AMD and Intel change their CPU specifications more often than they change the model names, so you cannot rely on the model name alone to tell you whether a chip will (a) be the speed you want or need, or (b) fit your particular motherboard.

● **Figure 2.2**   Two P4 chips with different PGA packages

Table 2.1	Comparison of CPU Speeds and Packages	
Make/Model	**Speed Range**	**Package**
Intel Pentium II	233–450 MHz	242-pin SEC
Intel P2 Celeron	266–433 MHz	242-pin SEC
Intel Pentium III	450–1266 MHz	242-pin SEC or 370-pin PGA
Intel P3 Celeron	300–766 MHz	242-pin SEC or 370-pin PGA
Intel Early Pentium 4	1.4–2 GHz	423-pin PGA
Intel Late Pentium 4	2–3 GHz	478-pin PGA
Intel P4 Celeron	800 MHz–2.2 GHz	478-pin PGA
AMD Athlon	500 MHz–1.4 GHz	242-pin SEC[1] or 462-pin PGA[2]
AMD Athlon XP	1.5–2.2 GHz	462-pin PGA
AMD Duron	600 MHz–1.3 GHz	462-pin PGA

[1]The AMD SEC cartridge was better known as Slot A and was not compatible with the Intel SEC CPUs.
[2]The AMD 462-pin CPU is more commonly known as Socket A.
[3]Athlon XPs use a model numbering system that gives the speed of an equivalent Intel processor instead of the true clock speed. For example, the Athlon XP 2800+ is touted by AMD to process as fast as an Intel Pentium 4 running at 2.8 GHz. The actual clock speeds for these processors are lower.

Five Ways to Identify a CPU

Identifying your CPU means knowing the manufacturer, the model, the speed, and the package. How do you get that information? Well, there are five ways to do this:

First, most versions of Windows have a **System Information tool**, which you can open by choosing Start | Programs | Accessories | Systems Tools | System Information. This will tell you some of the information you need to identify your CPU, though not all of it (see Figure 2.3).

Another way to find information on your CPU is to right-click the My Computer icon on your desktop and choose Properties; this opens the System Properties dialog box. The information here is often more complete. The System Properties dialog box in Figure 2.4 shows the make, model, and speed of the CPU. Unfortunately, not all processors reveal their speeds even here, as Figure 2.5 demonstrates.

Try This!

Comparing CPUs

AMD and Intel are in a constant battle to have the fastest and cleverest CPU on the market. One result is that computer system vendors have a range of CPUs for you to choose from when customizing a system. So, how do you know what you can and should choose? Try this:

1. Surf over to one of the major computer vendors' websites; `dell.com`, `gateway.com`, `hp.com`, and `ibm.com` all have customization features on their sites.

2. Select a low-end desktop from the available offerings and pretend you're considering purchasing it. Select the customization option and record the CPU choices you're given and the price differentials involved. Note which CPU comes as the default choice. Is it the fastest one? The slowest?

3. Now start again, only this time select a high-end model. Again choose to customize it as if you're a potential purchaser. Record the CPU choices you get with this model, the price differentials, and which choice is the default.

4. Finally, do an Internet search for benchmarking results on the fastest, slowest, and at least one other of the CPU choices you found. What differences in performance do you find? How does that relate to the differences in price?

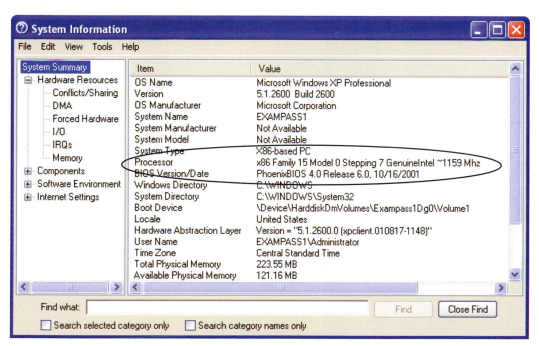

• **Figure 2.3**   The System Information tool provides some information about your processor.

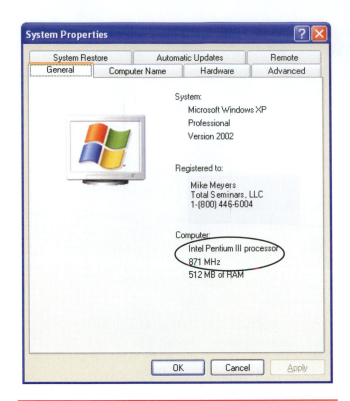

Figure 2.4 Informative System Properties dialog box (Windows XP)

Figure 2.5 Less informative System Properties dialog box (Windows 2000)

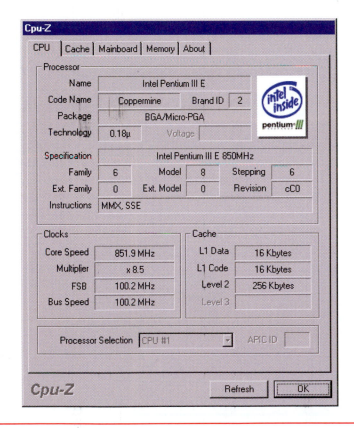

Figure 2.6 CPU-Z in action

Another approach is to shut down the PC, open the system unit, yank the fan off the CPU, and look at it. This is a bit of work, and not without risk, but it is definitive.

Yet another approach is to reboot the PC and watch for the CPU information to scroll by—modern PCs all display this information during the boot sequence. This, too, is not the most convenient way to receive detailed CPU information.

A fifth option is to use a CPU identification program. There are a number of these available. My personal favorite is CPU-Z, a handy piece of freeware that does a very nice job of identifying most CPUs. As shown in Figure 2.6, it will almost always tell you the manufacturer, model, speed, and package—plus a lot of other information that you'll probably never need. You can download a copy of CPU-Z at www.cpuid.com.

Introduction to PC Hardware and Troubleshooting

Identifying the Type of CPU in Your PC

Try to determine the type of CPU in your PC using the five methods just discussed. Then compare the results from these different methods to see which one worked best for your system.

To complete this exercise, you will need the following:

- A working PC running Windows
- Paper and pen or pencil
- Screwdrivers (Phillips and straight-slot) and an antistatic wrist strap if you do the optional Step 6.

Step 1

Write down the four pieces of information that you want to determine about your CPU: the manufacturer, the model, the speed, and the package. Create a table like the one here (or just use this one) on a blank sheet of paper, with a row for each of the four facts you need and a column for each of the five methods you will try.

	System Information	My Computer Properties	Physical Inspection	Reboot	CPU-Z
Manufacturer					
Model					
Speed					
Package					

Step 2

Choose Start | Programs | Accessories | System Tools | System Information to open the System Information tool. Fill in your chart with whatever information this gives you.

Step 3

Right-click the My Computer icon on your desktop and select Properties to open the System Properties dialog box (refer back to Figures 2.4 and 2.5 to see examples of this dialog box). Fill in your chart with the information provided there.

Step 4

Reboot your PC and watch for the CPU information to appear. This information may scroll by quickly, but most PCs will let you pause the boot process by pressing the Pause/Break key. Does your PC allow you to pause the reboot? If it doesn't, you may need to reboot more than once to record all of the information. Add to your chart all of the information you can get this way before you can't stand to reboot again.

```
PhoenixBIOS 4.0 release 6.0
Copyright 1985-2000 Phoenix Technologies Ltd.
All Rights Reserved


CPU = Pentium III  500MHz
640K System RAM Passed
47M Extended RAM Passed
USB upper limit segment address:  EEFE
Mouse initialized
```

Step 5

Launch your web browser and browse to www.cpuid.com. Download a copy of CPU-Z and install it on your computer. Installation consists of nothing more than unzipping the three small files that comprise the program into a single folder on your hard drive.

Double-click the executable (CPUZ.EXE) to run the program. Add the information you find to your chart.

Step 6

The final method mentioned is to shut down your PC, open the system unit, and inspect the CPU. However, removing a CPU can be a risky proposition. If you're not already familiar with how to do this, you should skip this step until you have read the CPU removal and insertion instructions later in this chapter. Even then, you should proceed with care and ask for assistance if you're not sure about something.

Step 7

Compare the results of the five methods. Did you get any contradictory information? Which method seems to be the most accurate? Which one was the easiest?

Motherboards

The typical motherboard supports a very limited number of CPUs. These limitations are based on the socket type, the CPU speed, and possibly other, more complex issues such as the CPU voltage. Failure to verify all of these will absolutely guarantee a rather nasty, smoky, and expensive CPU installation experience.

Read the Motherboard Book

The first place to check for information on a motherboard is the **motherboard book**. A motherboard book is a special booklet printed by the motherboard manufacturer that describes in great detail all of the technical aspects of the motherboard. If you purchase a new motherboard, you'll find the book inside the box with the motherboard. Most motherboard books come in a 5-inch by 7-inch format with a nice, shiny cover that advertises that specific motherboard. If the motherboard packaging does not include a manual, check the CD-ROM that came with the board.

If you don't have the motherboard book, open the system and look on the motherboard. In all but the rarest cases, motherboard makers print the make and the model of the motherboard on the board itself, though you may have to do a little searching and moving of cables to locate this text. There are a limited number of motherboard makers, so look for names like ABIT, Asus, Epox, Gigabyte, Iwill, MSI, and Tyan. If you locate one of these names, look for some numbers and letters nearby. That is the motherboard's model number. Write it down!

If you can locate the make and model number, you're in luck. Every motherboard maker provides excellent, if not downright exhaustive, documentation on each of its motherboards. If you cannot locate the make and model on the board, you're probably out of luck. Try taking the entire system to the place where you intend to buy the CPU to see if a professional can help you.

Inside Information

Motherboard Book Versus Instruction Manual

Don't confuse the motherboard book with the instruction manual or user's guide that comes with many OEM systems. The user's guide describes only issues like opening the system unit and installing a keyboard—it won't help with more complex issues like motherboard-CPU compatibility. If you can't find a motherboard book for your system, odds are good that either the motherboard book is lost, or you never got one in the first place. Most OEMs (Dell, Gateway, IBM, and so on) do not provide a motherboard book with their systems.

Determine What Type of CPU Your Motherboard Supports

Once you have the necessary documentation for your motherboard, your next step is to determine what type of CPU your motherboard supports. Every motherboard made since the mid-1990s supports *either* an AMD *or* an Intel CPU. Each maker has unique sockets used only for their CPUs, so the brand and socket type are closely connected. Check your motherboard documentation—it will clearly advertise the brand and socket type that your motherboard supports.

6VMM Motherboard

Summary Of Features	
Form Factor	• 20.6 cm x 24.4 cm Micro ATX size form factor, 4 layers PCB.
CPU	• Socket 370 processor Intel Pentium® *!!!* 100/133MHz FSB, FC-PGA Intel Celeron™ 66MHz FSB, FC-PGA VIA Cyrix® III 100/133MHz FSB, CPGA • 2nd cache in CPU (Depend on CPU)

• Brand/socket information as found in a motherboard book

Be sure to check the socket type of the CPU you're considering. Many makes and models of CPUs come in two or more socket types, so you cannot rely entirely on the make and model of a CPU to determine whether your motherboard supports it. The Pentium 4, to take an example from Table 2.1, comes in two completely incompatible socket types: the older Socket 423 and the more recent Socket 478. Too many techs have glanced through a motherboard book, seen the words "Pentium 4," and gone out and purchased a CPU that won't fit in their motherboard. Not only is this a really embarrassing mistake, but if the store has a restocking charge, it can be an expensive one too.

Just as some CPU chips come in more than one socket type, some sockets accept more than one model of CPU. For example, during the time when the Intel Pentium III and the equivalent Celeron were popular, they both used the venerable Socket 370, and many—but not all—motherboards would accept either one. The bit of motherboard book documentation shown in Figure 2.7 displays a motherboard that can support quite a few different processors.

Once again turn to your documentation, this time to verify the range of CPU speeds that your motherboard can handle. Most motherboards accept only a rather narrow range of speeds.

Speed is a very dangerous area because all CPUs actually have two speed settings: the motherboard speed and the CPU multiplier. Most motherboards handle these two speed settings automatically. However, some motherboards provide the ability to set these two values manually using jumpers or switches on the motherboard. If your motherboard documentation starts to mention settings like these, verify that the jumpers are set to something with a name like "automatic," "jumperless," or "jumperfree." Failure to set the speed correctly could at best cause the CPU to fail, and at

Most stores that sell CPUs will also install one for a nominal charge.

If you take a peek around the typical computer store, you may see CPU-conversion devices that enable a motherboard to accept a CPU with a different socket type than that the one it was designed to use. Although these devices do work, they are often problematic. In my opinion the results are not worth the effort. You still won't be able to use an AMD CPU in an Intel system, or vice versa.

Chapter 1 Introduction
Summary of Features

Form Factor	• 30.4cm x 20.5cm ATX size form factor, 4 layers PCB.
Motherboard	• GA-7VTXE/GA-7VTXH Motherboard
CPU	• Socket A processor

AMD Athlon™/Athlon™ XP/ Duron™ (K7)
128K L1 & 256K/64K L2 cache on die
200/266MHz FSB and DDR bus speeds (PCI 33MHz)

• Supports 1.4GHz and faster

• **Figure 2.7**   This motherboard can accept many different CPUs.

worst literally send it up in smoke. Proceed with caution—or if you need to do so, give the CPU to a professional to install.

Step1-1: CPU Speed Setup

The clock ratio can be switched by CK_RATIO and refer to below table.

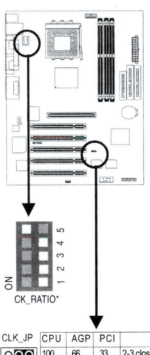

O: ON / X :OFF

RATIO	1	2	3	4	5
AUTO(Default)	X	X	X	X	O
5x	O	O	X	O	X
5.5x	X	O	X	O	X
6x	O	X	X	O	X
6.5x	X	X	X	O	X
7x	O	O	O	X	X
7.5x	X	O	O	X	X
8x	O	X	O	X	X
8.5x	X	X	O	X	X
9x	O	O	X	X	X
9.5x	X	O	X	X	X
10x	O	X	X	X	X
10.5x	X	X	X	X	X
11x	O	O	O	O	X
11.5x	X	O	O	O	X
12x	O	X	O	O	X
>=12.5x	X	X	O	O	X

CK_RATIO*

CLK_JP	CPU	AGP	PCI	
1 O O O	100	66	33	2-3 close
1 O O O	133	66	33	1-2 close

The system bus frequency can be switched at 100/133MHz by adjusting system jumper (CLK_JP). (The internal frequency depend on CPU.)

• Manual jumper settings. Note the Auto option.

Most motherboards no longer provide jumpers or switches to let you manually change these settings. Instead, most motherboards provide manual speed settings in your System Setup program—read all about your System Setup program in Chapter 4.

Almost all motherboards set the voltage for you automatically, but you will run into the occasional motherboard that provides manual voltage settings.

Be warned: Improper voltage settings can *destroy* a CPU! Check for manual settings, and if you find them, either set them to "automatic" or, better yet, find a professional to set them.

3. HARDWARE SETUP

2) Voltage Settings (VIO/VIO1)

VIO allows you to select the voltage supplied to the clock generator and VIO1 (for overclocking only) allows you to select the voltage supplied to the chipset and DDR DIMM modules. The default voltage should be used for better system reliability.

Setting	VIO1		Setting	VIO
2.7 Volt	[1-2] (default)		3.30 Volt	[1-2] (default)
2.9 Volt	[2-3]		3.56 Volt	[2-3]
2.8 Volt	[3-4]		3.45 Volt	[3-4]

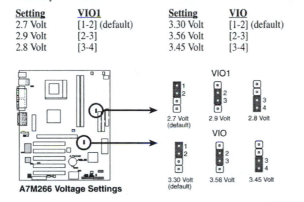

A7M266 Voltage Settings

WARNING! Using a higher voltage may help when overclocking but may result in the shortening of your computer component's life. It is strongly recommended that you leave these settings on their default.

- Voltage settings on an older Athlon motherboard

There is one final issue to consider when making a CPU upgrade decision for an existing system: Is it worth it? In most cases, upgrading the CPU in an existing motherboard offers only a small improvement in performance. Additionally, it is often difficult or impossible to even find a replacement CPU for an older system (anything pre–Pentium III).

 Many motherboards can be coaxed into using a CPU with a higher speed or different voltage by flashing the BIOS. You will learn all about the BIOS and how to flash it later in this book.

■ Installing and Upgrading CPUs

When installing or upgrading the CPU on a motherboard, you must check four features: the brand and socket type, the model, the speed, and the voltage. The CPU you choose to install must match the motherboard in these four respects for the CPU to work in your system.

To make a CPU functional in the PC requires installation of both the CPU itself and the proper cooling assembly to avoid overheating. This section walks you through CPU installation; the next section completes the picture, walking you through the procedure to attach a heat sink and fan assembly. Let's get to work!

 The first Athlon processors that fit Slot A and the Pentium II processors for Slot 1 came with an attached heat sink and fan. That made installation a snap!

Installing a CPU

Installing a new CPU is a pretty straightforward affair, requiring only a little research (for compatibility, as noted earlier) and common sense. Upgrading an existing PC with a new processor requires you to remove the old CPU as well.

To complete this excercise you will need the following:

- A PC with a CPU and motherboard
- A straight-slot screwdriver if removing an older CPU fan and heat sink assembly
- An antistatic wrist strap
- Some antistatic plastic or foam

Step 1

First, you must remove the fan and heat sink assembly. Some CPU fan and heat sink assemblies, like the one shown in the following illustration, can be removed relatively easily by flipping two release levers. Other assemblies require a screwdriver and some serious force to pry them off the connectors.

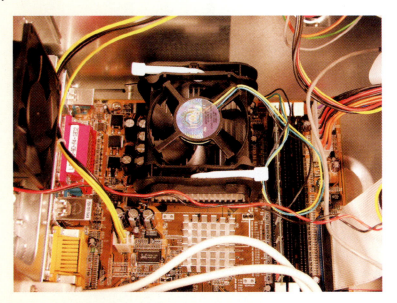

I'd love to show you how to remove every type of CPU fan and heat sink assembly available, but given that there are literally hundreds of different methods, that's impossible. Here you can see an assembly that would need to be removed using a screwdriver.

Most slot-style CPUs come with an attached fan and heat sink assembly. Although you can remove the fan from most such assemblies, there's usually little reason to do so.

As you remove the CPU fan assembly, you may notice a white paste on the top of the CPU chip, as shown in the illustration. That is **thermal compound**. This compound is designed to improve heat transfer between the CPU and the fan assembly. Try to avoid getting any on you (something that's all too easy to do).

Step 2

After you have removed the CPU fan and heat sink assembly, carefully unplug the fan's power connector from the motherboard. This step works the same for both socketed and slotted CPUs. Make a mental note of where the connector goes because you'll soon plug in the new CPU fan's power connector in that same spot.

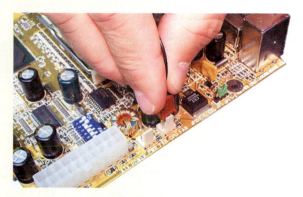

Step 3

Once the CPU fan and heat sink are off, the next step is to remove the CPU itself. If by any chance you took off the fan without a wrist strap, by all means put one on now!

To remove a socketed CPU, pull the small lever arm on the side slightly away from the CPU and then pull up. The arm should move easily slightly past 90 degrees. Once the arm is all the way up, grab the edges of the CPU and lift straight up, keeping the CPU

as horizontal as possible. Twisting the CPU as you lift it will cause the pins underneath to bend or (gasp!) break off, rendering the CPU useless. Set the CPU down *gently* on some antistatic plastic or foam.

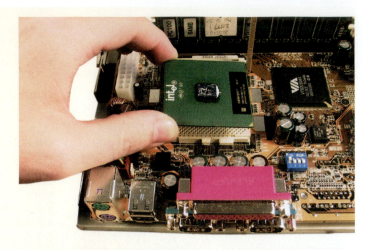

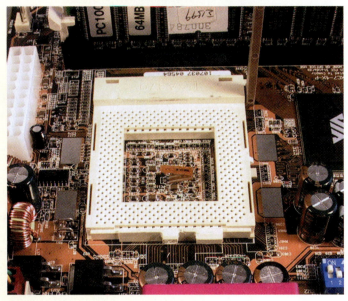

Many slotted CPUs are snapped into a bracket, as shown in the following illustration. The CPU has a pair of small latches on a brace that you need to flip to unlock the brackets. Other slotted CPU motherboards have no bracket, and you simply lift out the CPU. Brackets or not, the CPU should come out fairly easily. Just grab the edges of the processor and gently rock the CPU lengthwise while you exert upward pressure.

Step 4

Store the old CPU in a safe place—you never know if you might need it again, and at the very least you now have the beginnings of an old CPU collection, virtually a requirement if you aspire to become a computer hardware geek. Now you're ready to install a new CPU.

Step 5

Begin the installation process by taking the new CPU out of its carrying case or plastic bag. Hold the CPU by the edges—*do not touch any of the pins or contacts.*

Sockets and slots have guides to help you orient the CPU properly. On the sockets, look for some missing pinholes on one or two of the corners. Slots have an off-center ridge. It is thus impossible to install a CPU incorrectly, although you can push really, really hard and break something.

Orientation corners
on a socketed CPU

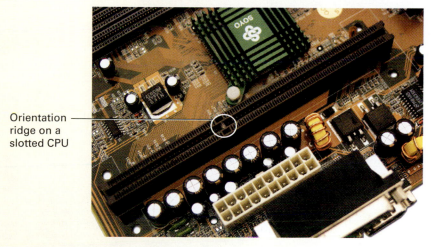

Orientation
ridge on a
slotted CPU

Step 6

To insert a socketed CPU, gently align the pins on the chip with the holes in the socket, using the missing pins in the corner as your guide. When you have the CPU lined up, gently *drop* it into the socket. Again, if you do this right, you don't have to push.

If you aligned the pins properly, the CPU will be flush against the socket, with no pins visible. If you can see pins, or if the CPU is not completely flush, *gently* slide the CPU around until it drops in. If the CPU still has not dropped into the socket, double-check the location of the corner with the missing pins and try again. If the chip still won't drop in, inspect it to see if there are any bent pins. Use a mechanical pencil (with the lead removed!) to straighten up any bent pins *very gently*. Once the CPU is in, resecure the lever arm.

To insert a slotted CPU, orient the slot ridge with the CPU notch and then push down firmly. Some slots have brackets that snap around the CPU automatically once you get the CPU fully in, but others have no brackets and are secured by the slot itself.

Note: If your slotted CPU came with a detached fan and heat sink assembly, a fairly rare occurrence, read the next section before you do this step! You need to install the fan and heat sink on slotted CPUs before you insert the CPU into the slot on the motherboard.

You should have no exposed contacts on the CPU. Do a visual check. If you see contacts or otherwise have trouble inserting the CPU, check the orientation to make certain you're installing it properly and then use a little more force when you push down to install. At this point, you're done with the installation of the CPU. Your next stop is cooling, so read on!

■ Select and Install the Proper Heat Sink and Fan Assembly

Because all Intel and AMD microprocessors run too hot for their packaging to handle, you need to install a cooling system after you install the processor. For mainstream computers, the cooling system of choice is a combination of two components: a heat sink to pull excess heat away from the CPU core and a fan to draw the heat from the heat sink.

Intel retail CPUs come with a decent heat sink and fan combination, but most OEM Pentium III, Celeron, and Pentium 4 processors come bare. All AMD processors, retail or OEM, come bare. You therefore need to know how to select the right heat sink and fan for your processor.

A good heat sink and fan combination combines sufficient airflow with a relatively low noise output. You'll find plenty of solutions (and opinions) on either side of the noise debate, but I tend to fall in the middle. I want the CPU cooled enough not to cause problems and quiet enough not to be annoying.

Although both Intel and AMD processors have automatic shutdown features that kick in if the processors get too hot, these technologies don't always work—and when they fail, the CPU goes up in smoke. Selecting the proper cooling system for a CPU and installing it correctly are essential skills all techs must master. Even a small error in installation can cause a CPU to overheat a little bit and cause random system crashes and general instability. I can't stress how important it is to get this right.

Heat Sinks

A heat sink snaps into place directly on top of the CPU and draws heat from the core of the processor up copper or aluminum vanes to be dissipated by the fan. Two basic styles of heat sink currently compete in the market: traditional fat-vaned models and the newer thin-vaned ones. The advantage of the fatter vaning is greater strength and lower cost. The thin-vaned heat sinks dissipate more heat, but cost more and are very delicate; it's disturbingly easy to bend or break them.

Aside from the technology, you need to consider two factors when selecting a heat sink: form factor and installation.

Because the heat sink snaps directly onto the socket or CPU, you must use a heat sink designed for the particular processor you have chosen. Snapping a Socket 370 heat sink onto a Socket 462 AMD Duron, for example, will crack the CPU. This is not a good thing. The only way to make sure that

Thermal compound is known by many names among techs, such as thermal paste, heat dope, and, my editor's favorite, *nasty white goo*. Manufacturers of the product generally call it thermal compound.

you have the right heat sink for your motherboard and processor is to check the manufacturer's labeling. Most heat sinks do not carry markings indicating which sockets or CPUs they fit. Read the label!

Installation involves two issues. First, you sometimes have to use a remarkable amount of force to attach a heat sink and fan assembly to a socket. Be ready to flex some muscle *without* sacrificing control—otherwise you can find yourself stabbing your motherboard with the screwdriver you're trying to use as a lever. Second, you should make certain to apply a small amount of evenly spaced thermal compound between the processor core and the heat sink. Failure to do this will create a less-than-optimal connection between the CPU and the heat sink and can cause the CPU to overheat and create system instability or, in the worst-case scenario, die.

Although you can purchase a heat sink as a separate unit, most people buy a heat sink and fan combination or package. So let's look at fan issues and then get to installation.

Fans

Fan specs encompass three basic measurements: size, airflow, and noise. Most fans for socketed processors are 60 mm in size, although you can find high-performance fans that are 70 or even 80 mm. Fans for Slot 1 and Slot A processors generally run smaller, more like 50 mm, although you can certainly find 60-mm ones as well. Bigger fans are more expensive than smaller fans, but generally move more air. Your first consideration is getting a fan of the correct size for your heat sink; then if you have options, you can select the one that works best with your budget.

The defining purpose of a fan is to move air, so not surprisingly, fans are rated according to the amount of air they can move, measured in **cubic feet per minute (CFM)**. A typical fan for socketed CPUs pushes air at 22 CFM; high-performance models can crank out 45 CFM or even more. Slotted CPU fans are more modest, moving 10 to 12 CFM on the average.

It seems like a no-brainer to go for the higher-performance fans because the price difference is not that much ($15 as opposed to $5, for example), and you'll run less risk of overheating the processor. More is better, right? Unfortunately, the more air pushed by a fan, usually the more noise the fan generates.

Fan noise is measured in A-adjusted **decibels (dBA)**. A relatively silent fan puts out about 20 dBA, whereas a noisy fan can pump out double that or more. Many system designers consider 39 dBA the magic upper limit for the whole PC, including the CPU fan, so the fans at the high end of air flow will burst through this ceiling all by themselves. Walking into the office of an enthusiast is sometimes akin to walking into a vacuum cleaner showroom!

The best of the fan/heat sink assemblies offer heat sensors with variable-speed fans. When your system is working away at something not particularly taxing, such as word processing, web surfing, or a game of solitaire, the fan runs slowly and quietly. When your system is doing phenomenally complex computing, such as pipelining in Tony Hawk's Extreme Skateboarding game, the fan will crank up to match the increased heat output by the CPU. Cool!

A decibel is a unit to measure noise. dBA is an acronym for decibels on the A scale, which is weighted to simulate how we perceive sound in the middle range. A change in volume of 5 dBA is considered noticeable. An increase of 10 dBA over existing noise levels is perceived as doubling the loudness. The U.S. EPA identifies 85 dBA as the threshold of risk for potential hearing loss.

Comparing CPU Coolers

Knowing what size and type of CPU cooler assembly to choose for your system can be a challenge, but if you value the life of your expensive new CPU chip, it's important to be able to choose well. Try this:

1. Do a couple of online searches on the topic of CPU coolers for sale. Search on "CPU coolers" as well as "CPU fan" and "CPU heat sink" and finally, add "overclocking" to one of your searches. See if you can find one for under $10, and one for over $35.

2. Identify the two most common materials found in the heat sink part of the assembly. See if you can find a cooler assembly that doesn't have a cube-shaped heat sink.

3. Compare at least four different fans that are part of a CPU cooler assembly. Can you find one with a noise level under 20 dBA? Over 50 dBA? Examine the noise level in relation to the fan's other specs, in particular its fan speed (RPM) and airflow (CFM). Can you see any correlation?

Step-by-Step 2.3

Installing a Fan and Heat Sink Assembly

In Step-by-Step 2.2, you installed a CPU into a socket or slot on a motherboard. Now you're ready to take the installation to its conclusion, installing a heat sink and fan assembly.

To complete this exercise, you will need the following:

- A PC with a motherboard with a socketed CPU installed
- A heat sink and fan
- A straight-slot screwdriver
- An antistatic wrist strap

| **Step 1** | Attach the antistatic wrist strap to the power supply or a bare piece of metal on the frame of the system unit. Make certain that the power is disconnected from the AC outlet before continuing. |

| **Step 2** | Double-check that your heat sink and fan work with the specific model and speed of CPU installed in the motherboard. As mentioned earlier, using the wrong heat sink and fan assembly can physically break a CPU. |

| **Step 3** | Installing heat sink and fan assemblies can be quite tricky and require a lot of force. Attaching the metal clips to the socket takes a bit of practice to perfect. To minimize potential difficulties, do a test run of the installation first to see how the fan fits before trying it with the CPU chip in place. |

Next, with the CPU in place, check to see if the heat sink has come pre-doped with a small bit of thermal compound. If it has, you may need to remove a protective bit of tape to be sure. If the fan isn't pre-doped, you'll need to acquire some thermal compound. Many OEM fans come with a small tube, which should be plenty for one installation. You can also buy compound at any computer or electronics store.

To apply the thermal compound, spread a *thin* film over the top of the CPU—not the entire CPU, just the center part that sticks up higher than the rest. That's the area where the actual circuitry is, and thus the area that needs maximized heat transfer. You could put the heat dope on the fan, but if you're applying it yourself, it's more accurate to apply it directly to the CPU, rather than guessing where on the heat sink the CPU will touch. If you put on too much thermal compound, it will squish out the sides and make a mess.

After you've applied the thermal compound, install the heat sink and fan assembly on top of the CPU. For socketed CPUs, get your screwdriver and attach the fan to the clips on the socket. Make certain that you have the heat sink fully over the CPU core; otherwise, your CPU may overheat at a time of peak performance.

Slotted CPUs usually have four connection points for the heat sink and fan assembly. Simply align the points and push them through.

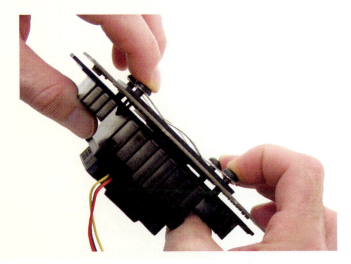

Step 6

Once the assembly is secured, plug the fan's power cable into the proper connector on the CPU. The connector will be close to the CPU socket and is often conveniently marked on the motherboard with the words *CPU fan*. The fan's connector is designed so that you should not be able to install it improperly.

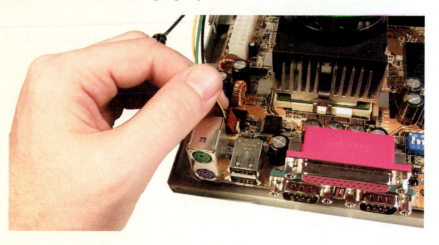

Step 7

Now for the acid test: reboot the system. If you've installed the CPU correctly, the system will boot properly. Don't worry if the fan starts to spin, stops for a moment, and starts again—most PCs have a thermostat that controls the fan's spinning. If the system runs for more than a minute or two and the fan still doesn't start, turn off the system and check to make sure you have properly connected the fan's power.

All modern motherboards have safety features to prevent a CPU from cooking in the case of fan failure, as mentioned earlier. Most have an audible alarm—you'll know the sound when you hear it!

If the fan is spinning but the computer doesn't boot, check to make sure you don't have any jumpers set to manual. Finally, check to be sure you didn't somehow manage to install the CPU incorrectly—that's hard to do, but not impossible.

Chapter 2 Review

■ Chapter Summary

After reading this chapter and completing the exercises, you should understand the following facts about the CPU.

Describe the function of the central processing unit (CPU)

- A CPU is an electronic device that takes input and performs hundreds of different types of functions on that input. The collection of all the functions that a CPU can perform is called the CPU's instruction set. Commands sent to the CPU to tell the CPU to do something are called programs.

- Programs are loaded into RAM from the hard drive, and then the very fast RAM gives the CPU access to the programs.

- Any time multiple wires are used to connect two or more devices, those wires are called a bus. The bus that interconnects the CPU, Northbridge, and RAM is called the frontside bus.

Identify the right CPU for any motherboard

- To identify a CPU, you must know four key facts: the manufacturer, the model, the speed, and the package.

- Currently two companies compete virtually alone in the CPU business: Intel Corporation and Advanced Micro Devices, better known as AMD.

- The model is the name or number that the CPU maker gives a CPU with a particular set of characteristics. The latest Intel CPUs are the Pentium III, Celeron, Pentium 4, and Itanium. The latest AMD CPUs are the Athlon, Duron, Athlon XP, and Athlon MP.

- The clock chip is a crystal that oscillates at a certain frequency when electricity is applied to it, providing the system speed. Typical system speeds are 100 MHz and 133 MHz. Almost everything runs at some factor or multiple of the system speed.

- A modern CPU runs at a multiple of the speed of the system crystal. The original Pentium 4, for example, ran internally at 1.5 GHz on a 100 MHz system clock, a multiple of 15.

- "Package" is the computerese word for the form factor of a chip—that is, its shape, size, and

external features. CPUs have come in a wide assortment of packages, but two currently dominate the marketplace: SEC and PGA.

- Each of the different CPU packages has a name, as do the different types of sockets you snap them into. The names of modern sockets usually reflect the number of pins in the corresponding packages.

- You can identify the type of CPU in your computer in five ways: use the System Information tool, look in the System Properties dialog box, open the case and physically inspect the chip, read the information displayed on your screen during the boot process, or run a third-party utility such as CPU-Z.

- The typical motherboard supports a very limited number of CPUs. These limitations are based on the socket type, the CPU speed, and possibly other more complex issues such as CPU voltage. Read the motherboard book to verify the types of processor it supports.

Install and upgrade a CPU

- A CPU is extremely sensitive to ESD. Don't even think about performing work on a CPU without an antistatic wrist strap!

- The average motherboard provides a number of different voltages to support multiple CPU models. Almost all motherboards set the voltage for you automatically, but a few provide manual voltage settings. Be extremely cautious about setting these because improper voltage settings can destroy a CPU.

- When you remove a CPU from its carrying case or plastic bag, always hold the chip by the edges—do not touch any of the pins.

- Use the missing holes on one corner of the CPU socket to help orient the CPU properly when you insert it. Use the ridge near the center of the slot for slotted processors.

- If a CPU chip has bent pins, you can use a mechanical pencil (with the lead removed) to very gently straighten them.

- Push down firmly on SEC-style CPUs, but allow PGA processors to drop gently into place.

Select and install the correct heat sink and cooling fan assembly

- Heat sinks draw heat from the core of the processor up copper or aluminum vanes to be dissipated by the fan. Make certain to use the proper heat sink for your processor package or you risk breaking the CPU.

- Fans move air at rates measured in cubic feet per minute (CFM). Generally there's a trade-off when choosing a computer fan between an acceptable level of airflow and an acceptable level of noise.

- When mounting a fan assembly on top of a CPU chip, be sure to apply a thin film of thermal compound to the raised area of the CPU to improve heat transfer between the CPU and the heat sink.

Key Terms

clock chip *(32)*	hertz (Hz) *(32)*	package *(33)*
cubic feet per minute (CFM) *(48)*	instruction set *(29)*	pin grid array (PGA) *(34)*
decibels (dBA) *(48)*	megahertz (MHz) *(32)*	single-edge cartridge (SEC) *(33)*
frontside bus *(30)*	motherboard book *(38)*	System Information tool *(35)*
gigahertz (GHz) *(32)*	Northbridge *(30)*	thermal compound *(43)*

Key Term Quiz

Use terms from the Key Terms list to complete the following sentences. Not all terms will be used.

1. The _____ controls the system speed.

2. The Windows _____, found in System Tools under Accessories on the Start menu, can provide information to identify a system's CPU.

3. The form factor of a chip—that is, its shape, size, and external features—is referred to as the _____.

4. One cycle per second is called a/an _____.

5. The processor type with lots of tiny wires coming out the bottom is called a/an _____, and the type on a card that fits into a slot is called a/an _____.

6. Noise from your CPU fan is measured in _____, whereas a fan's ability to move air is measured in _____.

7. A typical system speed is 100 or 133 _____.

8. The _____ chip sits in between the CPU and RAM; the wires that connect all three are the _____.

9. The collection of all of the functions that a CPU can perform is called the CPU's _____.

10. You should always remember to add a little _____ between the CPU and the heat sink.

Multiple-Choice Quiz

1. What should you use to repair bent pins on a CPU chip?
   a. Screwdriver
   b. Empty mechanical pencil
   c. Paper clip
   d. Tweezers

2. Abit, Asus, and Gigabyte are the names of what?
   a. Motherboard makers
   b. CPU makers
   c. OEM systems
   d. AMD CPUs

3. Jake has an aging Intel SEC Celeron processor and wants to upgrade. He notices that the Athlon XP processors have dropped dramatically in

price and get great reviews from techs. His friend Joy says he should upgrade to the Athlon XP. Jean says he must choose an Intel CPU, so he should get a Pentium 4. Joe says either choice will require Jake to replace his motherboard. Who's right?

   a. Joy

   b. Joe

   c. Jean

   d. None of them

4. If you were advising Jake about upgrading his processor, where would you suggest he start?

   a. Look in the motherboard book to see what processors his motherboard can handle.

   b. E-mail the manufacturer of his motherboard to see what processors his motherboard can handle.

   c. Surf the Internet to Intel's website to see if he can hot-rod his old Celeron.

   d. Surf the Internet to AMD's website to find out about converters.

5. Bill bought a secondhand PC advertised as fast, but it seemed rather sluggish when he ran a game. He suspects that the processor was not set up correctly. Amy advises him to watch closely when booting the computer to see the processor settings and then open the case, remove the CPU fan, and check the actual chip to see if they match. Jody says he should download CPU-Z and run that utility. Which method will work?

   a. Only Amy's method will work.

   b. Only Jody's method will work.

   c. Both methods will work.

   d. Neither method will work. He needs to use the System Information tool.

6. Pentium 4 CPUs can come in which of the following packages? (Choose the best answer.)

   a. Socket 370, Socket A

   b. Socket 370, Socket 423

   c. Socket 423, Slot 1

   d. Socket 423, Socket 478

7. Athlon XP processors come in which of the following packages?

   a. Socket 370

   b. Socket 423

   c. Socket 462

   d. Slot A

8. Harry installed a new processor in his system, being careful to avoid ESD and adding a small film of thermal compound between the CPU core and the heat sink. When he turned on the system, however, it started to boot but then crashed, and he could smell the horrible dead electronics smell. The CPU had cooked. What did he do wrong?

   a. He forgot to plug in the power connector for the CPU fan.

   b. He forgot to plug in the thermal protection utility.

   c. He put the heat sink on backwards.

   d. He didn't get enough thermal compound between the CPU core and the heat sink.

9. How should you remove an SEC-type CPU?

   a. Grip it in the center and pull straight up.

   b. Grip it on the edges and gently rock it lengthwise.

   c. Slip a straight-slot screwdriver into the slot and gently pry it up.

   d. You can't. SEC CPUs always come as part of the motherboard.

10. What happens to the CPU if you break off one of the pins?

   a. The CPU is rendered useless.

   b. The CPU will be fine but will not run as fast as labeled.

   c. The CPU will be fine after you solder on a new pin.

   d. Nothing. Most of the pins are redundant.

11. How do you determine the manufacturer of a particular CPU?

   a. Memorize the various form factors. You should be able to tell by the shape of the package.

   b. All CPUs have numbers marked on the surface. You can do an Internet search on those numbers, and the CPU manufacturer's name will appear.

c. All CPUs have the manufacturer listed on the surface.

d. Look in the motherboard book.

12. John notices that Cindy keeps playing solitaire on her computer during break times. Where is solitaire running during those private interludes?

    a. In BIOS

    b. In RAM

    c. On the hard drive

    d. On the monitor

13. What four factors identify a CPU?

    a. Manufacturer, speed, manufacturing process, form factor

    b. Manufacturer, model, speed, manufacturing process

    c. Manufacturer, model, speed, package

    d. Form factor, model, speed, package

14. Butch walked into your office bragging about his new computer with a 1,000-megabyte processor. What does that mean?

    a. Butch has a great system.

    b. Butch has a large hard drive.

    c. Butch has a 1-gigabyte processor.

    d. Butch doesn't know the difference between megabytes and megahertz.

15. Emily bought a new 3-GHz Pentium 4 computer to record music with, but she was bothered by the sound when she turned on the system. The PC ran nicely but had a fairly loud hum that her microphone kept picking up. What should she do?

    a. Upgrade the processor.

    b. Upgrade the heat sink.

    c. Check and possibly replace the CPU fan.

    d. Check and possibly replace the microphone.

■ Essay Quiz

1. Write a paragraph setting out in your own words the steps in the process of installing a CPU. Include any safety measures or other cautionary instructions that apply.

2. Write a short essay describing the crucial differences between AMD and Intel processors.

3. What advice would you give someone wanting to upgrade a CPU? Write a short essay with *helpful* advice.

Lab Projects

• Lab Project 2.1

Good news! Your class has just received grant money for new CPUs. The only catch is that the donor stipulated that all of money has to be for upgrades, not new systems. Using the motherboard book or markings on the motherboard, determine what upgrades your system can handle.

• Lab Project 2.2

Word just arrived from Washington that today is National Switch Day. For most folks, that means switching positions so that the managers can learn what the workers struggle with, and the workers can learn about management issues. In your case, however, you get to switch computers!

More specifically, find out which of your classmates has a motherboard capable of handling your CPU. Remove your CPU and give it to that classmate. When one of your other classmates gives you a CPU, install it.

Be sure you record the make, model, speed, package, voltage, and so on, and also watch out for ESD!

3 RAM

"You can never be too rich or too thin—or have too much RAM."

—Mike Meyers' corollary to the famous quote by Wallis Simpson, the Duchess of Windsor

In this chapter, you will learn how to:

- **Describe how RAM functions in a PC**
- **Identify various RAM technologies used in PCs**
- **Explain the various ways in which RAM is packaged for use in a PC**
- **Install RAM in a PC**

Many folks are aware that something called **Random Access Memory (RAM)** is at work in their PCs, but very few know what RAM actually does. Properly functioning RAM, like properly functioning electricity, labors on quietly and efficiently in the background of our lives, never giving us a reason to consider how important it is. When something *does* go wrong with a system's RAM, however, everything grinds to a halt until a fix is found.

This chapter looks at RAM in detail. You'll become familiar with the various types of RAM used in PCs both past and present, and you'll tour the many types of RAM packages. You'll see many examples of actual RAM chips in PCs, so that you will be able to recognize the package type that your system needs. Finally, you'll learn how to tell when the RAM in your system needs help, and how to handle RAM properly when you need to intervene.

■ What Does RAM Do?

The CPU uses RAM as its active workspace. Programs stored on the hard drive need to be loaded into RAM to enable the CPU to swap data in and out quickly. Without RAM, the modern PC simply does not function.

You can conceptualize RAM as the CPU's short-term memory. If you wanted to solve a complex mathematical problem—a daily occurrence, right?—you'd most likely need to look it up in a book, get it into your short-term memory, and then solve it using your brainpower. The hard drive acts as the book, the RAM as the short-term memory. As you'll recall from Chapter 2, the CPU uses a helper chip, the *Northbridge*, for all of its communication with RAM. RAM has no direct connection to either the external data bus or the address bus; the Northbridge chip acts as the intermediary for all data transfers between RAM and the CPU. The CPU sends requests for data stored in RAM to the Northbridge chip via the address bus, and the Northbridge chip retrieves the data from RAM and drops it onto the external data bus for pickup by the CPU.

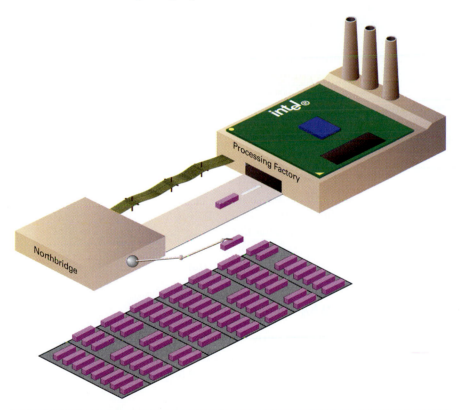

• The CPU uses the Northbridge to handle all communication with the RAM.

The CPU uses RAM to store active programs and data temporarily. As it changes data, the CPU tells the Northbridge to update that data in RAM. So, as you work on a document, such as a letter to your friend Sally, you can type merrily away and watch the data on the screen change to match what you're doing.

RAM does the job of storing programs just fine—but RAM also has a tiny problem! If your computer suddenly lost power, everything that you

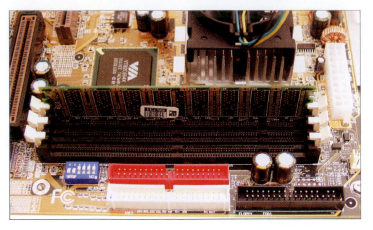

• **Figure 3.1** A motherboard with a stick of RAM. Two RAM slots are empty, allowing easy upgrading.

• Close-up of a stick of DRAM

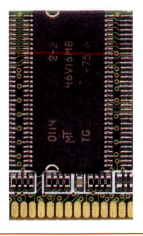

• Close-up of a RAM chip on a stick of RAM

typed would be irretrievably lost. RAM used in the PC is a *volatile* medium, meaning that it requires continuous electricity to hold data. Losing power for even a split second clears RAM completely.

To store data more or less permanently, you need to save it to some form of permanent, *nonvolatile* storage, such as a hard drive or a floppy disk. When you click the Save button in your word processing program, the CPU tells the Northbridge chip to send all that dynamically held data through the data bus to permanent storage on the hard drive.

RAM Sticks

Now that your recollection of how RAM operates in a PC has been refreshed, it's time to look at the actual physical manifestations of RAM in more detail. The RAM in a typical PC consists of one or more small circuit boards, called **sticks**, usually about 4 inches (13 cm) long. The average PC has at least one stick of RAM, although two, three, or four are not at all uncommon.

Figure 3.1 shows a cutout of a motherboard, with the green and gold backside of a RAM stick sitting in a slot.

If you look closely at those sticks of RAM, you'll see that they're covered with small chips. These chips are the actual physical location of the RAM. These chips work together to form the many millions of rows of 64-bit-wide RAM used in today's PCs.

RAM is structured in 64-bit-wide rows to optimize the flow of data into and out of the 64-bit-wide data bus on modern CPUs. The CPU tells the Northbridge to grab a row of RAM; then the Northbridge accesses all of the little chips on the RAM stick and places a 64-bit-wide chunk of data on the data bus.

Accessing RAM

Techs should understand the process of communication between the CPU and the Northbridge. You can't fix this, but memory addressing is handled in so many different ways in the PC that you should take a moment to grasp this cornerstone concept.

Given that RAM exists in the PC as millions and millions of 64-bit rows that can hold data, how does the CPU tell the Northbridge which row it wants at any given nanosecond? Anyone who answered "using the address bus!" gets a prize, but that's not the complete answer. To understand how the CPU uses the address bus, you need to know a *bit* of binary math (couldn't resist the pun!).

A Bit o' Binary

In the computer world, a device (a transistor, capacitor, wire, whatever) either holds or does not hold a charge. In most cases, a device holding a charge is said to represent a 1, and a device not holding a charge is said to represent a 0. This use of ones and zeros is a handy way to describe the state (charged or not charged) of devices in your system.

The CPU turns address wires on and off in certain patterns that represent specific memory addresses. The Northbridge interprets the signal, accesses the desired area of RAM, and places the data on the data bus. The possible combinations of on and off on three wires should help explain the concept. At any moment, the wires might all hold no charge, represented here as three zeros:

000

The wires might also all hold a charge, represented as three ones:

111

The three wires might also have a number of states other than all on or all off. Let's write all the possible combinations of on and off that might take place on three wires:

000
001
010
011
100
101
110
111

How many combinations are there for three wires? Eight. With only three wires, therefore, the CPU could tell the Northbridge to grab one of eight distinct rows of RAM, numbered from 0 to 7. If you use four wires, you double the number of combinations of on and off available. These possible four-wire combinations can be represented by the numbers 0000, 0001, 0010, 0011, and so on, up to 1111. So with a four-wire address bus, you get 16 distinct memory addresses. Got the concept?

I find the process of making a handful of separate chips manifest in the PC as millions of rows personally fascinating, but well beyond the scope of this book because the organization of RAM is not something you can fix. More importantly, current RAM works so well with modern motherboards that PC techs have almost no need to make fine adjustments to RAM settings unless they plan to tweak things for optimal performance. If you want to read more about such things, check out the Tech Files at my web site: www.totalsem.com.

Types of RAM Technologies

RAM manufacturers have developed many ways to hold data over the lifespan of the PC. Five technologies stand out because of their amazing longevity and market share; all are commonly known by their abbreviations: FPM, EDO, SDRAM, DDR SDRAM, and RDRAM. Although you'll find only the last three in any modern PC, as a tech you'll most likely be forced to deal with the earlier technologies as well.

Try This!

Working in Binary

It's very handy in the PC world to know the number of binary combinations for any given set of wires, transistors, and so on. The formula is $2^{(number\ of\ wires)} = Number\ of\ combinations$. For example, if you have 10 wires, you get $2^{10} = 1,024$ combinations.

Try using the Windows calculator to determine the maximum number of binary combinations for a given set of wires. For example, back in the previous chapter, we saw that most address buses have 32 wires. Each combination of ones and zeros on those 32 wires points to one byte of RAM. How many bytes of RAM can a CPU with 32 address bus wires support?

1. Fire up Windows Calculator by choosing Programs | Accessories | Calculator. When the application appears, you see the standard calculator, but a much more powerful one is available: choose View and select Scientific. The scientific calculator has about a million great uses for techs—calculating combinations is just one!

2. Because you want to know the number of combinations on 32 wires, you need to find out the answer to 2^{32}. Click the 2, then click the x^y button, then click 32, and then click = to see the answer.

It's useful for techs to understand the technologies of current RAM, if for no other reason than to be able to make informed recommendations to clients or potential clients when they solicit advice about computer purchases—plus the technologies make for scintillating conversations at geek parties!

We'll cover FPM and EDO memory technologies briefly as an introduction to the subject and to make the transition to later technologies easier to comprehend. You can't fix this stuff, but I promise it'll be interesting!

FPM RAM

RAM chips in early PCs were all 1 bit wide, but even then RAM commands had to be at least 8 bits wide. These early systems provided 8 bits at a time, with eight little RAM chips all nicely mounted on the motherboard. Every time the Northbridge asked for a byte of memory, each little RAM chip provided one of the necessary 8 bits.

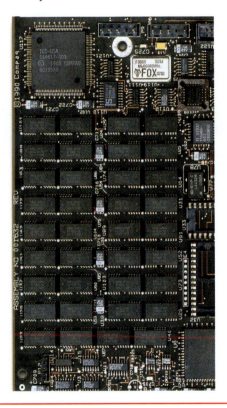

• Old RAM mounted on motherboard

On some older motherboards, you might see a ninth chip, the parity chip; it worked with the Northbridge to ensure data integrity.

Fast Page Mode (FPM) RAM enabled the Northbridge to access each bit of data very quickly, but required at least two clicks of the system clock to do so. The relatively low cost and high speed of FPM RAM compared to other technologies available at the time, however, made FPM RAM the dominant type of system RAM in PCs.

FPM RAM worked fantastically well for the first 10 years of the existence of the PC. But in the ongoing desire to make RAM faster, a number of technologies have appeared (and disappeared). The first of these FPM RAM replacements was Extended Data Output (EDO) RAM.

EDO RAM

The Northbridge chip accessed FPM RAM by engaging a pair of wires called the Row Array Strobe (RAS) and Column Array Strobe (CAS) in rapid sequence. To get a single row of RAM, the Northbridge needed to light up the RAS and CAS for each bit of data stored (hence, the need for multiple clock clicks per bit).

In this highly simplified example, if the Northbridge wanted row 5 on a RAM stick, it would light up in sequence: row 5, column 1; row 5, column 2; row 5, column 3; and so on until it got to the end of the row. This worked, but was not very efficient. The Northbridge kept lighting the same RAS wire while it lit different CAS wires.

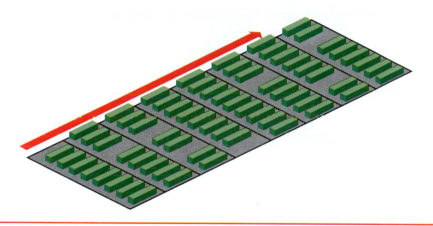

• The Northbridge accesses each row of RAM in sequence.

To remove this inefficiency, RAM makers invented a more advanced type of FPM RAM that lit the RAS wire only when the Northbridge moved to new row, speeding up RAM access substantially. That was EDO RAM: you could *extend* the amount of *data* you got *out* without relighting the RAS wire for each bit.

I'll bet you'd love to see a picture of an EDO chip. Well, it wouldn't do you a bit of good because EDO looked exactly the same as the older FPM RAM. This was a bit of a problem in the old days because motherboards used either one or the other—the different types of RAM were not interchangeable. We were very careful to put labels on our RAM back then!

Both FPM and EDO RAM shared one interesting feature: they were **asynchronous**, meaning they did not have a clock chip. When the CPU asked for a byte of information from RAM, the Northbridge chip would begin lighting the correct wires to get the data. This wire lighting was not an instantaneous process—it required the CPU to wait while the data was being fetched, usually around 10 to 30 clock cycles. The Northbridge couldn't force the data out of the RAM chips; it just waited until it saw the data appear on the data-out wires and then informed the CPU that the data was ready for it on the external data bus. What was the CPU doing while the data was being fetched? Nothing—nothing at all. The CPU was in a *wait state*.

Inside Information

Early Days

Way back when (before 1991), there was no chip called the Northbridge. The chip that acted as the interface between the CPU and RAM was referred to generically as the memory controller chip. The term Northbridge came into popular use after multiple chips on the motherboard were consolidated into two multi-function chips known as the Northbridge and Southbridge. The Northbridge has a number of jobs—taking care of RAM is only one. The Southbridge acts as the connection to other parts of the computer—we'll see more on the Southbridge in Chapter 5.

Both FPM and EDO RAM have long since been made obsolete by more advanced RAM types.

Back then, RAM came in a number of different speeds. Unlike a CPU, however, RAM had no clock, so RAM makers could not use terms like MHz to describe the speed of RAM; instead, they used the longest time that the user would have to wait for the RAM to produce data, measured in billionths of a second. A billionth of a second is a **nanosecond** (ns). A nanosecond is 1,000 times faster than a millisecond (ms). The smaller the speed in nanoseconds, the faster the RAM. The earliest FPM RAM used speeds in the 200 ns range; the last of the EDO RAM seen in PCs was as fast as 50 ns. This value was clearly printed right on the RAM chips (or on their storage bags).

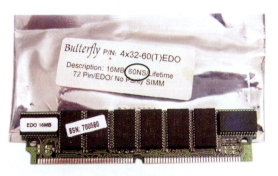

• RAM chips with ns rating printed on storage bag

Wait states were the bane of FPM and EDO RAM. The waiting alone was a total waste of CPU time—that part couldn't be helped—but in addition, there was no way to know *when* RAM would have the data ready. PC makers were forced to build in plenty of leeway to accommodate the longest possible time it might take for RAM to get the data—often far more than was needed. Because RAM wasn't tied to a clock like every other chip on the motherboard, there was no other way to handle this issue—until the introduction of SDRAM in the mid-1990s.

SDRAM

In the mid-1990s, RAM technology finally incorporated a clock, in **Synchronous Dynamic Random Access Memory (SDRAM)**. SDRAM shared the same organization as the earlier types of RAM, but for the first time the Northbridge could accurately predict the number of clock cycles needed for RAM to produce requested data, speeding RAM access dramatically.

As you might imagine, given that it has a clock speed, SDRAM speed is measured in hertz (Hz), just like CPU speed. SDRAM speeds generally matched the speed of the motherboard—that is, if the motherboard ran at 66 MHz, then you would need to use 66-MHz SDRAM. If the motherboard ran at 100 MHz, you would need 100-MHz SDRAM. This information was supplied with the motherboard documentation.

Memory	• 2 168-pin DIMM sockets.
	• Supports PC-100 / PC-133 SDRAM
	• Supports up to 1.0GB DRAM
	• Supports only 3.3V SDRAM DIMM

• Motherboard documentation showing the required SDRAM speed

DDR SDRAM

As its name implies, **Double Data Rate SDRAM (DDR SDRAM)** is SDRAM, but it can make two RAM accesses in each clock cycle, hence the "double." DDR SDRAM comes in four common speeds: 200, 266, 333, and 400 MHz.

DDR SDRAM is extremely popular today. Odds are good that unless you have a higher-end Intel Pentium 4 or better, the system you have in front of you uses DDR SDRAM. Again, the motherboard documentation will clearly state both the type of RAM and the speed it needs.

3. HARDWARE SETUP

3.5.1 General DIMM Notes
- DIMMs that have more than 18 chips are not supported on this motherboard.
- For the system CPU bus to operate at 200MHz/266MHz, use only PC1600-/PC2100-compliant DIMMs.
- ASUS motherboards support SPD (Serial Presence Detect) DIMMs. This is the memory of choice for best performance vs. stability.
- BIOS shows SDRAM memory on bootup screen.
- Single-sided DDR DIMMs come in 64, 128, and 256MB; double-sided come in 128, 256, and 512MB.

WARNING! Be sure that the DIMMs you use can handle the specified DDR SDRAM MHz or else bootup will not be possible.

- Motherboard documentation showing RAM type and speed

RDRAM

Way back in 1992, a company called Rambus invented a new type of memory technology called **Rambus Dynamic Random Access Memory (RDRAM)**. RDRAM is a very high-speed type of clocked RAM that runs at 400 or 533 MHz, achieving these high speeds by accessing RAM four times per clock cycle. RDRAM is more expensive than DDR SDRAM, so it tends to show up only in high-end systems that can use the slight advantage of RDRAM as compared to DDR SDRAM. Table 3.1 summarizes the various RAM technologies and their uses today.

There are a number of folks out there who say that DDR SDRAM is exclusively for AMD chips, and RDRAM is only for Intel chips. Not entirely true. You'll find plenty of Intel PCs using DDR SDRAM—but you won't find any AMD systems using RDRAM. RDRAM is used only on Intel systems.

▪ RAM Packages

Understanding RAM technologies enables you to make informed recommendations to clients, but techs work with hardware: selecting, installing,

Table 3.1	RAM Technologies Today
RAM Technology	**Typical CPU Today**
FPM	Obsolete; Pentium and earlier
EDO	Obsolete; Pentium II, Pentium, early Celeron and Athlon
SDRAM	All (Pentium and later)
DDR SDRAM	Later Celeron and Duron, Athlon XP, Pentium 4
RDRAM	Pentium 4

and configuring. Techs need to be able to pick up a stick of RAM, identify with a high degree of certainty what technology it is, and know which sorts of motherboards can use it. Second, you need to know certain quirks of RAM implementation, such as which type of RAM requires you to use a pair of RAM sticks rather than a single stick with a particular processor.

RAM comes in four basic *packages*, meaning physical form factors, known by their initials: SIMM, DIMM, SO DIMM, and RIMM. Each package has more than one variation in the number of pins it uses to connect to the motherboard, plus most can be used to implement one or two distinct RAM technologies as well, which adds up to quite a variety of RAM out there.

• An assortment of different RAM packages

This section starts with a brief discussion of the older technologies—both to introduce a couple of topics and because you'll still run into some of these older implementations in the field. RAM packages have amazing longevity because RAM used to be very expensive. In the early days, adding RAM often required painful soul searching: Would the cost of adding a few more megabytes of RAM be offset by the gain in system stability, speed, and performance?

SIMMs

Single Inline Memory Modules (SIMMs) came in two sizes, differentiated by the number of contacts used to connect to the motherboard: 30 pins or 72 pins. Both varieties had implementations of FPM and EDO technologies.

Motherboards were designed to handle one or both sizes, although not both technologies. In other words, you could have a motherboard that had both 30-pin and 72-pin SIMM sockets, but it would require you to use either FPM or EDO RAM. The motherboard in Figure 3.2 has both types of sockets.

Banking

All 30-pin SIMMs and most 72-pin SIMMs traveled in packs—you never saw them alone on a motherboard. On most PCs, 30-pin SIMMs had to be inserted in groups of four. You couldn't put in one, two, or three SIMMs; you had to insert four, or the computer would not recognize the RAM.

The number of SIMM sticks that must go into the motherboard as a group defines a **bank**. For instance, the following illustration shows an old 486 system that uses 72-pin SIMMs. In this system, there are two banks—each bank consists of one 72-pin SIMM. A bank that is empty is termed *unpopulated*; a bank with RAM installed is *populated*.

• 30-pin (above) and 72-pin (below) SIMMs

• A 486 motherboard with two banks

Although 30-pin SIMMs were much better than the old individual RAM chips, they had the single drawback of requiring multiple SIMMs to make a single bank. By the time the Pentium CPU became prevalent in the early to mid-1990s, most motherboards required eight 30-pin SIMMs just to make one bank! This created demand for an improved RAM package—in essence, four 30-pin SIMMs built into a new, larger SIMM: the 72-pin SIMM.

• **Figure 3.2**   This motherboard can use both 30-pin and 72-pin SIMMs.

One 72-pin SIMM was functionally the same as four 30-pin SIMMs. The vast majority of Pentium and Pentium II motherboards used this type of package. In most cases, two 72-pin SIMMs were required for a bank, although there were some exceptions.

• 72-pin SIMMs installed on a motherboard

Table 3.2 summarizes the application of the two SIMM types.

Table 3.2	SIMM Types	
SIMM Type	**Technology**	**Typical Processor Type Today**
30-pin	FPM, EDO	Obsolete; last spotted on ancient Pentium-class systems
72-pin	FPM, EDO	Obsolete; still seen on aging Celeron, Athlon, and Pentium II systems

DIMMs

Dual Inline Memory Modules (DIMMs) replaced the SIMM packages virtually overnight and remain the package of choice for most systems today. DIMMs come in two pin varieties, several technologies, and multiple speeds. Although it's pretty difficult to insert the wrong type of DIMM on a motherboard, you can and probably will insert the wrong speed of DIMM in a motherboard. This is bad because, as mentioned at the beginning of the chapter, if the CPU attempts to use the wrong type of RAM, the system will be buggy and crash-prone. Techs need to know their DIMMs! Table 3.3. shows the DIMM implementations typical today.

DIMMs fill up a bank all by themselves; you do not have to worry about banking in current systems.

168-Pin DIMMs

The ubiquitous 168-pin DIMM provides system memory for a very large percentage of modern systems, although that is slowly changing. Introduced with the Pentium-class CPUs, 168-pin DIMMs sport SDRAM technology. The following illustration shows a 168-pin DIMM. Note the notch just off the center of the connectors? That provides orientation for installation—a DIMM inserts into the motherboard slots only one way.

• 168-pin DIMM

SDRAM comes in three speeds: 66 MHz, 100 MHz, and 133 MHz. When SDRAM first appeared, it had a few compatibility problems, so Intel came up with a standardization system called PC66, PC100, and PC133.

184-Pin DIMMs

The 184-pin DIMM package provides the DDR SDRAM technology for a large portion of the current RAM market, from low-end PCs all the way to

Table 3.3	DIMM Implementations Common Today		
DIMM type	**Technology**	**Speeds (MHz)**	**Typical Processor Type Today**
168-pin	SDRAM[1]	66, 100, 133	All; implemented on every type of processor board, from Pentium class up to Pentium 4 and Athlon XP
184-pin	DDR SDRAM	200, 266, 333, 400	Athlon XP, Pentium 4, some later Duron and Celeron

[1]Very early implementations of 168-pin DIMMs used EDO technology, but these were few and far between. The SDRAM variety of DIMM has been dominant since the beginning and is all you're likely to see in the field.

state-of-the-art systems. Physically the same size as a 168-pin DIMM, the 184-pin DIMM has a slight variation in packaging so you simply cannot put an SDRAM DIMM into a motherboard that needs DDR SDRAM and vice versa. The following illustration shows a 184-pin DDR SDRAM DIMM and a 168-pin SDRAM DIMM (the 184-pin DIMM is on the top). Do you see the little notches in both DIMMS? See how they are in different locations? That's to prevent you from putting the wrong type of RAM in the motherboard.

• 184-pin (top) and 168-pin (bottom) DIMMs; note the different notches along the contacts.

DDR SDRAM Speed Ratings   Like SDRAM, DDR SDRAM also has a speed rating, but just to spice things up, the memory business uses two totally separate nomenclatures for measuring DDR SDRAM speed—what I call the tech way and the marketing way. The *tech* way describes the DIMM in terms of double the bus speed of the motherboard. DDR SDRAM runs at twice the motherboard speed: DDR200, DDR266, DDR333, and DDR400. That makes sense, right?

The *marketing* way to describe the speed of DDR SDRAM uses the number of bits per second that the DIMM can theoretically put on the data bus. That way, the marketing department gets to use a *bigger number*!

Because the CPU will always ask for at least a single byte (8 bits) of RAM, you multiply the speed of the DDR SDRAM by 8 bits to get the bits per second throughput. For example, a piece of DDR200 runs at 200 MHz; 200 x 8 = 1,600 Mbits per second. So the other name for DDR200 is PC1600. I'll leave the calculations for the other DDR RAM speeds for an exercise.

• DDR SDRAM showing speed

This dual speed rating system has caused most DDR SDRAM makers to throw up their hands and to slap labels on their RAM that include both nomenclatures.

SO DIMM

The Small Outline (SO) DIMMs used exclusively in laptop computers come in three different types of packages and implement two different technologies—all at different speeds. I've never met a RAM manufacturer that didn't agree that variety adds spice to life!

Table 3.4 clarifies these many SO DIMM options. Note the three different pin packages, the choices of SDRAM and DDR SDRAM, and the many options for speed.

Introduction to PC Hardware and Troubleshooting

Figure Out the Alternate Nomenclature

Although most DDR SDRAM makers do clearly indicate their speeds with both nomenclatures, it's not at all uncommon for some RAM packages to display only one, requiring you to either memorize the numbers for both types or be able to do the calculation quickly. It's not that hard—just multiply the speed by 8 or divide the bits per second by 8. Try this:

1. Imagine you want to add 128 MB of RAM to your system. You check the motherboard book to see the speed you need. This motherboard either uses PC2100 or PC1600. It's fairly common for a motherboard to accept more than one speed.

2. You run to the store and proclaim, "I need one stick of 256-MB PC2100 DDR RAM, please!" Sadly, the salesperson is not as RAM savvy as you are (this happens more than you can possibly imagine) and says, "PC2100? What's that? All I have is DDR200 and DDR266. Which one do you want?"

3. Fortunately for you, you know that you just reverse the calculation you saw earlier: you need to divide by 8. You whip out your mighty calculator and divide 2,100 by 8—and you get 262.5. Hey! Wait a minute! That's not 200 or 266, is it? No, but it's close enough. Take the PC266 DDR SDRAM.

4. Following this example, go ahead and figure out the alternate nomenclature for these: DDR200, DDR266, DDR333, and DDR400.

RIMMs

RDRAM also uses DIMMs—at least in everything but name. The Rambus folks decided to call their RAM packaging **RIMM**. What does RIMM stand for? Not a thing! Rambus just liked the name. The standard RDRAM RIMM has 184 pins (just like the DDR SDRAM DIMM), but because of the careful placement of notches on RIMMs, you'll never accidentally put a RIMM where you should be placing a DIMM.

 See the interesting metal plate that covers the individual chips on the RIMM? This is a heat spreader, used to disperse the tremendous heat generated by the RIMM.

• RDRAM RIMM

Table 3.4	SO DIMM Implementations Common Today		
Variant	**Technology**	**Speeds (MHz)**	**Processor Type**
72-pin	SDRAM	66, 100, 133	All pre–Pentium 4 laptops
144-pin	SDRAM	100, 133	Pentium III and Athlon laptops
200-pin	DDR SDRAM	200, 266, 400	Athlon and Pentium 4 laptops

RDRAM takes a rather different approach to RAM banking and requires that you always use two RIMMs. You'll never see a single RIMM in a PC. In addition, every bank on a motherboard that uses RDRAM must be populated. Rambus specifies special bank fillers called Continuity RIMMs (CRIMMs) that you must place in all unused banks on the motherboard. CRIMMs are not RAM; they are needed to, in essence, "complete the circuit" because RDRAM needs all banks filled.

• A typical CRIMM

My primary work PC, shown here, uses RDRAM. One bank is populated with a pair of RIMMs, and the other, unused bank has two CRIMMs—a very common setup for an RDRAM system.

• The inside of the author's system, showing RIMMs and CRIMMs

RDRAM speeds are explained exclusively in terms of the bits per second measurement explained in the previous section. Currently, the only speeds of RDRAM are PC600, PC700, PC800, and PC1066. A quick check of the motherboard documentation will tell you what speed you need.

	4Mbit Firmware Hub (FWH)	**14**
	Low Pin Count (LPC) Multi-I/O Chipset	**16**
Main Memory	Maximum 2GB support	
	4 RIMM Sockets	**3**
	Dual Channel PC800/PC600 RDRAM support	

• A motherboard book page showing RDRAM speed recommendations

RDRAM also addresses the needs of laptops by providing a 160-pin RIMM. Up to now, these modules have had very little impact on the laptop market. All current Pentium 4 laptops use either SDRAM or DDR SDRAM. RDRAM manufacturers are going to have to do some work to punch into the laptop market.

Adding and Upgrading RAM

Adding RAM to a PC can turn a floundering, sputtering lug of a PC into a lean, well-oiled machine—as long as you do it right. Adding the wrong RAM won't hurt anything except your pocketbook and possibly your pride because the system simply won't work. Adding RAM that's *almost* right, however, can create stability problems that cause your system to crash or reboot. Every tech needs to know when and how to install RAM properly. This is one of the core skills you'll be called on to use frequently.

Try This!

Shopping for RAM

This exercise requires you to make a trip to your local computer supply store. Although you can go to any popular chain store (such as Fry's or Micro Center in the U.S.), you'll often find that small mom-and-pop stores are likely to give you more of their time to "play."

1. In a local computer store, go to the motherboard section and look at the types of RAM the motherboards need. You'll see motherboards that use SDRAM, DDR SDRAM, and RDRAM.

2. Make a quick estimate of the percentage of motherboards that use each type of RAM. For example, at my local store, about 25 percent use SDRAM, 50 percent use DDR SDRAM, and 25 percent use RDRAM. Motherboard makers tend to make motherboards that use the most popular types of RAM.

3. Open up a few boxes if you can, or check out the display models to see how many RAM slots a typical motherboard provides. Note that the RDRAM motherboards always have even numbers of slots (they must be paired), whereas DDR SDRAM motherboards may have two, three, or four slots.

4. Check a few motherboard books and see if you can determine the exact type of RAM they need. Be patient; it's not always obvious where to look in those motherboard books!

5. After looking at the motherboards, select two different boards and take them to the counter. Tell the salesperson that you are considering these boards but you're not sure what RAM to use. Have the salesperson produce the RAM needed for those motherboards and then compare what the salesperson shows you to what you think you need. Are they the same?

This section starts with a discussion of reasons to add or upgrade RAM in a PC. Then it turns to the nuts and bolts of removing and installing RAM, following a three-stage process of researching, installing, and verifying.

Why Add RAM?

Adding or upgrading the RAM on a PC can make a dramatic difference in performance. Most people add RAM to increase the capacity of a PC so they can open more programs at once, but they don't realize that getting RAM to a sufficient level for a particular operating system can increase not only system performance but, more importantly, system stability.

One question I get asked all the time is "How do I know when adding RAM is a good idea?" Well, that's a good question—but unfortunately, in most cases, there's not a clear answer. Basically, my response boils down to this: your computer needs RAM to run programs. Every time a program starts, it uses RAM.

If you load too many programs, you'll reach a point where you run out of RAM. When you run out of RAM, your computer will begin to use a special part of the hard drive as RAM. The PC automatically begins to swap the less-used programs out of RAM to the hard drive to make room for the most-used program. This process is known as using **virtual memory**. The special part of the hard drive that stores the programs is called the **swap file**, and swapping is a normal process of your PC. If you didn't have a swap file, a very nasty error would occur.

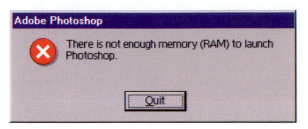

• Out-of-memory error

Every version of Windows is designed to use at least a little bit of your hard drive as virtual memory, especially as you switch between multiple, large applications or big picture files. It's painfully obvious when your PC is overusing the swap file—the computer slows to a crawl, the mouse pointer pops in and out of the hourglass state, and the hard drive audibly works very hard. In addition, the hard drive LED on the front of your PC seems to stay continuously lit; this is the biggest single clue that you need more memory.

Hard drives make noise when data is being accessed or written—this is normal. Excessive swap file accesses and writes create a long (3 to 10 seconds), rather unusual scratching sound. This sound is commonly called a *hard drive thrash*. Too much hard drive thrashing is another sign you need more RAM.

Step-by-Step 3.1

Checking Your System Resources

You begin to notice that your system is running slowly, and you suspect that it might be using the swap file too often. Is there a way to verify this? Sure! There are a large number of utilities that you can use to check this. For example, Windows 2000 and XP come with the handy Task Manager.

To complete this exercise, you will need the following:

■ A PC running Windows XP or Windows 2000

Step 1   Access the Task Manager by pressing CTRL-ALT-DEL and clicking the Task Manager button.

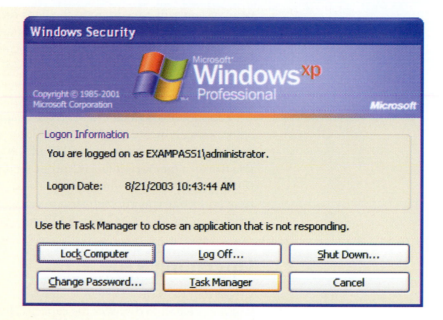

Click the Performance tab to see the memory usage. This window contains a great deal of information, but the only information of interest for memory usage is in the Physical Memory section. Note that this system has roughly 384 MB of RAM (Total Physical Memory), with almost 200 MB free (Available). This system is in fine shape; you would have to load a lot more programs before the system would start accessing the swap file excessively. This PC has lots of RAM. Most PCs today have 64 to 256 MB of RAM.

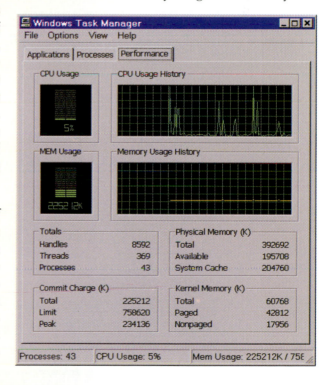

Note: If you're using versions of Windows other than XP or 2000, you can still complete this exercise. You just need to find a third-party program to help you. There are hundreds of memory programs you can use, but my personal favorite is Sandra by SiSoftware. You can download an evaluation copy of Sandra at www.sisoftware.com.uk.

Some Suggested Minimums

More than any other program, the operating system must have enough RAM to run efficiently. A portion of the OS loads into RAM when you boot a computer, but there's a twist. Microsoft designed Windows to load into RAM in pieces—so the more RAM you have, the more pieces of the OS can load at one time. The more pieces of the OS you have in RAM, the less likely your system will have to go to the hard drive and grab other pieces of the OS, thus improving your overall performance. That's a nice benefit!

Microsoft sets RAM minimums at ridiculously low levels. Sure, Windows XP will run on a system with 64 MB of RAM, but the computer would have to access the swap file so frequently that it would run like a three-legged dog. Table 3.5 suggests reasonable minimum- and moderate-level RAM requirements.

You should also factor in the types of applications you plan to run when determining how much RAM a specific system should have. Running Windows XP Professional with 256 MB of RAM is just fine, for example, until you fire up a memory-intensive program like Adobe Photoshop (minimum RAM: 128 MB) or Macromedia Dreamweaver MX (minimum RAM: 96 MB). Heaven forbid you run the system with Microsoft Office loaded as well (minimum RAM: 128 MB plus 8 MB per open application).

Upgrading RAM

Upgrading RAM in a system is almost always a three-stage process. First, you do research to discover the capacity, technology, and package of RAM the system can handle. Second, you install the RAM. Third, you verify that the upgrade succeeded.

Research

Researching RAM requirements for a motherboard means opening up the motherboard manual and reading, opening the system unit to see what's already installed, and taking note of a few intangible quirks. In your search, you should discover the following information:

- Total quantity of RAM the system can handle
- Amount of RAM each slot will handle
- RAM technology required
- Packages the motherboard can handle
- Speed of RAM sticks supported

Determining RAM Capacity How can you tell, for example, a 64-MB 184-pin DDR SDRAM DIMM from a 128-MB 184-pin DDR SDRAM DIMM? Well, the quick and easy answer is: you can't! You cannot simply look at two SIMMs/DIMMs/RIMMs and tell the capacity of one from another. RAM makers know this, and they all print the capacity of the RAM on a label placed on the RAM itself, as shown in Figure 3.3.

Many discount RAM suppliers try to sell unlabeled RAM. If you're ever offered one of these RAM sticks, run away! It's probably not good-quality RAM.

Many older systems can use higher-capacity RAM if you upgrade the BIOS. See Chapter 4 for details on how to do this.

Table 3.5	Minimum- and Moderate-Level RAM Requirements	
Operating System	**Reasonable Minimum RAM**	**Moderate RAM**
Windows 98/SE	64 MB	128 MB
Windows Me	128 MB	256 MB
Windows 2000	128 MB	256 MB
Windows XP (Home or Professional)	256 MB	512 MB

Beware capacity issues—older motherboards can rarely handle the highest-capacity RAM sticks. The motherboard documentation will state the largest-capacity sticks that the system can handle, but this information is not always easy to find in the motherboard documentation. Look at Figure 3.4. This documentation says that the system can support a maximum of 256 MB in each of the three slots. So do the math: 256 times 3 equals 768 MB. This system can handle RAM sticks totalling more than 768 MB.

If the documentation isn't clear, it's safe to gamble and try a larger-capacity stick to see what happens. If the system can't handle the capacity, it simply won't recognize the RAM; you won't cause any damage. I've guessed many times!

• **Figure 3.3**   Capacity marked on two different RAM sticks

Choosing Single- or Double-Sided Sticks   All SIMMs and DIMMs come in one of two types: single sided or double sided. Single-sided sticks have RAM chips on one side; double-sided sticks have chips on both sides.

Both of these types of RAM are perfectly functional, but some older systems may have problems with double-sided sticks. Before you use double-sided RAM, verify that your system will accept it.

Assessing the Number of Available Slots   Remember that your motherboard has a limited number of slots. A friend recently asked me to add a 128-MB stick of RAM to his system. When I opened his PC, I saw that he had three slots for RAM, all populated with 32-MB RAM sticks. For me to add RAM to his system, I would have to remove one of the three existing RAM sticks. I purchased a 128-MB RAM stick, yanked out one of the 32-MB sticks, and replaced it with the new RAM stick, giving his system a total of 32 + 32 + 128 = 192 MB of RAM. My friend was angry! In his view, I had lost 32 MB of RAM (he thought he would have 96 + 128 = 224 MB of RAM). It took a little bit of explanation about slots, but he finally understood.

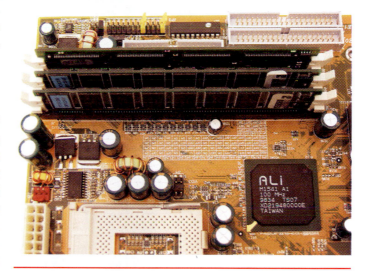

• How can you add RAM to this system?

Determining the Speed   All motherboards require a certain speed of RAM to function. However, it is very common to add RAM with a higher speed rating than you need. This does not make your system run any faster, but it gives you the ability to use this RAM in a faster system a year from now when you decide to upgrade the CPU or get a new motherboard. I always purchase the fastest RAM my wallet can handle, not because I need it now, but because I'll probably need it later.

Bank	Memory Module	Total Memory
Bank 0, 1 (DIMM1)	8MB, 16MB, 32MB, 64MB, 128MB, 256MB	8MB ~ 256MB
Bank 2, 3 (DIMM2)	8MB, 16MB, 32MB, 64MB, 128MB, 256MB	8MB ~ 256MB
Bank 4, 5 (DIMM3)	8MB, 16MB, 32MB, 64MB, 128MB, 256MB	8MB ~ 256MB
Total System Memory		8MB ~ 768MB

• **Figure 3.4**   Maximum of 256 MB per stick

Installation

Compared to what you need to go through to determine the right RAM for your system, the physical removal and installation of RAM is so simple as to be anticlimactic. SIMMs and DIMMs/RIMMs differ slightly, so we'll treat them separately.

Step-by-Step 3.2

Removing and Installing SIMMs

Unless you like to work with really old computers, odds are pretty good that you'll never have to mess with SIMMs. However, enough of this RAM is still out there to motivate us to give it our attention.

To complete this exercise, you will need the following:

- A motherboard with SIMM slots
- SIMM sticks
- An antistatic wrist strap

Step 1

If you look at a 30-pin or 72-pin SIMM in its slot, you'll notice two metal tabs on the ends. Gently pull these tabs away from the SIMM, and the SIMM will fall sideways—it will tilt at a small angle.

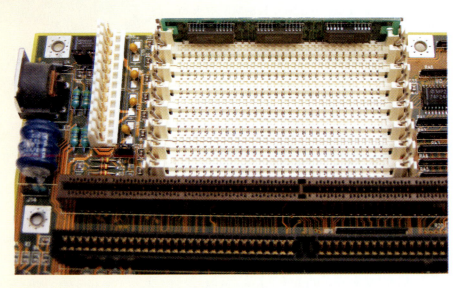

Step 2

Once the SIMM has tilted in the slot, grab the SIMM by the edges and remove it—do not touch anything metal on the chip. Store it in an antistatic bag. Remember that 30-pin SIMMs almost always come in banks of four, so you'll need to take out all four. Most 72-pin SIMMs come in banks of two; be sure to get both!

Now that you've removed the SIMM sticks, reinstall them in the motherboard. Holding a stick by the edges, gently insert the contacts into the slot at a mild angle, such as 60 degrees or so, aligning the notch in the stick with the raised part of the slot. Push the stick firmly into place; then tilt it up until it sits vertical in the slot. When you have it correctly in place, you should see and hear the silver tabs on the sides snap into place.

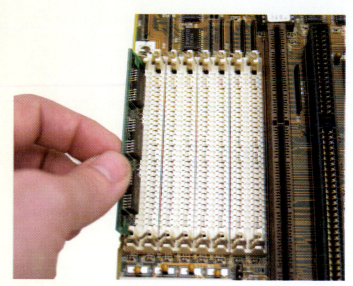

Step 4

Examine the SIMM after you've installed it. Does it look properly aligned? If it doesn't, there's a good chance it is not completely inserted (a very common occurrence). Just remove the SIMM and try again.

The key points to remember when installing a SIMM are to take care to avoid ESD, to avoid touching the contacts on the stick, and to align the stick properly. Practice, if possible, with a motherboard outside a case; this will teach you the skill without fear of scraping your knuckles.

Now let's turn to a process you're much more likely to encounter today: removing and installing DIMMs and RIMMs.

Step-by-Step 3.3

Removing and Installing DIMMs and RIMMs

The process of removing and installing DIMMs and RIMMs is even easier than that for SIMMs. To complete this exercise, you will need the following:

- A motherboard with DIMM or RIMM slots

- DIMM or RIMM sticks appropriate for the motherboard

- An antistatic wrist strap

Step 1

To remove a DIMM or RIMM, just pull the plastic tabs on the sides away from the DIMM or RIMM until it lifts out of the slot; then pull it straight out, remembering to hold it by the edges.

Step 2

Installation is just as easy, but you may need to exert a tad more force than you think should be necessary. First make

sure that the side tabs are pulled back as far as they can go. Then just press the DIMM or RIMM straight down into the slot until the tabs snap up into the locked position.

Step 3

After the stick is snapped down, check your handiwork. Does the DIMM or RIMM appear to sit evenly in the slot? If it doesn't look even, you probably haven't inserted it correctly, or you're trying to put the wrong type of RAM in the slot.

Verification

Now that you have the RAM inserted, it's time to test. The test is simple: try to start the system. If the system doesn't boot, you can be virtually certain that you made one of the following mistakes:

- You failed to insert the RAM properly (if the system makes a long beeping noise, then this is absolutely the problem).
- The motherboard uses multiple sticks for banking, and you didn't fill a bank.
- You installed RAM that is too slow for your system.
- You installed RDRAM, but you forgot to add CRIMMs.
- You have a bad stick of RAM.

In all of these cases but the last, a simple double-check will resolve the problem. The chances of a bad RAM stick are incredibly small, but if you're sure that you handled all of the other issues correctly, take the stick back to where you bought it—without removing it from your system. Be prepared for a humbling experience when you show the tech the system, and he or she just snaps down the RAM you could have *sworn* you checked carefully. If the tech charges you 20 bucks, consider it a cheap lesson in double-checking. In the rare instance that the RAM stick actually is bad, the tech can replace it right there.

The next place to watch for trouble is the boot screen—no, not the pretty Windows screen, but that ugly text that appears *before* the Windows screen. As your system boots, you will see a RAM check take place. Figure 3.5 shows the RAM check on a typical system.

If the computer sees the RAM during the RAM check, you are done. Windows will also see the new RAM, and you can relax and enjoy your faster PC. Watch out for a classic issue with RAM counts. RAM is counted in true millions of bytes, not megabytes. A megabyte is not one million; a megabyte is 1,048,576 bytes, so if your computer has 256 MB of RAM, the RAM count will

```
PhoenixBIOS 4.0 Release 6.0
Copyright 1985-1998 Phoenix Technologies Ltd.
All Rights Reserved

DELL Inspiron 7500 C400LT BIOS Rev A13     (037A)

CPU = Pentium III   600 MHz
0640K System RAM Passed
0127M Extended RAM Passed
0512K Cache SRAM Passed
Mouse initialized
Fixed Disk 0: FUJITSU MHG2102AT
DVD-ROM: TORiSAN DVD-ROM DRD-U624
```

● **Figure 3.5**   RAM check in action

show that as 256 x 1,048,576, or 268,435,456 bytes. No, you're not getting extra RAM; the discrepancy occurs simply because the RAM count is expressed in millions of bytes, but we buy RAM in megabytes—different units, same amount of RAM. Don't let the difference confuse you.

Here is one other issue that may arise during the RAM count. Remember my buddy with the 32-MB sticks and the 128-MB stick? Well, when I added the 128-MB stick and booted the system, the RAM count showed only 64 MB of RAM—the system didn't initially see the added RAM. If this happens to you, check for these problems:

- The RAM is not inserted correctly.
- The BIOS needs updating (see Chapter 4).
- The system can't use double-sided RAM.
- The RAM stick is faulty.

With my friend's system, we updated the BIOS and rebooted, and the RAM worked.

In general, installing RAM is simple and is an easy way to improve the performance of a slow system. The biggest mistake that most folks make is failing to install the correct RAM into their systems because they don't take the time to read the motherboard documentation. Be patient, read the documentation, and use a little common sense, and you'll have no problems with RAM.

Chapter 3 Review

■ Chapter Summary

After reading this chapter and completing the exercises, you should understand the following facts about RAM.

Describe how RAM functions in a PC

- RAM is the workplace where the CPU stores programs that are running.

- Dynamic RAM enables the CPU to update data rapidly, but it holds the data only temporarily. Without electricity, RAM cannot hold anything.

- The CPU directs the Northbridge chip to update and retrieve data—RAM does not directly connect to the address bus or the data bus.

Identify various RAM technologies used in PCs

- Fast Page Mode (FPM) RAM was the original type of RAM used in PCs. It is now obsolete.

- Extended Data Output (EDO) RAM was an improvement over FPM RAM, allowing extended access to a particular RAS wire. It, too, is now obsolete. FPM and EDO RAM were asynchronous. That is, unlike the CPU, they did not use a clock.

- Asynchronous RAM speeds are measured in nanoseconds. Synchronous DRAM does have a clock speed.

- Intel defined standards for SDRAM that specified how to make SDRAM run at certain speeds. These standards were the PC66, PC100, and PC133 standards.

- DDR SDRAM is an advanced, double-speed type of SDRAM. DDR SDRAM comes in four common speeds: DDR200/PC1600, DDR266/PC2100, DDR333/PC2700, and DDR400/PC3200.

- RDRAM is a proprietary type of RAM that is a direct competitor to DDR SDRAM. RDRAM is used in higher-end systems running Intel processors. RDRAM comes in four speeds: PC600, PC700, PC800, and PC1066.

Explain the various ways in which RAM is packaged for use in a PC

- There are two sizes of SIMMs: 30-pin SIMMs and 72-pin SIMMs.

- On many systems, SIMMs need to be installed in groups of two or four. This minimum number of sticks is known as a bank.

- SDRAM and DDR SDRAM use DIMMs. SDRAM uses a 168-pin DIMM. DDR SDRAM uses a 184-pin DIMM.

- Both SDRAM and DDR SDRAM also come in special SO DIMMs that are used almost exclusively in laptops.

- RDRAM uses a special DIMM called a RIMM. Unlike with all other types of RAM, all of the slots on an RDRAM motherboard need to be filled. Any unused slots must be filled with a special stick called a CRIMM.

Install RAM in a PC

- Every time you load a program, it takes up some of your RAM. When you run out of real RAM on your PC, your PC will use a special part of your hard drive, called the swap file, as if it were RAM. This process is called using virtual memory.

- Using virtual memory too much causes the system to slow down and the hard drive to thrash. These symptoms are the primary signs that you need to add RAM to your computer.

- Unless a RAM chip is labeled, it is impossible to tell its capacity simply by looking at it.

- Make sure that you have the right speed of RAM for your system.

- Always handle RAM very carefully to prevent ESD.

- Use the RAM count at bootup as your primary test to determine whether the PC recognizes added RAM.

■ Key Terms List

asynchronous *(61)*

bank *(65)*

**Double Data Rate SDRAM
(DDR SDRAM)** *(63)*

**Dual Inline Memory Module
(DIMM)** *(67)*

nanosecond *(62)*

**Rambus Dynamic Random Access
Memory (RDRAM)** *(63)*

**Random Access Memory
(RAM)** *(56)*

RIMM *(69)*

**Single Inline Memory Module
(SIMM)** *(64)*

sticks *(58)*

swap file *(72)*

**Synchronous Dynamic Random
Access Memory (SDRAM)** *(62)*

virtual memory *(72)*

■ Key Term Quiz

Use terms from the Key Terms list to complete the following sentences. Not all terms will be used.

1. Individual RAM chips are soldered to small circuit boards known generically as _____.

2. Both EDO and FPM RAM are _____, meaning they do not have a clock input.

3. The special part of the hard drive used as if it were RAM is the _____.

4. RDRAM is always sold in a package called a/an _____.

5. On most modern systems using SDRAM or DDR SDRAM, you need only one stick to make a _____.

6. The first type of synchronous RAM was called _____.

7. 72-pin SIMM speeds are measured in _____.

8. The process of using the hard drive to emulate RAM is called _____.

9. _____ gets its name from the fact that it accesses memory twice every clock cycle.

10. _____ is the only common proprietary type of RAM.

■ Multiple-Choice Quiz

1. The _____ chip is the primary interface between the CPU and RAM.
   a. Eastbridge
   b. Southbridge
   c. Northbridge
   d. RAMBUS

2. How many binary combinations can be made using 6 bits?
   a. 128
   b. 64
   c. 32
   d. 16

3. Tom says that he has 64 megabytes of RAM in his computer. What is the exact number of bytes of RAM he has?

   a. 67,108,864
   b. 64,000,000
   c. 65,536,428
   d. 62,324,982

4. How much is a kilo (K) in binary terms?
   a. 1,000
   b. 1,012
   c. 1,020
   d. 1,024

5. Which of the following RAM types is likely the fastest?
   a. FPM
   b. EDO
   c. DDR SDRAM
   d. SL-RAM

6. Which one of the following RAM types are you least likely to see in a modern motherboard?

   a. EDO RAM

   b. SDRAM

   c. DDR SDRAM

   d. RDRAM

7. The idle clock cycles that occur while the CPU waits for input from RAM are called _____.

   a. System stalls

   b. Wait cycles

   c. Wait states

   d. System states

8. Which of the following asynchronous clock speeds is the fastest?

   a. 50 ms

   b. 60 ns

   c. 100 ns

   d. 120 ms

9. SDRAM speeds are measured in _____.

   a. KHz

   b. GHz

   c. PHz

   d. MHz

10. Which are the two most common sizes of SIMMs?

    a. 15-pin and 72-pin

    b. 30-pin and 70-pin

    c. 30-pin and 72-pin

    d. 15-pin and 70-pin

11. Small versions of DIMMs known as _____ are often used in laptop systems.

    a. SO DIMMs

    b. Mini-DIMMs

    c. Mobile DIMMs

    d. PCI DIMMs

12. How many 30-pin SIMMs do you need to make a bank in most systems?

    a. 1

    b. 2

    c. 4

    d. 8

13. Which of the following is a legitimate speed designation for a DDR SDRAM chip?

    a. DDR100

    b. PC2700

    c. 100 ns

    d. PC1066

14. What does RIMM stand for?

    a. Random Inline Memory Module.

    b. Rambus Inline Memory Module.

    c. Rendering Inline Memory Module.

    d. It doesn't stand for anything.

15. A system that uses RDRAM also probably has a/an _____ CPU.

    a. AMD

    b. Intel

    c. Cyrix

    d. Novell

■ Essay Quiz

1. You have been asked to increase the RAM in an old 486 computer. What would you tell the user about the age and type of the RAM? What would be some strong arguments against upgrading? What would be some good arguments in favor of upgrading?

2. You go to the local PC parts store to purchase some new RAM for your system. You have a total of three slots, two of which are populated with PC2100, 64-MB DDR SDRAM sticks. You want to upgrade to a total of 256 MB of RAM. When you arrive, the store does not have the 128-MB sticks in stock. However, it has some 128-MB sticks of PC1600 and PC2700 RAM. It also has some PC2100 64-MB sticks on sale. Describe what you could do with the sticks that the store has available to increase your RAM by at least 128 MB.

3. You have just snapped some new RAM into your PC. It installed easily, yet when you boot the system, you notice that the new RAM is not listed. What steps should you take to try to make the system recognize the RAM?

Lab Projects

• Lab Project 3.1

When it comes to upgrading RAM, many techs forget an excellent source of free RAM: other computers in the organization. Suppose you are in charge of an organization with 30 computers, and you want to add RAM to speed up one of the systems.

1 How would you determine the exact type of RAM needed, including the package, quantity, and speed?

2 Develop an inventory system to keep track of the RAM in all 30 systems.

3 You don't want to take away RAM from a system that needs all the RAM it has. What tools could you use to determine how much RAM each system needs? How would you add that information to the inventory?

• Lab Project 3.2

RAM prices fluctuate dramatically depending on many factors. RAM prices also fluctuate based on brand name and perceived quality.

1 Track the price for 128-MB PC2100 DDR SDRAM sticks daily for one month. What is the total price variance? A variance of 15 to 20 percent in one month is not uncommon.

2 Like many products, RAM is sold under certain brand names or you can get cheaper generic RAM. There are big arguments among techs over whether to use brand-name RAM or cheaper generic RAM. Check out the four RAM companies at these web sites:

www.crucial.com
www.kingston.com
www.corsairmicro.com
www.micron.com

Call each sales department and ask what makes that company's memory better than that of other companies. There are also a number of suppliers of generic memory sticks. Go to some of the popular online computer parts stores and compare the prices of generic memory and name-brand memory. Decide for yourself if you prefer the quality assurance of a brand name over a lower price.

• Lab Project 3.3

Time to experiment! Your boss has decided to upgrade the RAM in the employee systems because too many employees are complaining that their programs take too long to perform simple and necessary tasks. He's asked you to test a standard system with a series of different RAM capacities to determine where the sweet spot lies between performance and cost.

Strip your system to the least amount of RAM needed to run your operating system. Then perform common tasks, keeping notes on the time it takes to accomplish them.

Keeping good documentation, add more RAM and run the tests again. Keep adding RAM and running tests until the performance gains become less dramatic. That's your sweet spot!

Motherboards and BIOS

*"Motherhood is a necessity for
all invention."*

—Unknown quipster

In this chapter, you will learn
how to:

- **Identify the parts of
a motherboard**
- **Identify types of motherboards**
- **Install a motherboard in a system**
- **Describe the function of the
system BIOS and access the
System Setup utility**

Everything in the PC directly or indirectly plugs into the **motherboard**. A properly configured and functioning motherboard provides a solid foundation for all the other hardware in the system. The converse of this statement is equally true. No PC with a poorly configured or poorly functioning motherboard will ever be stable, solid, or dependable. Techs need to know motherboards in detail because every PC starts here!

In this chapter, you will learn how motherboards work to unite all of the different system components into one harmonious system. You will learn to identify the parts that make up a motherboard and to identify the various motherboards you may run into out in the real world. You will also learn how to install a motherboard in a system. Finally, you'll learn about the function of the system BIOS and how to configure the System Setup utility, the tool for mastering the BIOS needed by devices that connect to the motherboard. So roll up your sleeves and prepare to meet the component that binds the whole system together: the motherboard.

Common Motherboard Features

Companies that build motherboards follow general guidelines for the placement of connectors, CPU sockets, ports, CPU fan connections—even screw holes. Although companies can make *proprietary* motherboards that work only with system units that they make, most use the standard guidelines—called **form factors**—for the motherboard. Using standard form factors enables companies to market their motherboards to a wider audience and thus thrive in the intensely competitive PC hardware market.

The *ATX* form factor dominates the current PC landscape, so a tour of the typical placement of ports, connectors, and so forth on an ATX motherboard will provide you with solid fundamental knowledge. Variations exist within the ATX form factor, and of course other form factors are on the market; we'll look at the variations in the second section of this chapter.

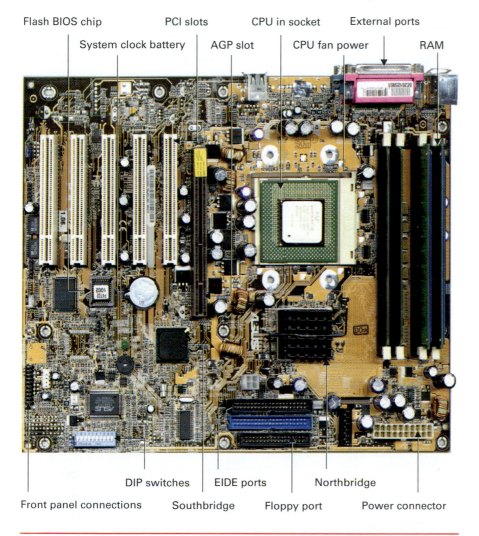

• A typical ATX motherboard with nothing connected

Your Personal Tour of the Motherboard

ATX motherboards have many parts working together to keep your computer running. It's important to know just what these various parts are, so this section will take you on a visual tour of the motherboard. Strap into the guide boat and prepare for the newest ride in our theme park: Mike Meyers' Motherboard Wilderness Ride. Please keep your hands inside the boat, and above all, don't panic.

CPU Socket/Slot

Although clearly central to any PC, the CPU doesn't sit anywhere near the center of an ATX motherboard. The CPU inserts into the motherboard near one corner, on the opposite end from the expansion slots. Recall from Chapter 2 that CPUs come in two flavors: *slotted*—for the older Athlon, Celeron, and other processors—and *socketed*—for the current Pentium 4, Athlon XP, and other offerings from Intel and AMD. Figures 4.1 and 4.2 show the corresponding slots and sockets on motherboards.

Recent motherboards have one of four socket sizes, three for Intel CPUs and one for AMD CPUs. The number on the socket identifies the type, such as Socket 423 for Intel Pentium 4 CPUs and Socket 462 for AMD Athlon XP processors. When buying a motherboard, make sure that it supports the type of CPU you want to use.

CPU Fan Power Connector   As you read earlier in this book, a CPU needs cooling to work properly. Most CPUs will bake nicely if they are without a fan for long. Because it takes at least a special *CPU fan* to keep a CPU cool, that fan will need to have a power source to run while the computer is on.

Most motherboards have a small, three- or four-wire power connector near the CPU for the fan (Figure 4.3). It's often labeled as such, quite conveniently. The connector has a flimsy plastic tab to help techs avoid plugging in the fan backward, although it's easy to make that mistake if you're not careful. Plugging in the fan power connector incorrectly will cook the fan or short the power connector, neither of which is a good thing.

> Need to refresh your memory about CPU socket types? Jump back to Chapter 2 and reread the information about CPU socket types.

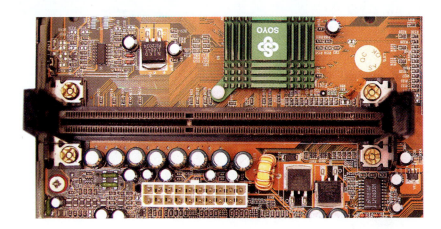

● Figure 4.1   A slot for a CPU on a motherboard

Introduction to PC Hardware and Troubleshooting

● Figure 4.2   A socket for a CPU on a motherboard

● Figure 4.3   Power connector for the CPU fan

Memory Slots

ATX motherboards have two, three, or four black slots near the CPU for memory (Figure 4.4), as you may recall from Chapter 3. These are called **memory slots** generically, although techs know that they're called *DIMM slots* for 168-pin SDRAM and 184-pin DDR SDRAM DIMMs, and *RIMM slots* for 184-pin RDRAM sticks. The slots have latches on each side to keep the DIMM or RIMM from coming loose.

Power Connector (P1)

A motherboard would be nothing without power going to it. There must be a connection between the outlet in your wall and the CPU and other components of your computer. On an ATX motherboard, this connection is through the **P1 power connector** (Figure 4.5).

Keep in mind that the P1 power connector powers the objects on the board such as the CPU and memory, but it does not power the hard drives, CD-ROM, or floppy drives. Additional power connectors run from the power supply in the computer to those devices.

● Figure 4.4   Memory slots on an ATX motherboard

● Figure 4.5   P1 power connector

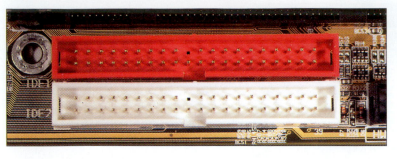

• **Figure 4.6**   EIDE ports

Chapter 8 discusses EIDE controllers, cabling, and drives in great detail.

EIDE and FDD Ports

Along the edge of the motherboard near the RAM slots, you'll see three or five ports with many wires poking up. These are the Enhanced Integrated Drive Electronic (EIDE) ports (Figure 4.6) and floppy disk drive (FDD) port (Figure 4.7) connections. EIDE provides a standardized interface for hard drives, CD-media drives, and other EIDE devices. Each 40-pin EIDE port can support two EIDE devices. Each 34-pin FDD port can support two floppy disk drives.

Many manufacturers use colored ports to denote different EIDE technologies supported. The colors are not standardized in the industry, however, so the same technology might be denoted by red on one motherboard and blue on another. The FDD port usually remains black. Both EIDE and FDD ports are *keyed*, with a notch in the middle of the port. This prevents you from inserting the FDD and EIDE cables incorrectly.

Chipset

The two chipset chips facilitate communication between the CPU and other devices in the system and so are relatively centrally located on the motherboard. The *Northbridge* chip helps the CPU work with RAM, as mentioned in Chapters 2 and 3. Current Northbridge chips do a lot and thus get pretty hot, so they usually get their own heat sinks (Figure 4.8).

We haven't discussed the Southbridge chip yet; it comes into play when the expansion bus comes onto the scene, in Chapter 5. The Southbridge handles some expansion devices and mass storage drives, such as hard drives and floppy disk drives. It sits between the expansion slots and the EIDE and FDD controllers on most ATX motherboards and often shows the manufacturer of the chipset, such as VIA Technologies (Figure 4.9).

Expansion Slots

You should have noticed a bank of similar slots sitting near one side of your motherboard. Those are part of the expansion bus. One of the early strengths of the IBM-compatible PC was its recognition that not everyone wanted the exact same computer. Rather than including every possible option as a part of the motherboard, the PC's designers allowed

• **Figure 4.7**   FDD port

• **Figure 4.8**   A VIA Northbridge chip on a motherboard. The tech is holding its heat sink.

Introduction to PC Hardware and Troubleshooting

you to customize your computer by adding components through the expansion slots (Figure 4.10).

This turned out to be a wonderful idea, particularly because expansion options such as sound and video tend to change more quickly than CPUs. Expansion slots allow the user to increase the capabilities of a computer without having to buy an entire new system every time an innovation appears.

ATX motherboards have one medium-sized brown slot next to some number of white slots—usually five, but the number can be anywhere from one to six—and possibly a much smaller brown slot. These are the AGP, PCI, and CNR expansion slots, respectively.

The **Accelerated Graphics Port (AGP)** slots (Figure 4.11) provide exclusive 32-bit, 66-MHz connections for video cards. AGP slots always sit closer to the Northbridge than any other expansion slot.

Peripheral Component Interconnect (PCI) slots are general-purpose, 32-bit, 33-MHz slots—you will see a wide variety of expansion cards in these slots, which are designed to enable quick communication between internal hardware add-ons and the CPU. Communication and Networking Riser (CNR) slots, on the other hand, are not nearly as common as PCI slots and are used only for network cards and modems, devices that enable you to connect a computer to the Internet and to smaller networks. Figure 4.12 shows both the white PCI slots and the small, brown CNR slot.

• **Figure 4.9**   A VIA Southbridge chip on a motherboard

Chapter 5 covers expansion slots in detail; Chapter 11 revisits AGP slots and goes into the subtle varieties of these slots—so stay tuned to this channel for more.

Date and Time Battery

Most ATX motherboards have what appears to be a watch battery stuck somewhere on them (Figure 4.13). This is *not* the source of your computer's power! The battery enables your system to retain accurate date and time settings in the event of a complete power outage. Every so often, I run into a system that needs a battery replacement, but that's exceedingly rare with modern motherboards.

Flash ROM

Every motherboard comes with a small set of code that enables the CPU to communicate properly with the devices built into the motherboard. This programming is called **basic input/output system (BIOS)** and is stored in a small chip called the flash ROM chip. You will find the flash ROM chip in almost as many different locations as there are motherboard manufacturers, although it often resides near the expansion slots. It usually has a small, silver label with the programming company's name listed, such as AMI or Award BIOS (Figure 4.14). You'll learn about the details of this chip later in this chapter.

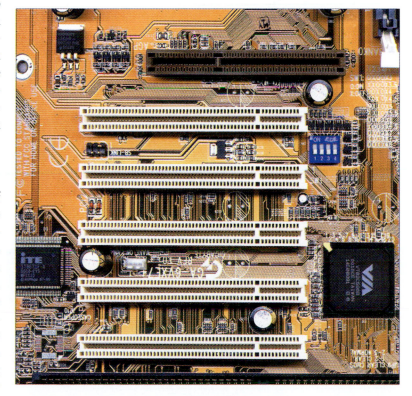

• **Figure 4.10**   Expansion slots on an ATX motherboard

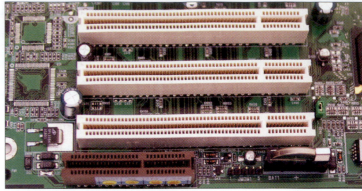

• Figure 4.11   • Figure 4.12   White PCI slots and brown CNR slot

• Figure 4.13   A watch battery!

Front Panel Connectors

Every motherboard has several connectors for various items on the front of the system unit, such as the power and reset buttons, the power and hard drive activity lights, and the tiny PC speaker. These connectors usually appear in a two-wire-wide row of about 8 to 10 wires along the edge of the motherboard opposite the expansion bus (Figure 4.15).

Although you can sometimes tell which leads plug in where by the tiny writing on the motherboard, it is far easier to consult the motherboard manual.

Jumpers and DIP Switches

Every motherboard comes with one or more configuration switches that enable you to make certain changes to important motherboard settings. One of the most important switches, for example, enables you to restore all motherboard settings to the factory default—very useful when something goes horribly wrong with a configuration.

• Figure 4.14   AMI and Award flash ROM chips

• Figure 4.15   Front panel connectors on a motherboard

Introduction to PC Hardware and Troubleshooting

These configuration switches come in two forms—jumpers and DIP switches—and a motherboard may have one or both options. A **jumper** is a pair of wires that you enable (turn on) or disable (turn off) by placing a small plastic and metal *shunt* over both wires. The metal in the shunt connects the two jumper wires, making a proper *circuit*. You'll find jumpers labeled on the motherboard as JP#, where # is any whole number, such as JP1, JP23, and so on. Figure 4.16 shows a three-pin jumper on a motherboard. You can place the shunt in one of two positions: over pins 1 and 2 or over pins 2 and 3.

A DIP switch is a little plastic box, often blue, with tiny white switches (Figure 4.17). Flipping a switch from off to on enables that switch. Despite the difference of form, there is no difference in function between jumpers and dip switches.

• **Figure 4.16** 3-pin jumper on a motherboard, with a shunt over pins 2 and 3

External Ports

ATX motherboards have a series of external port connections attached to one edge that poke through the back of the PC case when the motherboard is installed. These connectors enable you to attach external devices to the PC, such as a mouse and keyboard. Different motherboards vary in the number and type of some of the connectors, but most have a fairly standard set. Figure 4.18 shows the ports for a Pentium 4 motherboard.

> **Try This!**
>
> **What Does Your Motherboard Look Like?**
> Motherboard layouts and options vary greatly from one manufacturer's model to another's, so try this:
>
> 1. Open your PC case and examine the layout of your motherboard. What connections does it have?
>
> 2. Check the connections against the connections discussed in this section and note any differences. Then check your neighbor's motherboard for variations.

PS/2 Ports The two small round ports on the edge closest to the CPU are *mini-DIN* ports, more commonly called **PS/2 ports**. You plug a keyboard into the one closest to the motherboard surface, colored purple; a mouse plugs into the green port (Figure 4.19). Although the color coding is nice, it's

• **Figure 4.17** DIP switch on a motherboard

> **Inside Information**
>
> **Keyboard and Mouse Connections**
> *In the real world, you will likely run into an older AT-style connector for a keyboard. It's round, like a mini-DIN connector, but bigger. You can easily find an AT-PS/2 adapter, which will enable you to plug an old AT keyboard into a PS/2 port.*
>
> *Conversely, as more and more mice move from PS/2 to USB, you may need to buy a special USB-PS/2 adapter if you don't want your mouse taking up a USB port. These, too, are easy to find. As a technician, you may want to keep a few lying around just in case.*

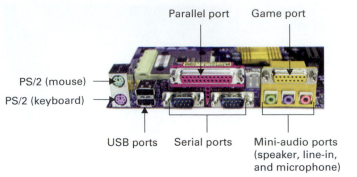

Parallel port   Game port

PS/2 (mouse)

PS/2 (keyboard)

USB ports   Serial ports   Mini-audio ports
(speaker, line-in,
and microphone)

• **Figure 4.18** Typical external connectors on a motherboard

• **Figure 4.19** Green for the mouse, purple for the keyboard—how easy is that!

sometimes tough to see the colors when a PC sits below a desk. Just remember that the keyboard goes on the bottom, and you'll do fine.

Parallel Port and Serial Ports   The **parallel port** is a 25-pin, D-shaped female port used to attach a printer, scanner, or other parallel device. The two 9-pin male **serial ports** below enable you to connect older serial devices, such as external modems. The serial port used to be the home of the mouse, but most mice now come as PS/2 or USB devices. Figure 4.20 shows both the parallel and serial ports.

USB   As the use of computers boomed, so did the number of gadgets that could be added on to them. It used to be that a mouse, printer, keyboard, and monitor made a complete computer system; there was nothing extra to add.

Now there are scanners, web cams, PDAs, and other devices that add fun and function to a system. However, this abundance presented a problem: where to plug in so many devices, especially with no easy way to switch between devices. With only a single parallel port and two serial ports to plug devices into, what could you do if you needed to use more than three devices at the same time?

Enter the **Universal Serial Bus (USB)**. It enables you to plug in up to 127 different devices at the same time. Most (if not all) ATX motherboards include two USB plugs just underneath the PS/2 ports. In fact, some computer users are not even using their PS/2 ports anymore because USB mice and keyboards are now available.

• **Figure 4.20** Parallel port (top) and serial ports (bottom)

Network Port   Many modern motherboards come equipped to connect directly to a local network or to the Internet via a standard *RJ-45* port. You'll learn all about those in Chapter 15. Figure 4.21 shows an RJ-45 port directly above two USB ports.

Sound and Game Ports   More and more ATX motherboards are offering extra goodies. The most common add-on for motherboards is sound. Motherboard manufacturers build a sound card into the motherboard that can handle the sound needs of most users.

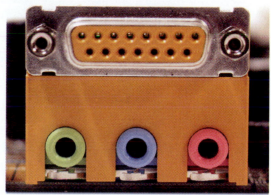

• **Figure 4.21** RJ-45 port above two USB ports

• **Figure 4.22** Standard sound ports below a game port

As you can see in Figure 4.22, a typical ATX motherboard offers the standard green 1/8-inch jack for speakers, plus two 1/8-inch jacks for a microphone (pink) and for a line-in (blue) to connect a stereo system to the computer.

In addition, a game port is available for joysticks and other game controller devices. The game port is a 15-pin, two-row, female, D-shaped port. You can even connect a special cable from this port to a MIDI controller to connect musical devices.

If you opt to use the built-in sound and have a CD-ROM drive on your system, you will undoubtedly want to play music CDs though your computer speakers. To do this, you will need to connect a special thin audio cable to the motherboard from the CD-ROM (Figure 4.23).

You will see a special port on the motherboard itself labeled CD_IN, as shown in Figure 4.24. All you need to do is plug in the cable from the CD-ROM to this port to be able to enjoy music from your CD-ROM on your computer.

Now that you're learned a bit about the features of motherboards in general, let's take a stroll down motherboard lane and learn how to identify types of motherboards.

• **Figure 4.23** Special audio cable for a CD-ROM drive

• **Figure 4.24** CD_IN audio port for a CD-ROM drive

■ Types of Motherboards

Motherboards come in variations of two standard form factors—AT and ATX—as well as in a substantial number of proprietary formats. Different form factors offer different features and sizes for a computer system, and most PC cases are designed to work with only one form factor. To perform motherboard upgrades and provide knowledgeable recommendations to clients, techs need to know their form factors.

This section looks at the common motherboard variations, starting with the AT family—Full AT and Baby AT—and then covering the ATX family—Full ATX, microATX, and FlexATX. The section finishes with a discussion of issues related to proprietary motherboards that techs need to know.

• **Figure 4.25**   AT-style motherboard

AT Motherboards

The old-style computer motherboards followed a form factor called **AT**. The AT form factor, invented by IBM in the early eighties, was the predominant form factor for motherboards for a long time. The AT type of motherboard has a large keyboard plug, called a **DIN** connector, in the same relative spot on the motherboard, and it has a split P8/P9 style of power socket (Figure 4.25).

The AT motherboard has a few size variations, ranging from large to very large. The original AT motherboard was almost as large as two pieces of paper laid side by side. Because the technology was new, a lot of space was needed for the various chips that ran the components of the PC, such as the keyboard.

Baby AT

As technology improved and the PC flourished, the demand for smaller PCs increased. After all, an old-style PC with an AT motherboard took up quite a bit of desk real estate. Need drives the PC industry, so a smaller motherboard was created, dubbed the **Baby AT**. The original AT motherboard was then called the Full AT, Regular AT, or sometimes just AT. The Baby AT became and remained the most popular AT form factor for quite a while.

Figure 4.26 shows AT and Baby AT motherboards for comparison. Note that the keyboard connector on each falls in the same spot, and though it's hard to see here, the holes for connecting the boards to a system unit also line up. This standardization of permanent elements enabled people to swap one motherboard for another, as long as they stayed within the AT standard.

There is also some slight variation in size among Baby ATs. The standardization of the AT and Baby AT motherboards, however, demanded that the keyboard port and expansion slots stick to the form factor specifications.

The AT form factor dominated the PC industry for many years; however, as technology and needs changed, a number of problems arose with the AT motherboards. The single greatest problem was the lack of external ports.

When PCs were first invented, the only devices plugged into the average PC were a monitor and a keyboard. That's what the AT was designed to handle—the only dedicated connector on an AT motherboard is the keyboard plug (Figure 4.27). Initially, if you wanted to add connectors for anything else, you had to do so through the expansion slots. This included connections to serial and parallel ports.

Over the years, the number of devices plugged into the back of the PC has grown tremendously. Mice, printers, and other devices created a need for a new type of form factor, one with more dedicated connectors for more devices.

• **Figure 4.26**   AT motherboard beneath a Baby AT motherboard

ATX Motherboards

ATX has achieved a strong position in motherboard form factors and today is the standard. Although there are variations among manufacturers, ATX provides a standard for manufacturers to adhere to. ATX motherboards are relatively small (particularly compared to the large, older AT motherboards), meaning that computers, although more powerful, take up less desk space than ever.

ATX motherboards offer a substantially improved number of external connectors designed to support the increasing demands of PC users and their peripherals. Other improvements, such as placing the RAM closer to the Northbridge and CPU than on AT boards, offer users enhanced performance as well. Figure 4.28 shows an AT and an ATX motherboard—note the radical differences in placement of internal connections.

• **Figure 4.27**   DIN connector for the keyboard on an AT motherboard

• **Figure 4.28**   ATX and AT motherboards are organized quite differently.

microATX

The microATX form factor was developed as a natural evolution of the ATX form factor to address new market trends and PC technologies. microATX is to ATX what Baby AT was to AT. While offering the same benefits as the ATX form factor, the microATX was designed to further reduce the price of motherboards.

A microATX motherboard has a smaller physical size—called a *footprint*—than a full ATX motherboard and usually has three or four expansion slots rather than six to eight. microATX cases require special microATX motherboards, but most microATX motherboards will fit inside a regular ATX case. Not all microATX motherboards have the same physical size.

Notice how motherboard sizes just get smaller and smaller? Well, get ready to meet the smallest ATX motherboard of all: the FlexATX.

FlexATX

In 1999, Intel created a variant of the microATX called the FlexATX. FlexATX motherboards have maximum dimensions of just 9 by 7.5 inches, which makes them the smallest motherboards in the ATX standard.

FlexATX was created to reduce the size of the lowest-cost computers. Because FlexATX motherboards greatly limit the expansion of a PC, the FlexATX standard is not terribly popular with PC enthusiasts. FlexATX is limited to use with socketed processors only.

Motherboards come in a wide variety of form factors. Go to your local computer store and check out what is on display. Note the different features offered by ATX, microATX, and FlexATX motherboards. Does the store still stock any AT motherboards?

Introduction to PC Hardware and Troubleshooting

Proprietary Motherboards

Several major PC makers, including Hewlett-Packard and Sony, make motherboards that work only with their cases. These *proprietary* motherboards enable these companies to create systems that stand out from the generic ones and, not coincidently, push you to get service and upgrades from their authorized dealers. Some of the features you'll see in proprietary systems are riser boards—part of a motherboard separate from the main one, but connected by a cable of some sort—and unique power connections. If you work on one of these systems, keep in mind that all PCs function similarly, regardless of how they look. You might not be able to figure out the specific power connection right away, for example, but you know that the proprietary system *needs* power!

Step-by-Step 4.1

Removing a Motherboard from a PC Case

What form factor is your motherboard? Let's take it out of the case so you can examine it properly and, of course, get some hands-on practice removing motherboards.

Removing a motherboard requires only a few steps, but you need to take a couple of precautions to avoid damaging any of the components inside the system unit, or yourself. First, beware of ESD. Wear your grounding strap! Second, the insides of many PC cases have sharp edges that can give you some annoying cuts if you're not careful. Watch where you put your hands, and you'll be all right.

To complete this exercise, you will need the following:

- A PC with a motherboard and common devices installed
- An antistatic wrist strap
- A Phillips-head screwdriver
- A small container, such as a bowl, in which to keep screws
- An antistatic mat or some antistatic bags

Step 1

Open the side of the PC case. Usually you will need to unscrew two or three screws on the left side of the PC case (as you face it). Remove the side of the case and place all screws inside a bowl or container. Be sure to unplug all of the cables on the back of the computer, including the power cable.

Note: Refer to Chapter 1 to refresh your memory regarding the many ways to open PC cases.

Step 2

Lay the PC on its side and attach your antistatic wrist strap to the power supply or to an exposed metal part of the frame. I know this is more a little skip than a full step, but I wanted to emphasize good practice for avoiding ESD. Ground thyself!

Step 3

Unplug all of the wires connected to the motherboard. Unplug the cables running from the hard drive and CD-ROM. Then unplug the power connector from the P1 connector on the motherboard. Leave the CPU and fan on for the moment. Document the positions of the little wires for the speaker, power switch, power LED, hard drive LED, and reset button for when you need to reinstall them.

Step 4

Remove all of the expansion cards in the AGP and PCI slots. Be sure to unscrew them from the PC chassis first. Place all of the screws in your screw container. Be sure to handle the cards on the edges only. Place them to the side on the antistatic mat or in antistatic bags.

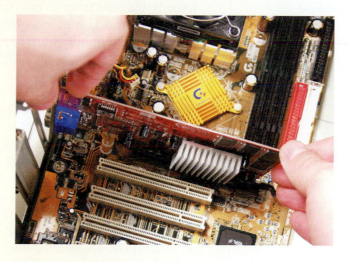

Step 5

Unscrew the motherboard from the case and place the screws that secured it—often as many as 10—in your bowl. *The motherboard will not simply lift out.* You definitely need to unscrew it from the case. The motherboard is sometimes also mounted to the case with plastic connectors called standouts that slide into keyed slots at the bottom of the box. Use your fingers to pinch the standouts and then lift the motherboard gently past the standouts. Be sure to handle the motherboard by the edges. The bottom side of a motherboard can sometimes have sharp solder points that can sting if you grab them with any force.

Step 6

At this point, you have the motherboard to examine at your leisure. Here are some of the issues you might want to consider:

What form factor is your motherboard? What internal connections does it have? External? How does your motherboard differ from your classmates' motherboards?

■ Installing a Motherboard

Motherboard installation is one of the fundamental tasks in building a PC. Although quite a few techs enjoy a bare-bones, caseless PC, most clients seem to need things in a nice, tidy package. With that in mind, let's put your PC together.

Installing a motherboard requires four things: research, preparation, common sense, and patience. The research part is pretty straightforward—you need to make certain that you have the correct case for your motherboard form factor. Once you've determined that the motherboard and case will fit together, then you're ready for the main event.

The other things you need are common sense and patience, just as for most other PC installation duties. Using common sense means not forcing something if it doesn't seem to want to go in easily. Check and double-check your connections to make certain that they line up, that the parts are oriented properly, and so on. Finally, installation of some motherboards simply takes time to do correctly. Take the time—and have fun.

Step-by-Step 4.2

Installing a New Motherboard

When you install a new motherboard, do not assume that you will put the screws and standouts in the same places as with your old motherboard. When it comes to the placement of screws and standouts, there is only one rule: anywhere they fit. Do not be afraid to be a little tough here! Installing motherboards can be a wiggly, twisty, scraped-knuckle process.

To complete this exercise, you will need the following:

- A motherboard (CPU and RAM installed is optional)
- A case that matches the form factor of the motherboard
- An antistatic wrist strap
- A Phillips-head screwdriver
- An antistatic mat or some antistatic bags

| Step 1 | Lay the empty PC case on its side. Attach your antistatic wrist strap to the power supply or the case frame. Then look for the bag of bronze-colored standout screws that came with your motherboard. These screws will fit between your motherboard and the metal plate, often called the motherboard plate, onto which you install the motherboard. |

| Step 2 | Before you mount the screws, you need to figure out where the motherboard will fit. The motherboard plate will seem to have many screw holes. This is to accommodate different ATX motherboard |

designs. Place your motherboard on the motherboard plate, with the external ports sticking out of the back of the PC case. Make a note of where the screw holes on the motherboard plate line up with the screw holes on the motherboard. When you've found the screw holes you want to use, attach the standout screws to the appropriate holes in the motherboard plate.

Step 3

You are now ready to mount the motherboard in the case. Place the motherboard over the standout screws you secured earlier. Those standout screws have screw holes on their tops that will enable you to secure the motherboard.

Make sure again that the external ports are sticking out of the back of the case. Use the proper-sized screws to secure the motherboard to the standouts. Just tighten the screws loosely at first, until you get all of the screws in place. Then tighten the screws snugly—there's no need to torque down too tightly, though.

Step 4

Plug the power lead from the power supply into the P1 power connector; then connect the front panel plugs to the motherboard. These usually include the connectors for the power button, reset button, speaker, power LED, and hard drive activity LED. Often the function of each set of front panel wires is printed on the connectors. If not, track each wire to the light or switch to determine its function, or break out the motherboard manual and find the diagram that shows which connectors fit on which pins.

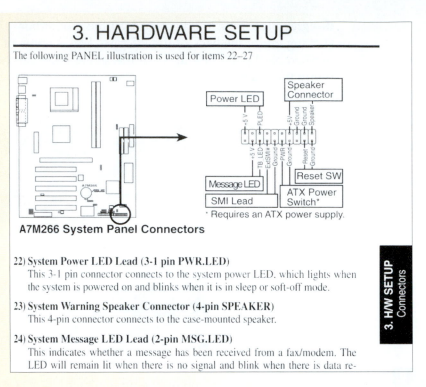

3. HARDWARE SETUP

The following PANEL illustration is used for items 22–27

A7M266 System Panel Connectors

22) System Power LED Lead (3-1 pin PWR.LED)
This 3-1 pin connector connects to the system power LED, which lights when the system is powered on and blinks when it is in sleep or soft-off mode.

23) System Warning Speaker Connector (4-pin SPEAKER)
This 4-pin connector connects to the case-mounted speaker.

24) System Message LED Lead (2-pin MSG.LED)
This indicates whether a message has been received from a fax/modem. The LED will remain lit when there is no signal and blink when there is data re-

There are a few rules to follow when installing these wires. The first rule is: The connectors have a positive and negative side; if they don't work one way, turn the connector around and try it the other. The second rule is: When in doubt, guess. More often than not, orienting the printed side of the connector toward the front of the case is the correct orientation.

At this point, you've installed the motherboard, and you're ready to test your system. To do that, you need to install three more items: the video card, a monitor, and power for the system. (This assumes that you had the CPU, CPU fan, and RAM installed already, of course.) Refer to Chapter 5 for instructions on installing expansion cards such as the video card, and to Chapter 11 for specifics on the monitor.

■ The System BIOS

A motherboard enables the different parts of a computer to communicate with one another, but not all motherboards are alike, and more importantly, the devices built into and attached to motherboards differ. You need to have some way to configure a system so that it understands all of its components and yet allows you to *change* that configuration to accommodate new and replaced devices. That's where the system BIOS comes into play. Let's look at input/output issues first and then turn to motherboard programming; we'll finish up by acessing the System Setup utility.

Why Do We Need BIOS in the First Place?

Here's the question: What's the process of going from *input* to *output*? You're working away in Microsoft Word and press the letter J—what happens? You know that the letter J will appear on the screen (unless you need a new keyboard), but *how* does that happen?

Inside Information

A Tale of Two Companies

Two companies—Award Software and Phoenix Technologies—write the vast majority of BIOS programs for motherboards. They customize the system BIOS programs for each model of motherboard.

First, you must have connectivity. Without a connection, there will be no J in the first place. When you press the J key, the keyboard sends data over the external data bus. The keyboard connects to the external data bus via the keyboard controller, called the *8042 chip*.

The keyboard constantly scans its keys, so when you press the J key, the keyboard translates that letter into a *scan code* and hands that code to the 8042. The 8042 puts the data into its registers, just like a CPU. Then, at some point, the CPU communicates with the 8042 and gets the data.

But wait! How does the CPU *know how* to talk to the 8042? Just like a CPU, the 8042 chip has a built-in code book. Just place those codes in the CPU's instruction set, and away we go!

Alas, there is another problem. There are many varieties of 8042 chips. It would be completely impractical to program *all* of those varieties into the CPU. The ideal solution would be to load some small program to teach the CPU how to talk to this *particular* 8042. This program concerns how the CPU handles input and output, and it's part of the *basic input/output system*, or BIOS.

Motherboards have quite a few built-in devices, all of which need BIOS. To make it practical for users and motherboard manufacturers, all of the important services are gathered together and collectively called the *system BIOS*.

The question now is where to put the system BIOS. This collection has to load every time the PC turns on; otherwise, the PC won't recognize any keystrokes from the keyboard or work properly with other devices.

We cannot store these programs in RAM. If RAM loses power, the system loses everything stored there. What kind of convenience would a PC give if you had to reprogram the system BIOS every time you started your computer?

We need updateable, nonvolatile memory to store this information. This means memory that stores data even when the power is off. Usually, non-volatile memory is a lot more expensive than volatile memory, but because the BIOS is very small, we don't need very much. We could use read-only memory (ROM), which works just like RAM but does not lose its data when the electricity goes away. But storing the system BIOS on a true ROM chip would make that data permanent and not easily upgradeable. That's not the goal, right?

Modern motherboards use a special kind of upgradeable nonvolatile memory called **flash ROM** to store the system BIOS. Most folks tend to lump the system BIOS (the programs stored in the flash ROM) together with the chip that holds the system BIOS under the term **flash BIOS**. Figure 4.29 shows an example of a BIOS chip of the sort you see on newer motherboards (compare this to the older oblong chips in Figure 4.14).

• How does the CPU talk to the keyboard controller?

• **Figure 4.29**   Flash BIOS chip on a motherboard

Certain devices fall into more than one category. Fancy keyboards with lots of extra keys and abilities, for example, belong in both the core group and the other devices group. The system BIOS handles the core functions, such as the typing of letters and numbers; the other, nonstandard features require device drivers. You'll learn more about these types of devices in Chapter 12.

Every Device Needs BIOS

Three types of devices need BIOS:

- **Unchanging system devices,** such as the keyboard controller and support chips on the motherboard. These are also called *core devices* because they form the core of your system. These get their BIOS programs from the system BIOS.

- **Changeable system devices,** such as the hard drive and floppy drive. These also get their BIOS programs from the system BIOS.

- **Other devices,** such as the sound card, network card, and so on. These devices require drivers or ROM chips built into the expansion card to bring their BIOS programs to the system. Chapter 5 discusses expansion devices and drivers in gory detail; this chapter concentrates on the core and changeable groups of BIOS programs.

The core group contains hardware that is essential for all PCs. Thus, we know that the list of core components won't change. One example of a core device is the 8042 keyboard controller chip. Other examples of core devices are parallel ports, serial ports, the PC speaker, and support chips on the motherboard. The flash BIOS, as mentioned earlier, provides a nonvolatile source for the CPU to access the BIOS for core devices. For the most part, technicians need never mess with the flash BIOS because it almost never fails without human intervention. We'll discuss making changes to the flash BIOS later in this chapter.

Changeable System Devices

Some devices in a PC are necessary and common, but have certain parameters that are changeable. Every PC, for example, must have RAM to operate, but the type, speed, and size of that RAM vary according to what is installed. The basic BIOS needed for assumed and necessary hardware—RAM, hard drives, floppy drives, video, and so on—is stored in the flash BIOS. However, if you change one of these items—for instance, upgrading a hard drive or adding a second hard drive—you must be able to change certain parameters to reflect those modifications to the hardware.

The flash BIOS programmers have provided a good interface that enables you to make changes to the setup and configuration of various changeable hardware devices without disturbing the underlying structure that keeps the core hardware working properly. This interface is called the **System Setup utility.**

Accessing the System Setup Utility

There are many ways to start the system setup utility—the method you use depends mainly on the brand of BIOS you have on your computer. Let me explain. When you fire up your computer in the morning, the first thing you see is the BIOS information.

This information shows you which brand of BIOS you are using—normally Award or Phoenix—as well as the hard drives and amount of

```
Award Modular BIOS v6.00PG, An Energy Star Ally
Copyright (C) 1984-2000, Award Software, Inc.

GREEN AGP/PCI/ISA SYSTEM

Main Processor : Pentium III 850MHz(100x8.5)
Memory Testing : 114688K

Award Plug and Play BIOS Extension v1.0A
Copyright (C) 2000 Award Software, Inc.
```

• A boot screen showing BIOS information

Introduction to PC Hardware and Troubleshooting

memory you have installed, among other things. BIOS manufacturers customize BIOS programs for motherboard models, as mentioned earlier, and they customize the means by which a tech can access the System Setup utility. This can cause problems, as seemingly identical System Setup utilities can be quite different from one another. Options that show up on one computer may be missing from another. Worst of all, it's not always clear how to access the utility in the first place.

Flashing the BIOS

Most motherboards have small programs called **BIOS updaters**. These programs give you the option of installing BIOS updates you download from the motherboard maker's website, as well as the ability to back up the current BIOS information.

Always be sure to make a backup copy of your current BIOS information before you update. You never know what can happen during a BIOS update, so it's best to be careful.

Try This!

Accessing the System Setup Utility

AMI, Award, and Phoenix each provide different ways to access the System Setup utility. Usually, you press the DEL key, but sometimes you need to press a function key. Try this:

1. Boot your system and turn on your monitor. Watch the information that scrolls by on the screen as your computer boots. Most BIOS makers include a line indicating what key to press to access the System Setup utility. Make a note of this useful information! You can also read your motherboard book to determine the process for accessing the System Setup program.

2. Reboot the system, and this time watch for information on the BIOS manufacturer. If you don't see it, and if it's okay to do so, open the system case and check the name printed on the system ROM chip. Make a note of this useful information.

3. Reboot one more time, and this time use the key you found to access the System Setup utility. Locate and make a note of the manufacturer, date, and version number of your PC's current BIOS.

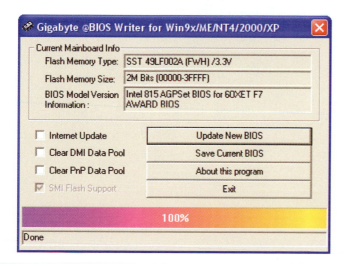

• BIOS updater program

The name of the BIOS backup file can be anything you want, though it should be something that describes the computer whose BIOS is being backed up. The BIOS information for many computers can be placed on one diskette.

Chapter 4 Review

■ Chapter Summary

After reading this chapter and completing the exercises, you should understand the following facts about motherboards and the BIOS.

Identify the parts of a motherboard

- Motherboards connect the diverse elements of a PC, enabling them to communicate with one another and work together.

- Motherboards have easily identifiable slots designed to fit the various PC components that need to communicate, including the CPU, memory, hard drive, and video card. Each component slot is easily identifiable.

- Motherboards have external ports that enable input devices such as mice and keyboards to communicate with the system.

Identify types of motherboards

- The ATX motherboard is the most common motherboard form factor.

- The ATX form factor was developed from the earlier AT form factor. AT motherboards were the original motherboards for PC systems.

- Baby AT motherboards were smaller, but did not solve the problematic issues with the AT design.

Install a motherboard in a system

- Installing a motherboard requires four things: research, preparation, common sense, and patience.

- Make certain that you have the proper case for your motherboard form factor, antistatic protection, and the standout screws and standard screws ready and waiting.

- Use common sense: don't force something if it doesn't seem to want to go in easily. Be patient and thorough; check and double-check your connections to make certain that they line up, and that you have the parts oriented properly.

- It is often easier on the tech and the motherboard to install the CPU, CPU fan, and RAM on a motherboard before installing the motherboard in the case.

Describe the function of the system BIOS and access the System Setup utility

- The BIOS determines how the various devices in the PC and the CPU communicate.

- The system BIOS is saved on a special chip on the motherboard called the flash BIOS chip.

- BIOS stored in the flash ROM can be updated. Updating enables a motherboard to access new technologies that it was not originally designed to support.

- You can use the System Setup utility to change variable BIOS information, such as the type of hard drive you have installed on your system.

- You can access the System Setup utility when you boot the computer. Just follow the on-screen instructions when you first power up.

■ Key Terms

Accelerated Graphics Port (AGP) *(89)*

AT *(94)*

ATX *(95)*

Baby AT *(94)*

basic input/output system (BIOS) *(89)*

BIOS updater *(105)*

DIN *(94)*

flash BIOS *(103)*

flash ROM *(103)*

form factor *(85)*

jumper *(91)*

memory slot *(87)*

motherboard *(84)*

P1 power connector *(87)*

parallel port *(92)*

Peripheral Component Interconnect (PCI) *(89)*

PS/2 port *(91)*

serial port *(92)*

System Setup utility *(104)*

Universal Serial Bus (USB) *(92)*

Key Term Quiz

Use terms from the Key Terms list to complete the following sentences follow. Not all terms will be used.

1. An ATX motherboard connects to the power supply via the _____.

2. The _____ expansion slot is made specifically for video cards.

3. The flash ROM and the system BIOS are often referred to collectively as the _____.

4. The mouse and keyboard connections on an ATX motherboard are called _____ ports.

5. _____ are small programs that the motherboard uses to install new BIOS information downloaded from the motherboard maker's website.

6. Before IBM came out with the PS/2 connector, the standard connection for a PC mouse was the _____.

7. _____ is currently the dominant motherboard form factor.

8. _____ controls the way that the CPU handles input and output.

9. You can use the _____ to change settings such as the types of hard drives your system uses.

10. The chip that stores the system BIOS is called the _____.

Multiple-Choice Quiz

1. The original form factor for a PC motherboard was the _____.
   a. AT
   b. Baby AT
   c. ATX
   d. LBX

2. What component, when added to the motherboard, protects the CPU from overheating?
   a. CPU fan
   b. CPU cooling unit
   c. Central cooling fan
   d. Central cooling unit

3. Which external port is usually used for printers?
   a. Serial
   b. Parallel
   c. Game
   d. Print

4. Which port allows simultaneous connection of up to 127 devices?
   a. USB
   b. Parallel
   c. Serial
   d. Game

5. Which port allows a CD-ROM to play music from a CD through a computer?
   a. Serial
   b. AUX_IN
   c. Parallel
   d. CD_IN

6. Which port on the motherboard provides a standardized interface for hard drives?
   a. FFD
   b. AGP
   c. PCI
   d. EIDE

7. Which expansion slot was designed to enable quick communication between internal hardware add-ons and the CPU?
   a. AGP
   b. Parallel
   c. PCI
   d. EIDE

8. When installing a motherboard, you first attach _____ to the motherboard plate so they line up with the holes on the motherboard.
   a. Standout screws
   b. Motherboard jacks

c. Plate connectors

d. Mounting risers

9. What portion of the motherboard connects to the power supply?

a. P8/P9 power connector

b. P1 power connector

c. P4 power connector

d. P1/P2 power connector

10. What portions of a motherboard can enable or disable some built-in devices?

a. Jump switches

b. Serial switches

c. Jumpers

d. Parallel switches

11. Which motherboard form factor was created to maintain all of the same connectors as the AT, but with a smaller size?

a. LBX

b. ATS

c. ATX

d. Baby AT

12. What is the generic name for DIMM slots and RIMM slots?

a. Memory slots

b. AGP slots

c. PCI slots

d. P8/P9 slots

13. What is the name of the keyboard connector on an AT motherboard?

a. Flex

b. PS/2

c. P8

d. DIN

14. What would you use to change the variable BIOS information in the system BIOS?

a. BIOS updater

b. System Setup utility

c. CMOS

d. System ROM

15. You want to access your System Setup utility. You hold down the DEL key during bootup, but that doesn't work. What should you do next?

a. Pressing DEL is the correct way to access System Setup. Try again and hold the key down longer.

b. You need to press a different key. You must watch your screen during bootup to find the information.

c. You need to press a different key. You must check your motherboard book to find the information.

d. You need to press a different key. Both answers b and c are valid ways to find the information you need.

■ Essay Quiz

1. Write a paragraph outlining the differences and similarities among the AT, Baby AT, and ATX types of motherboards. Why did motherboards evolve as they did?

2. Describe the location of each component of the motherboard and how each component pertains to your ability to use the PC.

3. Using your knowledge of CPUs and memory gained in previous chapters, write a brief essay about how these communicate with each other.

Be sure to incorporate a brief description of the purpose of the Northbridge chip.

4. Write a brief essay describing why system BIOS is necessary and how its information is stored on the motherboard.

5. Create a two-column list: on the left list all the types of external connectors on a motherboard, and opposite each type of connector, list the device(s) it serves.

Lab Projects

• Lab Project 4.1

Your class has recently won a grant, and your teacher has decided to upgrade the motherboards of your PCs. Safely remove your motherboard, exchange it for that of one of your classmates, and install the new motherboard in your system.

• Lab Project 4.2

When you are considering upgrading or replacing motherboard components, it's critical that you be able to identify key features and specifications of the motherboard itself. In this lab you will determine the various specifications and features of a motherboard. If possible, do this exercise using several different motherboards. When you can, determine the answers both through direct inspection of the motherboard and by looking in the motherboard book.

- **Layout**   Is the motherboard ATX or AT? Can you determine what variation of AT or ATX?

Does it have any special features advertised by the maker?

- **Make and model**   Who made the motherboard and what is the model number?

- **RAM**   Does it use SDRAM? DDR SDRAM? RDRAM? How many slots does it have? What is the maximum amount of RAM it will support?

- **CPU**   What is the socket/slot type? What type(s) of CPUs will it support?

Expansion Bus

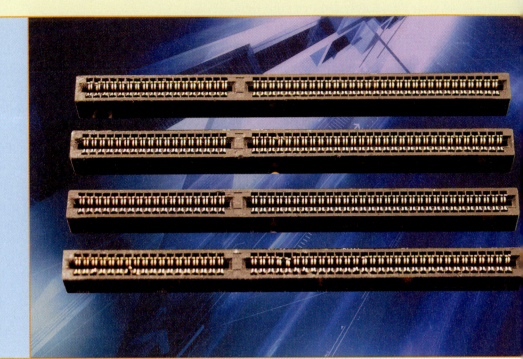

"C'mon baby,
take a chance with us,
And meet me at the back
of the blue bus."
—The Doors

In this chapter, you will learn how to:

- **Describe the purpose and basic functions of an expansion bus**
- **Recognize the different types of internal expansion buses used on PCs**
- **Install a Plug and Play expansion card**
- **Recognize the USB and FireWire bus technologies and know how to use them**

At its simplest, an expansion bus is nothing more than a slot or port that enables you to add devices to your computer. The concept of the expansion bus is one of the main reasons the PC has been able to achieve such an important place in today's society.

If you've ever looked inside a computer case, odds are good that you've already seen an expansion bus. Just take a look at any motherboard—the expansion slots usually take up more space on the motherboard than anything else.

This chapter begins by explaining why expansion buses exist and (without getting too technical) the basics of how they work. You will learn about the different types of expansion slots used on motherboards and go through the process of installing a typical expansion card in an expansion slot. Having conquered the inside of the PC, you will move on to USB and FireWire, two very popular external expansion buses.

• Expansion slots on a motherboard

■ Expansion Buses

In the old days, adding a piece of equipment to a PC was about two clicks below open heart surgery on the scary scale. Fortunately, adding devices to a modern computer (running Windows 98 or better) is in most cases fairly easy, assuming that you understand what you are doing. The reason? The wonderful, versatile expansion bus!

Why Expansion Buses Exist

The first step is to understand *why* expansion buses exist. Put simply, an expansion bus is a special connection on the motherboard that enables you to add hardware to your computer that didn't come with it. Expansion buses actually predate the PC. Mainframe computers had them, but with an important difference: if you wanted to add something to your IBM mainframe computer, you had to buy an IBM part. The multiple-vendor support that today allows us to install most devices without concern for the brand name did not exist.

In contrast, the expansion slots on a PC aren't specific to particular pieces of hardware. A PC's expansion slot is more like a light socket: you can plug in any compatible type and brand of device—any modem, sound card, or network card, for instance. Assuming everything else is done correctly, the installed device will work.

The Next Step Involves a Clock

Take a look at Figure 5.1. It shows a sound card, a device that enables your computer to record and play sound files. This sound card is designed to snap into any one of the white expansion bus slots on the motherboard shown in Figure 5.2. In fact, you can snap this sound card into just about any PC that has that type of expansion bus slot.

Let's consider this sound card for a moment. A quick glance confirms that it uses electronic chips, and these chips have a clock wire, just like the CPU. Therefore, the sound card needs to be pushed by a clock chip, just like the CPU—and just like every other chip on your PC. This all seems simple enough, except for one question: at what clock speed does the sound card run? If I snap it into an old AMD system with a 33-MHz motherboard, will it run at 33 MHz? What if I take the same sound card and snap it into a new Pentium 4 system with a 133-MHz motherboard—will it then run at 133 MHz? It turns out the answer to both questions is no—the clock speed of the expansion slots is separate and independent from the motherboard speed.

● Sound card inserted into an expansion slot on a motherboard

So how do you give a slow device like a sound card the ability to connect to the external data bus and the address bus? This is where the Northbridge (the part of a chipset on your motherboard that controls communication among the memory, CPU, external cache, and AGP bus) once again comes

- **Figure 5.2**   Close-up of PCI slots

into play. On modern systems, the Northbridge is in charge of the expansion slots on your motherboard. (Is this a busy chip or what?) The Northbridge provides a separate set of external data bus and address bus wires just for devices that are connected to expansion slots. This combination of special Northbridge wires and expansion slots is called the **expansion bus**. The number of wires on an expansion bus as well as the bus's speed depend on the *type* of expansion bus, and there have been quite a few over the years! We'll get to the hardware history later in the chapter, but first you need to understand how your computer makes this all work.

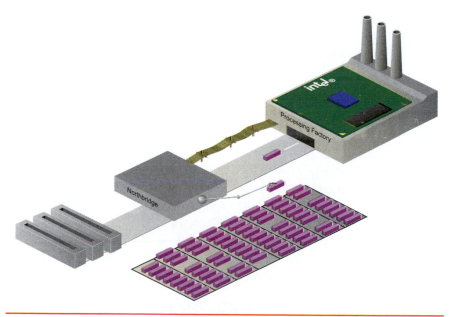

- The expansion bus connects to the Northbridge chip

• Typical video card with a device driver CD

Device Drivers

The simple act of putting a device into your computer is not enough to make the thing work. After the device is physically installed, the CPU needs some software it can use to communicate with the device. These programs are called **device drivers**. Device drivers normally come on a CD or floppy disk packaged with the device; they must be loaded when you install the device.

Although most device drivers are installed from a floppy or CD-ROM, some devices are so common that the device drivers are stored on the system ROM chip (that's the system BIOS discussed in Chapter 4). Certain devices such as the keyboard, the hard drives, and the floppy drive are *always* supported via BIOS stored in the system ROM. When you install a hard drive, you don't need to install a device driver—the system BIOS will be configured to see the hard drive, and the CPU can run the BIOS from the system ROM chip when it needs to talk to the hard drive.

So how do you know which devices need software device drivers and which are supported by the system BIOS? As a general rule, the following devices are supported by the system BIOS:

  Many hard drives do come with drivers on floppy disks, but they are provided in case you have a system with an older BIOS. You'll learn more about this in Chapter 8.

- Hard drives
- Floppy drives
- Keyboard
- RAM
- Chipset

Pretty much every other device in your PC needs a software device driver. Throughout the rest of this book, I will be discussing the installation of many different devices, and by the time you're done reading, you should have a solid grasp of what needs a software driver and what does not. For now, just remember that every device needs some type of support program, and that if the device isn't supported by the system BIOS, you will need to install the software driver yourself.

System Resources

A device inside your computer normally needs to do three things. First, it needs to communicate with the CPU. Second, it needs to inform the CPU that it has performed some action so that the CPU can initiate communication. Third, it needs to request RAM space for storage of the program code and data it's using and generating. These needs inherent to devices are known collectively as **system resources**. Let's look at each of these resources in turn and then explore how to examine the system resources of a Windows system using the Device Manager.

Communicating with the CPU: I/O Addresses

It's time to confess: I've told you only part of the story about the address bus. Up to now, I've discussed the address bus as the communication link between the CPU and the Northbridge that allows the CPU to access RAM. Well, that's true, but it's not the whole truth. The address bus also handles another critical job: I/O addressing. You see, the address bus doesn't just run between the CPU and the Northbridge; it also connects to the expansion slots.

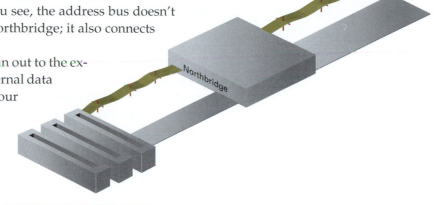

Now why does the address bus run out to the expansion slots? Well, although the external data bus may be the main *data* path on your PC, the address bus is the main *communication* path between the CPU and every device in your computer. When the CPU wants to talk to a device, it places a charge on a special wire called the **IO/MEM wire**. Everything in your computer is connected to this wire. Devices that the

• The address bus also goes to the expansion slots

CPU is currently using check the IO/MEM wire for the presence of a charge. If the devices find no charge on the wire, they know that the CPU is using the address bus to talk to RAM, so they can ignore the signals from the CPU on the address bus. When the CPU places a charge on the IO/MEM wire, the devices know that CPU is now using the address bus to communicate with one of them, so they'd better pay attention.

Every device in your computer is identified on the address bus by up to 16 different patterns of 16 ones and zeros. Each of these patterns of ones and zeros sent by the CPU over the address bus to a device is called an **I/O address**, and each I/O address corresponds to a command. For example, the keyboard uses four I/O addresses. Let's separate the 16 address wires into 4 groups of 4 to make the patterns more obvious. Note that the examples here do not replicate the exact keyboard commands, but they are close enough to illustrate the concept.

- 0000 0000 0110 0000 = Send the last key pressed to the external data bus, but do not erase it from the keyboard memory.

- 0000 0000 0110 0001 = Send the last key pressed to the external data bus and erase it from the keyboard memory.

- 0000 0000 0110 0010 = Check the status of the CTRL and ALT keys.

- 0000 0000 0110 0011 = Check the status of the keyboard LEDs.

Hmmm…all of these ones and zeros are confusing. I think it's time to make a short digression to talk about…(cue the drum roll) the Dreaded Hexadecimal System.

The Hexadecimal System   The hexadecimal system is really pretty simple once you understand the secret. The hexadecimal system, also known as base-16 mathematics, is a complete numbering system based on 16 instead of 10 digits. You can add, subtract, and even do trigonometry with hex. The only part of hex you need to know as a tech, however, is the part that the PC world uses.

To help you understand hex, I will use the address bus commands as examples. When the CPU turns on the IO/MEM wire, it can then use the first 16 address bus wires to talk to the devices in the computer. These 16 wires can either have voltage or no voltage on them. As you've seen before, a wire with

Only the first 16 wires of the address bus are watched by the devices when the IO/MEM wire is lit. Even though modern address buses use (at least) 32 wires, the original design used only 16 wires to signal devices. As is often the case with computers, this original design continues to affect the way things work—the other 16 wires are simply ignored during this operation.

voltage represents a 1, and a wire with no voltage represents a 0. Using 16 wires, you have 65,536 different possible combinations of ones and zeros, from 0000000000000000 through 1111111111111111.

Each combination of charged and uncharged wires represents a pattern that the CPU can send down the address bus to talk to a device. The problem for your basic human trying to deal with this is that it's really annoying to have to say, "The command to tell the hard drive controller to display its error status is 000000111110000." Although your computer is good at talking in ones and zeros, human beings find it very difficult. We need some kind of shorthand, some way to talk about ones and zeros so that human beings can easily follow what's being said. As you may have guessed, the hexadecimal system can be very useful in this regard. In the PC world, hex is used as shorthand to describe sets of binary values.

Pretend that you have a computer with a four-wire address bus. How many different patterns could you create? With four wires, you can create the following patterns of ones and zeros: 0000, 0001, 0010, 0011, 0100, 0101, 0110, 0111, 1000, 1001, 1010, 1011, 1100, 1101, 1110, and 1111.

So four wires give you 16 different possible patterns. No computer has only a four-wire address bus, but just about every bus in your computer has some *multiple* of four wires. Because four is the largest common denominator of all the different address bus sizes, you can create shorthand by substituting a single number for any group of four binary digits. Because there are 16 possible combinations of ones and zeros, the natural choice for this shorthand is—you guessed it!—a base-16 numbering system, a.k.a., hexadecimal. Table 5.1 shows this hex shorthand.

When referencing a particular pattern of ones and zeros being sent to a device on the address bus, you would not use a binary sequence like 0000000111110000. This is where you'd use the hex shorthand instead.

Table 5.1	Binary and Hexadecimal Values for Four Address Bus Wires	
Binary Number	**State of Wires (On or Off)**	**Hexadecimal Value**
0000	All wires off	0
0001	Only fourth wire on	1
0010	Only third wire on	2
0011	Third and fourth wires on	3
0100	Only second wire on	4
0101	Second and fourth wires on	5
0110	Second and third wires on	6
0111	Only first wire off	7
1000	Only first wire on	8
1001	First and fourth wires on	9
1010	First and third wires on	A
1011	Only second wire off	B
1100	First and second wires on	C
1101	Only third wire off	D
1110	Only fourth wire off	E
1111	All wires on	F

Let's walk through the process. First, mentally break the 16 binary digits into four sets of four. In this example, the four sets would be 0000, 0001, 1111, and 0000. Next, give each four-character set its own hex shorthand using the information in Table 5.1. Thus, 0000 becomes 0; 0001 becomes 1; 1111 becomes F; and 0000 becomes 0. Now instead of rattling off a string of ones and zeros, you can refer to this pattern by saying "01F0." All of the possible I/O addresses can be represented by four-digit hexadecimal values, starting at 0000 and ending at FFFF.

Now let's return to the keyboard example and use Table 5.1 to convert the binary I/O addresses for the keyboard into hexadecimal shorthand:

- 0000 0000 0110 0000 = 0 0 6 0, which is written as 0060h (the small "h" on the end shows it's a hex value)

- 0000 0000 0110 0001 = 0061h

- 0000 0000 0110 0010 = 0062h

- 0000 0000 0110 0011 = 0063h

Did you get it? Remember that the hex number has the same numerical value as the binary version. Translating the number simply makes it easier to write down and recall.

Back to the Address Bus   Now that you have a basic understanding of the hexadecimal system and understand that it is nothing but a handy shorthand for describing long chains of ones and zeros, I can return to the business at hand: I/O addresses. To recap, every device in your PC has multiple I/O addresses—we prefer to say a *range* of I/O addresses—and each pattern is really a command that the CPU can send to the device. The I/O address range for the keyboard is 0060h–0063h. Back in the bad old days (before Windows 95), you had to set the I/O address on a device manually. No two devices could simultaneously use the same I/O address, so getting this wrong could really cause trouble.

- Setting I/O addresses manually on a pre–Plug and Play (legacy) card

Fortunately, today's systems use a wonderful little feature called **Plug and Play (PnP)**. PnP means that when you snap in an expansion card, it talks to the BIOS and the operating system and automatically sets itself to an unused I/O address range. If you have a PC that is not PnP, you have a collector's item! The days of manual configuration are over. Long live PnP!

Talking to the CPU: Interrupts

When you move your mouse, you expect the mouse pointer to move to the new position. For the mouse pointer to move to the new location, the CPU must know which I/O address to light. To find out, it must run the correct device driver program, which will tell it. All well and good, but how does the CPU know that the mouse has been moved in the first place? That's the job of special wires called **interrupt request wires**, also known as **IRQs**.

IRQs are designated by the numbers 0 through 15. The same PnP programs that set up I/O addresses also assign IRQs to devices as needed. No two devices can use the same IRQ simultaneously. Back in the days before PnP, IRQs, like I/O addresses, had to be set manually. Pre-PnP, IRQ conflicts (two devices accidentally using the same IRQ) were the number-one cause of heartburn for PC folks. Hooray for PnP!

Requesting RAM

The final resource that devices need is RAM space in which to store the data and instructions they're using. There are two primary ways to get this: have the CPU assign the needed memory to the device or let the device access RAM directly.

Assigned Memory   Some devices—the most obvious example being video cards—need some memory assigned to them to function properly. In modern computers, PnP knows how to coordinate this access and does so automatically.

DMA   Some devices also like to access memory directly, without the intervention of the CPU. This process is known as **Direct Memory Access (DMA)**. To prevent two devices from accessing memory directly at the same time, the computer assigns each device that wants to access memory directly a DMA number from 0 to 7. Yet again, PnP handles this automatically for the few devices that still use DMA.

Device Manager

Even though you'll probably never need to deal with system resources today, you can still examine the system resources of a Windows system by accessing the **Device Manager**.

Step-by-Step 5.1

Checking Device Drivers

The folks who make cards for PCs often update drivers, adding extra functionality or stability. It's good practice to check occasionally to make sure that your drivers are the latest and greatest. This is especially true for video cards. The video card in my computer has gone through seven driver revisions in the past 18 months!

There are two methods for checking whether you have the latest driver: using the Windows Update utility, and checking manually. In this Step-by-Step exercise, you will check for drivers in both ways.

To complete this exercise, you will need the following:

- Two systems: one running Windows 9x/Me and the other Windows 2000 or XP. If you have access to only one or the other, follow the instructions for that OS only.

- Internet access.

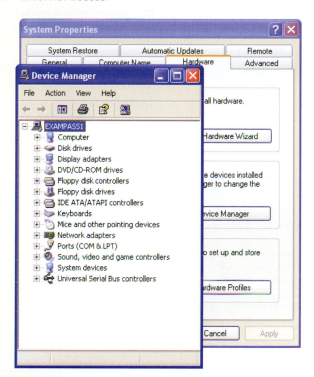

Step 1

If you're using a Windows 9x/Me system, open the Device Manager by alternate-clicking (right-clicking) the My Computer icon on the desktop, choosing Properties, and clicking the Device Manager tab. If you're using a Windows 2000 or XP system, alternate-click My Computer, choose Properties, click the Hardware tab, and then click the Device Manager button. The illustration at the right shows the Device Manager in Windows XP.

Step 2

To view the resources assigned to a device, click one of the small plus signs to the left of that type of device in the Device Manager list. This reveals the listing for the specific device.

The next step depends on the operating system. In Windows 9x, click to highlight the device and then click the Properties button; for Window 2000 and XP, alternate-click the device and choose Properties from the context menu that pops up. In the Properties dialog box, click the Resources tab to see what resources this device is using.

Step 3

Now click the Driver tab. If you have a Windows 2000 or XP system, the driver version and maybe a date will be displayed here. If you have a Windows 9x/Me system, you may need to click the Driver File Details button to see the revision number.

Write down this information. Note that the Drivers tab has an Update Driver button; this is not commonly used, and you won't use it for this exercise.

Step 4

Close the Device Manager. Open a browser and surf to the video card manufacturer's website. Find the drivers—usually they're on the Support or Downloads page. Locate the downloadable driver for your card and compare its date to the date of the version you're running to see which one is more recent.

Step 5

If you find a newer version of your driver online, download it. To make it easy to find, save it on your Windows desktop. Normally, the download will be a self-executable file. Double-click it to run the self-executing program and follow manufacturer's directions to update your driver.

Windows Update

The Windows Update tool that comes with later versions of Windows 98 and with Windows Me, 2000, and XP does a fairly good job of informing you of driver updates available online. The nicest thing about Windows Update is its simplicity. However, not all card makers subscribe to Microsoft's Update scheme, so to be completely sure, you have to check manually.

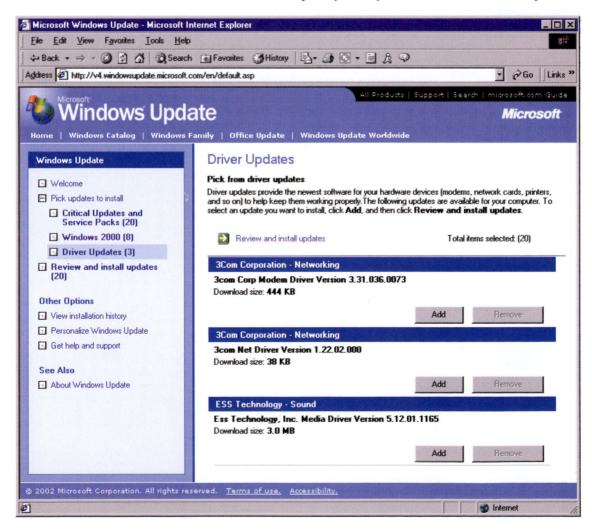

■ Internal Buses

Internal buses are much older than external buses, so I will discuss internal buses first. This approach allows you to follow the evolution of the technology over the years as buses become faster and cleverer.

8-Bit ISA

Imagine going back to IBM in the late 1970s, when the idea that became the IBM Personal Computer was being born. Almost every part of the original IBM PC came from other projects, including the expansion bus. The first PC used a piece of hardware that IBM called the PC expansion bus, but it is much better known as the Industry Standard Architecture (ISA) bus.

Try This!

Using Windows Update

Windows Update is as simple to use as it is useful. Try this:

1. Start Windows Update. Windows 98/Me systems provide shortcuts to Windows Update on the Start menu and under Settings. On Windows 2000/XP systems, open the Add/Remove Programs applet in the Control Panel, click the Add New Programs button on the left, and then click the Windows Update button. You can also find Windows Update at the top of the Windows XP start menu.

2. Allow Windows Update to scan your system.

3. If Windows Update finds any updates, it will show them to you. Then it's up to you to select and download the updates you want to apply.

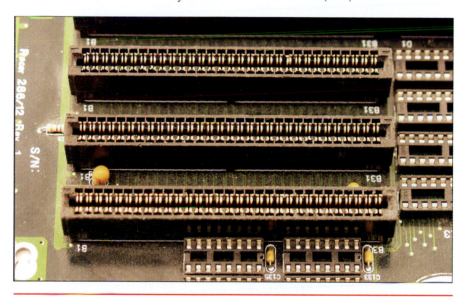

• 8-bit ISA bus slots

The first version of the ISA bus was a whopping 8 bits wide. Because early CPUs only had 8-bit-wide external data buses, however, that was big enough. The ISA bus ran at the (then) blazingly fast speed of about 7 MHz.

16-Bit ISA

The second generation of PCs ran Intel 80286 CPUs with 16-bit external data buses. IBM redesigned the 8-bit ISA slot by adding a small extension to the end of it, creating the venerable 16-bit ISA expansion bus. A 16-bit ISA card can be distinguished from an 8-bit card by the small, separate extension that makes it fit into the full length of the 16-bit ISA slot. There is no substantial difference between the 8-bit and 16-bit ISA slots other than their width in bits. Both buses ran at roughly 7 MHz; both were "stupid" in that you couldn't just snap them in and immediately expect them to work as you can with today's cards.

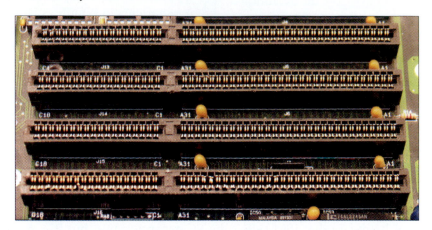

• 16-bit ISA bus slots

• 16-bit ISA network card

MCA

ISA was the only expansion bus for the first six to eight years of the PC's existence. Then, as 386 processors started to appear on the scene, IBM wanted to completely redesign the expansion bus to make it faster, wider, and

Introduction to PC Hardware and Troubleshooting

smarter. IBM came up with the (at the time) very impressive MicroChannel Architecture, better known as MCA.

MCA buses were up to 32 bits wide, matching the external data bus of the 386 and 486 CPUs. MCA devices ran at 12 MHz, much faster than ISA. Not only was MCA faster and wider, but microchannel devices were self-configuring. You simply installed the card and popped a special floppy disk into your floppy drive, and the device automatically configured itself. Back in the late 1980s, this was incredible. Unlike it did with ISA, IBM chose not to release MCA to the public domain, instead collecting a license fee from anyone using the technology on a motherboard or expansion card. As a result, MCA slowly died over the next five years.

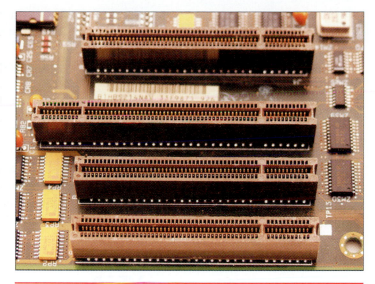

• MCA bus slots (the longer slot is a 32-bit slot; the others are 16-bit slots)

EISA

The PC world wasn't happy with IBM's attempt to charge for what had been free, and in retaliation, the major clone makers such as Compaq and Dell worked together in the late 1980s to invent their own improved expansion bus, called the Extended Industry Standard Architecture (EISA) bus. EISA had all the wholesome goodness of MCA: it was 32-bits wide, it ran at 8.33 MHz—a bit faster than ISA—and it was self-configuring. In addition, EISA had something MCA lacked: backward compatibility. MCA did not support the older ISA cards. By contrast, EISA defined a unique two-layered pin layout—the top layer was for ISA cards, and the bottom layer was for EISA cards.

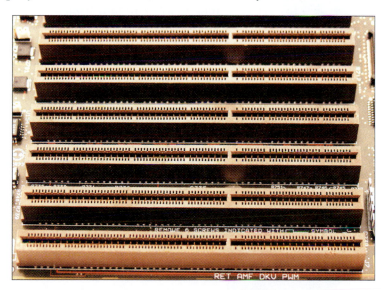

• EISA bus slots

Even though EISA was public-domain technology, two factors kept it from being used extensively. First, there was little demand back then for devices with 32-bit-wide data paths. The modems, hard drives, and keyboards of the late 1980s just didn't need that much bandwidth. The second issue was cost. EISA, though powerful, was very expensive to implement. Thus, the first 386 and 486 PCs, and even some early Pentium PCs, whose speeds by this time approached 100 MHz, were stuck using the ancient, narrow, and slow ISA bus.

This raised the question: how does a computer with a 32-bit-wide external data bus use a 16-bit-wide expansion bus? Figure 5.3 shows the answer: make a Northbridge that *terminates* 16 of the wires that run to the expansion slots. Most software was designed to send and receive data only in 16-bit chunks anyway. Also at this time everyone was still using DOS for an operating system, which can only handle 16-bit commands.

To distinguish the two parts of the bus, the part of the external data bus that ran at the speed of the motherboard was called the local bus, and the part that included the expansion slots kept the name expansion bus.

VESA Local Bus

Up until 1990, non-Apple computers were all running DOS, a *text-based* operating system. In 1990, Microsoft unveiled the first popular version of Windows.

• VESA VL-bus slots

Windows' Macintosh-like graphical user interface (GUI) was simply too much for the ISA video cards of the time to handle. The initial solution, developed in the late 1980s, was the VESA Local Bus (VL-Bus).

The VL-Bus was a parasitic bus. Placed directly behind an ISA slot, it relied on the ISA bus for the initial communication with the CPU, after which it pumped data directly to and from the local bus. Their long series of ISA and VL-Bus pin connectors give VL-Bus cards a distinctive appearance. The VL-Bus was incredibly popular from the late 1980s until about 1996, when a breakthrough type of bus called PCI became popular.

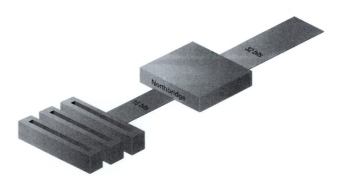

• **Figure 5.3**   The Northbridge terminated 16 of the 32 external data bus wires

Introduction to PC Hardware and Troubleshooting

PCI

Cheap, well understood, and reliable, the ISA bus dominated the market during its heyday. Eventually, though, the advance of CPU technology doomed ISA to the computer museum. ISA couldn't handle the faster Pentium and early Pentium II chips, and in 1990, the chipmaker Intel unveiled a revolutionary new expansion bus called **Peripheral Component Interconnect (PCI)**.

The PCI expansion bus has all the good aspects of both MCA and EISA. It is 32 bits wide (there's even a 64-bit version), is totally self-configuring, and runs at 33 MHz. Intel did not release PCI to the public domain, but it did make licensing so incredibly inexpensive that PCI immediately became a very attractive choice for motherboard makers.

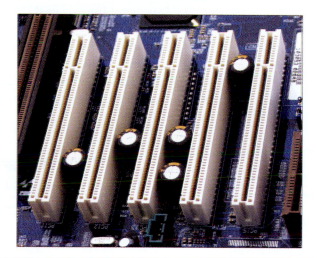

- PCI bus slots

PCI's most appealing feature is that it's a **mezzanine bus**. A mezzanine bus is an expansion bus that does not have to be the only expansion bus on the motherboard. Unlike ISA, EISA, and MCA, PCI was explicitly designed to coordinate with—the common term is *host*—other types of expansion buses. Thus, a motherboard with a mezzanine bus can have both PCI and ISA slots, or both PCI and EISA slots. The older buses don't have to know how to work with a PCI bus because the PCI bus handles things for both of them. In most systems, the Northbridge supports the PCI bus, and the Southbridge supports the hosted bus.

Now you can see just how busy the Northbridge really is. So where is the local bus now? There really isn't a local bus any more. The Northbridge really has four different buses, each with a specific function: one connects to the CPU, one to RAM, one to the PCI slots, and one to the Southbridge chip. To keep all of these different

Cross Check

PCI and Backward Compatibility

Why was PCI's mezzanine bus feature so important to the development to the PC? Reread the discussions of the features of ISA, MCA, and EISA earlier in this chapter. Think about the need for motherboard manufacturers to adopt the PCI bus without losing backward compatibility.

After reading about PCI's Southbridge, see if you can find any reference on the Internet to PCI-to-EISA bridges or PCI-to-MCA bridges. You probably won't find much. Although these types of bridges are possible to make, PCI's most common Southbridge chip was a PCI-to-ISA bridge. Why do you think this is the case?

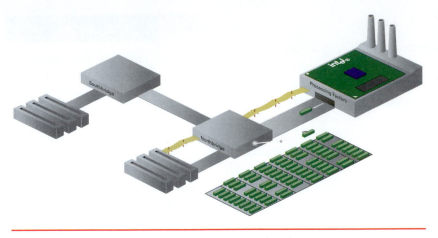

• Northbridge and Southbridge connected to expansion slots

buses straight, we need to give them specific names. The buses running from the Northbridge to RAM and the CPU are known collectively as the frontside bus. The bus running to the PCI slots is the PCI expansion bus, and the bus running to the Southbridge has so many different names that I'll just refer to it as the Southbridge bus.

Of course, nothing in the PC business stays the same. Recognizing that modern motherboards no longer have ISA slots, Intel's latest chips move the PCI connection to the South- bridge and have an optional third chip called the ICH that handles all of the onboard functions such as the keyboard, mouse, hard drive, and floppy drives. The ICH can also handle ISA slots, although this is almost never needed today.

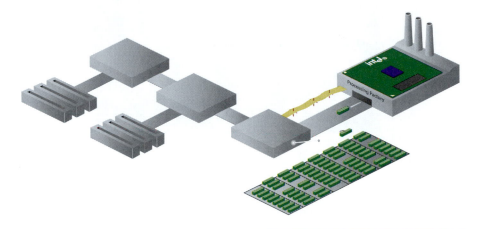

• Northbridge, Southbridge, and ICH on an Intel system

PCI has now completely taken over the motherboard world. If your motherboard has expansion slots, some or all of them will be PCI slots. When PCI first came on the scene, it was common to see motherboards with both PCI and ISA slots (Figure 5.4). As PCI became more prevalent, motherboards with only one or two ISA slots became common. Today, most motherboards have dropped ISA altogether. After almost 20 years, we are finally past the ISA world. PCI is the king of the expansion slots.

If you were paying close attention, you may have noticed two other types of slots on the motherboard: a long brown one and another tiny one. Guess what—those are PCI slots too! However, they are very special types of PCI slots, called AGP and AMR/CNR slots.

AGP

Have you seen some of the amazing computer games available today? These new graphically intense games cause the same problem for PCI cards

Introduction to PC Hardware and Troubleshooting

• **Figure 5.4**   Motherboard with PCI and ISA slots

that Windows caused for the old ISA cards: PCI cards can't handle the greater requirements. To support programs that use high-end graphics, Intel invented a super PCI slot called the **Accelerated Graphics Port (AGP)**. An AGP slot is a PCI slot, but one with its own personal connection to the Northbridge. AGP slots are only for graphics—don't try to snap a sound card or modem into one. You'll learn much more about this fascinating technology in Chapter 11.

• AGP slot (next to PCI slots)

The End of IRQs?

PCI devices are intelligent and don't require IRQs, but they still get IRQs assigned to them for backward compatibility. However, in most cases, all of the PCI devices share the *same* IRQ! Through a process called **IRQ steering**, one IRQ is assigned to all PCI devices, not for their sake, but to allow the PCI devices to coexist with older IRQ-dependent components. Try the following to see if your system is using IRQ steering.

1. Determine what PCI devices are installed in your PC. If necessary, open the PC and inspect the cards.

2. Open the Device Manager. Select any of the PCI devices. Check the resources for that device. Write down the IRQ number assigned to it. If that device does not show an assigned IRQ, try another one.

3. Now check the resources for a different PCI device. Is it using the same IRQ as the first one? You can repeat this process for however many PCI devices you have. In most cases, you will find that they are all using the same IRQ.

AMR/CNR

I'll bet you've listened to an AM radio station while driving in an automobile. Have you ever noticed that when you pass under power lines you hear a rather nasty humming sound? When the radio receiver in your car passes through the electrical field of the power lines, it interprets that energy as sound. In the electrical business, that unintended electrical sound is called *noise*. Many PCs suffer from the same phenomenon.

To counter this, sound cards and network cards contain noise-limiting devices; however, many motherboards also have a special PCI slot just for these types of devices, called a Communications/Networking Riser (CNR) slot. This tiny slot is present on about 25 percent of today's motherboards. The Audio/Modem Riser (AMR) is an older, visually identical, version of CNR. These slots are used by system makers, who purchase special riser cards to support sound or networking. These cards are not for sale on the retail market, so unless you bought a system with a riser card installed, you'll never deal with these slots.

• CNR slot

Mini PCI

One more type of internal expansion bus that you'll see is the **Mini PCI** slot. These slots are used only in laptops. Laptops, unlike desktop computers, haven't had a standard internal port that third-party makers could design devices to use. If you wanted a modem in your laptop, you either bought a laptop with a modem already built in or used a PC Card modem. Mini PCI has changed this by offering a standard internal port that anyone can make devices to use. Mini PCI offers an extremely convenient way to add modems, sound cards, or network cards to a portable computer.

• Mini PCI card and slot

Step-by-Step 5.2

Checking the Expansion Bus

To complete this exercise, you will need the following:

■ A system running Windows 98, Me, 2000, or XP with a PCI or AGP video card installed

■ If possible, a similarly equipped partner

Step 1

Shut down the system and open the case of the system unit. If possible, remove all of the expansion cards. Be careful doing this; most cards have at least one wire or cable connected to them that must first be removed. Be sure to document the location and orientation of these cables and wires *before* you remove any card!

Step 2

If you have a partner, hold up the different cards and make sure that you can identify the type of expansion bus they match. With the cards removed, check to be sure you can identify the different types of empty expansion slots on the motherboard.

Step 3

Make a list of all of the expansion slots on the motherboard. How many PCI slots are there? How many AGP slots? Are there any ISA slots? Do you have a CNR slot? If you have an old system—386, 486, or Pentium—you probably won't find an AGP slot, and you may not even have PCI slots, but you'll certainly have ISA slots. Check to see whether they're 8-bit or 16-bit ISA.

Step 4

Leaving the cards uninstalled, reconnect the power and reboot the PC. You will hear a beeeep-beep-beep-beep sound. That's the PC telling you that it cannot find a video card. Shut down the system and reinstall *only* the video card.

Step 5

Reboot the system and open the Device Manager. Try to locate the entries for the devices whose cards you have removed. Document what does and doesn't show up in the Device Manager.

Step 6

Shut down the system again and reinstall one of the cards you removed. Reboot the PC and check the Device Manager for that device. Document what you find. Do the same for the rest of the cards you removed until all devices are reinstalled.

■ Installing a Plug and Play Expansion Card

Installing a card into a PC is a relatively straightforward and simple process, but one that requires several specific and important steps. For this discussion, I'll use examples involving a network card, but of course this process also applies to many other types of expansion cards.

Picking the Right Card

There are many types of network cards. There are also many types of sound cards. In fact, there are dozens of different options for just about any general type of card, both in terms of functions and connection type. At this moment don't concern yourself with this issue, as I have saved it for other chapters. For example, I discuss the many sound card options in Chapter 13, "Sound."

Picking the Right Bus

Don't be embarrassed if you buy a card and take it home only to discover that it doesn't fit in your expansion slots. Always take a moment to consult your PC manual or, if necessary, open the computer case before you head to the store to make sure you know the type of slots you have available. The virtual monopoly of PCI these days makes slot fit less of an issue than it was in the past, but new expansion bus types are always coming out, so it still pays to check. When you get to the store to buy your card, be aware that all card makers print the bus type right on the box.

Getting the Correct Drivers

To be sure you have the best possible driver you can get for your device, you should always check the manufacturer's website. The drivers that come with a device may work well, but odds are good that you'll find a newer and better driver on the website. How do you determine if the drivers on the website are newer? First, take the easy route: look on the CD because sometimes the version is printed right on the CD itself. If it's not printed on the CD, you're going to have to load the CD in your CD drive and poke around.

Inside Information

Returns

When you first start buying your own cards, there's a better than average chance that you'll make the wrong purchase for one reason or another and need to return the card. I've been buying cards for almost 20 years, and I still find myself running back to the store because of some aspect of the card's installation or function I didn't notice.

Returns are a normal routine for those intrepid enough to go into their system units and install components. However, a nasty little "gotcha" is becoming all too prevalent in the PC supplier world: restocking fees. Many suppliers will try to charge you 10 or 15 percent of the purchase price as a restocking fee for returned items in good working order. This is, in my opinion, a rip-off. Before you buy, always check the return policy, and buy only from dealers with a no-questions-asked return policy!

Many driver disks have an autorun screen that advertises the version. If there's nothing on the autorun screen, look for a Readme file.

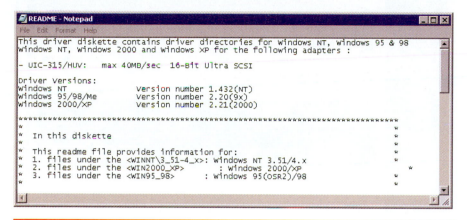

```
README - Notepad
File  Edit  Format  Help
This driver diskette contains driver directories for windows NT, windows 95 & 98
windows NT, windows 2000 and windows XP for the following adapters :

- UIC-315/HUV:   max 40MB/sec  16-Bit Ultra SCSI

Driver versions:
windows NT              Version number 1.432(NT)
windows 95/98/Me        Version number 2.20(9x)
windows 2000/XP         Version number 2.21(2000)

**********************************************************************
*                                                                    *
*   In this diskette                                                 *
*                                                                    *
*   This readme file provides information for:                       *
*   1. files under the <WINNT\3_51-4_x>: Windows NT 3.51/4.x     *    *
*   2. files under the <WIN2000_XP>     : windows 2000/XP             *
*   3. files under the <WIN95_98>      : windows 95(OSR2)/98         *
*                                                                    *
```

• Part of a Readme file showing the driver version

Removing the Old Drivers

Some cards—and this is especially true with video cards—require you to remove old drivers of the same type before you install the new device. To do this, you must first locate the driver in the Device Manager. In Windows 9x/Me, simply select the device driver you want to uninstall and click the Remove button. In Windows 2000/XP, alternate-click the device driver you wish to uninstall and select Uninstall. Many devices, especially ones that come with a lot of applications, will have an uninstall option in the Add/Remove Programs applet on the Control Panel.

• Uninstalling a device

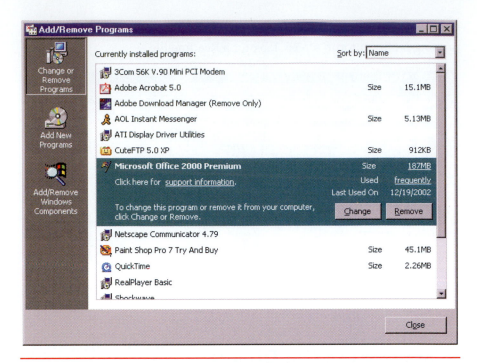

● Uninstall option (Remove button) in Add/Remove Programs

Step-by-Step 5.3

Installing a Plug and Play Card

Installing a card in a PC requires a number of specific and important steps. This exercise leads you through the process of installing a PCI expansion card in an empty slot. To imitate an upgrade scenario, you will also, if possible, remove a currently installed card from the PC and install the new card in the vacated slot.

To complete this exercise, you will need the following:

■ A computer with a Plug and Play BIOS and a PCI slot

■ A PnP PCI expansion card

■ An antistatic wrist strap

■ A Phillips screwdriver

■ An antistatic bag

Step 1

Whenever possible, don't handle a card without using an antistatic wrist strap. You should always be thinking about static, even if you don't have an antistatic wrist strap handy. Turn off the PC and unplug it from the wall and remove the cover of the case. If you don't have a wrist strap, touch the power supply to put you and the PC at the same potential.

Step 2

To use an empty slot, first remove the shim (or *slot cover*) covering the slot. You can choose any shim to remove, as long as it's lined up with the right type of expansion slot. Shims (and cards) are held in place with a screw at the top of the plate, which you must unscrew. The screws are almost always ¼-inch hex heads with a Phillips slot.

Note: Although cards will work even if they're not secured with a screw, it's not a very safe thing for the card or your PC. Always use screws to secure expansion cards.

Step 3

If you have an installed card you can remove from its expansion slot, first remove the screw from its back plate. Then carefully grab the outside of the card with one hand and the back edge of the card with the other, slowly wiggling it out. A well-seated card can take some serious tugging—be not afraid! However, do be sure to touch only the edges of the card. Handling the chips on the board can cause them to fail. The following illustration shows both the correct (left) and the incorrect (right) way to handle a card.

Step 4

Place the card you've removed in an antistatic bag. Ideally, a card should always be either in a PC or in an antistatic bag. Remove the new card from its antistatic bag. Holding it by the edges, line it up as best you can with the slots and the shim opening and push the card slowly but firmly into place in the slot. If it resists at all, check that the pins are properly aligned with the slot. When fully inserted, the contacts on the expansion card will fit completely into the slot. You should see no silver or gold showing!

Step 5

Screw the card into place. Attach any connectors it requires. Before you close the case, reboot the computer and complete the next Step-by-Step exercise to make sure that the new card is working properly.

Inside Information

Test Before Putting the Cover On!

There's an old adage in the PC business: "If you put the cover back on the case without testing a new card, the card will always fail." Common sense may tell you that this is impossible, but the empirical evidence is overwhelming. Don't put the cover on until the driver is loaded and you're convinced that the card works properly.

Never throw away the antistatic bags! In fact, never throw away any card packaging for at least a few months. If you return a card in its original box with all the trimmings, the store will be much more likely to take it back.

Installing a Driver for a New Expansion Card

In this exercise, you learn what steps to take when Windows doesn't already have the correct drivers for a device you've just installed.

To complete this exercise, you will need the following:

■ A Windows system that hasn't yet been rebooted following the installation of a new expansion card

Step 1

After you've installed the expansion card in Step-by-Step 5.3, reboot your system. If the device already has a driver, the Windows PnP function will automatically install it. In most situations, however, Windows will not find a suitable driver, and you'll get a message that prompts for a driver disk. Direct Windows to look for a driver on the CD or floppy disk that came with the device, but even if (as is likely) it finds one, don't install it yet. Press Cancel instead and then reload the CD.

Step 2

About 10 percent of the time, you will need to run a setup program on the installation disk before you can install drivers, but first you have to *find* the executable file that contains the setup program. When you reload the CD, you will usually see a friendly pop-up screen, courtesy of the autorun feature. If your CD doesn't have this feature, you may have to search the folders on the CD to find the correct drivers. View the contents of the CD in My Computer or Windows Explorer. It should look something like the following illustration. Note the large number of folders.

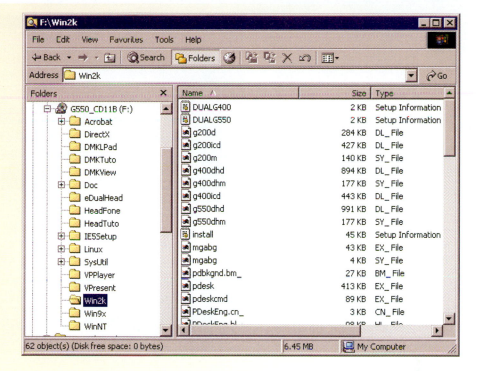

Step 3

On some very basic installation disks, you won't find any executable files at all. The following illustration shows the contents of a disk I recently got from a manufacturer. The important file to notice here is the setup information file—in this case the file named TRM3X5 with the icon that looks like a pad of paper with a small gear on the front. These **INF files** are the cornerstones of all device installations.

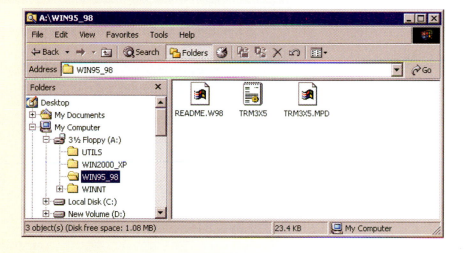

Step 4

There are several ways to use INF files to install drivers, but the best approach is to use the Device Manager. First make a note of where on the disk the INF file is located and then open the Device Manager. Open the Properties for the device, select the Driver tab, and click the Update Driver button.

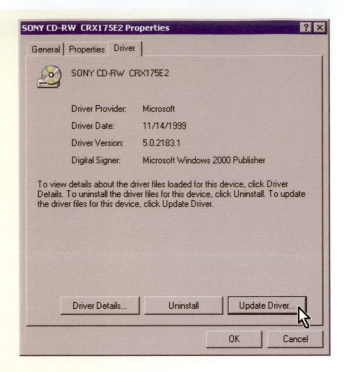

Step 5

What you see next depends on your version of Windows. In Windows 9x/Me, the Update wizard will ask whether you want Windows to look for a driver (and recommends this method), or whether you want to specify a location. The Windows 2000/XP screen, shown below, is very similar.

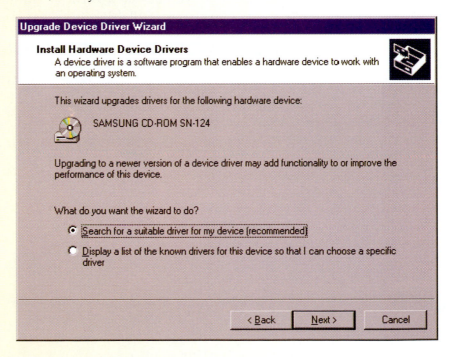

For this exercise, instead of letting Windows choose, select the option to specify a driver, browse to the location that you so cleverly wrote down, highlight the driver's INF file, and tell Windows to install it.

| Step 6 | The next-to-last step in device installation is to open the Device Manager and check to make sure that Windows recognizes the new device and can talk to it. Assuming that you just installed a modem correctly, for example, you would see a Device Manager display like the one shown here. | 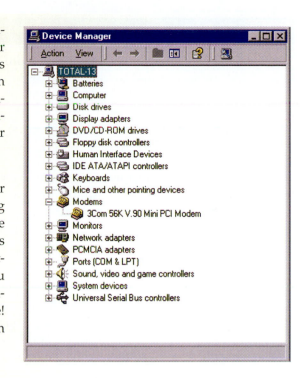 |

| Step 7 | Assuming that the Device Manager indicates that the device is working properly, your next step is to test the device by making it do whatever it is supposed to do. If you installed a network card, get on the Internet; if you installed a sound card, play some music. If everything works, you're done! If it doesn't, read the next section, on installation problems. |

Installation Problems

Many times after you install a new device, the Device Manager tells you there's a problem. Sometimes, it may not show the new device at all. In that case, your first step should be to verify that you inserted the device properly and that the device has power, if it needs it. Next, run the Add/Remove Hardware wizard and see if Windows recognizes the device. If the Device Manager still doesn't recognize the device, you have one of two problems: the device is physically damaged and you will have to replace it, or the device driver is incorrect or has a problem.

The Device Manager rarely fails to see a device. More commonly, device problems manifest themselves in the Device Manager via error symbols: a black !, a red **X**, a blue **I**, or a green or yellow **?**.

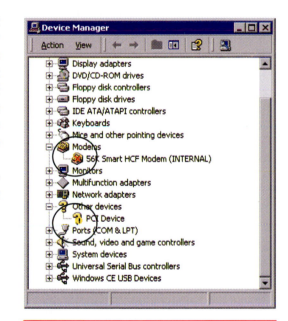

• Sample Device Manager errors

- A black ! on a yellow circle indicates that a device is missing, that Windows does not recognize the device, or that there's some sort of device driver problem. The device may still work with this error.

- A red **X** indicates a disabled device. This usually points to a system resource conflict or a damaged device. The device will not work with this error. You should have a professional computer technician fix it.

- A blue **I** on a white field indicates a PnP device for which someone has configured the system resources manually. This symbol merely provides information and does not indicate an error.

Try This!

Troubleshooting the ! Error Symbol

The ! is the most common error symbol, and the problem it signifies is usually the easiest to fix. If you have double-checked that the device is properly inserted and used the Update Driver feature with a driver you downloaded from the manufacturer's website, but none of this solves your problem, research can sometimes be your salvation. Try this:

1. Surf to the manufacturer's website and consult the online support documentation. Although the quality of such documentation varies, it's always a great place to start. See what sorts of troubleshooting assistance you can find there.

2. No matter what problem you have, there are always other people who have had the same one, and many of them will know how to solve it. Search the Internet to locate newsgroups or bulletin boards where people discuss device driver installation problems and see what kinds of help you can get by asking people how you can fix your driver problem.

- A green **?** indicates that Windows does not have the correct driver, but has successfully installed a *compatible* driver. The device will work but may not perform certain functions. This error symbol appears only in Windows Me.

- A yellow **?** means that Windows sees that the device has been installed, but the correct driver isn't installed. The yellow **?** is usually accompanied by a black **!** symbol. This error often appears when something goes wrong during the driver installation.

External Expansion Buses: USB and FireWire

For many years, PCs used only internal expansion buses. Of course, even the oldest PCs have connections for devices such as keyboards, but those external connectors are designed to support only one type of device. You would never plug a mouse into a keyboard port, for example, nor could you plug two keyboards into that port. Even ports for serial and parallel devices—which do support a variety of devices—support only one device at a time.

When I talk about external buses, I mean buses that can support multiple devices of multiple types from a single port. These types of buses did not come into broad use until the advent of USB in the mid-1990s.

USB

Installing expansion cards in a PC is a pain. At best, it requires you to turn off your PC, open the system unit, install the card, close the system unit, and turn the system back on. At worst, it can be a nightmare of hellish proportions. Beyond this, consider the fact that many times you may want to install a device, but not permanently. For example, you might want to borrow a scanner to scan a few photos and then return it, or temporarily plug in a joystick to enjoy a flight simulation game. Look at Figure 5.5. These are all devices that I *sometimes* connect to my system. Notice that I didn't include my keyboard, monitor, or mouse—those I use *all* the time.

USB Details

Computer users needed a form of external expansion bus that enabled them not only to add and remove devices easily, but also to do this while the

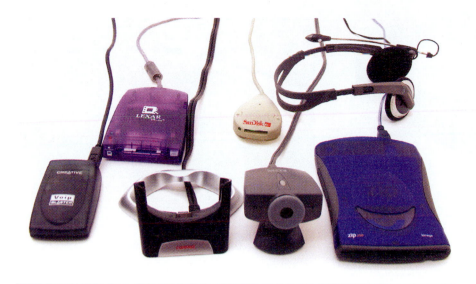

• Figure 5.5   Lots of devices that aren't connected permanently

computer was running, without having to reboot. A device that can function in this way is called **hot-swappable**. Salvation came in the form of the **Universal Serial Bus (USB)**. USB appears on systems in the form of one or more distinctive connectors, usually on the back of your PC case. Figure 5.6 shows a typical USB setup: two USB ports on the back of a PC. Note their rectangular shape—no other port on your PC looks like a USB port.

USB devices all come with special USB plugs (Figure 5.7). You simply plug the USB device into a USB port on your computer, Windows recognizes the arrival of a new USB device, and as long as Windows has the proper drivers for it, the device immediately works.

The real power of USB comes from its ability to daisy chain devices. Many—though not all—USB devices feature their own USB port, where you can install a second USB device. Figure 5.8 shows a USB keyboard that has USB ports. USB keyboards are popular because they enable you to plug the mouse into the keyboard instead of using one of the USB ports on the back of the PC.

USB devices can also plug into USB hubs. The usual setup with a USB hub involves plugging the hub into one of the USB ports on your PC and then plugging other USB devices into the hub. In this way, multiple devices can use a single USB port.

In theory, up to 127 devices can be connected through a single USB port. In reality, USB's 12 Mbps maximum throughput limits most USB port sharing to three or four devices, depending on their functions. USB ports also supply power to connected devices, so too many devices in a single USB chain can overtax its power capabilities.

There are two versions of USB: USB 1.1 and USB 2.0. USB 1.1 devices run at one of

• Figure 5.6   Two USB ports

• **Figure 5.7** USB Type A plug

• **Figure 5.8** USB keyboard with USB ports

Many USB 2.0 devices display this icon. Look for this icon either on the box or printed directly on the USB 2.0 device.

• USB 2.0 icon

• **Figure 5.9** USB B connector

two speeds: a low speed of 1.5 Mbps and a high speed of 12 Mbps. Some low-speed devices don't like to share a port with high-speed devices. Fortunately, most systems that support USB also provide more than one USB port. USB 2.0 devices run at a blistering 480 Mbps, making USB 2.0 a viable option for large data storage (for instance, hard drives).

USB 2.0 is physically identical to USB 1.1 and is fully backward compatible. In other words, if you plug a USB 2.0 device into a USB 1.1 port, it will work—but at the slower speed. If you install a USB 1.1 device in a USB 2.0 port, it will also work—but again only at USB 1.1 speeds. If you want USB 2.0 speeds, you need a USB 2.0 device and a USB 2.0 port.

There actually two different USB connectors. The one shown in Figure 5.7 is the USB A connector. There's also another, smaller type called a USB B connector (Figure 5.9), which is quite popular for devices like digital cameras that need a smaller connector than the A type.

USB has a maximum cable length of 5 meters, although you can extend this distance by adding a powered USB hub every 5 meters. Although most USB devices never get near this maximum, many devices such as digital cameras try to use 5-meter cables, which can cause problems. Personally, I stick to cables no longer than 2 meters.

USB Drivers

In theory, you simply install a USB device, and it works. Remember, however, this most important rule: Always install drivers *before* you install a USB device. Why? It's unrealistic to expect to be able to plug in a USB device and just assume that the system already has the drivers. Sure, there are exceptions to this rule. However, I'm teaching you how to deal with the mainstream, not the exceptions.

Don't relax yet, though, because often it's these core drivers that get you into trouble. USB is designed to try to install alternate drivers when it doesn't have the exactly right ones. This is why you must install the correct drivers first. If you don't, Windows will often install an incorrect driver following the "close enough" approach, and once a wrong driver is installed, it's a real pain to remove.

Introduction to PC Hardware and Troubleshooting

FireWire

The emergence of PC multimedia in the 1990s created an intense demand for a low-cost, high-speed, bidirectional cabling standard to replace the aged and notoriously slow serial communication mode. This demand led to the amazing **IEEE 1394** standard, better known by the name **FireWire**. Apple Computers designed FireWire, and the IEEE standardized it at the end of 1995. Even though FireWire has existed as a standard for many years, the standard has only recently been widely adopted.

A FireWire cable is a special six-wire cable with a unique FireWire connector, as shown in Figure 5.10. Sony Corporation has also developed a smaller, 4-pin version. The 6-pin connection provides power as well as data transfer. Devices that use the 4-pin version must use a separate power supply. You can purchase cables that convert the Sony 4-pin to the standard 6-pin connection.

Most devices use the larger, standard connector; the smaller one is found on devices such as digital video cameras. In fact, digital video camera input is one of the most popular uses for FireWire. Any single FireWire cable can be no longer than 5 meters, often referenced as 15 feet in the United States. FireWire supports daisy chaining, allowing up to 63 devices to run from a single controller.

IEEE 1394 allows devices to run at speeds of 100, 200, and 400 Mbps. Virtually all FireWire devices now use the 400 Mbps speed. FireWire is totally hot-swappable, runs at full duplex, and is fully compliant with Plug and Play, making it amazingly simple to use.

● **Figure 5.10**   FireWire connector

● FireWire ports

FireWire or USB?

At first glance, FireWire and USB 2.0 seem virtually identical—and in many ways, they are—so which one should you choose? Well, the easy answer is simply stick to one or the other, but personally, I think we're soon going to have both USB 2.0 and FireWire in all of our systems. Why? Because USB and FireWire are basically complementary technologies, each with its own strengths—higher performance with FireWire, lower cost with USB.

PC Card

Laptops have always had one big disadvantage compared to desktop computers: no expansion bus. Nowadays, laptops use USB and FireWire extensively to compensate for this. What did laptops do before these relatively new inventions? They used the Personal Computer Memory Card International Association (PCMCIA) card interface, better known in recent years by the name **PC Card**. This is a bus interface that enables your laptop to accept a special card that contains the additional functionality. Although the PC Card is much older than either USB or FireWire, its massive installed base guarantees that it will be a part of all laptops for some time to come.

> **Inside Information**
>
> **USB 2.0 vs. Firewire Speeds**
> *Firewire offers* sustained *data transfers at up to 400 Mbps;* USB *can reach those speeds, but only in* burst mode. *Thus, for short file transfers, USB 2.0 does well; but for bigger jobs, go with Firewall for serious speed.*

• PC Card samples

PC Cards and their associated slots come in three thicknesses: Type 1 is the smallest and least used, Type II is in the middle and is the most common, and Type III is used almost exclusively for PC Card hard drives. Most laptops come with two Type II slots.

To be completely accurate, a PC Card does not meet all of the criteria for an expansion bus because PC Card devices do not daisy chain. PC Cards do, however, create a separate bus, and devices are hot-swappable, so the PC Card is close enough to be considered an external expansion bus. The same rules apply to PC Cards as to USB—especially the rule that you should install drivers before you install the PC Card.

One small drawback to PC Card technology was its 16-bit bus. A few years ago, the PC Card consortium released a new type of PC Card called CardBus. CardBus is a 32-bit, backwardly compatible PC Card technology that has rapidly gained wide acceptance.

Chapter 5 Review

■ Chapter Summary

After reading this chapter and completing the exercises, you should understand the following facts about expansion buses.

Describe the purpose and basic functions of an expansion bus

- An expansion bus is a slot or port on the motherboard that enables you to add hardware to your computer that didn't originally come with it.

- The clock speed of expansion slots is separate and independent from the motherboard speed.

- The Northbridge provides a separate set of external data bus and address bus wires just for devices that are connected to expansion slots. This combination of special Northbridge wires and expansion slots is called the expansion bus.

- The CPU needs device drivers to communicate with devices. Certain devices—keyboards, hard drives, floppy drives, RAM, and the chipset—are *always* supported by BIOS programs stored in the system ROM.

- Every device in your PC has a range of I/O addresses, and each pattern is really a command that the CPU can send to the device. PnP programs can tell devices to assign themselves to unused I/O addresses.

- Special wires called interrupt wires, also known as IRQs, signal the CPU that a device wants attention. IRQs are designated by the numbers 0 through 15. No two devices can use the same IRQ simultaneously. The same PnP programs that set up I/O addresses also assign IRQs to devices as needed.

Recognize the different types of internal expansion buses used on PCs

- The first version of the ISA bus was 8 bits wide and ran at roughly 7 MHz. To accommodate new CPUs with 16-bit external data buses, IBM added a small extension to the end of the 8-bit ISA slot to create the 16-bit ISA expansion bus. There is no substantial difference between 8-bit and 16-bit ISA slots other than their width in bits.

- The Peripheral Component Interconnect (PCI) bus is 32 bits wide (there's even a 64-bit version), is totally self-configuring, and runs at 33 MHz. Most of the slots on a modern motherboard are PCI slots.

- The Northbridge has four different buses, each with a specific function: one connects to the CPU, one to RAM, one to the PCI slots, and one to the Southbridge chip. The bus running to the PCI slots is called the PCI expansion bus.

- To support programs like computer games that use high-end graphics, Intel invented a super PCI slot called an Accelerated Graphics Port (AGP), with its own personal connection to the Northbridge. AGP slots are only for graphics.

- Mini PCI slots are used only in laptops. They provide an extremely convenient way to add modems, sound cards, or network cards to a portable computer.

Install a Plug and Play expansion card

- Before you install an expansion card, be sure you have the right card, both in terms of function and connection type, and that you have the type of slot needed by the card.

- Check the manufacturer's website to make sure that you have the best and most recent driver you can get for your device.

- Some cards, especially video cards, require you to remove old drivers of the same type before you install the new device.

Recognize the USB and FireWire bus technologies and know how to use them

- The two dominant types of external buses are Universal Serial Bus (USB) and FireWire. The older PC Card interface continues to be common on laptops.

- USB devices are hot-swappable and can be daisy-chained. USB devices can also plug into USB hubs, enabling multiple devices to use a single USB port. USB has a maximum cable length of 5 meters, although you can extend this distance by using powered USB hubs.

- The IEEE 1394 standard, better known as FireWire, was designed by Apple Computer as a low-cost, high-speed, bidirectional cabling standard to replace serial communication. The 6-pin version provides its own power; the smaller, 4-pin version provides only data transfer.

- The PCMCIA card interface, better known now by the term PC Card, is a bus interface that enables a laptop to accept a special card that adds specific functionality, such as a modem, hard drive, or video input device.

■ Key Terms List

Accelerated Graphics Port (AGP) *(127)*
device driver *(114)*
Device Manager *(118)*
Direct Memory Access (DMA) *(118)*
expansion bus *(113)*
FireWire *(141)*

hot-swappable *(139)*
IEEE 1394 *(141)*
INF file *(135)*
interrupt request wire (IRQ) *(118)*
I/O address *(115)*
IO/MEM wire *(115)*
IRQ steering *(128)*
mezzanine bus *(125)*

Mini PCI *(128)*
PC Card *(141)*
Peripheral Component Interconnect (PCI) *(125)*
Plug and Play (PnP) *(118)*
system resources *(114)*
Universal Serial Bus (USB) *(139)*

■ Key Term Quiz

Use terms from the Key Terms list to complete the following sentences. Not all terms will be used.

1. A charge on the _____ tells devices that the CPU is speaking to one of them using the address bus.

2. The only *internal* expansion bus standard for laptops is called _____.

3. Both _____ and _____ support daisy chaining.

4. ISA was the first _____ used on PCs.

5. The software that comes with a device that enables the device to communicate with the CPU is called the _____.

6. PCI is a/an _____, which enables it to support other bus types on the same motherboard.

7. The different patterns of 16 ones and zeros used by the CPU to talk to devices over the address bus are called _____.

8. The process whereby a device accesses memory directly, without the intervention of the CPU, is known as _____.

9. _____ technology predates both USB and FireWire and uses small cards that insert into a laptop.

10. All devices to be installed in a Windows system must have a setup information file, also known as a/an _____.

■ Multiple-Choice Quiz

1. Which of the following are all considered system resources on a Windows system?

   a. IO/MEM, DMA, and IRQ

   b. Memory, DMA, and PCI

   c. I/O address, DMA, and IRQ

   d. I/O address, DMA, and MCA

2. What is the technology called that enables devices to automatically install themselves?

   a. Autorun

   b. Plug and Play

   c. PCI

   d. Ready Install

3. Which of the following offers the quickest way to determine whether a device is properly installed on a Windows system?

   a. My Computer

   b. System Info

   c. Device Manager

   d. Control Panel

4. Which of the following is a feature of USB?

   a. Hot-swappable

   b. No device driver needed

   c. Not Plug and Play

   d. Reboot ready

5. What type of expansion bus is used exclusively for video cards?

   a. ADG

   b. AMD

   c. AFP

   d. AGP

6. Which two chips normally make up the chipset on a PC?

   a. NorthPCI and SouthPCI

   b. Northchip and Southchip

   c. Northbus and Southbus

   d. Northbridge and Southbridge

7. Which two buses are you most likely to see on a motherboard today?

   a. PCI and ISA

   b. PCI and AGP

   c. PCI and CNR

   d. PCI and MCA

8. Which of the following is the most important single rule to remember when installing USB devices?

   a. Install the device first.

   b. Shut down the system first.

   c. Install the driver first.

   d. Reboot the system first.

9. At what speed does the PCI bus run?

   a. 33 MHz

   b. 133 MHz

   c. 32 MHz

   d. 64 MHz

10. Which of the following buses is the fastest?

   a. ISA

   b. MCA

   c. EISA

   d. VL-bus

11. The IEEE 1394 bus standard is more commonly known by what name?

   a. EISA

   b. Parallel

   c. FireWire

   d. USB

12. What is the theoretical maximum number of devices that USB supports on a single controller?

   a. 16

   b. 64

   c. 127

   d. 255

13. The CNR bus is designed primarily to eliminate what common problem of sound cards and network cards?

   a. Noise

   b. IRQ splitting

   c. Dirt

   d. IRQ conflicts

14. What is the term for the process by which all of the PCI devices on a PC share a single IRQ?

   a. IRQ sharing

   b. IRQ splitting

   c. IRQ allocation

   d. IRQ steering

15. What was the name of the parasitic bus that required an ISA slot?

   a. EISA

   b. VESA VL-bus

   c. MCA

   d. PCI

■ Essay Quiz

1. Put yourself back in the days when the dominant expansion bus was ISA. You work for a motherboard maker, and your company is considering whether to adopt the brand-new PCI bus technology. What are the advantages of moving to PCI? What is your biggest concern about making this change?

2. You are in the IT department of a corporation that wants to adopt a large number of special devices that come in FireWire and USB formats. You are asked to determine which type of bus would best satisfy the needs of your organization. Write a brief memo explaining the various factors the corporation should consider when making this decision.

3. You are working on the help desk at a university. A faculty member calls in complaining that he can't get his new USB device to work. In answer to your question, he admits that he inserted the device without first installing the driver from the CD that came with it. Following your instructions, he checks the Device Manager, where the device is not displayed as it should be. You know that the Windows system recognized the USB device incorrectly, which is why the professor cannot use the device. Outline in detail the steps the professor must take to fix his driver problem and explain why these steps are necessary.

4. You are a tutor for a computer class, and your students are learning about I/O addresses and hex. Write a brief set of step-by-step instructions explaining how to convert hexadecimal I/O addresses back to binary code.

5. Write a brief essay explaining in non-technical terms the role of expansion buses in PCs. What problems were they created to solve? What new problems did they create? In basic terms, how do they work with other parts of a PC?

Lab Projects

• Lab Project 5.1

ABC Corporation wants to donate a large number of PCs, as follows:

- 43 Pentium 100 systems with ISA buses, no USB
- 26 Pentium II systems with 2 PCI and 4 ISA buses, no USB
- 63 Pentium II systems with 1 PCI and 6 ISA buses, no USB
- 22 Pentium II systems with 6 PCI and 1 ISA bus, no USB
- 72 Pentium II laptops with PCMCIA, no Mini PCI, no USB
- 12 Pentium III laptops with PCMCIA and USB, no Mini PCI
- 6 Pentium III laptops with PCMCIA, USB, and Mini PCI
- 26 Pentium III systems with AGP, PCI, no ISA, and USB

All of these systems work. All have a video card but no modem or network card.

❶ The very thankful recipient tells you that the organization can use only systems that can accept a brand-new modem. Which ones would you give to the organization and why? Create a list of the PCs you would give to the organization and add any instructions you might give to the organization's IT people.

❷ The recipient also wants to add network cards to as many systems as can accept them. Make a list of the systems that could accept a modern network card and add any instructions you might give to the organization's IT people.

• Lab Project 5.2

Inventory the systems around you (in the classroom, at your business, at a swap meet, and so on), using the following table to document the systems. Write down the number of slots of each type in each system. The first two rows are filled in as an example.

1 Use this inventory to catalog all of the systems you find. Which of these systems could take a modern modem or network card? Which can have RAM upgraded? Which can take an AGP video card?

2 Go to your local computer store and compare the available video cards, network cards and modems against what you felt were the correct answers. Use this information to determine what systems you would want to support versus the ones you would dispose of.

CPU Type	RAM	AGP	PCI	ISA	Other	USB	FireWire	PCMCIA
486	4MB	0	0	0	MCA	0	0	0
P III	32MB	1	4	1	0	1	0	0

Power Supplies and Cases

"Power to the people, right on."

—JOHN LENNON

In this chapter, you will learn how to:

- **Choose a computer case for a PC system**
- **Remove and install a PC power supply**
- **Identify ways to cool your PC system**

Computer cases and power supplies? At first, this may seem like a strange combination, but in reality these two parts of your system are closely related. When you get a case, you almost always get a power supply, too. Power supplies have a nasty habit of occasionally failing—you need to know what to look for and, if necessary, how to install one in your computer. Cases protect your PC from harm. You need to know what choices you have in cases to make solid buying decisions. In this chapter, you will learn about PC computer cases and the various types that are available. You will learn about the different parts of a case and the purpose of each, and you will learn what type of motherboard is compatible with what type of computer case.

Next, you will learn about power supplies and computer cases and the role of the power supply in a PC. You will learn how to remove and replace a power supply, as well as how to select a replacement model if your power supply should fail. You will also learn about the different kinds of power connectors that come with a power supply.

Finally, you will learn why it is so important to keep the inside of your computer case cool, and you will be introduced to the several technologies available to help keep your computer components from baking.

■ Case Form and Function

CPUs, memory, motherboards—all of these have to fit *somewhere*. That somewhere is in a computer case. A computer case is the first thing you notice when you see a computer. Made of metal (or sometimes plastic), it's the box that houses all of the components and devices that make up a computer.

Computer cases come in a variety of shapes and sizes. Different manufacturers try to establish unique looks through minor color and styling modifications. Despite aesthetic differences, computer cases usually fit into one of a few distinguishable categories. Whether the computer is being used as a child's machine in a home or as a file server in an office, the design of the computer's case has a significant impact on the computer's ability to do its job.

There are no official, exact size specifications for the different types of PC cases. The categories of cases discussed here are only general concepts; it's not uncommon for two PC techs to disagree on the name for a particular size of case.

External Size

One of the first issues to consider when selecting a case is the external dimensions. The case you choose depends on several interrelated factors:

■ Do you plan to upgrade the system at a later date?

■ Who will be using the system?

■ What will be the final location of the system (for example, on top of or beneath a desk)?

If you're planning to upgrade your system at a later time, then you'll want a case that has several easy-access features. You'll want a case that has lots of interior room so you can work in it easily, as well as enough space to add plenty of other components. If you're planning to give the system to a person with basic computer needs, who probably won't need upgrades or add-ons, you can choose a simpler case with fewer easy-access features because the case probably won't need to be opened and shut frequently.

Let's start by discussing the different case sizes.

Only the most serious computer enthusiast would want a full-tower case. Its huge size is major overkill for almost everyone else.

Full-Tower Cases

A **full-tower case** (Figure 6.1) is likely to be the largest PC case you will see (except for the massive server-style cases described later). At least two feet tall, a full-tower case provides a maximum amount of interior space for a variety of drives and expansion cards, as well as plenty of room for your hands to reach past one component to easily access another. Because of its substantial size, a full tower must usually be placed on the floor rather than on a desk.

Why get a full-tower case? Expandability, that's why. If you want to build a "hot rod"

● **Figure 6.1** Full-tower case

● **Figure 6.2**   Mid-tower case

📄 Mini-towers generally have the smallest desktop footprint, so if you want a computer that you can tuck into a small space, a mini-tower may be the case for you.

● **Figure 6.3**   Mini-tower case

computer with all the latest components that money can buy, then you will need a full-tower case.

A full-tower case should have at least four externally accessible drive bays for CD-ROM, CD-RW, and DVD-ROM drives as well as two external floppy disk drive bays. Internally, however, is the where the tower case really shines. Most full-tower cases have internal space for at least three, and sometimes as many as five, hard drives.

Mid-Tower Cases

For those of you who like expandability but don't need as many extra drives, there is the **mid-tower case** (Figure 6.2). The mid-tower case is very common because of the flexibility of the mid-tower design. It is small enough to sit atop a desk without making a desk seemed cluttered.

A mid-tower case usually stands about 20 inches high and has an average of three external drive bays and one external floppy drive bay. It has fewer internal drive bays than does a full-tower case, but it can sometimes hold a pair of hard drives. A mid-tower has plenty of room for most ordinary computer users.

Mini-Tower Cases

A **mini-tower case** (Figure 6.3) is usually smaller and a little wider than a mid-tower case. Mini-towers provide the least amount of interior cooling, a topic you will learn about later, so they are not the best choice if you want to build a high-performance computer. Most mini-towers have only two external drive bays and one internal bay. Because the mini-tower design does not offer a lot of working room on the inside, it's also not a good choice if you plan to do a lot of upgrading.

Desktop Cases

Unlike tower cases, which stand up on their thinner side, a **desktop case** (Figure 6.4) lies flat on its larger side. Desktop cases are so named because they are designed to sit on your desk with a monitor resting on top of them. Desktop cases were once the most common type of case, but in recent years, they've been eclipsed by mid-towers. A desktop case usually doesn't provide much capacity for expansion, and it's most commonly used for prebuilt computers that are not meant to be upgraded.

Server Cases

On the other end of the spectrum from the mini-tower case is the **server case** (Figure 6.5). Built to accommodate the greater space and expandability needs of servers, server cases are usually quite large, with plenty of bays and expansion slots. Rather than favoring a rectangular design like tower cases, server cases tend be square. Far larger and more expensive than even a high-end home user needs, the server case, with its large interior cavities, makes installing new components a breeze.

Other Case Types

Another type of computer case is the **rack-mount case**. Rack-mount cases are used exclusively by businesses that need a space-efficient way to organize large numbers of servers. Computer companies create powerful computers specifically for this purpose, cramming them into special cases that are made to be stacked on a matching vertical rack.

Rack-mount cases are sized by the **unit**, or **U** in computer jargon. A single rack unit is 1.75 inches high. Rack-mount cases are described according to the number of U's (multiples of 1.75 inches) high they are. For example, a 3U case is 5.25 inches high (3 × 1.75).

• **Figure 6.4**   Desktop case

Drive Bays

All cases are equipped with special areas, called drive bays, to hold storage drives. Unless you are planning never to upgrade your machine, the number of drive bays available should be one of your primary considerations when selecting a case.

There are two types of bay: external and internal. You must open the case to access an internal bay. External bays have openings that enable them to be accessed from outside the case. External bays are used for components like floppy disk drives and CD-ROM drives. Internal bays are used for components like hard drives that you don't need to access once they're installed. External bays come in two widths: 3½ inches and 5¼ inches.

> Even though rack-mount cases have different heights, they are always 19 inches wide to fit into standard equipment racks.

3½-Inch Bays

Larger cases come with both external and internal **3½-inch drive bays** (Figure 6.6). The external 3½-inch bay normally is used for a floppy drive, which, of course, must be accessible from outside the case. The internal 3½-inch drive bays are for hard drives, which these days are usually the same width as floppy disk drives.

5¼-Inch Bays

The **5¼-inch drive bay** (Figure 6.7) dates back to the days when computers used only 5¼-inch disk drives. Although the 5¼-inch floppy disk drive is gone, the bays remain because drives for optical media like CD-ROMs and DVD-ROMs require 5¼-inch bays. Older hard drives also used the wider drive bays. Currently, you can buy special cages that adapt 5¼-inch bays so they can hold modern 3½-inch hard drives.

• **Figure 6.5**   Server case

Chapter 6: Power Supplies and Cases

151

• **Figure 6.6**   Internal 3½-inch drive bay with hard drive installed

Rails

Most modern cases come with an easy solution to the tiresome chore of mounting new devices in drive bays: drive bay rails (Figure 6.8). These rails are the computer equivalent of the items that make your kitchen drawers slide in and out. They are often included on higher-end cases to facilitate drive installation. When installing drives in drive bays without rails, you have to attach the drive directly to the drive cage on the inside of the case. This involves getting several tiny screws and screwdrivers as well as large fingers into the small spaces around the drive bays.

For this reason, many tower cases now include drive rails. To install a drive using rails, you simply affix the rails to the sides of the drive and then slide the drive rails into matching channels built into the drive bay. Your drive is snug and secure, but it's easy to install and remove!

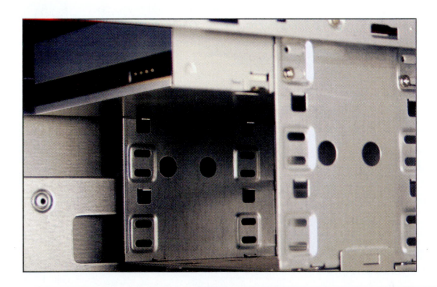

• **Figure 6.7**   5¼-inch drive bays with CD-ROM drive installed in top bay

● **Figure 6.8**   Drive bay rails

Back Plates

On the back of every case is a metal plate punched through with a specific set of holes. These holes are designed to allow various external connectors on the motherboard to poke through the back of the case. This punched metal plate, shown in Figure 6.9, is referred to as the back plate of the computer case. Even though your case will come with a back plate, you will usually remove that one and instead use the one that comes with your motherboard.

Not all cases accept all motherboard designs. One way of determining whether a computer case will accept the type of motherboard you plan to use is by looking at the back plate to see if the holes match your motherboard's external connectors.

● **Figure 6.9**   Back plate of a computer case

Inside Information

Drive Rails

Drive rails are not standardized. Every PC case that uses rails comes with its own set, and if you lose those rails, or if you throw them away, you will have a tough time finding replacements. Sure, you might be lucky and find a set of drive rails from another case that works with your system, but this is the exception more than the rule. Always keep all of the drive rails that come with your case. If you don't need them today, you'll need them tomorrow!

• A selection of computer screws

• Two common types of stand-off screws

Screws and Stand-offs

As you quickly learn when you start to work on computers, it takes a lot of tiny fasteners, usually screws, to hold a computer case together. Each component of the computer, from the motherboard to the expansion cards to the various drives, has to be attached to the case, and the parts of the case have to be attached to each other.

The various types of screws for a computer are fairly easy to identify. There are mounting screws with coarse or fine threading, and there are several types of stand-off screws for mounting the motherboard to the chassis of the computer case.

Fine-threaded screws are used almost exclusively for mounting CD media drives. All other devices use coarse-threaded screws, which usually come in large and small sizes. Usually, larger mounting screws have a hexagonal head with notches for a Phillips-head screwdriver. The smaller mounting screws usually have either hexagonal or rounded heads. However, what matters in selecting an appropriate fastener is the threading, not the size.

Special stand-off screws are designed to be attached to the inside walls of the case and fit through holes in the motherboard. The most common type is designed to screw into pre-positioned holes in the side of the case. Sometimes they are designed to be pushed through holes from the outside of the case and held in place by their tight fit.

To attach a motherboard to a case, first you install the stand-off screws; then you place the motherboard on top of them so they poke up through matching holes in the motherboard. The stand-off screws are concave so that standard large-threaded screws can be screwed into them to hold the motherboard securely in place.

Case Form Factors

Cases are usually designed with a specific type of motherboard in mind. The main issue is the number of expansion slots on the motherboard that require corresponding slots on the back of the case. As you will see, the type of case you buy depends on the type of motherboard you want to use. When building a computer, you should first choose a motherboard and then a case of the corresponding form factor to go along with it.

There are four main form factors for cases and motherboards: AT, ATX, microATX, and FlexATX.

AT

Because the AT motherboard has been rendered obsolete by the ATX type, not many cases are built for AT motherboards anymore. For a long time, however, virtually all motherboards and cases were built in the AT type (Figure 6.10) or the smaller, so-called Baby AT type. You are likely to encounter this form factor in older computers, but you'll most likely never see it in a new computer case.

ATX

ATX motherboards are the most common form factor found in modern PCs, and not surprisingly, there are a wide variety of compatible case designs to

● **Figure 6.10**   AT case with a large keyboard connector (bottom center)

choose from. An ATX motherboard can fit into any tower case, as well as into desktop and some larger rack- mount cases. ATX motherboards can even fit into server cases.

microATX

microATX cases are available in form factors ranging from mid-tower and mini-tower cases to desktop cases. Lately, microATX cases are being designed specifically to have a small footprint to accommodate businesses that want a small, out-of-the-way computer for use as a file server.

Often you will find mid-tower and mini-tower cases that can accept both ATX and microATX motherboards. This is no great feat because the external connections on the two motherboard form factors are identically arranged.

FlexATX

FlexATX is the smallest ATX form factor. The FlexATX mother-board form factor was created specifically for 1U rack-mount cases. Many FlexATX cases will also accept microATX motherboards.

Connections

Most of the external connections on a motherboard are located in a very inconvenient place: the back of the computer. The connections were originally placed in the back to keep the cords out of the way. With the advent of fast and removable connections like USB, easy access to these connections has become very important. More and more cases now have front-mounted USB (Figure 6.11) and FireWire ports.

■ Power Supply

The term **power supply** is a bit of a misnomer: a PC's power supply does not actually supply any power. Just as with any electrical appliance, the power for a PC is supplied by the wall socket,

● **Figure 6.11**   Front-mounted USB ports

which is connected to your local electric grid, which is supplied electricity by a power company. What the power supply in a PC actually does is act as a step-down transformer. That means that it converts high-voltage (115 volts in the U.S.) alternating current (AC) into low-voltage (12, 5, and 3.3 volts) direct current (DC). Generally, a PC uses 12-volt current to power motors on devices like hard drives and CD-ROM drives, and 5-volt and 3.3-volt current to support onboard electronics.

• Power supply

Two types of power supply, AT and ATX, comprise over 99 percent of all power supplies installed in personal computers. AT is the older style; it held sway from the early days of the PC but is rarely used now. Most modern PCs use an ATX power supply, which is matched to an ATX (ATX, microATX, or FlexATX) form-factor motherboard and case.

Whether AT or ATX, all power supplies share a number of features:

■ **Power connection**   Power supplies must plug into a power outlet.

■ **Motherboard power**   There must be some connection to provide power to the motherboard.

■ **Peripheral connections**   There must be connectors to provide power to internal devices.

■ **Fan**   This critical component both cools the inside of the power supply and provides a cooling airflow throughout the case.

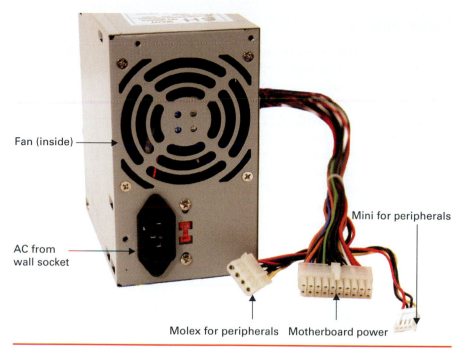

Fan (inside)

AC from
wall socket

Mini for peripherals

Molex for peripherals   Motherboard power

- Common features of power supplies

Every component in your PC—CPU, RAM, hard drives, and CD-ROM drives—requires electricity to operate. All PC power supplies provide specialized connections to the motherboard to provide the correct DC electricity in several voltages to feed the needs of the many devices.

What constitutes a good power supply? There are a number of specifications, but the two most important are the wattage and type of connectors. These two aspects help to determine the quality of a power supply. Let's look first at the wattage.

Wattage

Power supplies are rated in watts. A **watt** is the standard measurement unit of power, or energy/time. A PC requires sufficient wattage for the machine to run properly. If it doesn't receive the necessary amount, several problems can occur:

- The PC will fail to complete the power-on self-test (POST).
- The PC will complete the POST but will fail to load the operating system.
- The PC will complete the POST and load the operating system, but it will reboot spontaneously once a load is applied to the CPU or other hardware.

Play it safe and use at least a 400-watt power supply. This is a very common wattage and will give you plenty of extra power for bootup as well as for whatever other components you might add to the system in the future.

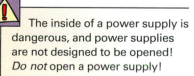 The inside of a power supply is dangerous, and power supplies are not designed to be opened! *Do not* open a power supply!

Connectors

All the wattage in the world is useless without the proper connectors to the parts of your computer that need power. There are many different types of power connectors that you might encounter, depending on the type of power supply in a computer. Among these are power connectors for providing a motherboard with power (P8/P9 and P1 connectors) and for powering peripheral devices (Molex and Mini connectors).

Note that all power connectors have some sort of safety feature built into their design that should prevent you from plugging in these connectors improperly. However, these safety features are not foolproof, so you should take special care to ensure that you have the connectors oriented properly before applying the small amount of force that is usually required to plug in a power connector. If you plug a power connector into a device or motherboard improperly, an incorrect voltage can be supplied to the device, causing it to smoke and burn.

> ⚠️ Remember this rule when dealing with P8 and P9 connectors: Keep the black wires together! Failure to do so will result in a fried motherboard.

P8/P9 Power Connectors

An AT power supply plugs into an AT motherboard using **P8/P9 power connectors** (Figure 6.12). P8/P9 connectors must be plugged in with the black wires next to each other. These connectors are faced and keyed, which is to say that they have different front and back faces and a small guide or key on

● Figure 6.12   P8/P9 power connectors

● **Figure 6.13**   P1 power connector

one side so you cannot install them backward. The key also helps hold the connector in place. Sometimes you have to angle the connectors in before snapping them down all the way, to accommodate the row of small teeth on one side of the plugs.

P1 Power Connectors

A modern ATX power supply plugs into an ATX motherboard using a single **P1 power connector** (Figure 6.13) instead of the P8/P9 connectors. The P1 connector plugs into its own special socket on an ATX motherboard. P1 connectors include a 3.3-volt wire along with the standard 5V and 12V wires. Look for the white P1 socket standing out clearly on the motherboard. A P1 connector has a key on one side that prevents you from inserting the connector incorrectly.

Molex Connectors

The most common type of power connection for devices that need 5 or 12 volts of power is the **Molex connector** (Figure 6.14). The Molex connector has notches, called chamfers, that are supposed to guide its installation. The tricky part is that Molex connectors do require a firm push to plug in properly, but the chamfers can be defeated if you push too hard, so *always* check for proper orientation first!

 As with any power connector, plugging a Molex connector into a device the wrong way will almost certainly destroy the device. Check twice before you plug one in!

● **Figure 6.14**   Molex connector

● **Figure 6.15** Mini connector

Mini Connectors

Most systems also provide a **Mini connector** (Figure 6.15). Floppy drive makers adopted the Mini as the standard connector on 3½-inch floppy drives, so most PCs have at least one. Often these Mini connectors are referred to as floppy power connectors.

Be extra careful when plugging in a Mini connector! Whereas Molex connectors are extremely difficult to plug in backwards, you can insert a Mini incorrectly with very little effort; as with a Molex connector, this will almost certainly destroy the device.

Pentium 4 Power Supplies

System designs based on Pentium 4 processors require a different type of power supply. This new type, an ATX12V power supply, is a superset of the original ATX power supply specification. Its extra 12-volt power connector enables the delivery of more power to motherboards designed for the Pentium 4 processor. The two types of ATX power supplies are nearly identical in appearance; only the presence of the extra 12-volt, 4-pin connector indicates that the power supply is an ATX12V rather than a regular ATX power supply.

> With the P1 connector, the P4 connector, and the auxiliary connector, most P4 systems need three power plugs.

The new motherboard connection for the ATX12V power supply is a 12-volt DC connector, commonly referred to as a **P4 power connector** (Figure 6.16). Additionally, the ATX12V power supply has a 6-pin auxiliary power connector (that looks exactly like one of the old AT P8/P9 connectors) that supplies 3.3- and 5-volt DC current.

Athlon Processors

Athlon processors require a great amount of power to operate. When building an Athlon system, choose a high-wattage power supply. AMD recommends at least a 400-watt power supply for the AMD Athlon XP processors. Athlon power supplies do not have the P4 or auxiliary power connectors seen on power supplies designed for Pentium 4 CPUs. However, it's very common to see an Athlon system using a Pentium 4 power supply—it just doesn't use the P4 and the auxiliary connectors.

Server Power

Computers that "serve" documents and/or applications to computer users, called (logically) servers, require significant processing power, large amounts of memory, and even larger amounts of storage space. Because servers are very powerful machines, they are power hungry as well. A good-sized server can require a power supply of 550 watts or more. It's not unusual to find a server equipped with more than one power supply, as shown in Figure 6.17.

Power Switches

Every PC turns on and off by means of a power switch. Power switch use is one of the major differences between AT and ATX power supplies. AT power switches simply turn the system on or off. On ATX power supplies,

● **Figure 6.16** P4 connector

● **Figure 6.17**   Server with multiple power supplies

however, the power switch interacts with the power supply using a feature called soft power, which requires a little extra explanation.

The AT power switch came first, so let's start by discussing some of the problems with AT power. In particular, you'll find out that AT power supplies lack support for current system needs such as power management.

AT Power Switches

AT power switches come in two common and interchangeable types: rocker and plunger. Each has four tab connectors that attach to four color-coded wires leading from the power supply. Both types of AT power switch can handle 120 volts of power. Figure 6.18 shows a plunger-style AT power switch with its four color-coded wires.

● **Figure 6.18**   Plunger-style AT power switch

AT Power and Power Management

The AT form factor and AT power supplies do not mix well with any type of power management. Most modern systems have the ability to shut down hardware not currently needed by the system. Most PCs also have the ability to go into a **hibernate mode** (sometimes called sleep mode) where every device, including the CPU, either shuts down or goes into a frozen, hibernation-like state.

A system in hibernate mode looks like it is shut down, but it's not. Therein lies a problem for an AT system: When a user runs off to get a cup of coffee, or maybe even leaves for the day, he or she may well leave programs running and documents open and unsaved. Then another user (or maybe the same user, bleary-eyed the next morning) walks up to the system, which, because it's in hibernate mode, appears to be turned off, and presses the on/off switch to turn it on. When you do this to an AT system, the system turns off immediately, without any second chances. Turning off a Windows system without first performing a proper shutdown procedure can cause problems, not to mention the possibility of losing unsaved data. The ATX soft power feature was developed in part to solve this problem.

ATX Soft Power

The soft power feature of ATX motherboards and power supplies handles power management issues quite nicely. Basically, **soft power** works by keeping the system from ever completely shutting off. As long as an ATX system is receiving AC power from the wall socket, the ATX power supply puts a 5-volt charge on the motherboard.

For years, techs bickered about the merits of leaving a system plugged in or unplugged while it was being serviced. ATX settles this issue forever. Remember that an ATX power supply *never turns off*. As long as that power supply stays connected to a power outlet, as mentioned earlier, the power supply will continue to supply 5 volts to the motherboard, regardless of the current power state of the system. Therefore, you should always *unplug* an ATX system before you do any work. Many ATX power supplies provide a real on/off switch on the back of the system (Figure 6.19). You can use this switch to shut off power to the motherboard, but remember that it is always safer to completely unplug the computer from the power outlet on the wall.

Power Supply Fans

The **power supply fan** provides the basic cooling for the PC. It not only cools the voltage regulator circuits *within* the power supply; it also provides a constant flow of outside air throughout the interior of the computer case. A dead power supply fan can rapidly cause tremendous problems, even equipment failure. If you ever turn on a computer and it boots just fine, but you notice that it seems unusually quiet, check to see if the power supply fan has died. If it has, quickly turn off the PC and replace the power supply.

 AT systems don't support power management well, but that doesn't mean they don't support power management at all. Many of the last generation of AT systems supported some basic power management functions, although the fact that you could always turn off an AT system kept AT power management from developing very far. Real power management had to wait for the introduction of ATX.

• Figure 6.19   ATX power supply with real on/off switch

Step-by-Step 6.1

Removing a Power Supply

Power supplies can and do die, especially if they get hit by a power surge, so it's important to know how to replace one. In this Step-by-Step exercise, you will remove an old power supply from a case. In the next Step-by-Step exercise, you will install a power supply.

To complete this exercise, you will need the following:

■ A PC with a power supply installed

■ A Phillips-head screwdriver

■ An antistatic wrist strap

■ A small bowl or container to hold screws

Step 1

Power down and unplug the computer. Remove all exterior cables, noting which cables plug in to which connections. Place the computer on a flat, open workspace with plenty of light.

Step 2

Be sure to attach yourself to the computer using the antistatic wrist strap. Then open the computer case. If your case has a U-shaped cover, first grab your Phillips-head screwdriver and remove the screws around the edges on the back of the case; then carefully remove the cover. If you have a case with a removable side panel, check carefully to determine which screws, if any, you actually need to remove. As you remove screws, place them in the small container so they won't roll off into a dark corner to hide.

Step 3

Before you can remove the power supply, you must unplug all of its connections. Remove the interior power connections carefully. Start with the connections to the drives; be sure to unplug the motherboard power connector.

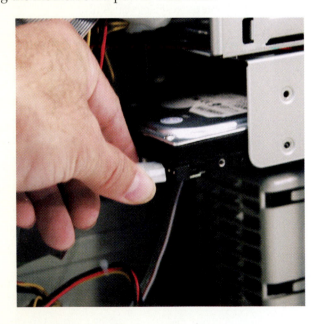

Step 4

After all of the power connections are removed, look at the back of the case. You will see four screws where the power supply rests against the back of the case. Those screws hold the power supply in place. As you remove them, be sure to support the power supply by keeping a hand underneath it.

Step 5

After you've freed the power supply from the case wall, carefully lift the power supply out of the case, making sure that the cables remove easily. This is easier to do in some cases than in others. Just take your time and be careful.

Once you get the power supply completely removed, you are ready to replace it with a new one. In most cases, you will install a new power supply at the same time you remove one, so in the next Step-by-Step, you will install a power supply.

Installing a New Power Supply

In the previous Step-by-Step exercise, you learned how to remove a power supply. In this Step-by-Step exercise, you will either reinstall the power supply you removed (if there's nothing wrong with it) or install a new power supply.

To complete this exercise, you will need the following:

- A PC with the power supply removed
- A power supply that matches the PC's motherboard type (AT or ATX)
- A Phillips-head screwdriver
- An antistatic wrist strap
- A small bowl or container to hold screws

Step 1

Be sure to attach yourself to the computer using the antistatic wrist strap.

Position the power supply in the appropriate corner of the case. Using the Phillips-head screwdriver and four screws, secure the power supply to the back of the case.

Step 2

Once the power supply is secured to the case, run the power cables back into the case and reattach the power connectors. If you're not sure what goes where, consult the notes you took when you removed the power supply. Start by reconnecting the Molex and Mini connectors to the various drives. Then plug in the motherboard power connector. (If you'd prefer, plug in the motherboard power connector first—it doesn't matter.) Make sure that all the connections are firmly seated.

Before you close the case, plug in the computer and reboot it to ensure that everything is correctly and securely attached. If everything works, power down and unplug the system; then replace the cover or side panel and reattach any screws you removed.

■ Cooling

Heat and computers are not the best of friends. Cooling is therefore a vital consideration when building a computer. Electricity equals heat. Computers, being electrical devices, generate heat as they operate, and too much can seriously damage a computer's internal components.

The CPU generates the greatest amount of heat, but it is not the only computer component in danger of overheating. Hard drives and memory are susceptible to damage from extreme heat as well. Heat from any source reduces the lifespan of your components. Although computer components are cheaper than they used to be, they are not so cheap that you'd want to have to replace them frequently due to damage by overheating.

Older, slower computers could keep cool with a single CPU fan plus the fan in the power supply. As computers become faster and faster, however, cooling becomes more and more of an issue. For this reason, an entire segment of the computer industry is devoted to discovering new ways to cool computers.

Power Supply Fan

As you can imagine, the components of the power supply can get quite toasty after running awhile. That's why every power supply has a built-in fan (Figure 6.20) to help keep its components cool. This fan actually does double duty: in addition to cooling the power supply itself, the power supply fan helps circulate air inside the case to cool the rest of the components.

• **Figure 6.20**   Power supply fan

Heat Sinks and Fans

You learned in Chapter 2 that all CPUs require a special heat sink and fan unit to operate properly. If this device is not properly secured and operating normally, a modern CPU can reduce itself to a pile of molten silicon in a matter of seconds.

The fan that sits atop a heat sink also plays a role in circulating air inside the computer case. You should keep the following in mind when considering heat sinks and fans:

■ You can theoretically keep your computer case cooler by putting a larger fan on the CPU heat sink. However, large fans are often very noisy.

■ Without proper airflow through a case, a heat sink fan may simply recycle the same heated air over and over, possibly raising the temperature of the CPU rather than lowering it.

Although almost every computer comes with a perfectly fine fan and heat sink on the CPU, you may sometimes need more cooling. That's where case fans really make a difference.

Case Fans

Case fans (Figure 6.21) are large, square fans that snap into special brackets on the case, providing extra cooling for key components. Most cases don't come with a case fan, but no modern computer should really be without one.

Larger cases with multiple bays and slots usually have more spaces for case fans because extra devices mean extra heat. If your system will have a

Introduction to PC Hardware and Troubleshooting

large number of devices and drives, you should add as many fans as the case will accommodate.

The single biggest issue related to case fans is where to plug them in. Most case fans come with standard Molex connectors, which are easy to plug in, but other case fans come with special three-pronged power connectors that need to connect to the motherboard. If you need to, you can get adapters to plug three-pronged connectors into Molex connectors or Molex connectors into three-pronged connectors.

Step-by-Step 6.3

Installing a Case Fan

Installing a case fan is a relatively easy task. You should be familiar with the procedure if you ever plan to add components to a system. Case fans are readily available at a modest cost from your local computer store.

To complete this exercise, you will need the following:

■ A PC case with a place to install a case fan

■ A case fan that matches the case (make sure that the case fan has power connectors that work with your motherboard!)

■ A Phillips-head screwdriver

■ An antistatic wrist strap

■ A small bowl or container to hold screws

Depending on your case, you may or may not actually need the Phillips-head screwdriver. Many mid- and full-tower cases have special plastic slots that let you snap in a fan without using screws.

Step 1   If you haven't already done so, power down and unplug the computer and remove all exterior cables, noting which cables plug in to which connections. Place the computer on a flat, open workspace with plenty of light.

Step 2

Remove any panels so that you can access the internal parts of the system unit. Attach yourself to the computer using the antistatic wrist strap. Locate the fan mount, usually on the inside of the back wall of the case. Remove the case fan from any packaging and position it over the fan mount.

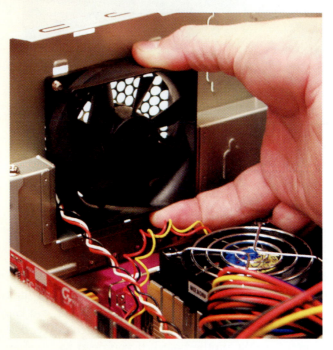

Step 3

Depending on the type of case you have, either snap the case fan into the plastic fan slot or use the Phillips-head screwdriver and four mounting screws to secure the fan to the case.

Step 4

Connect the case fan to the power supply with the appropriate connector. As mentioned earlier, some case fans use a three-wire connector that plugs into a connection on the motherboard. Look for a small, three-pronged plug on the motherboard labeled something like POWER FAN, AUX(ILIARY) FAN, or SYS(TEM) FAN. Some larger case fans come wired with standard Molex connectors. Be sure to orient the connector properly before plugging it in to the power supply.

Step 5

Don't close the case yet! Reattach the connectors on the back, plug the system back in, and power up! As the system powers up, look at the various fans to verify they are all running. Then close the case and make sure that all the screws are back in their designated holes.

Airflow

A computer is a closed system, and that feature of computer cases helps the fans keep things cool: everything is inside a box. Although many tech types like to run their systems with the side panel of the case open for easy access to the components, in the end they are cheating themselves. Why? A closed case enables the fans to create *airflow*. This airflow substantially cools off interior components. When the side of the case is open, you ruin the airflow of the system, and you lose a lot of cooling efficiency.

An important point to remember when implementing good airflow inside your computer case is that hot air rises. Warm air always rises above cold air, and you can use this principle to your advantage in keeping your computer cool.

In the typical layout of case fans for a computer case, an intake fan is located near the bottom of the front bezel of the case. This fan draws cool air in from outside the case and blows it over the components inside the case. Near the top and rear of the case (usually where the power supply is located), an exhaust fan is located. This fan works the opposite of the intake fan: it takes the warm air from inside the case and sends it to the outside.

Why not just put two fans side by side, with one blowing into the case and one blowing out? That might work to some extent, but this approach wouldn't be nearly as efficient as the layout just described. Recall the statement "hot air rises"; then you can see why the positioning of case fans is so important. The intake fan on the lower part of the case draws in cool air. This cool air enters the case and immediately begins to absorb heat from the electrical components. Some is sucked in by the heat sink fan and blown over the processor, cooling the processor—and heating the air. The newly heated air rises, where it is met in the top of the case by the exhaust fan.

Slot Covers

Another important part of maintaining proper airflow inside the case is ensuring that all empty expansion bays are covered by **slot covers** (Figure 6.22). To maintain good airflow inside your case, you shouldn't provide too many opportunities for air to escape. Slot covers not only assist in maintaining a steady airflow; they also help keep dust and smoke out of your case.

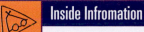

Inside Infromation

Other Ways to Cool Your Computer

If you are unhappy with the fans and airflow in your computer case, you can keep your computer cool in other ways. Among these options is water cooling your computer. Water cooling? Let me explain. In a water-cooled computer, water runs through a plastic hose to a hollow copper or aluminum block that sits on top of the CPU, just like a heat sink and fan would do. The water passing through the block cools the CPU, just like the air blowing from the fan across a heat sink, but it does a far better job than any fan can do. Water cooling relies on a closed system—a system where nothing can enter or exit the cooling loop. This means that the system must be completely free from leaks.

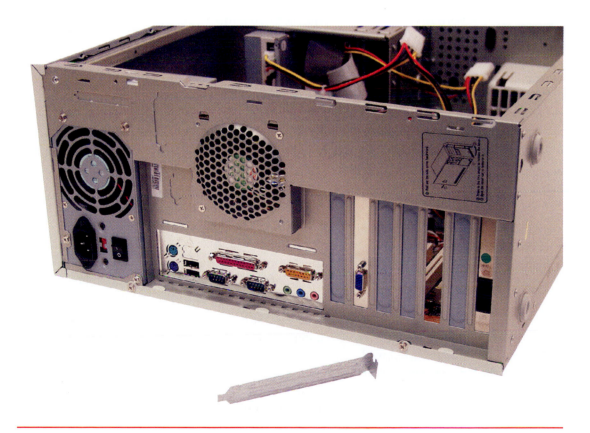

● **Figure 6.22**   Slot cover lying next to a case with an uncovered slot

Chapter 6 Review

■ Chapter Summary

After reading this chapter and completing the exercises, you should understand the following facts about cases and power supplies.

Different case forms have different functions

- A computer case is the box that houses all of the components and devices that make up a computer.

- Cases come in a variety of form factors: full-tower, mid-tower, mini-tower, desktop, server, and rack-mount. Rack-mount cases are sized by the unit (U), which is 1.75 inches high. The case's form factor is closely related to its intended function, location, and upgrade potential.

- Computer cases are equipped with special areas, called drive bays, to hold storage drives. Drives in external bays can be accessed from outside the case, so they are used for components such as floppy disk drives and CD-ROM drives. They come in two widths: 3½ inches and 5¼ inches. Internal bays aren't accessible without opening the case; they are used for components such as hard drives.

- Modern cases come with drive bay rails to facilitate drive installation. When installing drives in drive bays that don't have rails, you need to attach the drive directly to the drive cage on the inside of the case. To install a drive using rails, you affix the rails to the sides of the drive and then slide the drive rails into matching channels built into the drive bay.

- On the back of every case is a metal plate, called a back plate, punched through with a set of holes for various external connectors on the motherboard.

- Computer components attach using mounting screws with coarse or fine threading. Fine-threaded screws are used almost exclusively for mounting CD media drives. All other devices use coarse- threaded screws.

- Special stand-off screws are designed to be attached to the inside walls of the case and fit through holes in the motherboard. Stand-off screws are concave so that standard large-threaded screws can be screwed into them to hold the motherboard securely in place.

- Cases are usually designed with a specific type of motherboard in mind. There are four main form factors for cases and motherboards: AT, ATX, microATX, and FlexATX. Because the AT motherboard has been rendered obsolete by the ATX type, not many cases are built for AT motherboards anymore.

Understand the power supply

- The power supply in a PC doesn't supply power; it acts as a step-down transformer, converting high-voltage (115 volts in the U.S.) alternating current (AC) from the wall socket into low-voltage (12, 5, and 3.3 volts) direct current (DC).

- Power supplies have connectors to provide power to the motherboard and various internal devices. These include P8/P9 (for AT) or P1 (for ATX) connectors to supply power to the motherboard, special P4 connectors for Pentium 4 support, and Molex and Mini connectors for powering peripheral devices.

- System designs based on Pentium 4 processors require an ATX12V power supply, with an extra 12-volt, 4-pin connector to supply extra power to the motherboard.

- Power supplies are rated in watts. A watt is the standard measurement unit of power, or energy/time. A modern computer needs at least a 400-watt power supply to run safely.

- Power switch use is one of the major differences between AT and ATX power supplies. To better support power management and hibernation, ATX power supplies have a soft power feature. Soft power works by keeping the system from ever completely shutting off.

Ensure proper cooling

- Heat from any source reduces the lifespan of your components. Ensuring adequate cooling is a vital consideration when building a computer.

- A computer is a closed system, and that feature of computer cases helps the fans create airflow to keep things cool.

- The power supply fan not only cools the power supply, but also provides a flow of outside air throughout the interior of the computer case.

- The fan that sits atop the CPU's heat sink also plays a role in circulating air inside the computer case.
- Case fans are large, square fans that snap or screw into special brackets on the case, providing extra

cooling for key components. Most case fans use standard Molex connectors, but some use special three-pronged power connectors that plug directly into the motherboard.

■ Key Terms

3½-inch drive bay *(151)*	mini-tower case *(150)*	rack-mount case *(151)*
5¼-inch drive bay *(151)*	Molex connector *(159)*	server case *(150)*
desktop case *(150)*	P1 power connector *(159)*	slot cover *(171)*
full-tower case *(149)*	P4 power connector *(160)*	soft power *(162)*
hibernate mode *(162)*	P8/P9 power connectors *(158)*	unit (U) *(151)*
mid-tower case *(150)*	power supply *(155)*	watt *(157)*
Mini connector *(160)*	power supply fan *(162)*	

■ Key Term Quiz

Use terms from the Key Terms list to complete the following sentences. Not all terms will be used.

1. AT power supplies connect to the motherboard using _____.

2. A/an _____ is used to connect hard drives and CD-ROM drives to the power supply.

3. When a computer shuts down all its devices temporarily, it goes into _____.

4. A/an _____ is a tall, roomy computer case with plenty of interior space for adding multiple drives and expansion cards.

5. A/an _____ is designed to lie flat on its larger side with a monitor sitting on top of it, most commonly used for prebuilt computers that are not meant to be upgraded.

6. To maintain good airflow inside a case, an empty expansion bay should be sealed off from the outside using a/an _____.

7. Both an ancient large floppy drive and a modern optical drive must be mounted in an external _____.

8. A/An _____ is the standard measurement for a unit of power.

9. A modern ATX power supply plugs into an ATX motherboard using a single _____.

10. A/An _____ is a small computer case not recommended for systems requiring efficient case cooling and room for added drives and expansion cards.

■ Multiple-Choice Quiz

1. How many watts minimum should a power supply be for a modern computer?
   a. 250 watts
   b. 300 watts
   c. 350 watts
   d. 400 watts

2. What kind of power connector should you use with a 3½-inch floppy drive?
   a. P1 power connector
   b. Molex connector
   c. P4 connector
   d. Mini connector

3. The feature of ATX power supplies that keeps a motherboard from turning off all the way by feeding it a trickle charge of 5 volts, thus enabling it to be awakened by a remote command, is called _____.
   a. Soft power
   b. Rocker switch
   c. Hibernate mode
   d. Plunger switch

4. The _____ provides the basic cooling for the PC; if it stops turning, tremendous problems and equipment failure can occur.

   a. Power supply fan

   b. Bay fan

   c. CPU fan

   d. Case fan

5. A rack-mount case that is 4U is _____ inches high.

   a. 1.75

   b. 3½

   c. 5¼

   d. 7

6. The _____ has holes designed to allow various matching external connectors on the motherboard to poke through the computer case.

   a. Back area

   b. Back plane

   c. Back plate

   d. Back plain

7. Which type of case stands about 20 inches high and has an average of three external drive bays and one external floppy drive bay?

   a. Full-tower case

   b. Mid-tower case

   c. Mini-tower case

   d. Server case

8. What type of drive bay is used by modern floppy drives and hard drives?

   a. 5¼-inch bay

   b. 3½-inch bay

   c. 1.75-inch bay

   d. 1U bay

9. Almost all devices except CD media drives use what sort of screws?

   a. Fine-threaded

   b. Hex-headed

   c. Small-headed

   d. Coarse-threaded

10. What devices are often included in higher-end cases to facilitate mounting new devices in drive bays?

    a. Fans

    b. Housings

    c. Rails

    d. Bay fasteners

11. What are large fans that snap into special sections of a tower case, providing extra cooling for some key components, called?

    a. Case fans

    b. Power supply fans

    c. CPU fans

    d. Component fans

12. Which of the following cases would usually be the largest?

    a. Desktop case

    b. Mid-tower case

    c. Server case

    d. Full-tower case

13. What do you attach to the inside walls of the case and fit through holes in the motherboard to secure it to the case?

    a. Motherboard mounts

    b. Stand-off screws

    c. Riser mounts

    d. Two-head screws

14. Which is the smallest ATX form factor?

    a. FlexATX

    b. microATX

    c. Slim-ATX

    d. Rack-ATX

15. Which of the following connectors is unique to an AT power supply?

    a. Molex

    b. P1

    c. P8/P9

    d. P4

1. You are teaching a course on computers. In your next lecture, you want to explain to your students how power gets from the outlet in the wall to the various components of the computer. Write several paragraphs of a lecture explaining the process. Describe what hardware the power has to pass through and what happens to the power on its journey.

2. Your boss wants you to build a set of computers for yourself and your two officemates (a bit crowded, yes, but space is at a premium in this office). He has talked to a couple of his buddies and gotten conflicting suggestions on what case to choose. He knows he wants to use a relatively new CPU chip and to include the latest types of connectors, like FireWire and USB-2. He also wants the flexibility to have different employees use different sets of external drives and to change the sets of the drives they're using. Write a brief memo setting out the various case form factors. Discuss which cases support which motherboards. Explain what form factor you recommend and why. Include a discussion of your boss's criteria and any additional factors you think are relevant.

3. A friend sent you an e-mail telling you that she just won a new ATX motherboard, complete with CPU and RAM, at a local charity event. She wants to put it in her old AT system. Send an e-mail back telling her what this job will entail.

4. You get a call from a friend who tells you that his young son's computer won't start. Your friend thinks they have a bad power supply. What questions would you ask to troubleshoot this issue? What would you ask your friend to check first before you have him replace the power supply? (Think simple here!)

5. A friend who knows you're taking a course on PC hardware calls to ask for advice about his new computer. He wants to build a powerful gaming system, and has purchased a full-tower case with a 400-watt power supply; a top-of-the-line P4 CPU and motherboard; two large, fast hard drives; and serious, gamer-quality sound and video cards. He read somewhere on the Internet that serious gamers have to worry about overheating more than the average computer user, and he wonders if you have any advice about this. Write an e-mail explaining what he needs to consider in configuring his system. Include an explanation of why and how to create good airflow, which components he already has to help with cooling, and which ones he might want to add.

Lab Projects

• Lab Project 6.1

Inventory all of the computers in your immediate area. Create a list that gives the model, maker, wattage, and types of connectors (Molex, P1, and so on). Count the number of Molex and Mini connectors and add that information to the list, too.

• Lab Project 6.2

Assume that you want to purchase a new case for your computer. Here are the URLs of the manufacturers of some popular high-quality cases:

Aberdeen: www.aberdeeninc.com

Antec: www.antec-inc.com

Lian Li: www.lianli.com

Check out the different cases each company has for sale. Find the case you want based on size or power supply wattage. Then look at the other options, such as color, windows, USB ports, and any other features that interest you. Now look at the prices—good cases are expensive! Compare your choice to the choices of other students.

Removable Media

In this chapter, you will learn how to:

- **Identify, install, and troubleshoot floppy drives**
- **Identify and install Zip drives and SuperDisk drives**
- **Identify modern tape drive technologies**
- **Select and implement an appropriate tape backup strategy**

Your PC's primary storage device is the hard drive. Hard drives are fast and store a tremendous amount of data, but for all their capacity and speed, hard drives lack one important ability: they can't easily be removed from your system, making simple tasks like sharing a document with a friend or making a backup copy of your latest epic poem impractical. The need to move files from one system to another motivated us to use removable storage devices. These devices come in two distinct pieces: a drive mounted on the system unit, and a removable media disk. This class of devices is called **removable media**.

In this chapter, you will learn about the many types of removable media available for the PC, beginning with the oldest and most common type of removable media, the **floppy disk** and its associated drive. Then I will focus on more recent technology: the Iomega Zip drive and its only serious competition, the LS-120 SuperDisk.

After looking at floppy drives and their assorted progeny, we'll turn our attention to **tape backup devices**. All tape backup devices use a reel-to-reel cassette-type tape technology, which enables them to store massive amounts of data—up to 100 gigabytes—on a single cassette. The last section of this chapter covers the various tape backup strategies.

▪ Identifying, Installing, and Troubleshooting Floppy Drives

Of all of the types of removable media covered in this chapter, floppy drives are the only type that came with the original IBM PC. In fact, early PCs didn't even have hard drives—all programs and data were read from and stored on floppy disks. It was a big deal back then when systems appeared that had *dual* floppy drives because you could leave the program disk in one drive while you used the other drive for your data.

Although floppy drives have been with PCs from the beginning, they have gone through a number of changes over the years. Let's start by looking at some of the older types of floppy drives and how they evolved into the floppy drives we use today.

How Floppy Drives Work

All floppy disks are coated with a metallic film capable of holding a magnetic charge. The magnetic coating on a newly made floppy disk has no charge until it is formatted, which these days usually happens before the floppy leaves the factory. **Formatting** means placing organizational information on the floppy disk so that it can store data in a useful way. During the formatting process, magnetic charges are placed on the disk to create special storage areas, called **sectors**. Each sector can store up to 512 bytes of data. Don't bother trying to open a floppy disk to see these sectors—they're nothing but magnetically charged areas on the disk.

• Ancient PC with only floppy drives

> 💡 Some floppy disk makers do sell unformatted floppy disks. See Step-by-Step 7.2 to learn how to format a floppy disk.

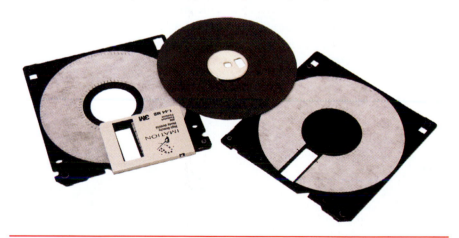

• Innards of a modern floppy drive

On the very outside edge of the floppy disk is a special group of sectors known as the file allocation table, or FAT (see Chapter 8 for more information on the FAT). The FAT is the card catalog for the files stored on the disk, keeping track of which files are stored in which sectors.

• Front of a floppy drive

When you insert a floppy disk into a floppy drive, the protective slide opens, revealing the magnetic media inside the plastic casing of the floppy disk. A motor- driven spindle snaps into the center of the drive to make it spin. A set of read/write heads then moves back and forth across the drive, reading or writing tracks on the disk as needed (Figure 7.1).

Whenever your system accesses a floppy disk in its floppy drive, a read/write LED on the outside front of the drive will flash on. You should not try to remove the floppy disk from the drive when this light is lit! That light means that the read/write heads are accessing the floppy drive, and pulling the disk out while the light is on can damage the floppy disk. When the light is off, you can push in the small release button on the front of the drive to eject the floppy disk.

Although the way that floppy drives work hasn't changed much since the days of the first floppy drives, the size of floppy disks and drives has shrunk over the years, and data capacity has grown. Let's look at the evolution of the floppy from its beginnings over 20 years ago.

For technical accuracy, I must mention that floppy drives actually predate the PC. They were commonly used in many earlier computers, including mainframes. These ancient floppy drive technologies are simply too far back in the misty past to discuss here; however, if you're a fan of old computer technology, there are a number of good websites to feed your curiosity: www.obsoletecomputermuseum.org www.computerhistory.org www.computer-museum.org

The History of Floppy Disks

Early PCs didn't need a lot of storage. Early PCs ran DOS as their primary operating system. DOS was very simple compared to Windows or Linux, and of course, it was not a graphical interface. This meant that many early PCs could and did run perfectly well with only 64 K of RAM and a single floppy drive. You booted the computer from a DOS floppy disk, and then you removed that floppy and inserted a floppy that stored the program you wanted to run. When it was time to store or access data, you took out the program disk and inserted your data disk; then you took that out and put the program disk back in, and so on.

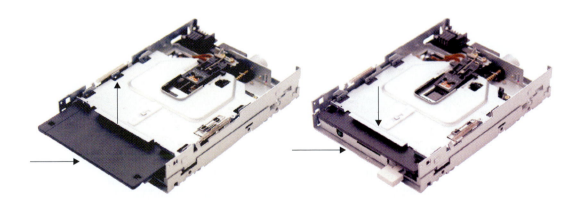

• Figure 7.1   Read/write heads on a floppy drive accessing a floppy disk

Introduction to PC Hardware and Troubleshooting

The first floppy drive to come with the original IBM PC was 5¼ inches in diameter and stored a whopping 360 K bytes of data. This disk was referred to as a 5¼-inch, 360 K, double-sided, single-density floppy. By the time the 286 computers came out, the floppy disk of choice was an improved version of the 5¼-inch disk: it was double-sided and double-density and had a data storage capacity of 1.2 MB. **Double-density** means that the tracks—the magnetic circles where the data is stored on the floppy disk—are packed together twice as closely as the tracks on a single-density disk.

The problem with 5¼-inch disks was that they were, well, too floppy. If you held one up and waved it, the semi-rigid plastic casing flopped back and forth, leading to its rather odd name. More importantly, you could easily bend a 5¼-inch floppy with your hands or by sitting on it—people found many creative, albeit accidental, ways to render them useless as data storage devices.

• 5¼-inch floppy drive and floppy disk

In the late 1980s, IBM unveiled a new type of floppy disk and drive for the PC that solved all three problems inherent with the earlier floppy drives. They replaced the floppy casing that covered the old disks with a totally rigid plastic shell, making the delicate magnetic insides far less vulnerable to accidental damage. They also made the new floppy disks smaller.

These new disks originally had a data storage capacity of 720 KB (double-sided, double-density). These were quickly replaced with the now universal 1.44 MB (double-sided, high-density) floppy disks. These 3½-inch floppy disks and drives are in virtually every PC made today. A 2.88 MB (double-sided, extra high-density) 3½-inch disk appeared briefly, but it never really caught on due to cost and lack of support by computer makers—it fell into that huge trash heap of unused technologies that litter the history of the PC world.

Floppy Drive Cables

All floppy drives need cables to connect to the PC. A PC can support a maximum of two floppy drives—no big deal because one is plenty for almost all PCs. Floppy disks connect to the motherboard via a **34-pin ribbon cable**. Most floppy drive ribbon cables used today have one connector for the drive. If for some reason you want to use two floppy drives, you'll need a cable with a second drive connector.

The ribbon cables that support two floppy drives have a twist in between the two drive connectors. This twist determines which floppy drive gets which drive letter. The floppy drive installed on the end of the cable becomes the A: drive, and the floppy drive installed on the second connector is the B: drive. If you're installing only one floppy, make sure you install it in the A: drive position or your system won't be able to boot to it!

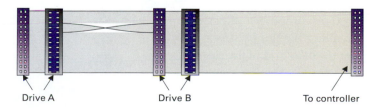

Drive A   Drive B   To controller

• A floppy drive ribbon cable

Installing a Floppy Drive

In this Step-by-Step exercise, you will install a typical 3½-inch floppy drive in a PC. To complete this exercise, you will need the following:

- Computer system running any version of Windows with the floppy drive removed
- 3½-inch floppy drive
- Floppy drive ribbon cable

Step 1

The first step in installing a floppy drive is deciding where to install it. Most cases have several 3½-inch bays available for adding drives. Install the floppy into the drive bay. (Refer back to Chapter 6 if you're unsure about how to install a drive into a drive bay.)

Step 2

Next, you install the ribbon cable on the back of the floppy drive. The trick here is to make sure you insert the ribbon cable the right way; your guide is the colored stripe running down one side of the cable, which you must orient to pin number 1 on the floppy drive connector. This sounds straightforward—but how do you tell which pin on the connector is number 1? If you're lucky, the number 1 pin is actually labeled on the floppy drive. If you're *really* lucky, your floppy drive has a connector with a special notch that permits you to insert the cable only one way.

Step 3

Don't panic if you have to guess about the number 1 pin on the floppy drive. If by chance you install the floppy cable backwards, when you boot the system the floppy won't work, but you won't cause any damage. The big clue that this is what's happened: the floppy's read light will come on as soon as you boot the system, and it won't ever go off. To fix the problem, just turn off the PC, reverse the cable, and reboot.

Step 4

After you've inserted the ribbon cable in the floppy drive's connector, place the floppy drive into the drive bay and plug a handy "mini" power connector into the floppy drive. Be careful when plugging in the power cable—it is difficult, but (as many hapless techs have proven) not impossible to insert the power connector upside down or even off to the side. Incorrectly attaching the power cable may destroy the floppy drive!

Step 5

Got everything plugged in properly? Super! You're almost done installing the floppy drive. Your next step is to plug the *other* end of the ribbon cable into the floppy drive controller's connection on the motherboard. The same rules as before apply: make sure you match the colored

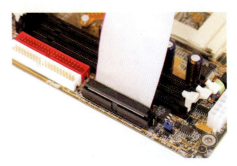

stripe on the cable to the number 1 pin on the connector. Fortunately for you, almost all motherboards not only label the number 1 pin; they also have a notch in the connector to help ensure you attach the cable right.

Step 6

After you've finished connecting the ribbon cable, you're done installing the floppy drive. Insert a formatted floppy disk, preferably one with files on it, and try to view the contents using My Computer or Windows Explorer, to make sure Windows can successfully access the floppy disk.

At this point, you might be tempted to ask, "What about the System Setup program? Don't I need to go in there and change settings?" Excellent question, but in this case the work has most likely been done: every PC made in the past five or six years *automatically* assumes that your A: drive is a 3½-inch, 1.44-MB floppy drive.

Care and Feeding of Your Floppies

Floppy drives and floppy disks are probably the most abused parts of the average PC. The drives are repeatedly exposed to dirt, smoke, and other foreign elements that eventually clog the floppy drive and dirty the read/write heads. Floppy disks tend to get sat upon, chewed on, covered in maple syrup, and otherwise trashed in more ways than the average mind can fathom. To borrow shamelessly from Smokey the Bear, "Only you can prevent floppy abuse!" This section discusses ways to avoid these problems, and what to do when they (inevitably) happen anyway.

Caring for Floppy Drives

The single most important action you can take to protect your floppy drive is to keep it clean. Head out to your local computer or electronics store and pick up a floppy drive **cleaning kit**. Now here's the real secret: It's not enough to simply possess the kit. As yet, none have been created that can exert a cleaning influence from within their protective packaging. Thus,

• Typical floppy drive cleaning kit

for optimum effect, you should actually unwrap it and *use it* about once a month.

Foreign objects run a close second to dirt as a source of floppy drive problems. As a floppy drive ages, the mechanical release button on the drive tends to wear out. After the release button fails, users desperate to remove their floppy disks will try to pry them out using paper clips, hairpins, X-Acto blades, and all manner of other creative tools. This display of initiative not only tends to damage the floppy disks in question, but the tools often end up disappearing inside the drive. This is a *bad thing*, and it will require surgical intervention in most cases.

When floppy drive surgery is required, you should first shut down the system and take off the front faceplate (*gently*—you'll want to replace it later). Removing the faceplate before you operate does two good things. First, it gives you easier access to the inside of the floppy drive as you work to remove the foreign object. Second, in the case of a drive with a weak release button, it makes popping out the disk somewhat easier. If necessary, you can remove the floppy drive entirely and upend it. A pair of tweezers can help to grab small objects, or just to hold the door open so things can fall out.

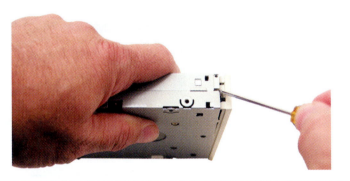

• Removing the front faceplate of a floppy drive

Fixing Broken Floppy Drives

You don't *fix* broken floppy drives, you *replace* them. A standard floppy drive sells for less than $20 (US). However, before you spend even that much money, you should be aware that a floppy drive that appears to be broken often isn't. Here are a few tips for dealing with a floppy drive you think may have gone bad.

How do you know when a floppy drive has a problem? The symptoms will be evident when you try to access a disk in the floppy drive. A number of different errors indicate a problem with the floppy drive, but there's no need to memorize them—just look for errors that sound like they involve floppy disks or the A: drive. Here are some examples:

■ Data error reading drive A:

■ Drive is not accessible. Access is denied

Introduction to PC Hardware and Troubleshooting

- There is no floppy in the drive. Please insert a formatted floppy and try again.

- The floppy in drive A: is not formatted. Format now?

Suppose you get one of these floppy-related error messages—what should you do? First check whether the floppy icon appears in My Computer. If it does, you know that Windows recognizes the drive and that the drive's electronics are in good order. If it doesn't appear, perform a mental reinstallation, which involves verifying that the drive has power, the ribbon cables are connected correctly, and the system setup is configured properly.

• Sample floppy disk error message in Windows

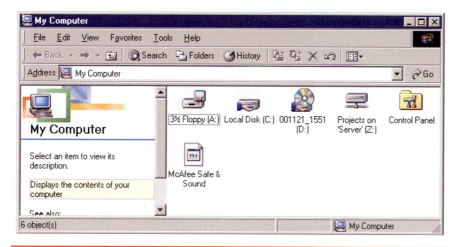

• If you can see the icon for the floppy drive, the drive is probably okay.

Second, try some other floppy disks—can the system read them? If it can, you can blame the floppy disk rather than the drive. If it can't, you probably are suffering from the most common source of floppy drive failure: **radial misalignment**.

When you read or write data on a floppy disk, small motors in the drive move read/write heads back and forth over concentric tracks on the disk, calculating the correct distances from a predetermined zero point near the center. Because the distances involved are quite tiny, if the actual starting position of the head shifts even fractionally off this zero point, the head may have trouble reading data and may even partially overwrite data on nearby tracks when it performs a write function. Radial misalignment can be caused by normal wear and tear over time or by damage from foreign objects, including dust and grit blown in by the case fans. If your floppy drive fails to read three or four known good floppy disks, you almost certainly have a radial misalignment and should replace the drive.

If multiple floppy drives fail at the same time, the situation can get really complicated: "I can read Bob's floppy disks but not Sally's or Ted's. Sally can read mine—sometimes—and can always read Bob's and Ted's." What's causing this odd situation? All of these floppy drives are afflicted with radial misalignment, but to different degrees. The solution? Replace *all* of them!

Bootable Floppy Disks

When you start a computer, it automatically goes through the process of looking for an operating system. Most PCs are configured to look for an operating system first on a floppy disk in your floppy drive, next on the hard drive, and sometimes also on a CD-ROM drive. Normally you want to load the operating system on the hard drive, but there are a few situations where

Inside Information

Floppies and Booting

It's very common to leave a floppy disk in the computer when you shut it down. If you boot a system with a nonbootable floppy disk in the floppy drive, the system will attempt to boot off that floppy and, finding no actual operating system, will respond with an error message similar to this:

```
Non-system Disk or
Disk Error
Replace and press any
key to reboot
```

If you get this or a similar error message, smack yourself in the forehead (okay, that part's optional), pop out the floppy disk, and press any key to let the system start normally. Not that I have ever done this myself, of course!

you might want to boot from a specially formatted floppy disk (or disks) called, with admirable clarity, a bootable floppy. Some operating systems call them startup disks.

Try This!

Creating a Windows 98 Startup Disk

If you have a computer system running Windows 98, you should have a startup disk you can boot from when your computer locks up and won't boot normally. Grab a blank floppy disk and try this:

1. Open the Control Panel from the Start menu. Double-click on the Add/Remove Programs icon to start that applet. Select the Startup Disk tab and click the Create Disk button.

2. Insert a floppy disk when prompted. Windows will create a bootable floppy by formatting the disk and adding certain key files that will enable Windows to boot from it. When the process is finished, remove the floppy and label it *Windows 98 Startup Disk*.

3. Restart the system with the Startup disk inserted. You should see a Windows startup screen with several boot options. Select *Start Computer with CD-ROM* support, and watch the boot process progress to the A:\> prompt. Remove the startup disk and reboot into Windows.

Step-by-Step 7.2

Formatting Nonbootable Floppy Disks

In this Step-by-Step exercise, you will learn how to format a nonbootable floppy disk. Formating regular (nonbootable) floppy disks is a quick and handy way to erase their contents. In addition, formatting a floppy disk gives you a cleaner result than just deleting the files. Formatting a floppy disk is generally a fairly simple operation, but you may run into a few quirks depending on what you want to do.

To complete this exercise, you will need the following:

- A computer system running any version of Windows with a functioning floppy drive

- A floppy disk that is either blank or contains only files that you can destroy

Step I

Boot the computer (if it's not already running) and then insert the floppy disk into the floppy drive. Open My Computer. Locate the floppy icon (A:\). Alternate-click (right-click) the icon and select Format. The Format dialog box appears.

Introduction to PC Hardware and Troubleshooting

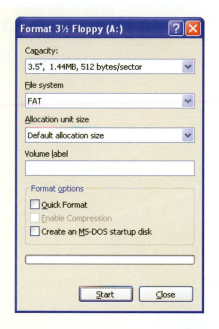

Step 2

Locate the Quick Format check box in the lower half of the dialog box. If this option is *not* checked, Windows will perform a Full format operation. If you are formatting a floppy drive that has never been formatted (once a common way to buy floppies, but rare now), you *must*

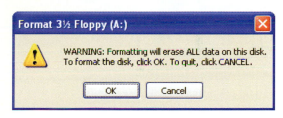

use the Full format option. Leave the Quick Format box unchecked and click the Format button to start the Full format process. Windows will ask you to confirm that you understand that formatting will destroy all data on the disk. Click OK to let the format operation proceed.

Note: The Full format option prepares the floppy for use and then checks the entire floppy for errors. The Quick format option only prepares the floppy for use.

Step 3

When formatting is completed, Windows pops up a small dialog box to let you know. Click OK to return to the Format dialog box. Check a clock and note how long the Full format operation took.

Step 4

If the floppy is already formatted and you just want to eliminate the data, you need to perform only a Quick format. Using the same floppy disk you just formatted, perform a Quick format operation. Select the Quick Format check box to check this option; then click Format. Check a clock again and note the difference in the length of the formatting processes.

Step 5

Now that the floppy is formatted, you can close the dialog box. Remember to remove the floppy from the drive!

■ Identifying and Installing Zip Drives and SuperDisk Drives

For many years, the only true read/write removable media option on the PC was the floppy disk. 1.44 MB seemed like a lot of data back in the days when the typical hard drive might store 40, 80, or if you were really smoking, 200 MB; however, by the mid-1990s the growing size difference between the floppy and the hard drive created demand for a new type of easy-to-use removable media that could store substantially more than the typical floppy.

A number of manufacturers made attempts to come up with a removable media solution, but none of them caught on, until a little company called Iomega (www.iomega.com) developed a special type of removable media drive called the **Zip drive**. The first Zip drives could store up to 100 MB of data—as much data as a *box* of floppies! Iomega introduced the Zip drive in the mid-1990s.

Iomega made sure its Zip drives were easy to install and simple to use. The company was rewarded, as storage-starved users made Zip drives extremely popular virtually overnight. Zip drives are very common today, and Iomega is the king of the disk-type removable media market. What set Iomega Zip drives apart from other removable drives produced around the same time was the fact that Iomega drives and disks were cheap and easy to install and use.

Let's look at the Iomega Zip drive now as well as the only serious competitor to Zip: the SuperDisk.

• 100-MB Iomega Zip drive with Zip disk

Zip Drives

It would be an overstatement to say that Iomega owns the removable media market, but it's probably fair to say that Iomega Zip drives own the lower end of the market, for drives that store less than 1 GB. One of the great aspects of Zip drives is that Iomega gives you so many ways to connect them to your PC. Zip drives come in two types: internal drives that you install inside the system case, and external drives with a cable that you plug into a port on the system case.

• Internal Zip drive

• External Zip drive

Internal Zip drives are ATAPI devices. As you'll learn in Chapter 8, ATAPI devices are designed to install like a hard drive. The external drives have more flexibility; you can purchase an external Zip drive that plugs into a parallel port, a USB port, or an external SCSI port.

Although Zip drives are quite popular, they cannot totally replace a floppy drive. Motherboard makers have not been willing to create a BIOS that supports a bootable Zip drive (although a few now do), and more importantly, Zip drives cannot read regular 1.44-MB floppy disks. If you were to replace your floppy drive with a Zip drive, you would not be able to read any of your floppy disks. Seeing the need for a large-capacity drive that could both read floppy disks and be a true replacement for the venerable floppy drive, in 1997 Imation Corporation, an offshoot of 3M, invented the **LS-120**, better known as the **SuperDisk**.

Zip drives and disks come in three capacities: 100 MB, 250 MB, and 750 MB. Think about the type and amount of data you want to store on your Zip disks before choosing a size. A factor to keep in mind: 750-MB Zip drives will not write to 100-MB disks; otherwise, however, Zip drives can read and write to any smaller-sized Zip disk.

SuperDisk Drives

The SuperDisk drive has all the benefits of the Zip drive, plus it can read and write to a standard floppy disk. When it came out, it was greeted with quite a bit of fanfare as the true floppy drive replacement option. Unfortunately, for reasons that are not totally clear, the SuperDisk drive has never achieved wide adoption, but it does enjoy enough market share to make it worth knowing about.

Imation now makes two versions of the SuperDisk: the LS-120 with a storage capacity of 120 MB, and the LS-240 with a storage capacity of 240 MB. Like Zip drives, SuperDisk drives come in internal and external versions. Also like the Zip drives, internal SuperDisk drives install like hard drives; external SuperDisk drives come in parallel and USB versions.

• Internal LS-120 SuperDisk drive

• LS-120 disk

Both Zip and LS-120 seem to be starting to fade slowly from the PC market, due to the influx of USB and FireWire removable media drives that equal or approach hard drives in size and speed. On the other hand, we are now starting to see motherboards that allow you to boot to either Zip or LS-120 drives—could this mean the end of floppy drives and a new lease on life for these drives?

Cleaning Zip and SuperDisk Drives

SuperDisk drives need to be kept clean. Cleaning kits are readily available for these drives, but you may need to go to the Imation website (www.imation.com) to find a SuperDisk cleaning kit. Interestingly, Iomega does not support the cleaning of Zip drives; in fact, the company warns that attempting to clean a Zip drive will damage the read/write heads.

Step-by-Step 7.3

Booting to a Floppy, Zip, or SuperDrive Disk

You don't absolutely have to have a Zip drive or LS-120 drive to complete this Step-by-Step exercise, but it makes it a bit more fun. The goal of this exercise is to see what you can do in your system setup to change the order in which your PC tries to boot to its different devices. These include not only floppy and Zip drives but also the hard drive and maybe even a CD-ROM drive.

To complete this exercise, you will need the following:

- A computer system running Windows with a functioning floppy drive and CD-ROM drive

- If possible, an installed Zip or SuperDrive drive, either external or internal

- A nonbootable floppy disk and a nonbootable CD-ROM, both either blank or containing only files you can destroy

- If you have the matching drive, a nonbootable Zip or SuperDrive disk that is either blank or contains only files you can destroy

Step 1

Shut down and reboot your system, holding down the appropriate key to enter the System Setup utility. Find the screen that enables you to set your PC's boot device sequence. On most systems, the boot sequence list will show the A: (floppy) drive first, followed by the C: (hard disk) drive, followed by perhaps a CD-ROM drive, Zip drive, or SuperDrive. Make a note of the boot device sequence.

Step 2

Check whether your System Setup utility supports Zip or LS-120 drives in the boot sequence. If it does, follow the setup program's instructions to make the Zip or LS-120 drive the first boot device and your floppy drive the second boot device. If you don't

Introduction to PC Hardware and Troubleshooting

have a Zip or LS-120 drive, set the floppy to be the first device. Finally, set the CD-ROM to be the third boot device (the second device if you don't have a Zip or LS-120 drive).

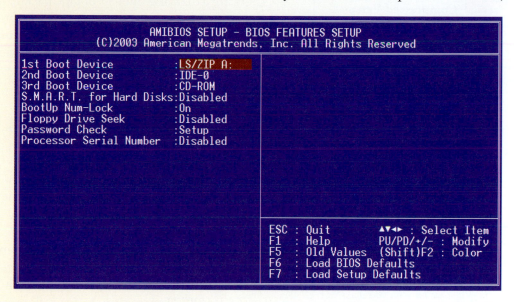

Step 3

Boot the system with a Zip disk in the Zip drive or SuperDisk in the LS-120 drive, a floppy disk in the floppy drive, and a CD-ROM in the CD-ROM drive. (If you don't have a Zip or LS-120 drive, just use a floppy and a CD-ROM.) See what error message you get when the system tries to boot to the Zip or LS-120 disk. Press any key to continue the boot process. See what error you get when the system tries to boot to the floppy disk. Press any key to continue the boot process. See what error you get when the system tries to boot to the CD-ROM. Press any key to continue the boot process.

Step 4

Reboot the system again and go back into the System Setup utility. Return the boot device sequence to its former working state, referencing your notes if necessary. Make sure the system boots properly.

■ Modern Tape Drive Technologies

When it comes to storing multiple megabytes of data, nothing beats good old tape drives. Tape drives aren't as fast as other options like CD media or other removable drives, but they are great for cheap and dependable data backup.

The problem with tape drives isn't a lack of usefulness—it's deciding which type of drive to use. There are three different types of tapes, each with a number of different capacities, and it can be tough to decide which tape drive option best fits your needs.

Tape Drive Options

Magnetic tape is the oldest of all methods for storing computer data, and even today nothing can beat magnetic tape's ability to store phenomenal amounts of data cheaply and safely. Remember the computers on old 70s TV shows, with huge banks of reel-to-reel tapes spinning away industriously?

Thanks to hard drives, reel-to-reel tape is no longer a primary storage medium. Now it's pretty much relegated to the job of backup storage.

There are a dizzying number of tape backup options, each with its own advantages and disadvantages. They basically break down into three major groups: QIC, DAT, and DLT. All three types use **cartridge tapes**—square tapes, like fat audio cassettes—but the physical cartridge size, data capacity, recording method, tape length, and tape speed vary enormously.

QIC

Quarter-Inch Cartridge tape, or **QIC tape**, is an old standard, rarely used in any but the smallest of networks. QIC was one of the first standards used for PC backups, and it has gone through much evolution over the years in an attempt to keep up with the demand for increased capacity. The earliest versions of QIC could store about 40 MB—fine for the days when tiny hard drives were the rule, but unacceptable today. QIC capacity eventually reached 2 GB, but QIC has fallen out of favor and is no longer a desirable tape standard. Imation Corporation created an improved QIC format called **Travan**, with a capacity of around 10 GB. Travan is quite popular, again on smaller networks. Under the Travan banner, QIC lives on as a tape backup option. Older QIC/Travan drives used a floppy connection, but EIDE and SCSI connections are more common today.

• Tape showing compressed and uncompressed sizes

DAT

Digital Audio Tape, or **DAT**, was the first tape system to use a totally digital recording method. DAT was originally designed to record digital audio and video, but it has moved easily into the tape backup world. DAT is currently the most popular tape type. DAT media have much higher storage capacities than QIC/Travan tapes—up to 24 GB—and are popular for medium-sized networks. DAT drives use a SCSI connection.

DLT

Digital Linear Tape, or **DLT**, is quickly becoming the tape backup standard of choice. DLT is a relatively new standard that has massive data capacity (up to 200 GB). DLT drives use a SCSI connection. DLT is very fast, incredibly reliable, and—here's the downside—quite expensive compared to earlier technologies. When the data is critical, however, the price of the tape backup may well be considered insignificant. Figure 7.2 shows the kind of DLT drive I use in my server.

Tape Backup Strategies

The goal of data backup is to ensure that when a system dies, a recent copy of the data will be available that you can use to restore the system. You could simply back up the complete system at the end of each day, or at whatever interval you feel is prudent to keep the backup fresh, but complete backups can

• **Figure 7.2**   DLT tape drive with tape

be a tremendous waste of time and materials. A single backup may consist of one tape or more, and if a backup needs more than one tape, a person must be present to switch out the tapes as the backup program requires.

Instead of backing up the entire system, a better plan is to take advantage of the fact that not all files will have been changed in any given period. Most of the time, you really need to back up only the files that have changed since your last backup. Recognizing this, most backup software solutions have a series of options available beyond the old Complete (usually called Full or Normal) backup.

The key to understanding backups other than Full backups is a little fellow called the **Archive bit**. All files have little 1-bit storage areas called **file attributes**. The most common attributes are Hidden (hidden from the operating system), System (a critical file for the system), Read-Only (a file that can't be erased), and Archive. These attributes were first used in DOS but, with the exception of Hidden, are still completely supported today by all versions of Windows. The Archive bit is the attribute you need when making backups.

The Archive bit basically works like this: Whenever a file is saved, the Archive bit is turned on. Simply opening a file affects the current state of the Archive bit. A backup program will usually turn off the file's Archive bit when it is backed up. In theory, if a file's Archive bit is turned off, there is a current backup of that file on some tape. If the Archive bit is turned on, that file *has been changed* since the last backup. Archive bits are the tool used to perform backups that are not full backups.

These are the most commonly supported types of backup:

- A **Normal backup** is a full backup. Every file selected will be backed up. The Archive bit will be turned off for every file backed up. This is the standard "back it all up" option.

- A **Copy backup** is identical to a Normal backup with one big exception: The Archive bits are not changed. This strategy is used (although not often) for making extra copies of a previously completed backup.

There are a large number of variations on the basic backup strategies, but if you understand the backup methods explained here, you'll understand all the others, too.

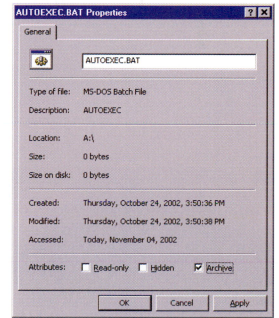

• The Archive bit is on because the file has been changed.

- An **Incremental backup** backs up only files whose Archive bits are turned on. An Incremental backup copies only the files that have been changed since the last backup. It then turns off the Archive bits.

- A **Differential backup** is identical to an Incremental backup, except that a Differential backup doesn't turn off the Archive bits.

- A Daily backup, better known as a **Daily Copy backup**, backs up all files that have been changed that day. It does not change the Archive bits.

Any time you do any type of backup, you will use one or more tapes. Even if you have enough room on a single tape for more than one backup job, you invariably still use a different tape. Keeping each backup job on its own tape (or set of tapes) prevents confusion. Once you no longer need a particular backup, there's no reason not to reuse those tapes. If you do a full backup every day, you can keep using the same set of tapes over and over again. In most such situations, there's no reason to keep the previous week's backup.

Backups are necessary but also a chore. The key is to do them in such a way as to minimize the number of backups you do, or to limit the number of tapes you use for each backup. Incremental and Differential backups serve these goals. The motivation for choosing between Incremental and Differential backups is not always clear because they seem so similar. Let's assume that a company that performs a Normal backup every Monday and either an Incremental or a Differential backup Tuesday through Friday. A Differential backup is a cumulative backup. Because the Archive bits are not set, it keeps backing up all changes since the last Normal backup. Clearly, the backups will get progressively larger through the week as more files are changed, usually on the same tape. The Incremental backup, in contrast, backs up only the files changed since the last backup. Each Incremental backup will be small, but also totally different from the previous backup. An Incremental backup uses more tapes (one every day) than a Differential backup (just one backup that is updated daily).

Depending on the backup strategy you choose, you may find either Incremental or Differential backup more appropriate for your site. The greater the number of days between Normal backups, the more Incremental backups you need to restore. A Differential backup will always require only two backups to restore. Looked at this way, the Differential backup looks like the better choice. On the other hand, a big benefit of Incremental backup over Differential backup is backup size. Differential backups will be massive compared to Incremental backups. The backup strategy you choose will depend on the specifics of your situation—just make sure you're doing something!

Backup Programs

Unlike floppy drives, Zip drives, and SuperDisk drives, tape backup units do not appear as a drive letter (for example, D: or E:) in My Computer. Because you can't access

Cross Check

Incremental Versus Differential Backup

Assume for a moment that you have a system that you back up using either an Incremental or Differential backup strategy. Suppose the system was wiped out during the day on Thursday. How would you restore the system? From how many tapes would you need to restore data? With an Incremental backup, you would first have to restore the weekly backup, then the Tuesday backup, and then the Wednesday backup before the system was restored. If you used a Differential backup, on the other hand, you would need only the weekly backup and then the Wednesday backup to restore the system.

tape drives directly, you must use a backup program to back up a PC to a tape drive. Many backup programs are available; one of the most common is the Microsoft Backup utility that comes with almost every version of Windows.

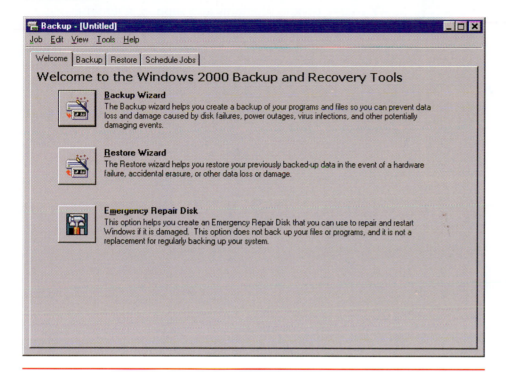

• Windows Backup on a Windows 2000 system

All backup programs work in roughly the same way. First, they automatically try to detect the presence of a tape backup system. If they don't find one, they will usually inform you rather bluntly.

• "No backup devices were found" error message in Windows 98

You are then presented with some type of Windows Explorer–like interface so you can select the files you want to back up. Because of this, users commonly place all of their critical data in just a few Windows folders—this makes it much easier to select the files and folders to back up. The most common backup procedure is to back up the same set of files every day or week, so all backup programs allow you to create a *backup job*, which is simply a set of backup instructions specifying what to back up and when and how

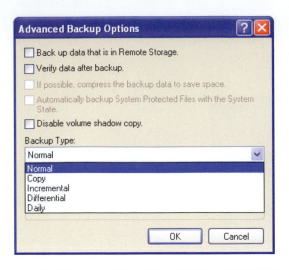

(the backup strategy): for instance, "Perform a Daily Copy backup on all the files in the My Documents folder Monday through Friday at 6 p.m." As shown in Figure 7.3, the Windows XP Backup utility is quite clear about your choice of backup type.

Of course, backup programs also support restoration of data. In most backup programs, you must specify the backup job or catalog that you want to restore, and then the backup program does the rest for you. Although the backup program will first look for a tape backup, more advanced backup programs will also let you back up to a file on your hard drive. If you have a copy of Windows Backup, try creating a small backup job that backs up a few files.

● **Figure 7.3**   Windows XP backup choices

Step-by-Step 7.4

Working with Attributes

Attributes may not be visible when you look at a file in My Computer or open a file to work on it, but they are present if you know where to look. In this Step-by-Step exercise, you will find and change several file attributes so you can see them in action.

To complete this exercise, you will need the following:

■ A computer system running Windows XP (Other versions of Windows will also work for this exercise, but be prepared for subtle differences in text, dialog boxes, and so on.)

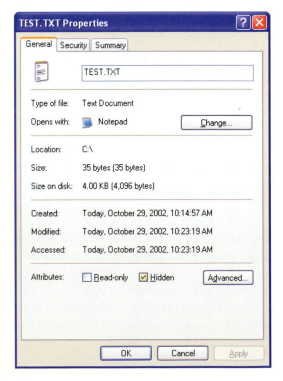

Step 1

Open My Computer and double-click the C: drive to view the contents. Select any arbitrary file and alternate-click it. Select Properties to open the File Properties dialog box. Click to put a check in the check box next to the Hidden attribute; then click OK. Look at the My Computer window and notice that the file is no longer visible.

Step 2

From the Tools menu, choose Folder Options to open the Folder Options dialog box. Select the View tab. You'll see an option to show or not show Hidden files. By default, Hidden files are not displayed. Select Show Hidden Files to display the files. Look at the My Computer window again; the Hidden file should be dimmed but visible.

Step 3

Open the Folder Options dialog box again, select the View tab, and this time select the option to have Windows hide files marked as Hidden. Look at the My Computer window again; now the Hidden file has disappeared.

Step 4

Open the Folder Options dialog box yet again, select the View tab, and change the view option back to Show Hidden Files. In My Computer, find the file you've been working with, alternate-click it, and select Properties to reopen the File Properties dialog box. Uncheck the box next to the Hidden attribute; then click OK to set the file back to its original state.

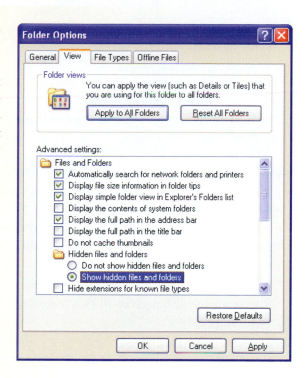

Note: In the old DOS days, activating a file's Read-Only attribute prevented the file from being deleted, but Windows ignores this attribute and still lets you delete the file.

Chapter 7 Review

■ Chapter Summary

After reading this chapter and completing the exercises, you should understand the following facts about removable media.

Identify, install, and troubleshoot floppy drives

- The first floppy drives used in PCs were 5¼ inches in diameter. Today's floppy drives use a 3½-inch format. Although the 3½-inch drives have come in capacities ranging from 720 KB to 2.88 MB, 1.44 MB is the de facto standard.

- All PCs are designed to support up to two floppy drives, although most PCs use only one floppy drive.

- Floppy drives use a 34-pin cable. This cable may have a twist and a second connection for a second floppy drive.

- Floppy drives get their drive letters from their position on the cable. The drive connected on the end is A:, and the one connected in the middle is B:.

- Floppy drives need a Mini power connector.

- Always match the colored stripe on the ribbon cable to the number 1 pin on the drive and on the motherboard.

- Use a floppy drive cleaning kit to keep floppy drives clean.

Identify and install Zip drives and SuperDisk drives

- Iomega Zip disks come in three sizes: 100 MB, 250 MB, and 750 MB.

- SuperDisks come in two sizes: 120 MB and 240 MB.

- Both SuperDisk drives and Zip drives are available in external and internal versions.

- SuperDisk drives can read standard floppy disks, but Zip drives cannot.

- Internal drives usually install like hard drives (ATAPI).

- External drives most commonly plug into parallel ports or USB ports.

- It is a good idea to clean SuperDisk drives but not Zip drives.

Identify modern tape drive technologies

- QIC is the oldest tape standard; in its Travan form, it stores up to roughly 10 GB.

- Most tapes are sold in compressed and uncompressed sizes. The compressed size is only an estimate and is simply double the uncompressed size.

- DAT tapes store up to 24 GB. They are very popular as backup media.

- DLT tapes store up to 200 GB. DLT is becoming the backup standard of choice.

Select and implement an appropriate tape backup strategy

- The four attributes associated with every file are Hidden, Read-Only, System, and Archive. Archive bits are turned on whenever a file is created or changed.

- There are five common backup strategies:

  - Normal performs a full backup; the Archive bit is turned off for every file backed up.

  - Copy is identical to Normal except the Archive bits are not changed.

  - Incremental backs up only files that have the Archive bit turned on; it then turns off the Archive bits.

  - Differential is identical to Incremental, but Differential doesn't turn off the Archive bits.

  - Daily (or Daily Copy) backs up all files that have changed that day; it does not change the Archive bits.

- It's not necessary to make a complete backup every time you back up a system.

- A standard backup strategy includes a weekly Normal backup and daily Differential or Incremental backups.

■ Key Terms

34-pin ribbon cable *(179)*

Archive bit *(191)*

cartridge tape *(190)*

cleaning kit *(181)*

Copy backup *(191)*

Daily Copy backup *(192)*

Differential backup *(192)*

Digital Audio Tape (DAT) *(190)*

Digital Linear Tape (DLT) *(190)*

double-density *(179)*

file attribute *(191)*

floppy disk *(176)*

formatting *(177)*

Incremental backup *(192)*

LS-120 *(187)*

Normal backup *(191)*

Quarter-Inch Cartridge tape (QIC tape) *(190)*

radial misalignment *(183)*

removable media *(176)*

sector *(177)*

SuperDisk *(187)*

tape backup device *(176)*

Travan *(190)*

Zip drive *(186)*

■ Key Term Quiz

Use terms from the Key Terms list to complete the following sentences. Not all terms will be used.

1. Hidden, System, and Archive are all examples of _____.

2. _____ is the oldest tape media still used in PCs.

3. Iomega invented the _____ drive.

4. Floppy drives use a _____ to connect the floppy drive to the motherboard.

5. Given the choice between Differential and Incremental backups, a/an _____ does not reset the Archive bit.

6. A/An _____ backs up all of the files that have been changed on a given day.

7. The _____ is turned on whenever a file is created or changed.

8. A/An _____ or _____ drive can also read standard floppy disks.

9. _____ and _____ are two modern types of digital tape.

10. Read-Only is an example of a/an _____.

■ Multiple-Choice Quiz

1. What determines whether a floppy drive is designated drive A: or drive B:?
    a. Whether there is only one floppy drive or two.
    b. Whether it is plugged in on the end or in the middle of the ribbon cable.
    c. Whether it is a 3½-inch or a 5¼-inch floppy drive.
    d. Whether it is an internal or an external floppy drive.

2. The colored (usually red) stripe on a floppy drive ribbon cable should always be oriented toward which pin?
    a. Number 1 pin
    b. First available pin
    c. Primary pin
    d. System pin

3. Most desktop PCs have BIOS support for a maximum of how many floppy drives?

    a. 1
    b. 2
    c. 4
    d. 127

4. What is the capacity of the standard 3½-inch floppy drive used in almost all computers?
    a. 720 KB
    b. 1.2 MB
    c. 1.24 MB
    d. 1.44 MB

5. Which of the following is most likely to result if you install a floppy drive ribbon cable backwards?
    a. You will short out the floppy drive the first time you try to use it.
    b. The drive will seem to work, but it will destroy any floppies you try to read.

c. The drive's System Setup settings will be cleared each time you reboot.

d. The drive won't work as long as the cable is reversed, but it won't be damaged.

6. Which of the following is a classic symptom of a floppy ribbon cable that's been installed backwards?

   a. The system will not boot.

   b. The error message "Data error reading drive A:" appears.

   c. The floppy drive read light comes on and doesn't turn off.

   d. When you try to insert a floppy disk, the drive automatically ejects it.

7. Which of the following is an advantage that SuperDisk drives have over Zip drives?

   a. SuperDisk drives can read standard floppy disks.

   b. SuperDisk drives are faster.

   c. SuperDisk drives hold over twice as much data as Zip drives.

   d. SuperDisk drives can read Zip disks.

8. Which of the following is a standard size for a Zip disk?

   a. 1.44 MB

   b. 120 MB

   c. 240 MB

   d. 250 MB

9. What type of drive should never be cleaned, according to its manufacturer?

   a. LS-120

   b. Zip

   c. Floppy

   d. System

10. John installed a 3½-inch 1.44-MB floppy drive in his system. It works perfectly, even though he never went into the System Setup program to configure the A: drive. Which of the following is the most likely reason for this?

    a. The A: drive normally is set by default as a 3½-inch 1.44 MB floppy drive.

    b. Someone else went into the System Setup program and configured it for him.

c. Most systems automatically detect the floppy drive and configure the system accordingly.

d. The A: drive is set by default as a 3½-inch 720 KB floppy drive, so the drive works, but until John configures it in System Setup, it will read only the first 720 KB of data.

11. Which file attribute do backup programs use to determine whether a file has been changed?

    a. Copy

    b. System

    c. Backup

    d. Archive

12. What tape format is an improved version of QIC tape, with a capacity of around 10 GB?

    a. DLT

    b. DAT

    c. Travan

    d. L-120

13. Which type of backup is identical to a Normal backup except that the Archive bits are not changed?

    a. Daily Copy

    b. Differential

    c. Copy

    d. System

14. Assume that you perform a Full backup on Mondays and another type of backup daily. If you lose all of your data to a crash on Thursday, which of the following backup types would restore your data using the *fewest* tapes?

    a. Daily Copy

    b. Differential

    c. System

    d. Incremental

15. Assume that you perform a Full backup on Mondays and another type of backup daily. If you lose all of your data to a crash on Thursday, which of the following backup types would restore your data using the *most* tapes?

    a. Copy

    b. System

    c. Incremental

    d. Differential

■ Essay Quiz

1. Your four-system office uses lots of floppy disks to share data among the systems. Everyone can read and write to their own floppy drives, assuming that they first format the disks they use. John's system is an exception—his system can read floppies right out of the box. John's system can read Jane's and Dave's floppies, but not Debbie's. Jane can read John's, but not Dave's or Debbie's. Debbie cannot read anyone's floppies. Dave can read only John's floppies. What strategy would make it possible for everyone to read everyone else's floppy disks? Write a brief memo explaining your recommendation to your boss.

2. Your boss has just discovered Zip drives and wants you to install them in 16 systems in the graphics department to use for storing files at the end of each workday. Half of the systems create two or three massive graphics files, easily 150 MB each, during a day. Four of the systems usually create 40 to 50 graphics files in the 2 to 3 MB size range. The other four systems occasionally create files larger than 100 MB but normally create about half a dozen files between 10 and 50 MB each. Write a memo to your boss recommending the best sizes of Zip drives for the three different groups of systems.

3. You're a contractor for a government agency that wants to replace 130 old 386 systems with modern computers. All of the 386 systems use 5¼-inch floppy drives, and you estimate that the office has close to a thousand 5¼-inch floppy disks that are actively being used to store data. Although all of the files on these floppies are around only 300 K, in many cases the users need 10 to 20 disks just to save one group of related data files. Users need to continue to pass data among themselves using some type of removable media. Create a step-by-step action plan that describes how you will upgrade these systems while preserving their existing data and still give the users a way to share data.

4. You have decided to add a tape backup device to your server at your rapidly growing firm. Your average backup is roughly 20 GB. Write an argument for the type of tape backup you want to buy.

5. You have a tape drive installed on your server. Your average backup is about 20 GB. Which tape backup strategy would you use? You want to perform as few backups as possible in case you ever need to restore data.

Lab Projects

• Lab Project 7.1

Your small network server recently crashed, and your company lost almost a week re-creating lost data. The total amount of lost data was roughly 4 GB. The owner of the company asks you to install a tape backup system.

1 Using any PC, have one person act as the user and another as the computer support. Review the critical data on the system with the user. Where are the data files?

2 Start Windows backup and create a backup job that backs up those data files.

3 Assume that the user will have a QIC tape backup system with a tape capacity large enough to back up all data files. Present to the user a tape backup strategy. Discuss with the user what to do if the data reaches a point where more than one tape cartridge is needed.

• Lab Project 7.2

Check all of the computers in your classroom to determine whether every system can read every other system's floppy disks.

1 First go to each system with a new box of floppy disks and determine which systems can read the disks. Try copying files to and from a floppy on each system.

2 Format a floppy disk on one system and then go to every other system in the room to see if they all can read that floppy disk. Try copying a file and reading that file on each system you test.

3 Make a table outlining your results.

Hard Drives

"Back up my hard drive?
How do I put it in reverse?"

—INFAMOUS TECH JOKE

In this chapter, you will learn how to:

- **Describe how hard drives store data**
- **Physically install a hard drive in a PC**
- **Configure a newly installed hard drive**
- **Maintain and troubleshoot a hard drive**

I think by now you appreciate that every PC runs programs—lots of programs—and every PC needs a place to store all of those programs so they are available when you need them. This big storage area on a PC is the hard drive. Hard drives can hold a tremendous amount of information—current drives store over 200 GB of data!

You'll begin this chapter by taking a look inside a hard drive to see how it works and to learn some important terms, like EIDE and SCSI. After that, you'll learn how to install a hard drive in a typical system. Finally, you'll find out what it takes to keep your hard drive running at top efficiency and what you can do to fix some of the more common hard drive issues you're likely to encounter.

How Hard Drives Store Data

The hard drive is the great paradox of the PC. Incredibly complex devices, hard drives are also fairly simple to install and use. They store extremely sensitive data, yet they can withstand an amazing amount of punishment. No larger than a small book, a single hard drive can store many thousands of books. Let's begin by examining the insides of these incredible devices to get a sense of how they perform their amazing feats.

If you open a hard drive, you'll see what seems to be a fairly simple apparatus: a number of shiny disks with some read/write armatures at each side of each drive.

If you flip a hard drive over and look at its underside, you'll find that it's covered by a computer circuit board. This board contains most of the logic that controls the movement of the disks and read/write arms inside the drive. This board is called the *hard drive controller* circuit board.

⚠️ Opening a hard drive will destroy it. *Never* open a hard drive if you ever intend to use it again!

• Internal and external views of a typical hard drive

• Controller board on a typical hard drive

The disks, read/write arms, and controller circuitry work together to do one thing: store ones and zeros—lots and lots of ones and zeros. The data on the drive must be *organized* in some way that enables the PC to *retrieve* all those stored ones and zeros. That organization is based on an electronic division of the drive, which is called the drive's **geometry**.

Geometry

Have you ever taken a close look at a music CD? No matter how hard you look, you can't tell whether it actually contains any music until you drop it into your CD player. The moment you start playing the CD, however, you know *something* is on that CD. The music on the CD is stored as a series of microscopic pits arranged in distinct, concentric circles on the disc. You can say that the physical placement of those circles of tiny pits is the CD's *geometry*.

Hard drives also have a geometry. Unlike a CD, a hard drive uses microscopic magnetic spots on a **platter** instead of the tiny pits found on a CD, but in both cases the "marks" form concentric circles. Thus, a hard drive's geometry is similar to that of a CD, even though the medium is quite different.

Geometry determines where a hard drive stores data on its stacks of disks. Just as with the music CD, if you opened up a hard drive, you would not see the geometry. Unlike the CD, however, each model of hard drive has a *different* geometry. We describe the geometry of a particular hard drive with a set of numbers that refer to three unique values: the number of heads, the number of cylinders, and the number of sectors per track.

Heads

The heads of a hard drive are its **read/write heads**. Every platter requires two heads: one to read the top side and one to read the bottom side. If a hard drive has four platters, for example, it needs eight heads.

Because every platter needs two heads, you might assume that hard drives always have an even number of heads, but you'd be mistaken. Most hard drives have an extra head or two for their own use. These extra heads help guide the read/write heads into the correct position, as well as perform other jobs unique to that drive. Therefore, a hard drive can have either an even or an odd number of heads.

Cylinders

The second element of hard drive geometry is the cylinder. To visualize a cylinder, imagine removing both the top and bottom ends of a soup can, washing off the label, and cleaning out the inside. Now imagine sharpening the rim of the soup can so it easily cuts through the hardest metal. Visualize placing the soup can over the hard drive and pushing it down through the drive. The can will cut an identical circular hole through every stacked platter in the drive. Of course, real hard drive platters don't have holes in them—but they do have circles on them where the can would cut the platters: one on the top of the platter, and a matching one on the underside. Each of these circles is called a **track**, and tracks are where you store data on a hard drive.

Each platter has tens of thousands of concentric tracks on each side. Interestingly, the individual tracks themselves are not directly part of the drive geometry. Our interest lies in only the *groups* of tracks of the same diameter (think of the can cutting each platter in the same place). Each group of tracks of the same diameter going vertically completely through the drive is a called a **cylinder**.

A hard drive contains more than one cylinder! Get yourself about a thousand more cans, each a different diameter, and push them through the hard drive. A typical hard drive has thousands of cylinders.

Sectors per Track

Imagine cutting the hard drive like you would a round birthday cake, slicing each track into a number of tiny arcs. Each arc is called a sector, and each sector stores 512 bytes of data.

• Four platters = eight heads

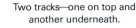
Two tracks—one on top and another underneath.

Every head has many hundreds of tracks on each side.

• Tracks on hard drive platters

• A cylinder is a group of tracks of the same diameter.

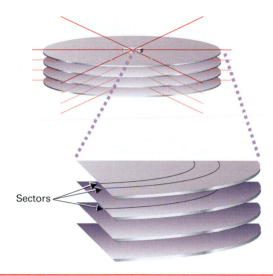

- A sector is a section of a track.

The sector is the universal atom of all hard drives: you can't divide data into anything smaller than a sector. Although sectors are important, the number of sectors is not a geometry value. The sectors geometry value is actually the **sectors per track**, often written sectors/track. The number of sectors in each track is equivalent to the number of "slices" in the hard drive.

Working with Geometry

Hard drive geometries are premade at the factory. The only thing you need to do is to make sure that the PC knows the geometry when you install a new hard drive into a computer. You'll learn how to do that in the section "Installing a Hard Drive" later in this chapter.

If a sector is the smallest storage area on your drive, what about a file that is smaller than 512 bytes? It still uses an entire sector. Nobody said computers were completely efficient! On the other hand, how do you store a file that is *larger* than 512 bytes? That's the job of the next two parts of the hard drive system you're going to learn about: partitions and file systems.

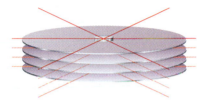

- Six sectors per track (sectors/track)

Partitions and File Systems

Can you imagine a world where every time you tried to save or retrieve data, you had to point the computer to the exact cylinder, head, and sector you wanted to use? Nobody else could either! Long before any hard drive ever made it into a PC, people realized that most of the details of the storage and retrieval process were going to have to be hidden from the users if hard drives weren't going to be impossibly difficult to use. One solution to this problem was the **partition**. A partition is a discrete electronic chunk of a hard drive used as an underlying structure for organizing data on the drive. Each partition has, in effect, its own personal card catalog, called a **File Allocation Table (FAT)**. The job of this "card catalog" is to keep track of the location of all files on a given partition.

Partitions

Windows PCs use two types of partitions. The type of partition a hard drive uses depends on the operating system. Every hard drive must have at least one partition. The most common type is the **primary partition**. The other type is the **extended partition**. In most cases, a hard drive is configured with one primary partition, which is assigned the drive letter C:, but there are plenty of exceptions.

Primary partitions differ from extended partitions in two very important ways. First, *only* primary partitions are bootable—your computer will automatically look for a primary partition at boot time. If you plan to boot to an operating system on a hard drive, you must install that operating system in a primary partition. Extended partitions are not required, and are not bootable. Second, primary partitions are assigned a drive letter, but extended partitions are not, at least not directly. Once created, extended partitions must be divided into one or more **logical drives**, and it is these logical drives that have drive letters associated with them. On my computer, I have a 100-GB hard drive. Instead of having one big primary partition, I created a 50-GB primary partition and a 50-GB extended partition. I then divided the extended partition into two logical drives of 25 GB each. The primary partition is drive C:, and the two logical drives are D: and E:.

Why didn't I just make my entire hard drive a single 100 GB partition? I certainly could have, but dividing the drive like this makes backup easier. The operating system lives on the C: drive, and I store all of my critical data on one of the logical drives, which I back up regularly. I keep copies of all of my drivers on the second logical drive, for emergency access in case the C: drive fails. On most computers, however, you will find the entire drive formatted as one big primary partition, labeled the C: drive. That's fine for many users, but now you know you have options if you need them!

So where is all this partition information stored? All partition information is stored in a specific place on the hard drive called the boot sector. The boot sector consists of five distinct pieces: the **Master Boot Record (MBR)** and the four partition information areas. The MBR is simply a tiny bit of code that helps the operating system load the correct partition.

When you boot your computer, the PC automatically starts reading the boot sector, looking for a primary partition from which to boot. The boot sector information directs the PC to begin reading the operating system from the primary partition, enabling your system to boot. In theory, you can have up to four primary partitions on a single hard drive, each loaded with a different operating system. In practice, about the only time you'll see more than one primary partition is when someone has loaded multiple operating systems on a single hard drive.

Suppose you were sufficiently geeky to have four different operating systems to choose from on your hard drive; how would the MBR know which partition to boot from? That's where the *active partition* comes into play. The MBR always boots to the active partition. Only one primary partition at a time can be set as the active partition. In most cases, this doesn't matter, though, because in most cases there is only one primary partition, which is automatically set as the active partition.

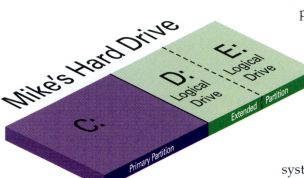

• Partitioning of Mike's hard drive

File Systems

To store files in a partition, your PC needs a filing system that defines the names of the files, as well as a system to track which sector stores which file. Additionally, you want to be able to create folders so that you can organize the contents of the drive. Over the years, Windows has used a number of different file systems, but they all have the same function. Essentially, they work like the card catalogs in libraries, which tell you where a particular book can be found on the shelves: that is, file systems tell the software where to find the data files stored on the hard drive. Let's look at the three generations of "card catalogs" used by Windows PCs.

A single primary partition or logical drive can use only one file system

FAT16 The oldest of the Windows file systems is called FAT16. FAT stands for File Allocation Table, and the number 16 refers to the fact that this file system allocates 16 bits to store the address of each sector. The File Allocation Table of a FAT16 file system is stored at the beginning of the partition, before any other data.

The first versions of FAT16 (going *way* back to the DOS days here) had a limitation: the largest partition that FAT16 could handle was only 32 MB. Now keep in mind that at this time, hard drives held only 5 to 10 MB, so the first version of FAT worked just fine. However, as hard drives grew, it became obvious that a new and improved version of FAT16 was needed.

When DOS 4.0 came out in the late 1980s, a new version of FAT16 came out as well. This new version grouped sectors together into a new "atom" called a *cluster*. The number of sectors in a cluster depended on the size of the partition. The larger the partition, the more sectors per cluster. This improved FAT16 could support partitions of up to 2 GB.

Even though FAT16 is now considered obsolete, it is still supported by every version of Windows, emphasizing yet again how important backward compatibility is to computer makers!

FAT16 was the only choice for later versions of DOS, Windows 3.1 (the version of Windows before Windows 95), and the first versions of Windows 95. However, the constant increases in hard drive size motivated Microsoft to come up with a new file system.

FAT32 As hard drives began to approach and pass the 2 GB limit of FAT16, Microsoft recognized the need for a new file system that could handle larger partitions. Microsoft introduced a new type of file system called FAT32. As its name implies, FAT32 uses 32 bits to address each cluster. This didn't just double the maximum partition size, however, because the math involved is exponential: instead of 2^{16} x 512 bytes per sector, a partition could hold 2^{32} x 512 bytes per sector, raising the capacity from 32 *mega*bytes to a whopping 2 *tera*bytes (in theory—however, Windows 2000 supports FAT32 partitions of up to only 32 *giga*bytes). FAT32 is the file system of choice for all versions of Windows 9*x* with the exception of the very first version of Windows 95. If you have a system running a later version of Windows 95, any version of Windows 98, or Windows Me, it has a FAT32 file system.

NTFS Windows NT, 2000, and XP all use the vastly more powerful, robust, and flexible **NT File System (NTFS)**. What makes NTFS so great? Well, let's just say that NTFS is virtually indestructible, provides ultrahigh security for files, on-the-fly file and folder compression and encryption, and a wealth of other features. NTFS uses a super-FAT called the **Master File Table (MFT)** that builds substantially on the FAT concept. Unlike FAT16 and FAT32, NTFS enables users to adjust the cluster sizes, although people rarely do so. NTFS supports partitions of up to 2 terabytes.

So Many File Systems! With so many file formats, how do you know which one to use? In almost all cases, you want to use the best file format your operating system supports. If you have a Windows 9*x* system that supports FAT32, use it. If you have Windows 2000 or XP, use NTFS. Sometimes you may encounter systems that use NTFS as the primary file system, but have an extra FAT32 partition for backward compatibility or dual-boot purposes.

Step-by-Step 8.1

Identifying Your File System

Every version of Windows has some method to enable you to identify the file system used by your hard drives. In this exercise, you will learn how to identify your file system using both Windows 98 and Windows XP. The Windows 98 procedure works for any Windows 9*x* system, and the XP procedure also works for Windows 2000 systems. Windows 9*x* systems provide two ways to determine the type of file system being used: you can run a program called

FDISK, or you can check the properties of the drive in My Computer. Windows 2000 and XP also let you check the properties of the drive in My Computer, and you can use the Disk Administrator tool.

To complete this exercise, you will need the following:

- A computer system running Windows 98
- A computer system running Windows 2000 or XP

Step 1

Boot the computer running Windows 98. Choose Start | Run and type **command** to open a command prompt window. Type **FDISK** and press ENTER to run the FDISK program. Select Yes if prompted to choose large disk support. Select option 4, Display Partition Information. Make a note of the partition information that you see.

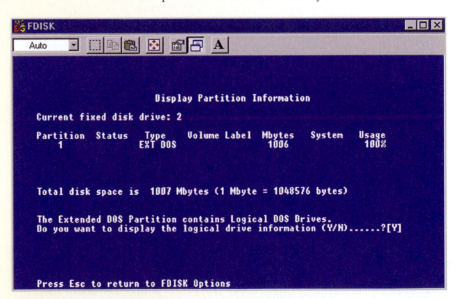

Step 2

Press the ESC key to return to the main FDISK screen. If you have more than one hard drive, select menu option 5 and then select the other hard drive. Again select option 4 to display the partition information and then make a note of it. Close FDISK and then close the command prompt window.

Step 3

Now try the second method. Open My Computer. Select the primary hard drive, alternate-click (right-click) the icon and select Properties. In the Drive Properties dialog box, examine the General tab, which should be displayed by default. Look for the FAT16 or FAT32 file system designation. Make a note of it. Close the dialog box and My Computer.

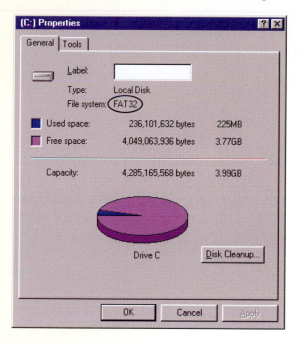

Step 4

Now boot the computer running Windows 2000 or XP. Open My Computer. Select the primary hard drive, alternate-click the icon and select Properties. In the Drive Properties dialog box, examine the General tab, which should be displayed by default. Make a note of the file system designation, which in this case should be NTFS. Close the dialog box and My Computer.

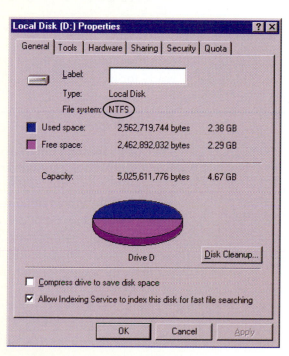

Step 5

Open the Control Panel, double-click to open Administrative Tools, and then open the Computer Management applet. Click Disk Management to display information on all fixed drives, including the file system type of each partition. Note whether your hard drive has one or multiple partitions, and whether you have any FAT32 partitions (probably you don't). Close the applet and the Control Panel.

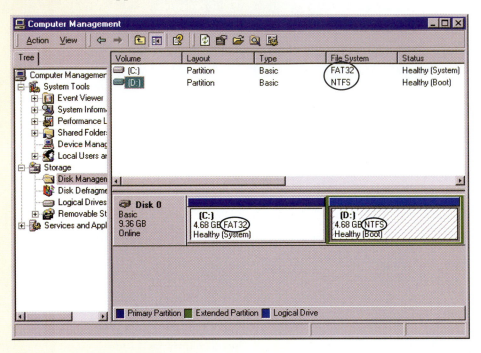

■ Installing a Hard Drive

Now that you know about the physical hard drive, partitions, and file systems, you are ready to install a hard drive. This section presents the issues to consider and steps to follow to install a new hard drive in your system unit, ready for work.

<table>
<tr><td>⚠</td><td>Everything you are about to learn can and will *wipe out all data* on a hard drive. Don't perform any of the steps in this section on a drive that contains data that you want to keep!</td></tr>
</table>

EIDE Versus SCSI

Two totally incompatible drive technologies are used in PCs. In this chapter, you will work with the far more common technology, **Enhanced Integrated Drive Electronics (EIDE)**. EIDE drives are used in over 95 percent of all computers and are almost certainly the type of drive you'll want to know how to install. The other type of drive technology, called small computer systems interface (SCSI), gets its own chapter later in the book. It's easy to tell a SCSI drive from an EIDE drive; drive makers learned a long time ago to advertise the drive technology on the drive itself, so all you need to do is read the back of the case.

You can also look at a drive's connections. EIDE drives use a unique 40-pin connector, whereas SCSI drives use either a 50-pin connector or, more often these days, a high-density (a nice way to say that it has tiny pins), 68-pin connector.

Hard Drive Terminology

No one can outdo the hard drive industry in creating confusing acronyms. Here are some of the terms you'll run into:

- **ATA**   Advanced Technology Attachment, or ATA, is the real family of standards behind IDE or EIDE. The ATA umbrella includes a number of standards that define everything from the physical connections to the speed of the drives. These standards span ATA-1 through ATA-7.

- **ATAPI**   The ATA Programmable Interface, or ATAPI, standard was introduced as part of the ATA-2 standard. The ATA-2 standard was remarkable in that it allowed storage devices other than hard drives (CD-ROMs, Zip drives, tape drives) to use the ATA connections.

- **EIDE**   EIDE was a marketing term invented by Western Digital about 12 years ago to reflect their adoption of the ATA-2 standard. It added slightly to the standard by allowing a maximum of four ATA devices. The term EIDE is used universally to describe all drives under the ATA-2 through ATA-5 standards.

- **IDE**   More correctly called ATA-1, IDE was the predecessor of EIDE. It uses the same cables but much slower drives. Actual IDE drives are obsolete, and you are unlikely to encounter one, but you will still hear the term used as shorthand for EIDE technology. IDE systems supported a maximum of two hard drives.

- **PIO**   Programmable Input/Output, or PIO, was the original method for transferring data between the hard drive and RAM in early versions of ATA. It was replaced by UDMA and is now obsolete.

- **UDMA**   Ultra Direct Memory Access, or UDMA, is the current method for transferring data between the hard drive and RAM. The term UDMA is rarely used, however; instead, you will see references to **ATA speed ratings**.

What you'll find interesting in the real world is how badly these terms are used. I often judge the knowledge of a computer person by the use of these terms. For instance, a tech who calls an EIDE drive an "ATA drive" shows that he or she is familiar with the terminology. Although ATA is more correct, EIDE is used so overwhelmingly that even I will use EIDE in this chapter. I encourage you to use these terms correctly in the real world—but also realize that these terms are largely interchangeable.

EIDE drives have different UDMA speed ratings. ATA speed ratings measure how fast the hard drive is capable of transferring data to the rest of the system, expressed in MBps. This is a maximum potential speed, which is not achieved under most conditions. The standard speeds are 33, 66, 100, and 133 MBps. The common terms for these speeds are ATA33, ATA66, ATA100, and ATA133.

These speed ratings are important for two reasons besides just performance. First, ATA33 uses an older 40-wire cable, whereas all the newer speed ratings use an 80-wire cable. Second, your motherboard is designed to use a certain speed of hard drive. If you match a slower hard drive controller with a faster hard drive or vice versa, the resulting data transfer speed will be that of the slower device. For best performance, match the speed rating of your hard drive to the speed rating that your motherboard is designed to support, and use the proper cable for that speed.

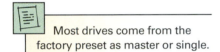

Most drives come from the factory preset as master or single.

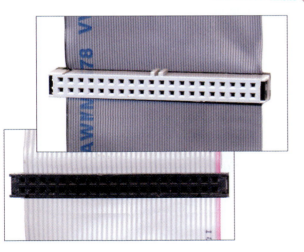

• **Figure 8.1**   EIDE controllers on a motherboard

• **Figure 8.2**   Comparison of 40-wire (bottom) and 80-wire (top) EIDE ribbon cables

A final terminology issue you should be aware of (before I dive into a discussion of EIDE cables) concerns the term *controller*. The actual controller for an EIDE drive is located on the drive itself; however, it is common to refer to the 40-pin motherboard connection at the other end of the drive cable (Figure 8.1) as a controller, too. Strictly speaking, this usage of the term is incorrect, but you need to recognize it when you hear it because, like many such errors, it has become a common reference.

EIDE Cables

Every EIDE controller can support two EIDE drives. EIDE cables have three connections: one for each drive and one for the controller. As mentioned earlier, there are two types of EIDE cables: the older 40-wire version and the newer 80-wire version (Figure 8.2).

Even though one cable has 80 wires and the other has 40 wires, they both have only 40 *pins*—so what happens to the extra 40 wires in the 80-wire cable? Because they're used only to reduce interference, these wires don't have pin connections. Instead, they simply terminate inside the connectors.

Master/Slave

When two devices share a single ribbon cable and both have their own onboard controllers, one device needs to be configured to handle the control work for both devices. The device that is doing the controlling is called the **master**. The other device's controller needs to be configured so it knows that the first controller is in charge. The device that's not in charge is called the **slave**. When you install a hard drive, you must configure these settings. Every EIDE drive has several small jumpers that are designed to let you configure it as a master or a slave.

So how do you know where to place the jumpers to make a drive a master or a slave? Well, all good drives will have this information printed clearly on the drive itself (Figure 8.3). Most EIDE drives have two different master settings. One master setting is for a master with a slave present, and the other setting is for a drive without a slave present. Again, the documentation on the drive itself will show you these settings.

On rare occasions, you may stumble across a drive that does not have these settings printed on it. In these cases, visit the support section of the manufacturer's website. As a rule, hard drive makers provide excellent documentation for their drives.

Remember that you must configure the master/slave setting properly if you want drives on the same ribbon cable to operate. If you have one drive, it must be set to master or single, depending on the manufacturer's requirement. If you have a second drive on the same ribbon cable, it must be set as a slave, and the first drive must be set as the master with a slave present if such a setting exists.

Introduction to PC Hardware and Troubleshooting

• Figure 8.3   Setting a jumper using master/slave information on a hard drive

ATA Speed Ratings

Where you place the master and slave drives on the cable doesn't matter on the older ATA33 drives that use the 40-wire cables. The master can be on the end of the cable or in the middle. However, on drives using more modern ATA speeds (ATA66 and faster), the location of the master and slave on the 80-wire cables is critical. The 80-wire cables have three color-coded connectors (Figure 8.4). The colored connector (usually blue but sometimes red) must attach to the controller on the motherboard. The black connector, on the end, must attach to the master (or single) drive. If you have a slave drive, it must attach to the gray connector, in the middle.

Nearly all motherboards come with two EIDE controllers. One controller is the primary controller, and the other controller is the secondary controller. On most systems, these are clearly marked as IDE0 (primary) and IDE1 (secondary).

On modern systems that use ATA66 or better, usually only the primary controller uses a high-speed connection, and the secondary connection uses the older ATA33 standard. Motherboards that follow this scheme often have one colored controller and one white controller (Figure 8.5). When you see this, you can start with the assumption that the colored controller is the primary one.

The first hard drive in a system should always be the master (or single) on the primary controller. A second hard drive is normally installed as the primary slave, but there's nothing intrinsically wrong with making the second drive a secondary master.

One issue that comes up often concerns the interchangeability of ATA33 and the faster standards. For example,

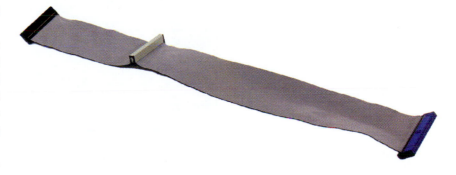

 • Figure 8.4   Colored connectors on an 80-wire cable

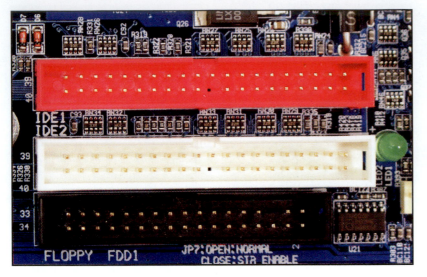

• **Figure 8.5**   Different-colored controllers on a motherboard

can you install an ATA100 hard drive on an old-style ATA33 controller using the older 40-wire cable? You certainly can! You just won't get the speed enhancement of the faster ATA100 standard, but the drive will work fine. So how about installing an ATA100 drive on an ATA66 controller with an 80-wire cable? That will also work, but the drive will run only at ATA66 speeds. Pretty much everything is interchangeable but will run at the speed of the slowest device.

BIOS Limitations

Once a drive is physically installed, you must configure its geometry so that the system can work with the drive. Back in the bad old days, that meant that you had to fire up the System Setup utility and manually punch in the geometry—and if you got one of the values wrong, the drive would not function. Fortunately, those days are long gone. Now every System Setup utility includes a special setting called Autodetect (or just Auto) that tells the system to query the drive at bootup to get all of the necessary geometry information (Figure 8.6).

Autodetect is a great tool when installing a new hard drive. After you've installed the drive, you can run Autodetect to see whether the system recognizes the drive. If Autodetect doesn't see the drive (Figure 8.7), you know you've made a mistake with the cabling, jumpers, or power.

People new to installing hard drives are sometimes confused because most System Setup utilities still provide settings, usually labeled User or Manual, that allow manual configuration of the geometry settings. These settings are there for a few rare situations and can be ignored.

• **Figure 8.6**   Autodetection at system setup

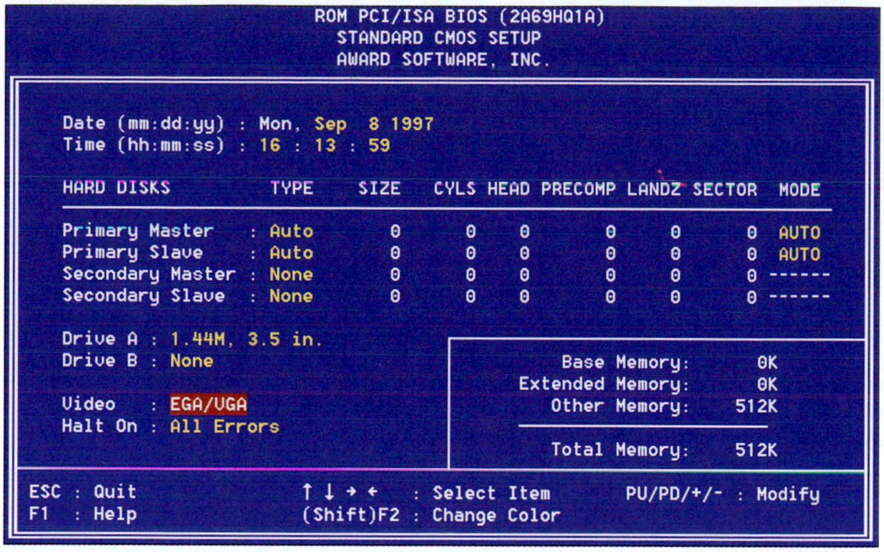

```
                    ROM PCI/ISA BIOS (2A69HQ1A)
                        STANDARD CMOS SETUP
                        AWARD SOFTWARE, INC.

    Date (mm:dd:yy) : Mon, Sep  8 1997
    Time (hh:mm:ss) : 16 : 13 : 59

    HARD DISKS          TYPE   SIZE   CYLS HEAD PRECOMP LANDZ SECTOR  MODE

    Primary Master   : Auto     0      0    0     0      0      0    AUTO
    Primary Slave    : Auto     0      0    0     0      0      0    AUTO
    Secondary Master : None     0      0    0     0      0      0    ------
    Secondary Slave  : None     0      0    0     0      0      0    ------

    Drive A : 1.44M, 3.5 in.
    Drive B : None               ┌─────────────────────────────────┐
                                 │    Base Memory:        0K        │
    Video   : EGA/VGA            │ Extended Memory:        0K        │
    Halt On : All Errors         │    Other Memory:      512K        │
                                 │    ─────────────────────────     │
                                 │    Total Memory:      512K        │
                                 └─────────────────────────────────┘

    ESC : Quit            ↑ ↓ → ←   : Select Item    PU/PD/+/- : Modify
    F1  : Help          (Shift)F2 : Change Color
```

● **Figure 8.7**   Screen when Autodetect does not find a drive

Just as operating systems over the years have evolved to support larger hard drive sizes, so has the BIOS. The earliest BIOS programs could not support drives larger than 504 MB. If you installed a new 50 GB hard drive and ran Autodetect, it would report a 504 MB drive. Back in 1990, a new standard called LBA increased the maximum supported drive size to 8.3 GB. Most drives today use a relatively new standard called INT13 Extensions that enables your BIOS to recognize drives of up to 137 GB. Unless you have a system that predates 1997, odds are good you have a BIOS with INT13 Extensions.

So what about hard drives bigger than 137 GB? There's a new standard called ATA-6 that introduces a new limit: a whopping 144 petabytes (144,000,000 GB). This new standard—better known, as peddled by Maxtor Corporation, as Big Drives—should keep us from worrying about maximum drive size for a while.

So what do you do if you install a drive in a system and Autodetect can't see the entire contents of the drive? The best option is to contact your motherboard maker and see if it has a BIOS update that will upgrade your BIOS so your system can recognize the drive. These days, this can be done pretty easily from most manufacturers' websites.

If your motherboard manufacturer doesn't have a BIOS upgrade, you can still use the drive, although the solution is not pretty. You can install a drive overlay program that, in essence, adds a little extra BIOS to your hard drive and enables your system to recognize the drive. Drive overlay programs usually come on floppy disks with new hard drives. Because, essentially, you're storing a BIOS on your hard drive, drive overlays are inherently risky. When you use an overlay program, file corruption may result in the loss of all data on the drive. However, if a BIOS upgrade isn't available, an overlay is your only option.

Every drive manufacturer makes its own drive overlays, and each has its own installation method. Most require a bootable floppy disk (good thing you

Many people want to know what capacity of drive they should buy. There's no formula to determine this. In most cases, you should simply purchase the largest-capacity drive you can afford. If you are going to be working with graphics and video, a large capacity is particularly important. I personally would never consider buying a drive smaller than 30 GB, but that's not saying much—it's hard to find a drive smaller than 20 GB on a new system nowadays.

• **Figure 8.8** Properly oriented ribbon cable plugged into an IDE controller

know how to make one of those!). Read the instructions carefully before you use a drive overlay!

Physically Installing a Hard Drive

Okay—armed with all of this knowledge, it's time for you to install your EIDE hard drive. The first step is to determine what speed of hard drive your motherboard can handle. A quick check of the motherboard documentation should give you that information.

Next, make sure that you get a drive with at least that speed—remember that faster drives are always backwardly compatible. It's not uncommon to see an old PC using a fast new hard drive, not because the system can use the speed but because that's all that's available.

The next step is to set the jumpers to single or master. Find those jumpers and set them correctly! Then plug the ribbon cable into the drive and into the controller on the motherboard. Remember that, as with all ribbon cables, you must orient the colored edge of the ribbon cable toward the number one pin (Figure 8.8).

Rounded hard drive cables can save you space inside the computer case, but they can be tricky to orient correctly. Many rounded cables have no colored stripe or other device to tell you where the number one pin is located. Worse, many rounded cables lack an orientation notch. In many cases, you simply have to guess which direction to orient the cable. Don't worry about guessing, though, because if you plug in the cable backward, you won't damage anything—you just won't see the drive when you use Autodetect. If you think you've installed the cable backward, shut down the system and reorient the cable; then restart the system and see if Autodetect works. After you install the ribbon cable, insert a power connector in the drive (Figure 8.9).

A good approach is to avoid permanently mounting a new hard drive until after the drive passes autodetection. It's too easy to make little mistakes that require you to remove and reinsert the drive. Instead, just slide the drive into a mount, or even leave the drive dangling until Autodetect sees the drive.

After the drive is physically installed, it's time to fire up the system and head into the System Setup program to see whether it recognizes the drive. You can sometimes skip this step because most BIOS programs by default set the primary master drive to Auto; if you watch the boot process carefully, you may see the system recognize the hard drive at bootup.

Many BIOS programs report the hard drive by its model number—good thing you know the model number of your hard drive!—but this is not a perfect test because many others don't report this information. Additionally, if a BIOS has a manual User setting, it will repeatedly report the manual settings and ignore the newly installed drive. Unless your BIOS reports the new drive by model number, the safe course of action is to enter the System Setup utility and run the Autodetect feature.

• **Figure 8.9** Installing power for a drive

Adding a Second Drive

Adding a second hard drive to an existing system is one of the most common system upgrades. This exercise uses a hardware configuration found on most PCs.

To complete this exercise, you will need the following:

- A computer system (with any operating system)

- A single hard drive installed in the system and configured with one primary partition (C:)

- A second hard drive compatible with the system

- A 40-wire or 80-wire (depending on the hard drive) ribbon cable to connect the second hard drive when you install it

- A Phillips screwdriver sized for the computer screws

- Motherboard documentation for the system, if available

Step 1

First, power down and unplug the system if you haven't already done so. Take antistatic precautions and set up a neat work area. Open the case, carefully setting aside any screws in a small container. Now inspect the system to see what hard drive *speed* the motherboard can handle. If you see an 80-wire cable on your system, you know that the primary controller will accept at least ATA66, but play it safe anyway and check the motherboard documentation.

Step 2

Determine the maximum hard drive *size* the system can handle. You can make a pretty good guess by noting the size of your existing drive. If the drive in the system is 10 GB, you can feel pretty confident that the system is running INT13 Extensions, in which case it can handle a drive of up to 137 GB.

Step 3

Once you've selected a hard drive to install, you must select the controller on which you will install it. The best place to install a second hard drive is on the primary controller, as a slave. Set the jumpers on both drives. Usually, to change the jumpers on the master drive, you will need to remove the drive from its mount so you can see the jumpers and read the jumper documentation. Remember that many hard drives have separate settings for single master and master with slave. As always, put the screws in a container so they won't fall in the case or roll under the furniture.

Step 4

Reinstall the cable, making sure to orient it correctly to the number one pin and to insert the master and slave at the correct locations on the cable. You'll probably need to install the slave drive at this point because there won't be enough cable to let it dangle as you test. Plug in the power cables to both drives, making sure to get them all the way in.

Step 5

Give your installation efforts a final check and then boot the PC. Run Autodetect to verify that *both* drives are recognized by the system. If there's a problem, recheck each step, remove all the connectors and then plug them all back in, and try again. After the system recognizes the drives, *gently* attach them to the drive bays with the screws you carefully set aside for this purpose; then close the case.

■ Configuring a Hard Drive

Once a drive has been physically installed and recognized by the BIOS, you need to partition the drive and to add a file system. The process of creating partitions is called *partitioning,* and the process of adding a file system is called *formatting*. In this section, you will learn the tools and the techniques needed to partition and format hard drives under both Windows 98 and Windows XP. There's a strong motivation for showing you two operating systems here. Windows 95, 98, and Me use one method to partition and format, and Windows NT, 2000, and XP use a completely different method. If you want to work with Windows computers, you need to know both methods.

Partitioning

One of the main differences between Windows 9*x* and Windows NT/2000/XP is their treatment of hard drive partitioning. In the Windows 9*x* world, all partitioning is handled by the command prompt program FDISK. Windows NT/2000/XP do not use FDISK; instead, they rely on a graphical tool called Disk Administrator.

Windows 98 Installation

To install Windows 98 onto a blank hard drive, you need a way to access the installation program, which means that you need an installation program that you can boot from somewhere other than the hard drive. Windows 98 takes care of this by making the Windows 98 installation CD bootable. By going into the System Setup utility and setting the system to boot from the CD-ROM before the hard drive, you can begin the installation of Windows 98 directly from the CD itself.

This book does not cover the Windows 98 installation process in detail, but you should become familiar with a few of the screens that tell you that the installation program is handling the partitioning and formatting job for you.

At some point during the installation process, Windows 98 will notice that you have a blank hard drive and will then begin the partitioning process. By default, it will make the entire hard drive a single primary partition using the FAT32 file system. Windows indicates this by setting the Large Drive Support parameter to Yes. If you change this selection to No, the system will create a FAT16 file system. This brings up an interesting point: you determine the file

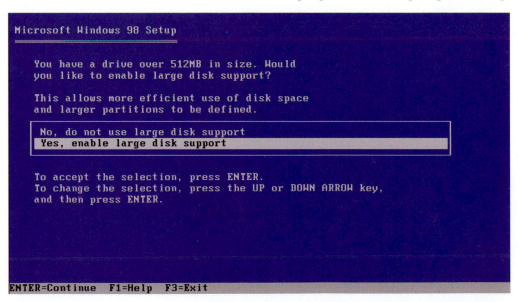

• Selecting Large Disk Support during Windows installation

system at the *partitioning* stage, not the formatting stage. This is true with all partitioning methods.

After you select FAT32 by choosing Large Disk Support, the installation program informs you that it is about to restart your computer. Be happy—you just created a primary partition and set it as active! Whenever any changes are made to partitions in Windows 9*x*, you must restart the system, but you don't have to worry about it because the Windows installer handles this task for you. You'll learn how the Windows 98 installation process handles formatting in the next section.

Windows 98 and FDISK For manual partitioning, FDISK is the tool to use. From the early DOS days through Windows Me, the FDISK program was the only means of partitioning a hard drive. All versions of Windows 9*x* continue to use FDISK. FDISK is text-based, non-intuitive, and easy to misunderstand, but fortunately the most recent versions, the ones that came with Windows 98 and Me, have an automated mode that makes them easier to use.

FDISK is traditionally run from the Windows 98 startup disk. The assumption behind this is that if you are running FDISK, you must not yet have any drive partitioned, so you will need to run FDISK from a floppy disk. You can also run FDISK from Windows using a command prompt, however, and this is the usual way you install a second hard drive. This example will assume that you're running FDISK from a bootable floppy. To start FDISK, simply type **FDISK** at the A:\> prompt and press ENTER.

If FDISK detects a hard drive of greater than 504 MB, it will prompt you to see if you want large disk support (Figure 8.10). As explained earlier, the program is really asking whether you want to use FAT16 or FAT32. You should respond to this by accepting the default, Y, to use FAT32.

The main FDISK screen provides four menu options: Create DOS Partition or Logical DOS Drive, Set Active Partition, Delete Partition or Logical DOS Drive, and Display Partition Information (Figure 8.11).

In most cases, you have a new, blank drive for which you want to create one large partition. You can see the blank drive in FDISK by selecting option 4,

```
Your computer has a disk larger than 512 MB. This version of Windows
includes improved support for large disks, resulting in more efficient
use of disk space on large drives, and allowing disks over 2 GB to be
formatted as a single drive.

IMPORTANT: If you enable large disk support and create any new drives on this
disk, you will not be able to access the new drive(s) using other operating
systems, including some versions of Windows 95 and Windows NT, as well as
earlier versions of Windows and MS-DOS. In addition, disk utilities that
were not designed explicitly for the FAT32 file system will not be able
to work with this disk. If you need to access this disk with other operating
systems or older disk utilities, do not enable large drive support.

Do you wish to enable large disk support (Y/N)...........? [Y]
```

● **Figure 8.10**   Prompt for large disk support

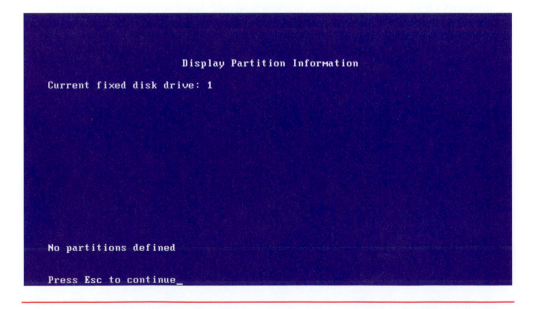

```
                    Microsoft Windows 98
                  Fixed Disk Setup Program
              (C)Copyright Microsoft Corp. 1983 - 1998

                        FDISK Options

  Current fixed disk drive: 1

  Choose one of the following:

  1. Create DOS partition or Logical DOS Drive
  2. Set active partition
  3. Delete partition or Logical DOS Drive
  4. Display partition information


  Enter choice: [1]




  Press Esc to exit FDISK
```

● **Figure 8.11**   Main FDISK screen

Display Partition Information. To do this, simply press the 4 key and then ENTER. In this example, FDISK reports, "No partitions defined." As shown in Figure 8.12, this is a blank hard drive.

If you want to make just one primary partition, you can use FDISK's automated tool for this purpose. Press ESC to return to the main FDISK screen and then press the 1 key and ENTER to display the Create DOS Partition or Logical DOS Drive screen (Figure 8.13).

At this screen, press 1 to create the primary partition. When you do so, the system asks whether you want to use the maximum available size for a primary DOS partition and make the partition active. If you press ENTER (for Y), FDISK will create a single primary partition on the hard drive (Figure 8.14), and the system will prompt you to restart.

```
                      Display Partition Information

  Current fixed disk drive: 1








  No partitions defined


  Press Esc to continue_
```

● **Figure 8.12**   FDISK showing a blank drive

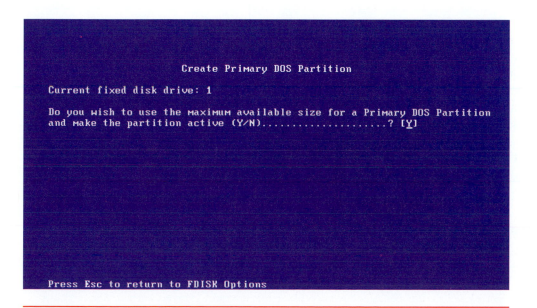

```
                 Create DOS Partition or Logical DOS Drive

Current fixed disk drive: 1

Choose one of the following:

1.  Create Primary DOS Partition
2.  Create Extended DOS Partition
3.  Create Logical DOS Drive(s) in the Extended DOS Partition




Enter choice: [1]




Press Esc to return to FDISK Options
```

● Figure 8.13   Create DOS Partition or Logical DOS Drive screen

After the drive is partitioned with FDISK and the computer has rebooted to the Windows 98 startup disk, the new drive letter C: appears. Until the drive is actually formatted, however, you won't be able to access the drive. You'll learn about the formatting process in the next section.

Windows XP Installation

Windows XP also uses a bootable CD-ROM and includes a hard drive setup procedure early in the installation process. The inclusion of NTFS makes the process a bit more complex than the FAT32 process of Windows 98, so it warrants a separate discussion.

> The process for Windows XP discussed here also applies to Windows NT and 2000 installations.

```
                 Create Primary DOS Partition

Current fixed disk drive: 1

Do you wish to use the maximum available size for a Primary DOS Partition
and make the partition active (Y/N).....................? [Y]











Press Esc to return to FDISK Options
```

● Figure 8.14   Automated partition creation tool in action

Try This!

Using FDISK

You can run FDISK on any Windows 9x system to inspect the current partitions on any drives on the PC. Try running FDISK on a Windows 9x system to determine the number and size of the partitions on the hard drive. Changing anything using FDISK will destroy data, so you should only tour the existing partitions *without* making any changes. If possible, use a system with *two* installed hard drives.

1. Select Start | Run, type **COMMAND** in the text area, and click **OK** to open a command prompt window. Type the command **FDISK /STATUS** and press ENTER. A screen appears showing the status information.

2. Now run FDISK without the /STATUS switch, to display the standard FDISK menu screen. If the system has two hard drives, you will see a fifth menu option, which enables you to select the drive to partition.

```
                Microsoft Windows 98
               Fixed Disk Setup Program
        (C)Copyright Microsoft Corp. 1983 - 1998

                    FDISK Options

Current fixed disk drive: 1

Choose one of the following:

1. Create DOS partition or Logical DOS Drive
2. Set active partition
3. Delete partition or Logical DOS Drive
4. Display partition information
5. Change current fixed disk drive

Enter choice: [1]




Press Esc to exit FDISK
```

• FDISK with five options

3. Select option 4 (Display Partition Information) to see how the first drive is partitioned. Make a note of what you find. If the system has two drives, select option 5 (Change Current Fixed Disk Drive) and choose the second drive; then use option 4 again to see how the second drive is partitioned. Again note what you find. Exit FDISK.

Let's briefly review the process that the Windows XP installation program uses to partition a blank hard drive. When you boot to the installation CD, Windows XP will notice that there are no partitioned hard drives on the system and prompt you to proceed. As instructed, press the letter C. The installation program will search the hard drives and report back. Windows XP then combines completion of the partition with some formatting, prompting you to choose NTFS or FAT.

Windows XP and Disk Management
Windows NT, Windows 2000, and Windows XP no longer use FDISK for partitioning, so you must either partition the drive during the initial installation or use the Disk Management utility once you have installed Windows. Of course, you shouldn't change the partition where Windows itself is installed, but Disk Management does a fine job when you need to add a second drive. You will learn to use Disk Management to partition a second drive in Step-by-Step 8.3.

Formatting

All versions of Windows offer multiple ways to format a drive and thus make the drive capable of holding data. Most users choose to use one of the graphical methods of formatting in Windows. In Windows 9x, after you've partitioned a new drive using FDISK, the drive will show up in My Computer, but if you try to access it by clicking it, you'll get an error—preparing a drive takes two steps, remember: partitioning and *formatting*.

You can format a hard drive by typing **FORMAT X:** at a command prompt, where X is the letter of the drive you want to format. If you are already running Windows 98, simply alternate-click on the drive letter in My

• **Figure 8.15** Windows 98 Format dialog box

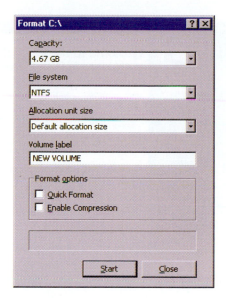

• **Figure 8.16** Windows 2000 Format dialog box

Computer and select Format to get the standard Windows 98 Format dialog box (Figure 8.15). The procedure here works the same way in Windows 2000 and XP, although the Format dialog box looks a bit different (Figure 8.16).

The Disk Management tool that comes with Windows 2000 and XP also performs disk formatting, but its capabilities reach way beyond formatting and partitioning.

Disk Management

The Disk Management tool that comes with Windows NT/2000/XP is the one-stop, do-it-all utility for working with hard drives using these operating systems. If there's something you want to do to a hard drive, Disk Management is the tool to use to get it done.

Windows 2000 and XP enable you to do some amazing things with your drives. For instance, you can change the drive letters assigned to various devices, something Windows 9x doesn't allow. Even more amazing, Windows 2000 and XP enable you to implement a very special type of drive organization called **Redundant Array of Independent Disks (RAID)**. To allow this, Windows assigns a *drive signature* to each drive when it is installed. Windows then uses this drive signature—invisible to you—to keep track of each of the drives installed in the system.

The first time you install a drive in a particular Windows 2000 or XP system and run Disk Management, Windows opens the Write Signature and Upgrade Disk wizard (Figure 8.17). The wizard asks if you want to put a signature on the drive—no question about it, you want to! It then asks if you want to upgrade the drive to a dynamic disk. In certain cases, you will want to choose Yes here also. For Windows to implement RAID, you must configure the drives as dynamic disks.

The Disk Administrator tool that comes with Windows NT lacks some of the features that are a part of the Windows 2000 and XP versions of the tool.

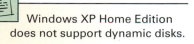

Windows XP Home Edition does not support dynamic disks.

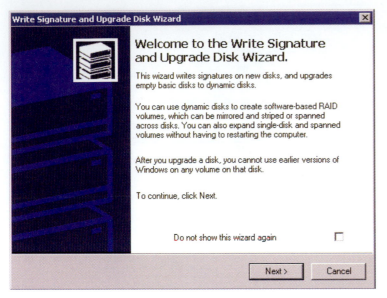

Welcome to the Write Signature and Upgrade Disk Wizard.

This wizard writes signatures on new disks, and upgrades empty basic disks to dynamic disks.

You can use dynamic disks to create software-based RAID volumes, which can be mirrored and striped or spanned across disks. You can also expand single-disk and spanned volumes without having to restarting the computer.

After you upgrade a disk, you cannot use earlier versions of Windows on any volume on that disk.

To continue, click Next.

Do not show this wizard again ☐

Next >   Cancel

● **Figure 8.17**   Write Signature and Upgrade wizard

⚠️ Once a drive has been upgraded to a dynamic disk, there is *no way* to return it to a basic disk without losing all the data on the drive. Make sure you want to upgrade before you act—there's no turning back!

Inside Information

Dynamic Disk Compatibility

Windows 2000 and Windows XP are the only operating systems that can read a dynamic disk, so you should be very sure that these are the only operating systems you'll be using before you upgrade from a basic disk to a dynamic disk. Never upgrade to dynamic disks on systems configured to boot more than one operating system, for instance. Also note that if you need to remove a drive and put it into a system with an older operating system, if the drive is a dynamic drive, you won't be able to access the data.

Dynamic Disks

Dynamic disks are a storage type unique to Windows 2000 and XP. You can do some cool things with dynamic disks, such as turn two separate hard drives into a single partition. Dynamic disk drives allow you to enlarge their partitions without first deleting the partition or losing data—something previously impossible without specialized third-party tools.

Regular drives are known as basic disks, to distinguish them from dynamic disks. Once you convert a drive from a basic to a dynamic disk, there are no longer any such things as primary and extended partitions; dynamic disks are divided into *volumes* instead of partitions.

RAID

RAID arrays are multiple hard drives that work together to act as one drive with a single drive letter. There are seven types of RAID, numbered RAID 0 through RAID 6. Of those seven types, only three, RAID 0, RAID 1, and RAID 5, are commonly used. These RAID types correlate with various types of dynamic disks.

Dynamic disks support different types of volumes:

- A **simple** volume uses space on a single disk; basically, it acts just like a primary partition.

- A **spanned** volume is a simple volume spread across multiple disk drives; it acts like a single partition with one drive letter.

- A **striped** volume is also known as RAID 0. Striping spreads out blocks of each file across multiple disks. Using two or more drives in a group called a *stripe set*, striping writes data first to a certain number of clusters on one drive, then on the next, and so on. Striping speeds up data throughput because the system has to wait a much shorter time for a drive to read or write data. The drawback of striping is that if any single drive in the stripe set fails, all data in the stripe set is lost.

- A **mirrored** volume is also known as RAID 1. Using two drives, all data written on one drive is simultaneously written to the second drive. If one of the drives fails, the other can take its place. Mirroring is a very good way to preserve data if a drive fails, but throughput is slow because two read/write operations are required every time the drives are accessed. Data on mirrored drives is duplicated on two physical disks.

- **RAID 5** is also known as striping with parity; it combines the best of RAID 0 and RAID 1. RAID 5 requires at least three hard drives. Basically, RAID 5 is striping using three or more disks, with fault tolerance added in the form of parity bits, which are also striped across the disks. If one of the disks fails, its portion of the striped data can be re-created from the remaining data and the parity bits, as long as only of one of the disks fails. Because it is rare for more than one disk drive to fail at a time, RAID 5 offers safety while still allowing speedy drive access.

The benefits you receive from dynamic disks depend partly on the type you use. Striping enables faster access to your data, but because striped disks are optimized for speed, they're no more fault tolerant than basic disks. Mirrored disks provide wonderful fault tolerance but eat up large amounts of disk real estate. RAID 5 is the most broadly used type of dynamic storage because it combines the speed of striping and the fault tolerance of mirroring, but in a more space-efficient way using parity bits.

Upgrading to Dynamic Disks

To turn a basic disk into a dynamic disk, you can use the Upgrade wizard that starts automatically when you open the Disk Management utility after you install a new drive. You can also start the utility manually by alternate-clicking the drive and selecting the Convert to Dynamic Disk option (Figure 8.18). After upgrading, the Disk Management tool will indicate that the drive is a dynamic drive, as shown in Figure 8.19.

Dynamic drives are a type of storage, not a type of file system. Just like basic drives, dynamic drives can use FAT16, FAT32, and NTFS file systems.

Third-Party Tools

A number of excellent third-party tools are available to help you with partitioning and formatting chores. One of the most popular third-party tools is PowerQuest's PartitionMagic. PartitionMagic and other very advanced

Inside Information

RAID 5

Windows 2000 comes in several versions: Professional and three different server versions. Only the server versions allow you to create RAID 5 arrays. RAID 5 is such a powerful tool for protecting data that in many companies, some non-server systems (for example, a programmer's workstation) run Windows 2000 Server just to take advantage of RAID 5. But you don't have to own Windows Server to get the benefit of RAID 5. Many companies, such as Promise Technology (www.promise.com), sell special controller cards that enable you to protect your valuable data using RAID 5.

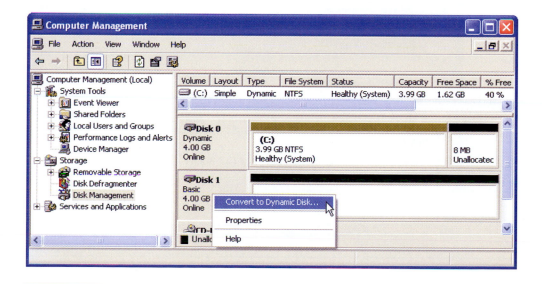

● **Figure 8.18**   Convert to Dynamic Disk option

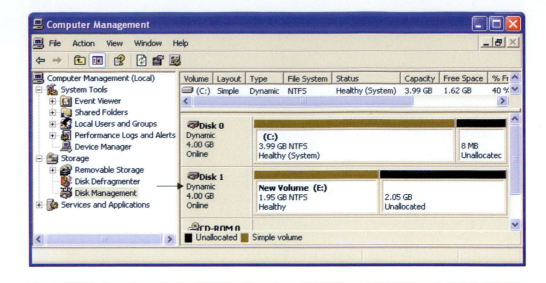

● **Figure 8.19**   Disk Management indicating Disk 1 is now a dynamic drive

third-party tools are the Swiss Army knives of the drive partitioning and formatting world. Literally anything you need done to your drives, they can do—and best of all, without destroying your data!

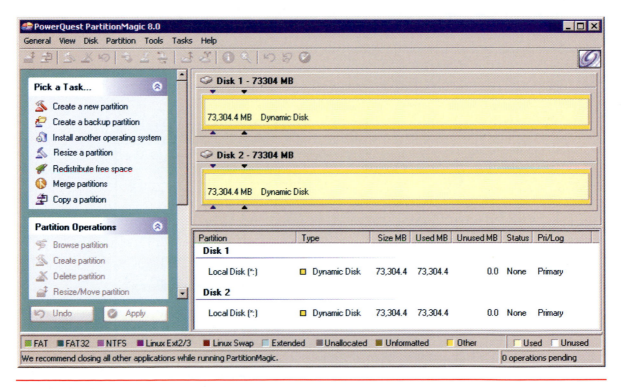

● PartitionMagic

Working with Partitions Using the Disk Management Utility

Dynamic disk storage is the business standard these days, so it's something any good PC tech should be comfortable implementing. In this Step-by-Step exercise, you will use the Disk Management tool that comes with Windows 2000 and Windows XP to set up a disk with two partitions and then convert the basic disk partitions to dynamic disk volumes.

To complete this exercise, you will need the following:

- A computer system running Windows 2000 or Windows XP Professional with a second hard drive installed but *not* partitioned or formatted

Step 1

Have your system up and running in Windows. Go to the Control Panel and double-click on the Administrative Tools icon; then double-click on the Computer Management icon. In Computer Management, select Disk Management from the available utilities. Because you've installed a new, unformatted drive, the Windows wizard will appear. You're going to perform this task manually, so click Cancel. The Disk Management tool will display the new drive, but with a white bar on a red circle to indicate that it does not yet have a signature.

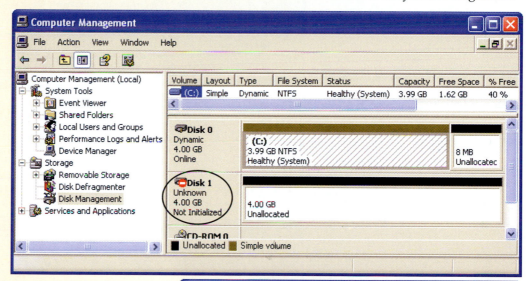

Step 2

Alternate-click the new disk and select Initialize Drive. After the drive is initialized, again alternate-click the disk, and this time select Convert to Dynamic Disk. After Disk Management converts the drive, alternate-click in the black area to the right of the disk area and select New Volume. This will start the New Volume wizard. Click Next on

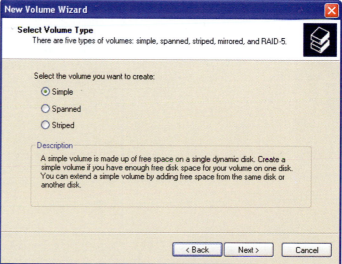

the first screen to display the partition types.

Step 3

Select Simple and click Next to display the Select Disks dialog box. This dialog box has two parts. The left side lists the available drives, and the right side lists the selected drives. By default, the disk you originally alternate-clicked is selected. At the bottom of the dialog box is the partition size selector. By default, it selects the entire drive. Reduce that amount by roughly half.

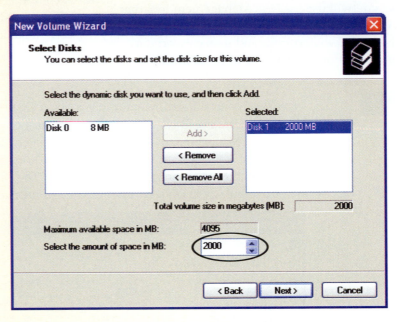

Step 4

Click Next to assign the new partition a drive letter. This is one of the more interesting screens. You can give the new partition a traditional drive letter, or you can make the new partition a *folder* on an existing partition. For this exercise, just accept the drive letter suggested and click Next.

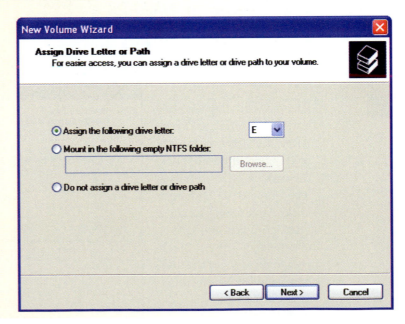

The final screen of the wizard prompts for the type of file format. Because you're running Windows 2000 or XP, NTFS will be selected by default. Accept NTFS and click Next. The wizard will display a summary screen. Click Next, and the new partition will appear.

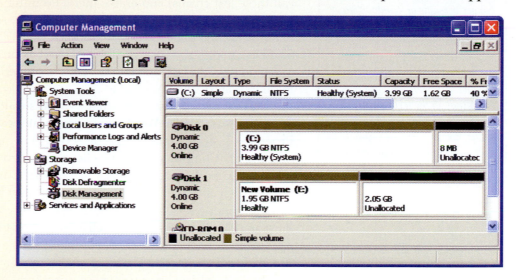

Hard Drive Maintenance and Troubleshooting

Hard drives are complex mechanical as well as electrical devices. With platters spinning at thousands of rotations per minute, they also generate heat and vibration. All of these factors make hard drives susceptible to failure. In this section, you will learn some basic maintenance tasks that will keep your hard drives healthy, and for those inevitable instances when a hard drive fails, you will also learn what you can do to repair them.

Hard Drive Maintenance

Hard drive maintenance can be broken down into two distinct functions: checking the disk occasionally for failed clusters and keeping data organized on the drive so that it can be accessed quickly.

ScanDisk

Individual clusters on hard drives sometimes go bad. There's nothing you can do to prevent this from happening, so it's important to check occasionally for bad clusters on drives. The tool used to perform this check is called ScanDisk. When it finds bad clusters, it puts the electronic equivalent of orange cones around them so that the system won't try to place data in those bad clusters. ScanDisk is one of the oldest utilities ever made for the PC market—ScanDisk was around back in the DOS days, and it continues to do its thing in the latest versions of Windows.

Error-checking

Newer versions of Windows no longer call the disk-checking tool ScanDisk. Instead, Microsoft has relegated this important tool to a button called Error-checking in the Drive Properties dialog box. Even though the term ScanDisk has disappeared from the program name, however, most PC people still use it to refer to any of Windows' hard disk error-checking programs.

ScanDisk does far more than just check for bad clusters. It goes through all of the drive's file names, looking for invalid names and attempting to fix them. It looks for clusters that have no file names associated with them (we call these lost chains) and erases them. From time to time, the underlying links between parent and child folders are lost, so ScanDisk checks every parent and child folder. With a folder such as C:\TEST\DATA, for example, ScanDisk makes sure that the folder DATA is properly associated with its parent folder C:\TEST, and that C:\TEST is properly associated with its child folder C:\TEST\DATA.

The best part of ScanDisk is that it works so automatically. The trick is to know how to start it! In Windows 9x, you locate ScanDisk by choosing Start | Programs | Accessories | System Tools. You can also start ScanDisk by opening My Computer, alternate-clicking the drive you want to check, and selecting Properties to open the Drive Properties dialog box. Select the Tools tab and then click the Check Now button to start ScanDisk.

The Windows 9x version of ScanDisk gives you a choice between Standard and Thorough testing, as well as an option to have it automatically fix any errors it finds (Figure 8.20). For maintenance purposes, it's fine to use the Standard check. The Thorough check takes a long time, so you'll normally use it only when you suspect a problem. As a rule, you should also always check the Automatically Fix Errors check box.

To access Error-checking (a.k.a. ScanDisk) on a Windows 2000/XP system, open My Computer, alternate-click the drive you want to check, and select Properties to open the Drive Properties dialog box. Select the Tools tab and click the Check Now button (Figure 8.21) to display the Check Disk dialog box, which has two options. Check the box next to Automatically Fix File System Errors, but save the option to Scan for and Attempt Recovery of Bad Sectors for times when you actually suspect a problem.

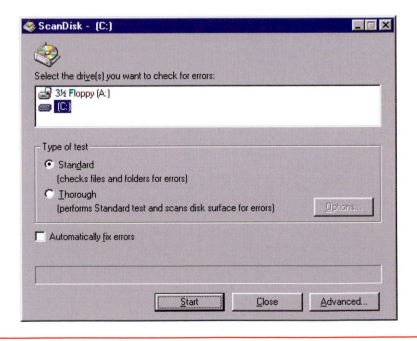

• **Figure 8.20**   ScanDisk options

Now that you know how to run ScanDisk, your next question should be, "How often do I run it?" A reasonable maintenance plan would include running ScanDisk about once a week. ScanDisk is fast (unless you use the Thorough option), and it's a great tool for keeping your system in top shape. However, disk checking isn't the only thing ScanDisk can do. As you're about to see, it's a powerful tool that can help you when things go wrong on a hard drive.

Defragmentation

Hard drives store files in clusters. Normally, the clusters used to store a file are contiguous (one right after the other), but as files get erased and rewritten, there are fewer and fewer contiguous clusters to write to. If your system cannot write files to contiguous clusters, it will save chunks wherever it can find empty clusters, often chopping a file into a large number of non-contiguous clusters. The FAT or MFT will keep track of the location of each cluster, but having to fetch pieces from all over the hard drive slows down access to your files. The solution to this is a process known as **defragmentation (defrag)**. Defragmentation is just what you'd think: file clusters are rearranged to minimize file fragmentation—that is, to maximize the number of files stored in contiguous clusters.

• **Figure 8.21** Tools tab and Check Now button in Disk Properties in Windows 2000

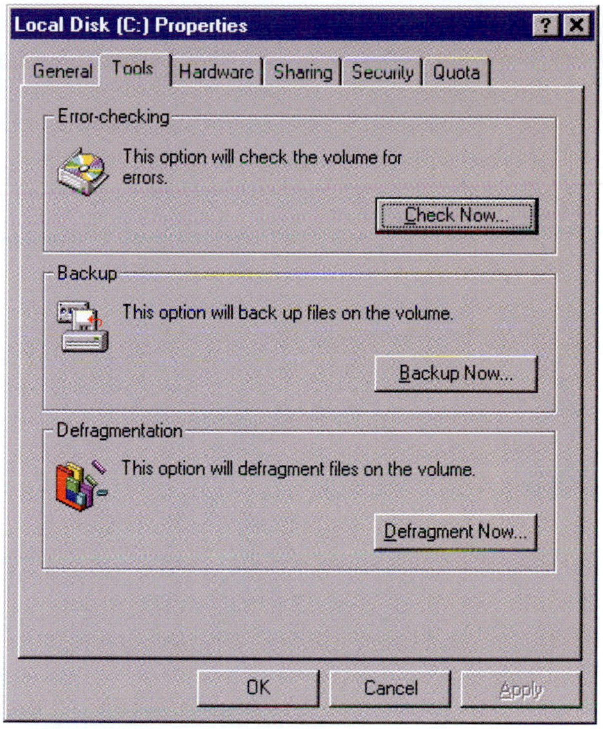

To access the Windows 98 Defrag program, choose Start | Programs | Accessories | System Tools | Disk Defragmenter. You'll be prompted to select the disk you want to defragment. Once you've selected a disk, the

Try This!

Comparing ScanDisk to Competing Tools

A good PC tech is an informed PC tech. A number of companies make third-party tools that they claim are better than ScanDisk. Try this:

1. Research these two competing products: SmithMicro's CheckIt utility (`www.checkit.com`) and Symantec's Norton Utilities (`www.symantec.com`). Look through these websites and gather information on the products' features. How can these products help you maintain and repair hard drives?
2. Call or e-mail each company's sales department and ask this question, "Why should I buy your product when I already have ScanDisk?" Print the e-mail message, or if you call, write down the response.
3. Write a brief report outlining the similarities and differences among the three programs (including ScanDisk) and the advantages and disadvantages of each. Rate the programs; which seems the best buy and which the worst?

Inside Information

Defrag

In the computer world, it's important to be familiar with the prevailing jargon. When discussing defragmentation, almost everyone refers to the process using the term defrag, as in, "I really need to defrag this disk—it's getting sooo slow!" Defrag utilities are almost as old as ScanDisk—you can find defrag programs beginning with the later versions of DOS. The DOS program was called DEFRAG, which is why PC techs use that term, and so does this book.

defragging begins. Defragmentation takes quite a while. If you want to watch the process, click the Show Details button to see the clusters get rearranged. It's fascinating to watch—kind of like watching paint dry to some, but sort of mesmerizing, too.

• Selecting the drive to defragment

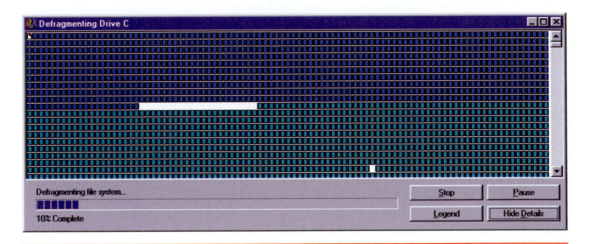

• Defrag running in Show Details mode

Simply running Defrag with the default settings is fine in most situations, but there are some specialized settings that you may want to employ. The Select Drive screen has a Settings button. Clicking this displays the settings choices you can use. The one option of interest is the Start Programs Faster option. This option tells Defrag to put all of the directory information at the beginning of the drive, which makes files load more quickly.

The defrag tool that runs with Windows 2000 and XP is accessed via the Start button exactly as described for Windows 98. Although functionally equivalent, it does look a bit different. No worry, though—it does the same job.

Defrag and ScanDisk are the two maintenance tools that everyone should run on their systems. As with ScanDisk, you should run Defrag once a week.

Disk Cleanup

Did you know that the average hard drive is full of trash? No, I'm not talking about the junk you intentionally put in your hard drive like the 23,000 e-mail messages that you refuse to delete from your e-mail program. I'm talking about all the files that you never see that Windows keeps for you. Here are a few examples:

■ **Files in the Recycle Bin** When you delete a file, it isn't really deleted. It's placed in the Recycle Bin just in case you decide you need the file later. I just checked my Recycle Bin and found 3 GB worth of files. That's a lot of trash!

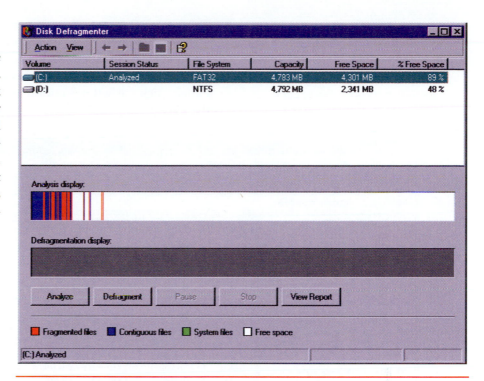

• Defrag in Windows 2000

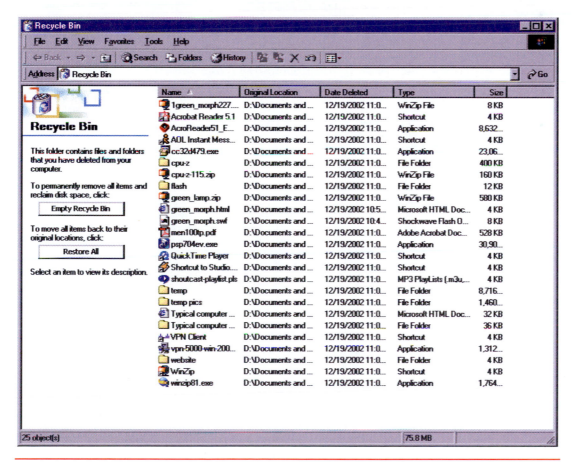

• Mike's Recycle Bin

- **Temporary Internet Files**   When you go to a website, Windows keeps copies of the graphics and other items so that the page will load more quickly the next time you access the page. You can see these files by opening the Internet Options applet on the Control Panel. Click the Settings button on the General tab and then click the View Files button.

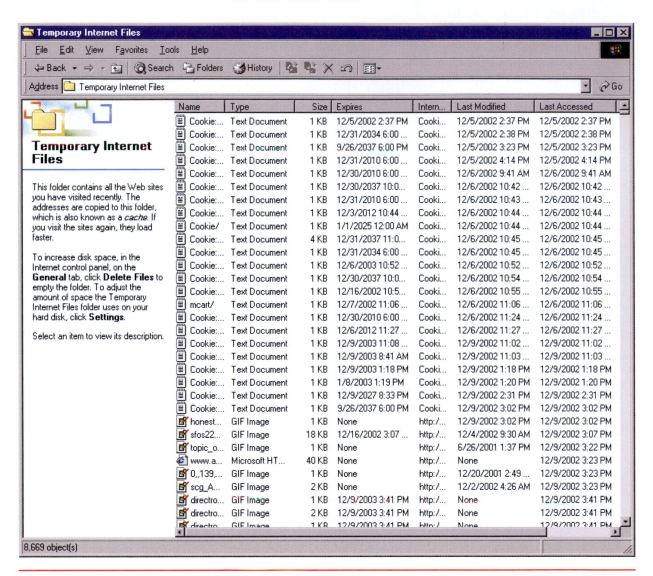

• Temporary Internet Files in Windows 2000

- **Downloaded Program Files**   Your system always keeps a copy of any Java or ActiveX applets that it downloads. You can see these in the Internet Options applet by clicking the View Objects button on the General tab. You'll generally find only a few tiny files here.

- **Temporary Files**   Many applications create temporary files that are supposed to be deleted when the application is closed. For one reason or another, these temporary files sometimes aren't deleted. The location of these files varies with the version of Windows, but they always reside in a folder called TEMP.

Every hard drive will eventually become filled with lots of unnecessary trash. All versions of Windows tend to act erratically when the drives run out of unused space. Fortunately, all versions of Windows starting with Windows 98 have a powerful tool called Disk Cleanup. You can access Disk Cleanup in all versions of Windows by choosing Start | Program | Accessories | System Tools | Disk Cleanup.

• Disk Cleanup in Windows 2000

Disk Cleanup gets rid of the four types of files just described. Run Disk Cleanup once a month or so to keep plenty of space available on your hard drive.

Troubleshooting

There's no scarier computer problem than an error that points to trouble with a hard drive. In this section, we look at some of the more common problems that occur with hard drives. These issues can be divided into three categories that correspond to the tasks for installing a drive: physical problems, system setup problems, and partitioning and formatting problems.

Physical Problems

Physical problems are rare but devastating when they happen. If a hard drive is truly damaged physically, there is nothing that you or any service technician can do to fix it. Fortunately, hard drives are designed to take a phenomenal amount of punishment without failing. Physical problems manifest themselves in two ways: either the drive works properly but makes a lot of noise, or the drive seems to disappear.

All hard drives make noise—the hum as the platters spin and the occasional slight scratching noise as the read/write heads access sectors are normal. However, if your drive begins to make any of the following sounds, it is about to die:

- Continuous high-pitched squeal
- Series of clacks, a short pause, and then another series of clacks
- Continuous grinding or rumbling

Back up your critical data and replace the drive.

You'll know when a drive simply disappears. If it's the drive that contains your operating system, the system will lock up. When you try to restart the computer, you'll see this error message:

```
No Boot Device Present
```

If it's a second drive, it will simply stop showing up in My Computer. The first thing to do in this case is to fire up the System Setup program and see if Autodetect sees the drive. If it does, then you do not have a physical problem with the drive. If Autodetect fails, shut off the system and remove the ribbon cable, but leave the power cable attached. Restart the system and listen to the drive. If the drive spins up, you know that the drive is getting good power. In most cases, this is a clue that the drive is probably good. In that case, you need to look for more mundane problems such as an unplugged power cord or jumpers incorrectly set. If the drive doesn't spin up, try another power connector. If it still doesn't spin up and you've triple-checked the jumpers and ribbon cable, you have a problem with the onboard electronics, and the drive is dead.

System Setup Problems

Electrical surges can cause your System Setup program to lose the hard drive information. Just reboot the system to verify that Autodetect still works and save the system settings.

Partitioning and Formatting Problems

Partitioning and formatting problems are by far the most common cause of hard drive errors. These problems sometimes manifest themselves in system lockup, but more often they manifest themselves in errors that seem to indicate a hard drive problem. Here are some examples:

- Data error reading drive C:
- Cannot copy file…
- Error copying file to drive D:
- No disk present

There are literally hundreds of these types of errors. The important thing to appreciate is simply that they are hard drive errors. When you have a formatting problem, the first tool to try is ScanDisk. Run ScanDisk in the Thorough mode. ScanDisk will fix most formatting errors. In fact, Windows will often run ScanDisk automatically if it detects a problem, most often after an unplanned shutdown.

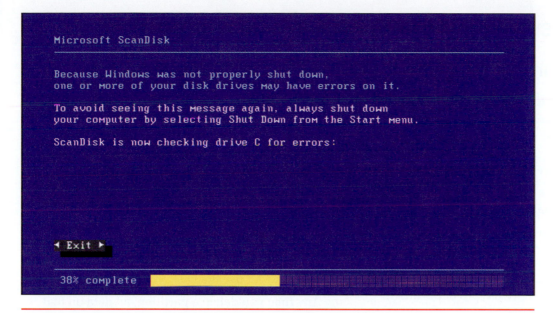

```
Microsoft ScanDisk

Because Windows was not properly shut down,
one or more of your disk drives may have errors on it.

To avoid seeing this message again, always shut down
your computer by selecting Shut Down from the Start menu.

ScanDisk is now checking drive C for errors:




◄ Exit ►


38% complete  ████████████
```

• ScanDisk running automatically after an unplanned shutdown

If the problem persists after you run ScanDisk, go to the website of your drive's manufacturer and download the diagnostic tool for your type of drive. These tools, known as low-level formatters, always run from a bootable floppy. They will often fix a problem that gets by ScanDisk.

 Cross Check

ScanDisk and Floppy Disks

ScanDisk also works perfectly well on floppy disks and other removable media. Try running ScanDisk on a floppy disk.

1. What are some of the differences in the way ScanDisk runs on a floppy as compared to a hard drive? Why do you think that you can't run FDISK on a floppy disk?

2. Reread the discussion of floppy drive maintenance and repair concepts in Chapter 7, in the "Care and Feeding of Your Floppies" section. How would you incorporate ScanDisk into your floppy disk and drive troubleshooting?

 When running a low-level formatting tool, read all of the directions very carefully—incorrect use can destroy a drive!

Chapter 8 Review

■ Chapter Summary

After reading this chapter and completing the exercises, you should understand the following facts about hard drives.

Describe how hard drives store data

- All hard drives have a make and a model, and this is important information to know.

- The smallest storage area on a hard drive is called a sector. Every sector stores 512 bytes.

- All hard drives must be partitioned.

- Windows systems have two types of partitions: primary and extended.

- Each partition has in effect its own personal card catalog, called a File Allocation Table (FAT).

- Three file systems are used on Windows PCs: FAT16, FAT32, and NTFS.

Physically install a hard drive in a PC

- EIDE is the most common drive technology used in PCs today. EIDE drives use 40-pin cables.

- ATA66 and higher-speed drives need a special 80-wire cable. Even though the cable has 80 wires, it still has only 40 pins.

- The actual drive connection on the motherboard is almost universally called the controller, although in reality it is only a connector for the EIDE cable.

- One EIDE controller can support a maximum of two ATA devices. If two EIDE drives are on the same controller, one must be set as master and the other as slave.

- Almost all hard drives have two EIDE controllers on the motherboard. They are called the primary and the secondary controllers. This allows a maximum of four ATA devices in a single PC.

- Almost all System Setup programs have an Autodetect feature that tells the BIOS all of a drive's geometry settings.

- The original IDE standard supported a maximum drive size of 504 MB. The LBA standard increased the maximum drive size of 8.3 GB. The INT13 Extensions standard increased the maximum drive size to 137 GB. The ATA-6 (Big Drives) standard increased the maximum drive size to 144 petabytes.

Configure a newly installed hard drive

- You partition hard drives during the installation of the operating system. Windows 9*x* systems use the FDISK utility to partition drives. Windows NT, 2000, and XP use the Disk Management program.

- Any time you delete a partition, all data on that partition is lost.

- FAT16 supports a maximum partition size of 2 GB. FAT32 supports up to 2 terabytes. NTFS also supports partitions up to 2 terabytes.

- Windows 2000 and XP Professional have a new type of drive configuration called dynamic disk. Dynamic disk drives must be used if you want to take advantage of special features such as RAID or drive spanning.

- The three most important types of RAID are RAID 0, RAID 1, and RAID 5. RAID 0 is also known as a striping. RAID 1 is also known as mirroring. RAID 5 is known as striping with parity.

Maintain and troubleshoot a hard drive

- ScanDisk and Defrag are the two most important tools for maintaining a healthy hard drive.

- ScanDisk primarily looks for bad clusters. ScanDisk also looks for invalid file and folder names.

- Defragmentation is a process in which file clusters are rearranged to minimize file fragmentation. All versions of Windows have a utility with this capability.

- All versions of Windows since Windows 98 have a tool called Disk Cleanup to remove unneeded files that accumulate during normal operation of the PC.

■ Key Terms

ATA speed ratings *(209)*
cylinder *(202)*
defragmentation (defrag) *(229)*
dynamic disks *(222)*
Enhanced Integrated Drive Electronics (EIDE) *(208)*
extended partition *(204)*
File Allocation Table (FAT) *(203)*

geometry *(201)*
logical drive *(204)*
master *(210)*
Master Boot Record (MBR) *(204)*
Master File Table (MFT) *(205)*
NT File System (NTFS) *(205)*
partition *(203)*
platter *(202)*

primary partition *(204)*
read/write head *(202)*
Redundant Array of Independent Disks (RAID) *(221)*
ScanDisk *(227)*
sectors per track *(203)*
slave *(210)*
track *(202)*

■ Key Term Quiz

Use terms from the Key Terms list to complete the following sentences. Not all terms will be used.

1. _____ is a tool that checks for bad clusters and lost chains on a hard drive.

2. _____ are multiple hard drives that work together to act as one drive with a single drive letter.

3. The best file system used by Windows XP is _____.

4. Each partition has its own personal card catalog, called a/an _____.

5. The _____ is a tiny piece of code that helps the operating system load the correct partition.

6. A group of tracks of the same diameter going completely through a hard drive is a called a _____.

7. The circular paths where data is stored on a hard drive are called _____s.

8. A/an _____ is a discrete electronic chunk of a hard drive that is used as an underlying structure for organizing data on the drive.

9. A drive's _____ determines where it stores data on its stack of disks.

10. Extended partitions must be divided into one or more _____s.

■ Multiple-Choice Quiz

1. What are the three components of hard drive geometry?
   a. Cylinders, platters, and heads
   b. Heads, tracks, and sectors
   c. Cylinders, heads, and sectors per track
   d. Sectors, platters, and cylinders per track

2. What is the maximum number of primary partitions that Windows XP allows on a single hard drive?
   a. 1
   b. 4
   c. 8
   d. 32

3. What obsolete file system was used by DOS and Windows 3.1?
   a. FAT8
   b. FAT16
   c. FAT32
   d. FAT64

4. What term is used universally to describe all drives in the ATA-2 through ATA-5 standards?
   a. ATAPI
   b. ATA
   c. IDE
   d. EIDE

5. When two devices share a single ribbon cable, one of those devices must have its controller turned off. What is that device called?
   a. Secondary
   b. Passive

c. Slave

d. Dependent

6. What is the name of the tool used to partition a disk manually on a Windows 9*x* system?

a. FDISK

b. Defrag

c. Partition

d. ScanDisk

7. What type of dynamic disk storage is known as RAID 0?

a. Striped

b. Segmented

c. Mirrored

d. Spanned

8. Which RAID level uses striping with three or more disks and fault tolerance added in the form of parity bits?

a. RAID 0

b. RAID 1

c. RAID 4

d. RAID 5

9. How many read/write heads would a hard drive with 12 platters require?

a. 12

b. 24

c. 48

d. 60

10. Each sector on a hard drive stores how many bytes of data?

a. 1

b. 16

c. 32

d. 512

11. The Master Boot Record looks for what partition to boot from?

a. Primary

b. Secondary

c. Active

d. Extended

12. What is the name of the super-FAT used by the NTFS file system?

a. NT File Allocation Table

b. Master File Table

c. Extended File Allocation Table

d. NT File Administrator

13. What is the current method for transferring data between a hard drive and RAM?

a. Ultra Direct Memory Access

b. Programmable Input/Output

c. Advanced Memory Attachment

d. Integrated Drive Access

14. How many drives can a single EIDE controller support?

a. 1

b. 2

c. 3

d. 4

15. How many wires are there on the two types of ATA cables?

a. 34 and 50

b. 40 and 40

c. 40 and 80

d. 50 and 80

■ Essay Quiz

1. Write a set of instructions laying out the basic steps involved in partitioning and formatting a hard drive. Be sure to cover the steps in order, and explain your terms.

2. You are assigned to handle maintenance for your boss's computer. Part of this responsibility involves keeping her hard drive in good working order. Write a memo detailing the various hard drive maintenance tasks you wish to perform. Explain why you need to do each one, and how often.

3. Your coworker comes to you for help. He just changed offices and set up his computer on his new desk. When he opened My Computer to access his second hard drive, it wasn't there! Write an essay explaining how you would troubleshoot this problem. Include any questions you would ask your coworker.

4. You have just given four of your coworkers new PCs. Each of the PCs has the hard drive partitioned into a C: drive and a D: drive. Your coworkers have never seen a drive with two partitions and are confused. Create an e-mail message explaining the two partitions and the benefits they might provide.

5. As the new PC technician at your company, you are shocked to discover that your predecessor did all of the hard drive defragging and disk scanning herself, spending hours moving from one drive to the next. Create a short e-mail message explaining to the users that they can use these two tools themselves and provide a series of steps to show them how to run these programs.

Lab Projects

• Lab Project 8.1

Partitioning can be a far more complex affair than the basic single primary partitioning described in this chapter. Placing multiple partitions on a single drive allows you to organize your data more effectively and makes backup easier. Using a system with a hard drive that you can erase, try some of the more complex types of partitioning.

1 Add one extended partition to the hard drive and then create two logical drives in the extended partition.

2 Add two extended partitions to the hard drive and create a single logical drive in each one.

3 Add one extended partition to the hard drive and create four logical drives in it.

• Lab Project 8.2

You should occasionally check a drive to see if it needs maintenance. This process often allows you to catch small errors on the drive before you begin losing data. Check the hard drive on a computer in your classroom to see if it needs maintenance.

1 Run ScanDisk on the hard drive. Record the results.

2 Have the Defrag program analyze the drive. Record the percentage of the drive it reports as fragmented.

3 Compare your results with those of other students. Are the classroom systems well maintained?

4 Create a maintenance plan for the classroom systems to keep the hard drives in good condition.

CD Media

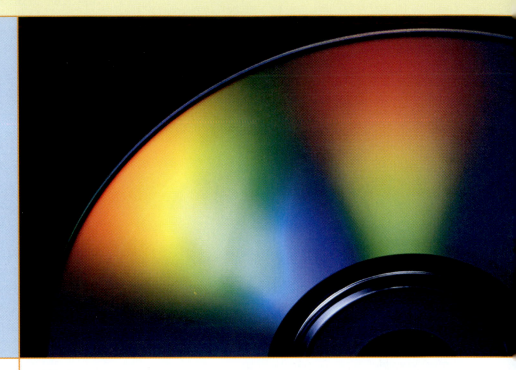

"You have a CD drive? Yeah, well, I have an EF drive! Ha!"

—THE AUTHOR'S FOUR-YEAR-OLD
(AT THE TIME) DAUGHTER

In this chapter, you will learn how to:

- **Identify the various types of CD technologies**
- **Install a CD media drive in a Windows PC**
- **Use and maintain a CD media drive in a Windows PC**
- **Troubleshoot basic CD media problems**

Once upon a time, in the late 1980s, floppy disks ruled the PC world as the only media available for transferring files. They were also the only choice for installing software. This was fine because at that time, one or two 1.44 MB floppy disks were adequate for most purposes. By the mid-1990s, however, operating systems and applications had become much larger and more complicated—when Windows 95 came along, it required a staggering 27 floppy disks for installation! It was clear that some new solution was needed. Enter an invention called the **compact disc**, or **CD**.

Originally designed more than 20 years ago as a replacement for vinyl records, the CD reigns today in the computer world as the primary method of long-term storage for sound, video, and data. It has made software installation from floppy disks a thing of the past. Although at one time, all CD media for computers were referred to by the term **CD-ROM** (Compact Disc–Read-Only Memory), these high-capacity discs now cover a range of technologies such as CD-R, CD-RW, and DVD. For simplicity, all of these technologies are referred to with the umbrella term **CD media**.

This chapter introduces the CD-ROM and all of the other offshoot CD media technologies. You'll learn how to install a CD-ROM drive in your computer, how to use and maintain CD media drives and discs, and how to perform some basic troubleshooting for those drives and discs. Let's get spinning by taking a look at what CD media can do for you.

■ Understanding CD Media Technologies

Philips and Sony developed compact discs in the late 1970s and unveiled the technology in 1981 as a replacement for vinyl records. The first CDs—the ones you still see today at your local music store—were designed only for storing musical data. These discs are called **CD Audio** or **CD Digital Audio (CDDA)**. These audio CDs did not, and still do not, have any type of formatting to support the storage of computer files; they store only sounds in a digital format. Over the years, a number of new standards have been developed to take CDs from simple vinyl record replacements to the data storage powerhouses they are today.

CD Data Storage

All CD media store data in the same basic way: as a series of microscopic pits on a plastic disc. A laser beam scans these pits to read the data. The pits are aligned in a long spiral, similar to the groove on a vinyl record.

The bottom side of the CD is coated with a reflective substance. Whenever the laser comes across a tiny pit in the reflective surface, it reads that as a 0. When it comes to a spot without a pit (called a *land* in the CD media industry), the laser interprets that as a 1.

All CDs are divided into 2,352-byte sectors. Don't confuse these unique CD sectors with the sectors on a hard drive—there are no FATs or other file formats that can store data on these CD audio sectors. Instead, each sector on an audio CD represents 1/75 of a second of high-quality stereo sound. The standard audio CD stores 74 minutes of sound. An audio CD can accept up to 99 separate tracks of sound (usually a track is a single song). At the center of the audio CD sits the table of contents, or TOC, which contains all of the track information, including the names of the songs and other details.

Land
Pit

• Pits and lands on a CD

CD-ROM

It didn't take the CD media folks too long after the introduction of audio CDs to come up with a way to store computer files on a CD. In 1989, a new standard file format called **ISO9660** was introduced. This standard gave CDs additional information to enable them to store standard computer files. These are the data CD-ROM discs that are so common today.

Be careful with your terms here—the term ISO9660 is almost never used to describe these data CDs. Instead, use the term CD-ROM, or *data CD*. In fact, if you look on the Windows properties of a typical data CD-ROM, you'll see the file system described as *CDFS* (CD File System). The standard data CD stores 650 MB of data.

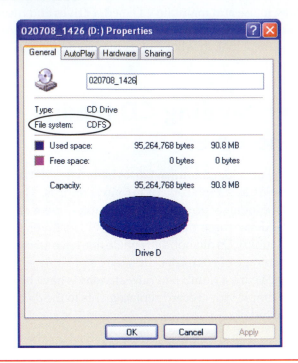

• Properties of a data CD in Windows XP

A data CD looks identical to an audio CD, but the similarity ends there. In terms of how they store data, these are very different discs, and Windows treats them as such. Before we explore the differences between audio and data CDs, let's take a moment to look at the device used to play both of them: the CD-ROM drive (Figure 9.1).

CD-ROM drives first began to appear in PCs in the early 1990s. The folks who developed CD-ROM drives had a problem: the first CD-ROM drives could read only data CDs. If you inserted an audio CD into an early CD-ROM drive, nothing happened. It would take a number of years before sound cards and CD-ROMs were developed that could talk to each other.

• **Figure 9.1**   Typical CD-ROM drive

So what did the early audiophiles do to listen to music CDs on their CD-ROM drives? The answer lies in the headphone jack and volume knob located on the front of the drive. In fact, a CD-ROM drive can play music through its headphone jack—a throwback to the early days of CD-ROMs. The few people who still have computers with no sound card can use this jack to listen to music played on the CD-ROM drive. The volume knob adjusts the volume on the CD-ROM drive's headphone jack only; it does not affect anything passing through the sound card.

• The CDDA emblem on an audio CD

Speeds and What They Mean

The first CD-ROM drives processed data at roughly 150,000 bits per second (150 KBps), copying the speed from the original CDDA standard. Although this speed is excellent for playing music, the CD-ROM industry quickly recognized that installing programs or transferring files at 150 KBps was the electronic equivalent of watching paint dry. So since the day the first CD-ROM drives for PCs hit the market, there's been a push to speed them up to increase their data throughput.

Each increase in speed is measured in multiples of the speed of the original 150-KBps drives. Faster drives are given an x number, known as a **multiplier**, to show their speed relative to the first (1x) drives. Here's a list of the common CD-ROM multipliers and speeds, including most of the early speeds that are no longer used.

CD-ROM Speed	Transfer Rate
1x	150 KBps
2x	300 KBps
4x	600 KBps
6x	900 KBps
8x	1,200 KBps
10x	1,500 KBps
12x	1,800 KBps
16x	2,400 KBps
24x	3,600 KBps
32x	4,800 KBps
36x	5,400 KBps
40x	6,000 KBps
48x	7,200 KBps
52x	7,800 KBps
60x	9,000 KBps
72x	10,800 KBps

Keep in mind that these speeds are maximums and are rarely met in real-life operation—a 52x CD-ROM drive will never run continually at 7,800 KBps—but you can use these speeds as a relative gauge of CD media performance; you can count on a 32x drive reading data faster than an 8x drive. As multipliers increase, though, many other factors also come into play, so that telling the difference between a 52x and a 60x drive (for example) becomes difficult.

Lots of Standards

The audio CD format has not changed since the mid-1980s, but data CD formats have gone through a large number of changes and improvements. Many of these formats were never widely adopted, but CD makers are aware that you might try to use a CD with one of these formats. As a result, if you read the box that comes with a modern CD-ROM drive, you'll see a list of the various file formats that the drive can read. Don't worry; the odds that you'll use a CD with an obscure format are small.

CD-R and CD-RW

The process of making audio CDs or data CD-ROMs requires specialized, expensive equipment and substantial expertise, making the creation of CD-ROMs the province of a relatively small number of CD-ROM production companies. From the time the first CD-ROMs came to market, however, ordinary PC users clamored for a way to create their own audio and data CDs. This demand motivated the creation of two more CD media technologies: CD-R and CD-RW.

• Top view of a typical CD-R disc

CD-R

In the mid-1990s, the CD industry introduced the **CD-R** (CD-Recordable) standard. The CD-R standard enables inexpensive CD-R drives to add data to special CD-R discs. Any CD-ROM drive can then read the data stored on the CD-R, and all CD-R drives can read regular CD-ROMs.

All CD-R drives have two lasers: a lower-powered one for reading and a higher-powered one for writing. When a CD-R writes data, the **writing laser** actually makes tiny burns on the shiny CD-R disc, mimicking the pits and lands of a CD-ROM drive. You can easily see the burned part of a partially burned CD-R disc.

The process of placing data on a CD-R (or CD-RW, which I discuss next) is known as **burning**. You burn data onto a CD using special burning software. For years, software for burning CDs was available only as third-party programs, which you either purchased separately or received with your CD-R. Today, users of Windows XP get CD burning capacity built right into the operating system.

• Bottom view of a partially burned CD-R disc (the arrows point to the end of the burned section of the CD-R)

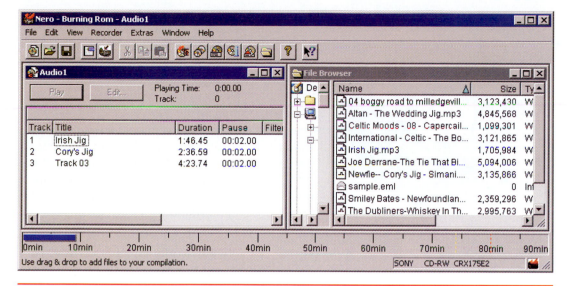

• Ahead's Nero Burning ROM, a popular burning program

CD-R burning requires special CD-R discs, which come in two varieties: 74-minute discs that hold about 650 MB, and 80-minute discs that hold about 700 MB (Figure 9.2). Note that a CD-R burner must be specifically designed to support the longer 80-minute CD-R format, which is currently the most common form sold. CD-R discs look exactly like CD-ROMs, except that the bottom side is colored instead of silvery. Most CD-Rs are clearly labeled as such on the printed side of the disc.

CD-R drives have two multiplier values: a **read speed**, which is the speed at which the drive can retrieve data, and a **write speed**, which is the speed at which the drive can burn data. If you see a CD media drive with two speeds listed, you automatically know that the device is a CD-R drive. CD-R drives (but not CD-R discs) have become obsolete due to the popularity of CD-RW.

CD-Rs also come in a special version called music CDs. These CD-Rs are designed to be used in stand-alone home CD recorders, and they include a small amount of code that prevents these home recorders from making copies from the CDs. You can copy *to* a music CD—you just can't copy *from* it. You can use these CDs in your PC's CD media drive, which just ignores the extra code.

• **Figure 9.2**   80-minute, 700-MB CD-R

• Top and bottom view of a CD-RW disc

CD-RW

The problem with CD-Rs stems from the fact that anything burned onto a CD-R is set in stone; it cannot be changed. This is fine for many uses, such as archival storage. However, what if you wanted to change information burned onto a disc? How can you delete that one embarrassingly silly picture on an otherwise excellent collection of family photos sitting on a stack of 24 CD-Rs, ready for a Christmas mailout? You can't! Your only option is to burn another set of discs with the correct information. What a waste!

CD-RW (CD-Rewritable) technology enables PC users to burn data onto a disc and then change it later—add to it, delete it, and so on. CD-RW drives require special CD-RW discs, which—like CD-Rs—look exactly like CD-ROM discs, with the exception of a colored bottom side. With these special discs, CD-RW technology makes CD media the equivalent of 650 MB floppy disks.

CD-RW drives also have two lasers: one for reading and the other for writing and erasing. CD-RW media are designed with a special substance that crystallizes under a certain amount of heat. The write/erase laser heats spots and crystallizes them, creating the equivalent of the lands of a CD-ROM. The substance on the CD-RW decrystallizes (becomes amorphous) at a higher heat. Thus, to erase the disc, the laser temperature is turned up, creating the equivalent of a pit.

CD-RW drives can read multiple types of CD media—CD-ROM, CD-R, CD-RW, and so on. Moreover, they can write to both CD-RW and CD-R discs. This versatility made CD-R drives obsolete virtually overnight and gave users a great set of data storage options. You can burn the family photo album on CD-RW discs—just in case!—and add to them later. You can burn a CD-R full of your favorite music tracks to enjoy as you drive to work.

Even though CD-RW drives read CD-ROM discs, many systems have both a regular CD-ROM drive and a CD-RW drive. With a dual CD drive setup such as this, you can make fast copies—just place a disc in the CD-ROM drive and a CD-R or CD-RW disc in the CD-RW drive and run special software such as Roxio's Easy CD Creator to create exact replicas of the original disc (Figure 9.3).

CD-RW drive specs have three multiplier values. The first shows the write speed, the second shows the **rewrite speed** (the speed at which the drive can overwrite existing data), and the third shows the read speed (Figure 9.4). You will learn more about these speeds later in this chapter. There's tremendous variance among these drives; here are a few representative samples:

2 x 2 x 24
4 x 2 x 20
4 x 4 x 24
8 x 4 x 32
12 x 10 x 32

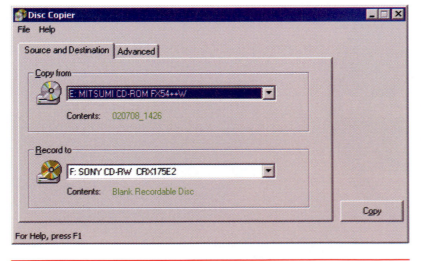

• **Figure 9.3** Easy CD Creator's Disc Copier screen

Introduction to PC Hardware and Troubleshooting

CD-RW drives fulfill functional needs that CD-R drives did not handle nearly as well. The best example is backups—not the archival, "put it on the disc and stash it in the closet" type of backup, but rather the daily or weekly backups that most of us perform for our systems. Using CD-R discs for these backups is wasteful—once a disc fills up, you can't use it for the next backup and instead must use a new disc, throwing the old disc away. However, you can use the same set of CD-RW discs time and again to back up your system.

● **Figure 9.4** Front of a CD-RW drive with its speeds listed

DVD

The **DVD** (Digital Versatile Disc) was developed by a large consortium of electronics and entertainment firms during the early 1990s and released in 1995. At first glance, DVD discs look exactly like all other CD media (Figure 9.5)—but looks are deceiving.

The DVD standard used to show movies is called *DVD video*. DVD video discs store 135 minutes on each side of the disc—yes, unlike all the other CD media, DVDs can be double-sided. The DVD video standard includes the use of menus, multiple languages, letterboxing, and high-quality sound.

DVD has become the fastest-growing media format in history and will almost certainly totally replace VHS tape in the coming years as a video format. To play DVD discs on your computer, you need a special DVD drive, plus third-party DVD player software. A number of free players are available today, and most (perhaps all) DVD drives come bundled with a DVD player program. If you have Windows XP, you can play DVD movies using the built-in Windows Media Player.

● Windows Media Player playing a movie

DVD drives have become moderately popular in desktop computers. Not surprisingly, many people would prefer to watch DVD movies on their

● **Figure 9.5** DVD video disc

There are a number of combination DVD/CD-RW drives on the market—so a single drive can now read, write, and rewrite data and play DVDs!

large television screens instead of on their comparatively tiny PC screens, and excellent DVD players are available that connect to most television sets. The one place where DVD has gained great popularity in the PC world is in laptop computers. I recently took an overseas flight and loaded my laptop with four movies I'd been wanting to see. It sure beat the stuff the airline was showing!

• Typical DVD drive

Although DVDs have had a huge impact on the video business, DVD has not made significant inroads into the data storage realm. Only one well-accepted standard currently exists for DVD: DVD-ROM. DVD-ROM discs, like CD-ROM discs, can be made only on specialized devices, and as their name implies, they're read-only. A DVD-ROM disc can hold up to 4.37 GB per side. Double-sided DVDs can support twice as much data, up to 8.74 GB, but you do have to remove the DVD, flip it over, and re-insert it to get to the other side. The typical DVD drive used in today's PCs supports both DVD video and DVD-ROM. Even though a DVD drive may support DVD-ROM discs, there aren't too many folks distributing data on DVD—not yet, at least.

A number of DVD standards are in the works that will enable writing and rewriting of DVDs, but they are currently incompatible with each other and still not fully debugged. Until the DVD world settles on a single writable/rewritable DVD standard, the best use of your DVD drive will be playback of DVD videos and the occasional DVD-ROM disc.

Try This!

Investigate DVD Data Standards

The superior capacity of DVDs compared to other CD media has led to a scramble by a number of manufacturers for a DVD standard that supports data. In addition, the popularity of CD-RW has motivated the industry to produce a similar product for DVD. In the haste to bring product to market, a number of incompatible standards have been developed, creating frustration for those who would like to take advantage of their DVD drives for something other than watching movies.

1. Search the Web for the following DVD standards:
    a. DVD-ROM
    b. DVD-RAM
    c. DVD-R
    d. DVD-RW
    e. DVD+RW

2. Answer the following questions:
    a. What is the capacity per side of each technology?
    b. Which of these technologies enables you to write data to a disc?
    c. Which of these technologies enables you to rewrite data on a disc?
    d. Of the DVD standards that allow rewriting, do any allow you to interchange their type of media for the media of the others? For example, can a DVD-RAM drive read a DVD-R disc?
    e. Can you find any DVD drives for these media available from online vendors?

■ Installing CD Media Drives

Installing or replacing a CD media drive is a fairly common task and one that's not too hard to do as long as you don't mind digging into your system. One of the best reasons to upgrade is to enhance your system's capabilities. If you have a CD-ROM drive, you can replace it with a CD-RW drive, or keep the CD-ROM drive and add the CD-RW drive and have two drives. Another good reason to upgrade is speed; you might want to consider replacing any CD-ROM drive slower than 32x with a faster drive. Regardless of your reasons, installation is just a matter of breaking the job into parts: physical installation, driver installation, and application installation.

Physical Installation

Almost all internal CD media drives are ATAPI drives that connect to your system via the EIDE bus. The same 40-pin cable that you use to connect hard drives to your computer can also connect a CD media drive.

You'll need to set the master/slave jumpers on your drive, just as you did with hard drives in the last chapter. When connecting your CD-ROM drive to your computer for the first time, you can choose whether to make the CD-ROM drive a slave to your primary hard drive, or to make the CD-ROM drive a master on the second IDE bus. On the back of the CD-ROM drive, just as on IDE hard drives, you can set the jumper for master, slave, or cable select (Figure 9.6).

Some CD-ROM drives can slow down a hard drive if they are placed on the same controller. To avoid this, the best practice, if you have only one hard drive, is to make the CD-ROM drive the master of the second IDE controller. If you plan on populating your computer with multiple hard drives and CD-ROM drives, set the hard drives as masters and the CD-ROM drives as slaves.

● **Figure 9.6** Jumpers on the back of the CD-ROM drive

Audio Cables

If you want to play audio CDs through your sound card, you need a special cable that runs from your CD media drive to the sound card. These cables have been around for a while, but the connectors were not standardized—for years, you had to use the one that came with your sound card and just hope that it would connect to your CD drive.

Today, a connector called MPC2 is quite standard, and cables usually come with CD media drives, not sound cards. To accommodate the many other types of connections that are still out there, a special cable called a **universal audio cable** is also available.

Universal Audio Cables   Universal audio cables (Figure 9.7) have a set of connectors to enable a CD-ROM drive to connect to any sort of audio card. Universal audio cables were important when CD-ROM audio connections were not standardized.

MPC2/SoundBlaster Cables   The early SoundBlaster line of audio cards from Creative Labs came with a small, proprietary connection for CD-ROM drives. Because SoundBlaster dominated the field of sound cards for many years, you'll still run into audio cables with an MPC2 connector on one end and a SoundBlaster connector on the other end. Current SoundBlaster cards use a standard connector.

MPC2/MPC2 Cables   As technology has progressed, the connections between audio cards and CD-ROM drives have become standardized. Now you'll most commonly find MPC2 connections and **MPC2/MPC2 cables** (Figure 9.8). This cable will probably be the type included with any new CD-ROM drive you buy.

Inside Information

Cable Select?

Ever get tired of having to keep track of which drive is the slave and which is the master on an IDE bus? Just like with hard drives on the IDE bus, many manufacturers of CD media drives offer the cable select option. Cable select enables the machine to automatically tell which drive is the master and which is the slave according to the position of the drive on the cable.

For cable select to work properly, you need motherboard support for the feature, both drives must be set to cable select, and you need a cable select cable. When you have all the components singing in unison, cable select can make drive installation a snap!

• **Figure 9.7** Universal audio cable

• **Figure 9.8** MPC2/MPC2 cable

Power

All devices need electricity to function, and CD media drives are no exception. Every CD media drive needs a power connection. Like hard drives, CD media drives use Molex connectors from the power supply.

• A Molex connector supplies power to a CD media drive.

Figure 9.9 shows all of the connections properly installed on the back of a CD-ROM drive. Note the three connections: the EIDE cable that runs to the motherboard, the power cable, and the audio cable that runs to the sound card.

Driver Installation

Every hardware device needs some type of driver to operate. This is one area where all versions of Windows shine—they all come with all the CD media drivers you'll ever need. Assuming that you've installed the CD media

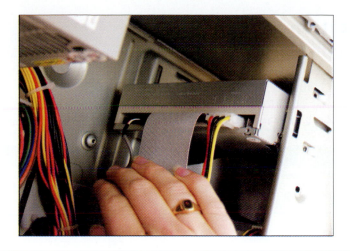

• **Figure 9.9**   Properly installed CD media drive

drive correctly, it will automatically appear in both Device Manager and My Computer.

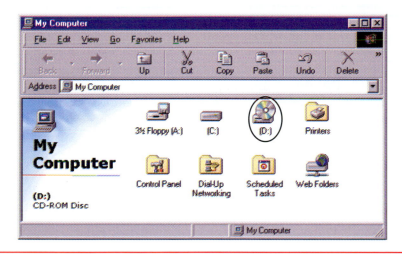

• CD-ROM drive in Windows 98

Windows 98 doesn't differentiate among the different types of CD media. If you want to burn a CD with your new CD-RW drive or watch a movie with your DVD player, you're going to need some applications. Windows XP does a really nice job with CD media drives; not only does it have the drivers, but it also recognizes the type of drive and shows it to you in My Computer.

• CD-ROM drive displayed in My Computer in Windows XP

Application Installation

After the CD media drive is installed and appears in both My Computer and the Device Manager, your last step is to make sure you have the proper applications installed for that device.

If you have a CD-ROM drive, you don't need any special applications. Just insert your CD-ROM discs and access their contents via My Computer.

• Accessing a CD-ROM disc via My Computer

CD-R/CD-RW drives need software to enable them to burn CDs. If you're running any version of Windows before Windows XP, you're going to need some type of burning software. Three popular burning programs for PCs are Nero Burning ROM, Easy CD Creator, and Disc Juggler. Ahead Software's Nero Burning ROM—my favorite—has handy wizards that enable you to create audio or data CDs with very little effort.

Installing an application is one thing, but actually using it is another. We explore what you can do with your CD media drives and your applications in the next section.

Step-by-Step 9.1

Installing a CD-ROM Drive

Installing a CD-ROM drive is as easy as installing a hard drive. A CD-ROM drive is a vital component of your computer system, so you need to know how to install or replace one as needed. All you need are the right tools.

To complete this exercise, you will need the following:

■ Computer system running Windows 98 or later, with no devices installed on the secondary EIDE controller

■ A Phillips-head screwdriver

■ An antistatic wrist strap

■ A CD-ROM drive

■ A 40-pin IDE cable (usually included with the drive)

■ An 18-inch MPC2/MPC2 audio cable (usually included with the drive)

■ Mounting screws (usually included with the drive)

Step 1

Make sure that your computer is shut down and unplugged. Open your computer case as you have done in previous chapters. Be sure to observe all of the antistatic procedures you have learned so far in this book.

Step 2

Remove the plastic plate over a 5¼-inch drive bay. Some cases cover the bay with a metal plate as well; if you see such a plate, remove it. You may need to use a bit of force to remove the metal plate; this is the case itself, however, so a little force shouldn't do any harm.

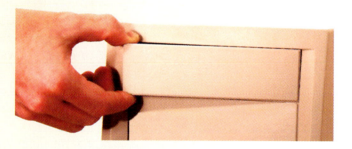

Step 3

Before you install your CD-ROM drive, be sure to verify that the master/slave/cable select jumpers are set the way you want them. The setting will depend on your computer's configuration. For the purpose of this exercise, set the CD-ROM drive as the master.

Step 4

Place the CD-ROM drive into the 5¼-inch drive bay. Align the CD-ROM drive so that it is level with the face of the case; from there, you can keep it in place with the mounting screws usually provided with the CD-ROM drive. Mount the CD-ROM drive with those screws.

Plug the IDE cable into the back of the CD-ROM drive. Then attach the other end of the cable to the secondary IDE controller, which should be the empty IDE controller. Attach the Molex power connector to the back of the CD-ROM drive.

Step 6

Attach the MCP2/MCP2 cable to the back of the CD-ROM drive, as shown in the illustration. Plug the other end into either the built-in CD_IN port on the motherboard or your audio card.

Step 7

Reboot your computer and make sure that the CD-ROM drive is visible during the system's bootup routine. If you don't see your CD-ROM drive, check the BIOS. If the drive is not visible in BIOS, then go over the previous steps and make sure that all of the connectors are plugged in.

```
PhoenixBIOS 4.0 Release 6.0
Copyright 1985-2002 Phoenix Technologies Ltd.




CPU = Pentium 4  1500 MHz
640K System RAM Passed
63M Extended RAM Passed
Mouse initialized
Fixed Disk 0: IDE Hard Drive
ATAPI CD-ROM: IDE CDROM Drive
```

Step 8 Let the system boot to the operating system. If your computer has speakers, insert an audio CD and play the CD using Windows Media Player to verify the installation.

■ Using CD Media

After you have your CD media drive installed, it's time to start enjoying it. CD media have a number of capabilities and functions that aren't obvious when you first learn about them. In this section, we look at a number of aspects of CD media drive use.

Audio Files Versus Audio Tracks

One area that tends to confuse people greatly is sound: in particular, the difference between audio files and audio tracks. Most digital music is stored on your hard drive in sound file formats such as WAV, MP3, and WMA. Each of these files contains a single song. MP3 and WMA are special compressed formats, and WAV files are uncompressed. These audio files look like any other file on your hard drive. Audio tracks, however, are not files. They are the raw digital data that is designed to be read by audio CD players.

When you put audio files on a CD, you must decide whether you want to store them as data files or convert them to audio tracks. If you want to play these sounds on a standard audio CD player, you need to convert them to audio tracks (don't worry; this process is pretty much automatic today). If you store them as files on a data CD, you'll be able to play these CDs only on a PC or a special device such as an MP3 player.

In Chapter 13, you'll learn about the various file formats and special drivers called *codecs* that convert compressed files into an uncompressed format. You may want to take a trip to your local audio store and see what types of players can play audio CDs and which can play data CDs—you may be surprised to see that most modern players support both!

Mixed-mode CDs store both audio and data. They are fairly rare because many older audio CD players get very unhappy when such discs are inserted in them. Avoid mixed-mode CDs whenever possible.

Autoplay

The folks who make installation CDs long suffered from a problem: How do you get people to start the right program or programs after they insert an

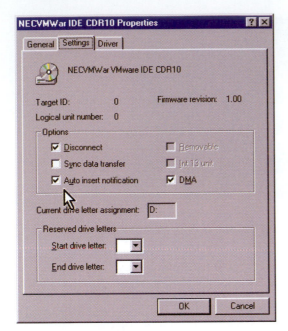

• Auto Insert Notification option in Windows 98 drive properties

• CD Player

• Autoplay in action on Windows XP

installation CD? It's a bit ambitious to expect less-than-experienced users to understand that they have to open My Computer, access the CD, and then start a certain program to begin installation, install a driver, or upgrade software. To make life easier, Microsoft introduced the concept of **autoplay** (also known as Auto Insert Notification) with Windows 95.

Autoplay works very differently in Windows 98 than it does in Windows XP, so we'll look at both scenarios.

Autoplay in Windows 98

Autoplay in Windows 98 is a fairly simple tool. When a CD is inserted, Windows looks for a special file called AUTORUN.INF on the CD. AUTORUN.INF includes a command that tells Windows what program to start automatically. On most installation CDs, the AUTORUN.INF file starts a menu program that shows the user all that the CD has to offer at once.

In most cases, autoplay is a convenient, handy tool, but there are times when it can get in the way. For example, I like to play a computer game called Age of Empires (the Conqueror's Expansion Pack *rocks!*), but to play, I must have the original CD in the CD-ROM drive. The problem is that every time I insert the CD-ROM, autoplay kicks in, asking me if I want to install. The solution to this little problem is easy: turn off autoplay.

Turning off the autoplay feature in Windows 98 requires a few clicks. First, alternate-click (right-click) on My Computer and select Properties to open the System applet. Click the Device Manager tab, select the CD media drive, and open Properties. Select the Settings tab and you'll see a check box for Auto Insert Notification. Uncheck it to turn autoplay off—in the future, you can check it again to turn autoplay back on.

Autoplay also works for audio CDs. In Windows 98, the built-in CD Player tool starts a CD automatically. If you have the MPC cable installed, you'll hear the CD play.

Autoplay in Windows XP

Windows XP takes the concept of autoplay to a new level. If you insert a CD that contains an AUTORUN.INF file, Windows XP runs the autoplay program just like Windows 98 does. If you insert a data CD without an AUTORUN.INF file, Windows XP automatically opens an Explorer window showing the contents of the CD. If XP detects any other type of disc in the drive, it opens a dialog box that lists the programs on the PC that can run that type of disc, and you can choose which program to use. You can also select a program to run automatically when you insert discs in the future.

To turn off autoplay on a Windows XP system, open up My Computer, alternate-click the CD media drive, and select Properties. Click the AutoPlay tab to display a dialog box similar to the one you saw for Windows 98. Choose the type of file you're working with. This is also the place to go if you choose a particular program to run automatically but then change your mind.

Introduction to PC Hardware and Troubleshooting

• AutoPlay tab in Windows XP

Autoplay, especially the ultrapowerful autoplay that comes with Windows XP, makes playing your CD media easy—just put the CD in the drive and enjoy! But what do you do when you want to make your own CDs? That's when you turn to your burning software.

Burning CDs

Before Windows XP, burning CD-Rs and CD-RWs seemed to require almost a kind of black magic. You needed a third-party utility—the burning software—which you used to perform some mysterious functions to turn a blank CD-R or CD-RW disc into a data or audio CD.

Windows XP comes with built-in burning functions, making additional applications unnecessary unless you need more advanced features. If you don't have Windows XP, though, you still need a burning program. We'll explore how to create audio and data CDs in both ways: using a third-party burning tool (with Ahead's Nero for demonstration), and using the built-in burning capabilities of Windows XP.

Before you dive into CD burning, make sure that you understand the types of CDs that you can burn, as well as some of the interesting burning strategies you can use to make CDs. You'll normally create basically three types of CDs: audio CDs, data CDs, and mixed mode (audio and data) CDs.

To recap, audio CDs consist of music or other sound stored in individual tracks. Audio CDs are the ones everyone plays in their home stereo systems and cars. Data CDs store files just like a hard drive does.

CD-to-CD copies are just what they sound like: complete direct copies of one CD to another. You don't have to have a second CD media drive to make copies, but the process is faster if you do. If you have a second CD drive, you can place the original in one drive and copy directly to the other. If you have

Inside Information

CD Images

Disk images are something used quite often in the CD burning world. A CD image, more commonly known as an ISO image, is a complete CD stored as a single massive file on your hard drive. It is common practice to use your burning software to create an ISO image and then use that ISO image to make multiple copies of an audio or data CD. However, Windows XP currently does not support the creation or burning of ISO images—which is one reason many people with Windows XP still use third-party burning programs.

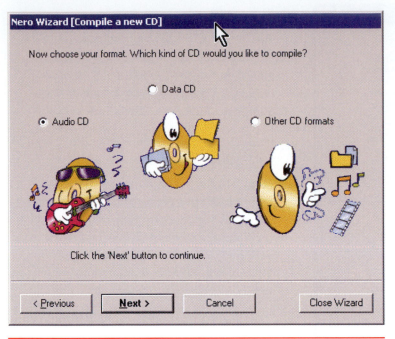

• Nero wizard in action

only one drive, the burning software will usually create an ISO image of the original, prompt you to switch media, and then burn the copy.

Working with Ahead's Nero

There's a reason that Nero is such a popular CD burning program: it's so darned easy to use! Nero comes with all kinds of advanced tools, but by default it starts in a very handy wizard mode that guides you through the process of creating any kind of CD you want. When you start Nero, the wizard pops up, asking you if you want to copy a CD or compile your own CD.

If you opt to compile a new CD, the wizard will ask what type of CD you want to make. Let's say you want to create an audio CD. The wizard will display two windows: a file browser for your system and a compilation window that enables you to drag in sound files. These sound files are automatically converted to sound tracks as you drag them into the compilation window. Once you've chosen the songs you want to burn, click the Burn button, and the program will burn the songs for you.

Working with Windows XP

Windows XP includes the burning interface directly in Windows Explorer, so you don't even need to start any kind of program to burn a CD. Just drag the files you want to burn into the CD's window and click *Write These Files to CD* to open the CD Writing wizard.

• CD Writing wizard in Windows XP

Introduction to PC Hardware and Troubleshooting

If you copy sound files to the CD, Windows XP asks if you want to burn them as audio files or as data files.

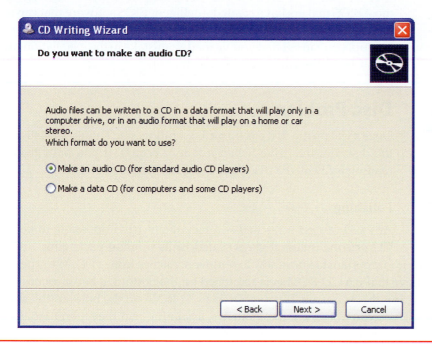

- Windows XP prompting you to specify audio or data files

Windows XP makes the burning experience simple by eliminating the need for a separate program and enabling you to drag and drop files onto the CD drive. This ease of use, however, comes at the cost of certain handy features and tools that come with the third-party burner programs, such as direct CD-to-CD copying and ISO image features. Many people who burn lots of CDs prefer to purchase a CD burning program, even though they have Windows XP, to take advantage of these enhanced capabilities.

■ CD Media Troubleshooting

In general, a CD media drive is an amazingly reliable piece of equipment. CD-ROM, CD-R, and CD-RW are mature technologies, so the odds that your CD drive will fail are small. CD media problems generally fall into one of two categories: drive problems or (far more commonly) disc problems.

Drive Problems

The single biggest problem with CD media drives, especially in new installations, is the connections. Your first clue that a drive isn't installed properly will be that the drive does not appear in My Computer. A few of the more common problems are an unplugged power connector, a cable that has been inserted backward, and misconfiguration of jumpers or switches. The test for an improper physical connection is always the same: using the BIOS or your operating system's device drivers, check whether the system can see the CD media drive.

How the BIOS detects a CD media drive depends on the system. Most CD media drives used today are the ATAPI type. Knowing this, most BIOS makers have created intelligent BIOS software that can see an installed CD media drive. If the CD-ROM drive fails to appear at bootup, you can bet that you've made a mistake in the installation process. Check everything and try again.

Disc Problems

Once a CD media drive is up and operating, you should first suspect the disc, not the drive, when a failure occurs. If you have trouble reading a CD media disc, here are a few issues to consider.

Polishing

● **Figure 9.10** CD polishing device in action

Any CD can get scratched—in fact, it's nearly impossible to keep a CD pristine unless it stays sealed in its original packaging. This is why it's important to know how to remove scratches from a CD. Many people believe that if a CD-ROM gets scratched on the bottom, it becomes unreadable, but this is untrue. If you scratch a CD-ROM on the bottom (the shiny side), you can polish out the scratches, assuming that they aren't too deep, and then read the CD. A number of companies sell inexpensive CD-ROM polishing kits (Figure 9.10).

Scratches on the top of a disc can wreak havoc on CD-ROMs because that's where the pits and lands actually reside on the disc. Avoid writing on the top of a CD with anything other than a soft-tipped pen—and certainly don't scratch the top!

● CD-RW disc showing the multiplier

Burn Speeds

One of the major causes of burn failure is mismatched burn speeds between the CD drive and the CD media. Most good-quality CD media are designed to be read at a certain multiplier speed, which is clearly advertised on the media itself. CD-R and CD-RW discs are also designed to burn at a certain speed. The problem occurs when you try to burn a CD-R or CD-RW disc

---

 Try This!

Repairing a Compact Disc

Every tech should have access to a CD polishing kit and be familiar with its operation. Try this:

1. If possible, obtain a CD polishing kit from a computer store. Otherwise, use a kit provided by your instructor.

2. Take a disc *that you don't mind potentially ruining* and make light scratches on the bottom of the CD. Be sure not to scratch too heavily; just try to replicate everyday wear and tear. If the disc is already lightly scratched, that's even better.

3. Use the CD polishing kit. Follow the instructions provided exactly.

with a lower multiplier using a CD media drive with a higher multiplier. The resulting burns usually create discs that are unreadable and useless— except as drink coasters. Although some failed burns are due to disc quality (we'll discuss quality issues next), usually they're due to mismatched multipliers. To prevent bad burns, all third-party burning programs allow adjustment of the burn speed to accommodate slower CD media.

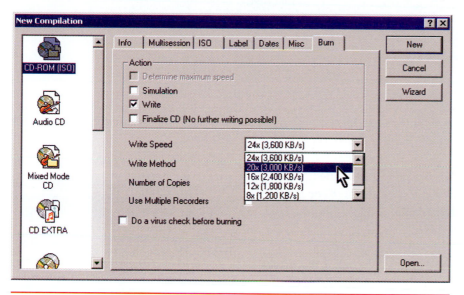

• Burn multiplier adjustment in Nero

Quality Issues

The best recommendation in choosing CDs is to find a brand you like and stick with it. Two factors contribute to media quality: media speed and ink. Media makers often have two product lines: a high-quality line, which is guaranteed to work at a certain speed, and a generic line, where you take your chances. As a rule, I buy both—I primarily use cheap discs but always have a stash 5 to 10 good-quality discs in case I run into a problem.

CD-R and CD-RW discs use various organic inks as part of the burning process. Some techs love to talk about which color gives the best results. Ignore them—the color by itself guarantees nothing as far as results go. Instead, try a few different brands of discs when you first get your drive to determine what works best for you.

Firmware

Almost all CD media drives have an upgradeable flash ROM chip that carries essential BIOS for the drive. If you run into problems reading certain media, check the manufacturer's website for updated *firmware* (the BIOS programs written on ROM chips, remember?). It is a common practice to upgrade the flash chip to increase the capabilities of a CD media drive or to fix problems with the drive.

Step-by-Step 9.2

Breaking Your CD-ROM Drive

So far, everything in this chapter has taught you how to take care of your CD-ROM drive. Now, at the end of the chapter, you're going to see what your CD-ROM drive looks like when it no longer works.

    To complete this exercise, you will need the following:

- A working computer with a CD-ROM drive installed
- An antistatic wrist strap
- A Phillips-head screwdriver

Step 1   If your computer is running, shut it down. Open your computer case to expose the case interior. Be sure that you are wearing your antistatic wrist strap and that you observe all of the safety rules discussed in earlier chapters of this book.

Step 2   Reach into the case and unplug the CD-ROM drive's Molex power connector. Keep the IDE cable and audio cable plugged into the back of the CD-ROM drive.

```
PhoenixBIOS 4.0 Release 6.0
Copyright 1985-2002 Phoenix Technologies Ltd.



CPU = Pentium 4  1500 MHz
640K System RAM Passed
63M Extended RAM Passed
Mouse initialized
Fixed Disk 0: IDE Hard Drive
```

Step 3   Reboot your computer. Watch for the drives to be listed after the memory check during the bootup routine. Does the CD-ROM drive appear?

Step 4   Power down your computer and plug the Molex power connector into the CD-ROM drive. Unplug the audio cable from the back of the CD-ROM drive.

Step 5   Reboot your computer and watch the BIOS after the memory check. Does the CD-ROM drive show up during the BIOS check? Surprised? Let the system boot to the operating system.

Step 6   Assuming that your system has speakers or headphones and a sound card installed, insert an audio CD in your CD-ROM drive and play it using Windows Media Player or some other media player. Do you hear any sound? Data on a CD-ROM can still be accessed without the audio cable. The audio cable is there only to enable you to use your CD-ROM drive as an audio CD player through your sound card.

Step 7   Unplug your speaker or headphone cord from the sound card and plug it into the headphone jack on the front of the CD player. Play the audio CD. Are you hearing music? A CD-ROM is still capable of playing music through the headphone jack on the front of the CD-ROM player. The volume knob adjusts the volume on the CD-ROM drive only. It does not affect anything passing through the sound card.

Step 8   Shut down your computer. With the computer turned off, reattach the audio cable to the back of the CD-ROM drive. Take care not to accidentally loosen any of the other cables in the box.

Chapter 9 Review

■ Chapter Summary

After reading this chapter and completing the exercises, you should understand the following facts about CD media.

Identify the various types of CD technologies

- All CD media can be categorized as either audio CDs or data CDs. Audio CDs were developed in the early 1980s as a replacement for vinyl records. Their format has not changed since they were invented.

- Audio CDs normally store up to 74 minutes of sound on separate tracks.

- Data CDs have gone through many versions, but the predominant version used today is the ISO9660, or more commonly, the CD-ROM or data CD.

- A standard CD-ROM stores up to 650 MB of data.

- All CD media have a read speed based on a multiple of the original 150 Kbps read speed of the first CD-ROMs.

- CD-R discs can be burned, but you can't change the data burned on them. CD-R drives have two speeds: a read speed and a write speed.

- CD-RW discs can be written and erased many times over. CD-RW drives have three speeds: a read speed, a write speed, and a rewrite speed.

- Although CD-R drives are no longer made, CD-R discs are still commonly used in CD-RW drives.

- Both CD-R and CD-RW media come in 74-minute, 650 MB versions and 80-minute, 700 MB versions. Your CD-RW drive must be able to support the larger discs if you want to use them.

- The process of placing data on a CD-R or CD-RW disc is called burning. The term *burning* is appropriate because the writing laser heats up the surface of the CD.

- Before Windows XP, a third-party burning program was needed to burn CDs. Windows XP comes with built-in burning software.

- DVD is a very popular standard for video, but it has not yet had much impact on data storage because there are many competing standards.

Install a CD media drive in a Windows PC

- Almost all internal CD media drives are ATAPI drives that install just like a hard drive.

- ATAPI drives have master, slave, and cable select settings.

- CD media drives are typically placed on the secondary EIDE controller in single–hard drive systems.

- To play music through your sound card, you must install the audio cable. These cables come in three types: universal audio, MPC2/SoundBlaster, and MPC2/MPC2.

- All CD media drives need a power connection.

- You should never have to install a driver for a CD media drive in Windows, as all Windows operating systems have built-in CD media support.

- CD-ROMs do not need any special application to run. The contents of the CD-ROM simply appear in My Computer.

- CD-R and CD-RW drives require a burning program. You can get third-party programs, or if you have Windows XP, you can use the built-in burning program.

Use and maintain a CD media drive in a Windows PC

- Windows' ability to detect and respond to the presence of an inserted CD disc is called autoplay, or Auto Insert Notification.

- Most CD burning programs can create an ISO image—the entire contents of a CD packed into one huge file. You can use an ISO image to make many copies of the same CD.

- You can also make direct CD-to-CD copies. This works best when your system has both a CD-ROM drive and a CD-RW drive.

Troubleshoot basic CD media problems

- The biggest single problem for CD media drives is incorrect installation. If a newly installed CD drive fails to work, verify your installation to see if an error was made.

- Many CD-ROM drives have built-in firmware that can be updated. These updates enable that drive to work with newer operating systems and clear up any possible issues with the drive.

- If you have any problems accessing a CD, be sure to check the CD for scratches or damage first. Then check the connections of the CD-ROM drive.

- Watch the burn speed when making your own CDs. CD media are usually rated for a certain burn speed, so make sure that the speed of the CD matches that of your CD drive. If the CD does not show the speed, check the box that the CD came in—or just try the CD and see if it works.

■ Key Terms

autoplay *(256)*

burning *(244)*

CD audio *(241)*

CD Digital Audio (CDDA) *(241)*

CD media *(240)*

CD-R *(244)*

CD-ROM *(240)*

CD-RW *(246)*

compact disc (CD) *(240)*

DVD *(247)*

ISO9660 *(241)*

MPC2/MPC2 cable *(249)*

multiplier *(243)*

read speed *(245)*

rewrite speed *(246)*

universal audio cable *(249)*

write speed *(245)*

writing laser *(244)*

■ Key Term Quiz

Use terms from the Key Terms list to complete the following sentences. Not all terms will be used.

1. The type of drive that can access CD-ROM discs and write only once to a disc is called a/an _____ drive.

2. A/An _____ drive can write and erase data from the corresponding CD media, using the CD like a floppy disk.

3. The rate at which a CD-ROM drive can access information on the CD media is called the drive's _____.

4. Writing information to a CD with a laser is called _____.

5. The _____ is quickly replacing videotape as the most common medium for movies.

6. Data CDs are formatted according to the _____ standard.

7. The _____ is a speed rating based on a multiple of the original CD speed standard.

8. The _____ is the audio cable most prevalent in today's computers.

9. The _____ etches through the organic ink on a CD-R or CD-RW disc, creating marks that mimic the pits and lands found on a CD-ROM disc.

10. Audio CDs store data under the _____ standard.

■ Multiple-Choice Quiz

1. Which two companies developed the CD media standard in the early 1980s?
   a. Panasonic and Magnavox
   b. Philips and Sony
   c. Sony and Microsoft
   d. Panasonic and Philips

2. How much information can the highest-capacity CD-R discs hold?
   a. 650 MB
   b. 700 MB
   c. 750 MB
   d. 800 MB

3. How many minutes of sound can a standard audio CD hold?
   a. 650 minutes
   b. 43 minutes
   c. 74 minutes
   d. 300 minutes

4. Which of the following is a legitimate multiplier value for CD media?

   a. 8.3x

   b. 400x

   c. .16x

   d. 32x

5. What kind of drive might be described as 12 x 10 x 32?

   a. CD-ROM

   b. CD-R

   c. CD-RW

   d. DVD

6. At what speed does a CD-ROM 1x drive transfer data?

   a. 600 KBps

   b. 450 KBps

   c. 300 KBps

   d. 150 KBps

7. What kind of CD-ROM audio cable is specifically designed to handle a connection between a CD-ROM drive and an older Creative Labs sound card?

   a. Universal audio cable

   b. MPC2/SoundBlaster cable

   c. MPC2/MPC2

   d. IDE cable

8. Internal CD-ROM drives are connected to the motherboard via which port?

   a. IDE

   b. USB

   c. Parallel

   d. PCI

9. Which version of Windows comes with built-in burning functions?

   a. Windows NT

   b. Windows 98

   c. Windows 2000

   d. Windows XP

10. What information is contained in the AUTORUN.INF file?

    a. CD drive letter

    b. Boot information

    c. Instructions to run a certain program automatically

    d. Capacity of the CD-ROM

11. What might you do to eliminate scratches from the surface of a CD?

    a. Wipe the CD with bleach.

    b. Use a polishing kit.

    c. Place the CD in the dishwasher.

    d. Use a pencil eraser.

12. You install a CD-RW drive and discover that it is not working properly with your operating system. What could you do to solve this problem?

    a. Update the firmware.

    b. Replace the CD-RW drive.

    c. Reverse the IDE cables.

    d. Reinstall the CD-RW drive.

13. Which organic ink color provides the best write for a CD-R?

    a. Blue

    b. Green

    c. Gold

    d. The ink color doesn't matter.

14. How can you quickly tell that a system has recognized your CD-ROM drive after installation?

    a. Watch the BIOS check at bootup.

    b. Boot to the operating system from the CD-ROM drive.

    c. Select Safe Mode when booting to Windows.

    d. You cannot tell until you are in the operating system.

15. What is an ISO image?

    a. The complete contents of a CD stored as a file

    b. The directory of all the tracks on a CD

    c. The file format used on a CD-ROM

    d. Microsoft's version of the ISO9660 format

Essay Quiz

1. Your boss just told you to purchase 250 MB external SCSI Zip drives as backup tools for users. You know that you can get CD-RW drives at roughly the same price as the Zip drives. Zip 250 disks cost about $12 each, whereas CD-RW discs cost less than a dollar each. Write a memo to your boss to convince her that you should instead purchase CD-RW drives. Consider the installation of the drives, the size of the media, the costs involved in purchasing Zip drives versus CD-RW drives, and any other factors you find worth mentioning.

2. You have been tasked with purchasing 50 desktop and 25 laptop systems for your company. Both the desktop systems and the laptops you are considering come with CD-ROM drives as standard equipment. CD-RW and DVD drives are offered as options at extra cost. You allowed each user of the new systems to order his or her own custom system, and almost everyone ordered both the CD-RW and the DVD drives, sending you over your budget. Write a letter to the users explaining that only users with valid reasons may have one or both of the add-on options. Give them some factors they should consider when deciding which of the two drive options they want. Also create a sample response letter from a user who will be getting a laptop.

3. A fellow IT tech e-mails you for advice on how to handle a request for assistance from the publishing department. This department has a dedicated PC that it uses to burn CDs for shipment to the printer, and the staff members are having trouble producing good copies of the files on the hard drive. They have a brand-new CD-RW drive and a value-pack of name-brand CD-RW discs they got at a discount warehouse, which they are repeatedly turning into coasters. Write a response reviewing the possible reasons for their problem and suggesting troubleshooting steps. Be sure to include all of the possibilities that the tech should consider, not just the ones you feel are most likely.

4. Your brother, knowing that you're now a computer tech whiz, e-mails you asking for help with his new computer game on his new Windows XP computer. He explains that when he installed it, he could get right into it and play the first time, but now every time he inserts the CD-ROM to try to play the game again, it seems to want him to reinstall. He has reinstalled twice now and is getting pretty tired of it! He wants to know whether he has a defective CD that he should return to the store, or whether something else is wrong and, if so, how to fix it. Compose a reply that explains the autorun feature to him, discussing why it's actually a good thing most of the time, and then detail how he can turn the feature off so he can go right to his game when he wants to.

5. Your mother has a computer with a basic CD-ROM drive. She wants to be able to burn CDs, both as part of her weekly backup procedure and to carry documents back and forth between home and her office so she can edit them in both places and always have the most recent copy with her. She went to the computer store and saw that it had both CD-RW drives and DVD-RAM drives for sale. The clerk told her she should get the much more expensive DVD-RAM drive because then she can burn DVDs, but she wants your opinion before she buys. Write a note to your mother explaining the differences between the two types of drives and the two types of media. Tell her what you recommend she get, and why.

Lab Projects

• Lab Project 9.1

Every computer in your company has a CD-RW drive installed. Up to this point, you have allowed users to make their own purchases of CD media, but your boss has asked you to reduce the cost of CD media by at least 20 percent. You've noticed that everyone seems to be purchasing the same name brand of CD-RW discs at around a dollar each. CD-R discs are around 25 cents each, but no one uses those; only the more expensive CD-RWs are being purchased. You begin to do a study of what the CD-RWs are used for by department and come up with the following facts:

Accounting uses about 50 CD-RWs every week for personal backups. This department keeps a copy of every backup created for a year. Accounting also uses roughly 120 CD-RWs every quarter to back up quarterly data.

The sales department uses 250 CD-RWs a month to back up sales information on each customer. Each customer's data (never more than 75 MB) is stored on an individual CD-RW. These CD-RWs are stored in a large file cabinet, sorted by customer.

The shipping department uses about 50 CD-RWs each month to archive all deliveries to all customers. This information is stored for a year and then discarded.

1 Create a table that analyzes the monthly CD-RW usage for the company. This table should have the departments as columns and the usage as rows. Look at the way discs are being used and create rows with names like "Reusable" and "Archival." Add Total columns at the end of the table to determine total usage.

2 Using your table as a guide, consider the ways that the CD-RWs are used and come up with a plan to reduce CD-RW usage by using CD-Rs when possible or by using CD-RWs more efficiently. Using your recommendations, calculate the total savings to the company each month.

• Lab Project 9.2

You've been asked to install a second CD media drive in a customer's system. For this lab, you will need a Windows 98 or XP system with a CD media drive installed, plus an extra CD media drive.

1 Shut down the system and inspect the installation of the existing CD media drive.

   a. Is the CD drive on the primary or secondary EIDE controller?

   b. Is the CD drive set as master or slave?

   c. Based on what you see on the system, what options do you have for installing the second CD media drive? Primary slave? Secondary master? Secondary slave?

2 Once you have decided on an installation option, install the CD media drive. Boot the system and verify that the new CD drive is visible in My Computer.

3 Remove the drive and try one of the other installation options. Boot the system again and verify that the CD drive shows up in My Computer.

SCSI

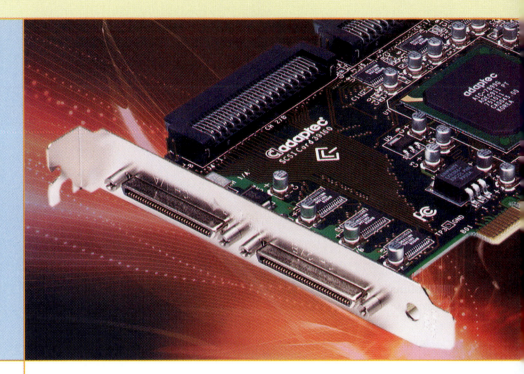

"It works better if you plug it in."

—SATTINGER'S LAW

In this chapter, you will learn how to:

- **Describe the major SCSI components**
- **Identify the different flavors of SCSI**
- **Install SCSI devices on a Windows PC**
- **Perform basic troubleshooting of a SCSI implementation**

The small computer system interface, better known as SCSI, can best be described as a private expansion bus of devices used by your PC. These devices are connected to each other in a process called daisy-chaining. Any type of device can be built as a SCSI device, but SCSI is most often used with storage devices such as hard drives and CD-ROM drives. Other common types of SCSI devices include tape backup units, removable hard drives, and scanners.

So what is SCSI? SCSI is a standard that describes how to make devices that work together. The term SCSI covers a large number of hardware and software standards that have evolved dramatically since SCSI first appeared on the scene. We begin this chapter with a look at how SCSI works. Then we branch out and take a tour of the many types of SCSI standards—these different standards are also known as flavors—to see how they differ and how they're alike. Then we grab some SCSI equipment and go through the process of making SCSI devices work on a Windows XP system. Finally, we look at some basic troubleshooting issues that are unique to SCSI.

■ Major SCSI Components

There are many standards for SCSI devices, but in this section, we concentrate on the one that's most common today: Wide SCSI-2. If you took a trip to the computer store today, most of the SCSI equipment you'd find would be Wide SCSI-2. You'll learn SCSI using Wide SCSI-2 and then go back and learn about the different flavors of SCSI. Let's get started!

SCSI Chains and Host Adapters

SCSI devices are **daisy-chained** to form a string of interlinked devices called a **SCSI chain**. The SCSI chain connects to the PC through a device called a **host adapter**. Some high-end motherboards come with a SCSI host adapter (Figure 10.1) built into the motherboard, but most SCSI host adapters are PCI cards that you snap to the motherboard. If you want to use SCSI devices, you must have a SCSI host adapter.

● **Figure 10.1**   SCSI host adapter

Look at the sample SCSI host adapter in Figure 10.1. Note that the card has two connections. The first connector, at the left of the figure, is for *external* SCSI devices, or those on the outside of the PC. The second connector, at the top of the figure, is for inside, or *internal*, SCSI connections.

All SCSI devices can be divided into two groups: external and internal. External devices stand alone outside the system unit and are hooked to the external connector of the host adapter. An external device (Figure 10.2) will often have a second connector, which enables another external device to connect to it and make a daisy chain.

> Although SCSI allows for both internal and external devices, you are not required to use both. It is common for SCSI to be used for just internal or just external devices.

Internal SCSI devices are installed inside the PC and connect to the host adapter through the internal connector. Figure 10.3 shows an internal SCSI device, in this case a CD-ROM drive.

Internal devices connect to the host adapter and to each other by attaching to a 68-pin ribbon cable, so they don't need a second connection to daisy-chain. An internal SCSI chain may consist of a single device and a host adapter, or it may consist of many devices—plus the host adapter, of course.

Multiple internal devices can be connected together simply by using a cable with enough connectors. Whereas EIDE cables always come with three connections—one for the controller and two for the drives—SCSI cables come with many different numbers of connectors. A SCSI cable may have only two connectors, or it may have up to 15 connectors.

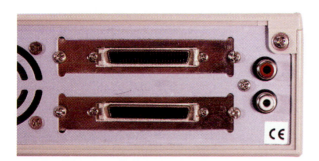

● **Figure 10.2**   Back of external SCSI device showing two connectors

● **Figure 10.3**   Internal SCSI CD-ROM drive

External SCSI devices connect to the host adapter through the host adapter's special SCSI external connection. Be aware that some cheap host adapters do not have external connections, so you cannot put external devices on them.

SCSI IDs

If you're going to connect a number of devices on the same chain of cable, you must provide some way for the host adapter to tell one device from another. To differentiate devices, SCSI uses a unique identifier called the SCSI ID. The SCSI ID number can range from 0 to 15. SCSI IDs are similar to many other PC hardware settings in that a SCSI device can have any SCSI ID, as long as that ID is not already taken by another device connected to the same host adapter.

• **Figure 10.4**   SCSI Zip drive with sliding switch to set SCSI ID

Every SCSI device has some method of setting its SCSI ID. The trick is to figure out how as you're holding the device in your hand. A SCSI device may use jumpers, dip switches, or even tiny dials; every new SCSI device is a new adventure as you try to determine how to set its SCSI ID. Figure 10.4 shows a SCSI Zip drive—note the small sliding switch between the connectors used to set the Zip drive to SCSI ID 5 or 6, typical SCSI hard drive ID jumper settings.

Most internal SCSI devices use four jumpers to set the SCSI ID. Unfortunately, these jumpers work in different ways depending on who made the device, and—lucky you!—you get to figure out the method in each case. To determine how to set jumpers, check the documentation that came with the device or get the documentation from the manufacturer (Figure 10.5 shows an example). In many cases, a device will have a label on one side that clearly shows which jumpers to short for various SCSI IDs. Shorting means placing a tiny plastic and metal piece, called a shunt, over two jumper pins to create an electrical circuit.

> ⚠️ Use caution when installing SCSI devices! Whereas if you plug in an EIDE device wrong, it simply won't work, you can severely damage a SCSI device by plugging it in incorrectly. Be careful and install SCSI devices properly the first time. You'll learn how to install them later in this chapter.

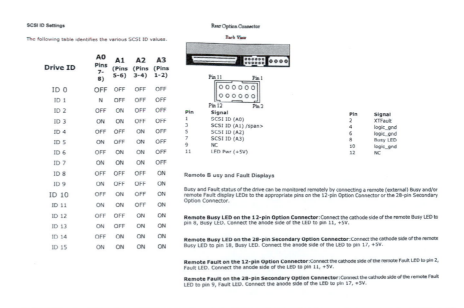

SCSI ID Settings

The following table identifies the various SCSI ID values.

Drive ID	A0 Pins 7-8)	A1 (Pins 5-6)	A2 (Pins 3-4)	A3 (Pins 1-2)
ID 0	OFF	OFF	OFF	OFF
ID 1	N	OFF	OFF	OFF
ID 2	OFF	ON	OFF	OFF
ID 3	ON	ON	OFF	OFF
ID 4	OFF	OFF	ON	OFF
ID 5	ON	OFF	ON	OFF
ID 6	OFF	ON	ON	OFF
ID 7	ON	ON	ON	OFF
ID 8	OFF	OFF	OFF	ON
ID 9	ON	OFF	OFF	ON
ID 10	OFF	ON	OFF	ON
ID 11	ON	ON	OFF	ON
ID 12	OFF	OFF	ON	ON
ID 13	ON	OFF	ON	ON
ID 14	OFF	ON	ON	ON
ID 15	ON	ON	ON	ON

Rear Option Connector
Back View

Pin	Signal		Pin	Signal
1	SCSI ID (A0)		2	XTFault
3	SCSI ID (A1) /span>		4	logic_gnd
5	SCSI ID (A2)		6	logic_gnd
7	SCSI ID (A3)		8	Busy LED
9	NC		10	logic_gnd
11	LED Pwr (+5V)		12	NC

Remote Busy and Fault Displays

Busy and Fault status of the drive can be monitored remotely by connecting a remote (external) Busy and/or remote Fault display LEDs to the appropriate pins on the 12-pin Option Connector or the 28-pin Secondary Option Connector.

Remote Busy LED on the 12-pin Option Connector: Connect the cathode side of the remote Busy LED to pin 8, Busy LED. Connect the anode side of the LED to pin 11, +5V.

Remote Busy LED on the 28-pin Secondary Option Connector: Connect the cathode side of the remote Busy LED to pin 18, Busy LED. Connect the anode side of the LED to pin 17, +5V.

Remote Fault on the 12-pin Option Connector: Connect the cathode side of the remote Fault LED to pin 2, Fault LED. Connect the anode side of the LED to pin 11, +5V.

Remote Fault on the 28-pin Secondary Option Connector: Connect the cathode side of the remote Fault LED to pin 9, Fault LED. Connect the anode side of the LED to pin 17, +5V.

• **Figure 10.5**   Documentation showing jumper settings for SCSI IDs

Not all jumpers on SCSI devices are used for setting the SCSI ID. The hard drive documented in Figure 10.5, for example, has six jumpers, but only the last four jumpers are used to set the SCSI ID.

SCSI IDs must also be configured for external SCSI devices. Many external SCSI devices are actually just SCSI internal devices "in a box." For example, Figure 10.6 shows an external SCSI hard drive that is really just an internal hard drive in a hard plastic enclosure. You still set this drive's SCSI ID by setting jumpers.

Locating the ID setting for true external SCSI devices (as opposed to internal devices in a box) is often easier than for internal devices. The device shown in Figure 10.7 has a handy ID number display with clicker buttons above and below to change the SCSI ID.

Try This!

Use Jumpers to Set a SCSI ID

There's a bit of practical math to these four jumpers. Each jumper is assigned a value: 8, 4, 2, and 1 respectively. As you short each jumper, the device takes that value. For example, if you short the 4 and 2 jumpers, you set the SCSI ID to 6; if you short 8 and 1, the SCSI ID is 9. It really is that straightforward!

Use the following table for this exercise.

Jumper Name	J0	J1	J2	J3
Jumper Value	8	4	2	1

Write down the names of all of the jumpers you would need to short to get the following SCSI IDs:

3 _____   11 _____

5 _____   13 _____

7 _____   15 _____

9 _____

• **Figure 10.6**   This external SCSI device is just an internal device in a box!

• **Figure 10.7**   Setting the SCSI ID on an external device

• **Figure 10.8**   SCSI Zip drive

Finally, not all SCSI devices are designed to use every SCSI ID. For example, the Iomega Zip drive shown in Figure 10.8 can be set only to SCSI ID 5 or 6.

Termination

Whenever you send a signal down a wire, some of that signal reflects back up the wire, creating electronic chaos. This is called *reflection*. SCSI chains are long strings of wire that are vulnerable to reflection. To prevent reflection on SCSI chains, the SCSI standards call for the use of termination. Termination simply means putting devices on the ends of a SCSI chain to prevent this echo. These devices are called **terminators**.

The rule with SCSI is that you *must* terminate *only* the ends of the SCSI chain. Do *not* terminate devices that are not on the ends of the cable, or you'll cut off communication with any devices farther along the cable. Figure 10.9 shows some examples illustrating where to terminate SCSI chains.

Because any SCSI device might be on the end of a chain, most manufacturers build SCSI devices that can self-terminate. Some devices detect when they are on the end of the SCSI chain and automatically terminate themselves. Most devices, however, require you to set a jumper or switch to enable termination.

You can set termination in a number of ways. Figure 10.10 shows two ways that SCSI hard drives can be terminated: one uses a jumper, and the other uses a removable resistor.

Many SCSI hard drives are not capable of terminating themselves, so they need a separate terminator piece.

Be careful when you are terminating! Improper termination can damage SCSI hard drives.

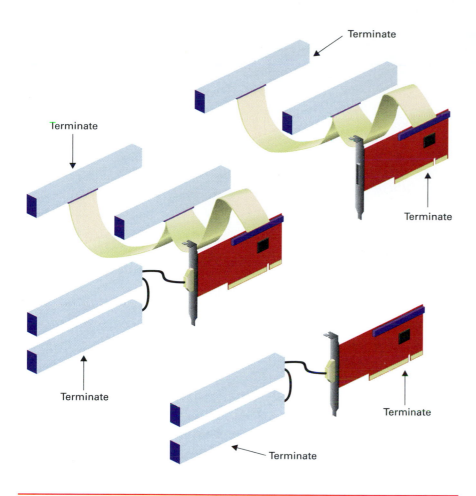

● **Figure 10.9**   Location of terminated devices

● **Figure 10.10**   Setting termination using a jumper (left) and a removable resistor (right)

Working with SCSI Chains

SCSI chains are incredibly flexible, allowing the installation of many devices on a single chain. However, knowing where to place termination may be a bit of a challenge. In this exercise, you'll work with multiple devices to determine where to terminate a SCSI chain.

To complete this exercise, you will need the following:

- Nine 3 x 5-inch index cards
- A dark marker

Step 1

On the top of each card, use the marker to write one of the following terms:

- Host adapter
- Internal drive A
- Internal drive B
- Internal drive C
- External Zip drive A
- External Zip drive B
- External CD-ROM drive
- Terminator
- Terminator

Step 2

Make notations on the cards based on the following parameters:

- The host adapter has an internal and an external connection.
- The host adapter must use SCSI ID 7.
- The Zip drives can use SCSI IDs 5 and 6.
- The CD-ROM drive can use SCSI IDs 4, 5, 6, and 7.
- The internal drives can use SCSI IDs 0 through 15.
- Only the host adapter has built-in termination.

Step 3

Now use the cards to make a model of a SCSI chain, staying within the parameters set forth in Step 2. Place the terminator cards as appropriate and use paper strips, yarn, or some other creative means to represent the cabling. When you have the cards arranged in a workable SCSI chain model, assign SCSI IDs and write them lightly on the cards.

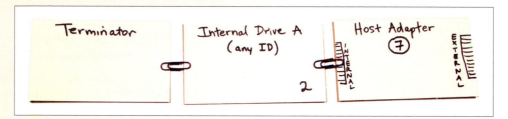

Step 4

Now cross out those SCSI IDs and try to build each of the following chains. Discuss each configuration and verify that it is valid. Be aware that not all of these configurations are possible—make sure you understand why!

1. Make a SCSI chain using two internal drives.
2. Add one external SCSI Zip drive to the chain.
3. Add the CD-ROM drive and remove a hard drive.
4. Add all of the devices.

■ The Different Flavors of SCSI

Any technology that survives more than 20 years must constantly improve or risk being replaced by newer technologies. SCSI has avoided extinction by evolving dramatically since its inception in 1979. SCSI was invented by a company called Shugart Associates, but was given over to the IEEE in the early 1980s. Before that time, there was no single standard of SCSI, so devices made by various manufacturers were rarely, if ever, compatible with one another. This incompatibility came to an end with the first official standard for SCSI, called SCSI-1.

SCSI-1

SCSI was already a mature technology by the time the first SCSI standard was approved in 1986. However, the **SCSI-1** standard did a lot to make devices more interchangeable by defining once and for all standard connections, cable lengths, and signaling characteristics. SCSI-1 was not a complete standard, but compared to what existed before—that is, no standard at all—it was a good start.

SCSI-1 is distinguished by its use of **internal 50-pin connector** cables. The internal device cables looked virtually identical to EIDE cables except they were a bit wider.

External devices used 50-pin Centronics connectors, similar to the ones used on printers but a bit wider. Even though SCSI-1 had 50 wires, only 8 wires (8 bits, or 1 byte) were used to move data. This flavor eventually came to be known as **Narrow SCSI**. The SCSI-1 standard also defined a 25-pin DB connection that was identical to the parallel connection used on the back of PCs.

• 50-pin SCSI cable

• External SCSI-1 cable with a 25-pin DB connector and a 50-pin Centronics connector

SCSI-1 specified a maximum of only eight devices on a single SCSI chain. These devices ran at a 5-MHz clock rate. Given that SCSI-1 was narrow (1 byte), it had a data throughput of 5 MBps.

SCSI-1 had some serious limitations. The biggest single limitation was that although it defined the types of signals (voltage, speed, and so on) that went on the wires, it didn't define what these signals would say. This was similar to inventing a telephone system and then having each person who used it speak a different language. This problem, combined with enhancements in speed and new SCSI technologies, led to a new SCSI standard.

SCSI-2

The **SCSI-2** standard, finalized in 1990 but not officially adopted until 1994, was the first SCSI standard to address every aspect of SCSI in detail. Up until this time, getting two SCSI devices from different manufacturers to work together was challenging and often impossible; this was due not to physical problems, but to the way devices communicated. The SCSI-2 standard solved this problem by defining very carefully exactly what a device could "say" on the SCSI chain.

The SCSI-2 standard also made substantial changes to the cabling and connectors. First, SCSI-2 defined a new type of signaling that moved data in chunks of 2 bytes instead of just 1 byte. This was called **Wide SCSI**, and it called for new devices, new cabling, and new connections. Internal Wide SCSI devices used a 68-pin cable with a new D-shaped **high-density (HD) 68-pin connector**. As odd as it might seem, the new HD 68-pin Wide SCSI connector was physically narrower than the 50-pin Narrow SCSI cable!

The SCSI-2 standard still used the 50-pin ribbon cable for the internal narrow connections, but dumped the big external Centronics connector for a **high-density 50-pin** connection (Figure 10.11).

Not only was SCSI made wider, it was also made faster. The speed doubled from 5 to 10 MHz, creating four versions of SCSI: Slow/Narrow(5 MBps), Fast/Narrow (10 MBps), Slow/Wide (10 MBps), and Fast/Wide (20 MBps). By the time the SCSI-2 standard was completed, no one was making Slow SCSI anymore, so Fast/Narrow and Fast/Wide were the standards that actually appeared on shelves.

During the time that SCSI-2 was working toward adoption, two more versions of Fast SCSI were invented, called **Fast-20** (also called **Ultra**) and

Even though the SCSI-2 standard wasn't adopted until 1994, SCSI manufacturers were already using the entire SCSI-2 standard by 1991. Official SCSI standards always lag far behind the actual adoption of the technologies.

Many manufacturers incorrectly call the Wide 68-pin connector a *SCSI-3 connector*.

Although Centronics cables are rarely seen on modern equipment, they are still used in some SCSI installations. There's even a 68-pin wide Centronics connector that's used on occasion.

Introduction to PC Hardware and Troubleshooting

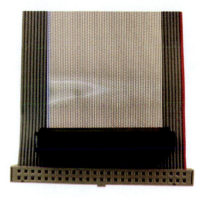

• **Figure 10.11**   50-pin and 68-pin internal SCSI connectors (left), and an external high-density 50-pin connector (right)

Fast-40 (also called **Ultra2**). These two standards also came in Narrow and Wide varieties, making for a rather long list of different types of SCSI. Table 10.1 lists all of the SCSI-2 standards (SCSI-1 has been added for comparison).

Termination wasn't forgotten in SCSI-2. Fast SCSI needed a new type of termination, called **active termination**. Whereas the old termination (called **passive termination**) used little more than tiny resistors, active termination uses more complex circuitry.

• Active and passive SCSI terminators

Table 10.1	SCSI-1 and SCSI-2 Standards			
Version	Name	Speed (MHz)	Width (bytes)	Throughput (MBps)
Slow SCSI-1	None	5	1	5
Fast SCSI-2	Fast SCSI	10	1	10
Fast/Wide SCSI-2	Wide SCSI	10	2	20
Fast-20 SCSI-2	Ultra	20	1	20
Wide/Fast-20 SCSI-2	Wide Ultra	20	2	40
Fast-40 SCSI-2	Ultra2	40	1	40
Wide/Fast-40 SCSI-2	Wide Ultra2	40	2	80

SCSI-3

The **SCSI-3** standard, only recently approved, is incredibly complicated. All of the SCSI cabling and connections you have seen to this point are part of a single technology called Parallel SCSI. The name Parallel SCSI refers to the fact that multiple wires simultaneously send data along the cable. That makes sense because we know that Narrow SCSI is 8 bits wide and Wide SCSI is 16 bits wide—but the new SCSI-3 standard addresses many other types of cabling options. For example, it defines a number of different physical connections for SCSI, including FireWire (which was discussed in Chapter 5) and other technologies such as fiber channel and Serial SCSI. The complete SCSI-3 standard is way outside the scope of this book!

Let's ignore the more advanced SCSI physical options and instead concentrate on the ways Parallel SCSI cabling has improved to fit this standard. First, SCSI-3 does not define any new types of parallel cabling or connectors; we continue to use the cables already discussed in this chapter. However, SCSI-3 speeds up the data throughput substantially by using faster signaling as well as more advanced terminators.

The speed improvements manifest as two new standards: Fast-80 (Ultra160) and Fast-160 (Ultra320). These two new speed standards run at 80 MHz and 160 MHz, respectively, and manage to pack two signals into each clock cycle. Both of these standards come only in Wide versions. Table 10.2 summarizes these standards.

Moving data at these very high speeds requires the use of more powerful terminators, called **low voltage differential (LVD)** terminators. LVD terminators use two wires for each signal, greatly increasing both the speed and the maximum length of the SCSI cables. LVD is the most common termination method used in SCSI chains. LVD terminators are clearly marked as such.

• LVD terminator

Table 10.2	Parallel SCSI-3 Standards			
Version	Name	Speed (MHz)	Width (bytes)	Throughput (MBps)
Fast-80	Ultra160	80	2	160
Fast-160	Ultra320	160	2	320

Mixing Flavors

If all of these different SCSI flavors make your head spin a bit, don't worry—even experienced techs often have trouble keeping all of these standards clear. In any case, SCSI is very tolerant of mixed standards. For example, you can install an Ultra320-capable hard drive on a Fast/Wide SCSI-2 host adapter, and the drive will work just fine, although it will run at the slower speed of the host adapter.

Mixed connectors are also quite common. Consider Narrow SCSI for a moment. There are three types of external connectors: the old Centronics connector, the 25-pin DB connector, and the HD 50-pin connector. In almost all cases, you can use cables with one type of connector on one end and another type on the other.

You can also mix Narrow and Wide SCSI, although your chances of success diminish a bit here. There are plenty of conversion cables on the market to make the physical connection possible—just be prepared for an occasional failure when mixing these technologies.

■ Installing SCSI Devices

SCSI is rarely something you choose to install. More often than not, you install a SCSI device because that's what the device that you want to use happens to be. Fortunately, the steps for installing a SCSI device are pretty straightforward. Just don't be tempted to skip any steps.

Buying a Host Adapter

Folks who are new to SCSI often get a nasty shock when they realize that once they've purchased a SCSI device, they can't use it until they've spent more money to get a host adapter. Some devices do actually come with a cheap but functional host adapter, but usually you need to buy your own. The challenge, then, is deciding which one you need.

The most obvious step is getting a host adapter that uses the right connector. If you're installing a hard drive with a 68-pin HD connector, you need a host adapter with the same connector. If you're installing a tape drive with a 50-pin Narrow connector, make sure that the host adapter has a 50-pin connector, too. Pull the host adapter you're considering out of the box, so you can compare it with the device you're intending to connect to it.

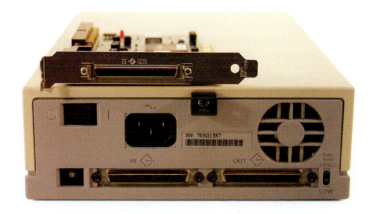

• Comparing a host adapter to a device

Then verify the speed at which the host adapter runs and verify that it will operate at the speed of the device. Check the documentation of both the device and the host adapter. This information is almost always printed on the box—although you may need to look closely!

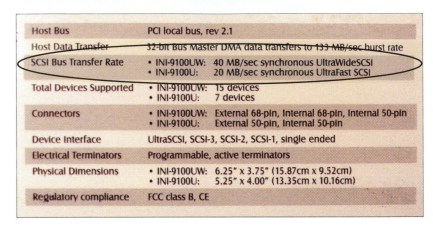

Host Bus	PCI local bus, rev 2.1
Host Data Transfer	32-bit Bus Master DMA data transfers to 133 MB/sec burst rate
SCSI Bus Transfer Rate	• INI-9100UW: 40 MB/sec synchronous UltraWideSCSI • INI-9100U: 20 MB/sec synchronous UltraFast SCSI
Total Devices Supported	• INI-9100UW: 15 devices • INI-9100U: 7 devices
Connectors	• INI-9100UW: External 68-pin, Internal 68-pin, Internal 50-pin • INI-9100U: External 50-pin, Internal 50-pin
Device Interface	UltraSCSI, SCSI-3, SCSI-2, SCSI-1, single ended
Electrical Terminators	Programmable, active terminators
Physical Dimensions	• INI-9100UW: 6.25" x 3.75" (15.87cm x 9.52cm) • INI-9100U: 5.25" x 4.00" (13.35cm x 10.16cm)
Regulatory compliance	FCC class B, CE

• Checking the box to find the speed

Remember that you can always buy a host adapter that runs faster than the device; this may save you money later if you decide to add a faster device.

Finally, make sure that the host adapter has an onboard BIOS, which is basically the same as your motherboard's system BIOS. However, the host adapter's BIOS has special programming just for the host adapter. Almost all host adapters do. The BIOS allows you to perform a number of handy tests without even booting to the operating system. Instead, when your PC boots, you'll see text something like that shown in Figure 10.12.

When you press the appropriate key or key combination, screens that look very similar to system setup screens appear. You'll learn what to do—or more to the point, what *not* to do—in the host adapter setup programs later. For now, just make sure you have a host adapter that includes a BIOS.

Once you have the right connections and the right speed, you'll probably want to make sure that you're not paying for extra features you won't use. Many host adapters are designed to support RAID and other options that the average user doesn't need. There are two ways to tell if the host adapter you need is too fancy: look at the price and look at the connectors. Figure 10.13 shows a typical high-end SCSI host adapter—check out the multiple internal connectors, a sure sign that this adapter is overkill for your needs. You can then look at the price tag: high-end SCSI host adapters usually cost three to four times as much as lower-end cards.

• **Figure 10.12**   Sample BIOS screen

● Figure 10.13   High-end SCSI card

SCSI Cables

Now that you have the right host adapter for your new device, it's time to head over to the SCSI cables. Before you buy a cable, take a moment to look in both the new SCSI device's and the host adapter's boxes. Internal devices usually come with internal cables, and external devices sometimes come with an external cable, so you may not need to make a cable purchase.

If you need to buy an internal cable, don't be afraid to buy one that has multiple connections, even though you may need only one for now. An internal cable with a few extra connectors won't cost much more than a cable with the exact number of connections you need. It's not a problem to have unused connectors on a SCSI chain.

Termination and SCSI IDs

Next, you'll need to check on termination. Although you can buy a separate terminator, almost all SCSI devices, including host adapters, have built-in termination. Take some time to make sure the devices on the end of your chain are terminated.

Your last step is to set the SCSI IDs for both the device and the host adapter. The host adapter will be preset to SCSI ID 7, and no SCSI device maker will ever preset a device to SCSI ID 7—so odds are good that you can ignore the SCSI IDs. However, it's a good idea to check the SCSI settings just to be sure; it will also make changing them easier if you ever add more devices.

With the host adapter, device, and SCSI cable in hand, do a test fitting of all the parts before you place anything inside the PC. Check all the connections as well as the settings—it's just too easy to make a mistake, and it's so much easier to fix problems before everything is bolted into the box.

 If the devices do not self-terminate, you will need to purchase an external terminator. When in doubt, always use an LVD terminator because it will work for SCSI chains that require either a passive or an active terminator.

• Plugging a cable into a SCSI device to make sure it fits

Installation and Host Adapter Settings

It's always best to start by installing the SCSI host adapter by itself, to ensure that the operating system recognizes the host adapter. Once you know that the host adapter is properly installed, you can add your SCSI device. Like most devices, the host adapter will probably come with a device driver CD.

SCSI support is one area where all versions of Windows really shine. In many cases, Windows comes with a driver that will fully support your host adapter. Even so, it's always a good idea to take a quick peek at the manufacturer's website to see if a more up-to-date driver is available.

After the host adapter shows up properly in Windows, restart the system and watch for the screen that enables you to access the SCSI BIOS. You'll need to keep a close eye on your monitor, as these screens are visible only for a moment! When you access the SCSI BIOS, you'll see a screen that gives you some options. Figure 10.14 shows a sample SCSI BIOS screen.

All SCSI BIOS programs have at least four functions. One function, often called Adapter Settings, enables you to set the SCSI ID and the termination for the host adapter. The second setting, often called Show Devices, scans the SCSI chain to see what devices are present. The third setting, Disk Utilities, lets you configure SCSI hard drives. The fourth option, which usually goes by a name like Device Setup, lets you perform special configurations for each device on the SCSI chain. No two SCSI BIOS programs are alike; you need to be patient and take some time to become familiar with your system's program to find these tools.

The names of the BIOS settings used here are in no way universal. Understand the functions, rather than memorizing the names, as the host adapters you encounter may call them something totally different.

Adapter Settings

The Adapter Settings screen is often the only place in the entire SCSI BIOS where you'll need to make changes. This is where you can change the SCSI ID

● **Figure 10.14**   Sample SCSI BIOS screen

of the host adapter and set its termination. In most cases, you should use the Automatic option if it is available. The boot device ID is the SCSI ID of a hard drive you want to boot from. Because even if you install a SCSI hard drive, you're likely to keep one or more EIDE drives in your system as well, you'll normally be booting to your EIDE drive and can ignore this option (unless you remove all of your EIDE drives or do something in the system setup program—see the discussion of EIDE and SCSI that follows). Parity checking is on by default, providing error checking for data on the SCSI chain.

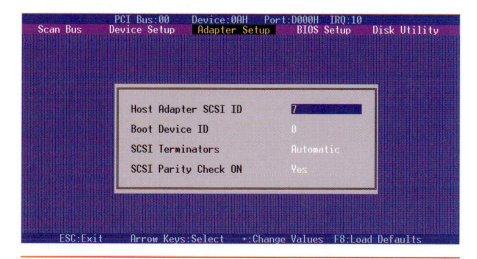

● Adapter Settings screen for a SCSI BIOS

Show Devices

The Show Devices option, also often referred to as Scan Bus, is the handiest tool that comes with the SCSI BIOS. Show Devices scans the SCSI chain and displays the names of all properly configured devices. In many ways, this option can be compared to the Autodetect feature in the system BIOS.

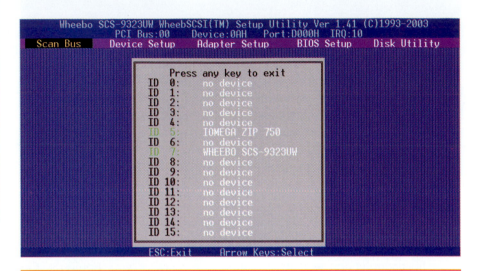

Inside Information

SiSoftware Sandra

Using the SCSI BIOS requires you to reboot your computer. You can save yourself a reboot if you use third-party tools that include the scan function. My personal favorite is SiSoftware Sandra. The professional version scans your host adapter and provides very detailed information about all of the devices on the SCSI chain. Tools like these are standard equipment for people who work with SCSI.

If the Show Devices option lists a SCSI device, you know that the SCSI chain is properly terminated, the SCSI IDs are all unique, and the SCSI device in question has power.

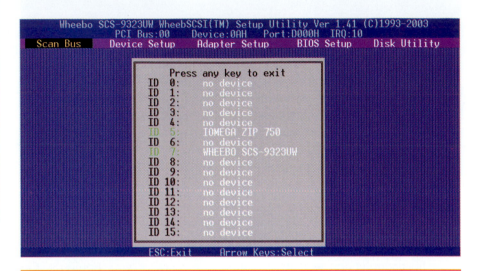

• Show Devices screen for a SCSI BIOS

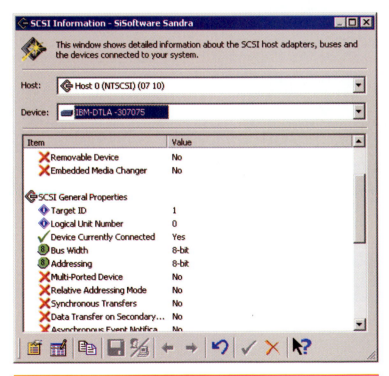

• SiSoftware's Sandra SCSI scan at work (say that five times fast!)

Disk Utilities

The Disk Utilities option is used only for SCSI hard drives, and even then only rarely. The Disk Utilities option provides further options, usually called Verify Disk and Format Disk, or something similar. The Verify Disk option ensures that the disk is ready to receive data; it does not wipe out any data when run. The Format Disk command here is not like the one you learned in the hard disk chapter; rather, this option performs low-level formatting to clean up SCSI drives that may be acting badly, usually when they are first installed. If you perform this low-level formatting, you lose all data on the drive.

Device Setup

Of the four main SCSI BIOS options, Device Setup is the one you are least likely to use. This option provides a single place where you can configure a number of specialized settings for each device on the chain. You'll generally make changes here only when a technical support person tells you to do so.

Introduction to PC Hardware and Troubleshooting

Drivers

Do you remember how one of the biggest problems with SCSI-1 was that the standard didn't include a defined language for the devices to use? Well, SCSI-2 defined that language, and it quickly became apparent that this language would have to be based on classes of devices.

The entire SCSI world of devices is divided into just a few classes, and each class of device uses the same drivers. For example, every SCSI CD-ROM drive needs the same identical drivers. This is nice because you need only a few different drivers to run every SCSI device, and all versions of Windows come with all of them! This means that if you physically install a SCSI device properly, it will always show up in Device Manager.

However, that doesn't mean that the default Windows driver is always the best driver. Most SCSI devices still come with drivers that provide extra functions. The Iomega Zip drive is a great example. If you use the default Windows drivers, you will have a removable drive that works fine, but if you install the enhanced Iomega drivers, you get lots of extra functions such as password protection of the disk.

Remember that when you install a SCSI chain, you'll need at least two drivers: one for the host adapter and one for the SCSI device. Like SCSI devices, Windows systems (especially Windows 2000 and XP) have a broad repertoire of drivers preinstalled, so in many cases a new SCSI host adapter doesn't need a driver disk or CD. Check the documentation to see if you need to install a driver for your version of Windows.

Inside Information

EIDE RAID

A number of drive makers have begun to introduce specialized EIDE RAID controllers. These specialized controllers can support up to eight EIDE drives, making EIDE more practical for RAID than it ever has been before. However, these specialized controllers are very expensive— about the same price as a high-end SCSI controller.

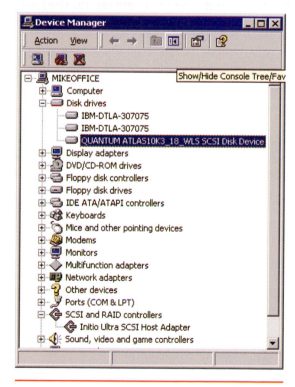

• SCSI device in Device Manager

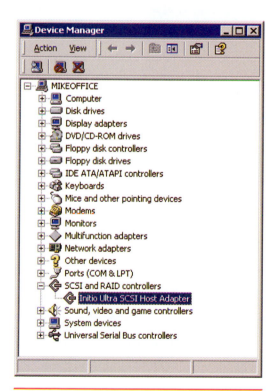

• Properly installed host adapter in Device Manager

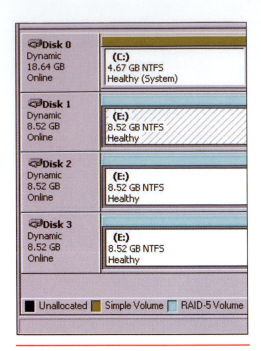

Disk 0
Dynamic
18.64 GB
Online
(C:)
4.67 GB NTFS
Healthy (System)

Disk 1
Dynamic
8.52 GB
Online
(E:)
8.52 GB NTFS
Healthy

Disk 2
Dynamic
8.52 GB
Online
(E:)
8.52 GB NTFS
Healthy

Disk 3
Dynamic
8.52 GB
Online
(E:)
8.52 GB NTFS
Healthy

■ Unallocated ■ Simple Volume □ RAID-5 Volume

● **Figure 10.15**   RAID array on a system

EIDE and SCSI

A standard PC with onboard EIDE will easily support SCSI hard drives. Typically, a system will first try to boot to the EIDE drives; if it can't find any EIDE drives, it will then try the SCSI drives. If the system goes to the SCSI chain to find a primary partition, it will first look at SCSI ID 0.

Some systems have a single EIDE drive that stores the operating system, while the SCSI host adapter has three or more drives (often running as a RAID array) that store critical data. Figure 10.15 shows a detail from the Disk Management program on my file server. This file server is using three SCSI hard drives in a RAID-5 configuration; note how all three drives share the same drive letter. In this case, C:\ is an EIDE drive that stores only the operating system, while all of my important data is saved on the RAID array.

Step-by-Step 10.2

Installing SCSI Devices

The procedure for installing a SCSI device is much like the procedures you've used to install similar non-SCSI devices. The key differences lie in the device configuration, including termination.

To complete this exercise, you will need the following:

- ■ A Windows system
- ■ A SCSI host adapter
- ■ Two internal or two external SCSI devices with all necessary cables and drivers
- ■ Terminators as needed

Step 1   Install the SCSI host adapter and any drivers that are needed. Check Device Manager to verify that the host adapter is working.

Step 2   Install both SCSI devices and install any drivers that are needed. Make sure the two devices show up properly in Device Manager.

Step 3   Shut down the system and remove the termination from one end of the chain. Boot to the SCSI BIOS, run the Show Devices utility, and see if any devices show up. Many SCSI devices have auto-termination, so don't be surprised if they appear.

Step 4   Turn off the termination from the host adapter, reboot, and reenter the SCSI BIOS. Again run the Show Devices utility. Note whether the devices show up now.

Step 5	Reestablish the proper termination. Reboot the system and check Device Manager to verify that all of the SCSI devices are once again functional.
Step 6	Shut down the system and intentionally set the two SCSI devices to share the same SCSI ID. Boot to the SCSI BIOS, run the Show Devices utility, and see if any systems show up. Do you see multiple instances of a single device?

■ Basic SCSI Troubleshooting

Sometimes people who are just starting to work with SCSI think that these devices are going to work differently just because they're SCSI devices. This is just plain wrong! If you install a SCSI hard drive, you will still need to partition and format it to use it. If you have a SCSI CD-ROM drive, it will automatically appear in My Computer just as an EIDE CD-ROM drive will automatically appear. If you have a SCSI tape backup device, it will appear in the Windows Backup program just like any other tape drive.

So when it comes time to test a newly installed SCSI device, you treat it just as you would any other device. If you install a SCSI hard drive, see if you can partition the drive. If you install a removable media drive, see if you can drop in a disk or CD and access it via My Computer.

The vast majority of SCSI problems take place at installation. If a newly installed SCSI device fails to function, the first place you should turn is the Show Devices utility in your SCSI BIOS, where you can see whether you physically installed the device correctly. You'll generally see one of three problems here: no devices show up, only some of the installed devices show up, or there are multiple copies of the same device.

• Multiple copies of the same device reported in the device scan

If multiple copies of the same device appear, you've probably given two devices the same SCSI ID. Carefully double-check all of the devices to find the two that share the same ID. If no devices show up, then you've made a mistake in the termination. If only some of your devices show up, odds are good that either the missing devices don't have power, or you terminated the chain between the host adapter and the missing device.

Chapter 10 Review

■ Chapter Summary

After reading this chapter and completing the exercises, you should understand the following facts about SCSI.

Describe the major SCSI components

- SCSI devices are daisy-chained to form a string of interlinked devices called a SCSI chain.
- SCSI chains connect to the PC through the host adapter.
- SCSI devices are either internal or external.
- Every device on the SCSI chain must have a unique SCSI ID.
- The ends of a SCSI chain must be terminated.

Identify the different flavors of SCSI

- There are three SCSI standards: SCSI-1, SCSI-2, and SCSI-3.
- SCSI-1 devices run at 5 MHz on an 8-bit bus and have a throughput of 5 MBps.
- SCSI-1 devices use a 50-pin internal cable similar to an EIDE cable.
- SCSI-1 defines a maximum of eight devices per SCSI chain.
- SCSI-2 defines two widths: 8-bit Narrow and 16-bit Wide.
- SCSI-3 requires the use of LVD termination.

Install SCSI devices on a Windows PC

- Make sure the host adapter has the proper connections and speed to connect to your SCSI devices.
- Host adapters always default to SCSI ID 7.
- Always test-fit parts to ensure proper connections before installing them into a system.
- Even though Windows almost always has a functional driver for SCSI devices, the manufacturer's driver will usually provide better functionality.

Perform basic troubleshooting of a SCSI implementation

- Most SCSI problems take place during installation.
- The Show Devices option (or an option with a similar name, depending on your SCSI BIOS) is the single best tool for diagnosing SCSI problems.
- If multiple copies of the same device appear in Show Devices, two devices probably have the same SCSI ID.
- If no devices are visible in Show Devices, you probably have not terminated the devices properly.
- If some devices are missing in Show Devices, the missing devices may not be powered, or a terminator may have been set between the missing devices and the host adapter.

■ Key Terms

active termination *(277)*
daisy-chain *(269)*
Fast-20 *(276)*
Fast-40 *(277)*
high-density 50-pin connector *(276)*
high-density 68-pin connector *(276)*
host adapter *(269)*
internal 50-pin connector *(275)*
low voltage differential (LVD) *(278)*
Narrow SCSI *(275)*
passive termination *(277)*
SCSI chain *(269)*
SCSI-1 *(275)*
SCSI-2 *(276)*
SCSI-3 *(278)*
terminator *(272)*
Ultra *(276)*
Ultra2 *(277)*
Wide SCSI *(276)*

Key Term Quiz

Use terms from the Key Terms list to complete the following sentences. Not all terms will be used.

1. Fast-20 is also known as _____ SCSI.

2. All versions of _____ are 8 bits wide.

3. The SCSI chain connects to the PC via the _____.

4. The _____ standard defines Wide SCSI.

5. _____ allows for a maximum of 16 devices on a SCSI chain.

6. There must be a/an _____ at each end of a SCSI chain.

7. Centronics connectors were introduced in the _____ standard.

8. Ultra160 and Ultra320 are part of the _____ standard.

9. SCSI-1 devices use _____ on the ends of the SCSI chain.

10. When in doubt, you should always use _____ termination.

Multiple-Choice Quiz

1. Narrow SCSI allows a maximum of _____ devices on a single SCSI chain.
   a. 4
   b. 8
   c. 16
   d. 255

2. Ultra320 requires _____.
   a. Passive termination
   b. Active termination
   c. CVD termination
   d. LVD termination

3. If a hard drive uses three jumpers to set the SCSI ID, it is almost certainly a/an _____ SCSI drive.
   a. LVD
   b. Wide
   c. Narrow
   d. Active

4. What is the speed for Ultra320 SCSI?
   a. 80 MHz
   b. 4 MHz
   c. 160 MHz
   d. 320 MHz

5. Internal Wide SCSI-2 devices use a _____ cable.
   a. 25-pin
   b. 48-pin
   c. 50-pin
   d. 68-pin

6. SCSI-1 devices run at what speed?
   a. 5 MHz
   b. 5 GHz
   c. 5 Hz
   d. 5 KHz

7. Fast/Wide SCSI-2 has a throughput of _____ MBps.
   a. 10
   b. 20
   c. 40
   d. 80

8. Which of the following SCSI flavors absolutely requires LVD termination?
   a. Fast/Wide SCSI-2
   b. Ultra SCSI
   c. Fast-80 SCSI
   d. Ultra2 SCSI

9. Jane has two SCSI hard drives on her SCSI chain. She installs a third device. When she runs the Show Devices utility in her SCSI BIOS, she sees none of the devices. Which of the following is the most likely reason?

   a. None of the devices have power.

   b. She gave two devices the same SCSI ID.

   c. She didn't set her drive speed correctly.

   d. She didn't terminate the devices properly.

10. John installed a SCSI CD-RW drive in his Windows XP system. After installation, he checks Windows Device Manager and sees that the drive has been installed without any errors. What should he do next?

    a. Check for a better driver on the manufacturer's website.

    b. Nothing—he can now use the drive.

    c. Add any applications that came with the CD-RW drive.

    d. This is impossible; CD-RW drives do not come in SCSI versions.

11. Tammy is installing a new Narrow SCSI hard drive in her system. Of the following, which would be the best SCSI ID to use?

    a. Channel A

    b. 0

    c. 7

    d. 12

12. The _____ standard defines the use of SCSI with nonparallel connections such as FireWire.

    a. SCSI-1

    b. SCSI-2

    c. SCSI-3

    d. SCSI-4

13. A SCSI host adapter most commonly appears _____.

    a. As a PCI card

    b. On the motherboard

    c. As a CNR card

    d. Off the EIDE controller

14. External SCSI devices usually have _____ connections for the SCSI chain.

    a. 1

    b. 2

    c. 4

    d. 8

15. What is the fastest SCSI standard discussed in this chapter?

    a. Ultra2

    b. Ultra4

    c. Ultra320

    d. Ultra640

■ Essay Quiz

1. Half of the systems in your office have single 8 GB SCSI drives. All of the systems with SCSI drives also support EIDE, but there are no EIDE drives in the systems. You want to upgrade all of these systems to 20 GB or larger drives. Go online and compare the cost of SCSI and EIDE drives of the same capacity. Should you go with EIDE or SCSI? Write a memo to your boss giving your recommendation.

2. Your boss has just discovered Zip 750 drives and wants you to install them in 16 systems in the graphics department; eight of these systems already have external Narrow SCSI CD-ROM drives. The boss has found a great deal on bare (no cables or host adapters) external Zip 750 Wide SCSI drives and wants your written opinion on whether the company should take advantage of this deal. Write a memo to your boss with your recommendation regarding whether to get these Zip drives. Give your boss alternatives if you feel that is necessary.

3. Your organization has four file servers. Each file server has four 30-GB Ultra320 SCSI hard drives used in a RAID-5 array. All of the arrays are starting to fill up, and you need to replace the drives. Each server boots to an EIDE drive and also has an EIDE CD-ROM drive. A co-worker has forwarded a memo to your boss suggesting

replacing all of the SCSI drives with EIDE RAID controllers. How would you respond to this employee's idea about replacing the SCSI RAID with the EIDE RAID? In particular, address the issue of cost.

4. You have roughly 100 brand-new Windows XP systems. Not all of the systems are currently functional due to shipping damage. You need to determine how many of them have SCSI host adapters. Describe a host adapter to your employees so they can look for them inside the system units.

5. Your company just took over another company, and you just received a fax from one of your coworkers telling you that she found a large number of hard drives "just lying in a closet" and wants to know if you need them. You need EIDE and Wide SCSI-2 drives badly. You won't be able to talk to her on the phone (you're heading out of town), so write her an e-mail message telling her what to look for to determine whether she has any drives you might need.

Lab Projects

• Lab Project 10.1

Gather any SCSI equipment that you may have handy. If you don't have any SCSI equipment, search the Web for SCSI devices, host adapters, and so on. Write down the connection and speed for these devices on 3 x 5-inch cards and use them instead.

1 Have one person hold up a SCSI host adapter (or a card that describes the SCSI host adapter).

2 Have a second person take a SCSI device (or a card that describes the SCSI device) and stand next to the person holding the host adapter.

Discuss the issues necessary to connect this device to the host adapter:

a. How would they connect?

b. How would you set the SCSI ID?

c. Where and how would you terminate the SCSI chain?

3 Repeat Step 2 with more SCSI devices (or cards) until you run out, or until the chain is full.

• Lab Project 10.2

Start the System Setup utility on a PC and check the boot sequence options to see if they offer a way to boot first to a SCSI device and then to an EIDE device. Do not make any changes to the system setup.

1 Install a SCSI host adapter.

2 Connect a SCSI hard drive to the host adapter. Set it to whatever SCSI ID the host adapter needs to make it a boot device (almost always SCSI ID 0).

3 Make sure the SCSI drive appears in My Computer. Partition and format the SCSI drive if needed.

4 Go back to your System Setup utility and set the system to boot first to the SCSI drive.

5 Document your results.

chapter 11

Video

"Video killed the radio star."

—The Buggles

In this chapter, you will learn how to:

- Select the right monitor for the situation
- Select and install the correct video card
- Install and configure video software
- Troubleshoot typical video problems

The term *video* encompasses a complex interaction among numerous parts of the PC, all designed to put a picture on the screen. The monitor shows you what's going on with your programs and operating system. It's the primary output device for the PC, as discussed in Chapter 1. The video card or display adapter handles all of the communication between the CPU and the monitor. The operating system needs to know how to handle communication between the CPU and the display adapter, which requires drivers specific for each card and proper setup within Windows. Finally, each application needs to be able to interact with the rest of the video system.

The first three sections of this chapter walk you through the selection and setup of the three layers of a computer's video system: the monitor, display adapter, and software, including the operating system and applications. You'll learn how each individual component works and how it's installed and configured. In the final section, you will master the art of troubleshooting the video system of a personal computer.

■ Selecting the Right Monitor

Monitors today come in two basic flavors—CRT and LCD—with lots of variation within those types. Learning to differentiate between a good monitor and a bad monitor of either type is a critical skill for any person who's going to use a monitor. Nothing—and I mean truly nothing—you purchase relating to a PC will last longer than the monitor. Making a poor choice can put you in the unenviable position of either shelling out more cash for a better monitor later, or worse, suffering from excess fatigue, eyestrain, and even *permanent* eye damage if you stick with the poor choice. Good techs don't mess around with this issue, but instead master the jargon, features, and options available and select the right monitor. Let's get you there!

CRTs

When most folks hear the word *monitor*, they picture the traditional, bulky, beige **Cathode Ray Tube (CRT)** displays. Similar in design and function to a television, CRT displays grace the desks of most computer users.

Although the CRT is under assault by the new, skinny, flat-panel monitors (see "LCDs" later in this chapter) for the hearts (and money) of computer consumers, CRTs are so common that all techs need to know a lot about them. Most techs do not work on the insides of CRT monitors, but knowing the technology involved helps you make smart decisions about the quality and features of any particular unit.

How CRTs Work

CRTs have a central vacuum tube (the cathode ray tube) with electron guns at one end and a phosphor-coated screen at the other end. The unit has electronic controls and magnets to help aim and focus everything.

Refresh Rate   When struck by light from the electron guns, the phosphor coating covering the inside of the CRT screen glows briefly and then fades. When struck rapidly enough, however, the dots appear not to fade. The electron guns write the screen according to what the CPU says to do, writing from left to right many times per second, refreshing the dots (officially called phosphors). The number of times that the electron guns can write and then refresh all of the phosphors in a single second is called the **refresh rate**. Refresh rates are measured in **hertz (Hz)**, or cycles per second. The faster the monitor, the faster the refresh rate it can achieve. In the United States, 60 Hz is considered acceptable, whereas the European standard puts the refresh rate minimum at 72 Hz. Most monitors can handle refresh rates as low as 43 Hz and up to around 120 Hz.

The phosphor coating inside the screen of the monitor is arranged in a pattern of red, green, and blue phosphors, each corresponding to a specific electron gun. The blue electron gun, for example, is supposed to strike only the blue phosphors, whereas the red gun is supposed to strike only the red phosphors.

CRT electron guns are *not* super-precision devices, however. Left to themselves, the electron guns would bleed all over colors other than their own. What makes the technology work and still remain affordable is the **shadow mask**.

• Typical CRT

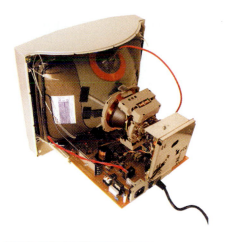

• Inside a CRT

 Most techs do not work on the inside of a CRT monitor for a simple reason: the electricity stored inside can kill you—dead...dead...dead. This electricity stays at lethal levels *even after the CRT is unplugged!* Don't open monitors for any reason. Leave them to the professional monitor techs.

Shadow Mask The blue electron gun does not bleed onto nonblue phosphors because a thin metal grill with tiny holes poked through it, called generically a shadow mask, is anchored in front of the phosphor coating on the monitor. The blue electron gun is angled so that any stray fire hits the grill.

• Shadow mask

> Working on a PC with the refresh rate set too low (<60 Hz) can cause *permanent damage to your eyes*. Note, though, that a refresh rate set too high for the monitor to handle will shorten the life of the monitor.

Dot Pitch In general, the finer the shadow mask, the sharper the picture on the monitor. This fineness is expressed in **dot pitch**. Dot pitch in the traditional sense is the distance, in millimeters, from the center of a dot to the center of the closest same-color dot. A typical monitor has a shadow mask with a dot pitch of 0.25 mm from one red dot to another on the diagonal. Today's CRTs dot pitches range from roughly 0.17 to 0.28. The smaller the dot pitch, the sharper the image.

• Dot pitch

Pixels As the electron gun sweeps across the phosphors on the CRT, the electrons strike groups of red, green, or blue dots in rectangular patterns. Each rectangular grouping is called a **pixel**. The image you see on your monitor is a mosaic of pixels. Pixels are not fixed in size—you can increase or decrease the number of pixels (and therefore their size) on the screen. The number of pixels on the screen at a given moment is called the **resolution**. The higher the resolution, or number of pixels, the smaller the pixels will be, and the higher the picture quality. Figure 11.1 illustrates two pixel configurations for the same screen, one with a low resolution and one with a high resolution. Note that the phosphors remain the same regardless of the pixel size.

The video industry has defined standard resolutions that reflect the 4:3 aspect ratio of the typical CRT. The standard low resolution is 640 pixels wide by 480 rows of pixels, written as 640 x 480. The resolution in a typical work environment is 1,024 pixels wide by 768 rows of pixels, or 1,024 x 768. You'll learn more about resolution when you get into the other parts of the video process later in the chapter.

Introduction to PC Hardware and Troubleshooting

Variation Among CRTs

All CRTs may function similarly on the inside, but an informed tech or consumer knows that CRTs vary from model to model and company to company and include different features. Important variables are monitor size, viewable image size, tube type, and multimedia options.

Monitor Size The size of a monitor is measured in three ways: the size of the screen, measured diagonally; the dimensions of the entire monitor, such as how high it sits and how deep it is; and the actual size of the screen that you can work with, called the viewable image size (VIS). All CRTs are sold by their diagonal measurement.

The standard consumer or home-use monitor has a 17-inch screen, whereas the typical office model has a 19-inch screen. Professional graphics and design folks (and gamers) will often go for even more screen real estate, such as a 21-inch screen.

The trade-off in screen size is that bigger in one way almost invariably means bigger in every other way as well. As a general rule, the diagonal width of the screen equals the depth of the monitor, or at least the amount of space you'll need from the monitor face to the wall if your desk abuts a wall.

Viewable Image Size The **viewable image size (VIS)** is the part of the screen that actually displays pixels. The VIS for CRT-style monitors is substantially less than the diagonal size. A typical 19-inch monitor, for example, has a VIS of less than 18 inches diagonally. All CRTs have a small black rim around the screen that eats up valuable glass space. Although you can adjust the size of this rim, as you'll see in a moment, you'll always lose some screen space to the black rim.

Tube Type Lots of manufacturers make CRT monitors, but only a handful of companies make the CRT—the tube inside the monitor—itself. All CRT tubes can be categorized into one of two types: traditional curved-screen CRTs and CRTs that are often referred to as *perfect flat*—using a new kind of vacuum tube that has a completely flat screen and no bending around the edges. The perfect flat screens offer a wider viewing angle than standard CRT screens. About the only negative to the perfect flat screens is that they tend to lack true black, so pictures seem just shy of a natural richness of color and contrast.

Multimedia Options A lot of monitors are billed as multimedia monitors, offering features such as built-in stereo speakers, microphone, and even a USB hub in the base. Figure 11.2 shows one of these fancy monitors.

For the most part, you'll probably find that the built-in components lack in performance, and you'll want to go with external peripherals. The speakers tend to sound tinny and weak, the microphones catch way too much external noise and deliver poor-quality audio, and the USB hubs are mostly superfluous because most newer PCs come with plenty of USB sockets.

Built-in Controls

Because of the nature of the manufacturing and shipping process and the toll taken by time and use, no monitor is always perfect. Manufacturers know

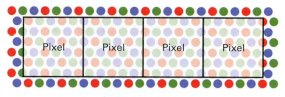

Lower resolution

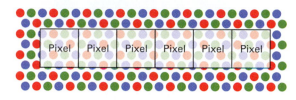

Higher resolution

• **Figure 11.1** High resolution versus low resolution

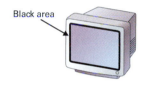

Black area

• Wasted viewing space on a typical CRT

● **Figure 11.2**   Fancy multimedia monitor

● **Figure 11.3**   Front-panel buttons and built-in functions on a CRT monitor

this and so include built-in electronic controls for adjusting both the common display elements—brightness, contrast, color saturation—and the less common—such as pincushioning and keystoning. Pincushioning occurs when the image bulges or shrinks in the middle, making a pincushion shape. Keystoning occurs when the top and the bottom of the image are different sizes, making a keystone shape. There are many other less common display elements that you may be able to adjust.

Figure 11.3 shows front-panel buttons on a typical CRT and the built-in electronic controls displayed on the screen. Not all models work the same way, of course.

Enough discussion! Let's connect a monitor to the system.

Step-by-Step 11.1

Installing and Configuring a CRT

At this point, you're ready to install and configure a CRT monitor. A monitor is not a stand-alone component; you need an installed and fully functional video card and operating system to make the monitor anything more than a big paperweight. As mentioned at the beginning of this chapter, all of the video components must work together.

To complete this exercise, you will need the following:

- Monitor (exercise assumes one new in box)
- PC with properly installed video card and drivers

Step 1

Take a sharp object and gently slice the tape that holds the box flaps together on top of the monitor box. Open the four flaps fully. Fold one of the flaps down so it's flush against the outside of the box. Gently tip the monitor box onto that side, guiding it the entire way. Next, tip the monitor another 90 degrees so the open top of the box faces the ground. Now you can grab the box flaps and lift the box off the monitor.

Introduction to PC Hardware and Troubleshooting

Warning: Many people will reach in and try to pull the monitor up and out of the box. Unless you're very strong, this does not work well—your position is awkward, monitors are heavy for most folks, and you may hurt your back or drop the monitor once you get it out of the case. Don't pull out the monitor this way!

Step 2

Place the monitor on the desk or table and remove the twist-ties from the three-prong power cable and the system cable. If you have extra multimedia cables with your monitor, ignore them for now or turn to Chapter 12 for information on connecting them to the sound card or built-in sound element on the motherboard.

Step 3

Find the three-row DB-15 port on the back of your PC case and orient the system cable connector from the monitor so that the flatter side of the D aligns with the flatter side of the DB-15 on the case. Note that you can't force a monitor cable onto a DB-15 incorrectly; the connector simply won't go in. If you have trouble aligning the connector with the port and the connector does not go on smoothly, rotate the cable end in your hand and try inserting it again.

Step 4

Once you have good connectivity, push gently but firmly to ensure that the connector is seated completely. Connect the retaining screws to the sockets on the video port, screwing them in firmly. Now insert the three-prong power cable into a properly grounded wall outlet and press the power button on the front bezel of the monitor. You should see a small, orange LED light up, indicating good power.

Step 5

When monitors are first installed, most will not provide an optimal display at your preferred settings. Use the built-in controls on the monitor to make adjustments. Push the menu button or equivalent on your monitor to bring up the built-in tools. Select the brightness control and check the setting. Use the left-right arrows or equivalent controls to adjust it. Do the same with the contrast setting.

LCDs

Liquid Crystal Display (LCD) monitors offer PC users an alternative display, one that takes up very little desk space and theoretically takes advantage of the digital nature of the PC. LCDs have taken the PC world by storm and seem poised to replace CRT monitors in the hearts—and on the desktops—of PC users.

Well-informed PC techs need to understand LCD monitors to support the increasing number of such monitors in the workplace and home and to make informed choices for themselves and clients selecting LCD monitors.

This section begins with a brief overview of the technology of LCD monitors and then explores some of the variations among models, connectivity issues, and maintenance and troubleshooting. Let's get to work.

How LCDs Work

LCD monitors combine three essential groups of components to make the display work: the display, a backlight, and control electronics. The display has layers of filters, liquid crystal, and transistors that provide the individual red, green, and blue dots on the screen. The cold fluorescent backlight provides a more or less uniform brightness for the display. Finally, the control electronics do what you would expect, making everything happen properly.

Inside Information

Loose Connections

A loose connection between the monitor and video card can cause the display to degrade spectacularly. This problem can catch the uninformed tech by surprise and lead to some embarrassment. (Not that it's ever happened to me, of course!) When you see skewed colors, distortions, and graininess on a display, always check the connection first before jumping to the conclusion that the monitor or video card is dying.

Fixed Resolution   Each LCD panel has a default, fixed resolution. A typical 15-inch LCD, for example, has a resolution of 1024 x 768. You can make such a monitor emulate other resolutions, with more or less success. Generally, emulated resolutions appear blurred or fuzzy.

Backlight   LCD monitors usually have one or two cold fluorescent lights, called backlights, that provide the brightness for the monitor. The brightness is measured in **nits**, with 100 nits on the low end and 300 or more on the high end.

The potential problem with this technology arises from the nature of light shining through an object. What do you get when you look at a flashlight behind a piece of paper? A bright spot where the center of the beam hits the paper, and then increasing darkness out toward the edges. Light works in LCD monitors in the same way: many, if not most, are brighter in the center and darker along the edges.

LCD Options and Variations

LCD panels come in a variety of sizes, shapes, and levels of quality. An informed tech or consumer needs to understand four variations: size, brightness, contrast ratio, and interface.

Size   Unlike CRT manufacturers, LCD monitor manufacturers practice truth in advertising. A 15-inch LCD has a VIS of 15 inches when measured on the diagonal. LCD screens extend edge to edge on the monitor face, with no framing of blackness. Common sizes are 15, 17, 18.1, and 20 inches. You'll definitely get the best quality on the smaller screens, although the manufacturers have stepped up efforts to improve quality.

Brightness (Backlight)   Providing a uniform brightness level has proven tricky for manufacturers, and you'll find many LCD models that have good brightness in the center but are dim around the edges. One mid-level model I have around the office has one too-bright spot about a third of the way down from the top on the left side. Make sure the LCD you choose has a backlight you can tolerate.

Contrast Ratio   A big drawback of LCD monitors is that they don't have nearly the color saturation or richness of contrast that CRTs do. A good contrast ratio—the difference between the darkest and lightest spots that the monitor can display—is 450:1, but much lower levels (250:1 or 200:1) are common in LCDs.

Interface   The connection between the video card and the monitor has traditionally been analog because CRTs require an analog signal. LCD monitors, in contrast, are digital devices, meaning that they use 1s and 0s just like the PC. To make the transition to LCD panels as easy as possible for consumers and businesses, most LCD manufacturers give their monitors an analog interface. That way, Joe Consumer does not have to think about connections; he can simply unplug his CRT and plug in his new LCD, and all is well.

Figure 11.4 shows you the traditional analog connector for CRTs: a 15-pin DB connector that goes by the name **Video Graphics Array (VGA)**.

Although this approach works, it's a bit silly to have the video card convert the signal from digital to analog and then have the monitor convert it back from analog to digital. Wouldn't it make more sense to use a digital

● **Figure 11.4**   VGA connector

Introduction to PC Hardware and Troubleshooting

interface on both the video card and monitor? Of course! And manufacturers know this. The new connection and interface is generically called the **Digital Video Interface (DVI)** and is shown in Figure 11.5.

So now a new LCD monitor may come equipped to use either a DVI or a VGA connector. This is fine as long as you appreciate that your video card also may come with either a DVI or a VGA connector, and that you make sure that both ends match so you can connect your video card to your monitor.

● **Figure 11.5**   DVI connector

■ Selecting the Right Video Card

The video card, commonly known as the display adapter, provides the connection between the CPU and the monitor; receiving commands from the CPU and translating them into commands understandable to the monitor so that the information you desire is displayed on the screen. Unlike most of the hardware discussed in this book, video cards have a large number of options and adjustments. Understanding how video cards work thus is critical to ensuring that your screen displays a great image every time.

As a good tech, you should understand how the display adapter works inside—even though you can't fix the hardware—to provide clients with the proper advice or fixes. As you'll see in the next few pages, often a video problem is the result of asking too much of an otherwise perfectly functioning video card, rather than any flaw in the hardware. Tech or user ignorance can create phantom video problems such as a card that can't display a particular effect or that displays the desired effect but not with the desired results, or a high-resolution setting that works fine in Windows, but wreaks havoc in a high-demand application, such as a game or drafting program.

Inside the Display Adapter

Everything displayed on your screen starts with the CPU. The CPU processes the commands necessary to carry out your wishes (open a window, start a video, and so on), and then it sends commands to the video card. The commands travel through the data bus to the expansion bus and into the video card. Every video card has RAM. The video card's RAM stores the data that will become your screen image.

Until the late 1980s, video cards were not "smart"—it was up to the CPU to tell the video card exactly what to place in the video RAM. Today's video cards have their own processors, so the CPU can give the video card much simpler commands, and the video card's onboard processor can then take over at that point. Once the image is placed in the video RAM,

Try This!

Install and Configure an LCD Monitor
You know the concepts of LCD monitor setup from your study of CRT installation and configuration. The steps are the same, although the connectors may be DVI as well as VGA. In addition, the built-in controls may be very different—but nothing that you can't handle.

1. Connect the power and data cables to the electrical outlet and PC, respectively.

2. Adjust the resolution to the native resolution of the LCD. Note that you don't have to set the refresh rate because this doesn't matter on an LCD.

3. Check out the built-in controls to see what options you have.

the video processor sends that data to the monitor. This data is either sent directly to a fully digital LCD monitor, or through a specialized chip called a RAMDAC that converts the digital data in the video RAM to an analog signal.

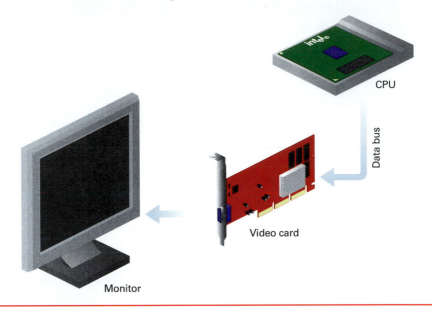

• The display process

Graphics Processor

The graphics processor handles the heavy lifting of taking commands from the CPU and translating them into coordinates and color information that the monitor understands and displays.

When we talk about video cards, we discuss their manufacturer, model number, graphic processor, and amount of video RAM. An example of a typical video card name is the ATI All-in-Wonder Radeon 8500 128 MB—ATI is the manufacturer, All-in-Wonder is the model, Radeon 8500 is the name of the graphics processor used on the card, and 128 MB is the amount of video RAM.

There are many companies that make the hundreds of different video cards on the market, but only three companies produce the vast majority of graphics processors found on video cards: nVidia, ATI, and Matrox. ATI and Matrox produce complete video cards as well as the graphics processors; both ATI and nVidia sell their chips to third-party manufacturers, who then design, build, and sell video cards under their own branding. Figure 11.6 shows an nVidia GeForce4 Ti 4600 on a board made by VisionTek.

Your choice of graphics processor is your single most important decision in buying a video card. Low-end graphics processors will usually work fine for the run-of-the-mill user who wants to write letters or run a web browser. High-end graphics processors are designed to support the beautiful 3D games that are so popular today.

A Word on Games   Your PC is capable of providing you with hours of incredible entertainment via a huge number of popular games that immerse you in 3D environments full of light, shadows, explosions, and other amazing effects that create a fun and beautiful gaming experience. However, these 3D games have special needs to be able to do all this amazing stuff. One need is textures. A **texture** is a small picture that is tiled over and over again on walls, floors, and other surfaces to create the 3D world. Take a look at the wall in Figure 11.7. The wall is made up of only three textures that are repeated over and over again on the surface.

Games also use hundreds of lighting effects such as transparency (water), shadows, reflection, and bump mapping—the process of laying multiple textures on the same spot to give a more textured (bumpy) look to the surface. These games are where the higher-quality graphics processors really shine.

The problem is deciding what graphics processor to choose—the video industry is constantly coming out with new graphic processors. One of the best guides is price. For years, the best (and newest) graphics cards usually cost around $400. The cheapest cards cost around $60. I usually split the difference and go for a card priced around $180 to $200—such a card will have most of the features you want without breaking your bank account.

If you use your computer only for 2D programs (most office applications, such as word processors, e-mail, and web browsers, are 2D), then almost all of the features of the more advanced graphics cards will do you little good. If you're not a gamer, then think cheap; the low-end video cards will more than suffice for your needs.

• **Figure 11.6**   An nVidia GeForce4 Ti 4600

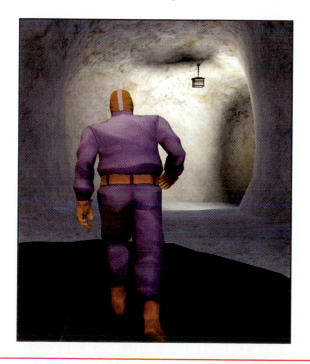

• **Figure 11.7**   Wall of textures

• Video card with four onboard RAM chips

Video RAM

At its most basic, the RAM on the video card stores the image that is currently on the screen. However, video cards use the video RAM for far more than just the current image. For example, if Lara Croft (aka, the Tomb Raider) is running down a long stone tunnel, it makes more sense to have the textures that make up the tunnel walls stored on the video card's RAM than to have the CPU process them and send them through the data bus. The onboard video also stores the hidden parts of Windows and keeps an image of the mouse pointer for fast updating of the screen.

For many PCs, a modest amount of video RAM—such as 16 MB—suffices, but gamers, artists, and designers (who tend to use very large monitors) usually need substantially more video RAM. Some video cards geared toward gamers have 128 MB of RAM or more. The amount of video RAM on the video card also affects the price.

RAMDAC

Every video card capable of running a CRT or analog LCD has a **RAM Digital-to-Analog Converter (RAMDAC)** chip to take the commands from the graphics processor and turn them into the analog signals used by CRTs. Digital video cards that use only DVI connectors don't need to convert their digital signals to analog and as a result do not have a RAMDAC chip.

Expansion Bus Interfaces

Video cards come with one of two types of expansion buses: PCI or AGP. Let's take a look at both of these.

PCI

PCI video cards (Figure 11.8) used to be all the rage, but since the invention of the AGP bus, any PCI video cards still on the market are primarily for adding a second monitor to your system (see "Multiple Video Cards for Multiple Monitors" later in this chapter). PCI video cards connect to PCI slots on the motherboard, just like any other expansion card.

AGP

The primary video card in PCs today connects to the rest of the system via a specialized, video-only **Accelerated Graphics Port (AGP)** expansion slot.

Inside Information

Who Gets the Old Computer?

A big mistake people often make when they purchase a second computer for the home is deciding that "the kids can have the old computer." If you're going to purchase a second computer, give it to the kids and keep the old one for yourself. Kids play these 3D games and can take advantage of the better video cards that come with a new system. If you're just using your PC for e-mail, web browsing, and other nongraphics-intensive tasks, you'll never need the extra power of a more advanced video card.

Introduction to PC Hardware and Troubleshooting

As you should recall, AGP is an advanced form of PCI slot that provides much higher speeds than PCI and also adds a number of video-specific options to make the image on your screen look great. Two AGP standards currently exist, named AGP 2.0 and AGP 3.0. (I haven't a clue what happened to version 1.)

The reason you need to know any of this is that the slots on the motherboards and the connectors on the AGP video card vary according to the version and model, and they are *not* all compatible. Some AGP 3.0 cards will physically plug into AGP 2.0 slots, for example, but they won't work. Figure 11.9 shows two different AGP slots.

Some motherboard manufacturers make a universal slot that can accommodate multiple versions. If you're buying a new video card, you need to know what type of AGP slot your system uses so you can get a video card that works in your system.

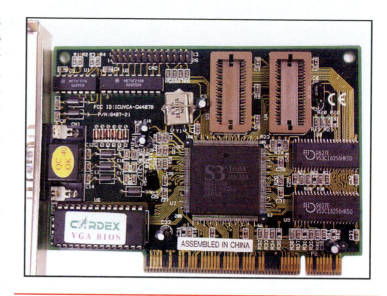

• **Figure 11.8**   PCI video card

Video Card Ports

You can find all sorts of ports on the back of video cards, from standard three-row, 15-pin DB VGA (also called analog) ports to DVI ports. These you'll recall from the monitor discussions earlier in the chapter. In addition, many video cards have an S-video port for plugging into a television and even RCA jacks for assorted fun and games. Some cards even enable you to capture video directly from a camcorder or VCR. Sweet!

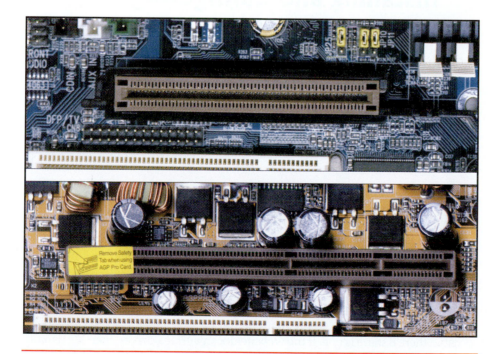

• **Figure 11.9**   Different AGP slots

• Typical dual monitor setup

Multiple Video Cards for Multiple Monitors

It's becoming increasingly popular to connect multiple monitors to a single system. Starting with Windows 98, you can install two or more video cards in one computer and expand your Windows desktop across them. Multiple monitors are a great way to work with multiple programs or programs that need as much screen space as you can give them, such as graphics and video editing programs. I use dual monitors to allow me to see multiple programs running without have to switch windows.

You don't have to do anything special to take advantage of multiple monitors—just install a second video card and plug a monitor into the card, and Windows does the rest for you. One problem with a dual-monitor setup arises from the fact that one video card in the system normally will be an AGP card, so—because the motherboard has only one AGP slot—the other card will have to be PCI card, and PCI video cards are hard to find these days. If you want to try dual monitors without using a second video card, a number of single video cards do support two or more monitors. Figure 11.10 shows a typical video card that supports two monitors.

Once you've properly installed the video card and connected it to the monitor, you've conquered half the territory for making the video process work properly. You're ready to tackle the operating system and drivers, so let's go!

• **Figure 11.10** Video card with two monitor outputs

■ Installing and Configuring Video Software

Once you've physically installed the video card, attached the monitor, and thrown a little electricity into the mix, you're ready to teach the system how to talk to that specific video card and optimize it in Windows. This is usually a two-step process. First you need to load drivers for the video card. Then you need to open the Control Panel and go to the Display applet to make your adjustments. Let's explore how to make the video card and monitor do Windows.

Drivers

Just like any other piece of hardware, your video card needs a driver to function. Video card drivers install pretty much the same way as all of the other drivers we've discussed thus far: either the driver is already built into Windows or you must use the installation CD that comes with the video card.

Video card makers are constantly updating their drivers. Odds are good that any video card more than a few months old will have at least one driver update. If possible, check the manufacturer's website and use the driver located there if there is one. If the website doesn't offer a driver, then it's usually best to use the installation CD. Try to avoid using the built-in Windows driver as it tends to be the most dated.

We explore driver issues in more detail after we discuss the Display applet. Like so many things about video, you can't really fully understand one topic without understanding at least one other!

Using the Display Applet

With the driver installed, you're ready to configure your display settings. The Display applet on the Control Panel is your next stop. The Display applet provides a convenient, central location for all of your display settings, including resolution, refresh rate, driver information, and color depth.

The default Display applet in Windows XP (Figure 11.11) has five tabs: Themes, Desktop, Screen Saver, Appearance, and Settings. The first four tabs have options that enable you to change the look and feel of Windows and set up a screen saver; the fifth tab is where you make adjustments that relate directly to your monitor and video card. Let's take a close look at the Settings tab.

Settings Tab

The Settings tab (Figure 11.12) is the place to optimize monitors and video cards. At the bottom of the dialog box you'll see two options: Screen Resolution and Color Quality. By moving the Screen Resolution slider you can change—you guessed it!—the resolution of the screen. Resolution is measured in pixels. A system running with a resolution of 800 x 600 displays 800 pixels horizontally and 600 pixels vertically. The most common resolutions are 640 x 480, 800 x 600, 1,024 x 768, and 1,280 x 1,024. Keep in mind that these are only the most common resolutions—your system may have more or fewer resolution options.

Everyone has a favorite resolution, and higher isn't always better. Especially for those with trouble seeing small screen elements, higher resolutions can present a difficulty—those 20-pixel-square icons are *much* smaller at 1,024 x 768 than at a basic VGA resolution of 640 x 480. Try all of the resolutions to see which you like.

The color quality is the number of colors displayed on the screen. Techs don't talk in terms of number of colors, but in terms of the **bit depth**. Use Table 11.1 to decode the correspondence between bit depth and number of colors. Not every computer is able to support all of these bit-depth options. Except for the highest bit-depth option, the correspondence with the number of colors displayed is actually simple

Try This!

Install a Video Card

You know how to install an expansion card from your reading in earlier chapters. Installing a video card is pretty much the same. Try this:

1. Follow the instructions in Step-by-Step 5.3 to install the video card.

2. Plug the monitor cable into the video card port on the back of the PC and power up the system. If your PC seems dead after you install a video card, or if the screen is blank but you hear fans whirring and the internal speaker sounding off *long-short-short-short*, you probably did not seat the video card correctly. Unplug the PC and try again.

Especially useful to LCD monitor users, including folks with portable computers, is the Effects button on the Appearance tab of the Display Properties dialog box. The second option gives you a choice of font smoothing techniques, and many users have been heard to exclaim joyously after they change the default from Standard to Clear Type.

• **Figure 11.11** Display Properties dialog box in Windows XP

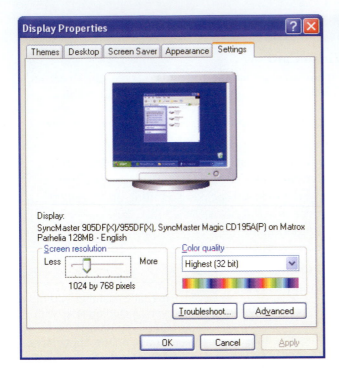

Display Properties

Themes | Desktop | Screen Saver | Appearance | Settings

Display:
SyncMaster 905DF(X)/955DF(X), SyncMaster Magic CD195A(P) on Matrox Parhelia 128MB - English

Screen resolution
Less _____ More
1024 by 768 pixels

Color quality
Highest (32 bit)

Troubleshoot... | Advanced

OK | Cancel | Apply

• **Figure 11.12**   Settings tab in Windows XP

math: the number in the right column of Table 11.1 is equal to 2 to the power of the bit-depth value; thus, 4-bit color produces $2^4 = 16$ colors. However, 32-bit color doesn't use the extra 16 bits to add more colors, but rather to give the display additional abilities. You can change the screen resolution with a simple slider and adjust the color depth from 4-bit all the way up to 32-bit color.

Because even a young, healthy pair of human eyes has trouble distinguishing more than 16.7 million colors, running at 24-bit color is sufficient for most applications. Running at 32-bit color gives a nice realistic tone to images, and many games insist on it. Up until about four years ago, many lower-end video cards required the system to run at lower bit depths, but unless you have a an older video card or a significant video speed issue, you'll probably set your system for 32-bit color and never touch this setting again.

Clicking the Advanced button opens another dialog box with four or more tabs. Your monitor model serves as the title of the dialog box. Your video card driver determines which tabs show up here. You can ignore most of these tabs, but the Monitor tab is a handy place to adjust your refresh rate.

The Monitor tab gives you details about the currently installed monitor and enables you to make changes to the driver and the refresh rate. Click the Properties button to display the driver details for the monitor. In the Monitor Settings section of the Monitor tab, you can change the refresh rate using a drop-down dialog box (Figure 11.13).

Note the option Hide Modes That This Monitor Cannot Display. If you have a video card that's substantially superior to your monitor, you could clear this check box to reveal a whole lot more refresh rates. However, you can toast a monitor by driving it too fast even in a relatively short length of time, so don't do this!

Working with Drivers

Now that you know the locations of the primary video tools within the operating system, it's time to learn about fine-tuning your video. You need to know how to work with video drivers from within the Display applet, including how to update them, roll back updates, and uninstall them.

Table 11.1	Correspondence Between Bit Depth and Number of Colors	
Bit Depth	**Number of Colors**
4-bit	16
8-bit	256
16-bit	65,536
24-bit	16.7 million
32-bit	16.7 million

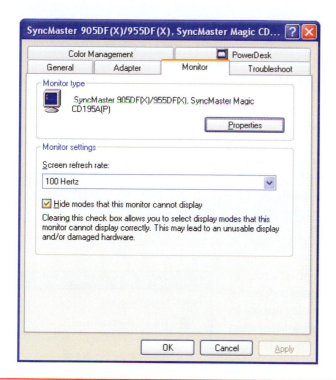

• Figure 11.13   Monitor tab

Windows is very persnickety when it comes to video card drivers. You can crash Windows and force a reinstall simply by installing a new video card and not uninstalling the old card's drivers. This doesn't happen every time, but certainly can happen. As a basic rule, always uninstall the old card's drivers before you install drivers for a new card.

When you update the drivers for a card, you have a choice of uninstalling the outdated drivers and then installing new drivers—which makes the process the same as for installing a new card—or if you're running Windows XP, you can let it flex some digital muscle and install the new ones right over the older drivers.

Updating

To update your drivers, go to the Control Panel and double-click the Display applet. In the Display Properties dialog box, select the Settings tab and click the Advanced button. In the Advanced button dialog box, click the Adapter tab and then click the Properties button. In the Properties dialog box for your adapter (Figure 11.14), select the Driver tab and then click the Update Driver button to run the Hardware Update wizard.

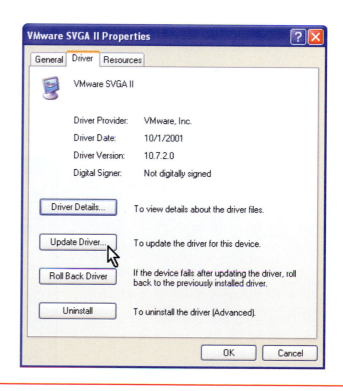

• Figure 11.14   Adapter Properties dialog box

Updating Video Drivers the Right Way

Updating drivers the right way requires quite a few steps: getting information about your current drivers; finding the latest drivers on the video card manufacturer's website; deciding whether to download beta drivers, the latest fully supported drivers, or Microsoft-approved drivers; downloading and unpacking or unzipping the drivers; testing the drivers; and if necessary, rolling back to the old drivers. This exercise will take you through all of these steps.

To complete this exercise, you will need the following:

- A working Windows computer with a video adapter
- An Internet connection

Step 1

Your first task is to determine what driver you're currently using. Open the Control Panel and double-click Display applet. In the Display Properties dialog box, select the Settings tab and click the Advanced button. In the Advanced Settings dialog box, click the Adapter tab and then click the Properties button to open the adapter's Properties dialog box.

Step 2

Select the Driver tab to display the provider (the company that wrote the drivers), date, version, and digital signer, if any (here, digitally signed means approved by Microsoft). In this example, the Matrox card has old drivers installed, listed as version 5,13,1,1000. How do you know they are old? Just check the Matrox website to see the version number for the latest driver.

Step 3

Your next task is to acquire the new drivers. This process can be more complicated than simply downloading a file. To find out the make and model of your video card, press and hold down the Windows key on your keyboard and then press the Pause key to open the System Properties dialog box. Release both keys and select the Hardware tab. Click the Device Manager button to open the Device Manager; click the plus sign next to Display Adapters and select your video card. Double-click it to see its properties.

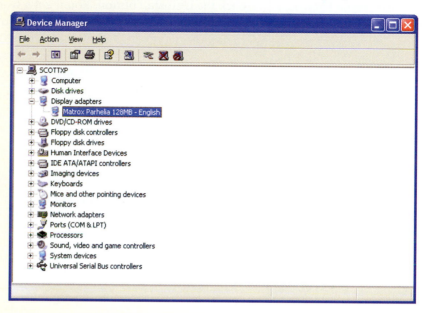

Step 4

Once you've determined the make and model of your video card, go to the website of the video card manufacturer and find suitable drivers for your video card. For this exercise, download the latest supported—but not necessarily Microsoft-approved—drivers.

Step 5

Once you download the drivers, you need to install them. Look for an executable file, such as SETUP.EXE, and double-click it.

Step 6

Now it's time to test your new drivers. The best way to do that is to run your video card through its paces. Play a game and do some web browsing—does everything seem okay?

Try This!

Run 3DMark

3DMark is a benchmark program that tests primarily your video card and CPU, although system RAM is important as well. You get a numerical score overall as well as a breakdown of performance in the individual tests.

1. You have learned how to download drivers from manufacturers' websites. If your lab doesn't have a copy of 3DMark, go to www.madonion.com and download a copy. Use 3DMark2001 SE or a later version.

2. Load 3DMark2001 SE or a later version onto your machine and run the software. Note your scores for the video card and overall performance using your current drivers.

3DMark pushes your system very hard, staggering even high-end systems on some tests. It can also crash your system if the hardware cannot handle the calls. To optimize scores and stability, turn off all other programs—including background applications, such as antivirus software—before running 3DMark.

Uninstalling Drivers

When you change video cards, good practice encourages you to uninstall the current drivers before you install the new video card or drivers. Some aggressive or exceedingly temperamental video cards will require you to uninstall the current drivers just to upgrade drivers for the same card!

In any case, open the Drivers property sheet for the display adapter and click the Uninstall button. You'll get a warning, but that's about it.

Think about this for a moment: if you uninstall the video card drivers, then the video card won't work, correct? Well, when you uninstall a video card driver, Windows automatically replaces it with a generic VGA adapter so you can at least see what's on the screen. When you click the OK button to uninstall the drivers, you're on your way to turning your video card into Standard VGA.

DirectX

In the old days, many applications communicated directly with much of the PC hardware and, as a result, could crash your computer if not written well enough. Microsoft tried to fix this problem by placing all hardware under the control of Windows, but programmers balked because Windows added too much work for the video process and slowed everything down. For the most demanding programs, such as games, only direct access of hardware would work.

This need to "get around Windows" motivated Microsoft to unveil a new set of protocols called **DirectX**. Programmers use DirectX to take control of certain pieces of hardware and to talk directly to that hardware; it provides the speed necessary to play the advanced games so popular today.

DirectX is not only for video; it also supports sound, network connections, input devices, and other parts of your PC. Each of these subsets of DirectX has a name like DirectDraw, Direct3D, or DirectSound.

DirectX is installed as a separate component in your Windows PC. All versions of Windows since Windows 98 have some version of DirectX, but you should be sure to install the version needed by your game. Every game will clearly indicate the version of DirectX it needs.

You can quickly determine the version of DirectX on your system using the handy DirectX diagnostic tool. To access the DirectX diagnostics, choose Start | Program Files | Accessories | System Tools | System Information. In the System Information utility, click the Tools menu and select DirectX Diagnostic Tool to open it.

If your current game needs a newer version of DirectX, first check on the game's installation CD—usually, the game itself comes with the version you need. If the version is not

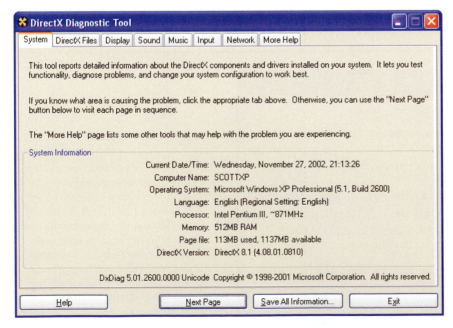

If you want to uninstall a video card that Windows installed drivers for by default, you'll need to uninstall the drivers and then turn off the system. Remove the video card, insert your replacement, and then boot the machine normally.

there, download the newest version of DirectX from the Microsoft website, at http://www.microsoft.com/windows/directx/default.asp.

The Dxdiag utility does far more than just tell you the version of DirectX you are running. It also comes with a number of diagnostics that let you test your DirectX installation. You can use the diagnostic utility to get information about your hardware, or you can simply click the Display tab and test the features. Let's walk through the process.

Step-by-Step 11.3

Testing DirectX on Your System

In this exercise, you will run diagnostic tests on your video subsystem, specifically to see how well it handles DirectDraw and Direct3D, the two video parts of the DirectX protocol.

Step 1

Choose Start | Run, type **dxdiag**, and click OK to open the DirectX diagnostic tool. In the DirectX Diagnostic Tool dialog box, select the Display tab. There are two buttons related to testing: Test DirectDraw and Test Direct3D.

Step 2

Click the Test DirectDraw button to start testing. When you are prompted to proceed, click the Yes button. Perform all of the DirectDraw tests; then do the same thing with the Direct3D option.

Step 3

Most DirectX problems stem from video driver issues or an improper DirectX installation. Always be sure to check you video card manufacturer's website for any special actions you may need to take to get DirectX working for you.

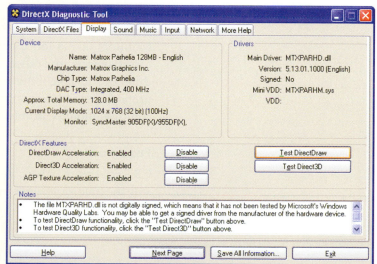

■ Maintenance and Troubleshooting

With proper configuration, the right drivers, and proper maintenance, your video system can run for years without giving you any problems. To keep everything running smoothly, follow the advice presented here.

Caring for Your Monitor

If all monitors were perfect, this section would be unnecessary, but alas, such is not the case. Monitors get scuffed, jostled, slimed, dusted, smoked, and generally abused. Let's take a look at cleaning issues, environmental concerns, and onscreen adjustments.

Cleaning

Keeping CRTs clean is important, but they're pretty robust creatures as long as you don't drop them! To keep your CRT clean, dust it regularly with a computer vacuum and clean fingerprints off the front screen. Dusting is good for your monitor and your general well being, so do it! You can clean the screen with any glass cleaner and a soft, nonabrasive cloth.

The screen of most LCD panels is covered with a fairly fragile antiglare coating and thus requires care when cleaning. Here's the scoop: The conventional wisdom on LCD screens is that you should never use Windex or any other commercial window cleaning solution; you'll melt the coating on the screen, a very expensive *oops*! Instead, use the manufacturer's recommended cleaning methods for your specific model of LCD.

Environmental Concerns

Pollution and interference from other electrical equipment can shorten the life of your monitor and cause it to look bad in a big hurry. Avoid smoking around your monitor.

Interference can be caused, for example, by running a hair dryer on the same circuit as your monitor. It can also be caused by something more insidious, such as a nearby magnet that bends or warps the display.

> ⚠️ I said this at the beginning of the chapter, but I have to say it again: *never* open a monitor for repair! Take it to a qualified monitor repair center. Check the manufacturer's website for one close to you.

Troubleshooting Monitor Problems

Monitors take a lot of abuse. They are in the direct line of fire for spills, tossed objects, and other abuse that any device exposed to humans must endure. In addition, if the monitor is a CRT, it uses vacuum tubes, and as your grandfather can tell you, all tubes eventually fail. Here are a few of the more common monitor problems and what you can do about them.

Fuzziness

CRT screens may become fuzzy or out of focus when the electron guns inside the tube move out of alignment. A quick trip to the repair shop will often fix this.

Missing Color

If your monitor suddenly stops showing red, green, or blue, the video cable is likely slipping out of the video card, and a quick reinsertion should fix it. If this doesn't help, you need to take your monitor in for repair.

Missing Pixels

Missing pixels can happen on either a CRT or an LCD monitor. If it happens on an LCD, live with it; all LCDs have a few missing pixels. If it happens on a CRT, you have a video RAM problem. Most video cards do not have replaceable RAM, so that means a new video card.

Dim Screen

All monitors have brightness adjustments. If your screen seems dim, first turn up the brightness. If the brightness is all the way up and the screen is still dim, you have a problem. A dim screen on a CRT means that the electron guns are wearing out and that the monitor needs replacing. A dim screen on an LCD means the backlight is wearing out—a surprisingly inexpensive repair, in most cases.

No Image

When no image appears on the screen, the number-one reason is that the monitor is unplugged from the video card or not turned on—so plug it in and turn it on! Also check the brightness knob and make sure it is turned up. If there's still no image, try another monitor. If another monitor works, take yours in for repair—although be prepared to hear that it will cost more to fix than it does to buy a new monitor.

Troubleshooting LCD Monitors

LCD monitors bring a set of unique issues for techs to troubleshoot, beyond those they share with CRTs. Common issues are connectivity, white or black speckles, and ghosting. Let's take a look.

Connectivity

I recently plugged an LCD monitor into a new video card, DVI to DVI, but when I powered on the PC, all I saw on the screen was a jumble of colored lines. I couldn't even access the on-screen controls. It turned out that I had the wrong cable/connector combination. If nothing appears when you plug in the monitor, check your cables first.

Speckles

Right out of the box, you may notice bright white or pure black speckles on the screen. There's nothing you can do about this problem except return the monitor and try another one. Note that two monitors of the same make and model can have different white or black spots on them—this is simply a manufacturing issue.

Inside Information

Ugly Games

You buy some cool new game and install it only to discover that the game seems incredibly ugly and pixilated—what gives? This is a common problem; most DirectX games don't automatically start using DirectX, so you need to look for something in the game that will turn on DirectX. Even if a game looks OK, you can often find nice tweaks in its DirectX settings that will make it look even better. However, this varies from game to game, so you may have to do a little poking around and experimenting to really make your game rock.

Ghosting

LCD monitors simply don't refresh as quickly as CRTs, and thus users often complain about ghosting. During action games or DVD playback, the screen will show a little motion blurring when a character moves too quickly for the transistors on the LCD to refresh. This phenomenon is called slow pixel response time, and you can't do anything to correct it.

Long cables, extenders, and splitters can also cause ghosting and other screen decay or artifacts. How long is too long? It depends on the model and the cable. If an LCD monitor known to be of good quality experiences excessive ghosting, check the cable first and replace or adjust it if necessary.

Video Card Problems

Video cards are incredibly robust and if treated well will probably last for the life of the system. When video cards do fail, they can be difficult to diagnose. Here are a few of the more common symptoms.

Beeping Dead PC

Many times video problems are caused by users asking too much of an otherwise perfectly functioning video card, rather than any flaw in the hardware. Ignorance of your hardware's design limitations can result in "phantom" video problems. A card may be unable to display a particular effect, or will display the desired effect, but not with the desired results. Sometimes a high monitor-resolution setting works fine for Windows activity, but wreaks havoc within a high-demand application, such as a game or drafting program.

If you start the system and the computer makes a series of beeps and fails to boot, the system most likely doesn't recognize the video card. This problem is most common on a new installation, but it can also occur when a video card is not screwed down. AGP slots in particular are very persnickety, and it's not uncommon to have to reseat an AGP card a few times before the system boots.

Bizarre Image

There's no other way to describe this: the screen just looks—bizarre. Strange bits of text appear and disappear. Ghost images appear and don't go away until you reboot, or wild designs appear on the screen and just get worse and worse. These symptoms all indicate bad video RAM. Get a new video card.

Decaying Image

An image that starts well but then begins to decay—goes black and seems to dissolve—usually points to an overheated video card. If the video card has a fan, check it and make sure it is working. If it's not, you may be able to get a replacement, depending on the manufacturer.

Troubleshooting Configuration Errors

The vast majority of video problems are the result of configuration errors. Your first clue that there's a configuration error is simply that the screen doesn't look right. Just how the screen looks wrong is a clue to the particular configuration error. Let's look at a few of the most common symptoms that point to configuration errors.

Misaligned Screen

A properly configured monitor should place the screen image in a nice rectangular pattern with a small (less than ½-inch) black border. Many times, particularly immediately after you change resolution or color depth, you'll find that the screen loses that nice rectangular shape. If this happens to you, don't worry. You simply need to adjust the monitor. This is where those controls on the monitor come in handy. With those controls, you can readjust your monitor so it looks right.

Flicker

Screen flicker is a huge problem with monitors. At the very least, it's an irritant; at worst, it causes eyestrain and nasty headaches. Don't put up with screen flicker. Go to the Display Properties dialog box as described earlier and increase the refresh rate until the flicker disappears. In fact, the higher the refresh rate, the easier the image is on your eyes. Most people find a refresh rate of around 72 Hz acceptable; I go as high as I can—my screen runs at 100 MHz, and I have a beautiful screen image and no headaches.

If you raise the refresh rate beyond what your screen can handle, you'll get either no image or a badly warped image. When you change the refresh rate, Windows displays a dialog box asking you if you want to keep this refresh rate. If you don't click Yes in a few seconds, it returns to the old settings. This feature is a lifesaver when you set your refresh rate too high—because you can't see anything on the screen! If you set your refresh rate too high, just wait until Windows returns to the old settings.

 Once an image is properly aligned on a CRT, it shouldn't change. However, if a properly aligned screen image begins to warp (usually at the top), this is a sign that the monitor is being pushed at too high a refresh rate. Reduce the refresh and readjust the image.

Chapter 11 Review

■ Chapter Summary

After reading this chapter and completing the exercises, you should understand the following aspects of the video system:

Select the right monitor for the situation

■ Monitors come in two basic flavors: the traditional analog Cathode Ray Tube (CRT) monitor and the digital Liquid Crystal Display (LCD) monitor.

■ CRTs come in a variety of sizes, with a 17-inch screen common for the home user and a 19-inch screen common for businesses.

■ Two types of CRT screens are produced currently: the standard, convex shape and the perfect flat screen that has no edge bending.

■ LCD panels offer a fine alternative to CRT displays. They take up substantially less space, require less electricity, and, frankly, look cooler on your desk.

■ Many LCDs use the analog VGA connector, the three-row, 15-pin DB connector, to plug into the video port. Some LCDs use the newer DVI connectors.

■ A monitor's refresh rate is measured in hertz (Hz), meaning cycles per second.

Select and install the correct video card

■ Video cards—also called display adapters—have several components that you now know: the graphics processor, video RAM, and RAMDAC. The processor interprets the code, swapping it in and out of the video RAM, and the RAMDAC takes the finished product and translates it from digital to analog. Note that a digital card with only a DVI output will not need or use RAMDAC.

■ The graphics processor chip also handles specific high-end functions, such as 3D effects and texture grabbing, thus freeing the CPU for other chores.

■ Video cards use the very fast AGP bus to communicate directly with RAM. AGP comes in two flavors: AGP version 2.0 and AGP version 3.0.

Install and configure video software

■ Video drivers enable the operating system and CPU to communicate effectively with devices. Be sure to get the latest drivers from the manufacturer.

■ The most common screen resolutions for monitors are 640 x 480, 800 x 600, 1024 x 768, and 1280 x 1024.

■ Use the Display applet to set up and optimize the operating system for the video subsystem. Use the Settings tab to set the resolution, refresh rate, color depth, and more for the video card and the monitor.

■ A monitor's color quality is the number of colors it displays on the screen. Techs don't talk in terms of number of colors, but in terms of the bit depth. 24-bit color is sufficent for most users.

■ Microsoft's DirectX protocols provide a standardized way for applications like computer games to access system hardware directly.

Troubleshoot typical video problems

■ Most video problems are simply configuration errors. The most common symptom of this is a misaligned or flickering screen image.

■ Common monitor problems include fuzzy or dim screens, missing colors or pixels, and no image at all.

■ Common LCD troubleshooting issues include connectivity, white or black speckles, and ghosting.

■ Common symptoms of a bad video card include a beeping, unbootable PC; strange-looking images on the screen; and an image that starts to decay after the computer has been running for a while.

■ Most monitor problems require you to take in the monitor for repairs. Never open a monitor yourself!

■ Key Terms

Accelerated Graphics Port (AGP) *(302)*
bit depth *(305)*
Cathode Ray Tube (CRT) *(293)*
Digital Video Interface (DVI) *(299)*
DirectX *(310)*
dot pitch *(294)*

hertz (Hz) *(293)*
Liquid Crystal Display (LCD) *(297)*
nits *(298)*
pixel *(294)*
RAM Digital-to-Analog Converter (RAMDAC) *(302)*
refresh rate *(293)*

resolution *(294)*
shadow mask *(293)*
texture *(301)*
Video Graphics Array (VGA) *(298)*
viewable image size (VIS) *(295)*

■ Key Term Quiz

Use terms from the Key Terms list to complete the following sentences. Not all terms will be used.

1. Two monitor types dominate the PC scene: the analog _____ and the digital _____.

2. Cindy Tech glanced at John's monitor and exclaimed, "You should change the _____ to 1024 x 768. You'll get more screen real estate that way!"

3. After Kathy complained about tired eyes and headaches at the end of the day four days in a row, Bill Tech finally deigned to appear at her cubical. He took one look at her computer setup and exclaimed, "Good heavens! See that screen flicker? Your _____ is set to 60 Hz, so no wonder you're not feeling great!"

4. The PC draws the screen on the monitor using a grid of blocks of red, green, and blue phosphors. Each block is called a/an _____.

5. The screen covered with tiny holes to help direct the electron beams to the phosphors on the CRT screen is called the _____.

6. Many video cards come with two ports: VGA for connecting analog monitors and _____ for connecting digital monitors.

7. The expansion bus slot designed exclusively for video is called the _____.

8. A small bitmap used to create the 3D environments in games is called a/an _____.

9. The distance between two phosphors of the same color on a CRT screen is called the _____.

10. Microsoft created _____ to enable more direct communication between applications and the video hardware.

■ Multiple-Choice Quiz

1. Which of the following is unique to LCD monitors?

   a. Shadow mask

   b. Refresh rate

   c. Dot pitch

   d. DVI

2. Which of the following is a common screen resolution?

   a. 650 x 840

   b. 900 x 300

   c. 1,024 x 768

   d. 2,096 x 1280

3. If you are running at a 16-bit color depth, how many colors will the screen display?

   a. 16

   b. 65,536

   c. 16.7 million

   d. 4.2 billion

4. Given the choices of video card drivers listed here, which would probably be the best one to use?

   a. The drivers that come with Windows

   b. The drivers on the video card's installation CD

   c. The drivers from the manufacturer's website

   d. The reference drivers for the graphics processor

5. Which of the following would tell you the version of DirectX that is running on your system?

   a. Dxdiag

   b. System Properties

   c. Display Properties

   d. Device Manager

6. Which of the following features is found only on a CRT monitor?

   a. Graphics processor

   b. VGA connector

   c. Shadow mask

   d. VIS

7. Why is it a bad idea to open a CRT?

   a. There's nothing that can be done inside the CRT.

   b. Once a CRT has been opened, it will no longer work.

   c. Opening a CRT can damage the internal components.

   d. The internal parts of a CRT are an electrical hazard

8. Which of the following is a valid refresh rate?

   a. 72 KHz

   b. 72 MHz

   c. 72 Hz

   d. 72 THz

9. Many LCD displays use a _____ video connector instead of the old VGA connector.

   a. DMI

   b. DVI

   c. DRQ

   d. D-video

10. An LCD panel's brightness is measured in _____?

    a. Hertz

    b. Pixels

    c. Angstroms

    d. Nits

11. To reduce screen flicker, you need to increase the monitor's _____.

    a. Contrast

    b. Brightness

    c. Refresh rate

    d. Voltage

12. After installing a new video card, the system at bootup has a blank screen but is making a strange beeping sound. This is a sure sign of _____.

    a. Insufficient voltage

    b. Flicker

    c. An improperly seated card

    d. A bad video driver

13. Increasing the resolution also increases the number of _____.

    a. Pixels

    b. Dot pitches

    c. VIS

    d. Colors

14. Digital video cards do not have a _____.

    a. Refresh rate

    b. Resolution

    c. RAMDAC

    d. BIOS

15. Current European standards recommend a minimum refresh rate of _____.

    a. 60 Hz

    b. 62 Hz

    c. 72 Hz

    d. 100 Hz

■ Essay Quiz

1. You have been asked to purchase some new CRT monitors for your department. Write a memo explaining some of the criteria that you would use to select the monitors. Include some parameters (for example, a dot pitch of 0.17 to 0.28—smaller is better).

2. Some of the people in your department want new video cards, claiming that the increased video RAM and more powerful processors will help in their jobs. Your department runs only basic 2D office applications. Write a memo to the users explaining why new video cards will not help.

3. Some of the people in your department (including you) want to use dual monitors. Your department runs only basic 2D office applications. Write a memo to your immediate supervisor explaining why you need dual-monitor setups.

Lab Projects

• Lab Project 11.1

When it comes to the quality of a monitor's image, different people may have very different opinions about any given monitor. With a partner (or group), look at the images on a number of different monitors. Rank each monitor's image quality from first to last. List reasons why you prefer one monitor over another. Compare your observations to other people's observations.

• Lab Project 11.2

Everyone has a different opinion as to the best settings for a given monitor. Adjust a monitor to the settings that you find comfortable (refresh rate, resolution, screen size, number of colors). Then have a partner adjust the monitor to the settings he or she likes. Compare the two. What settings are the same? Which are different? Did either of you change the other's opinion about which settings are best?

Input Devices

"A program is a spell cast over a computer, turning input into error messages."

—Anonymous

In this chapter, you will learn how to:

- **Install a keyboard on a Windows system**
- **Install and configure a mouse on a Windows system**
- **Identify some less common types of input devices**
- **Maintain and troubleshoot input devices**

In this chapter, you will learn about input devices, including a bit about their history. You will learn about some of the more popular options when choosing input devices and what the differences mean to you, the user and future tech. You will learn about the various connectivity options and why one option might be better than another. You will walk through the configuration of some standard devices, and you will learn how to modify settings to fit a user's style of working (or playing). Then you'll take a look at some nonstandard devices and learn their common uses. Finally, you'll learn what you should do to maintain input devices, as well as one or two things you shouldn't do.

■ Installing a Keyboard

Today's keyboards come in a huge variety of shapes and layouts, but they are, for the most part, more similar than not. They're so similar, in fact, that if you plug pretty much any of these many different keyboards into your computer, it should work immediately. Some keyboard manufacturers distribute specialized drivers to run the specialized tasks that they have built into their keyboards, but this isn't necessary to simply run your system.

What techs need to be aware of is that keyboards differ in two major ways: physical design—in particular, connections—and ergonomics. Connections are easy to understand—they're simply the many ways you plug a keyboard into your PC. **Ergonomics** is the art and science of human-friendly design, with the goal of making products comfortable, safe, and efficient. We explore a few of the most common options here.

Keyboard Ergonomics

The keyboards on the first IBM PCs had 83 keys and were cramped and not easy to use, especially for touch typists. In response, IBM altered the layout somewhat to produce the **84-key keyboard** layout (or AT keyboard). This still garnered some complaints, so in 1986 IBM brought out what was to become the standard layout for many years: the enhanced **101-key keyboard** layout. The most common keyboard today is based on the 101-key layout, but has a total of 104 keys. The three extra keys are provided to support

• 104-key keyboard

Windows functions—and are a very handy set of keys. Modern keyboards also tend to have small, fold-up legs on the bottom to adjust the angle at which you can type. Typical keyboards cost $15 to $20 and up at any computer store, and they are all you really need to run your system (except possibly a mouse; I'll get to that shortly).

Some otherwise standard keyboards are made with an eye toward sleek design. Some of these might even be considered substandard if they come with fewer features than a standard keyboard. Among these style-conscious models are solid black keyboards (Figure 12.1), transparent keyboards, and keyboards with curves and contours that set them apart from standard rectangular models.

A step up from the base keyboard for many is the natural keyboard, shown in Figure 12.2. These are becoming extremely popular with people who sit in front of their monitors for hours on end typing. Their V-shaped key layout is intended to position the typist's wrists in line with the forearms. Typists whose wrists can rest naturally while typing theoretically suffer less tendon and joint stress, reducing the risk of conditions such as carpal tunnel syndrome. You can also find keyboards with large print, big keys, and left-handed orientation.

• **Figure 12.1**   A black keyboard

• Figure 12.2   A natural keyboard

You can actually have more than one usable keyboard attached to your system at one time. If you connect a USB keyboard to a system that already uses a PS/2 keyboard, or if you connect two USB keyboards to one system, you'll have two active keyboards attached to your system. If you share a computer with someone but favor different keyboard types, you could use this setup to make everybody happy.

Making Connections

All keyboards, regardless of design, need some way to send and possibly receive data from the computer itself. This is where the different types of connectors come into play.

DIN

Starting at least with the IBM PC, the primary connection for a keyboard was what's known as a **DIN**-type, or AT-style, connector. You should recall from Chapter 4 that one of the primary ways you can tell an AT-style motherboard from a newer ATX-style is by looking at the keyboard connector or port. The AT-style keyboard plug, as shown in Figure 12.3, is larger than its modern replacement, the PS/2 connector.

Mini-DIN

When IBM came out with its PS/2 (or Personal System 2) computer in 1987, it also introduced a new connector for both the mouse and the keyboard. This connector is known as a **PS/2** connector, a **mini-DIN**, or an ATX-style mouse/keyboard connector. Figure 12.4 shows a PS/2 keyboard. As you learned in Chapter 4, these mouse and keyboard PS/2 ports come in standard colors. To refresh your memory, the mouse port is green, and the keyboard port is a nice purple. When these are combined with similarly hued mouse and keyboard plugs, it's easy to get the right connector in the right port.

USB

A more recent addition to the keyboard connector options is the **USB connector**. This connector has several features that make it extremely desirable. First, it is **hot-swappable**, which means that you can insert or remove it without restarting your system. Items with USB connectors can also be **daisy-chained** (that is, you can attach your USB mouse and USB media card reader to your keyboard and then attach your keyboard to the computer itself, and all will work). Finally, transmission through USB is faster than through the standard PS/2 serial ports,

• **Figure 12.3**   An AT-style keyboard with DIN connector

● **Figure 12.4**   An ATX-style keyboard with PS/2 (aka mini-DIN) plug

allowing faster data transfer between your keyboard, mouse, or any other input device and your system. Figure 12.5 shows a USB keyboard.

Wireless

For years, scientists and science fiction writers have envisioned a world in which everything worked without wires or cables. There's even a Japanese company that's exploring a way to set up solar panels on the moon and beam the resulting electricity back here to Earth. Do you hear something? You should—it's the sound of the future knocking at your door. The wireless craze has already begun, and it's probable that many future computers will simply be boxes with no plugs, connectors, or other cable outlets.

Wireless keyboards are becoming increasingly popular as the prices keep dropping and people try to limit the amount of clutter and cabling around their desks. Wireless technology is divided into two general types: infrared and radio frequency wireless systems. In both cases, the keyboard sends signals to a receiver that interprets them and passes them to the keyboard controller in your computer.

Both of these types of systems are limited in range, but the range of each is more than enough to allow your keyboard free movement around your desk and on your lap. If you're thinking about trying one, however, note that a system that supports one type of wireless keyboard won't necessarily

● **Figure 12.5**   A USB keyboard

support the other, so before you purchase a wireless keyboard, check the specs for your system to make sure it supports the type you intend to buy.

Step-by-Step 12.1

Installing a Keyboard

To install a keyboard, you simply plug it into the appropriate connector and—*poof*—you're done! Just make sure that you have a keyboard connector port available and be sure to plug in the connector correctly. In addition, you shouldn't connect or disconnect a serial connector while a computer is running.

To complete this exercise, you will need the following:

- A working computer with a PS/2 keyboard port and a USB port
- A PS/2 keyboard
- If possible, a USB keyboard
- If possible, an older computer with an AT keyboard port

Step 1

The first order of business is to identify the connector that's attached to the keyboard. If it's a DIN, or AT-type, connector, it will look like the black plug shown here. Look at the end of the connector to see the pattern of pins. When you plug in the connector, be careful to line up the pins and connectors. If your keyboard doesn't have an old connector, see if you can find an older system that does and examine the connector and port.

Step 2

If your connector is a mini-DIN, or PS/2, connector, it will look like the blue plug shown here. Again, look down the shaft of the connector to see the pin layout. It's a bit different from the DIN. A small rectangular key allows you to insert the connector only one way. The side closest to the key almost always displays a marking that indicates which side the key is on so you can see how to insert the connector with a just quick look or even by feel alone. Some of these connectors are flat on one side, others have a notch or arrow that you can feel, and still others have a series of grooves on one side of the connector. Insert the connector with this flat spot, notch, or grooved area aimed toward the middle of the case, away from the edge. Your system will most likely have a PS/2 keyboard connector, but if it doesn't, try to find one that does and examine the connector and port.

Warning: If you ever have to change out a keyboard attached the oldest way, be forewarned: you should not connect or disconnect a serial connector while the computer is on. The keyboard or mouse attached to the computer uses one of the pins in the serial port for power. Although in many cases nothing will happen, there have been enough instances where the motherboard or device itself has been damaged that you are well advised to power down the computer before attempting to insert or remove any serial connectors.

Step 3

If your keyboard has a USB connector, it will have a little symbol printed on one side like the one in the following illustration. A USB connector is meant to be installed only one way. When the connector is plugged in, this symbol should always point either up or toward the inside of the case (away from the edge). As long as you don't apply a lot of muscle to force the connector into the socket, you won't hurt anything if you position it wrong—the connector just won't go into the port. Again, if your keyboard isn't USB, try to find one that is and examine the connector and port.

Step 4

Once you've identified the connector on your keyboard, it's time to plug it in. Make sure the computer is turned off; then insert the connector into the correct socket. Now boot the computer. If you have a slow system, or if you watch very closely, you can see the boot program recognize the keyboard and load the driver.

Note: A USB keyboard can be connected or removed successfully without shutting down the system, but a PS/2 keyboard can't. Thus, whether you're replacing a PS/2 keyboard with a USB model or vice versa, you still need to power down and reboot.

Step 5

Every personal computer comes with a driver already built into the system that will run a standard keyboard. That's all that most users will ever need. At this point, therefore, you should have a working keyboard. However, if your keyboard has advanced features, they may not all work if you use the standard driver.

Step 6

Some specialized keyboards have custom drivers that need to be installed to make use of their nonstandard features. These drivers will come with the keyboard, usually on a floppy disk or CD. If you have a keyboard with its own drivers, follow the directions and load them. Try some of the features to verify that the drivers actually enabled them.

■ Installing and Configuring a Mouse

The modern mouse (or its equivalent) is as important to the basic operation of your computer as the venerable keyboard. All modern GUIs are designed to work with a pointing device of some sort, be it a mouse, trackball, touch pad, or any variety of other cursor-manipulation peripherals. For the purposes of this section, I lump all of these devices (unless otherwise noted) into the general category of mice.

Just like keyboards, mice come in a huge array of shapes and sizes, but they are, for the most part, all alike. Because a mouse driver is built into most systems, you can normally just plug in the little rodent and be off and running as soon as the operating system boots. As with keyboards, ergonomics and connectors are the primary areas where commercially available mice differ.

Ah, the Choices!

Mice come in a dizzying array of packages, all dedicated to moving that pointer or cursor across your screen and clicking virtual buttons. The first mouse was created by a team working for Doug Engelbart in the late 1960s and debuted in December 1968. It was a hollowed-out wooden block with a button on top. Two wheels below set at a 90-degree angle from one another enabled the user to move the cursor vertically and horizontally (Figure 12.6).

• **Figure 12.6** The first mouse

Configure Your Keyboard

Modern keyboards provide many ways to fine-tune their operation and characteristics to suit a wide variety of users. These changes are handled by the **Keyboard applet** on the Control Panel. However, most people never take the time to tweak their keyboard settings. Try this:

1. Open the Control Panel and run the applet that controls your keyboard settings.

2. Make your cursor blink faster.

3. Configure the SHIFT key to turn off caps lock.

4. Configure your keyboard so it can bring your computer out of standby mode

Since that time, many new designs have emerged, but the standard mice all share the same architecture, and in fact, all pointing devices have at least these things in common: a way to manipulate the pointer on the X and Y axes and at least one button that allows the user to click the virtual buttons on the computer screen.

Standard-Issue Mouse

Today's standard PS/2 mouse consists of two finger-operated buttons, a small wheel between the buttons, and a cable connecting the mouse to the computer. These mice can be found at any store that sells anything computer related and cost $10 and up. They aren't indestructible, but with normal use and a little cleaning, the average mouse has a lifespan greater than the average system it connects to, and they're pretty foolproof to use.

• A standard mouse

More Ergonomics

Ergonomics plays a huge role in today's human-computer interaction. Every aspect of office and home life is being reconsidered, and products designed specifically to reduce fatigue, backaches, muscle cramps, and other injuries are becoming increasingly common.

The design of the mouse pointing device has been rethought and changed profoundly through the study of ergonomics. The most common changes from the standard mouse design are in the shape and the movement. Mice are available that are contoured to the shape of a hand and that require very little effort to move, greatly reducing fatigue. Many mice allow your hand to rest at a more comfortable angle, and they glide almost effortlessly on any surface. These improvements not only increase productivity but also substantially reduce the risk of carpal tunnel syndrome.

One other item to consider if you use a mouse is a pad on which to rest your wrist and/or mouse. These pads are designed to take the stress off your wrist and arm; many options are available, but some work better than others. I prefer the gel-filled pads (as opposed to the simple foam pads) for my wrist.

Trackballs

The **trackball** is an option for users who don't like to use a mouse. Many people, for instance, don't like flexing their wrists as much as it takes to manipulate a mouse. For these people, there are many styles of trackballs, one of which may fit them perfectly.

The most common trackball has a platform on which to rest the hand; two buttons (located where the hand naturally rests) and a wheel on that platform; and a ball, which is operated by the thumb, that contacts two small mechanical wheels that translate the trackball's movement to the pointer on

• A contoured mouse

• **Figure 12.7** Typical trackball

the screen. Many other types of trackball are also available, including some that allow the wrist to rest at a more natural angle, some that allow either the thumb or the forefinger to control the ball, some that are designed so you control the buttons with your thumb and middle or ring finger, some that are designed so you control the buttons with your first and middle fingers, and even some that are designed to be held in the fingers and not rested on the desk at all. Figure 12.7 shows a typical trackball. Generally, the primary difference between a mouse and a trackball is that you control a mouse by moving your hand, and you control a trackball by moving just one or two fingers.

Optical Mice

The latest popular innovation (though it's actually not that new) in mice is the **optical mouse**. These mice are quickly replacing the older style **mechanical mouse** that uses the rubberized ball and mechanical wheels. Instead, optical mice use a tiny camera that detects mouse movement by imaging the surface that the mouse moves over. An optical mouse takes between 1,500 and 6,000 images per second, depending on the manufacturer and the age of the mouse (the newer ones are faster). This means that there is no little ball to attract and collect dirt, and the user can use the mouse on virtually any nontransparent surface. Remember the *nontransparent* part, as optical mice tend not to work well on glass. An optical mouse also tends to provide a much smoother, more certain pointer action than a mechanical mouse. Because of this you can, for example, plug one of these mice into your laptop, sit down in a park, and navigate using your leg or the surface of the table where you're sitting (as long as it's relatively smooth).

• Bottom of an optical mouse

Touch Pads

The **touch pad** is mostly known through its use in laptop computers. It consists of a small pad across which the user runs a finger to manipulate the pointer or cursor. To click an on-screen button, the user either taps the pad or presses one of the buttons usually included above or below the pad itself.

Touch pads use a technology called field distortion sensing. Basically, under the top surface of the pad, two layers of electrical conductors in a grid arrangement create a field. When you touch the surface, your finger distorts the field at that spot. (This technology won't work with a stylus or pen. Only skin will work.) The exact spot that you touched is then calculated and passed to the computer. As you drag your finger across the surface, the pointer follows the same path.

Mouse Connections

Time for a brief review of mouse connections! In the past, the mouse was connected to systems with a standard 9-pin **serial connector**. When the ATX motherboard appeared on the scene, that changed. Just like the keyboard, the ATX board has a port reserved especially for the mouse. You will still find some older mice attached to AT-style systems, but these are now obsolete and quite rare.

PS/2

As with the keyboard, the modern standard connector for the mouse is the PS/2 connector, also known as a mini-DIN or ATX-style keyboard/mouse connector.

USB

Many mice come with a USB connector these days. These are exactly the same as the USB connectors described earlier: you plug in the device, and it works. Also as mentioned earlier, USB generally sends data faster than a serial PS/2 connection. This makes it a perfect mate for the optical mice and trackballs that work more quickly (and therefore more smoothly) than the standard mechanical mouse.

Wireless Mice

Just as there are wireless keyboards, there are also mice with no cords. Also just as with keyboards, these are available in two basic types: infrared and radio frequency. Infrared is the more established technology, but the radio frequency types are beginning to find their place in the market. One big difference between the two is that anything that works in the infrared part of the spectrum is pretty much limited to line-of-sight access to its intended receiver, whereas radio waves can transmit signals through furniture and walls. The downside of devices that rely on radio frequency is the possibility of interference, which can hamper reception and therefore performance.

Step-by-Step 12.2

Installing a Mouse

As with a keyboard, a large percentage of the time you can simply plug a mouse into its appropriate socket and it will work. All desktop systems come with a mouse driver built into them, and for a standard mouse, that's pretty much all most people will ever need.

To complete this exercise, you will need the following:

- A working computer with a PS/2 mouse port and a USB port
- A PS/2 mouse
- If possible, a USB mouse
- If possible, a mouse with a 9-pin DB serial connector

Step 1

As in Step-by-Step 12.1, your first order of business is to identify the connector. The PS/2 and USB connectors will look just like their counterparts on the keyboard. A pre-ATX-style 9-pin DB serial connector may look unique; however, this connector attaches exactly like every other DB connector.

Step 2

While the computer is off, plug the mouse into the correct port, carefully checking the orientation of the connector before pushing. Then boot your system to see if the mouse works.

Step 3

As with keyboards, modern Windows systems have a mouse driver built in. However, most mice come with customized drivers to take advantage of special features of the mouse. If you have such drivers, load them. The customized drivers should come with instructions you can follow to load them. After loading the drivers, use the Mouse applet on the Control Panel to configure your mouse's properties to take advantage of the advanced features.

Step 4

In this final step, you'll try something a bit more challenging. Shut off the system, unplug the mouse, and restart your computer, just for the experience. When your computer is finished booting, you should find yourself in Windows—with no mouse! Lucky for you, Windows also responds to keystroke combinations. Press CTRL-ESC and then use the arrow keys to navigate to the Shut Down option. (If you have it, you can also use the WINDOWS key, which is the one with the Microsoft Windows icon, next to the ALT key.) Press ENTER, make sure the Shut Down option is highlighted, and press ENTER again.

Configuring a Mouse

If you load a custom driver for your mouse, you will usually also have a custom configuration application to go along with it. Even if you use the built-in Windows driver, you can use the **Mouse applet** on the Control Panel to modify the way your mouse reacts, to suit your personal tastes and needs.

■ Identifying Less Common Input Devices

If you count the devices that have been created for custom applications, there are really dozens, if not hundreds, of devices that can be put under the heading "Input Devices." Trying to describe and explain them all would take a book in and of itself, but you should know about a few more general-use devices that you can expect to see.

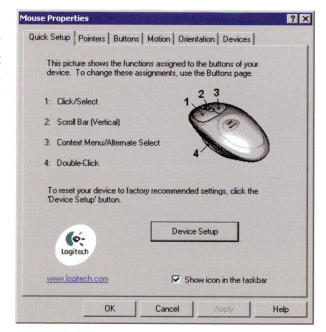

• Mouse applet

Try This!

Configure Your Mouse

Like modern keyboards, modern mice provide a variety of configuration options you can use to customize their interaction with you. Many people struggle unnecessarily to control their mice because they don't know, or don't know how, they can change the way the devices operate. Try this:

1. Open the Control Panel and run the applet that controls your mouse settings.

2. Set up your mouse for a left-handed person.

3. Change or customize the look of your cursor and pointer.

4. Change the speed with which your mouse traverses the screen.

• A joystick

Inside Information

Force Feedback

Force feedback refers to the action of an input device (such as a joystick) in response to changes in the game or device that it's controlling. For instance, if you were flying an F-16 in a flight simulator and you went into a virtual high-speed dive, the software might activate the force-feedback mechanism inside the joystick to make the joystick more difficult to pull back, creating a more realistic experience.

Game Ports

The personal computer is what it is today partially because of the popularity of computer games. A good portion of the computer industry is influenced by what sells games and what makes game players happy.

It should be no surprise, then, that the joystick and its cousins are so popular. In addition to the built-in mouse port and keyboard port, the vast majority of motherboards are sold with built-in serial game ports. In fact, the game port was one of the first add-on cards for the original IBM PC.

Types of Game Controllers

Game controllers come in three main types: joysticks, steering/racing wheels and pedals, and game pads. The common view is that joysticks are used for flight simulator and space flight games, steering wheels are used for driving games, and game pads are used for action games, but the lines are actually blurred. Some of the best virtual racers use a joystick instead of a steering wheel, and you can really use the game pad for just about any game you want.

Joysticks   The number of gaming devices that plug into the game port has grown dramatically over the years, but the joystick has been there in one form or another from the very beginning and is still the most common control device. You can find joysticks with seemingly hundreds of different options these days, from simple stick-and-trigger types to those with dozens of programmable buttons, another tiny joystick on top (called the hat switch), and force feedback support for games that offer it. Some joysticks even come equipped with pedals to use as rudder controllers for those totally realistic flight simulators, or another controller that acts as the throttle in many games.

It is important to note that games aren't the only uses for a joystick. Several training programs use them to simulate the manipulation of heavy machinery, and some people use them to operate remote equipment while sitting safely at a desk. Indeed, when IBM added the 15-pin female DB game port to the PC, the mouse wasn't the standard device that it is today. The engineers at IBM saw the joystick, particularly, becoming the hard-working input device that the mouse is today. Nevertheless, when you see a joystick on someone's desk these days, you can be fairly certain that it's used for hunting down the bad guys in a strange and wonderful virtual world far more than it's used for any—ahem—"useful" task.

Racing Wheels/Accelerator Sets   Probably the second most popular game controller for the PC is the steering wheel and accelerator set, also known as the racing wheel. Technically the computer still sees these as joysticks (in fact *all* game devices that plug into the game port are seen as and operate like joysticks), but they are different enough in their use to require separate mention.

Basically, these devices consist of a steering wheel that sits on or attaches to your desk, and often a set of pedals. The steering wheel functions as such in games that call for one, and the pedals function as a brake and accelerator.

• A racing wheel

Game Pads   When most people see or hear about a game pad, they first think about console gaming systems like the Microsoft XBox or the Sony PlayStation 2. However, game pads are also made that work (almost always through USB these days) with a standard PC and act as dedicated game controllers. These controllers tend to resemble those that come with the console systems, as shown here.

In general, game pads have multiple customizable buttons, some kind of multidirectional toggle or pad (called an analog controller or digital pad, respectively), and an ergonomic design that allows fatigue-free hours of gaming. Because they are mostly USB devices, there are few (if any) compatibility issues, and setup is generally easy.

• A game pad

Input Device Connections

You're probably aware by now of a running theme in input device connection: connections use either serial or USB ports. Even wireless controllers have a receiver plugged into one or the other type of port.

Serial   For game controllers, the serial port du jour is the game port (Figure 12.8) that is standard on all modern motherboards. This is a 15-pin female DB port that is almost always colored yellow.

Just like the mouse and keyboard, the game port has its own driver built into most modern operating systems, but because of the prevalence of specialized game controllers, you are much more likely to want to load a custom driver for these or to alter the configuration of the included driver to more personal specifications.

USB   USB, as mentioned before, is hot-swappable. This is a wonderful convenience when you've finished a long day of working from home and you want to fire up a virtual racecar for some fast-paced racing thrills. With USB, there's no need to turn off your system—just plug in your joystick and off you go! USB is also faster than a serial port, which is desirable for all uses of a joystick or game controller because a lot of information can be passing between

• **Figure 12.8**   A 15-pin female DB port

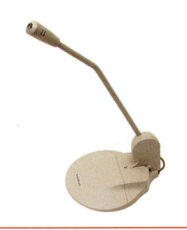

• A common microphone for the PC

the computer and the device in the middle of a game or while your multimillion-dollar submersible is probing the bottom of the ocean.

The only issue with USB is that it relies more on the CPU than the serial ports do, so if you're really asking a lot of the processor, your pointer may behave erratically. I haven't personally seen this, but I mention it as a possibility.

Microphones

Microphones are having more of an impact nowadays as online phone calls, virtual conferencing, and online presentations and seminars become more popular. As the bandwidth of interconnected networks has increased, sending live audio back and forth between multiple locations is becoming almost commonplace. I have several times hooked up a microphone to my PC and attended online seminars where more than 40 people were verbally asking questions of the presenter. For many large companies, online conference calls are a standard means of doing business across the continent or overseas, and for this purpose, a microphone is essential.

Many office programs can use voice recordings to add commentary to presentations. In fact, voice tools are all over your computer—just look for them!

Microphones are also being used to interact directly with the computer itself. Voice recognition software has improved dramatically since its earliest incarnations in the 1980s. Several companies make sophisticated programs that let you type documents, control program features, and even interact with Windows simply by speaking into a microphone. Software manufacturers are now building voice recognition capabilities directly into their word processing and other office products. This technology still has a long way to go before it reaches the *Star Trek* state of usability, but it's definitely the application of the future for the humble PC microphone.

Still and Video Cameras

Many online conference calls include either a still picture of the people involved or a live video feed along with the live audio feed. Live video can eat up a *lot* of bandwidth, but it is quite feasible and is becoming more common. Video is, of course, managed through the use of cameras connected to the sending and receiving computer systems. Windows 2000 and Windows XP both have applications built in that allow the user to simply plug a camera into the USB or FireWire port, configure it, and get underway.

In addition, thousands of computer users have small webcams mounted on their desks or computers and send out pictures by e-mail, or they link their cameras to their personal websites so people can see them.

Tablets

If you are a graphic designer, illustrator, or other user of high-end graphics software, you'll probably be familiar with the **art tablet**: a large, flat tablet that is accompanied by a pen device and usually also a mouse. These are

• A webcam

used in CAD drawing, animation, movie production, and other illustration or design tasks.

The pen that comes with the tablet is really a sensitive pointing device that interacts with a grid built into the tablet in much the same way as your finger interacts with a touch pad. These pens are extremely pressure sensitive; at least one I know of has 1,024 levels of touch sensitivity. The pen offers an experience similar to drawing with an ordinary pen or pencil in that you can exert pressure to alter the thickness of a line or paint splatter.

Touch Screens

The last input device we explore here is the **touch screen**. You've probably used one of these fairly recently, to make a deposit at an ATM perhaps, or to choose the tire or battery that is best for your car, or to buy movie tickets—touch screens are, quite literally, everywhere. You will see them in use when you buy food at a fast-food restaurant; many sit-down restaurants use them as well.

A touch screen allows users to enter information or operate a computer simply by touching a display screen. These devices can be used as easily as a mouse or touch pad. Unlike touch pads, however, touch screens work with pretty much anything that touches the screen, be it your finger or a pointer of some sort.

Many monitors are made with the touch screen aspect built in, but many of the touch screens you see are really standard monitors (either CRTs or LCDs) with touch sensors added in front. You can easily purchase a touch screen to mount over most monitors and transform your own monitor into a touch-interactive one.

• An art tablet

Step-by-Step 12.3

Installing and Configuring a Game Controller

The first step in getting a new joystick ready for serious action is to install the game controller. Then you need to configure it. These steps are not difficult, but how you complete them can make all the difference in your gaming experience.

To complete this exercise, you will need the following:

■ A working computer running Windows with some sort of joystick attached

■ Any custom software that requires a joystick

Step 1

Open the Control Panel. Locate the icon of a joystick and game pad with the title Gaming Options, as shown here. Double-click the icon to bring up the Gaming Options dialog box.

Step 2

Look at the Controllers tab, shown here, to see if it lists your game controller. If you don't see your game controller, click the Add button and scroll down the list until you see a description of your controller. Double-click your choice, and Windows will find the driver and load it. Fire up something fun that uses a joystick and try it out.

Step 3

Once you have loaded the game controller and your computer has acknowledged that it does indeed exist, you will want to configure it to your liking. The specific process will vary depending on your particular gaming hardware and software, but the basics remain the same. Open the Control Panel again and double-click the Gaming Options icon to bring up the Gaming Options dialog box.

Step 4

Make sure that the controller in question is highlighted and click the Properties button. This will bring up the Properties window for your controller, similar to the one shown here. Choose the Settings tab and click the Calibrate button. This feature permits you to adjust the performance characteristics of the joystick so that it reacts correctly to your input.

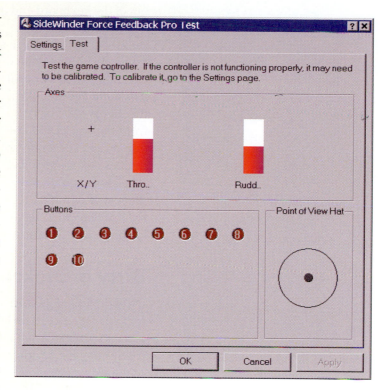

Step 5

If you have loaded software from the manufacturer, you will probably see a custom Properties window. In either case, follow the directions given to calibrate your toggle controllers and buttons. When you're done, try out the joystick and see how it now differs.

■ Maintaining and Troubleshooting Input Devices

Most devices need some form of maintenance, and input devices need more than most. These are the parts of the computer that regularly touch your skin. These are the parts that are most likely to collect dirt, dust, and food while you are absorbed in that annual report or busy blowing space rocks into microscopic particles. Without proper maintenance, your devices will eventually begin working erratically, and then not at all. There are actually two types of maintenance that users should perform: physical cleaning, and driver updating.

Cleaning

Cleaning procedures are specific to the device in question, but there are some basic points that you should know. First, soaking electronic parts in water is not a good idea, and probably for more reasons than the ones that may seem obvious. The local water in most locales isn't just water. It includes other chemicals that have been added either naturally or through human intervention. Many of these chemicals can leave a film or buildup on your electronic and mechanical components, altering the way they work or even destroying them. Individual parts are sometimes washable—the ball in a trackball, for instance, or the individual keys of a keyboard—but personally, I'm not going to pop all the keys off of my keyboard, put them in the dishwasher, and then replace them just because they're dirty. If you spill a soda on the keyboard, you can certainly pop the keys off and try to clean the mess out of the keyboard and off the keys, but many people will prefer just to buy a new keyboard.

To perform basic cleaning, use a damp (not wet) rag and clean the parts by gently wiping them down. For mice and track balls, take the ball out and clean the wheels or bearings that ride against the ball. Be sure to clean the ball itself. For an optical mouse, you need only wipe down the mouse with the damp rag. For keyboards, use a can of compressed air to blow out dirt from the cracks and crevices and then wipe the casing and the keys with a damp rag. The same holds true for the game controllers and other input devices—compressed air and a damp rag will usually do the job.

Before you do any of this, however, read the packaging or instructions that came with the device in question. Some manufacturers (such as those that make touch screens) recommend specific cleaning fluids or methods for keeping their products in excellent working order.

Dirty or Broken Devices

Dirty devices may work badly or not at all. If there seems to be a problem—for instance, if a certain key on the keyboard sticks or the pointer jumps from place to place instead of scrolling smoothly when you move your mouse—try cleaning the device thoroughly. This solves 80 to 90 percent of the problems with input devices.

Another possibility is that the hardware itself may be broken in some way. In this case, you might be tempted to open the device to determine the problem. However, you should be very careful about cracking open the case of one of these devices because not all of them are meant to be opened. Unless you know what you're doing or what needs to be fixed, you're likely to accomplish nothing except wasting your time.

Even though breakage does happen, most input devices are pretty hardy. You'll find keyboards and mice that are 10 years old and still work as well as they ever did. However, I do know of a situation where a man couldn't get his mouse to do *anything*. He went to see if it was plugged in properly and found that he had shut his metal desk drawer on the cable, severing it completely. The upside to a broken device is that most of these devices are cheap to replace, and the newer model will probably work better anyway. There is little reason to try to fix basic input devices, if for no reason other than cost: what's the point of spending an hour or more resuscitating a $15 mouse? If you do purchase an expensive device, however, be sure to send in that registration card and keep your proof of purchase and paperwork.

Driver Issues

Driver issues can be difficult to troubleshoot. If you have a driver problem, you may find that the device works badly or not at all, or that just a particular aspect of the device doesn't work. For instance, the specialized buttons on a joystick may not work while everything else works beautifully.

If you have taken apart your device (as much as is possible) and cleaned it, your next step is to go to the manufacturer's website and download the newest driver for your device. Then follow the directions the company gives for loading the driver onto your system. If this doesn't solve the problem, then dig up the number or e-mail address for tech support for your device or system. The tech should be able to help you determine if there's a conflict somewhere or if you should just get a new device.

■ Chapter Summary

After reading this chapter and completing the exercises, you should understand the following aspects of input devices:

Install a keyboard on a Windows system

- Keyboards come in a number of designs.

- The most common keyboard today is based on the 101-key model but has a total of 104 keys.

- Keyboards use DIN, mini-DIN (PS/2), or USB connectors.

- Windows has built-in driver support for almost all keyboards.

Install and configure a mouse on a Windows system

- Pointing devices such as touch pads and trackballs usually fall under the general heading of "mice."

- It is possible to plug devices into ports that weren't made for them (for instance, to plug a USB keyboard into a PS/2 port), but you must have an appropriate adapter to do so.

- Optical mice tend to work longer than mechanical (ball and roller) mice and need less maintenance.

- Mouse devices may use serial, DIN, mini-DIN (PS/2), or USB connections.

Identify some less common types of input devices

- In general, input devices connect through either some version of a serial connector or through a USB connection.

- Three types of less common input devices are joysticks, racing wheels, and game pads.

- The primary mouse, keyboard, and game serial ports are easily recognized and are usually color coded, and the connectors that go in them can be inserted in only one way.

- USB connectors are all the same, and any USB device can plug into any USB port.

Maintain and troubleshoot input devices

- Don't soak your devices or put them in a washing machine.

- Compressed air and a damp towel are the main tools for cleaning your devices.

- If you have a driver problem, you may find that the device works badly or not at all, or that just a particular aspect of the device won't work.

- After checking to be sure your hardware isn't the problem, check the manufacturer's website for updated drivers to download and install.

■ Key Terms

84-key keyboard *(321)*
101-key keyboard *(321)*
art tablet *(332)*
daisy-chained *(322)*
DIN *(322)*
ergonomics *(321)*
hot-swappable *(322)*

Keyboard applet *(326)*
mechanical mouse *(327)*
mini-DIN *(322)*
Mouse applet *(329)*
optical mouse *(327)*
PS/2 *(322)*
serial connector *(328)*

touch pad *(327)*
touch screen *(333)*
trackball *(326)*
USB connector *(322)*
wireless *(323)*

■ Key Term Quiz

Use terms from the Key Terms list to complete the following sentences. Not all terms will be used.

1. AT PCs used a _____ style keyboard connection.

2. PS/2 style connections are also known as _____.

3. The most common type of keyboard used today is based on the _____.

4. Working kind of like an upside-down mouse where you roll the ball with your hand, the _____ allows you to keep your hand still while manipulating the cursor.

5. If you can disconnect or connect a device without restarting the system and the device works properly, the device is _____.

6. Many _____ devices will work only if you touch them with your skin.

7. A/an _____ uses light to detect movement as opposed to a mechanical method.

8. Before they used DIN connectors, mice plugged into computers using _____.

9. Artists might use a/an _____ because it allows more control over input to the system, and it operates like a pencil.

10. Any keyboard configuration is handled by the _____.

■ Multiple-Choice Quiz

1. _____ was the man who invented the mouse.
   a. Charles Babbage
   b. Douglas Engelbart
   c. Herman Hollerith
   d. Steve Jobs

2. The most common keyboard today is based on the 101-key keyboard but has a total of _____ keys.
   a. 83
   b. 84
   c. 100
   d. 104

3. Which of the following connections would you be least likely to see for a keyboard?
   a. DIN
   b. Parallel
   c. Mini-DIN
   d. USB

4. Which port allows you to daisy-chain devices?
   a. Parallel
   b. Game
   c. Serial
   d. USB

5. How should you clean a keyboard?
   a. Soak it in a bathtub.
   b. Wash it in the dishwasher.
   c. Wipe it with a damp cloth.
   d. Spray heavy-duty cleaner on it and let the cleaner soak in.

6. Which of the following is an advantage of an optical mouse over a mechanical mouse?
   a. You can alter the configuration of an optical mouse.
   b. An optical mouse has a built-in port.
   c. An optical mouse is easier to keep clean.
   d. You don't have to move your wrist as much while using an optical mouse.

7. The science concerned with designing safe and comfortable machines for humans is called _____.
   a. Computing
   b. Aesthetics
   c. Industrial design
   d. Ergonomics

8. The PS/2 port was first introduced by _____.
   a. IBM
   b. Compaq
   c. MITS
   d. Apple

9. The _____ connector used to be common for mice but is now obsolete.
   a. 25-pin parallel
   b. 9-pin serial
   c. USB
   d. Mini-DIN

10. Force feedback is _____.
    a. What happens when a punch card is rejected
    b. The ability of a joystick to physically react to changes in a game or device that it's controlling
    c. What happens when you get an electrical shock from touching a mouse
    d. The ability of the USB port to eject a malfunctioning device

11. Optical mice are quickly replacing the older-technology _____ mice.
    a. Serial
    b. Magnetic
    c. Parallel
    d. Mechanical

12. The MIDI connector can also be used as the _____ port.

   a. Game

   b. PS/2

   c. DIN

   d. USB

13. You'll have a hard time trying to use an optical mouse on _____.

   a. Marble

   b. Glass

   c. Wood

   d. Plastic

14. If your mechanical mouse is starting to behave erratically, what most likely is the problem?

   a. Device driver failure

   b. Hardware failure

   c. User error

   d. Dirt

15. Where can you find the built-in applets that allow you to alter the configuration of the keyboard and mouse?

   a. Desktop Properties

   b. My Documents

   c. Control Panel

   d. Device Manager

■ Essay Quiz

1. While writing the specs for a major PC purchase for your company, you see that the mice are cheap mechanical ones. Write a memo to your boss explaining why the company should spend a bit more for optical mice.

2. After getting your boss to change the purchase specifications to include optical mice, you see that she has chosen a cheap, nonergonomic mouse. Write an addendum to the memo you sent earlier motivating the boss to purchase slightly more expensive ergonomic mice.

3. While searching through some old systems, you find a number of AT-style 84-key keyboards. The boss wants you to distribute these with some new PCs. Write a memo to your boss explaining why this is a bad idea.

4. You are the IT person for a department. Your office is composed of roughly half optical and half mechanical mice. You're getting tired of responding to mice problems caused by dirt in mechanical mice. Write a quick procedure sheet for determining whether a mouse is dirty and what to do if it is.

5. You have a number of new Windows XP systems with microphones. Write a brief note that you will attach to the new systems to motivate users to try to use the microphones.

Lab Projects

• Lab Project 12.1

Arguably the two most popular makers of better mice and keyboards are Microsoft and Logitech. Go to both the Microsoft (www.microsoft.com) and Logitech (www.logitech.com) websites and look at the many different mice and keyboards. As you investigate these mice and keyboards, create a list of features that are important to you for a mouse and a keyboard: color, ergonomics, mechanical versus optical, wired versus wireless, and so on. Choose a particular model of a mouse and of a keyboard. Present your reasons for choosing these models to others and compare your reasons to theirs.

• Lab Project 12.2

One subjective aspect of keyboards is the "feel" of the keyboard—the way the keys respond when you press them down. Try out a number of different keyboards (at a local computer store, for instance) and judge the feel of the different keyboards. Document the feel using descriptive adjectives such as "spongy" and "loose." Note the make and model of the keyboard you like best and compare your responses with those of others.

Sound

"This music mads me: let it sound no more."

—SHAKESPEARE, *THE TRAGEDY OF KING RICHARD THE SECOND*, ACT V, SCENE V

In this chapter, you will learn how to:

■ **Describe how sound works in a PC**

■ **Purchase the right sound card**

■ **Install a sound card in a Windows system**

■ **Perform basic sound card troubleshooting**

Racing down the virtual track, pixels flying across the screen, hearing the engine roar as you take another turn and press down the accelerator—or surfing the Web for lovely scenic nature photos with the sweet, mellifluous sounds of Mozart filling the room: sound has become an integral component of the computing experience, and setting up and optimizing sound for the personal computer have become integral skills for all computer techs.

Correctly setting up sound for a PC requires you to know about quite a few things; the sound process has many components. You need a properly installed sound card with the right drivers loaded, reasonably high-quality speakers, support software such as the right API for a particular game, and your application set up to use the features of the sound card properly. And every great tech needs to know troubleshooting to handle both routine and uncommon problems with sound.

How Sound Works in a PC

Like the ripples rolling across a pond when you drop a rock in the center, sound flows from a source in invisible but measurable waves that cause the membranes in your ears to vibrate in certain ways. The sophistication of the human ear enables most people to differentiate the melodious and the raucous, the loud and the soft. Computers aren't nearly as sophisticated as the human ear and brain, so very clear standards are necessary for converting music into a format that a PC can use to record and play sound.

 Computer folks use the terms *capture* and *output* instead of record and play.

Sound-Capture Basics

Virtually every PC today comes with four critical components for capturing and outputting sound: a sound card, speakers, microphone, and recording/playback software. Sound waves are captured (recorded) in electronic format through a process called **sampling**. In its simplest sense, sampling means capturing the state or quality of a particular sound wave a set number of times each second. The sampling rate is measured in units of thousands of cycles per second, or **kilohertz (KHz)**. The more often a sound is sampled, the better the reproduction of that sound. Most sounds in the PC world are recorded with a sampling rate of from 11 KHz (very low quality, like a telephone) to 128 KHz (ultrahigh quality, better then the human ear).

Sounds vary according to their loudness (amplitude), how high or low their tone (frequency), and the qualities that differentiate the same note played on different instruments (timbre). All the characteristics of a particular sound wave—amplitude, frequency, timbre—need to be recorded and translated into 1s and 0s to reproduce that sound accurately within the computer and thus out your speakers.

The most famous of all sound cards is Creative Labs' popular SoundBlaster series.

The number of characteristics of a particular sound captured during sampling is measured by the **bit depth** of the sample, the number of bits used to describe the characteristics of a sound. The greater the bit depth used to capture a sample, the more characteristics of that sound can be stored and thus re-created. An 8-bit sample of a Jimi Hendrix guitar solo, for example, captures $2^8 = 256$ characteristics of that sound per sample. It would sound like a cheap recording of a recording, perhaps a little flat and thin. A 16-bit sample, in contrast, captures $2^{16} = 65,536$ different characteristics of that same sound and reproduces all the fuzzy overtones and feedback that made Hendrix' unique sound.

The last aspect of sound capture is the number of different tracks of sound that are captured. Most commonly, we capture either a single track (monaural) or two tracks (stereo). There are more advanced captures that record many more sound tracks, but that's a topic for a more advanced sound capture discussion.

The combination of sampling frequency and bit depth determines how faithfully a digital version of a sound captures what your ear would hear. A sound capture is considered **CD quality** when recorded at 44 KHz, with 16-bit depth, and in stereo.

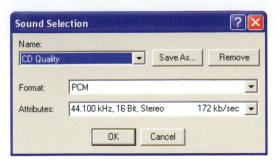

• **Figure 13.1** Sound Recorder settings

> WAV and MP3 are only two among a large number of file formats for sound. Not all sound players can play all of these formats; however, many sound formats are nothing more than some type of compressed WAV file, so with the right codec loaded, you can play most sound formats.

Most recording programs let you set these values before you begin recording. Figure 13.1 shows the configuration settings for the popular Windows Sound Recorder.

Hey, wait a minute! Did you notice the Format setting in Figure 13.1? What's that? You can save those sampled sounds in lots of different ways—and that's where the term *format* comes into play.

Recorded Sound Formats

The granddaddy of all sound formats is Pulse Code Modulation (PCM). PCM was developed in the 1960s to carry telephone calls over the first digital lines. With just a few minor changes to allow for use in PCs, the PCM format is still alive and well, although it's better known as the WAV format so common in the PC world. WAV files are great for storing faithful copies of sounds and music, but they do so at a price. WAV files can be huge, especially when sampled at high frequency and bit depth. A four-minute song at 44 KHz and 16-bit stereo, for example, weighs in at a whopping 40+ MB!

What's interesting about sound quality is that the human ear cannot perceive anywhere near the subtle variations of sound recorded at 44 KHz and 16-bit stereo. Clever programmers have written algorithms to store full-quality WAV files as compressed files, discarding unnecessary audio qualities of that file. These algorithms—really nothing more than a series of instructions in code—are called compressor/decompressor programs, or more commonly just **codecs**. The most famous of the codecs is the Fraunhoffer MPEG Layer 3 codec, more often called by its file extension, **MP3**.

Playing Sounds

A large number of programs can play sounds on a typical Windows computer. First, virtually every Windows computer comes with Windows Media Player, possibly the most popular of all sound players. However, many other players are available. This is good because not all sound players can play all sounds.

• Windows Media Player

MIDI

Every sound card can produce sounds as well as play prerecorded sound files. Every sound card comes with a second processor designed to interpret standardized **Musical Instrument Digital Interface (MIDI)** files. It's important to note that a MIDI file is not an independent music file. Unlike a WAV file, which will sound more or less the same on many different PCs, a MIDI file is a text file that takes advantage of the sound processing hardware to enable the PC to produce sound. Programmers use these small text files to tell the sound card what notes to play, how long, how loud, on which instruments, and so forth. Think of a MIDI file as a piece of electronic sheet music, with the instruments built into your sound card.

The beauty of MIDI files is that they're tiny in comparison to equivalent WAV files. The first movement of Beethoven's Fifth Symphony, for example, weighs in at a whopping 78 MB as a high-quality WAV file. The same seven-minute song as a MIDI file, in contrast, slips in at a svelte 60 *KB*!

MIDI is hardware dependent, meaning the abilities and quality of the individual sound card make all the difference in the world on the sound produced. Sound cards play MIDI files using one of two technologies: FM synthesis or wavetable synthesis.

FM Synthesis

Early processors used electronic emulation of various instruments—a technique often called **FM synthesis**—to more or less produce music and other sound effects. Software developers could tell the sound processor to reproduce a piano playing certain notes, for example, and a sound remotely resembling a piano would pour forth from the speakers. The problem with FM synthesis is that although the modulation sounds okay for a single note, such as middle C, it sounds increasingly electronic the farther up or down the scale you go from that prime note.

Wavetable Synthesis

To address the odd techno-sound of early sound processors, manufacturers began embedding recordings of actual instruments or other sounds in the sound card. Many modern sound cards use these recorded sounds to reproduce an instrument much more faithfully than with FM synthesis. When asked to play a C on a piano or on a viola, the sound processor grabs a prerecorded WAV file from its memory and adjusts it to match the specific sound and timing requested. This technique is called **wavetable synthesis**. The number of instruments stored in a sound card is called the polyphony of that card. Decent sound cards have 64 instruments stored, and better cards have 256, 320, or more—a veritable symphony orchestra on a chip!

Other File Formats

The WAV, MP3, and MIDI formats may account for the majority of sound files, but plenty of other less common formats are out there. Here are the extensions of some other sound file formats you may run into in the PC world:

- **ASX** One of the newest sound file types. You'll need the latest version of Windows Media Player to play these.
- **ASM, WMA** Compressed sound formats that are often seen on the Internet and used in streaming sound.

Inside Information

Compressing WAV Files to MP3 Format

Using MP3 compression, it is possible to shrink a WAV file by a factor of 12 without losing much sound quality. When you compress a WAV file into an MP3 file, the key decision is the bit rate. The bit rate is the amount of information (number of bits) transferred from the compressed file to the MP3 decoder in one second. The higher the bit rate of an MP3 file, the higher the sound quality. The bit rate of MP3 audio files is commonly measured in thousands of bits per second, abbreviated kbps. Most MP3 encoders support a range of bit rates from 24 kbps up to 320 kbps (or 320,000 bits per second). A CD-quality MP3 bit rate is 128 kbps.

MIDI files have the file extension .mid in the PC world.

MIDI files are much less popular than recorded formats on PCs. However, every Windows computer and every sound card still fully supports MIDI.

- **RM** These files play either just audio or audio and video. They are proprietary to RealMedia, a popular player often used on the Internet. You must have a RealMedia player to play these files.

- **AIFF** A popular sound format used on Macintosh computers. These files are often seen at websites, and you can use the well-known QuickTime player to play these files.

- **MOD, VOC** Two obsolete file formats promoted by Creative Labs in the early 1990s. They are rarely seen today; however, most sound players will still play these types of files.

- **AU** Another popular Macintosh format that is often seen in the Windows world. Many different players can play these files.

In no way is this list comprehensive. There are over 100 sound file formats, but the odds of seeing one other than these are pretty slim.

Video

Recorded audio files and MIDI files aren't the only files that play sounds on your computer. Video files also have sound built into them. However, to play the sound that accompanies the video, the video player program must support the particular video file format. The most common video formats in the PC world are AVI, MPEG, MOV, ASF, and RM.

Applications

Many applications, especially games, play sounds, too. In the not-too-distant past, a game or an application sometimes had its own sound format, but most applications and games today use standard WAV, MP3, or MIDI files.

Streaming Media

Streaming media is incredibly popular on the Internet. Streaming media is a broadcast of data that is played on your computer and immediately discarded. Streaming media has spawned an entire industry of Internet radio stations. The two most popular streaming media players are Windows Media Player and Winamp. The ASF and RM compressed audio/video file formats were created specially to stream over the Internet.

Try This!

Play Sounds in Windows

The typical Windows PC comes with a number of applications for playing sound files. Take a tour of a typical Windows system to see the applications available for playing sound files. Using a Windows system with a sound card, try this:

1. Using the file search feature in Windows, locate all of the files on your computer that have the extension .wav—all versions of Windows come with a number of WAV files. Double-click one of the files to play it. What program is associated with WAV files?

2. Repeat Step 1, but this time look for files with the extension .mid. Not all versions of Windows have MIDI files. Double-click one of the files to play it. What program is associated with MIDI files?

3. From the Start button, search for any sound programs that may be on your system. You'll almost certainly run into Windows Media Player and Sound Recorder, but also see if there are any third-party programs installed.

4. If possible, install the popular sound player Winamp on your system. You can get a copy of this free program at www.winamp.com. Check Winamp's Help feature to see what types of file formats Winamp supports—it supports a lot of file formats!

5. If you have an Internet connection, try running some streaming audio. If you have version 7 or later of Windows Media Player, find some music using its Radio Tuner. If you have Winamp, look for something you can dance to at www.shoutcast.com.

Purchasing the Right Sound Card

Sound cards have many capabilities built in, including two separate sound processors (one for all of the recorded formats like WAV and another for MIDI), support chips for joysticks and other pointing devices that plug into the game port, and recording capabilities. All sound cards, from the cheapest to the most expensive, can play music and drive a pair of speakers, so techs need to delve a little deeper to understand the crucial differences among low-, mid-, and high-end sound cards. Sound cards differ in five basic areas: processor capabilities, speaker support, recording quality, jacks, and extra features.

Processor Capabilities

Sound processor capabilities differ dramatically from the low end to the high end, much more than the difference in price would suggest. The sound processor handles the communication among the application, operating system, and CPU and translates commands into sounds coming out of the speakers. Low-end sound processors do little more than translate, which means that the CPU has to do the heavy lifting on the processing front.

Better sound processors, in contrast, shoulder much of the processing burden and bring a series of extra features to the table. By handling a lot of the processing onboard, these better sound processors free up the CPU for other duties and, both in effect and in name, *accelerate* the sound process. These decent sound processors also provide excellent sound reproduction, so your MP3s sound as awesome on your PC as they do on your stereo.

Most midrange and all high-end sound processors offer support for various surround-sound standards, enabling suitably equipped games and other applications to provide positional audio effects and detailed sound modeling—features that make PC gaming take on a whole new dimension. You'll learn about the various standards in detail in the "Speakers" section, later in this chapter, but for now let an example suffice. With properly implemented positional audio, when you're sneaking down the hall, ready to steal the Pasha's treasure, you will hear behind you the sounds of the guards marching up to capture you. Such added realism has many potential benefits beyond games, but games are currently the primary beneficiary of this technology.

Speaker Support

Every sound card supports two speakers or a pair of headphones, but many better sound cards support five or more speakers in discrete channels. These multiple speakers provide surround sound—very popular not only for games but also for those who enjoy playing DVDs on their PCs. The card in Figure 13.2, for example, has inputs for front speakers (Out 1) and rear speakers (Out 2).

Another popular speaker addition is a **subwoofer**. Subwoofers provide the amazing low-frequency tones that give all of your sounds, from the surround sound of a game to the music of a simple stereo MP3 file, an extra dimension. Better sound cards support both surround sound and a subwoofer and

Inside Information

Sound Cards

The hardware portion of sound-processing equipment in the PC either comes as a chip built into the motherboard or on an expansion card. Techs call both forms sound cards, even though technically the first type is not a card at all. Still, the generic term has stuck for the time being.

• **Figure 13.2**   A sound card with multiple speaker connections

advertise this with a nomenclature such as Dolby Digital, DTS, or **5.1**. The 5 denotes the number of speakers: two in front, two in back, and one in the center. The .1 denotes the subwoofer. Figure 13.3 shows one type of surround speaker system. You'll learn more about surround sound in the upcoming "Speakers" section.

Recording Quality

Almost every sound card has an input for a powered microphone, but the high-end cards record with substantially lower amounts of noise or other audible artifacts. The measure that describes the relative quality of an input port is the signal-to-noise ratio, expressed in decibels. The smaller the number, the worse the card is for recording because it's more likely you'll get noise. Most sound cards at the low end and in midrange have a signal-to-noise ratio of 30 to 50 decibels, which makes them unacceptable for recording. High-end cards offer a 96 to 100 signal-to-noise ratio, a level near what professional musicians use. Check the documentation before you buy or recommend a sound card for recording purposes.

• **Figure 13.3**   Surround speakers

SantaCruz™
6-channel DSP Audio Accelerator

Specifications

Advanced 3D Positional Audio Support:	Unlike other sound cards with simple 3D sound that positions the sound source to quad speakers, Santa Cruz uses Sensaura HRTF 3D positional audio technology to move sources in the X, Y and Z plane for true 360° positional effects that appear above, below and around you. The DSP accelerates 32 hardware and 16 software DirectSound3D streams. 3D audio is compatible with A3D™ 1.0, EAX™1.0/2.0, IA3D, MacroFX™, MultiDrive™, Virtual Ear™.
Audio Performance:	Frequency Response (A-A): 10Hz - 120KHz. (-3dB) SNR: > 96 dB FS A. THD+N: (-3dB): >91 dB FS (0.0027%). Crosstalk: 105 dB @ 100Hz.

• The Turtle Beach Santa Cruz advertises its excellent 96+-decibel signal-to-noise ratio (SNR) for recording

Jacks

Virtually every sound card comes with at least three connections: one for a stereo speaker system, one for a microphone, and one for a secondary output called line out. If you look at the back of a motherboard with a built-in sound card, you'll invariably see these three connections (Figure 13.4). On most systems, the line-out connector is green, the main stereo speaker connector is blue, and the microphone connector is pink.

However, you'll often find plenty of other connectors. Let's see what these connectors do for your sound card.

Line Out

As mentioned, the line out is a secondary connector, often used to connect to an external device such as a cassette or CD player to enable you to output sounds from your computer.

Line In

The line-in port connects to an external device such as a cassette or CD player to enable you to import sounds into your computer.

Rear Out

The rear-out connector connects to the rear speakers for surround audio output.

Analog/Digital Out

The multifunction analog/digital-out connection acts as a special digital connection to external digital devices or digital

• **Figure 13.4** Typical audio connections on a motherboard sound card

speaker systems, and it also acts as the analog connection to center and subwoofer channels (see the "Speakers" section later in this chapter for a discussion of surround sound).

Microphone

The microphone port connects to an external microphone for voice input.

Joystick

The joystick port connects a joystick or a MIDI device to the sound card.

• Lots of connections on a high-end sound card

Extra Features

With more motherboards now having built-in sound, expansion sound card makers have responded by adding a host of extra goodies and abilities to their cards that, for some folks, prove irresistibly tempting. These include a digital output to integrate the PC with a home entertainment unit, allowing users to add a DVD receiver and surround-sound speakers; a breakout box that adds recording and output ports in a 5¼-inch bay; and a FireWire connection for direct gaming, file sharing, and immediate MP3 playing from a portable MP3 device. Figure 13.5 shows a version of the Creative Labs' popular **SoundBlaster** breakout box. These features aren't for everyone, but they are compelling to many consumers.

Speakers

The sound card itself is only one part of the equation. You also need good-quality speakers if you have any intention of listening to music or enjoying some of the more advanced features such as surround sound. It always blows me away when I walk into someone's study and hear tinny music whining from a $10 pair of speakers connected to a $2,000 computer. If you listen to music or play games on your computer, a decent set of speakers can significantly improve the experience! Speakers come in a wide variety of sizes, shapes, technologies, and quality and can stump the uninformed tech who can't easily tell that the $50 set on the right sounds 100 times better than the $25 pair on the left.

• **Figure 13.5**   Breakout box for a SoundBlaster Live! Platinum sound card

• High-quality speaker (right) set versus another manufacturer's low-end speaker set (left)

Speaker Standards

The advent of surround sound in the computing world has created a number of speaker standards. You should know these different standards so that you can choose the speakers that work best for you.

Stereo Stereo is the oldest speaker technology that you'll see in the PC world. Stereo speakers are just what you might imagine: two speakers, a left and a right. The two speakers share a single jack that connects to the sound card. Most cheap speakers are stereo speakers.

2.1 Systems A **2.1** speaker system consists of a pair of standard stereo speakers combined with a subwoofer (Figure 13.6). The average 2.1 speaker system has a single jack that connects to the sound card and runs into the subwoofer. Another wire runs from the subwoofer to the two stereo speakers. If you want to enjoy great music and don't feel you need surround sound, you probably want a 2.1 sound system.

Surround Speaker Standards Going beyond standard two-channel (stereo) sound has been a goal in the sound world since the 1970s. However, it wasn't until the advent of Dolby Laboratory's **Dolby Digital** sound standard in the early 1990s that surround sound began to take off. The Dolby Digital sound standard is designed to support five channels of sound: front-left, front-right, front-center, rear-left, and rear-right. Dolby Digital also supports a subwoofer—thus, the term *5.1*. Another company, **Digital Theatre Systems (DTS)** created a competing standard that also supported a 5.1 speaker system. When DVDs were introduced, they included both Dolby Digital and DTS 5.1 standards, making 5.1 speakers an overnight requirement for home theater.

• Stereo speakers

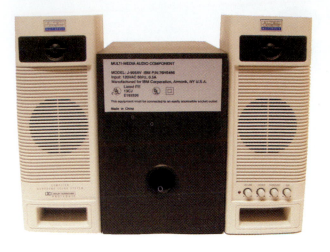

• **Figure 13.6**   Typical 2.1 speakers

If you want to enjoy your DVDs in full surround sound on your PC, you must purchase a full 5.1 speaker system. There are a number of 5.1 speaker systems for PCs. The choice you make is usually determined by what sounds best to you.

Many higher-end sound cards come with a special **Sony/Philips digital interface (SPDIF)** connector that enables you to connect your sound card directly to a 5.1 speaker system or receiver (Figure 13.7). Using a single SPDIF instead of a tangle of separate wires for each speaker greatly simplifies your sound setup.

Games can also take advantage of 5.1 speakers, but they use a totally different standard (one you should remember from Chapter 11): **DirectX**. DirectX offers numerous commands, also known as APIs, which issue instructions such as "make a sound on the right speaker" or "play music in both the right and left channels." DirectX simplifies the programming required to create sound and video: rather than having to program sounds in different ways for each sound card option, games can talk to DirectX; the hardware manufacturers simply have to ensure that their sound cards are DirectX compatible.

DirectX version 3 introduced **DirectSound3D (DS3D)**, which offered a range of commands to place a sound anywhere in 3D space. This is known as *positional audio*, and it fundamentally changed the way most PC games are played. DS3D could not handle all sound information, but it supported extensions to its instructions for more advanced sound features. This challenged the sound card designers to more fully develop the concept of positional audio. Creative Labs responded by rolling out **Environmental Audio Extensions (EAX)**. EAX gives developers the ability to create a convincing sense of environment in entertainment titles and a realistic sense of distance between the player and audio events.

Only a few 5.1 PC speaker systems come with SPDIF. In most cases, you'll have to use the regular audio outputs on the sound card.

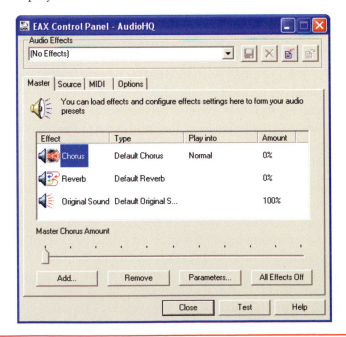

• EAX setup screen

● Figure 13.7   SPDIF connector

In late 2000, a number of EAX effects were incorporated into the DirectX audio component of the latest release, DirectX 8.0. This signaled the acceptance of EAX as the standard for audio effects in gaming. Shortly afterward, Creative Labs started releasing audio cards that are Dolby 5.1 compatible out of the box. Now you can plug a 5.1 speaker system directly into your sound card. The sound card automatically applies the Dolby/DTS standards when you play a DVD and the EAX standards when you play a game.

Speaker Features

Speakers also come with a few other features that you may find appealing.

Power   Many cheaper speakers use batteries. I hate batteries—they always seem to run out when I need them. Try to get speakers that use AC power.

Controls   All speakers have volume controls as well as an on/off switch. Get a system that provides easy access to those controls by placing them on an easy-to-reach speaker or on a special control box.

Headphone Jack   The problem with headphones is that you need to plug them into the back of the sound card and then tell Windows to output to them from the Sound applet on the Control Panel. Save yourself a lot of hassle and get a speaker system that has a handy microphone jack on one of the speakers or on a control box.

Many speaker systems and sound cards support more advanced speaker setups with names like 4.2, 6.1, and 7.1. Little support is available for these, and unless you're a serious audiophile or in the music business, in most cases these are a waste of money.

Installing a Sound Card in a Windows System

The installation process for a sound card is basically the same as the installation process for any other card. You snap the card into a slot, plug some speakers into the card, load a driver—and for the most part, you're done. Because so many disparate components are bundled into a single card, however, the sound card is one of the most complex expansion cards in a computer. Sound cards used to be the bane of hardware techs, but with Plug and Play, they're much easier to set up. Like most of the devices discussed in this book, sound card installation consists of three major parts: physical installation, device driver installation, and configuration.

Physical Installation

The physical installation of a sound card isn't really any different from the installation of any other card. Almost all sound cards use the PCI expansion bus, so any open PCI slot will work. The real trick to physical installation is deciding where to plug in the speakers, microphone, and so on. The surround-sound sound cards so common today feature a variety of jacks, so you will probably want to refer to your sound card documentation for details, but here are a few guidelines:

You cannot damage your speakers or sound card by inserting the wrong jacks into any of the connections on the back of the sound card, so don't be afraid to experiment when you're not positive where something plugs in.

- The typical stereo or 2.1 speaker system will use only a single jack. Look for the jack labeled Speaker or Speaker 1.

- Surround speakers use either a single digital (SPDIF) connection (which in most cases runs from the sound card to the subwoofer) or three separate cables: one for the front two speakers that runs to the Speaker 1 connector, one for the back two speakers that runs to the Speaker 2 connector, and a third cable for the center channel and subwoofer that runs to the Digital/Audio Out or Speaker 3 connector.

- Typical sound card

The best way to do learn how to install a sound card is to see the process in action.

Step-by-Step 13.1

Physically Installing a Sound Card

Now that you know what sound does for you, it's time to install a sound card in your machine. Sound cards are probably one of the easiest peripherals to install.

To complete this exercise, you will need the following:

- A Phillips-head screwdriver
- An antistatic wrist strap

- A Windows system with an open PCI slot and no sound card installed.
- A sound card
- An audio cable to connect to the CD-ROM
- A small hexagonal screw for securing computer hardware
- Computer speakers
- A microphone

Introduction to PC Hardware and Troubleshooting

| Step 1 | Shut down the computer and prepare to work in a well-lit, open area. Observe all antistatic safety procedures, such as connecting your antistatic wrist strap to the computer case. |

| Step 2 | Open the computer and position the sound card over an available PCI slot. Hold the sound card by the edges, being careful not to touch the gold teeth on the card that fit into the PCI slot. |

| Step 3 | Insert the sound card into the PCI slot. Make sure that the card is fully seated. Then take the small hexagonal screw and secure the sound card to the chassis. |

| Step 4 | Connect the CD audio cable to the back of the CD-ROM or DVD-ROM drive. Connect the other end to the CD Audio port on the sound card. Be careful to install the cable in the correct connector. Note that the sound card in the following illustration has three audio connectors: one for the CD, one for the DVD, and one for a modem. |

Now that the sound card is installed, close the PC case and return the computer to its workspace. Get the speakers and microphone ready. Before you fully restore the computer to its old position, you will need to install the speakers. Plug the speakers into the power strip or wall and take the speaker connectors in your hands.

Connect the speakers, making sure that each lead enters the right jack. Plug the microphone into your sound card as well. This completes the physical installation. Now you just need to install the drivers!

Installing Drivers

Once the sound card is installed, start the system and let Windows Plug and Play install the sound card's drivers. As you might expect by now, you'll probably have a choice between the built-in Windows drivers and the one that comes on a CD with your sound card. Just as with other cards, it's always best to use the driver that comes with the card. Most sound cards have easy-to-use autoplay-enabled installation CDs that step you through the process.

After your driver is installed, make a quick trip to Device Manager to make sure that the driver was installed correctly, and you're two-thirds of the way there. Installing the driver is never the last step for a sound card. Your final step is to configure the sound card using configuration programs and to test the sound card using an application. Most sound cards come with both special configuration programs and a few sound applications

Sound card drivers are updated occasionally. Take a moment to check the manufacturer's website to see if your sound card has any driver updates.

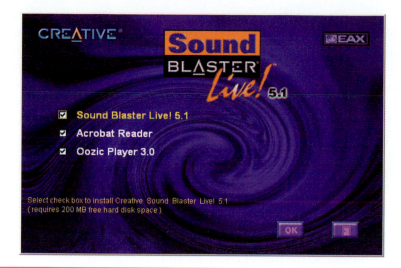

• Typical autoplay screen for a sound card

stored on the same CD that supplies the drivers. Let's look at these extra bits of software that I simply call sound programs.

Installing Sound Programs

You've already seen that you need a program to play sounds: Windows Media Player, Winamp, or something similar. However, two other classes of sound programs also reside on your computer: programs for the configuration of your sound card and special applications that may or may not come with your sound card.

Configuration Applications

Every Windows computer comes with at least one very important sound configuration program built right into the operating system: the **Sounds and Audio Devices applet** in the Control Panel in Windows XP, or Sounds and Multimedia in Windows 2000, or the two applets called Sounds and Multimedia in Windows 95 and 98. Whatever the name, this applet (or applets) performs the same job: it provides a location for performing most or all of your sound card configuration tasks. Let's use the Sounds and Audio Devices applet in Windows XP as an example; the applets in the other versions of Windows work roughly the same way, although they may have one control or another in a different place.

The Sounds and Audio Devices applet has five tabs: Volume, Sounds, Audio, Voice, and Hardware. The most interesting is the Volume tab. This tab adjusts the volume for the speakers, and it also provides access to an Advanced Audio Properties dialog box, from which you can set up the type of speaker system you have, as shown in Figure 13.8.

The Sounds tab allows you to add customized sounds to Windows events such as the startup of a program or

• **Figure 13.8** Advanced Audio Properties dialog box

Windows shutdown. The Audio tab (Figure 13.9) and Voice tab do roughly the same thing: enable you to specify the device used for input and output of general sounds (Audio tab) and voice (Voice tab). These settings are handy for folks like me who have a regular microphone and speakers but also use a headset with microphone for voice recognition or Internet telephone software. By telling Windows to use the microphone for normal sounds and to use the headset for voice recognition, I don't have to make any manual changes when I switch from listening to an MP3 to listening to my brother when he calls me over the Internet.

The Hardware tab isn't used very often, but it does have one interesting feature: it gives you access to a list of the audio and video codecs installed in your system (Figure 13.10). Not long ago, you had to manually install codecs in your system to play certain compressed file formats. Today, most audio players automatically detect whether a file is using an unrecognized codec and will download the proper codec for you.

Proprietary Configuration Applications

Many sound cards install proprietary software to support configuration features not provided by Windows. Figure 13.11 shows one such application. This is a special configuration application that comes with Creative Labs' sound cards to add a few tweaks to the speaker setup that the Sounds and Audio Devices Control Panel applet doesn't support.

Most sound cards come with some form of configuration program. Take some time to experiment with it—this is a great way to learn about some of the features of your sound card that you might otherwise not even know are there.

• **Figure 13.9** Audio tab (note the MIDI Music Playback option)

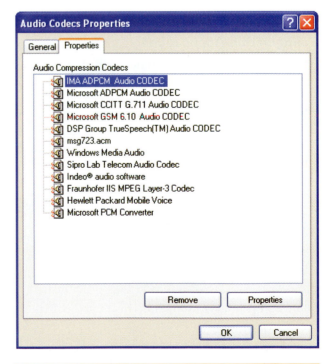

• **Figure 13.10** Audio codecs

Introduction to PC Hardware and Troubleshooting

• **Figure 13.11** Creative Labs' Remote Center

Installing Applications

Some sound cards—Creative Labs' sound cards are by far the most infamous for this—install one or more applications, ostensibly to improve your sound experience. Whether you'll agree with this or not is a matter of opinion. Personally, I'm not a big fan of, for example, an electronic keyboard program—but then you might be just the type of person who loves it. Either way, be sure to install at least the applications that come with your card. If you don't like them, you can easily uninstall them.

• Creative Labs' keyboard program

■ Troubleshooting Sound

The problems that you'll run into with sound seem to fall into one of two camps: those that are embarrassingly simple to repair, and those that defy any possible logic and are seemingly impossible to fix. This section divides sound problems into three groups—hardware, configuration, and application problems—and gives you some ideas on how to fix these problems.

Hardware Problems

Hardware problems are by far the most common sound problems, especially if your sound card has worked for some amount of time already. Properly installed and configured sound cards almost never suddenly stop making sounds.

Volume

The absolute first items to check when your sound dies are your volume controls. Remember that you have two places to set the volume: in software and on the speakers. I can't tell you the number of times I've lost sound only to discover that my wife turned down the volume on the speakers. If the speaker volume is okay, open the volume control in Windows (click the little speaker icon on the taskbar) and make sure that both the master volume and the volume of the other controls are turned up.

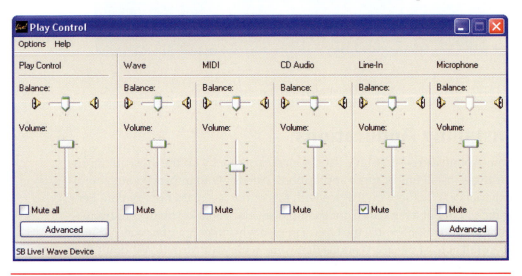

• Volume controls in Windows

Speakers

Your second place to look for sound problems is the speakers. Make sure that the speakers are turned on and are getting good power. Then make sure the speakers are plugged into the proper connection on the back of the sound card. If this all checks out, try playing a sound. If the sound *looks* like it is playing—maybe the application has an equalizer that is moving or a status marker that shows that the application is playing the sound—you may have blown speakers. Try another pair and see if the sound returns.

Configuration Problems

Configuration errors occur when the sound card is physically good but some setting hasn't been properly configured. I also include drive problems in this category. These errors happen almost exclusively at installation, but they can appear on a working system, too.

The first place to check is Device Manager. If the driver has a problem, you'll see it right there. Try reinstalling the driver.

If the driver doesn't show any problems, again try playing a sound and see if the player acts as though the sound is playing. If that's the case, you need to start touring the Sounds and Audio Devices applet to see if you've made a configuration error—perhaps you have the system configured for 5.1 when you have a stereo setup, or maybe you set the default sound output device to some other device. Take your time and look—configuration errors always show themselves.

Technically speaking, turning down the volume in the volume control program is a configuration problem, but it's just something I always check at the same time I check the volume on the speakers.

Application Problems

Application problems are always the hardest to fix and are the ones that do tend to occur on a system that was previously playing sounds without trouble.

First, look for an error message. If an error code appears, write it down *exactly* as you see it and head to the program's support site. Odds are very good that if you have an error text, you'll get the fix right away from the support site. Of course, you can always hope the built-in help has some support, but help systems tend to be a little light in providing real fixes.

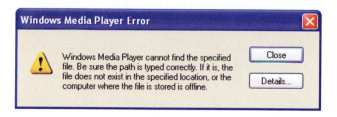

• Sample error message

Don't always blame the sound application—don't forget that any sound file might be corrupted. Most sound players will display a clear error message, but not always. Try playing the sound file in another application.

If nothing else has worked, a good approach almost always is to reinstall the application.

■ Chapter Summary

After reading this chapter and completing the exercises, you should understand the following aspects of sound:

Describe how sound works in a PC

- The process by which sounds are stored in electronic format on your PC is called sampling.

- Sounds are sampled thousands of times per second.

- The amount of information stored at each sampling is called the bit depth.

- The cornerstone of all file formats is Pulse Code Modulation (PCM). The popular WAV file format as well as most other recorded sound formats are based on PCM.

- Compression is a popular way to reduce the file size of recorded sounds. The programs that compress and decompress sound files are called codecs. The most popular compressed file type is MP3.

- To play sounds, you must have some form of player software.

- MIDI files are not recordings like WAV files. They are specialized text files that tell your sound card what notes to play.

- Sound cards use one of two methods to store notes for MIDI: FM synthesis or wavetable synthesis.

- There are a large number of other sound file formats. Not all players play all sound formats. Some file formats require their own proprietary players.

- Sounds can also be found in video formats, applications, and streaming media.

Purchase the right sound card

- The five major criteria for choosing a sound card are processor capability, speaker support, recording quality, jacks, and extra features.

- A 2.1 system consists of a pair of stereo speakers and a subwoofer. A 5.1 system has two front, two rear, and one center speaker, plus a subwoofer.

- Surround sound is popular for games and DVD. There are a number of surround-sound standards, but the most common are Dolby Digital and DTS.

- The Dolby Digital and DTS standards both require five speakers and a subwoofer. These speaker setups use the nomenclature 5.1.

Install a sound card in a Windows system

- Sound card installation can be divided into three major steps: physical installation, device driver installation, and configuration.

- Although the physical installation of a sound card is straightforward, knowing where to plug in multiple speakers can be a bit of a challenge.

- It is preferable to use the driver that comes with the sound card as opposed to the Windows built-in drivers.

- Look for configuration programs in two places: in the Control Panel Sounds and Audio Devices applet and in any proprietary applications that are installed with the sound card.

Perform basic sound card troubleshooting

- You can divide sound problems into three groups: hardware, configuration, and application problems.

- The two first places to check when you suspect a hardware problem are the volume controls and speaker connectivity.

- Configuration errors almost always take place at installation of the sound card.

- Application problems are often the most challenging of all sound problems. Your best hope is an error message; you can then check the programs' website for help.

■ Key Terms

2.1 *(349)*	**CD quality** *(341)*	**DirectSound3D (DS3D)** *(350)*
5.1 *(346)*	**codec** *(342)*	**DirectX** *(350)*
bit depth *(341)*	**Digital Theatre Systems (DTS)** *()*	**Dolby Digital** *(349)*

Environmental Audio
    Extensions (EAX) *(350)*
FM synthesis *(343)*
kilohertz (KHz) *(341)*
MP3 *(342)*

Musical Instrument Digital
    Interface (MIDI) *(343)*
sampling *(341)*
Sony/Philips digital
    interface (SPDIF) *(350)*

SoundBlaster *(348)*
Sounds and Audio
    Devices applet *(355)*
subwoofer *(345)*
wavetable synthesis *(343)*

■ Key Term Quiz

Use terms from the Key Terms list to complete the following sentences. Not all of the terms will be used.

1. A sound's sampling rate is measured in thousands of cycles per second, called _____.

2. _____ enables a sound card to simulate a number of different instruments.

3. _____ uses specialized text files that tell the sound card which sounds to play.

4. The best known of all sound cards is Creative Labs' _____.

5. 44.1 KHz stereo is also known as _____ audio.

6. _____ is the process of capturing the state or quality of a particular sound wave a set number of times each second.

7. The most common compressed audio format is _____.

8. A/an _____ is a series of instructions telling a computer how to read a compressed file.

9. _____ was developed by Microsoft as a means of simplifying commands to multimedia devices such as sound cards.

10. The Dolby Digital/DTS standards define six speakers using the terminology _____.

■ Multiple-Choice Quiz

1. The number of characteristics of a particular sound captured when sampling is measured by the _____.
   a. Sample rate
   b. Kilohertz
   c. Bit depth
   d. Quality rating

2. CD-quality sound samples are recorded at 44 KHz, with 16-bit depth and what else?
   a. Monaural
   b. Stereo
   c. 5.1
   d. 2.1

3. All recorded sound formats used in PCs today are derived from the _____ format.
   a. WAV
   b. Fraunhoffer
   c. MP3
   d. PCM

4. The most common compressed sound format is _____ .
   a. MP3
   b. WAV
   c. VOC
   d. TXT

5. Almost all sound cards use the _____ expansion bus.
   a. ISA
   b. AGP
   c. Internal
   d. PCI

6. Which sound format contains no actual sound recording, but only a series of commands stored in a text file for the sound card to interpret?
   a. WMA
   b. WAV
   c. MIDI
   d. MP3

7. Which audio/video compression format was created specifically to stream over the Internet?

   a. MP3

   b. MIDI

   c. WAV

   d. ASF

8. How many speakers are in a Dolby Digital 5.1 setup?

   a. Five speakers plus a subwoofer

   b. Six speakers plus a subwoofer

   c. Seven speakers plus a subwoofer

   d. Eight speakers plus a subwoofer

9. Which component of DirectX offered only a range of commands to place a sound anywhere in 3D space?

   a. DirectSound

   b. DirectSound3D

   c. EAX

   d. A3D

10. What is the name of the extensions to the DirectSound3D standard developed by Creative Labs?

    a. EAX

    b. MP3

    c. Positional audio

    d. Reverberation

11. What is the name of the direct competitor to Dolby Digital ?

    a. DirectSound

    b. DirectSound3D

    c. DTS

    d. Surround Sound

12. The ".1" in 5.1 or 2.1 refers to the _____?

    a. Volumetric sound positioning

    b. Subwoofer

    c. Subchannels

    d. Reverb positional matrices

13. What is the name of the standard digital connection that replaces many analog connections on some sound cards?

    a. CD Audio connector

    b. AUX connector

    c. TAD connector

    d. SPDIF connector

14. Which version of DirectX introduced DirectSound3D?

    a. Version 8.0

    b. Version 3

    c. Version 2

    d. Version 1

15. Jane's sound card is suddenly not making any sound. She suspects that the volume is turned down. She checks the speaker volume and sees that it is turned up. What should she check next?

    a. The volume control program

    b. The application

    c. The speaker power

    d. Device Manager

■ Essay Quiz

1. Detail in your own words how you think sound aided the evolution of the computer. What aspects of sound are necessary to computers? Why is sound needed?

2. Outline how you could use the connections provided on a modern sound card to create a multimedia home theater with your computer.

   Be sure to include hardware discussed in previous chapters, such as DVD-ROM drives.

3. Write an essay on the kind of sound card you would need for your computer. Detail what you personally would like to accomplish with your computer and how a sound card would help you.

Lab Projects

• Lab Project 13.1

Lately your sound card has been acting oddly. You suspect that the problem is in your audio drivers. You feel that somehow the files have been corrupted on your system. Uninstall and reinstall your audio drivers, as follows:

1 On your XP operating system, alternate-click (right-click) the My Computer icon and select Properties. In My Computer Properties, select the Hardware tab. Then click the Device Manager button.

2 In Device Manager, expand the Sound, Video, and Game Controllers section. Double-click your audio driver.

3 Select the Drivers tab at the top of the screen and then select Uninstall. This will uninstall your audio drivers.

4 Insert the driver CD supplied by your sound card manufacturer. Reinstall the audio drivers from the CD.

• Lab Project 13.2

You have successfully uninstalled and reinstalled your audio drivers, but the drivers supplied on the CD are probably not the latest available.

1 Visit your sound card manufacturer's website. Usually the sound card manual will tell you the link to the website. If it doesn't, do an Internet search on your make and model to locate the website.

2 Navigate the website until you find the drivers for your sound card.

3 Download the latest drivers to your hard drive. Use the Readme file or other information on the website to determine what the driver update is meant to change or fix.

4 Install the drivers. Test your sound card's performance. See if you can tell any difference.

Printers

*"Making duplicate copies and
computer printouts of things no
one wanted even one of in the
first place is giving America a
new sense of purpose."*

—ANDY ROONEY

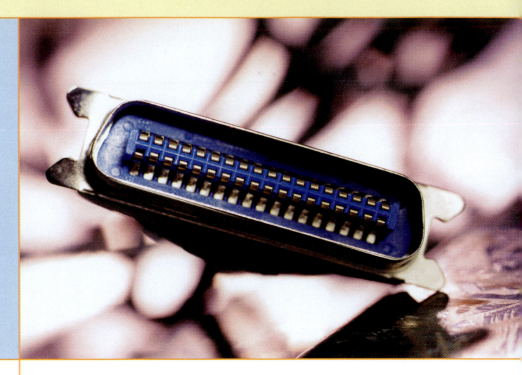

**In this chapter, you will learn
how to:**

- **Describe current printer
  technologies**
- **Install a printer on a Windows PC**
- **Perform basic printer
  maintenance**
- **Recognize and fix basic printing
  problems**

According to many a fallen computer pundit, printers shouldn't even exist next to your computer anymore. As early as 20 years ago, computer prophets began to envision a world where interconnected computers would share electronic documents, negating the need to do something as primitive as printing words and pictures on the crushed, bleached remains of primordial forests.

Well, seems they were wrong, or at least premature. Today, even though only 30 percent of computer documents created ever get printed, it is estimated that we produce some 3.6 *trillion* documents every year—that's a lot of printing and a lot of paper!

This chapter will guide you through the key challenges that today's printers present for the conscientious computer user. First, you must identify the current printer technologies so that you can purchase the right printer for your particular needs. Second, you have to install your printer and make sure that it prints properly. Third, because printers absolutely must have periodic maintenance to ensure years of reliable operation, you must know what maintenance to perform and how often. Finally, because all printers experience problems from time to time, an informed computer user should know how to deal with at least the most common problems.

■ Identifying Current Printer Technologies

No other piece of your computer system is available in a wider range of styles, configurations, and feature sets than a printer, or at such a wide price variation. During a recent visit to a local computer store, I counted 40 different printers for sale, priced anywhere from $90 to $1,500. So which one out of all these choices is right for you? Partly that depends on what you need the printer to do. The other part of the equation is what the printer can and can't do, which, in turn, is largely determined by the type of printer technology it uses—that is, how it gets the image onto the paper.

There are currently three dominant printer technologies: dot matrix, inkjet, and laser. Each has different strengths and weaknesses—that's why all three still coexist. Let's take a look at each, starting with the oldest, dot matrix printers.

This section covers three print technologies, but be aware that there are more than just these three. However, these three technologies account for roughly 99 percent of all printers sold today.

Dot Matrix Printers

Dot matrix printers (Figure 14.1) work by using a grid, or matrix, of tiny pins that strike an inked ribbon against the paper to print a character. Because they actually strike the paper in the manner of a typewriter, they are called *impact printers*. Dot matrix printers have either a 9-pin matrix or a 24-pin matrix. As you might imagine, the ones that use 24 dots of ink per character produce better-quality images than the ones that use only 9 pins.

The original IBM PC came equipped with a dot matrix printer, and for about the first 10 years of the PC age, dot matrix printers were extremely common. However, dot matrix printers have some serious limitations. The first stems from the use of tiny pins to print. Compared to the more modern technologies, dot matrix printers make very rough images: individual letters in text documents look ragged and unprofessional, and graphics are almost amusingly primitive. Second, dot matrix printers don't produce color images very well. The few color dot matrix printers that existed years ago are all long gone. Finally, dot matrix printers require a lot of maintenance to work well. These days, dot matrix printers are relegated to the one function at which they still excel: high-speed, multipart printing. Many things you see every day are printed using dot matrix printers. For example, dot matrix printers are used for paychecks, invoices, and the addresses in bulk mailings, and in hundreds of similar situations where speed and the ability to imprint text on multiple sheets of paper are more important than beauty.

Inkjet Printers

Today's most popular printer technology, especially for homes and small offices, is inkjet technology. **Inkjet printers** (Figure 14.2) work by squirting tiny droplets of ink from tiny nozzles, or jets, riding on a printhead that moves back and forth across

● **Figure 14.1**   Dot matrix printer

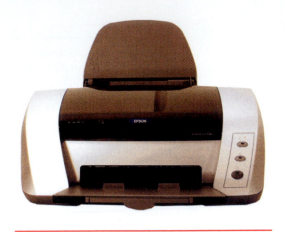

• **Figure 14.2**   Typical inkjet printer

the paper. These droplets are so tiny that they cannot be distinguished by the naked eye.

The first inkjet printers were not much better than dot matrix printers. Inkjet printer quality is measured in terms of the resolution, similar to the way monitors are measured by screen resolution. A printer's **resolution** is expressed as some number of **dots per inch (dpi)**, measured both vertically and horizontally. The first inkjet printers had a resolution of 150 x 150 dpi. This resolution produced a rather poor image. Over the years, inkjet resolution has dramatically increased. Today, a middle-of-the-road inkjet printer can produce images with a resolution of 2,880 x 720 dpi. A resolution of 2,880 x 720 means that every square inch of paper is filled with over 2 *million* individual dots of color! Today's inkjet printers have such a fine resolution that they require specialized papers to prevent the inks from bleeding together and making the image fuzzy.

Inkjet technology is a natural choice for color printing. Although the earliest inkjet printers had only a single **ink cartridge** that used only one color—black—modern inkjets have multiple jets, each with different primary colored ink, and each squirting different amounts of ink onto the same tiny part of the paper. Using this multiple-jet method, inkjets can produce amazingly high-quality color images.

The first color inkjet printers used three inks: cyan (blue), magenta (red), and yellow. Each color had its own jet and own ink cartridge that traveled on the printhead. They created black by combining all three colors—and the results didn't look very good. The second generation of inkjets allowed the user to swap a single black ink cartridge for a three-color cartridge, but as you might imagine, constantly swapping cartridges was a hassle and therefore unpopular. Most of today's inkjet printers come with four separate ink colors: black, cyan, magenta, and yellow. You can find inkjets that come with six or even seven colors; the extra ink colors significantly improve the quality of the resulting image.

• Different colored inks

Introduction to PC Hardware and Troubleshooting

The last important aspect of inkjet printers is speed—the amount of time the printer takes to print a page. Inkjet print speed is measured in **pages per minute (ppm)**. A typical lower-end inkjet will print around 15 ppm in black and white. Color printing will be much slower, often 1 ppm for the highest-quality output.

Laser Printers

When it comes to high-speed, high-quality, black-and-white printing, nothing beats **laser printer** technology. Contrary to popular myth, laser printers (Figure 14.3) do not use a **laser** to burn an image onto the paper. Laser printers use tiny lasers to scan a photosensitive drum. Then the drum is exposed to **toner** (think of toner simply as ink dust). The spots scanned on the **photosensitive drum** by the laser attract toner, creating the image. The toner-covered drum is then exposed to statically charged paper that attracts the toner. The toner is then sealed to the paper with heat and pressure, the static is discharged from the paper, and the finished sheet is discharged from the printer.

Laser printers have a resolution, just as inkjets do, measured in dpi. Very early, laser printers were able to generate 300 x 300 dpi, the resolution that most printing authorities say is needed for high-quality text printing. Modern laser printers can print at resolutions as high as 2,400 x 2,400 dpi, although most laser printers max out at 600 x 600 dpi—plenty for ultrahigh-quality text. Laser printers are very fast compared to inkjet printers. The average laser printer generates around 15 ppm, whereas higher-end laser printers can generate 50 ppm or more. Color laser printers are available, but they are significantly more expensive. Laser printers always cost more than inkjet printers; however, the cost per page for laser printer consumables—toner, for example, instead of ink cartridges—is often much lower than for inkjet printers.

 Most people use a color inkjet printer at home and a black-and-white laser printer at work.

Buying a Printer

Now that you have a basic understanding of the different printing technologies, you can tackle the job of actually going out and buying a printer. To find a printer that fits your needs, you need to answer three basic questions: What are you going to print? How fast do you want to print? How much do you want to pay?

What Are You Going to Print?

The single most important question you need to ask yourself when looking for a new printer is what are you going to be printing. Do you need color? Are you sure? Many home users are interested in printing digital pictures, for example, but in most office environments, 99 percent of the printing is black-and-white text documents, unless a specific business function requires color.

Another issue to consider is page size. Almost every printer can handle letter-size (8½ x 11) or legal-size (8½ x 14) paper, but you may have a specialized need to print on even

● **Figure 14.3** Typical laser printer

larger paper. There are plenty of large-format printers to choose from, but the cost goes up dramatically as your page size needs increase.

Many companies now produce specialized devices that combine printing, copying, and faxing capabilities in the same machine. These multifunction, all-in-one machines are very popular in small offices that don't want multiple machines taking up space. However, all-in-one machines do not always stand up well to heavy use. If you copy, print, and fax only a few times a day, consider one. Otherwise, buy a separate printer, copier, and fax machine.

How Fast Do You Want to Print?

Printing speed is probably the factor most overlooked by people buying printers. A printer that's too slow is both annoying and a drag on productivity, whereas buying a printer that's too fast is a waste of money.

The first speed factor is the obvious one: the ppm rating. Most printers have two ppm speeds: one for black-and-white text, and another (slower) speed for color printing. In general, a printer that generates text pages at 15 ppm is more than adequate for a single user in most situations. However, in a networked office environment, where several users share a printer—much cheaper than giving everyone a personal printer—you may need a faster speed.

How Much Do You Want to Pay?

Most people focus on the cost of a printer when they are choosing the one they want to buy, but initial cost is not the biggest expense of printer ownership. The biggest expense over time is not the printer itself, but the paper and ink it needs to work—the **consumables**. Laser printers store their toner in **toner cartridges** (Figure 14.4), and inkjet printers store ink in ink cartridges (Figure 14.5). As you useup the toner or the ink, these need to be replaced.

Toner and ink cartridges both are expensive. A typical toner cartridge costs around $100; for that money, you can buy three to nine inkjet cartridges, but most inkjets need a black cartridge and either one 3-color cartridge or three single-color cartridges. Some printers use consumables at a much faster rate than others, prompting the industry to rank printers in terms of their cost per page. An inexpensive printer (laser or inkjet) costs around 4 cents per page, whereas an expensive printer can cost more than 20 cents per page—a huge difference if you do any volume of printing. This hidden cost is particularly pernicious in the sub-$100 inkjet printer market. Their low prices often entice buyers, who then discover that the cost of consumables is outrageous.

Unfortunately, it's not always easy to determine which printers have a low cost per page, and which have a high cost per page. Printer models change every few

Try This!

Pages per Minute Versus Price

Printer speed is a key determinant of a printer's price, and this is an easy assertion to prove. Try this:

1. Fire up your browser and head over to the website of Hewlett-Packard (www.hp.com), Canon (www.usa.canon.com), Epson (www.epson.com), or Lexmark (www.lexmark.com). These four companies make most of the printers on the market today.

2. Pick a particular printer technology and check the price, from the cheapest to the most expensive. Then look for printers that have the same resolution but different ppm rates.

3. Check the prices and see how the ppm rate affects the price of two otherwise identical printers.

• **Figure 14.4**   Laser printer toner cartridge

• **Figure 14.5**   Inkjet ink cartridges

months, so it's impossible to find a single free source for this information. You can buy a subscription to the popular *Consumer Reports* magazine (www.consumerreports.com), or check your public library for the print version. Another option, free but not nearly as handy as *Consumer Reports*, is to search the Web using the phrase "printers review cost of consumables" and a specific model if you're considering a particular one. You'll find plenty of printer reviews, and with a little persistence, you can determine the printer that's best for you.

Step-by-Step 14.1

The Real PPM!

There is often a substantial difference between the advertised speed of a printer and the actual speed once it is put into use. Printer companies advertise only the best speeds—usually at the lowest resolutions and after the printer has warmed up.

In this Step-by-Step exercise, you will determine the advertised speed for your printer and then compare that to some actual printing tests of your own.

To complete this exercise, you will need the following:

- A computer running Windows 98, 2000, or XP
- An installed printer, preferably a color inkjet
- 30 sheets of paper

Step 1

Locate the performance information for your printer. This information may be found in the printer documentation, on the box that came with the printer, or at the manufacturer's website. Note the ppm rate for both text and graphics. Also note that the specification usually says "*up to*" some number of ppm.

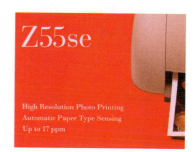

Z55se

High Resolution Photo Printing
Automatic Paper Type Sensing
Up to 17 ppm

Step 2	Turn off the printer and then turn it back on. Note that the printer goes through a reset process. This process can take a few seconds, or it can take a few minutes. Time this process. What would happen if you wanted to print immediately after restarting the printer?
Step 3	After the printer has completed its reset process, create a three-page document in any word processing program. Make sure that each page has only *one line of text*. Print the document and see how long the printer takes to print the page. How does that compare to the advertised speed?
Step 4	Create a second document, but this time fill the pages with text. Reprint the document. How does this print speed compare to the first?
Step 5	Open Microsoft Paint and draw a picture containing five or six geometric shapes of different colors. Print this. How does the print speed compare to the print speed for text? How does it compare to the advertised print speed for graphics?

■ Installing a Printer on a Windows PC

Okay, you've chosen a printer. Now it's time to install it. No worries—printer installation is very easy on a Windows system. You need to consider only a few things before you start printing.

Port Options

For years, there was only one standard way to connect a printer to your PC: via the parallel port. Parallel ports are still common on just about every computer, but today more and more printers connect to the PC via a USB port. There's not really a particular benefit to using one connection or the other, although USB is a great way to connect a second printer to a system when the parallel port is already being used. Let's take a look at both of these connections

Parallel Ports

Parallel ports date back to the original IBM PC. You can always recognize a **parallel port** by its **25-pin female DB connector** (Figure 14.6). On more recent PCs, the parallel port is a deep fuchsia color.

The parallel port on the printer looks completely different from the parallel port on the PC. The printer uses a **Centronics connector** (Figure 14.7). Centronics connectors usually have a wire wing on each side that snaps onto the parallel cable.

It's very rare for a parallel printer to come with a parallel cable, so you usually need to purchase one when you buy the printer. A number of parallel cables are available; just be sure to get one that is **IEEE 1284** rated (Figure 14.8). This ensures that it is compatible with modern printers.

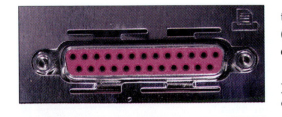

• **Figure 14.6** Typical parallel port

● **Figure 14.7**   Centronics connector

● **Figure 14.8**   IEEE 1284 cable

USB Ports

Unlike parallel printers, USB printers usually come with a USB cable.

USB printers plug into any USB port on your computer. Usually, the USB cable has a **USB type A** connector on one end and a **USB type B** connector on the other end (Figure 14.9). Some USB printers have two type A connectors. USB type A and B connectors were discussed in Chapter 5. USB type B connectors are much smaller. Whichever configuration your USB printer has, just plug in the USB cable—it's literally that easy!

Don't Forget Power!

All printers also need a power cable. Many printers use the exact same type of power cable used on most PCs, but some come with a special power cable permanently attached to the printer.

Unpacking and Assembly

Printers are rather delicate devices. The folks who make printers pack new printers using more foam, peanuts, spacers, and tape than you can imagine. This is great for making sure your new printer arrives undamaged, but if you're not careful, it's easy to miss some tiny bit of packing material clinging to the inside, and that can cause serious problems. All printers come with documentation that shows you how to properly remove all the packing bits—for your printer's sake, read it!

One of the last steps in setting up a printer is insertion of the toner cartridge or ink cartridges. Again, refer to the documentation that comes with the printer to ensure that you install these correctly. Although most cartridges install fairly easily, something as simple as failing to remove a piece of protective tape can turn your printing adventure into a nightmare.

Drivers

What would any piece of computer hardware be without drivers? Printers are certainly no exception to the "everything needs a driver" rule. When you

Inside Information

No Cheap Cables!
Some parallel cables are cheaper than the IEEE 1284 cables, but these may—or may not—work. Don't buy unnecessary hassles—just get an IEEE 1284 cable! Installing a parallel cable is a snap. Just insert the DB-25 pin connector into the parallel port on the back of the PC and insert the Centronics connector into the printer's Centronics port, and you're ready to go to press!

In almost all cases, you must install drivers before you plug a USB printer into your computer. You'll learn about installing printer drivers later in this chapter.

Many printers come with both a USB and a parallel connection, giving you the choice. These printers frequently don't come with either type of cable, so be sure to check what you need before you leave the store.

• **Figure 14.9**   USB cable with type A and type B connectors

unpack a new printer, you'll almost certainly find a CD-ROM disk packed full of software. Printers, unlike most other hardware, have a high probability of being installed by a user with very limited experience. The folks who make printers know this, and almost every printer comes with an incredibly easy-to-use installation CD.

• Typical printer installation menu

The only substantial trick to installing printer drivers is figuring out *when* in the process to install them. Some printers, mostly parallel printers, require you to physically install the printer first, *before* you install the driver. Other printers, usually USB printers, require that you install the *driver* first—but to add confusion, there are plenty of exceptions in both cases. Installing the driver at the wrong time will require you to start over, so read the installation instructions to make sure you do things right the first time.

Windows, especially Windows XP, comes with lots of built-in printer drivers that usually work just fine. When you buy a brand-new printer model, it's usually best to install the driver that comes with it, rather than relying on Windows. However, if you're installing a printer that was built before 2001, you can ignore the installation CD and just use the built-in Windows drivers. In that case, if Windows sees the printer when you install it, the printer will almost always work fine. After the installation process is complete, most printer installations give you the option of performing a test print—do so to ensure that the printer is working properly.

Between today's user-friendly printer installation CDs and the amazing power of Windows Plug and Play features, printer installation almost always proceeds without a hitch. However, there are a few cases where printer installation may not be quite so easy. For example, what if instead of a handy-dandy installation program, your printer comes with a bunch of INF files stored on a CD? What if you want to use a printer that isn't currently attached to your system? This happened to me once on a plane trip, when I and two other laptop users had to share a battery-powered printer to finish a presentation. Such situations aren't common, but they do occur. In those cases, you can always install the printer driver manually.

Windows handles manual printer driver installation with the Add Printer wizard. The Add Printer wizard is located in the Printers (Windows 98 and 2000) or Printers and Faxes (Windows XP) applet on the Control Panel.

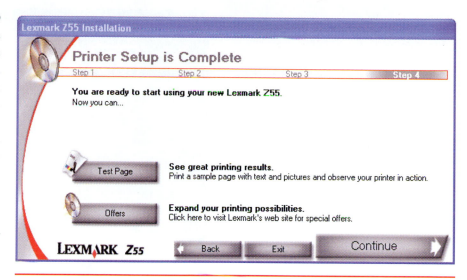

• Successful installation!

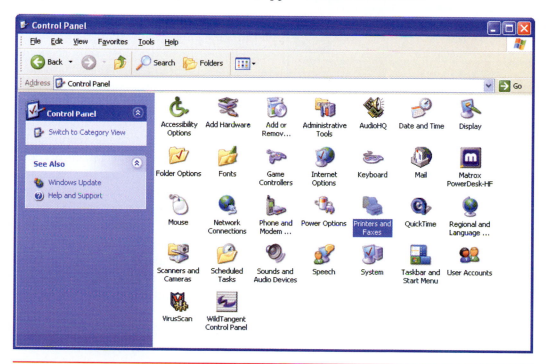

• Printers and Faxes applet on the Windows XP Control Panel

• Add Printer wizard in Windows XP

The Add Printer wizard displays an introductory screen, and then on the next screen, it asks you if you want to install a printer attached to your computer (a local printer) or to install a shared printer on a network. The same dialog box has a check box that you select if you want Windows to automatically detect and install a printer. Odds are good that if you are using this wizard, automatic installation didn't work, and in that case, you'll want to uncheck this check box.

If you tell the wizard that you're installing a local printer (the most common home and home office situation), the wizard next asks you to specify a printer port. The printer port it's asking for is not the hardware; rather, it is akin to a telephone number for the physical parallel connection. These ports are actually special sets of codes that tell the CPU how to talk to the printer. To make life simpler for the average computer user, the computer industry long ago decided to hide such settings from you and simply give the different combinations of settings names. Parallel printer ports have names like **LPT1** or **LPT2**. If your system has only a single parallel port, you can bet it's called LPT1.

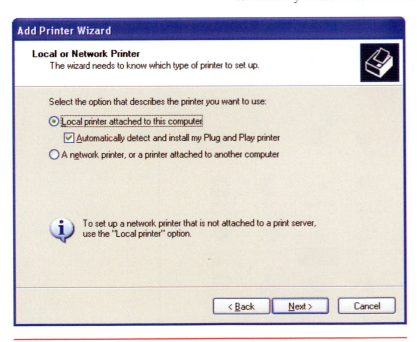

• Specifying a local or network printer

Introduction to PC Hardware and Troubleshooting

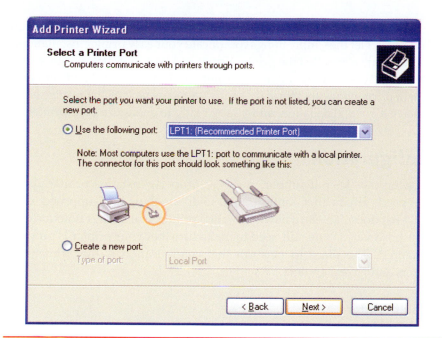

• Selecting the printer port

It is possible to go into your system setup and change the port associated with a parallel connection. You could, for example, change the parallel port from LPT1 to LPT2. However, because modern printers tend to use USB connections and you aren't likely to use more than one printer on a system, LPT2 is usually destined for irrelevance.

After you select the port, the Add Printer wizard will ask you what type of printer you want to install, by make and model. Windows comes with thousands of printer drivers. You can find the manufacturer name on the left side of the dialog box and then select the model on the right side.

If you have an installation disk, you don't need to find your printer in the list. Instead, you can click the Have Disk button and use the Browse button to locate the driver for your printer, which Windows will then install.

You should really use Windows' manual installation feature only as a last resort. Printer driver installation is usually automatic today, so you should almost never need to use it. Before you give up and perform a Windows manual installation, review the following list of common "oops" items:

■ Is the printer on?

■ Is the printer securely connected to the PC?

■ Did you unpack the printer correctly and install the ink or toner cartridge?

■ Do you have the right driver CD?

■ Did you follow the installation documentation correctly?

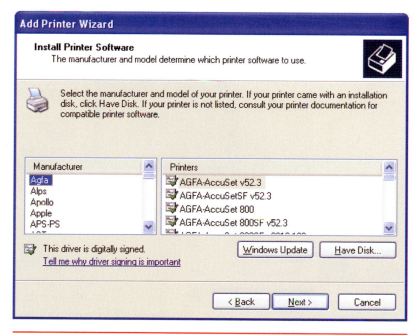

• Selecting the printer model

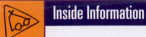
Most printer installations fail because the answer to one of these questions is "no." Don't let the simple things complicate your easy printer installation.

Once you've installed the printer driver and Windows has recognized the printer, head over to the Printers (or Printers and Faxes) applet and verify that the new printer appears there. If "Ready" appears next to the printer name, you have a good installation, and you're ready to configure your printer.

Configuration

Following the "keep it simple" policy, a properly installed printer almost never needs any further configuration to do the thing it is supposed to do: print. That doesn't mean a newly installed printer will always function optimally, however, so you still need to make sure that your printer is properly configured. The place to perform this configuration is the Printers (or Printers and Faxes) applet.

Default Printer

Windows always sets one printer as the default printer. This is the printer to which all applications will send their print jobs unless you specifically tell them to use another printer. You can easily identify the default printer by the check mark on the printer icon.

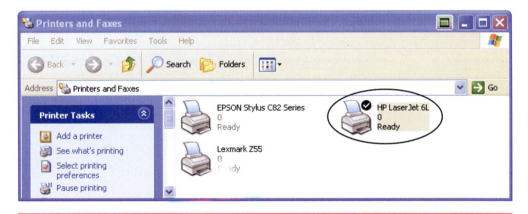

• Default printer in Windows XP

• Changing the default printer

If a PC has only a single printer installed, that printer will automatically be the default printer. However, if you have more than one printer, the most recently installed printer will normally be the default printer. To make a particular printer the default printer, you simply alternate-click (right-click) its icon and select the Set as Default Printer menu option.

Printing Preferences

All printers, and especially color inkjet printers, have a large number of printer settings that affect the overall quality of your printouts. Printer makers tend to configure their printer settings to defaults that cover the broadest range of possible printing situations, which pretty much guarantees that at some point you will need to know how to change your printing preferences to get the results you need.

The tool you use to make these changes is the Printing Preferences menu option, which you access by opening the Printers (or Printers and Faxes) applet on the Control Panel, alternate-clicking the printer you want to configure, and selecting Printing Preferences from the menu. The Printing Preferences dialog box varies dramatically among printers. When you install your printer driver, you are also installing the Printing Preferences dialog box. The Printing Preferences dialog box for Windows-supplied drivers tends to be rather simple, and the ones that come from the printer manufacturers tend to have more controls and an easy-to-use user interface.

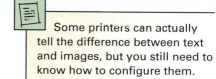

Some printers can actually tell the difference between text and images, but you still need to know how to configure them.

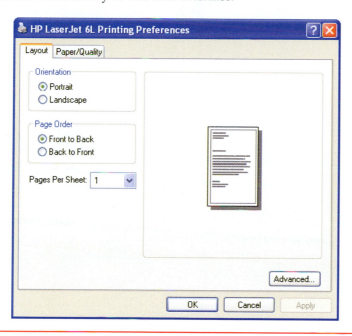

• Printing Preferences dialog box for a Windows-supplied driver

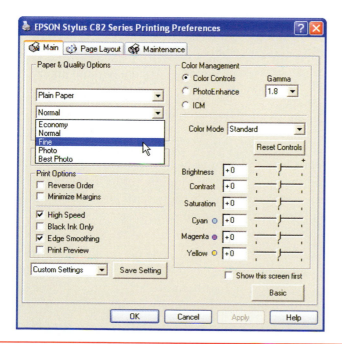

• Printing Preferences dialog box for a manufacturer-supplied driver

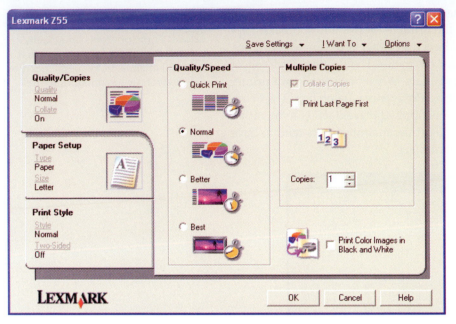

• Another Printing Preferences dialog box

Specific settings will vary according to the make and model of your printer, but you'll find certain items for almost every printer. The most important setting is usually called something like Print Quality. Print quality is especially critical on color inkjet printers, which invariably have four or five print quality settings, ranging from Draft or Quick to High Quality. The Draft setting uses minimal ink and prints very quickly; as you move to better-quality printouts, printing uses progressively more ink and takes longer.

The question you need to ask is: What do I normally print? If you're like most people, the answer is, "Quick and ugly text!" Most print jobs do not need to impress—they are meant to give quick information. You can both greatly improve print speed and stretch the lifespan of the ink or toner by setting your default printing preference to Draft. Whenever you want higher-quality output, you can easily change your printing preferences.

Step-by-Step 14.2

Installing a Printer

Different printers may require a different order of installation than the example presented here, but all printers will require all of these steps. If the printer's documentation mandates a different installation order than the one shown here, go ahead and change the order of the steps to fit your printer's needs.

To complete this exercise, you will need the following:

- A Windows system without an installed printer
- Any type of printer with cables, documentation, and installation CD

Step 1

If the printer is still in the box, unpack it now. Locate the documentation and installation CD and remove all packing materials. Clean off all the little clingy Styrofoam bits and stray pieces of tape. Locate the toner or ink cartridges. Make sure that you have an appropriate printer cable and, if necessary, a separate power cable.

Step 2

Turn off your PC and install the USB or parallel cable between the printer and the PC. Complete any printer assembly required, such as attaching printer trays. Insert the ink cartridges or toner cartridge, making sure to remove any protective strips (a common feature of ink cartridges). Plug in the printer and turn it on.

Step 3	Reboot your PC. Wait for Windows to see the new printer hardware and start the Printer Install wizard. You have an installation CD, so you should cancel rather than run the Install wizard. Insert the printer's installation CD and allow it to autoplay. Follow the instructions to install the printer driver.
Step 4	After the printer has been installed, the fun begins! Before you try any "real" print jobs, run a test print to verify that the printer is working properly. Most modern inkjets have Windows interfaces that let you perform tasks such as adjusting the printheads. For practice, do this if your printer is able. As a final test, try printing a document in your usual word processing program.

■ Performing Basic Printer Maintenance

If you want your printer to continue to give you clean, crisp printouts, you'll need to do some significant maintenance on an ongoing basis. No other part of your computer needs as much attention as your printer. Because printers use consumables—paper and ink—they have a tendency to get dirty over time. Without ongoing maintenance, you're asking for trouble!

 The number-one reason that printers fail is lack of proper maintenance.

Consumables

For many years, consumers have been the beneficiaries of an ongoing price and technology war among the main printer makers. As prices have plummeted, print quality has continued to rise, reaching the point where today you can purchase a very nice color inkjet printer for less than $100. However, the printer makers have learned a trick: they charge relatively little for the printer and then charge exorbitant rates for paper and cartridges. The single biggest printer expense is the cost of ink and toner cartridges.

 Despite tales to the contrary, simply using third-party replacement toner and ink cartridges does not void the printer's warranty. However, damage to your printer caused by faulty third-party toner or ink might void your warranty

Ink and Toner Cartridges

Ever since printers first appeared for PCs, printer makers and upstart third-party companies have battled for your ink and toner dollars. When Hewlett-Packard first came out with its popular LaserJet printers, you had to buy your replacement toner cartridges directly from Hewlett-Packard. However, within just a few years, companies began to provide toner refill services. This was quickly followed by companies selling refurbished cartridges. Today, third-party toner cartridge companies are very common, selling good-quality toner cartridges at substantially lower prices than the printer maker's same product.

The downside of third-party replacement cartridges is that the industry is made up of many thousands of small players, each with its own method of refilling and remanufacturing cartridges. There is no industry or government group that provides some level of quality control. So what do you buy? Well, I've had great success with remanufactured toner cartridges. A good remanufacturer will not only refill the toner, but will also replace certain internal components that tend to fail. Look for companies that provide

> Not all inkjet cartridges can be refilled and refurbished. Some manufacturers (Epson in particular) have created special cartridges that sense when they are empty and cease working, even if refilled. Keep this in mind when choosing an inkjet printer.

full warranties—and ask around! Word of mouth is your best guide when trying to find a local remanufacturer.

Third-party replacements aren't just for laser printers. Plenty of third-party brands of replacement ink cartridges are available for inkjet printers. Some, but not all, inkjet cartridges also can be refilled using refill kits. I'm not a big fan of refill kits. Most of the time they work fairly well, but I've had a couple of very messy experiences with them. If you want to save money on inkjet cartridges, consider letting a professional do the refilling and buy third-party refurbished ink cartridges.

Paper

Paper isn't nearly as big an issue as cartridges and toner. Both inkjet and laser printers do fine with general-purpose office paper, although inkjets do produce better-quality output using a slightly higher grade of paper, which is commonly marketed as being for inkjet printers. One case where better-quality paper does make a significant difference is color prints. You can purchase high-quality paper for printing photographs that will make a huge difference in the overall quality of your output. In fact, most inkjet printer preferences have special settings to tell the printer the paper quality, allowing the printer to adjust the print quality to match.

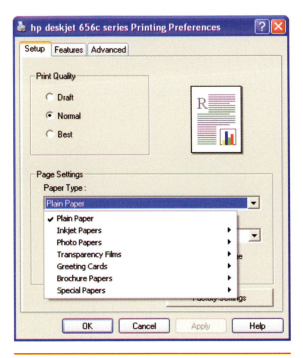

• Paper settings in Printing Preferences

Laser Printer Maintenance

Laser printers are complex devices and need thorough periodic maintenance. The following procedures will help you keep your laser printer in good working order.

Cleaning

Laser printers generate a fair amount of paper dust and excess toner. Most laser printers need a periodic vacuuming to get rid of this dirt. In most cases, you should vacuum about once every month or two. Don't use a regular vacuum cleaner! They generate static electricity that may harm your printer. Instead, use a special printer vacuum, available at most computer and electronics stores.

• Printer vacuum

Maintenance Kits

Most laser printers have parts that wear out over time and need replacing at certain intervals. Check with your printer manufacturer to see if a maintenance kit is available for your laser printer.

Professional Support

If you really want to keep your laser printer in top condition, get a maintenance contract with a local printer support company. These companies will come to your location at regular intervals and perform the exact maintenance that your printer needs at the times specified by the manufacturer.

Inkjet Printer Maintenance

Compared to laser printers, inkjet printers require little maintenance. Because of the low price of these printers, manufacturers know that people don't want to spend a lot of money keeping them running. Thus, inkjets tend to have built-in maintenance programs that you should run from time to time to keep your inkjet in good operating order.

Inkjet printers don't get nearly as dirty as laser printers, and most manufacturers do not recommend periodic cleaning. Unless your manufacturer explicitly tells you to do so, don't vacuum an inkjet.

Maintenance Applications

Inkjets generally do not have maintenance kits, but most inkjet printers come with extensive maintenance software. Usually, the hardest part of using this software is finding it in the first place. Look for an option in Printing Preferences, a selection on the Start menu, or an icon on your desktop. Don't worry—it's there!

All of these maintenance procedures described here are generalizations; be aware that every printer is particular about how maintenance tasks are performed. Check your printer documentation to see exactly how to perform any of these procedures on your printer.

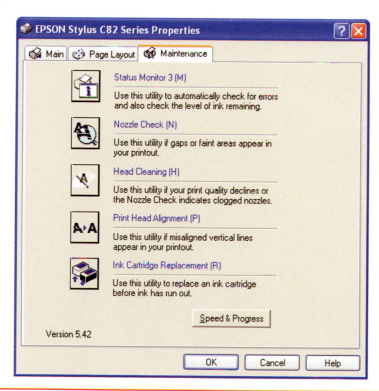

• Maintenance program

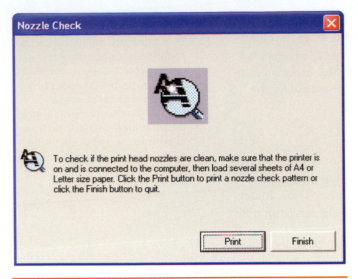

To check if the print head nozzles are clean, make sure that the printer is on and is connected to the computer, then load several sheets of A4 or Letter size paper. Click the Print button to print a nozzle check pattern or click the Finish button to quit.

Print   Finish

• Nozzle cleaning

Cleaning

Did I say that you never should clean an inkjet? Well, that may be true for the printer itself, but there is one part of your printer that will benefit from an occasional cleaning: the inkjet's printer nozzles. The printer nozzles are the tiny pipes that squirt the ink onto the paper. Their tiny size makes them vulnerable to clogging, especially if they haven't been used for a number of days.

Every inkjet has a different procedure for cleaning the nozzles. On older inkjets, you usually have to press buttons on the printer to start a maintenance program that clears the nozzles. On more modern inkjets, you can access a control screen from Windows that starts the maintenance program to clean the nozzles.

Step-by-Step 14.3

Maintaining an Inkjet Printer

Performing the proper periodic maintenance on your inkjet printer will save you time, money, and frustration, so it's a good idea to get familiar early on with how this is done on your specific printer model. This exercise is your opportunity to learn the proper care and feeding procedures for your faithful printer pal.

To complete this exercise, you will need the following:

- A Windows system
- An installed inkjet printer

Step 1   Open the Printers (or Printers and Faxes) applet on the Control Panel. Alternate-click the inkjet printer icon and select Printing Preferences from the menu.

Step 2   Locate the maintenance functions for this printer. If the Printer properties do not include maintenance functions, look on the Start menu or on the desktop for a maintenance application.

Step 3   Run the maintenance program to clear the nozzles. Check the printer documentation to see if you can run the maintenance program from the printer itself.

Step 4   Shut off the printer and then immediately restart it. Does the printer seem to go through the same maintenance check?

Recognizing and Fixing Basic Printing Problems

Nothing makes a computer technician more beloved than a printer problem—assuming they know how to fix it! This section discusses some of the more common printer problems and steps you can take to fix them.

Tools

Before you start looking at particular problems and how to fix them, you need to be aware of some handy tools that come with your printer. The first tool is the printer's user's guide. The user's guide lists a number of problems that may occur with your printer and offers solutions. Always turn first to the user's guide for help.

Your second handy tool is the maintenance program. Almost all printers have troubleshooting guides built into their maintenance programs, giving you a second place to look when your printer doesn't print correctly. All printer makers have excellent online troubleshooting guides, too.

The third tool is the printer test. All printers have the ability to print a test page from software. These test pages will make the printer print all of its colors and generate images and text to allow you to see if there are any print problems. Better inkjet and almost all laser printers have printer self-tests that you run from the printer itself, usually by pressing certain buttons, so you don't even need to have the printer connected to the PC to run the self-test. These self-tests are handy when you're not sure whether a problem is caused by the printer itself or by your drivers or connections.

Your fourth and final tool is the printer error warning system. All printers offer error warnings in some form. Windows may pop up an error message, usually for simple errors such as disconnection of the printer cable. Second, the printer itself provides error codes. On inkjet printers, error codes usually appear as different patterns of blinking LEDs. On laser printers, these error codes show up as text on a small screen.

Error codes can be confusing if you don't have your printer documentation. If you don't have documentation, go to the manufacturer's website for details on how to handle error codes.

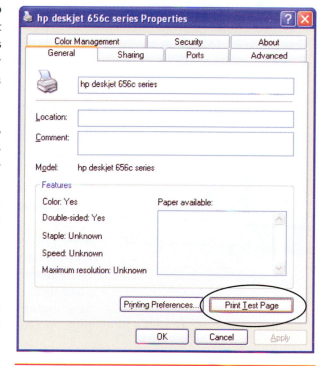

• Print test page

• Error code on a printer

No-Print Problems

Probably the most common printing problem is lack of output: you try to print a document, but nothing comes out. This type of problem can appear in two ways: either the printer seems to act like it's printing, but nothing comes out, or the printer doesn't do anything at all.

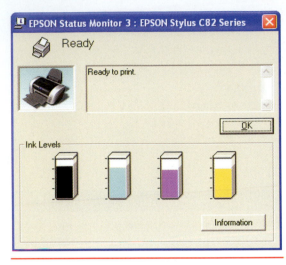

• Levels indicators

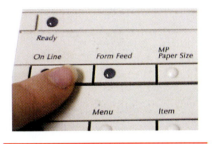

• Online button

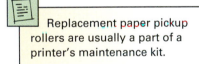
Replacement paper pickup rollers are usually a part of a printer's maintenance kit.

If the printer acts like it is printing, check for these problems first:

- Does the printer have paper?
- Does the printer have enough ink or toner?

Most printers now have a utility that shows you the current levels of ink or toner. Always look first for something simple; maybe the printer is simply out of ink.

If the printer doesn't act like it is printing, first make sure that the printer is connected and turned on. On some printers, look for an Online button. If your printer has an Online button, it must be enabled or the printer won't print. Also, watch for error codes. If the printer doesn't act like it is printing and an error code appears, the printer itself may be damaged.

Paper Problems

Printers often run into problems with paper. No matter how good the quality, all paper leaves some amount of paper dust, causing a number of problems on printers. The most common problem is paper jams. If your printer jams, take some time to check the documentation before you yank out the paper. Many printers have special hatches to help you remove the jammed paper.

The other big paper problem is in the paper pickup from the paper tray. If the printer won't grab a sheet of paper, check its pickup rollers to see if they are covered in paper dust. They should be cleaned or replaced—check the manufacturer's documentation for instructions on how to clean or replace them. Paper is also susceptible to humidity. If your printer starts grabbing multiple sheets of paper, open a new ream of paper and see if the problem persists.

Bad-Print Problems

Sometimes the printer may print a piece of paper, but the print is of poor quality. The solution depends on the type of bad-print output.

Streaks and Spots

If your printouts have streaks or spots (also called speckles), your first assumption should be a dirty printer. As laser printers get dirty, your first clue is spots on your printouts. Whip out that printer vacuum and start cleaning!

Streaks on an inkjet usually point to dirty nozzles. A quick run of the nozzle-cleaning program should clear up the problem. If streaks still appear, you probably have ink buildup on the print cartridge. Pull out the ink cartridge, grab a foam swab soaked in isopropyl alcohol, and dab that on the jets to remove the clog. Dry the cartridge with a cloth and reinsert it.

Fades

If your printouts appear faded, or if you see distinct round blank spots in your printouts, you need to check the following:

If the printout is faded evenly across the page, most likely your toner or ink is getting low. If you're using a laser printer, try removing the toner cartridge and shaking it side to side a few time to redistribute the toner. If you're using an inkjet, you need a new ink cartridge.

If the printout is spotted, your paper probably is too damp—a common problem in high-humidity areas. Try some paper from a newly opened ream to see if the problem goes away.

Fuzzy Printout

Fuzzy, unfocused printouts are common on color inkjet printers. This problem occurs when the different color nozzles get out of alignment. Most maintenance programs have an alignment program—if yours doesn't, then you'll need a trip to the repair shop. Fuzzy printouts on laser printers are rare and usually point to a serious problem requiring professional attention.

> ⚠️ It takes only a tiny amount of loose toner to mess up a perfectly nice shirt. Shake the cartridge as far away from you as you can to prevent a messy incident.

Step-by-Step 14.4

Exploring Printer Errors

Printer errors differ dramatically for each make and model of printer. In this Step-by-Step exercise, you will create some classic printer error situations and see how your printer responds. There is no one answer here. Look for errors signaled on the screen or by the printer's error codes.

To complete this exercise, you will need the following:

- A Windows system
- Any type of printer

Step 1

Verify that the printer is working correctly by running a test print. Unplug the printer cable from the back of the PC and try to print to the printer. What error messages do you see?

Step 2

Reattach the printer and run another test print. Turn off the printer and try to print to it. What errors messages appear? Turn the printer back on and run a test print.

Step 3

Turn off the printer and remove the ink or toner cartridge. Turn the printer back on. Do any error messages appear? Try printing to the printer. Do any error messages show up then?

Step 4

Reinstall the ink or toner cartridge and run a test print. Remove all of the paper from your printer and then try to print to it. What error messages appear now?

■ Chapter Summary

After reading this chapter and completing the exercises, you should understand the following aspects of printers:

Describe current printer technologies

- The three predominant printer technologies are dot matrix, laser, and inkjet.

- Dot matrix printers come in two varieties: 9-pin and 24-pin.

- The quality of a print image is called the resolution. The resolution is measured in dots per inch (dpi), which has two values: horizontal and vertical. An example of a resolution is 600 x 600 dpi.

- Printing speed is measured in pages per minute (ppm).

- Laser printers also have resolution. The maximum resolution for most laser printers is 600 x 600 dpi.

Install a printer on a Windows PC

- A printer may use either of two interfaces with the PC: a parallel connection or a USB connection.

- The parallel connector on the printer side is called a Centronics connector.

- The optimal parallel cable standard is called IEEE 1284.

- Almost anything you need to do to a printer can be performed from the Printers (or, in Windows XP, Printers and Faxes) applet on the Control Panel.

- Parallel connections have assigned settings called ports. The two most common parallel port names are LPT1 and LPT2.

- One printer will always be the default printer. If you have more than one printer installed, you can make any printer the default printer.

Perform basic printer maintenance

- You can save a substantial amount of money by using refurbished and refilled toner and ink cartridges.

- Laser printers need periodic cleaning. Be sure to use a special printer vacuum.

- Many laser printers have maintenance kits that you can use to replace worn parts.

- It's very common to hire a printer support company to perform all periodic maintenance for laser printers.

- Inkjet printers, due to their low price, rely on built-in programs to handle most of their maintenance needs.

- Inkjet printers need to have their nozzles cleaned from time to time. This is done by software or by pressing button combinations on the printer.

Recognize and fix basic printing problems

- A number of tools come with printers to help you perform basic repairs, including a user's guide, maintenance programs, self-test capabilities, and error codes.

- The printer's user's guide often provides troubleshooting help.

- The printer's maintenance program also has troubleshooting guides.

- There are two types of printer test: the Windows test in which you print a test page, and the printer self-test that runs from the printer itself.

- Printer error warnings appear on the screen as error messages or as error codes on the printer itself.

■ Key Terms

25-pin female DB connector *(370)*
Centronics connector *(370)*
consumables *(368)*
dot matrix printer *(365)*
dots per inch (dpi) *(366)*
IEEE 1284 *(370)*
ink cartridge *(366)*

inkjet printer *(365)*
LPT1 *(374)*
LPT2 *(374)*
laser *(367)*
laser printer *(367)*
pages per minute (ppm) *(367)*
parallel port *(370)*

photosensitive drum *(367)*
resolution *(366)*
toner *(367)*
toner cartridge *(368)*
USB type A *(371)*
USB type B *(371)*

■ Key Term Quiz

Use terms from the Key Terms list to complete the following sentences. Not all of the terms will be used.

1. You should always try to use a parallel cable with the _____ rating.

2. Most USB printers use a _____ connector on the printer.

3. A parallel printer connects to the parallel cable with a _____.

4. Laser printers use lasers to create the print image on a _____.

5. The two most common names for parallel ports are _____ and _____.

6. _____ are excellent for printing through multipart forms.

7. Most _____ print in color.

8. A _____ is the best choice when you need to print high-speed, high-quality text.

9. The resolution of a printer is measured in _____.

10. A printer's speed is rated in _____.

■ Multiple-Choice Quiz

1. Tammy needs to print color prints. Which printer technology would most likely be the best for her to use?

   a. Parallel

   b. Inkjet

   c. Laser

   d. Dot matrix

2. Dot matrix printers come in 9-pin and _____-pin versions.

   a. 6

   b. 16

   c. 24

   d. 32

3. Most of today's inkjet printers come with _____ colors of ink.

   a. 2

   b. 3

   c. 4

   d. 6

4. John is buying a new color inkjet printer. He has narrowed his selection to two printers of roughly the same resolution, speed, and price. What should he check next to help him determine which printer to buy?

   a. PPM

   b. DPI

   c. Power use

   d. Cost of consumables

5. The vast majority of printers use either a parallel or a/an _____ connection.

   a. USB

   b. PCI

   c. Serial

   d. VGA

6. Janet just bought a new Windows XP system. She wants to install her three-year-old inkjet printer on the new system but has lost the driver CD. She can't get on the Internet to download the latest drivers. What should she do for drivers?

   a. Install a driver for a similar printer.

   b. She's stuck until she can get on the Internet.

   c. She can use the built-in Windows drivers.

   d. She can install the printer without drivers.

7. If your computer has only a single parallel port, most likely it is preset to _____.

   a. COM1

   b. Primary

   c. USB

   d. LPT1

8. John just installed a second printer on his system. When he prints in Microsoft Word, the job goes to the wrong printer. What does he need to do to get print jobs always to go to one printer or the other?

   a. He needs to set the primary printer.

   b. He needs to set the main printer.

    c. He needs to set the default printer.

    d. He needs to set the system printer.

9. What is the name of the software tool used to set print quality for a printer?

    a. Printing Preferences

    b. Printer Properties

    c. Printer Settings

    d. Default Printer

10. Frank's color inkjet printer no longer prints the color yellow, though it prints all of the other colors just fine. The printer worked fine last month, the last time he printed in color. Which of the following is the most likely problem?

    a. He turned off the yellow nozzle.

    b. He has run out of yellow ink.

    c. He has a corrupt printer driver.

    d. His printer is set to black-and-white mode.

11. Beth's laser printer is printing tiny specks on the paper. What should she do first?

    a. Wipe the paper with bleach.

    b. Run the printer maintenance program.

    c. Clean the nozzles.

    d. Vacuum the printer.

12. Ursula's laser printer has stopped working and is displaying this error message: "Error 81 – Service." What should she do first?

    a. Update the printer's firmware.

    b. Reinstall the printer driver.

    c. Try to find the error in the user's guide or maintenance program or online.

    d. Turn off the printer and call the manufacturer's help line.

13. Kevin's inkjet printer isn't printing blue (cyan). He checks the ink levels and sees that there's plenty of ink. What should he consider next?

    a. A printhead is jammed.

    b. A laser is blocked.

    c. A nozzle is clogged.

    d. An ink cartridge is missing.

14. The output from Diane's laser printer is fading evenly. What should she suspect first?

    a. A laser is blocked.

    b. The printer is out of toner.

    c. A nozzle is clogged.

    d. Her printer is dirty.

15. Which of the following is a good reason to choose a laser printer over an inkjet printer?

    a. Speed

    b. Color

    c. Cost of the printer

    d. Resolution

■ Essay Quiz

1. Your department needs a number of color inkjet printers. However, at your organization all purchases are handled through professional buyers. Sadly, they know nothing about color inkjet printers. You need to submit a Criteria for Purchase form to your buyers. This is the standard form that your organization gives to buyers so they know what to look for in the products they buy. What are the top three purchasing criteria that you think they need to consider? Write the criteria as simply and clearly as possible.

2. You support 25 laser printers for your department as part of your job description. The printers take so much of your time that you often need to work overtime to keep them running. You're often criticized for shutting down printers that people need when you clean them. You've just been given a promotion and have been asked by your old boss to write a memo on how your old job can be improved. Recommend to your boss that a professional laser printer company should handle laser printer maintenance for your organization. Give as many compelling reasons as you can think of.

3. Interview a person who uses a computer for work. Ask the person what he or she does and then write a short description of the type of printer that would most suit that person's needs. Explain why this printer would be the best choice.

4. Dot matrix printers and multipart forms are an excellent match. Think of some businesses that

5. Describe the first printer you ever used. If you've never used a printer, ask another person about the first printer he or she used. Describe the printer, the technology, the size of paper it used, and the type of data that was printed. If possible, describe how the printer was maintained and serviced.

Lab Projects

• Lab Project 14.1

Laser printers often have rather complex maintenance procedures and schedules. For this lab, select a laser printer—preferably one that you actually have—and answer the following questions.

(1) Using the user's guide or online sources, determine the exact cleaning procedures for your laser printer. How often should it be vacuumed? Do any parts need to be removed for cleaning? Does the manufacturer recommend any specialized cleaning steps? Does your printer come with any specialized cleaning tools? Does the manufacturer have any recommended cleaning tools you should purchase?

(2) Based on the information you gathered, create a cleaning toolkit for your laser printer. Be sure to include a vacuum. Locate sources for these products and determine the cost of the toolkit.

(3) Determine the model number of the toner cartridge. Locate an online company that sells name-brand (such as Hewlett-Packard) toner cartridges. Locate an equivalent third-party toner cartridge. Assuming that the printer uses a toner cartridge every three months, what is your per system annual cost savings using third-party toner cartridges?

(4) All toner cartridges have a materials safety data sheet (MSDS). Locate the MSDS for your model of toner cartridge and read it. Note any potential hazards of the toner cartridges.

(5) Print the description of the cleaning kit you created as well as the manufacturer's cleaning instructions.

• Lab Project 14.2

Using the same laser printer you used in the first lab, locate and compile, on paper, all of the following information about your printer:

- User's guide
- List of error codes

- Troubleshooting guides
- Location of the latest drivers for Windows XP

Use this information to create a support book for the printer. Add your cleaning kit and cleaning instructions to your printer support book.

Networks

"There are three kinds of death in this world. There's heart death, there's brain death, and there's being off the network."

—GUY ALMES

In this chapter, you will learn how to:

- **Explain how networks work**
- **Install and configure a dial-up network**
- **Install and configure a Local Area Network**
- **Troubleshoot basic network problems**

Much of what makes modern computers so powerful is their ability to connect in small or large groups, or *networks*, and share files and resources. Every PC tech worth knowing knows the basics of networking. After all, why get into computing if you can't while away an afternoon gaming with your buddies, all from the comfort of your computer chair?

In this chapter, you will learn what comprises a network and what makes networks tick. You'll learn about some of the most common hardware used to create small networks and how the various hardware components interact. You'll also learn how to install a modem and network card and how to set up a basic network. Finally, you'll learn how to troubleshoot basic network problems.

How Networks Work

A network enables two or more computers to share data, hardware such as printers, and even applications. The computers must have some connectivity, of course: some way for the signal from one machine to reach the other. In addition, the hardware must be compatible and the software set up so that the receiving computer can understand what the sending machine sends. Think of two kids chatting over walkie-talkies as a network: for communication to occur, the hardware has to be in range for the signal, and it has to be from the same set, and the kids need to speak the same language. Networks work similarly.

Computers connect in two basic ways: in dial-up networks and in Local Area Networks. In a dial-up connection, your computer uses a telephone line to connect to an Internet Service Provider (ISP), which then gives you access to other computers, perhaps at your office or somewhere on the Internet. Computers in a Local Area Network, on the other hand, are connected to a central box—either by cables or by radio waves—through which they can communicate with each other and, if some machine on the network has the appropriate connection, with other computers on the Internet. Let's look at how both types of networks function before we turn to the nuts and bolts of installing and setting up networks.

Dial-Up Networks

The most common network connection consists of three pieces: a modem, a working telephone line, and an ISP. The **modem** enables the computer to communicate via phone lines. The phone line provides the link between the modem and the computers at the ISP. The ISP computers connect to the Big Kahuna of all networks, the Internet. Properly installed and configured, the modem-to-telephone line-to-ISP connection enables you to surf, shop, and otherwise explore websites hosted by computers all over the world. Tune in and turn on to dial-up networking.

The venerable modem has in recent years been challenged by two new consumer technologies for accessing the Internet: so-called "cable modems" and DSL (Digital Subscriber Line) service. Your computer's basic need for some kind of pipeline to communicate over hasn't changed—just the choice of pipeline and the way it's used. Both technologies take advantage of unused capacity on widely available transmission media.

Cable modems use the cables already in place in many homes for receiving cable TV signals as their pipeline to the Internet, rather than the telephone system. The cable TV companies take advantage of the fact that

• An internal modem

their cable TV signals occupy only a fraction of the capacity of the coaxial cables running into your home. Adding a cable modem to your computer enables it to use the cable TV connection as its pipeline to the Internet. Cable modems aren't actually "modems" at all in the sense that the signals they send and receive are entirely digital, but because they perform the same function, they go by the same name. You can install an internal type of cable modem as an expansion card, or connect an external cable modem to a port (usually USB) on your computer.

Is Your Modem Installed?

Does your computer have a modem installed? How can you tell? Is there a way to find out what kind? Some motherboards have built-in modems, but most modems come as expansion cards plugged into a PCI slot on the motherboard. To find out whether your system has a modem installed, try this:

1. Look on the back of your computer for a modem connection. Does your PC have a port that looks like the ports on the modem shown in the earlier illustration? If it does, then you know you have a modem installed.

2. To see what your system *thinks* it has installed, open the Modems applet in the Control Panel (called Modems in Windows 9x/Me; Phone and Modem Options in Windows 2000/XP).

3. Windows 9x will display a Modems Properties dialog box. Look on the General tab to see a list of the modem(s) your system believes are installed and on which COM ports. Windows 2000/XP displays a Phone and Modem Options dialog box; you must click on the Modems tab to see the list of installed modems and associated COM ports.

DSL, by contrast, still uses your telephone line as its pipeline, but it does so in a very clever way. The details are quite technical, but basically DSL exploits the fact that standard copper telephone lines can handle a much greater range of frequencies, or *bandwidth*, than what is needed to transmit your voice during phone calls. DSL uses this extra bandwidth capacity to send data over the telephone wires without disturbing their ability to carry voice conversations. This enables you to use a single phone line for both normal voice communication as you've always done and, at the same time, for digital data transmission between your computer and your ISP or other computers on the Internet.

The Internet itself is little more than a collection of smaller networks connected to form a bigger network. Communication between two PCs over the Internet still requires two functional computers that can understand each other. To open Microsoft's home page, for example, your browser software sends a request through your modem to the receiving computer at your ISP, which then forwards your request to the proper network to get it closer to the destination machine: the web server you want to access. This process can take many steps, with your request bouncing from machine to machine, network to network, until it lands in Redmond, Washington, home of Microsoft.

The Microsoft web server then responds to your request, giving your browser information to display. This process again can take many hops from computer to computer, network to network; until the Microsoft home page finally reaches your ISP and travels down your phone line and into your PC via the modem.

All of this activity happens so quickly for the most part that it seems almost like magic, but it isn't. For this process to work, a great deal of setup is required. You have to have a properly installed modem with the correct drivers loaded. You need properly set up software, and in this case, Windows' dial-up networking needs to be configured according to the details provided by your ISP. The ISP computers also need to be set up properly to receive your modem's call. If the ISP computers don't recognize your name and password, for example, you can call all day long and not get a connection to the world at large.

Local Area Networks

Dial-up networking provides users with a window on the larger world, but what if you want to connect two computers in the same room? It doesn't make sense that you should have to use two phone lines and call up an ISP to connect the machines, right? Of course not! You can connect the machines directly, in a **Local Area Network (LAN)**. A LAN is simply a group of networked computers that occupy a relatively small area, ranging from adjoining offices in a business to adjoining buildings on a campus. To make a LAN work, you need to ensure three things: connectivity, compatibility, and proper hardware and software setup.

To achieve connectivity, each computer has to have a **Network Interface Card (NIC)** installed. The NIC provides the basic link outside the box, much like a modem provides the link to the telephone line. The computers on a LAN connect to a central **hub**—usually over a cable, but also through the air, with a wireless LAN. Every PC that can send a signal to the hub can share data with every other PC on the hub.

Connectivity alone does not ensure a successful LAN, however. For a LAN to function properly, the hardware technology must be consistent within the system, following the same standards in everything from the cables to the connectors on the hub and the PC. Even with compatible hardware, you still need to answer a lot of other questions. It's one thing to issue a request such as, "Send a file from computer A to computer B," but how do you make sure that your request can be sent and read and fulfilled? Once you have established connectivity, you need to ensure that the networking hardware and software on the PCs work together.

- Network Interface Card (NIC)

If you're trying to share a big file between two computers, for example, you could chop up the data that comprises that file and move the data in discrete pieces from one PC to the other. But how does the receiving computer know how to put the data pieces back together? How do the two PCs negotiate to make the connection happen in the first place?

The protocols used with networking hardware and software answer all of the questions regarding compatibility. In computer networking, the term **protocol** describes any predetermined set of rules that defines how two devices or pieces of software should communicate with each other. Data that flows between computers is always split into smaller pieces, called **packets**, for efficiency. Protocols determine how the data is split and how it goes back together. Protocols specify what types of cabling and connectors should be used to connect networked PCs. Protocols control the way data packets are routed across a network, so when computer A sends them to computer B, they do get delivered to computer B, and they *don't* get delivered to computer C or D. To work together, computers on a network must share the same networking protocols, both as to their hardware and as to their software.

Finally, to create a successful LAN, everything must be set up properly: NICs must be installed with good drivers; wiring must be correctly installed to connect the PCs and the hub; matching network protocols must be correctly set up on every networked machine's operating system; and each system must be set up to enable sharing, so it can access shared resources on the other systems on the LAN and, in turn, the other systems can access shared resources on that system. This last step is crucial—if sharing is not enabled on each of the networked systems, the rest of your efforts will be for naught.

So that's the theory. Now it's time to move into action and look at the procedures for installing dial-up and Local Area Networks.

■ Installing and Configuring a Dial-Up Network

At some point in the early days of computing, some bright guy or gal noticed a colleague talking on a telephone, then glanced down at a personal computer, and then put two and two together: why not use telephone lines for data communication? The basic problem with this idea is that telephone lines use analog signals, whereas computers use digital signals.

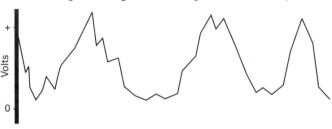

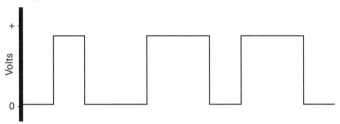

• Analog signals used by a telephone line versus digital signals used by the computer

Creating a dial-up network required equipment that could turn digital data into an analog signal to send it over the telephone line, and then turn it back into digital data when it reached the other end of the connection. Let's take a brief look at the technology before we turn to installation and software setup.

Modem Technology

The modem solves one of the problems with the use of analog voice lines to move digital data. Modems take incoming analog serial data—in this case, the signal coming over the telephone line—and turn it into digital serial data. Likewise, modems turn the digital signal flowing out of the PC into analog data than can be transferred over the telephone line. This process—called modulation/demodulation—provides the name for the technology: MOdulation/DEModulation, get it?

• Modem translating digital data into an analog signal, and vice versa

Phone lines have a speed based on a unit called a **baud**, which is one cycle per second. The fastest rate that a phone line can achieve is 2,400 baud. Modems can pack multiple bits of data into each baud; a 33.6 kilobits per second (Kbps) modem, for example, packs 14 bits into every baud: 2,400 x 14 = 33.6 Kbps.

It is technically incorrect to say, "I have a 56 K baud modem." You should instead say, "I have a 56 Kbps modem." However, people use the term *baud* instead of bps so often that the terms have become functionally synonymous.

Modern Modem Standards: V.90 Versus V.92

The fastest data transfer speed a modem can handle is based on its implementation of one of the international standards for modem technology: the V standards. Set by the International Telecommunication Union (ITU), the current top standards are V.90 and V.92. Both standards offer download speeds of just a hair under 56 Kbps, but differ in upload speeds: up to 33.6 Kbps for V.90, and up to 48 Kbps for V.92 modems. To get anywhere near the top speeds of a V.90 or V.92 modem requires a comparable modem installed on the other line, and connecting telephone lines in excellent condition. In practice, you'll rarely get faster throughput than about 48 Kbps for downloads and 28 Kbps for uploads.

Bells and Whistles

Although the core modem technology has changed little in the past few years, modem manufacturers have continued to innovate on many peripheral fronts—pardon the pun and the bad grammar. You can walk into a computer store nowadays, for example, and buy a V.92 modem that comes bundled with an excellent fax machine and a digital answering machine. You can even buy modems that you can call remotely that will wake up your PC. What will they think up next?

• Some of the many features touted by the manufacturer of the SupraMax modem

Modem Connections: PCI and USB

Modems connect to the PC in two basic ways: internally or externally. Almost all internal modems connect to a PCI expansion bus slot inside the PC, although cost-conscious manufacturers may use smaller modems that fit in a special expansion slot designed to support multiple communications features, including modems, NICs, and sound cards. On AMD motherboards this is called an ACR (Advanced Communication Riser) slot, whereas Intel motherboards use the extremely similar CNR (Communications/Networking Riser) slot. Finally, and least expensive of all,

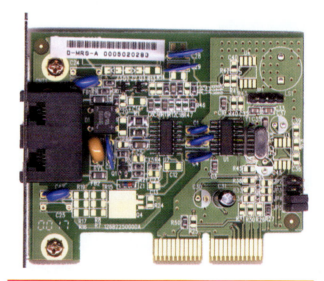

• CNR modem

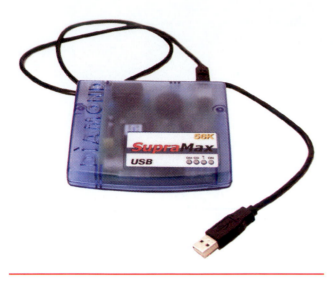

• USB modem

many current motherboards dispense with expansion cards entirely and come with the modem integrated into the motherboard.

External modems connect to the PC through an available serial port (the old way) or USB port. Many PCs come with two 9-pin serial ports, whereas most external modems designed to connect to a serial port come with a 25-pin connector. That means you will probably need a 9-to-25-pin converter, available at any computer store. Virtually all computers today have two or more USB ports in addition to the serial ports.

If you have the option, choose a USB modem, especially one with a volume control knob. The very low speeds of data communication over a modem make the physical type of the connection unimportant. Even the slowest interface—the aging serial interface—can more than adequately handle 56-Kbps data transfers. USB offers simple Plug and Play and easy portability between machines, plus such modems require no external electrical source, getting all the power they need from the USB connection.

Step-by-Step 15.1

Installing a PCI Modem

Installing any device in a PC requires three procedures. First, you must physically install the device. Second, you must assign it unused system resources, either manually or by using PnP (the Plug and Play setup utility) . Third, either you or the system (using PnP) must install the proper drivers for the card.

To complete this exercise, you will need the following:

- A PC with no modem installed
- A PCI modem
- A Phillips screwdriver
- An antistatic wrist strap

| Step 1 | Make sure the PC is unplugged and take proper ESD precautions. Remove the cover of the PC. Choose a free PCI slot, remove the back plate (if one exists), usually by gently bending it back and forth with a screwdriver. |

| Step 2 | Plug the card into the PCI slot. Physically inserting the modem into the PC is the easiest part of the task. Take care to avoid touching the pins or any of the chips on the modem. Once the card is inserted, |

secure it in the manner appropriate for your computer. Put the cover back on your computer and restart your system.

Step 3

Every modem comes with a set of drivers on a floppy disk or CD-ROM; locate the driver disk for your card. You might want to copy the drivers from the disk onto your PC's hard drive and then install them from there. That way, if you ever need the drivers again, you will not need to rummage around for the driver disk. You need to know exactly where you store the drivers, though, as you'll be asked to locate them during the load process. Remember that drivers are constantly being updated by their manufacturers, so check the manufacturer's website before using the driver disk. Along with the driver disk for your card, locate the installation CD for your operating system.

Step 4

As Windows boots, the Found New Hardware wizard should pop up. Click Next to continue. Select the option that directs Windows to search for a suitable driver for the new device and click Next. If the driver is on a floppy disk or CD-ROM, select that as the search location and insert that disk in the appropriate drive. If it's elsewhere, select the Specify a Location option. Click Next.

Found New Hardware Wizard

Welcome to the Found New Hardware Wizard

This wizard helps you install a device driver for a hardware device.

To continue, click Next.

< Back   Next >   Cancel

Step 5

If the driver is located on a fixed drive rather than an installation disk, click the Browse button and navigate to the file's location. If you don't find the file where you expected it to be, try searching for it using Windows Explorer or My Computer. Once you find the driver file, double-click to select it and return to the installation process. Click Next.

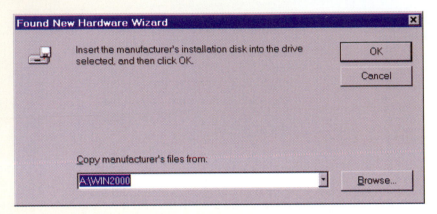

Step 6

If prompted, you may also need to insert your Windows CD. When the wizard is finished it will prompt you a final time. Click the Finish button and reboot your system. Your new modem is now properly installed.

Setting Up Software

Installing drivers completes only the most basic part of configuring your system for dial-up networking. You also need to set up dial-up networking in Windows to connect to your ISP properly. Let's look at the issues.

Dial-Up Networking

The software side of dial-up networks requires configuration within Windows to include information provided by your ISP. The ISP provides a dial-up telephone number or numbers, as well as your user name and initial password. In addition, the ISP will tell you about any special configuration options you need to specify in the software setup. The full configuration of a dial-up network is beyond the scope of this book, but you should at least know where to go to follow instructions from your ISP. Let's take a look at the Network and Internet Connections applet in Windows XP.

Network Connections   To start configuring a dial-up connection, open the Control Panel. Select Network and Internet Connections from the Pick a Category menu; then select Set Up or Change Your Internet Connection from the Pick a Task menu.

Windows 9*x* computers have a slightly different front end for configuring a dial-up connection, using the Dial-Up Network option in the Control Panel. This opens the Network Connections wizard, which offers many of the same options found in the dial-up settings in Windows XP. Microsoft has simplified the interface in its XP operating system.

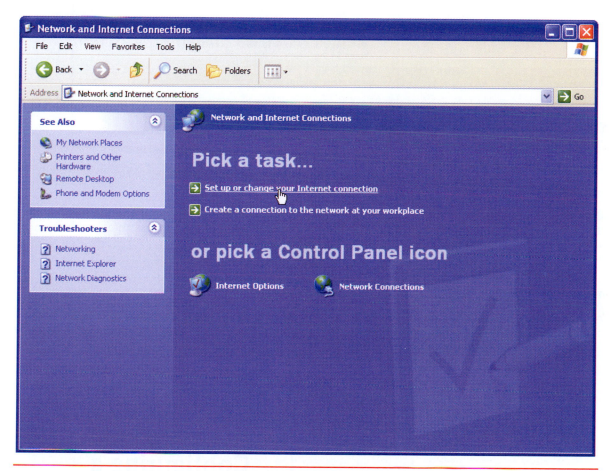

• Selecting the Set Up or Change Your Internet Connection option from the Pick a Task menu

The Internet Properties dialog box opens with the Connections tab displayed. All your work will proceed from here.

• Connections tab in the Internet Properties dialog box

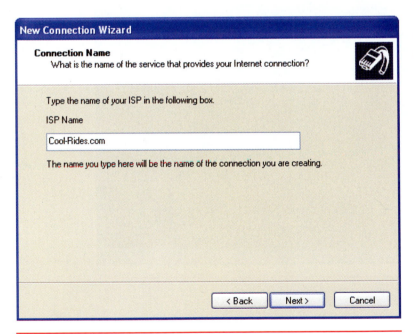

• New Connection wizard

Click the Setup button to run the New Connection wizard and then work through the screens.

At this point, you're going to need information provided by your ISP to configure your connection properly.

When you finish the configuration, you'll see a new Connect To option on the Start menu. Figure 15.1 shows the option to connect to a fictitious ISP, Cool-Rides.com.

■ Installing and Configuring a Local Area Network

Dial-up networking works well enough for accessing the Internet, downloading files and folders, and connecting to the world in general, but nothing beats a Local Area Network for fun and games or excellent productivity. Setup takes a few more steps than for dial-up networking, with more hardware and a little more software configuration required.

• **Figure 15.1**   Connection options on the Start menu

You need only a few pieces of networking equipment to set up a LAN: a couple of PCs with NICs properly installed, a hub to provide centralized connections, and a pair of cables to connect the PCs to the hub. You also need to set up the software on both PCs so they can communicate. Let's look at the technology involved in creating a LAN and then turn to the nuts and bolts of setup.

> The term **topology** refers to the physical or logical shape of a network.

Topology

Since the first networks were invented over 30 years ago, designers have tried many different wiring schemes to connect computers in a LAN. The topology of a network describes how the computers connect. The best topology for a specific situation depends on a variety of factors, including cost, speed, ease of installation, physical position of the PCs, and number of PCs in the network. One topology, however, has emerged as the favorite: the **Star Bus**.

A Star Bus network combines two separate topologies into a super topology that is much more robust than either of the individual topologies could be. A pure Star topology describes one aspect of the network: every computer on the network connects to a central box. However, this doesn't describe how data flows between the computers. We need one more part.

The *bus* in the first networks referred to the single cable that attached to every computer, enabling every computer to communicate with every other computer on the bus. This topology works, but has a fatal flaw. If something happens

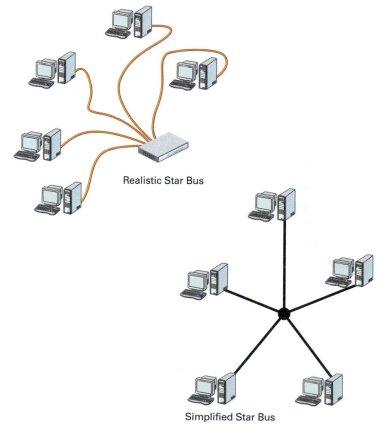

Realistic Star Bus

Simplified Star Bus

• A realistic Star Bus topology versus a simplified Star Bus topology diagram

• A hub

to the cable, the whole network goes down. A pure Bus topology lacks fault tolerance.

The basic Star Bus network consists of a central hub (which takes the place of the single cable) to which all of the devices connect via their own individual cables. Cheap and centralized, a Star Bus network does not go down if a single cable breaks. Only the machine directly attached to the broken cable is affected.

Early Star Bus networks functioned like big, live telephone party lines with many users connected. All of the users (or in this case, computers) had to listen to the line to see if it was in use before using it themselves. When computer A wanted to send an address to computer B, computer A checked to see if the line was in use and then, if it was free, placed its packet on the network cable. If the line was not available, the PC would have to wait. This early-style Star Bus network—still in use in millions of LANs, by the way—had limits on the number of machines that could be on the network and on the efficiency of communication between the machines. This was simply a function of the party-line technology.

Current Star Bus networks substitute a box called a **switch** for the earlier hubs, which in effect places each computer on the star into its own bus. This eliminates most of the problems and inefficiencies of the Star Bus network. A switch looks exactly like a hub, but the manufacturers kindly label it as a switch so techs know the difference.

Ensuring Compatibility: Ethernet

Theoretical connectivity is great, but you need to make certain that all of the pieces work together—everything from the cables, to the connectors on the switch, to the PC. Most current networks ensure compatibility of hardware and basic communication by using a series of standards called **Ethernet**. Ethernet comes in several flavors that are implemented with different cabling, connectors, and so on, but all of the flavors use the same type of data packaging. This enables you to mix and match flavors as long as you have the proper connectors.

Two implementations of Ethernet are most common today, called rather obscurely 10BaseT and 100BaseTX. They use the same cabling and connectors, so let's look at those elements first. Then we will get to the specifics about the two dominant flavors of Ethernet.

UTP Cable

Unshielded twisted-pair (UTP) cabling is the most common type of cabling used in networks today. UTP consists of, essentially, two to eight copper or aluminum wires—either stranded or solid core—twisted around each other and wrapped in a protective sheathing. The phone cords that connect the telephones in your house to the wall jacks are UTP cabling.

UTP cabling comes in categories that define the maximum speed at which data can be transferred over them (also called bandwidth), measured in megabits per second (Mbps). The major categories (CATs) are listed here:

- **CAT1**   Standard phone line
- **CAT2**   Data speeds up to 4 Mbps (ISDN and T1 lines)

• Typical UTP cable

Introduction to PC Hardware and Troubleshooting

- **CAT3**   Data speeds up to 16 Mbps
- **CAT4**   Data speeds up to 20 Mbps
- **CAT5**   Data speeds up to 100 Mbps
- **CAT5e**   Data speeds up to 100 Mbps
- **CAT6**   Data speeds up to 200 Mbps

The CAT level is usually clearly marked on the cable to minimize confusion.

The vast majority of networks today use **CAT5**, as these cables can handle data speeds up to 100 Mbps. Most new installations use the better-quality CAT5e (enhanced) or CAT6. CAT5e has less degradation of the signal than CAT5; CAT6 is even more robust.

• CAT5 cable

Most current Ethernet networks use only two of the four pairs of wires found in CAT5e and CAT6 cables, but virtually everybody installs four-pair UTP. The reason for this is simple: planning for the future. No one knows what network speeds will be common in the future or how many pairs of wires will be needed, so just about everyone is playing safe and installing four-pair CAT5e or better UTP.

UTP Connectors

To connect to the hardware, the cables usually have connectors attached. The two types of connectors used in computer networking are RJ-11 and RJ-45. **RJ-11** connectors are the ones that are attached to CAT1 phone lines in homes and offices. This type supports up to two pairs of wires, though most phone lines only use one pair. The other pair can be used to support a second phone line.

The **RJ-45** is the connector you'll see plugged into the NIC ports on computers and often connecting the main networking hardware together. If you examine an RJ-45 connector, you will see that it has connections for up to four pairs of wires; it also is visibly much wider than an RJ-11 (Figure 15.2).

The Electronics Industry Association/Telecommunication Industry Association (EIA/TIA) has developed two standards for determining which wires are connected to which pins on the connectors: EIA/TIA 568A and EIA/TIA 568B. Either of these standards is acceptable.

You will occasionally see a cable with EIA/TIA 568A on one end and EIA/TIA 568B on the other. With this sort of crossover cable, you can connect two PCs directly together, creating a tiny network of two. Figure 15.3 shows a wiring diagram for a crossover cable.

The "RJ" designation, short for *registered jack*, was invented by the Bell telephone company years ago and is still used today.

10BaseT

Until recently, the most common network was the Ethernet **10BaseT**. This standard (which falls under IEEE 802.3) defines Ethernet as running at 10 Mbps in some form of Star Bus topology over UTP cables.

The IEEE 802.3 standard specifies only two pairs of wires to run a 10BaseT network: one pair for sending and one pair for receiving. UTP cables that connect the PC to the switch can be no more than 100 meters long; if you use a longer cable, the signal will start getting weak, and data losses will occur.

• **Figure 15.2**   RJ-11 (left) and RJ-45 (right) connectors

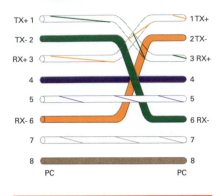

Crossover wiring standards used

T568A   **T568B**

TX+ 1	1 TX+
TX- 2	2 TX-
RX+ 3	3 RX+
4	4
5	5
RX- 6	6 RX-
7	7
8	8

PC   PC

• **Figure 15.3**   Crossover cable diagram showing UTP wire colors

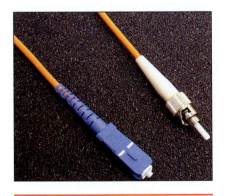

• Fiber-optic connectors

Fast Ethernet: 100BaseTX

Although 10BaseT Ethernet performs well enough for basic file and print sharing, today's more demanding network applications—such as the all-important category: games!—can quickly saturate a network running at a puny 10 megabits per second. Enter Fast Ethernet.

Fast Ethernet is not a single technology. The term **Fast Ethernet** refers to any of several Ethernet flavors that operate at 100 megabits per second. Rather than limiting Ethernet to a single high-speed solution, though, the IEEE endorsed multiple standards for Fast Ethernet and allowed the marketplace to choose among them. The major player in Fast Ethernet is **100BaseTX**.

A 100BaseTX network looks physically similar to 10BaseT network, using a Star Bus topology and connecting to hubs with UTP cabling. Just as in a 10BaseT network, the cable connecting a device to the hub may be no more than 100 meters long.

A 100BaseTX network requires at least CAT5 cabling to achieve 100 megabits per second speed using only two pairs of wires. It also requires a 100BaseTX switch if you want to get anywhere near the maximum data transfer rate between two properly equipped PCs.

Fiber-Optic Networks

One of the more exciting higher-end technologies is fiber optics; fiber-optic networks use pulses of light instead of electrical current to transmit data packets. Using light instead of electricity addresses the three key weaknesses of copper cabling. First, optical signals can travel much farther than electrical signals—up to 2 kilometers in some Ethernet implementations. Second, fiber-optic cable is immune to electrical interference, making it an ideal choice for high-interference environments. Third, fiber-optic cable is much more difficult to tap into than copper cable, making it a good choice for environments with security concerns.

The downside of this wonderful technology is that fiber-optic cabling is delicate, expensive, and can be easily damaged if it is not handled properly, so it is usually reserved for situations requiring its special characteristics, such as network backbones. The **backbone** is the main piece of Ethernet cabling to which all other hubs are connected. Backbones are used to connect the networks on multiple floors or in multiple buildings to one another. Many ISPs use fiber-optic cabling to connect to the Internet.

Wireless Networks

Wireless networking is a fascinating and quickly emerging technology that is becoming extremely popular. Already you can set up a wireless LAN in your home or office, and many groups are developing ways to create Wide Area Networks (WANs) using wireless technology. Wireless networks work just like cabled networks, except that where electrons would travel on a cable to bring data to your computer, that same information is sent via infrared or, more commonly, radio waves.

A wireless network usually consists of a box with a built-in transmitter/receiver that accepts the incoming cable-based signal and then disseminates it to special NICs connected to it by infrared (IR) or radio frequency (RF) waves.

This box is commonly called an access point, portal, or gateway, referencing the idea that the box receives the signal and then releases it into the air. Each computer attached to the network simply needs a special NIC that is compatible with the access point in use. Both IR and RF wireless devices do have fairly short ranges, but IR has an additional limitation. IR waves work on a line-of-site basis, limiting the amount of roaming away from the access point that you can do. RF waves, on the other hand, can go through walls and other barriers; you can move anywhere you like so long as you are within range of the signal.

One of the biggest issues facing wireless networks is security. IR and RF waves are free to the public, which means that anyone who is in range can access them at any time. The problems this could pose to any network are obvious.

• Wireless hub

LAN Hardware Connections

Now you know the basics of UTP and Ethernet; let's look briefly at the other two pieces of hardware you need to install a LAN: a network card and a hub or switch.

Network Interface Cards

A NIC is a collection of hardware (computer chips, traces, and so on) that translates the tiny electric pulses that make up machine code (1s and 0s) into more robust pulses (electric, light, infrared, or radio) that can be sent across long cables, and vice versa. Now you may ask, "But using that logic, isn't a modem also a NIC?" The answer is—yes! A modem is really just a NIC created to plug into and use a standard phone line.

The NIC provides the PC with a method of sending data to and receiving data from other systems by connecting the PC to the network's cabling structure. Every combination of networking technology and cabling has its own type of NIC. For the most part, these cards cannot be interchanged. Every PC in a 10BaseT network, for example, uses a 10BaseT card. Every PC in a 100BaseTX network uses a 100BaseTX card.

• A NIC

However, many NICs, called multispeed NICs, can operate at more than one speed using a single network technology. These NICs are very popular, especially those that can operate in the very common 10BaseT and 100BaseTX networks.

Most multispeed NICs automatically detect and adjust to the speed of the network without any configuration. These multispeed NICs are often referred to as autosensing NICs. If your network's PCs have autosensing 10/100BaseT NICs, you can change it from a 10BaseT network to a 100BaseTX

Try This!

Installing a NIC

The first step in setting up an Ethernet network is to install a NIC into a PC. Installing a NIC is like installing any other expansion device, such as the modem you did earlier. Try this:

1. Following the steps you learned in Step-by-Step 15.1, physically install the NIC in the system. Remember your ESD precautions!

2. Using the wizard Windows provides when it detects new hardware, install the correct drivers for your NIC. Using Plug and Play, Windows will assign the appropriate resources to the NIC.

3. If you have a network in place, connect your new NIC to the Ethernet cable for the network and test it out.

network simply by replacing the slower network hub with the faster model—assuming, of course, that the cabling is correct.

Buying NICs   When purchasing NICs, I have found that name brands seem a bit more robust than the cheapies. These devices generally are better made, have extra features, and are easy to return if defective. You can also more easily replace a missing or defective driver.

The speed of the NIC you should choose depends on your networking needs. Consider future needs and choose multispeed cards. Always try to stick with the same model of NIC when you are purchasing for multiple systems. Every different NIC means another set of driver disks to haul around. Sticking with the same model of NIC makes driver updating easier, too.

Hubs and Switches

A node is any device that is connected to a network; usually this means a PC, but other devices (such as some printers) can also be connected directly to a network.

The hub of a wheel is where all of the spokes come together. A network hub is the same thing, but with computers. All of the computers (also called **nodes**) on a multiple-node network plug into a hub to connect to each other. The hub's basic job is to accept packets from any of the computers on the network and send them to the other computers or other hubs attached to it.

The bottom line for making a 10BaseT or 100BaseTX network work properly is the use of the proper hub, or, more accurately with today's networks, the proper switch. Luckily, manufacturers make using the right hub or switch easy these days. Most 100BaseTX switches can handle 10BaseT cards and 100BaseTX cards with equal aplomb. These better switches are called 10/100 switches.

The maximum distance from the hub or switch to any 10BaseT or 100BaseTX device is 100 meters. No more than one PC can be connected to each Ethernet segment, and the maximum number of PCs that may be connected to any one hub is 1,024, though you will be hard pressed to find a hub with that many connectors. Most hubs come with 4, 8, 16, or 24 ports.

• 10/100 switch

Step-by-Step 15.2

Installing and Cabling a Hub

Installing a hub is really very simple. The biggest issue is keeping the cables arranged and in some kind of order; this is important because you'll eventually need to troubleshoot, and you will need to know which device is attached to which port on the hub.

To complete this exercise, you will need the following:

- At least two computers with NICs
- A network hub
- A network cable for each computer

Step 1

Place the hub in a centralized location so that all network cables can reach it while still being able to attach to their computers (you'd be amazed at how often this step is overlooked). Attach the hub's power cord and plug it into the surge protector. (You weren't going to plug it directly into the wall, were you? I didn't think so.)

Step 2

Attach a network cable to the NIC in each of the computers that you want to network. Then attach the network cables to the hub. Check for the green lights on the NICs—do you have a good connection?

Step 3

If all of the NICs are reporting a good connection, you're ready to share files and drives. That's all there is to it—you have now successfully set up your own basic network!

Once you've connected the NICs to the switch or hub, you've completed the proper physical connection. Now you need to turn to the last procedure involved in setting up a LAN: setting up the software correctly. Let's turn to protocols.

Ensuring Communication: Software Protocols

A network does much more than simply move data electronically from one machine to another; it must handle many other functions as well. For example, if a file is copied from one machine to another, it must keep track of all of the packets so that the data can be properly reassembled. If many machines are talking to the same machine at once, the network must keep track of which packets it sends to or receives from each PC.

Networking protocols essentially set the rules for communication in advance. However, there is no single protocol that allows computers and networks to interact. Even a simple exchange of data between two computers involves many distinct protocols. The most commonly used network protocols are IPX/SPX from Novell and NetBEUI from Microsoft, plus TCP/IP, developed for UNIX and the Internet.

IPX/SPX

Novell invented the Internetwork Packet Exchange/Sequenced Packet Exchange (IPX/SPX) protocol and built all versions of its NetWare software around it. The IPX/SPX protocol is speedy, works well with routers, and uses relatively little RAM when loaded.

NetBEUI

IBM's NetBEUI protocol could be a very annoying abbreviation to have to say, but almost immediately folks got around that by pronouncing it "Net Booey."

In the 1980s, IBM developed NetBIOS Extended User Interface (NetBEUI), which became the default protocol for Windows for Workgroups, LANtastic, and Windows 9x and NT. NetBEUI offers small size and a relatively high speed, but it can't be used for routing. This inability limits NetBEUI to networks smaller than about 200 nodes.

NetBEUI exists primarily to support Microsoft networking using Windows NT or Windows 9x. In essence, until the release of Windows XP, NetBEUI is what Microsoft operating systems used to communicate (copy files and so on) across routerless networks. TCP/IP is the new default protocol for XP.

TCP/IP

The Transmission Control Protocol/Internet Protocol (TCP/IP) was originally developed for the Internet's progenitor, the Advanced Research Projects Agency Network (ARPANET) of the U.S. Department of Defense. In 1983, TCP/IP became the built-in protocol for the popular BSD UNIX, and other flavors of UNIX adopted it as well. TCP/IP is becoming a preferred protocol for larger (more than 200 nodes) networks. In fact, the biggest network of all—the Internet—uses TCP/IP as its default protocol. Windows NT and later (2000 and XP) also use TCP/IP as a default. Compared to IPX/SPX and NetBEUI, TCP/IP takes up a lot of memory when loaded, but it is robust, well understood, and pretty much universally supported.

Making the Connection with TCP/IP

For any two computers to communicate properly, they must use the same protocols, and those protocols must be configured correctly. Protocol setup and configuration is beyond the scope of an introductory book like this one. However, a good tech at least knows where to enter information provided by a senior tech or network technician. A key task you must know how to do is enabling file and folder sharing.

Everything starts with the Control Panel, as usual. Open the Control Panel, select the Network and Internet Connections option, and then click the Network Connections icon to open the Network Connections system folder.

Double-click the Local Area Connection icon to open the Local Area Connection Status dialog box. Then click the Properties button to open the main network protocol configuration screen, the Local Area Connection Properties dialog box.

• Network Connections system folder

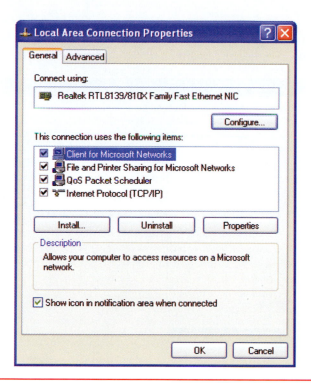

• Local Area Connection Properties dialog box

If you're using Windows XP, you should note two things. First, File and Printer Sharing for Microsoft Networks is installed and operational by default. This means that you're ready to share resources (files, folders, and so on) with another Windows XP machine connected to the same switch or hub. TCP/IP is likewise installed and enabled. If you're using an earlier version of Windows, you may have different protocols and options installed. Unless otherwise directed by a senior or network tech, leave these protocols alone!

You have but one more task to complete to share files and folders: share them. Let's walk through the process.

Step-by-Step 15.3

Sharing Resources and Accessing Shared Resources

To complete this exercise, you will need the following:

- Two Windows XP systems with 10/100 NICs running the TCP/IP protocol (You can substitute all 10BaseT or all 100BaseTX components in place of the multispeed type. This exercise will also work with Windows 9x

computers, but may take a little extra effort; I'll note where in the steps.)

- Computers connected to a 10/100 switch or hub with CAT5 or better UTP cable

- Default network configuration settings—most important, Workgroup should remain named Workgroup

Step 1

Open My Computer, double-click the C: drive, and create a new folder on the C: drive. Name it **Shared**. Alternate-click (right-click) the Shared folder and select Properties.

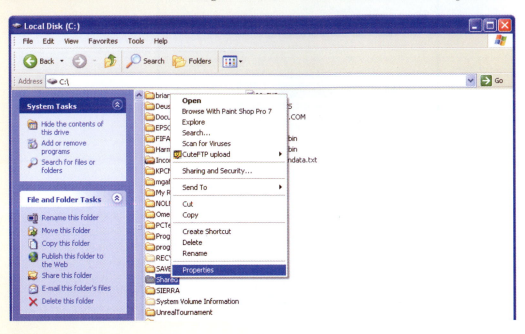

Step 2

In the Shared Properties dialog box, select the Sharing tab. Notice that the Do Not Share This Folder radio button is selected. Select the Share This Folder radio button. Suddenly you have more choices. You can set a maximum number of users and adjust permissions (for example, you can allow people to read or copy files in this folder, but not write to this folder), among other things. For this exercise, just share the folder in the default manner. Click Apply, and the computer you are linked to should be able to view your Shared folder.

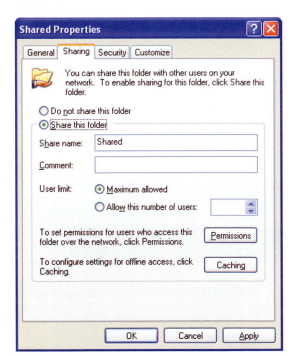

Step 3

Alternate-click My Network Places, which should be located on your desktop. Select Properties. Alternate-click your connection (look for a name like Local Area Connection) and again select Properties. In your Local Area Connection Properties dialog box, select File and Print Sharing for Microsoft Networks and click OK. If you don't see an option for File and Print Sharing, click Install and select a service and then click Add. Now select the File and Print Sharing option.

Step 4

Open My Network Places—double-click the icon—and select the Entire Network option under Other Places at the left of the window.

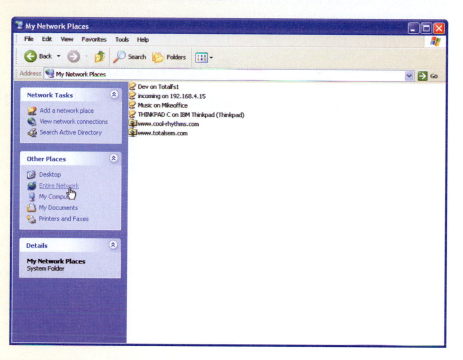

Step 5

In the main (right-hand) pane, you should see one or more options. Double-click the Microsoft Windows Network icon.

Step 6

You're now at the main network screen, where you should see what's called a workgroup. A workgroup is a basic group of computers connected to the same Ethernet network. Microsoft kindly names the default workgroup Workgroup; double-click Workgroup to see all of the computers connected to your Ethernet network.

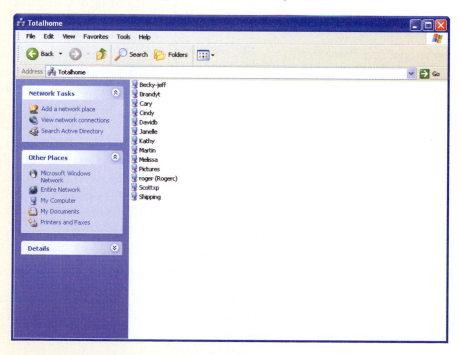

At this point, you can access any of the other computers and see what folders they have shared. If you don't see any computer but your own, don't fret. Wait a few minutes and refresh the screen. If you don't see any other computers, then it's time to turn to the next section of the chapter, "Troubleshooting Basic Network Problems."

You can share an entire drive the same way you share a folder. Simply alternate-click the drive in My Computer and follow the same steps. If the Share This Folder choice isn't available, you need to turn on File and Print Sharing.

■ Troubleshooting Basic Network Problems

Network troubleshooting tasks range from the very simple to the phenomenally complex. This section looks at the most common problems that occur in dial-up networks and Local Area Networks and how to fix them.

Dial-Up Networking Problems

When a dial-up network has a problem, it's usually for one of four reasons: there's something wrong with the telephone line, there's a modem problem—for instance, the modem isn't connected properly to the PC, or the wrong drivers are installed—the Network Connection settings are incorrect or have not been configured at all, or the ISP is experiencing problems.

In each case, the tech needs to test and then eliminate possibilities. Check the telephone line first. Is everything plugged in properly? Plug a phone into the jack to check for a dial tone.

Second, does the modem work? Windows XP comes with an excellent modem-testing utility. Open the Phone and Modem Options applet on the Control Panel, select the Modems tab, and click the Properties button. This opens the Modem Properties dialog box. Select the Diagnostics tab, and you'll see the Query Modem button. Click it! If a string of commands rolls through the little window, that's a good sign. Windows ran through some tests, and the modem responded properly.

With earlier versions of Windows, you need to use a third-party tool to run diagnostics. I suggest the popular shareware application Modem Doctor, written by Hank Volpe. Modem Doctor comes in DOS and Windows versions and is the best modem tester available for earlier versions of Windows.

Once you determine that the modem works, then go through the settings your ISP gave you and make sure you have specified them correctly, or simply call the ISP help line to have a support person walk you through the settings.

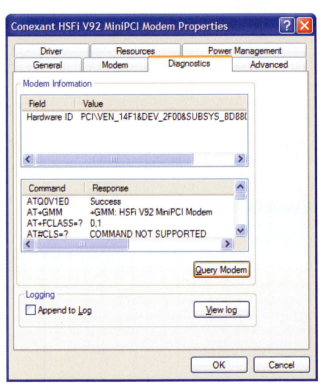

• Modem queried—the results may be incomprehensible to you, but the modem and the operating system understand each other—a very good sign!

LAN Problems

To troubleshoot LAN problems, you generally follow a four-step process, nearly the same process you went through to install the LAN. If you can't connect to other PCs, diagnose the NIC first. Second, check connections.

Is everything plugged in? Is the cable good? Third, check your software settings to make sure you're using the same protocols as the other PCs on the network, and that you've configured them properly according to instructions given by a senior technician. Finally, run a few diagnostic tests on the network.

Check the NIC

I have several times been told by Windows that my NIC was working properly when it didn't seem to be working at all. In cases like this, you can sometimes use a utility program on your NIC's driver disk. If your NIC comes with a diagnostic utility (this used to be common, but many modern NICs don't have such a utility), it may be included with the utility for setting system resources; poke around on the driver disk to see if you can find it.

Even if you don't have a diagnostic utility, all NICs provide a basic tester: get behind your computer and look for the lights on your NIC. These link lights tell you if your computer is connected to the network and if it's accepting packets. If you see a green light, your NIC is connected; a flashing green light means that your computer is exchanging packets with others.

Check the Cable

Make certain the network cable is plugged into the NIC on one end and into the hub or switch on the other. If it is connected, make sure the lights on the NIC and hub or switch are lit—if you do not see a light, you may have a bad cable, for example.

You can test a cable pretty readily by swapping out a suspect cable for one that works on another computer, which is called a *known-good* cable. You can also plug the cable into a relatively inexpensive machine called a cable tester. A cable tester enables you to determine if a particular cable is bad. "Bad" can be defined in a variety of ways, but it essentially means that the cable is not delivering the data for whatever reason: the cable is broken, crimped badly, or sits too close to a heat or electrical source.

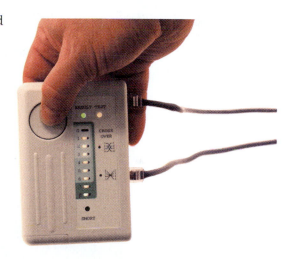

• Cable tester

Check the Protocols

If the hardware seems to be functional, but you still can't access shared resources on a machine connected to the same network, check the protocols. Make sure both machines have the same protocols installed and that both are set up according to directives from the senior technician or network technician.

Ping

Finally, if you have TCP/IP installed on both machines, you can use a whole range of software tools built into all versions of Windows. Almost all of these are beyond the scope of this book, but one is so commonly used that you definitely should know about it: Ping.

Ping is a TCP/IP utility you can use to determine whether a remote machine can be reached using the TCP/IP protocol. For example, let's say Bob can't access a shared folder on Cindy's machine. Because both Bob and Cindy have TCP/IP installed, Bob can *ping* Cindy. If Bob pings Cindy and

Ping can't locate her, then Bob or Cindy has a hardware, connectivity, or protocol problem. If Ping is able to locate Cindy's system on the network but Bob can't access the resources on her machine, then there is probably a protocol or sharing problem.

You run the Ping utility from the command line. To access the command line, choose Start | Run and type **cmd** in Windows 2000/XP or **command** in Windows 9*x*; then click OK.

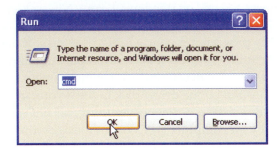

• Accessing the command line

Once the command line opens, you can type the ping command followed by the name of the computer you're trying to access, like this: **ping cindy**.

```
C:\WINDOWS\System32\cmd.exe

C:\>ping cindy

Pinging cindy.totalhome [192.168.4.4] with 32 bytes of data:

Reply from 192.168.4.4: bytes=32 time<1ms TTL=128
Reply from 192.168.4.4: bytes=32 time=1ms TTL=128
Reply from 192.168.4.4: bytes=32 time<1ms TTL=128
Reply from 192.168.4.4: bytes=32 time<1ms TTL=128

Ping statistics for 192.168.4.4:
    Packets: Sent = 4, Received = 4, Lost = 0 (0% loss),
Approximate round trip times in milli-seconds:
    Minimum = 0ms, Maximum = 1ms, Average = 0ms

C:\>_
```

• Ping at work

You can also do a lot more than just this with Ping, especially when you use it with other command-line utilities, but that discussion is beyond the scope of this book.

When you are troubleshooting a problem, you should also search the manufacturers' websites for information about your particular problem. Many hardware and software manufacturers offer searchable support databases where you can look for reports of problems similar to yours. You can then search the site for a fix or patch to download, a software or driver update, or lists of steps to take to correct the problem.

Chapter 15 Review

■ Chapter Summary

After reading this chapter and completing the exercises, you should understand the following aspects of networks:

Explain how networks work

■ A network enables two or more computers to share data, hardware such as printers, and even applications.

■ Computers connect in two basic ways: dial-up networks and Local Area Networks.

■ A standard dial-up network connection consists of three pieces: a modem, a working telephone line, and an Internet Service Provider (ISP).

■ To make a LAN work, you need to ensure three things: connectivity, compatibility, and proper setup of hardware and software.

■ Data is broken up and sent between computers in small chunks called packets and then reassembled.

Install and configure a dial-up network

■ Modems take incoming analog serial data—in this case, the signal coming across the phone line—and turn it into digital serial data. Likewise, modems turn the digital signal flowing out of the PC into an analog signal that can be transferred over a telephone line.

■ The current top modem speed standards are V.90 and V.92. Both offer download speeds of almost 56 Kbps, but differ in upload speeds: up to 33.6 Kbps for V.90 and up to 48 Kbps for V.92 modems.

■ Modems connect to a PC in two basic ways: internally, through the expansion bus, or externally, through either a serial port (the old way) or USB port. Almost all internal modems connect to a PCI slot.

■ There are three steps to installing dial-up networking on a computer: install a modem;

install drivers; and configure the Network Connections settings.

Install and configure a Local Area Network

■ The most common topology for networks today is the Star Bus.

■ In computer networking, the term *protocol* describes any predetermined set of rules that defines how two devices or pieces of software should communicate with each other. TCP/IP is the protocol used by the Internet. NetBEUI is an older Windows protocol. IPX/SPX is the Novell network protocol.

■ Unshielded twisted-pair (UTP) cabling is the most common type of cabling for networks today. UTP cabling comes in categories (CATs) that define the maximum speed at which data can be transferred, from CAT1 (standard telephone line) to CAT6. CAT5 is the type most widely used in networks today.

■ NICs, hubs, and cables make up the basic hardware of the vast majority of networks.

■ As long as you stay grounded and don't touch the pins, the physical installation of a NIC is the easiest part of the process.

■ In general, you should use the driver that comes with the device you purchased, not the one offered by your operating system, when loading a new piece of network hardware.

■ Once you have physically connected the computers in a network, you still must configure them so they will permit other computers to access their resources, before they can exchange data.

Troubleshoot basic network problems

■ When a dial-up network has a problem, it's usually for one of four reasons: there's something wrong with the telephone line, there's a problem with the

- modem, the Network Connection settings are incorrect or have not been configured at all, or the ISP is experiencing problems.

- Troubleshooting LAN problems generally follows a four-step process: diagnose the NIC, check the connections, check the software settings, and run diagnostic tests on the network.

- Ping is a TCP/IP utility used to determine whether a remote machine can be reached using the TCP/IP protocol.

- The link lights on your NIC can tell you if your computer is connected to the network and if it's accepting packets.

■ Key Terms

10BaseT *(403)*
100BaseTX *(404)*
backbone *(404)*
baud *(395)*
CAT5 *(403)*
Ethernet *(402)*
Fast Ethernet *(404)*
hub *(393)*

Institute of Electrical and Electronics Engineers (IEEE) *(402)*
Local Area Network (LAN) *(393)*
modem *(391)*
Network Interface Card (NIC) *(393)*
node *(406)*
packet *(393)*

protocol *(393)*
RJ-11 *(403)*
RJ-45 *(403)*
Star Bus *(401)*
switch *(402)*
topology *(401)*
unshielded twisted-pair (UTP) *(402)*

■ Key Term Quiz

Use terms from the Key Terms list to complete the following sentences. Not all of the terms will be used.

1. A/an _____ is a small chunk of data designed to be sent to other computers.

2. A/an _____ is a group of networked computers occupying a relatively small area.

3. The basic job of the _____ is to accept packets from any computer attached to it and send those packets to the other computers attached to it.

4. _____ is the connector used for phone communications.

5. A/an _____ converts analog data to digital data and vice versa.

6. The IEEE 802.3 standard defines the _____ network.

7. _____ are used to connect networks on multiple floors, or in multiple buildings, to one another.

8. An Ethernet network run over UTP cabling at 10 Mbps is also known as _____.

9. A/an _____ provides the PC with a method of sending data to and receiving data from other systems by connecting the PC to the network's cabling structure.

10. In computer networking, the term _____ describes any predetermined set of rules that define how two devices or pieces of software should communicate with each other.

1. The 802.3 committee is part of what organization?

   a. IEEE

   b. Ethernet

   c. InterNIC

   d. MI5

2. What category of UTP cabling is used in the vast majority of networks today?

   a. CAT1

   b. CAT3

   c. CAT5

   d. CAT7

3. The two standards created to determine which wires are connected to which pins on the connectors are the EIA/TIA _____ and _____.

   a. 10BASE-5, 10BASE-2

   b. Star Bus, Star Ring

   c. 568A, 568B

   d. CAT3, CAT5

4. The term _____ refers to any of several Ethernet flavors that operate at 100 megabits per second.

   a. Fast Ethernet

   b. Thinnet

   c. Fiber optics

   d. Routed network

5. The _____ topology is the most popular topology today.

   a. Star Ring

   b. Star Bus

   c. Ethernet

   d. Network

6. The maximum distance from the hub to any 10BaseT device is _____.

   a. 100 feet

   b. 185 meters

   c. 185 feet

   d. 100 meters

7. _____ cabling is delicate, expensive, and difficult to use, so it is mostly used for the network backbone.

   a. CAT5

   b. RJ-58

   c. UTP

   d. Fiber-optic

8. Wireless networks use a special transmitter/receiver that communicates with wireless NICs using _____ or _____ waves.

   a. Infrared, radio frequency

   b. Ultraviolet, infrared

   c. Waveband, radio frequency

   d. Waveband, ultraviolet

9. What technology enables you to use a single phone line for both analog voice communication and digital data transmission simultaneously?

   a. TCP

   b. TIA

   c. DSL

   d. ISP

10. CAT5 cabling can move data at speeds of up to _____.

    a. 100 Mbps

    b. 10 Mbps

    c. 16 Mbps

    d. 56 Kbps

11. _____ was the first type of cable used in a computer network.

    a. RJ-11 cable

    b. Coaxial cable

    c. UTP cable

    d. Fiber-optic cable

12. _____ is the protocol used by the Internet.

    a. IPX/SPX

    b. NetBEUI

    c. TCP/IP

    d. PPP

13. To determine if a cable is bad, you might use a _____.

    a. Cable tester

    b. Ping command

    c. Vampire connector

    d. Terminator

14. _____ is a TCP/IP utility used to determine if a remote machine can be reached using the TCP/IP protocol.

    a. DNS

    b. Ping

    c. Locate

    d. REMSYS

15. A modem is also considered a/an _____.

    a. NIC

    b. Proprietary technology

    c. Network gateway

    d. UTP

■ Essay Quiz

1. Your boss comes to you as his IT tech and tells you that he had lunch with a colleague who asked him what type of network topology his office uses. He was embarrassed not to know. You tell him that the office LAN uses a Star Bus topology. He asks you to write him a memo with a brief explanation of what "Star Bus topology" means and what he could say to explain and defend that choice at his next lunch.

2. You're the senior of two IT techs for a small office with a LAN that employees use to share data and access the Internet. You send your junior tech on a service call to help an employee who says he can't access the LAN. Outline for the junior tech all of the steps she might want to try to troubleshoot the problem.

3. You are helping your friend select components for a computer system that the local computer shop will assemble for him. He will have only dial-up access at home until next year, so he needs the system to include a modem. You've already selected a motherboard that doesn't have a built-in modem. Write a paragraph explaining what options and features your friend might choose, which ones you recommend, and why.

Lab Projects

• Lab Project 15.1

This lab exercise allows you to compare the issues involved in creating two different types of networks.

① Get a hub and connect to it as many computers as you have available for networking.

② Configure the computers connected to that hub to run the IPX/SPX protocol. Exchange several different types and sizes of files over the network. Access folders across the network. Copy files from remote folders across the network. Make notes on the speed and ease of network transfer and access (or lack there of) you encounter in these different tests.

③ Reconfigure your network so it uses TCP/IP instead. Perform the same file transfer and access tests outlined in Step 2. Again, make notes on your results.

④ Compare your notes from the two networks. What differences do you find in their performance? What similarities?

• Lab Project 15.2

This lab exercise simulates a common real-world situation: linking two LANs running different protocols.

1 Reassemble the two LANs you created in the previous lab.

2 Connect the two LANs together.

3 Try to move a file between the LANs. Note how IPX/SPX and TCP/IP interact.

4 Try to open a file on one LAN directly from a machine on the other LAN. Again, note how IPX/SPX and TCP/IP interact.

About A+ Certification

This book introduces you to microcomputer hardware and helps you build the skills you need to enjoy a successful career in the field of information technology. Over time, as you accumulate valuable experience and new skills, you'll find that many doors will open. But until then, while you're still just starting out in the IT field, one way to show potential employers that you have the skills to do the job is to earn an industry certification.

■ What's Certification?

A *certification* is a license that documents a certain level of skill and knowledge in a particular area of expertise. To attain a certification, you usually have to pass an exam. A lot of professions use certification as a way for individuals to demonstrate to potential employers that they have the necessary skills and knowledge to work in their field. For example, if you want a job in accounting, you need a Certified Public Accountant (CPA) certification. If you want to be an auto mechanic, you should get an Automotive Service Excellence (ASE) certification. These certifications are recognized by everyone in the industry as proof of a certain level of competence and ability.

Certification in the field of computer technology is particularly important because changes in technology happen so quickly. Even after you graduate from school, you'll need to keep up with changes in technology to advance your career. This doesn't mean that you need to keep going back to school every few months, but it does mean you should keep up with the latest changes. Certification is one way you can show that you're up-to-date on the latest technologies that matter to your profession.

There are many ways to study for a certification. You can buy a self-study guide at a bookstore, take a course at your local college or university, or find information online. There are also many vendor-specific certification programs you can use to prove your knowledge of a particular company's product. You can find information about vendor-specific certification programs at companies' websites. For example, Microsoft (www.microsoft.com) offers several certifications for its software. Microsoft Certified Systems Administrator (MCSA) and Microsoft Certified Systems Engineer (MCSE) are two popular certifications that experienced network administrators can get to demonstrate their ability to use and manage Microsoft Windows networking technologies.

■ A+ Certification

Most PC technicians and other computer specialists start by getting the *A+ Certification*, which is an industry-supported, vendor-neutral certification designed to demonstrate basic knowledge and skills in supporting microcomputers. A+ Certification is widely recognized by thousands of companies around the world, including IBM, Epson, Hewlett-Packard, Minolta, AT&T, Novell, Panasonic, Microsoft, and Sun Microsystems, to name just a few. A+ Certification requires passing two exams: one on hardware technologies, the other on operating system technologies. By passing both exams, you demonstrate the skills of a PC technician with at least six months of experience.

A+ Certification is part of a program developed by the Computing Technology Industry Association (CompTIA), which is a nonprofit trade organization with a membership of over 8,000 computer resellers, distributors, manufacturers, and training companies. In addition to A+ Certification, CompTIA offers certifications in other areas of the computer industry.

■ Preparing for the A+ Certification Exam

Although *Introduction to PC Hardware and Troubleshooting* is not a designed to be an A+ Certification study guide, it does provide a good foundation for learning how to use, configure, and troubleshoot personal computers. Most of the topics in the A+ Core Hardware Service Technician Exam Objectives are covered in this book. These exam objectives and the chapters that teach them are listed in the tables that follow. To prepare fully for the exam, I suggest you read my *A+ Certification All-in-One Exam Guide* (McGraw-Hill/Osborne), which provides thorough coverage of all A+ Certification topics in a fun and friendly style.

1.0 Installation, Configuration, and Upgrading

Objectives	Chapters
1.1 Identify basic terms, concepts, and functions of system modules, including how each module should work during normal operation and during the boot process.	1–14
1.2 Identify basic procedures for adding and removing field-replaceable modules for both desktop and portable systems.	1–14
1.3 Identify available IRQs, DMAs, and I/O addresses and procedures for device installation and configuration.	1–14
1.4 Identify common peripheral ports, associated cabling, and their connectors.	1–14
1.5 Identify proper procedures for installing and configuring IDE/EIDE devices.	8
1.6 Identify proper procedures for installing and configuring SCSI devices.	10
1.7 Identify proper procedures for installing and configuring peripheral devices.	1–6, 8, 10, 12
1.8 Identify hardware methods of upgrading system performance, procedures for replacing basic subsystem components, unique components, and when to use them.	1–14

2.0 Diagnosis and Troubleshooting

Objectives	Chapters
2.1 Identify common symptoms and problems associated with each module and how to troubleshoot and isolate the problems.	1–14
2.2 Identify basic troubleshooting procedures and how to elicit problem symptoms from customers.	1–14

3.0 Preventive Maintenance

Objectives	Chapters
3.1 Identify the purpose of various types of preventive maintenance products and procedures and when to use them.	1–14
3.2 Identify issues, procedures, and devices for protection within the computing environment, including people, hardware, and the surrounding workspace.	1–14

4.0 Motherboards, Processors, and Memory

Objectives	Chapters
4.1 Distinguish between the popular CPU chips in terms of their basic characteristics.	2
4.2 Identify the categories of RAM (Random Access Memory) terminology, their locations and physical characteristics.	3
4.3 Identify the most popular type of motherboards, their components and architecture (bus structures and power supplies).	4
4.4 Identify the purpose of CMOS (Complementary Metal-Oxide Semiconductor), what it contains, and how to change its basic parameters.	4

5.0 Printers

Objectives	Chapter
5.1 Identify basic concepts, printer operations, and printer components.	14
5.2 Identify care and service techniques and common problems with primary printer types.	14

6.0 Basic Networking

Objectives	Chapter
6.1 Identify basic networking concepts, including how a network works and the ramifications of repairs on the network.	15

The number in parentheses that follows each definition is the chapter in which the term is explained.

10BaseT LAN Ethernet standard (falling under IEEE 802.3) that supports data transfer rates of 10 Mbps using UTP cabling and RJ-45 connectors. (15)

100BaseT A popular implementation of the Fast Ethernet standard. (15)

101-key enhanced keyboard Keyboard layout that IBM introduced in 1986, which became the industry standard. This layout is the basis for the modern 104-key layout. (12)

2.1 Audio speaker nomenclature referring to a speaker setup with two standard stereo speakers and one subwoofer. (13)

25-pin female DB connector The signature connector of parallel ports, traditionally used to connect printers, scanners, and other devices to a PC. (14)

3½-inch drive bays Spaces in a PC case designed to hold floppy drives, hard drives, and any other storage devices that are 3½ inches wide. (6)

34-pin ribbon cable Type of cable used to connect a floppy drive to the motherboard. (7)

5¼-inch drive bays Spaces in a PC case designed to hold the old 5¼-inch-wide floppy disk drives. They're now used to hold optical media drives such as CD-ROM, CD-RW, and DVD-ROM drives. (6)

5.1 Audio speaker nomenclature referring to a speaker setup with five standard stereo speakers, used to produce a surround-sound effect, plus one subwoofer; used by Dolby Digital systems. (13)

50-pin connector A connector and cable type used with the SCSI-1 standard. (10)

50-pin high-density connector A connector and cable type used with the SCSI-2 standard. (10)

84-key keyboard Early PC keyboard design, designed by IBM for use with its AT computers. (12)

Accelerated Graphics Port (AGP) The slot on a modern motherboard that accepts the video card; generally brown in color, this is always the expansion slot closest to the Northbridge. (4, 5, 11)

active termination A type of SCSI termination that uses complex circuitry to prevent reflection on a SCSI chain. (10)

antistatic wrist strap Special device that electrically connects you to the computer. This device is used to avoid damage to the computer from electrostatic discharge. (1)

archive bit A file attribute that is turned "on" (set to a value of 1) when a file is created or modified. The status of a file's archive bit tells backup programs whether it was created or modified since the last backup. (7)

art tablet A large, flat tablet used in CAD drawing, animation, and other illustration tasks. The tablet is accompanied by a touch-sensitive, pen-shaped pointing device that provides a means of "drawing" directly into a graphics program. (12)

AT A motherboard form factor invented by IBM in the early 1980s that once dominated the PC market. It featured a large keyboard plug and the split P8/P9 power socket. (4)

AT power supply Older style of PC power supply, which is now rarely used. (6)

ATX The motherboard form factor that now dominates the PC market. It features a large number of external connectors, including PS/2 connectors for the keyboard and mouse and the P1 power socket. (4)

ATX power supply Newer style of PC power supply, used with an ATX motherboard. (6)

autoplay A feature that makes it possible for Windows to run a program on a CD automatically when the disc is inserted in a media drive. (9)

Baby AT A motherboard form factor that resembled AT but was smaller, to accommodate the demand for smaller PCs. (4)

back plate The metal plate on the back of a computer case, punched through with a specific set of holes to accommodate the various external connectors on the motherboard. (6)

backbone The main piece of Ethernet cabling to which all other hubs are connected. Backbones are used to connect the networks on multiple floors, or even in multiple buildings, to one another. (15)

bank Also called a memory bank. A bank defines the number of slots of RAM needed to fill up the data bus. Current systems using 168-pin and 184-pin DIMMs require one slot per bank. (3)

basic input/output services (BIOS) Programming code stored on a nonvolatile ROM or flash memory chip on the motherboard that enables the CPU to communicate with the basic devices in the computer, such as the keyboard, monitor, and hard drive. (4)

baud The number of signalling elements (bits or groups of bits) per second; the unit used to measure the speed of telephone lines. (15)

BIOS updaters Programs that enable you to install BIOS updates that you have downloaded from your motherboard manufacturer's website, as well as back up the current BIOS information. (4)

bit depth When discussing audio, the number of bits used to describe the characteristics of a sound. The greater the bit depth used to capture a sound sample, the better the reproduction of the original sound. When discussing video, the number of different colors that can be displayed on a monitor screen; the higher the bit depth, the higher the color quality. (11, 13)

burning The process of writing data to a CD-R or CD-RW disc. (9)

cartridge tapes Square or rectangular cassette-type tapes, such as those used for data backup. (7)

case fan A component that provides additional cooling for key components within the PC case. (6)

CAT5 High-performance networking cable consisting of twisted-pair conductors (usually four pairs), typically used in Ethernet networks running at 10 or 100 Mbps. (15)

Cathode Ray Tube (CRT) A common type of computer display that is similar in design to a television. (11)

CD The compact disc, an extremely popular type of removable optical media that was originally designed to store music. (9)

CD audio Also called *CDDA*; the original type of compact disc, designed to store only musical media. (9)

CD media The umbrella term for a variety of removable optical media, including CD-ROM, CD-R, CD-RW, and DVD. (9)

CD-quality Producing a quality of sound equivalent to a professionally recorded compact disc. A sound capture is considered CD-quality when recorded at 44 KHz, with 16-bit depth, and in stereo. (13)

CD-R Compact Disc–Recordable, a type of removable optical media that can be written to by a special drive as well as read by any CD-ROM drive. (9)

CD-ROM Compact Disc–Read-Only Memory, a type of removable optical media that's widely used for data storage. (9)

CD-RW Compact Disc–Rewritable, a type of removable optical media that can be written to, erased, and rewritten by a special drive as well as read by any CD-ROM drive. (9)

Central Processing Unit (CPU) Also called the microprocessor. The "brain" of the computer, the place where all the work gets done. Two companies currently control almost the entire PC CPU market: Intel and AMD. (1)

Centronics A type of connector used primarily on printers to connect a parallel cable. The Centronics port uses contacts instead of pins and uses wire wings to hold the cable in place. (14)

clock chip The timing chip on the motherboard that defines the system speed. (2)

codec A program that compresses and decompresses audio files using a particular compression algorithm. (13)

consumables Blanket term for products used by printers, such as paper, ink cartridges, and toner. (14)

copy backup A full backup of every file in the selected drive or directory. This kind of backup does not affect the Archive bit of those files that are backed up. (7)

Cubic Feet per Minute (CFM) Unit of measurement for the performance (cubic feet of air moved per minute) of CPU fans. (2)

cylinder A group of cylindrical tracks, each falling in the same location on one of the stacked platters in a hard drive. (8)

Daily backup   Better known as the Daily Copy backup. This type of backup includes all files that have been changed as of the day the backup is run. This kind of backup does not turn off the Archive bits for those files that are backed up. (7)

daisy-chaining   The process by which multiple devices, for example, SCSI and USB devices, are connected to each other and, in turn, to the PC. (10, 12)

DDR SDRAM   Double Data Rate SDRAM; RAM synchronized to the system bus that can make two RAM accesses in each clock cycle. (3)

decibels (dBA)   Unit of noise level; often used to describe the loudness of devices such as CPU fans. (2)

defragmentation (defrag)   A process that rearranges file clusters on a hard drive to minimize file fragmentation. (8)

desktop case   A type of PC case that is designed to lie flat, usually under the monitor, and generally offers little capacity for expansion. (6)

device drivers   Software that works with the OS to enable hardware devices to communicate with the CPU. They are normally included on the CD or floppy disk packaged with a device and must be loaded—either automatically or manually—when you install the device. (5)

Device Manager   A Windows tool that enables you to view or change the system resources and device drivers assigned to the various devices on your PC. (5)

Differential backup   A type of backup that includes only files for which the Archive bit is turned on. This kind of backup does not turn off the Archive bits for those files that are backed up. (7)

Digital Audio Tape (DAT)   The first tape system to use a totally digital recording method. Originally designed for audio and video use, this format has become very popular for data backup. (7)

Digital Linear Tape (DLT)   A type of backup tape that can store up to 200 GB of data. DLT drives use a SCSI connection. (7)

Digital Theatre Systems (DTS)   The company that created a popular sound standard that competes with Dolby Digital in supporting 5.1 speaker systems. (13)

Digital Video Interface (DVI)   A type of connector and interface used to connect a monitor to a video card without converting the digital signal to analog. (11)

DIMM   Dual Inline Memory Module; current-style RAM stick, which comes in 168-pin and 144-pin varieties. (3)

DIN   The name for both the port and connector, also called the AT-style connector. A DIN is used to connect a keyboard to an AT motherboard. (12)

Direct Memory Access (DMA)   A process by which a device can access memory directly, without the intervention of the CPU. To prevent two devices from doing this at once, DMA channels from 0 to 7 are assigned to specific devices. (5)

DirectSound3D (DS3D)   Part of DirectX versions 3 and later, this feature provides a set of commands for positioning sounds in 3D space. (13)

DirectX   An Application Program Interface (API) developed by Microsoft for creating and managing graphic images and multimedia effects. This set of Windows protocols enables modern PCs to achieve the speed necessary to play graphics-intensive games. (11, 13)

Dolby Digital   An audio standard developed by Dolby Laboratories designed to support five channels of sound: front-left, front-right, front-center, rear-left, and rear-right. Dolby Digital also supports a subwoofer. (13)

dot matrix printer   A type of printer that uses a grid, or matrix, of tiny pins that strike an inked ribbon against the paper to create text characters. (14)

dot pitch   A measurement that expresses the fineness of the shadow mask on a CRT monitor; the smaller the dot pitch, the sharper the image. (11)

dots per inch (dpi)   Measurement of the print resolution of a printer; measured both vertically and horizontally to obtain printer specs such as 2,880 x 720 dpi. (14)

double-density   A term used to describe floppy disks with double the storage capacity of the (obsolete) single-density floppy disk. (7)

drive bay rails   Metal components that you can attach to the sides of a computer drive, to enable you to move the drive into and out of a drive bay without repeated screwing and unscrewing. (6)

DVD   Digital Versatile Disc, a type of removable optical media developed to store movies in high-quality digital format. DVDs are unique among CD media in that they can store data on both sides. (9)

dynamic disks   A type of data storage that is unique to Windows 2000 and XP, required to implement RAID 5.

Dynamic disks are divided into volumes instead of partitions, so they can be reconfigured on the fly without rebooting. (8)

electrostatic discharge (ESD) The movement of static electricity from a charged source to a discharged source. ESD is far and away the number-one destroyer of PC components. (1)

Enhanced Integrated Drive Electronics (EIDE) Type of drive used in the vast majority of all modern PCs. EIDE drives use a unique 40-pin connector. (8)

Environmental Audio Extensions (EAX) A popular audio standard developed by Creative Labs to create realistic 3D soundscapes for applications such as computer gaming. Creative Labs' popular SoundBlaster sound cards use EAX. (13)

ergonomics The art and science of designing products that are human friendly. In the case of computer input and output devices, this involves minimizing the negative physical effects of the use of those devices, such as eyestrain and carpal tunnel syndrome. (12)

Ethernet A network architecture that uses a Bus or Star topology; developed by Xerox, DEC, and Intel in 1976. (15)

expansion bus A special set of external data bus and address bus wires in the Northbridge, dedicated to devices connected to the PC's expansion slots. (5)

expansion slots Special standardized ports on a motherboard that enable you to expand the capabilities of your system by adding components. (1)

extended partition A type of hard drive partition that is optional and not bootable. Extended partitions must be divided into logical drives, which can then be assigned drive letters. (8)

Fast-20 SCSI Also called Ultra SCSI. A version of Fast SCSI that moves data at 20 MBps. (10)

Fast-40 SCSI Also called Ultra2 SCSI. A version of fast SCSI that moves data at 40 MBps. (10)

Fast Ethernet A newer version of Ethernet that supports data transfer rates of 100 MBps. (15)

File Allocation Table (FAT) The organizing system for partitions on a hard drive that keeps track of the locations of all files on a given partition. (8)

file attributes One-bit storage areas that indicate various characteristics of a file. Common examples of file attributes are Hidden, System, Read-Only, and Archive. (7)

FireWire Another name for the IEEE 1394 standard, a high-speed, bidirectional cabling standard that runs at speeds of up to 400 Mbps and can support up to 63 hot-swappable devices on one port. (5)

flash BIOS A term that encompasses the system BIOS and the flash ROM chip used to store it. The key characteristic of flash BIOS is that it can be upgraded through software. (4)

flash ROM A special kind of upgradeable, nonvolatile memory used to store the PC's system BIOS. (4)

floppy disk A type of magnetic removable media protected by a plastic housing. (7)

FM synthesis A method of electronic emulation of sounds and musical instruments used by early sound processors on computers. (13)

form factors Standard guidelines for motherboard manufacturers. The form factor of a motherboard determines its size and shape and, to some extent, the location and orientation of its components. (4)

formatting The process of placing organizational information onto a disk so that the disk can store data in a useful way. (7)

frontside bus The bus that interconnects the CPU, Northbridge, and RAM. (2)

full-tower case A type of PC case that provides the maximum amount of interior space and many drive bays. At least two feet tall, this kind of case normally sits vertically on the floor, rather than flat on a desktop. (6)

geometry When discussing computer hard drives, geometry refers to the electronic division of a hard drive, usually described in terms of the numbers of heads, cylinders, and sectors per track. (8)

gigahertz (GHz) Billions of cycles per second; a common measurement of CPU speed. (2)

hard drive The hard drive is the PC's primary storage area for data and programs. It consists of platters that rotate at high speed. Modern hard drive storage capacity is measured in gigabytes. (1)

hertz (Hz) One cycle per second; a unit of measurement of electromagnetic wave frequency, used to express the refresh rate of a CRT. (2, 11)

hibernate mode   Also called sleep mode. A feature of power management that enables the PC to go into a frozen, hibernation-like state. (6)

high-density (HD) 68-pin connector   A type of connector used to connect internal Wide SCSI devices to their 68-pin ribbon cables. (10)

host adapter   A device through which a SCSI chain connects to a PC. (10)

hot-swappable   A term used to describe a device that can be added to and removed from a PC without the need to reboot. (5, 12)

hub   A connection point for networked devices, commonly used to connect LAN segments. (15)

IEEE 1284   A standard for parallel cables that ensures that those cables are compatible with modern printers. (14)

IEEE 1394   Another name for FireWire; a high-speed, bidirectional cabling standard that runs at speeds of up to 400 Mbps and can support up to 63 hot-swappable devices on one port. (5)

Incremental backup   A type of backup that includes only files for which the Archive bit is turned on. This process effectively backs up all files that have been changed since the last backup. This kind of backup turns off the Archive bit for every file backed up. (7)

INF files   Special text files used by Windows to install device drivers. (5)

ink cartridge   A container used to deliver ink to an inkjet printer. Modern inkjet printers use four different inks—cyan, magenta, yellow, and black—to achieve a nearly infinite range of print colors. (14)

inkjet printer   A type of printer that creates an image on the page by squirting droplets of ink from tiny nozzles, called jets. (14)

input/output (I/O)   The process of moving information into and out of the computer. The peripherals of your computer (keyboard, mouse, monitor, and so on) provide the I/O for your computer. (1)

Institute of Electrical and Electronics Engineers (IEEE)
A nonprofit technical-professional association best known for developing standards for the computer and electronics industry, including the widely followed IEEE 802 standards for LANs. (15)

instruction set   The collection of all of the functions that any processor can perform. (2)

interrupt request (IRQ) wire   A wire assigned to a specific device in a PC and used to initiate communication between that device and the CPU. (5)

I/O address   A unique pattern of ones and zeros used by the CPU to give instructions to a device on a PC. (5)

IO/MEM wire   A special wire that the CPU uses to inform devices that it's trying to communicate with one of them. (5)

IRQ steering   When enabled in BIOS, this feature enables Windows to dynamically assign PCI bus IRQs to PCI devices. On a PCI bus, the same IRQ can be assigned to one or more devices. (5)

ISO9660   The standard that gives CDs additional information to enable them to store standard computer files. (9)

jumper   A pair of wires that you turn on and off by using a shunt, which connects the wires to complete a circuit. (4)

keyboard   The typewriter-like peripheral that allows the user to enter character input into a computer. (1)

Keyboard applet   A program on the Control Panel in Windows that controls settings related to the keyboard. (12)

kilohertz (KHz)   Thousands of cycles per second; a unit often used to measure electromagnetic signal bandwidth. (13)

laser   Acronym for light amplification by stimulated emission of radiation. A device that produces a coherent beam of optical radiation. When discussing printers, the component of a laser printer that writes the image to be printed onto the photosensitive drum by draining the negative charge from portions of the drum. (14)

laser printer   A type of printer that creates an image on the page using a sophisticated system involving a laser beam, a photosensitive drum, and powder-fine toner. Laser printers deliver high print quality, but are used mainly for black-and-white printing. (14)

Liquid Crystal Display (LCD)   A type of monitor display that takes up very little desk space and uses fluorescent backlighting to create the display. (11)

Local Area Network (LAN)   A group of networked computers that occupies a relatively small area. (15)

logical drives   Portions of an extended drive partition that can be assigned drive letters and used to store files. (8)

low voltage differential (LVD)   A type of SCSI terminator that uses two wires for each signal, greatly improving both the speed capability and the maximum length of SCSI cables on a chain. (10)

LPT1 and LPT2   Names of the ports—basically sets of computer resources—used for parallel communication with printers. (14)

LS-120   Also known as the SuperDisk; a type of removable media that can use either specialized large-capacity disks or regular floppy disks. (7)

mainframe   Large computers that require a substantial number of people to run them. Unlike personal computers, mainframes are designed to be used by many people at the same time. (1)

master   When discussing hard drives, a term used to describe a drive that shares a ribbon cable with another device and handles the job of controlling both devices. (8)

Master Boot Record (MBR)   A tiny bit of code that contains the partition table, which helps the operating system load the correct partition. (8)

Master File Table (MFT)   The File Allocation Table used with NTFS. (8)

mechanical mouse   A type of pointing device that uses a rubberized ball and mechanical wheels to track movement over a surface. (12)

megahertz (MHz)   Millions of cycles per second; the common unit of measure for bus speeds. (2)

memory slots   Motherboard components that accept RAM sticks. Generally located near the CPU, they can be easily distinguished by the latches on either side that secure the DIMM or RIMM modules. (4)

mezzanine bus   An expansion bus that does not have to be the only expansion bus on the motherboard. (5)

mid-tower case   A popular type of PC case that combines flexibility with space-saving design. With an average height of about 20 inches, these cases can sit unobtrusively on a desktop, but they still offer enough drive bays to handle most users' needs. (6)

Mini connector   A common type of power connector; used to connect the power supply to a floppy drive. (6)

mini-PCI   A type of expansion slot used only in laptop computers. (5)

mini-tower case   The smallest type of PC case designed to stand upright. Although these cases are useful where desk space is limited, they limit the number of drives that can be installed in the system. (6)

Molex connector   A common type of power connector; used to connect the power supply to devices such as hard drives and CD-ROM drives. (6)

monitor   The television-like output peripheral common on all PCs. (1)

motherboard   The big printed circuit board that covers most of the bottom of the system unit. The motherboard's main job is to provide an area where all of the internal components of the PC can connect. (1, 4)

motherboard book   The instruction book that comes with all motherboards. (2)

mouse   The primary input device on a modern computer. The mouse enables you to interact with images on the monitor screen by controlling an on-screen icon called a cursor. (1)

Mouse applet   A program on the Control Panel in Windows that controls settings related to the mouse or other pointing device. (12)

MP3   The famous Fraunhoffer MPEG Layer 3 codec, more often called by its file extension: MP3. Because of their relatively small size, MP3 files are an extremely popular method of sharing of music files over the Internet. (13)

MPC2/MPC2 cables   A cable with standardized connectors; used to connect a CD-ROM drive to a PC's audio card. (9)

multiplier   A factor by which the original speed of CD-ROM drives (150 KBps) is multiplied to express the speed of newer, much faster optical drives; for example, a drive with a multiplier of 40 (written as 40x) runs at a speed of 6,000 KBps. (9)

Musical Instrument Digital Interface (MIDI)   A protocol for recording and playing back music supported by many computer sound cards. A MIDI file contains instructions that tell the sound card what notes to play from a set of prerecorded sound samples called a wavetable. (13)

nanosecond   A billionth of a second; common measurement for RAM access speed. (3)

Narrow SCSI   A type of SCSI interface that uses eight wires to move data. (10)

network interface   The interface that connects your PC to other PCs in a Local Area Network. (1)

Network Interface Card (NIC)   An expansion card that enables a computer to connect to a network. (15)

nit   The unit of measure for the brightness of an LCD monitor. (11)

node   Any device that is connected to a network; usually, this means a PC, but other devices, such as printers, can also be nodes. (15)

Normal backup   A full backup of every file in the selected drive or directory. With this kind of backup, the Archive bit of every backed-up file is turned off. (7)

Northbridge   Traditional name for the chip that serves as the interface for the CPU, RAM, and PCI bus. (2)

NT File System (NTFS)   A file system that is virtually indestructible and provides ultrahigh security, file and folder compression and encryption, and other popular features. (8)

optical mouse   A type of pointing device that uses light and a tiny camera to track movement over a surface. This kind of mouse is easy to maintain, as it doesn't collect dust and grime; it also doesn't require a specialized mousing surface. (12)

P1 power connector   A plug used to connect an ATX power supply to an ATX motherboard. (4, 6)

P4 connector   A plug used to connect an ATX12V power supply to a motherboard that supports a Pentium 4 processor. (6)

P8/P9 power connectors   A pair of plugs used to connect an AT power supply to an AT motherboard. (6)

package   The physical layout of a chip; most commonly used in reference to CPUs. (2)

packet   A piece of data transmitted over a network. (15)

pages per minute (ppm)   Measurement of the speed at which a printer can produce printed pages. (14)

parallel port   A 25-pin, D-shaped female port used to attach a printer, scanner, or other parallel device to a PC. (4, 14)

partition   A discrete electronic portion of a hard drive used as the underlying structure for the organization of data on the drive. (8)

passive termination   A type of SCSI termination that uses tiny resistors to prevent reflection on a SCSI chain. (10)

PC Card   A bus interface that enables a laptop computer to accept special cards that incorporate the functionality of the expansion bus. (5)

Peripheral Component Interconnect (PCI)   General-purpose, 32-bit, 33-MHz expansion slots on a motherboard; also, the expansion bus that serves these slots. (4, 5)

peripheral device   Any device that performs I/O functions for your PC. Typical peripherals include a mouse, keyboard, and monitor. (1)

personal computer (PC)   Officially a trademark of IBM Corporation, the term has come to mean any small, self-contained computer that is based on the original IBM PC design. (1)

photosensitive drum   A key component of a laser printer; this drum holds various electrical charges during the printing process, attracting toner, which is then transferred to the paper and fused in place. (14)

pin grid array (PGA)   The most common CPU package. The PGA has a number of subpackages. (2)

pixel   Term derived from "picture element." The smallest graphic unit of display on a computer screen. On a color monitor, a pixel's color is a blend of red, green, and blue color information. (11)

platter   An aluminum disk coated with a magnetic medium and used to store data on a hard drive. (8)

Plug and Play (PnP)   A feature used by Windows that enables you to plug a device into your computer and have the computer recognize that the device is there and automatically assign it appropriate system resources. The computer's BIOS and the device must be PnP-enabled for this feature to work. (5)

port   Generic term for any connection on the system unit. (1)

power supply   The component in a PC that converts high-voltage A/C electrical current into lower-voltage D/C current that the computer can safely use. The power supply then delivers this low-voltage power to the motherboard and all other components of the PC. (1, 6)

power supply fan   A component that supplies the basic cooling for the PC. This fan cools the power supply itself and also generates a constant flow of air inside the computer case. (6)

power switch   The button or toggle switch that turns a PC on and off. (6)

primary partition   The first partition that is created on a hard drive, normally assigned the drive letter C: and used to store the computer's operating system. Modern Windows versions (NT, 2000, and XP) can have up to four primary partitions, but only one of these can be set as the active partition from which the system boots. (8)

protocol   Any predetermined set of rules that defines the way that two devices or pieces of software should communicate with each other. (15)

PS/2   A type of port/connector also called a mini-DIN; used on modern PCs for the keyboard and mouse. The two small, round PS/2 ports are located on the edge of the motherboard closest to the CPU. (4, 12)

QIC tape   An early type of backup tape, no longer commonly used. QIC tape capacities range from 40 MB to 2 GB. (7)

rack-mount case   A type of computer case designed to fasten into a server rack; used by businesses as a space-efficient way to organize large numbers of servers. (6)

radial misalignment   A problem that can afflict a floppy drive, resulting from its read/write heads being slightly out of position. This causes problems with both the reading and writing of disks and is best addressed by replacing the drive. (7)

RAM Digital-to-Analog Converter (RAMDAC)   A type of chip used by video cards that can run CRT or analog LCD monitors. This chip converts commands from the graphics processor and turns them into analog signals that can be understood by these types of monitors. (11)

Random Access Memory (RAM)   The CPU's working memory. Just like facts stored in your short-term memory, data stored in RAM can be accessed very quickly, but it disappears when the power is turned off. (1, 3)

RDRAM   Rambus Dynamic Random Access Memory; system RAM used in high-end Intel Pentium 4 PCs. (3)

read speed   The speed at which an optical drive can retrieve data from a disc. (9)

read/write head   The mechanism that reads and writes data on the top and bottom surfaces of platters in a hard drive. (8)

Redundant Array of Independent Disks (RAID)   A type of storage in which multiple hard drives work together as one drive with a single drive letter. (8)

refresh rate   The number of times that the electron guns in a CRT can write and then refresh all of the phosphors in a single second. (11)

removable media   File storage media that aren't built into the PC, such as Zip disks and various optical media; also, the drives that accept these media. (7)

resolution   A measurement of the number of pixels visible on a CRT screen at a given moment; the higher the resolution, the higher the picture quality. Also used to describe the density of printing, expressed in dots per inch. (11, 14)

rewrite speed   The speed at which a CD-RW drive can overwrite existing data. (9)

RIMM   The current 184-pin RAM-stick style used exclusively with Rambus memory. (3)

RJ-11   A type of connector used for CAT1 (telephone) lines. It supports up to two pairs of wires, though most phone lines use only one pair. (15)

RJ-45   A type of connector used with CAT5/6 cabling for Ethernet networks. It supports up to four pairs of wires. (15)

sampling   Capturing the state or quality of a particular sound wave a set number of times each second. (13)

ScanDisk   A tool used to check for bad clusters on a hard drive. (8)

SCSI-1   A standard for SCSI devices, approved in 1986, that made these devices more interchangeable by defining standard connections, cable lengths, and signaling characteristics. (10)

SCSI-2   A standard for SCSI devices, officially adopted in 1994, that substantially changed the cabling and connectors used for SCSI. (10)

SCSI-3   A standard for SCSI devices that defines several new cabling options, including FireWire. (10)

SCSI chain   A series of SCSI devices daisy-chained together and connected to a PC by way of a SCSI host adapter. (10)

SDRAM Synchronous Dynamic Random Access Memory; used in most PCs as system RAM. SDRAM is synchronized to the speed of the bus. (3)

sector Special storage area on a magnetic disk. (7)

sectors per track A geometry value that expresses the number of sectors within each track on a hard drive. (8)

serial port A 9-pin or 25-pin male port used to attach older serial devices, such as external modems and serial mice, to a PC. (4, 12)

server case A type of computer case that's designed to accommodate the space and expandability needs of servers. These cases tend to be square, rather than rectangular like tower cases. (6)

shadow mask A thin metal grill with tiny holes that is anchored in front of the phosphor coating on a CRT monitor to prevent stray fire from the electron guns from causing the colors to bleed. (11)

SIMM Single inline memory module; older-style RAM stick that came in 72-pin and 30-pin configurations. (3)

single-edge cartridge (SEC) A card-type package that was popular on the Pentium II, Athlon, and early Pentium III CPUs; also known as single-edge contact cartridge (SECC). (2)

slave A term used to describe a drive that shares a ribbon cable with another device and allows that device to handle the controlling. (8)

slot cover Metal strip that screws into place on the back of the PC to cover an open slot behind an empty expansion bay. (6)

soft power A feature of ATX power supplies that keeps the PC from ever completely shutting off. As long as an ATX system is receiving AC power from the wall socket, the ATX power supply keeps a 5-volt charge on the motherboard. (6)

Sony/Philips digital interface (SPDIF) A special type of connector that enables you to connect your sound card directly to a 5.1 speaker system or receiver. (13)

sound card The peripheral that provides sound input and output for a PC. (1)

SoundBlaster Well-known modern brand of computer sound card, designed by Creative Labs, that supports modern 3D audio standards. (13)

Sounds and Audio Devices A Windows XP Control Panel applet, called Sounds and Multimedia in Windows 9x/2000, for configuring the system's sound card. (13)

Star Bus A popular network topology combining the Bus and Star topologies. (15)

stick A slang term for a circuit board populated with RAM. (3)

subwoofer A speaker designed to produce the lowest audio frequencies at an adequate volume. (13)

SuperDisk Also known as the LS-120; a type of removable media that can use either specialized large-capacity disks or regular floppy disks. (7)

swap file The special part of the hard drive that stores the programs placed in virtual memory. (3)

switch A device that filters and forwards packets between LAN segments. (15)

System Information tool A general-purpose utility that comes with most versions of Microsoft Windows. The System Information tool provides detailed information about the hardware and software on a PC. (2)

system resources A collective term for the I/O address, IRQ, and DMA: settings that enable each device on a PC to communicate with the CPU and request RAM space for its use. (5)

System Setup utility Often referred to as CMOS; the interface that enables you to specify parameters for various devices supported by the system BIOS. (4)

system unit The primary case for your computer that stores the RAM, CPU, motherboard, and other critical components that make up a PC. (1)

tape backup device A drive that uses magnetic tape on a reel-to-reel cassette to store massive amounts of data; usually used for backups. (7)

terminators Devices used on the ends of a SCSI chain to prevent reflection of electronic signals on the chain. (10)

texture A small picture that is tiled over and over again on walls, floors, and other surfaces in video game environments to create a three-dimensional look. (11)

thermal compound A white paste placed between the CPU and the CPU fan to improve the flow of heat away from the CPU. (2)

toner Ink powder used in laser printers. (14)

toner cartridge   The replaceable portion of a laser printer that contains not only the toner but also many other key printer components that wear out, such as the photosensitive drum. Much of the laser-printing process actually takes place inside this cartridge. (14)

topology   The physical or logical shape of a network. The most popular LAN topology is Star Bus. (15)

touch pad   A type of pointing device, commonly found on laptop PCs. To operate a touch pad, you run your finger across a touch-sensitive pad to move the cursor, and you tap the pad once or twice to click or double-click. (12)

touch screen   A device that enables you to interact with a computer simply by touching a display screen. (12)

trackball   A type of ergonomic pointing device consisting of a platform with a ball on top that the user manipulates with a thumb or finger. The trackball device remains in place on the desktop, instead of moving around on a pad like a mouse. (12)

tracks   Concentric circles on hard drive platters where data is stored. (8)

Travan   A type of backup tape that improved upon the QIC format, with a capacity of around 10 GB. (7)

Ultra SCSI   Also called *Fast-20 SCSI*; a version of Fast SCSI that moves data at 20 MBps. (10)

Ultra2 SCSI   Also called *Fast-40 SCSI*; a version of Fast SCSI that moves data at 40 MBps. (10)

unit   A way of measuring how much space a rack-mount case takes up in a server rack. One unit, or U, equals 1.75 vertical inches. (6)

universal audio cable   A cable that connects a CD-ROM drive to any sort of audio card. (9)

Universal Serial Bus (USB)   A technology that uses small, rectangular connectors to attach many different types of devices to a PC. A single USB port can support up to 127 devices at the same time, and USB devices are hot-swappable. (4, 5, 12)

unshielded twisted-pair (UTP)   The most common type of cabling used in modern networks, consisting of between two and eight wires, either copper or aluminum, stranded or solid core, twisted around each other and wrapped in a protective sheath. Telephone cords and CAT5 cables are examples of UTP cabling. (15)

USB type A   A type of connector used on USB cables. Most USB cables have a type A connector on one end, to attach to the PC either directly or indirectly through another device. (14)

USB type B   A type of connector used on USB cables. Most USB cables have a type B connector on one end, to plug in a device such as a printer, digital camera, or removable drive. (14)

video card   Also called a graphics adapter; the video card acts as the interface between the computer and the monitor. (1)

Video Graphics Array (VGA)   The video graphics standard that is the de facto common denominator for most modern computer monitors. It specifies characteristics such as screen resolution and refresh rate. (11)

viewable image size (VIS)   The part of a computer screen that actually displays pixels. (11)

virtual memory   The ability to swap the least-used programs in RAM to the hard drive to make room for the most-used program. (3)

watt   The standard unit of measure for power. (6)

wavetable synthesis   The technique of embedding recordings of actual instruments or other sounds in a sound card, where they can then be used to reproduce sounds much more faithfully than with FM synthesis. The set of embedded sounds is called a wavetable. (13)

Wide SCSI   A type of SCSI interface that uses 16 or 32 wires to move data. (10)

wireless   A term used to describe various PC devices, including keyboards, pointing devices, printers, and network cards, that communicate with the system or network without the use of cables. These devices use either infrared or radio waves to send and receive data. (12)

write speed   The speed at which a CD-R or CD-RW drive can write data on a disc. (9)

writing laser   A high-powered laser used in CD-R and CD-RW drives. It writes data onto an optical disc by actually burning tiny pits on the disc's shiny surface. (9)

Zip drive   A proprietary type of removable media drive created by Iomega Corporation. The first such drives used disks that could store up to 100 MB of data—a huge leap up from the then-popular floppy disk. (7)

■ Symbols and Numbers

! error symbol, in the Device Manager, 137, 138

1.44 MB (double-sided, high-density) floppy disks, 179

2D programs, 301

2.1 speaker system, 349, 350, 423

3½-inch drive bays, 151, 152, 423

3½-inch floppy disks, 179

3½-inch floppy drive, installing, 180

3-pin jumper, 91

3D games, 300–301

3DMark benchmark program, 309

86 aspect ratio, of the typical CRT, 294

4.1 system, 350

5¼-inch drive bays, 151, 152, 423

5¼-inch floppy drive and floppy disk, 179

5.1 speaker system, 349–351, 423

8-bit ISA bus, 121

9-pin matrix, 365

9-pin serial connector, for a mouse, 328

9-pin serial port, 13, 92

9-pin serial ports, connecting modems to, 396

9-to-25-pin converter, 396

10/100 switches, 406

10BaseT cards, 405

10BaseT Ethernet, 402, 403, 423

15-pin female DB port, 331

15-pin game port, 13

15-pin video port, 13

16-bit ISA bus, 121–122

16-bit ISA card, 121–122

17-inch screen, for a monitor, 295

19-inch screen, for a monitor, 295

21-inch screen, for a monitor, 295

24-bit color, 306

24-pin matrix, 365

25-pin female DB connector, 370, 423

25-pin parallel port, 13

30-pin SIMMs, 64–66

32-bit color, 306

34-pin ribbon cable, connecting floppy drives to the motherboard, 179, 423

40-pin motherboard connection, for the drive cable, 210

50-pin Centronics connectors, used in SCSI-1, 275, 276, 423

64-bit-wide data bus, 58

64-bit-wide rows, of RAM, 58

72-pin SIMMs, 64–66

compared to 30-pin SIMMs, 66

72-pin SO DIMM, 68, 69

80-wire cables, color-coded connectors, 211

84-key keyboard layout, 321, 423

100BaseTX cards, 405

100BaseTX Ethernet, 402, 404, 423

101-key keyboard layout, 321, 423

104-key keyboard, 321

144-pin SO DIMM, 68, 69

160-pin RIMM, 71

168-pin DIMM, compared to 184-pin, 68

168-pin DIMMs, 67

184-pin DIMMs, 67–68

200-pin SO DIMM, 68, 69

242-pin SEC package, 34

370-pin PGA package, 34

400-watt power supply, recommended, 157

423-pin PGA package, 34

462-pin PGA package, 34

478-pin PGA package, 34

640 x 480 resolution, 294

650-MB CD-R, 245

700-MB CD-R, 245

802.3 committee, of IEEE, 402

8042 chips, 103

8042 keyboard controller chip, 104

1,024 x 768 resolution, 294

2,352-byte sectors, on CDs, 241

■ A

A+ certification, 420–421

A scale, decibels on, 48

A-adjusted decibels. See dBA

ABIT, 38, 85

A/C current, converting into D/C current, 19

Accelerated Graphics Port expansion slot. See AGP expansion slot

access point, in a wireless network, 405

ACR (Advanced Communication Riser) slot, 395

active partition, 204

active termination, for Fast SCSI, 277, 423

Adapter Properties dialog box, 307

Adapter Settings function, of a SCSI BIOS program, 282–283

Add New Hardware Wizard, 134

Add Printer wizard, 373–376

Add/Remove Programs applet, 131, 132

address bus, 30

first 16 wires of, 115

identifying devices on, 115

as the main communication path, 115

Adobe Photoshop, minimum RAM requirements for, 74

A: drive, installing a floppy drive as, 179

Advanced Audio Properties dialog box, 355

Advanced Backup Options dialog box, 194

Advanced Micro Devices. See AMD

Advanced Technology Attachment. See ATA standards

AGP expansion slot, 126–127, 302–303, 423

on an ATX motherboard, 85, 89, 90

AGP video cards, 302–303

AIFF sound file type, 344

airflow

inside a computer case, 170–171

produced by CPU fans, 48

alignment program, for inkjet color nozzles, 385

all-in-one multifunction machines, 368

AMD (Advanced Micro Devices), 18, 31

AMD Athlon XP CPU, 29

AMD Duron, 32, 34

AMD processors, 31, 34

AMD SEC cartridge, 34

AMI, 105

amplitude, 341

AMR slot, 128

analog/digital-out connection, on a sound card, 347–348

analog interface, for an LCD monitor, 298

analog signals, compared to digital, 394

antistatic bags, placing cards in, 133

antistatic mat, placing a PC on, 8

antistatic plastic or foam, setting a CPU on, 43

antistatic wrist strap, 7, 423

Appearance tab, of the Windows XP Display Properties dialog box, 305

applications

installation for CD media drives, 252

installing for sound cards, 357

problems involving sound, 359

sounds played by, 344

Archive attribute, 191
Archive bit, 191, 423
ARPANET, 408
art tablet, 332–333, 423
ASM sound file type, 343
assembly language, 2
Assign Drive Letter or Path dialog box, in the New Volume Wizard, 226
assigned memory, for devices, 118
ASUS, 38, 85
ASX sound file type, 343
asynchronous RAM, 61
AT form factor, for computer cases, 154, 155
AT keyboard, 321
AT motherboards, 94, 95, 96, 423
AT power supply, 156, 423
AT power switches, 161
AT-PS/2 adapter, 91
AT-style connector, 91, 322
AT systems, power management and, 162
AT-type connector, 324
ATA-1. See IDE
ATA-2 standard, 209
ATA-6 standard, 213
ATA Programmable Interface. See ATAPI standard
ATA speed ratings, 209, 211–212
ATA standards, 209
ATA33, 209, 211–212
ATA66, 209
ATA100, 209
ATA133, 209
ATAPI devices, internal Zip drives as, 187
ATAPI standard, 209
Athlon motherboard, voltage settings on an older, 41
Athlon processors, power supplies for, 160
ATI, 300
attributes, working with, 194–195
ATX form factor, 85, 154–155, 423
ATX motherboards, 86, 95–96
ATX power supplies, 156, 162, 423
ATX soft power, 162
ATX-style keyboard/mouse connector, 328
ATX12V power supply, 160
AU sound file type, 344
audible alarm, for a CPU fan failure, 51
audio cables, for CD media drives, 249–250, 251
audio CDs, 241, 257
audio codecs, listing installed, 356
audio files, versus audio tracks, 255
Audio/Modem Riser. See AMR slot
audio ports, 13

Audio tab, of the Sounds and Audio Devices applet, 356
audio tracks, versus audio files, 255
Auto Insert Notification, 256
Autodetect setting, in the System Setup utility, 212–213, 214
automated mode, of FDISK, 217, 218, 219
automatic shutdown features, for processors, 47
Automatically Fix Error check box, in ScanDisk, 228
autoplay, 255–257, 423
AUTORUN.INF file, on a CD, 256
autosensing NICs, 405
Award Software, 102, 105

■ B

Baby AT motherboards, 94–95
back plates, of computer cases, 153, 424
backbone, of a network, 404, 424
backlights, for LCDs, 297, 298
backup programs, 192–194
backup strategies, 191–195
bad-print problems, 384–385
bad sticks, of RAM, 78
ball-type mice, 14
bandwidth, 124
        for cabling, 402
        exploited by DSL, 392
bank fillers, 70
banking, 424
        of RDRAM, 70
        of SIMMs, 65
bare processors, 47
base-16 mathematics. See hexadecimal system
basic components, of a PC, 10–11
basic disks, 222, 223
basic input/output system. See BIOS
baud, 395, 424
bays. See drive bays
B: drive, installing a floppy drive as, 179
beeping unbootable PC, 314
bent pins, straightening in a socketed CPU, 46
Big Drives standard, 213
binary combinations, for a given set, 59
binary I/O addresses, converting into hexadecimal shorthand, 117
binary quantities, 60
binary values, shorthand for describing sets of, 116–117
BIOS, 89, 103, 424
        device drivers stored in, 114
        devices needing, 104
        flashing, 105
        with INT13 Extensions, 213

support of larger hard drive sizes, 213
BIOS backup file, 105
BIOS chips, 103
BIOS updaters, 105, 424
bit depth, 305, 341, 424
bit rate, of an MP3 file, 343, 424
bizarre images, on the screen, 314
black keyboards, 321
black !, on a yellow circle in the Device Manager, 137, 138
black rim, around CRT screens, 295
"blippy" technology, 138
blue I on a white field, in the Device Manager, 137
blue line-in jack, for a stereo system, 93
boot device ID, on the Adapter Settings screen, 283
boot device sequence, 188
boot screen, 78–79, 104
boot sector, 204
bootable floppy disks, 183–184
bootable partitions, 204
booting
        to a floppy, Zip, or SuperDisk drive, 188–189
        a system with a nonbootable floppy in the floppy drive, 184
breakout box, for a sound card, 348
brightness, of LCD monitors, 298
broken input devices, 336
built-in controls, for monitors, 295–296
bump mapping, 301
burn speeds
        adjusting, 261
        mismatched, 260–261
burning, 424
        CDs, 257–259
        data onto a CD, 244
burning software, 244, 252, 257
bus, 30
Bus topology, 401–402
bus types, obsolete, 125

■ C

C++, 2
cable modems, 391
cable select jumper settings, for hard drives, 211
cable select option, for CD media drives, 249
cable tester, 413
cables
        checking a LAN's, 413
        purchasing for SCSI devices, 281
cabling options, for the new SCSI-3 standard, 278
calibration, of game controllers, 335
cameras, 11, 12

Introduction to PC Hardware and Troubleshooting

candela, 298
capacity, of RAM, 74–75
CardBus, 142
cards. *See* expansion cards
cartridge tapes, 190, 424
CAS wire, 61
case fans, 168–169, 424
    installing, 169–170
    positioning of, 171
cases. *See* computer cases
CAT levels, of UTP cabling, 402–403
CAT1 cabling, for standard phone
    lines, 402
CAT5 cabling, 403, 424
CAT5e cabling, 403
CAT6 cabling, 403
Cathode Ray Tube. *See* CRT (Cathode
    Ray Tube) displays
CD (compact disc), 240, 424
CD Audio, 241, 424
CD Digital Audio (CDDA), 241
CD media, 240, 424
    drivers, 250–251
    drives, 248–255
    problems with, 259–260
    reading multiple types of, 246
    standards, 244
    storing data, 241
    technologies, 241–248
    troubleshooting, 259–262
    using, 255–259
CD Player, in Windows, 256
CD quality sound capture, 341, 424
CD-R burner, 245
CD-R discs, 19
    varieties of, 245
    views of, 244
CD-R drives, multiplier values for, 245
CD-R standard, 244–245, 424
CD-ROM, 240, 241–243, 424
CD-ROM discs, 19
CD-ROM drives, 19, 242
    audio cable for, 93
    CD_IN audio port for, 93
    installing, 252–255
    speeds of, 243
CD-ROM polishing kits, 260
CD-RW discs, 19
    using for system backups, 247
    views of, 246
CD-RW drives, 246
CD-RW (CD-Rewritable) technology,
    246, 424
CD-to-CD copies, 257
CD Writing wizard, in Windows XP,
    258–259
CDDA. *See* audio CDs
CDFS (CD File System), 242
CD_IN audio port, for a CD-ROM
    drive, 93

CDs
    burning, 257–259
    quality issues with, 261
    removing scratches from, 260
    types of, 257
central processing units. *See* CPUs
centralized systems, mainframes as, 2
Centronics connector, 370, 371, 424
certification, 420
CFM (cubic feet per minute), 48, 424
chamfers, on Molex connectors, 159
changeable system devices, 104–105
CheckIt utility, 229
chips, on a stick of RAM, 58
chipset chips, on an ATX
    motherboard, 85, 88
chipset, supported by BIOS drivers, 114
circuit, making with a jumper, 91
classes, of SCSI devices, 285
cleaning
    inkjet printer nozzles, 382
    laser printers, 380
cleaning kit, for a floppy drive, 181–182
cleaning procedures, for input
    devices, 335–336
clock chip, 32, 424
clock speed, of expansion slots, 112
clone PCs makers, 5
clusters, 205
CMOS, 104. *See also* System Setup
    utility
CNR slots, 128
    on an ATX motherboard, 89, 90
    fitting modems into, 395
coarse-threaded screws, 154
COBOL, 2
codecs, 255, 424
Color Books, 244
color-coded connectors, on 80-wire
    cables, 211
color images, producing high-
    quality, 366
color quality, 305
colors, missing on monitors, 313
Column Array Strobe wire, 61
command line, accessing, 311, 414
commands, storing in RAM, 29
Commodore 64, 4
Communication and Networking
    Riser slots. *See* CNR slots
communication, between the CPU and
    the Northbridge, 58
compact disc. *See* CD
Compact Disc–Read-Only Memory.
    See CD-ROM
Compact Disc-Recordable discs. *See*
    CD-R discs
Compact Disc-Rewritable discs. *See*
    CD-RW discs

compatibility, of hardware within a
    LAN, 393
compatible driver, successful
    installation of, 138
complete backups, 191
Complimentary Metal-Oxide
    Semiconductor. *See* CMOS
components
    internal to a PC, 17–19
    of a modern PC, 10–15
compressed capacities, of tape
    drives, 190
compressor/decompressor programs.
    See codecs
computer cases, 148, 149
    back plates of, 153
    connection on, 155
    external sizes of, 149–151
    form factors for, 154–155
    manufacturers of popular, 176
    removing motherboards from,
        97–99
    for system units, 20
computer circuit board, in a hard
    drive, 201
Computer Management applet, 208
computer programs, 1. *See also*
    software
computer screws. *See* screws
computerphiles, 5
computerphobes, 5–6
computers. *See also* PCs
    cooling, 167–169
    short history of, 1–5
    shutting down without a
        mouse, 329
computing center, 2
configuration applications, for sound
    cards, 355–356
configuration errors, troubleshooting
    video, 314–315
configuration, of printers, 376–378
configuration problems, involving
    sound, 358
configuration switches, on
    motherboards, 90–91
connection points, 12
connections
    on computer cases, 155
    handling to PCs, 16–17
    for keyboards, 322–324
    for mice, 328
    removing a power supply's, 164
Connections tab, of the Internet
    Properties dialog box, 399–400
connectivity, achieving for a LAN, 393
connectors. *See also* plugs
    attaching to the motherboard, 102
    orientation of, 15
    on a power supply, 158–160

console gaming systems, 331
consumables, 424
  cost of, 367, 368, 379–380
contiguous clusters, 229
Continuity RIMMs (CRIMMs), 70
contoured mouse, 326
contrast ratio, of LCD monitors, 298
Control Panel
  Add/Remove Programs applet, 131, 132
  audio applets in, 355–356
  Display applet on, 305–306
  Internet Options applet, 232
  Keyboard applet, 326
  Local Area Connection Properties dialog box, 408–409
  Modems applet, 392
  Mouse applet, 329
  Network and Internet Connections applet, 399
  Network Connections system folder, 408
  Printers and Faxes applet, 373
controller board, on a hard drive, 201
controller cards, enabling RAID 5, 223
controller, for an EIDE drive, 210
Controllers tab, of the Gaming Options dialog box, 334
Convert to Dynamic Disk option, 223
cooling, computers, 167–169
cooling system, installing for a CPU, 47–51
copper cabling, weaknesses of, 404
Copy backup, 191, 424
core devices, 104
cost per page, ranking printers in terms of, 368–369
CPU-conversion devices, 39
CPU Socket/Slot, on an ATX motherboard, 85, 86
CPU-Z program, 36, 38
CPUs (central processing units), 18, 29, 424
  communicating with, 114–118
  detecting the use of input devices, 30
  fan power connector on an ATX motherboard, 85, 86, 87
  fans, 51, 100
  heat sinks and fans for, 168
  identification programs, 36
  identifying, 31–38
  information displayed during the boot sequence, 36
  installing, 41–47, 100
  internal processing speeds of, 33
  models of, 32
  multipliers, 39
  removing, 43

speed settings for, 39–40
speeds of, 32–33
storing in a safe place, 45
supported by a motherboard, 38
turning address wires on and off, 59
upgrading, 41–47
using Northbridge to handle all communication with RAM, 57
using RAM to store active programs and data, 57
Create DOS Partition or Logical DOS Drive option, on the FDISK screen, 217, 218, 219
CRIMMs, 70
crossover cable, 403, 404
CRT (Cathode Ray Tube) displays, 13, 293–297, 424
  cleaning, 312
  installing and configuring, 296–297
  missing pixels on, 313
  variations among, 295–296
CRT tubes, types of, 295
CTRL-ALT-DEL, accessing the Task Manager, 72
cubic feet per minute (CFM), 48, 424
cumulative backup, 192
cursor, 10
curved-screen CRTs, 295
cylinders, 202, 424

D

Daily Copy Backup, 192, 425
daisy-chained SCSI devices, 269
daisy-chained USB connectors, 322
daisy-chaining, 425
  supported by FireWire, 141
  USB devices, 139
DAT (Digital Audio Tape), 190, 425
data bus, 30
data CD formats, 244–248
data CD-ROM discs, 241
data CDs, 257
data recovery, from lost hard drives, 234
date and time battery, on an ATX motherboard, 85, 89, 90
dBA, measuring fan noise, 48, 425
DDR SDRAM, 63, 68, 69, 425
DEC VAX minicomputer, 3
decaying images, on the screen, 314
decibel, 48, 425
default printer, identifying and changing, 376
defragmentation (defrag), 229–230, 425
DEL key, accessing the System Setup utility, 105
Delete Partition or Logical DOS Drive, on the FDISK screen, 217, 218, 219

desktop cases, 150, 151, 425. See also computer cases
device drivers, 114, 425
  checking, 118–120
  determining the version of, 130–131
  getting the correct, 130–131
  removing old, 131–132
  updating, 120
Device Manager, 425
  accessing, 118–120
  checking for sound configuration problems, 358
  checking the installation of a device, 137
  displaying a SCSI device and host adapter in, 285
  error symbols in, 137
  installation problems indicated by, 137–138
  locating device drivers in, 131
  opening, 119
  using INF files to install drivers, 135–136
Device Setup function, of a SCSI BIOS program, 282, 284
devices
  holding or not holding a charge, 58
  identifying on the address bus, 115
  needs inherent to, 114
  viewing the resources assigned to, 119
diagnostic poking around, 6–7
diagnostic tests
  running on a network, 413–414
  running on a video subsystem, 311
diagnostic utilities, for NICs, 413
Diagnostics tab, of the Modem Properties dialog box, 412
dial-up connections, 391
dial-up networks, 391–392
  installing and configuring, 394–400
  problems with, 412
  setting up software for, 398–400, 401
Differential backup, 192, 425
Digital Audio Tape (DAT), 190, 425
Digital Linear Tape (DLT), 190–191, 425
digital signals, compared to analog, 394
Digital Subscriber Line (DSL), 391, 392
Digital Theatre Systems (DTS), 349, 425
digital video cards, using only DVI connectors, 302
Digital Video Interface connector, 299, 425
dim screen, on a monitor, 313

Introduction to PC Hardware and Troubleshooting

DIMM slots, 87
DIMMs, 67–68, 69, 425
    inserting the wrong speed of, 67
    removing and installing, 77–78
DIN connector, 322, 425
    identifying, 324
    on the AT motherboard, 94
DIP switches, on an ATX
    motherboard, 85, 90–91
Direct Memory Access (DMA), 118, 425
Direct3D, testing, 311
DirectDraw, testing, 311
DirectSound3D (DS3D), 350, 425
DirectX, 310–311, 350, 425
DirectX diagnostic tool, 310
dirty input devices, 336
disabled device, indicated by the
    Device Manager, 137
Disc Juggler, 252
Disk Administrator tool, with
    Windows NT, 221
disk cleanup, 231–233
Disk Cleanup tool, 233
disk drives, 12
Disk Management tool, 221
    upgrading to a dynamic drive,
    223, 224
    working with partitions,
    225–227
Disk Utilities function, of a SCSI BIOS
    program, 282, 284
display adapters, 299–302. See also
    video cards
Display applet, on the Control Panel,
    305–306
Display Partition Information, on the
    FDISK screen, 217–218
DLT (Digital Linear Tape), 190–191, 425
DMA (Direct Memory Access), 118, 425
Dolby Digital sound standard, 349, 425
DOS, running with one floppy
    drive, 178
dot matrix printers, 365, 425
dot pitch, 294, 425
dots per inch (dpi), 366, 425
Double Data Rate SDRAM. See DDR
    SDRAM
double-density floppy disk, 179, 425
double-sided DVDs, 248
double-sided, high-density floppy
    disks, 179
double-sided sticks, of RAM, 75
downloaded program files, 232
dpi (dots per inch), 366, 425
Draft setting, for a printer, 378
drive bays, 151–152
    rails for, 152, 153, 425
    types of, 151
drive overlay programs, 213
Drive Properties dialog box, 207
drive signature, 221

driver problems, with input
    devices, 336
Driver tab
    of an adapter's Properties
    dialog box, 308
    of the Properties dialog box, 119
    of the Properties window for a
    device, 135–136
drivers
    for CD media drives, 250–251
    for expansion cards, 134–137
    for keyboards, 325
    for printers, 371–376
    for SCSI devices, 285
    for sound cards, 354–355
    for USB devices, 140
    for video cards, 304–305,
    306–310
drives, sharing entire, 412
DS3D (DirectSound3D), 350, 425
DSL (Digital Subscriber Line), 391, 392
DTS, 349, 425
dual floppy drives, 177
Dual Inline Memory Modules. See
    DIMMs
dual speed rating system, for DDR
    SDRAM, 68
DVD (Digital Versatile Disc), 247–248,
    425–426
DVD drives, 247–248
DVD player software, 247
DVD-ROM, 248
DVD standards, in the works, 248
DVD video, 247
DVI (Digital Video Interface)
    connector, for an LCD monitor,
    299, 425
Dxdiag utility, 311
dynamic disks, 222, 223, 426
Dynamic RAM, 57

■ E

Easy CD Creator, 246, 252
EAX (Environmental Audio
    Extensions), 350–351, 426
EDO RAM, 61–62
Effects button, on the Appearance tab
    of the Display Properties dialog
    box, 305
EIA/TIA 568A and 568B standards, 403
EIDE, 209, 286, 426
EIDE cables, 210, 211
EIDE controllers, on a motherboard, 210
EIDE drives, 208
    40-pin connector, 208
    ATA speed ratings, 209
    configuring as master or
    slave, 210
    mixing with SCSI, 286

EIDE ports, on an ATX motherboard,
    85, 88
EIDE RAID controller, 285
EISA bus, 123–124
electrical charges, building up
    opposite, 7
electrical power cord, plug for, 12
electrical power, respecting, 7
electron guns, in CRTs, 293
electronic computer parts, handling,
    9–10
electrostatic discharge (ESD), 7–10, 426
Engelbart, Doug, 325
Enhanced Integrated Drive
    Electronics. See EIDE drives
Entire Network option, in My
    Network Places, 411
Environmental Audio Extensions
    (EAX), 350–351, 426
ergonomics, 321, 326, 426
Error-checking, on a Windows 2000/
    XP system, 228
error codes, supplied by printers,
    383, 385
error messages, involving sound
    applications, 359
error symbols, in the Device
    Manager, 137
error warning system, for a
    printer, 383
errors, involving floppy disks or the
    A: drive, 182–183
ESD (electrostatic discharge), 7–10, 426
Ethernet, 402, 426
Ethernet connector, 13
expandability, of a full-tower cases,
    149–150
expansion bus interfaces, on video
    cards, 302
expansion buses, 110, 111, 113, 426
    checking, 129–130
    external, 138–142
    internal, 121–130
    reasons for the existence of, 111
expansion cards, 18
    buying, 130
    handling, 21–22, 133
    installing drivers for, 134–137
    installing plug and play, 130–138
    removing from AGP and PCI
    slots, 98–99
expansion slots, 18, 426
    on an ATX motherboard, 85,
    88–89
    clock speed of, 112
    comparing, 22
    on a motherboard, 111
Extended Data Output RAM, 61–62
Extended Industry Standard
    Architecture bus, 123–124
extended partitions, 204, 426

external bays, 151
external expansion buses, 138–142
external modems, 19, 396
external ports, on an ATX motherboard, 85, 91–93
external SCSI devices, 269, 270, 271
external sizes, of computer cases, 149–151
external Zip drives, 186–187
extra features, provided by sound cards, 348
eyes, permanent damage to, 294

■ **F**

faced and keyed connectors, 158
faceplate, 20. *See also* front faceplate
fades, on printouts, 384–385
failed clusters, checking hard drives for, 227
fan and heat sink assembly, removing, 42
fan power connector
        on an ATX motherboard, 85, 86, 87
        unplugging from the motherboard, 43
fans, 48
        built in to power supplies, 167–168
        for CPUs, 168
        inside power supplies, 156, 157
Fast-20 SCSI, 276, 426
Fast-40 SCSI, 277, 426
Fast-80 (Ultra160) speed standards, for SCSI, 278
Fast-160 (Ultra320) speed standards, for SCSI, 278
Fast Ethernet, 404, 426
Fast Page Mode RAM. *See* FPM RAM
Fast SCSI, versions of, 276
FAT (File Allocation Table), 177–178, 203, 426
fat-vaned heat sinks, 47
FAT16 file system, 205
FAT32 file system, 205, 217
fault tolerance
        in RAID 5, 222
        in Star Bus networks, 402
FDD ports, on an ATX motherboard, 85, 88
FDISK program, 206, 217, 220
female connector, 16
fiber-optic networks, 404
field distortion sensing, 328
File Allocation Table. *See* FAT
file and folder sharing, enabling, 408–412
File and Printer Sharing for Microsoft Networks, in Windows XP, 409

file attributes, 191, 426
File Properties dialog box, in Windows XP, 194
file systems, 205–208
files, storing in partitions, 205
fine-threaded screws, 154
FireWire, 141, 426
firmware, 114, 261
first rule of PC hardware, 68
fixed resolution, of an LCD panel, 298
flash BIOS, 103, 104, 426
flash ROM, 103, 426
flash ROM chip, on an ATX motherboard, 85, 89, 90
flashing, the BIOS, 105
flat screen CRTs, 295
FlexATX form factor, for computer cases, 155
FlexATX motherboards, 96
flexing, the motherboard, 100
flicker, 315
floppies, 19
floppy disk drive ports. *See* FDD ports
floppy disk error message, in Windows, 182–183
floppy disks, 176, 426
        bootable, 183–184
        formatting nonbootable, 184–185
        history of, 178–179
        magnetic coating on, 177
        on the original IBM PC, 177
floppy drive cables, 179
floppy drives, 19, 177–178
        booting to, 188–189
        caring for, 181–182
        fixing broken, 182–183
        front of, 178
        installing, 180–181
        replacing, 182–183
        supported by BIOS drivers, 114
floppy icon, in My Computer, 183
FM synthesis, 343, 426
Folder Options dialog box, in Windows XP, 194–195
footprint, 96
force feedback, 330
foreign objects, as a source of floppy drive problems, 182
form factors, 426
        of chips, 52
        for computer cases, 154–155
        of heat sinks, 47
        for motherboards, 85, 94–97
Format dialog box, 184–185, 221
formats, for recorded sounds, 342
formatting, 426
        floppy disks, 177
        hard drives, 216, 220–223
FORTRAN, 2
Found New Hardware wizard, 397–398

four-pair UTP, 403
FPM RAM, 60–61
Fraunhoffer MPEG Layer 3 codec. *See* MP3 format
frequency, 341
front faceplate, removing from a floppy drive, 182
front-mounted USB and FireWire ports, 155
front panel connectors, on an ATX motherboard, 85, 90
front panel plugs, connecting to the motherboard, 101
frontside bus, 30, 126, 426
Fujitsu, 201
Full AT motherboard. *See* AT motherboards
Full backups, 191
Full format process, for a floppy disk, 185
full-tower cases, 149–150, 426. *See also* computer cases
functions, performed by a CPU, 29
fuzziness, of CRT screens, 312
fuzzy, unfocused printouts, 385

■ **G**

game controllers
        cleaning, 336
        connections for, 331–332
        installing and configuring, 333–335
        types of, 330–331
game pads, 330, 331
game ports, 13, 92–93, 330–332
games, 3D, 300–301
Gaming Options dialog box, 333–335
GB (gigabytes), 18, 60
geometry, of a hard drive, 201–203, 426
ghosting, on LCD monitors, 314
Gigabyte motherboard manufacturer, 38, 85
gigabytes (GB), 18, 60
gigahertz (GHz), 32, 426
grabber tool, retrieving screws, 22
graphics adapters, 19. *See also* video cards
graphics processor, 300, 310
green 1/8-inch jack, for speakers, 93
green ?, in the Device Manager, 138
green PS/2 port, 91, 322

■ **H**

hard drive controller circuit board, 201
hard drive errors, 234
hard drive thrash, 72
hard drives, 18, 176, 200, 201, 426
        adding a second, 215
        configuring, 216–227

formatting, 220–223
installing, 208–215
maintenance of, 227–233
make and model numbers of, 201
opening, 201
physically installing, 214
speed of, 29
supported by BIOS drivers, 114
terminology regarding, 209–210
troubleshooting, 233–235
hardware, 1
improper handling of, 6
problems involving sound, 357–358
proprietary for microcomputers, 4
hardware and software setup, in a LAN, 393
Hardware tab, of the Sounds and Audio Devices applet, 356
Hardware Update wizard, 307
hat switch, 330
Have Disk button, in the Add Printer Wizard, 375
headphone jack
on a CD-ROM drive, 243
on speakers, 351
heads, 202
heat dope. *See* thermal compound
heat sensors, offered by fan/heat sink assemblies, 48
heat sink and fan assembly, selecting and installing the proper, 47–51
heat sinks, 47
for CPUs, 168
styles of, 47
heat spreader, on RIMMs, 69
hertz (Hz), 32, 62, 293, 427
hexadecimal shorthand, converting binary addresses into, 117
hexadecimal system, 115–117
hibernate mode, 162, 427
Hidden attribute, 191, 194
Hidden files, displaying in Windows XP, 194–195
Hide Modes That This Monitor Cannot Display option, 306, 307
high-density 50-pin connection, 276, 277
high-density (HD) 68-pin connector, 276, 427
high-density floppy disks, 179
high-end graphics processors, 300
high-level languages, 2
high resolution, versus low, 294, 295
high-voltage alternating current (AC), converting into low-voltage direct current (DC), 156
history
of computers, 1–5

of floppy disks, 178–179
host adapters, 269, 427
buying, 279–281
checking the speed of, 280
drivers for, 285
installing, 282
preset to SCSI ID7, 281
host, mezzanine bus as the, 125
hot-swappable connector, 322
hot-swappable device, 139, 427
hot-swappable USB port, 331
hubs, 427
installing and cabling, 407
for LANs, 393, 406–407
Hz (Hertz), 32, 62, 293, 427

I

I/O addresses, 114–118, 427
IBM, 201, 408
IBM PC, 5
ICH chip, 126
IDE, 209
IDE0 (primary) controller, 211
IDE1 (secondary) controller, 211
IEEE (Institute of Electrical and Electronics Engineers), 402, 427
802.3 standard, 403
1284 cable, 370, 371, 427
1394 standard, 141, 427
images, not appearing on the monitor screen, 313
Imation Corporation, 187
impact printers, 365
IN jack, 13
incompatible DVD standards, 248
Incremental backup, 192, 427
individuals, software for use by, 3
Industry Standard Architecture (ISA) bus, 121
INF files, using to install drivers, 135, 427
infrared (IR) waves, in wireless networks, 404–405
infrared (IR) wireless mice, 328
ink cartridges, 366, 368, 369, 427
ink, current levels of, 384
inkjet cartridges, 380
inkjet printers, 365–367, 427
maintaining, 381–382
speed compared to laser printers, 367
inks, used as part of the CD burning process, 261
input device connections, for game controllers, 331–332
input devices, 11, 320
cleaning, 335–336
detecting the use of, 30

identifying less common, 329–335
maintaining, 335–336
troubleshooting, 335–336
input/output (I/O) functions, 11, 427
installation CDs
autoplay of, 256
for printers, 372
viewing the contents of, 134–135
installation problems, for devices, 137–138
installation program, accessing Window 98's, 216
Institute of Electrical and Electronics Engineers (IEEE), 402, 427
instruction manual, compared to the motherboard book, 38
instruction set, of a CPU, 29, 427
INT13 Extension, 213
Intel Corporation, 18, 31
Intel CPUs, 52
Intel Pentium 3 processor, 32
Intel Pentium II SEC package, 33
Intel processors, 34
versus AMD, 31
not compatible with sockets or slots for AMD processors, 34
Intel systems, RDRAM used only on, 63
interfaces, for LCD monitors, 298
internal 50-pin connector cables, used in SCSI-1, 275, 276
internal bays, 151
internal buses, 121–130
internal components, of a PC, 17–19
internal modems, 19, 395
internal SCSI chain, 269
internal SCSI devices, 269, 270
internal Zip drives, 186–187
International Telecommunication Union (ITU), 395
Internet Options applet, 232
Internet Properties dialog box, Connections tab, 399–400
Internet radio stations, 344
Internet Service Provider (ISP), 391, 399
Internet, TCP/IP as the default protocol of, 408
IO/MEM wire, 115, 427
Iomega, 186
IPX/SPX protocol, 408
IRQ steering, 128, 427
IRQs (interrupt request wires), 118, 427
ISA (Industry Standard Architecture) bus, 121
ISO image, 257
ISO9660 standard file format, 241, 427
ISP (Internet Service Provider), 391, 399
ITU (International Telecommunication Union), 395

J

jacks, provided by sound cards, 347–348
jammed paper, removing from printers, 384
Java, 2
joystick port, 13, 348
joysticks, 11, 12, 330
JP#, labeling a jumper, 91
jumper settings, manual, 40
jumpers, 427
    on an ATX motherboard, 90–91
    on a CD-ROM drive, 249
    setting for SCSI IDs, 270
    using for termination, 272, 273

K

Kbps (kilobits per second), 395
Keyboard applet, on the Control Panel, 326, 427
keyboard connection, 17
keyboard controller, 103
keyboard port, 12
keyboard PS/2 port, 91–92
keyboards, 10, 11, 14, 427
    cleaning, 336
    connectors for, 322–324
    ergonomics and, 321
    I/O addresses used by, 115
    installing, 321–325
    supported by BIOS drivers, 114
keyed cables and ports, 88
keyed EIDE and FDD ports, 88
keystoning, 296
KHz (kilohertz), 341, 427
kilobits per second (Kbps), 395
kilobyte, 60
known-good cable, 413

L

L1 and L2 cache, 57
LAN (Local Area Network), 391, 392–393, 428
    accessing, 19
    hardware required for, 405–407
    installing and configuring, 400–412
    setting up software for, 407–412
    technology involved in creating, 401–405
    troubleshooting, 412–414
land, 241
laptops
    bus interface for, 141–142
    slots used in, 128–129
Large Disk Support, selecting during Windows installation, 216–217
laser beam, scanning pits, 241

laser printers, 367, 380–381, 428
lasers, 244, 427
LBA standard, 213
LCD (Liquid Crystal Display) monitors, 13, 297–299, 427
    cleaning, 312
    missing pixels on, 313
    troubleshooting, 313–314
    variations of, 298
lighting effects, used by games, 301
lights, on NICs, 413
line-in port, on a sound card, 347
line out connector, on a sound card, 347
link lights, on NICs, 413
Liquid Crystal Display. See LCD monitors
Local Area Connection Properties dialog box, 408–409, 410
Local Area Network. See LAN
local bus, 124
local printer, installing, 374
logical drives, 204, 428
Logitech Web site, 339
loose connections, between monitors and video cards, 297
lost chains, 228
low-end graphics processors, 300
low-level formatters, 235
low-level formatting, on SCSI drives, 284
low resolution, versus high, 294, 295
low voltage differential (LVD) terminators, 278, 428
LPT1, 374, 428
LPT2, 374, 428
LS-120 or LS-240. See SuperDisk drives
luminance, 298
LVD terminators, 278, 281, 428

M

machine language, 2
Macintosh computers, 5
Macromedia Dreamweaver MX, 74
magnetic spots, on a platter, 202
magnetic tape, 189
mainframe computers, 2–3, 428
maintenance, of monitors, 312
maintenance kits, for laser printers, 380
maintenance program, for a printer, 383
maintenance software, for inkjet printers, 381
make and model number of a hard drive, 201
male connector, 16
manual jumper settings, 40
manual partitioning, in Windows 98, 217

manual printer driver installation, 373–376
manual voltage settings, for motherboards, 40–41
marketing way, to measure DDR SDRAM speed, 68
master, 210, 428
Master Boot Record (MBR), 204, 428
master drive, changing the jumpers on, 215
Master File Table (MFT), 205, 428
master/slave jumpers, on CD-ROM drives, 249
master/slave settings, configuring, 210–211
Matrox, 300
Mbps (megabits per second), 402
MBR (Master Boot Record), 204, 428
MCA (MicroChannel Architecture), 122–123
mechanical mouse, 327, 428
mega, 60
megabits per second (Mbps), 402
megabytes (MB), 18, 60
megahertz (MHz), 32, 63, 428
memory addressing, 58
memory bank. See banking
memory controller hub. See Northbridge chip
memory slots, 85, 87, 428
memory usage, viewing on the Performance tab of Task Manager, 73
metal frame, touching first, 8–9
mezzanine bus, 125, 428
MFT (Master File Table), 205, 428
MHz (megahertz), 32, 63, 428
mice. See mouse devices
microATX form factor, for computer cases, 155
microATX motherboards, 96
MicroChannel Architecture. See MCA
microchannel devices, self-configuring, 123
microcomputers, 4
microphone port, on a sound card, 348
microphones, 11, 12, 332
microprocessor, 18
microscopic pits, on a plastic disc, 241
Microsoft Backup utility, 193
Microsoft Office, minimum RAM requirements for, 74
Microsoft Web site, 339
.mid file extension, 343
mid-tower cases, 150, 428
MIDI, 343, 428–429
    controller, 93
    files, 343
    ports, 13, 332
millisecond (ms), 62
Mini connectors, 160, 428

mini-DIN connector
    for a keyboard, 322, 323
    for a mouse, 328
mini-DIN ports. *See* PS/2 ports
Mini PCI slot, 128–129, 428
"mini" power connector, 180
mini-tower cases, 150, 428. *See also*
    computer cases
minicomputers, 3
minimum RAM requirements, set by
    Microsoft, 74
Mirrored volume, 222, 223
misaligned screen, 314–315
mixed-mode CDs, 255
MOD sound file type, 344
model, of a CPU, 52
modem connections, 395
Modem Doctor shareware
    application, 412
modem port, 13
Modem Properties dialog box,
    Diagnostics tab, 412
modem technology, 394–398
modem-testing utility, in Windows
    XP, 412
modems, 19, 391
    installing into PCI slots, 396–398
    modern standards for, 395
Modems applet, in the Control
    Panel, 392
Modems Properties dialog box, 392
modulation/demodulation, 394
Molex connectors, 159, 250, 254, 428
monaural sound, recording, 341
Monitor tab, 306, 307
monitors, 10, 11, 13–14, 293, 428
    connecting multiple to a single
      system, 304
    maintenance of, 312
    optimizing with video cards, 305
    removing from the box, 296–297
    selecting, 293–299
    sizes of, 295
    troubleshooting, 312–315
motherboard book, 428
    brand/socket information
      found in, 39
    reading, 38
motherboard makers, 38
motherboard manuals, 85
motherboard manufacturers, 85
motherboard plate, 100
motherboard speed, 39
motherboards, 18, 84, 428
    allowing booting to either Zip
      or LS-120 drives, 187
    attaching to cases, 154
    brand and socket type of CPUs
      supported, 39–41
    common features of, 85–93
    CPUs supported by, 38

designed for a specific hard
    drive speed, 209
different-colored controllers
    on, 212
flexing, 100
installing, 100–102
matching the speed of, 62
modems integrated into, 396
mounting in cases, 101
parts of, 86
placing over standout screws, 101
removing from PC cases, 97–99
researching RAM requirements
    for, 74
with a stick of RAM, 58
traces in, 30
types of, 94–97
voltage settings for, 40–41
mounting screws, 154
mouse, 10, 11, 428
    installing, 328–329
    standard, 326
Mouse applet, on the Control Panel,
    329, 428
mouse connections, 16, 328
mouse devices, 14–15
    cleaning, 336
    configuring, 329
    installing, 328–329
    installing and configuring,
      325–329
mouse pad, 14
mouse port, 12
mouse PS/2 port, 91–92
MP3 format, 255, 342, 343, 428
MPC2 connector, 249
MPC2/MPC2 cables, 249, 250, 428
MPC2/SoundBlaster cables, 249
multimedia monitors, 295, 296
multipart printing, 365
multiple-jet method, 366
multiple monitors, connecting to a
    single system, 304
multipliers, 243, 428
multispeed NICs, 405
music CD, geometry of, 201–203
Musical Instrument Digital Interface.
    See MIDI
My Computer
    checking the properties of a
      Windows 98 disk drive, 207
    floppy icon in, 183
My Network Places, selecting Entire
    Network option, 411

■ N

nanosecond (ns), 62, 429
Narrow SCSI, 275, 278, 429
natural keyboard, 321–322

Nero Burning ROM program, 245,
    252, 261
Nero Wizard, burning CDs, 258
NetBEUI, 408
NetWare software, 408
Network and Internet Connections
    applet, in Windows XP, 399
Network Connections system
    folder, 408
Network Connections wizard, 399
network interface, 13, 429
Network Interface Cards. *See* NICs
network port, on an ATX
    motherboard, 103, 104
networking equipment, required to
    set up a LAN, 401
networking protocols, 407–408
networks, 390, 391
    fiber-optic, 404
    topology of, 401
    troubleshooting, 412–414
    wireless, 404–405
New Connection wizard, in Windows
    XP, 400
New Volume wizard, 225–227
NICs (Network Interface Cards), 19,
    393, 405–406, 429
    link lights on, 413
    purchasing, 406
    testing, 413
nits, 298, 429
"No backup devices were found"
    error message, 193
No Boot Device Present error
    message, 234
no-print problems, 383–384
nodes, 406, 429
noise
    electrical sound, 128
    generated by a fan, 48
non-contiguous clusters, tracking, 229
nonbootable floppy disks, formatting,
    184–185
nontransparent surface, required for
    an optical mouse, 327
nonvolatile memory, needed for the
    BIOS, 103
nonvolatile storage, 58
Normal backup, 191, 429
Northbridge chip, 30, 31, 85, 88, 429
    bus functions of, 125–126
    controlling expansion slots,
      112–113
    handling all communication
      with RAM, 57
    interpreting address signals
      from the CPU, 59
    terminating 16 of the 32 external
      data bus wires, 124
Norton, Peter, 230
Norton Utilities, 229

Novell, IPX/SPX protocol invented by, 408
nozzles
aligning on an inkjet printer, 385
cleaning on inkjet printers, 382
ns (nanosecond), 62, 429
ns rating, for RAM chips, 62
NTFS, 205, 429
nVidia, 300
nVidia GeForce4 Ti 4600, 300, 301

■ O

obsolete bus types, 125
on/off switch
on an ATX power supply, 162, 163
for a monitor, 13
trusting on a system unit, 7
onboard BIOS, on a host adapter, 280
Online button, on a printer, 384
operating system
developed for microcomputers, 4
installing on a primary partition, 204
RAM required by, 73–74
optical mouse, 15, 327, 336, 429
organic inks, used as part of the CD burning process, 261
orientation corners, on a socketed CPU, 45
orientation, of connectors, 15
orientation ridge, on a slotted CPU, 45
Osborne 1, 4
OUT jack, 13
out-of-memory error, 72
output devices, 11

■ P

P1 power connectors, 85, 87, 159, 429
P4 chips, with different PGA packages, 34
P4 power connector, 160, 429
P8/P9 power connectors, 158–159, 429
packages, 429
for CPUs, 33–34
of RAM, 63–71
packets, 393, 429
pads, for mice, 326
page sizes, printing larger, 367–368
pages per minute. See ppm
paper
problems related to, 384
selecting for printers, 380
paper dust, 384
paper jams, 384
paper pickup rollers, replacing, 384
paper settings, in Printing Preferences, 380
parallel cables, 370, 371

parallel ports, 13, 92, 370, 429
Parallel SCSI, 278
parasitic bus, 124
parent and child folders, checking underlying links between, 228
parity bits, 222
parity checking, data on the SCSI chain, 283
parity chip, 60
partition information, stored on the boot sector, 204
partitioning
hard drives, 216–220
using the Disk Management utility, 225–227
partitioning and formatting problems, with hard drives, 234–235
PartitionMagic, 223–224
partitions, 203, 429
storing files in, 205
types of, 204
passive termination, 277
PC Cards, 141–142, 429
PC cases. See computer cases
PC components
handling electronic, 9–10
number-one destroyer of, 8
proper procedures for handling, 6–10
PC connections, handling, 16–17
PC hardware
first rule of, 68
improper handling of, 6
PC screws. See screws
PC speaker. See also speakers
connector for, 90
PC systems, warranties for, 18
PC66 SDRAM, 67
PC100 SDRAM, 67
PC133 SDRAM, 67
PC600 RDRAM, 70
PC700 RDRAM, 70
PC800 RDRAM, 70
PC1066 RDRAM, 70
PCI connections, for modems, 395
PCI devices, one IRQ assigned to all, 128
PCI expansion bus, 125–126, 127
PCI expansion cards, 132–133
PCI slots, 429
on an ATX motherboard, 85, 89, 90
close-up of, 113
installing modems into, 396–398
PCI video cards, 302, 303
PCM format, 342
PCMCIA card interface, 141
PCs (personal computers), 5, 429. See also computers
basic components of, 10–11

connecting modems to, 395
connecting to a network's cabling structure, 405
identifying internal components of, 17–19
identifying major components of, 10–15
installing printers on, 370–379
as a registered trademark, 5
safeguarding, 5–10
shutting down without a mouse, 329
PCs, number-one destroyer of, 8
Pentium 4
incompatible socket types of, 39
power supplies, 160
perfect flat screen CRTs, 295
performance, improving by adding RAM, 71–72
Performance tab, of the Task Manager, 73
Peripheral Component Interconnect slots. See PCI slots
peripheral devices, 11, 429
Personal Computer Memory Card International Association (PCMCIA) card interface, 141
personal computers. See PCs
PGA packages, 34, 429
phantom video problems, 299
Phillips screws, for system unit cases, 20
Phoenix Technologies, 102, 105
phosphors, 293
photosensitive drum, 367, 429
physical design, of keyboards, 321
physical installation
of CD media drives, 249–250, 251, 252–255
of a sound card, 351–354
Physical Memory section, in Task Manager, 73
physical problems, with hard drives, 233–234
physical size, reducing for CPUs, 33
pin grid array package, 34, 429
pin number 1, on a floppy drive connector, 180
pincushioning, 296
Ping utility, 413–414
pink 1/8-inch jacks, for a microphone, 93
PIO (Programmable Input/Output), 209
pixels, 294, 313, 429
platters, magnetic spots on, 202
Plug and Play (PnP), 118, 429
plugging and unplugging, PC connections, 16–17
plugs, 13. See also connectors

Introduction to PC Hardware and Troubleshooting

plunger power switches, 161
PnP (Plug and Play), 118
poking around, 6–7
polishing kits, for CDs, 260
polyphony, of a sound card, 343
populated bank, 65
port options, for connecting printers, 370–371
ports, 12, 429
positional audio, 345, 350
POST (power-on self-test), 157
power. *See* electrical power
power and hard drive activity lights, 90
power and reset buttons, connectors for, 90
power cables, for printers, 371
power connections
    on CD media drives, 250
    on monitors, 13
power connectors. *See also* connectors
    on ATX motherboards, 85, 87
    connecting improperly, 158
    inserting in a hard drive, 214
    unplugging the fan's from motherboards, 43
power cord
    disconnecting, 16
    plugging back into the system unit, 16
power input, 12
power lead from the power supply, plugging into the P1 power connector, 101
power management, AT systems and, 162
power-on self-test (POST), 157
power supplies, 19, 148, 155–156, 429–430
    connectors for, 158–160
    features shared by, 156
    installing, 166–167
    removing, 163–165
    for servers, 160, 161
    touching first, 8–11
    types of, 156
    wattage of, 157
power supply fans, 162–163, 167–168, 430
power switches, 160–162, 430
ppm (pages per minute), 367, 429
ppm rating, of a printer, 368
pre-doped heat sink, 50
primary controller, 211
primary partitions, 204, 430
print quality, setting for, 378
printer drivers, installing manually, 373
printer port, specifying, 374–375
printer self-tests, 383
printer technologies, identifying current, 365–367

printer test, 383
printers, 12, 12
    advertised versus actual speed of, 369–370
    buying, 367–369
    configuring, 376–378
    installing, 378–379
    installing drivers for, 371–376
    installing on Windows PCs, 370–379
    maintenance of, 379–382
Printers and Faxes applet, on the Control Panel, 373
printing needs, 367–368
printing preferences, changing, 376–378
printing problems, recognizing and fixing, 383–385
printing speed, requirements for, 368
processor capabilities, of sound cards, 345–348
processor packages, 33–34
processors
    models of, 32
    on video cards, 299–300
professional support, for laser printer maintenance, 381
program code, sample of, 1
Programmable Input/Output (PIO), 209
programs, 29
Properties dialog box, opening for a video card, 308
Properties window for a controller, 335
proprietary configuration applications, 356–357
proprietary motherboards, 97
protocols, 393, 430
    checking on a LAN, 413
    for networking, 407–408
PS/2 connector, 430
    for a keyboard, 14, 322, 323
    for a mouse, 14, 328
PS/2 mouse, 326
PS/2 plug, 16
PS/2 ports
    on an ATX motherboard, 91–92
    both the keyboard and mouse ports as, 17
PS/2-to-DIN adapter, 323
Pulse Code Modulation (PCM) format, 342
pure Star topology, 401
purple PS/2 port, 91, 322

Q

QIC (Quarter-Inch Cartridge) tape, 190
Query Modem button, in the Modem Properties dialog box, 412

Quick Format check box, in the Format dialog box, 185
QuickTime player, playing AIFF files, 344

R

racing wheels/accelerator sets, 330–331
rack-mount cases, 151, 430
radial misalignment, 183, 430
radio frequency (RF) wireless mice, 328
radio frequency (RF) wireless networks, 404–405
RAID, 221, 222, 430
RAID 0, 222
RAID 1, 222
RAID 5, 222, 223
RAID arrays, 222–223, 286
rails, for drive bays, 152, 153
RAM (Random Access Memory), 18, 57, 430
    accessing, 58
    adding and upgrading, 71–79
    bad sticks of, 78
    as the CPU's short-term memory, 57
    determining the capacity of, 74–75
    installing into a motherboard, 100
    measuring the speed of, 62
    physical manifestations of, 58
    purchasing the fastest affordable, 75
    reasons for adding, 71–72
    requesting, 118
    storing commands in, 29
    supported by BIOS drivers, 114
    technologies in current use, 63
    testing, 78
    unlabeled, 74
    upgrading, 74–76
    in video cards, 299, 302
    volatility of, 30, 58
RAM check, on the boot screen, 78–79
RAM chips, in early PCs, 60
RAM Digital-to-Analog Converter chip. *See* RAMDAC chip
RAM packages, 63–71
RAM sticks, 19, 58, 75
RAM technologies, types of, 59–63
Rambus Dynamic Random Access Memory. *See* RDRAM
RAMDAC chip, 300, 302, 430
Random Access Memory. *See* RAM
range, of I/O addresses, 117
RAS wire, 61
RCA jacks, on video cards, 303
RDRAM, 63, 70, 430
RDRAM RIMMs, 69

Read-Only attribute, 191, 195
read speed, of a CD-R drive, 245, 430
read/write heads, 178, 202, 430
read/write LED, on the front of a
    floppy drive, 178
README files, 372
RealMedia player, 344
rear-out connector, on a sound
    card, 347
reboot, pausing, 37
recorded sound formats, 342
recording quality, of sound cards,
    346–347
Recycle Bin, files in, 231
red X, in the Device Manager, 137
Redundant Array Of Independent
    Disks. See RAID
reel-to-reel tape, 190
reference drivers, 310
refill kits, for inkjet cartridges, 380
reflection, 272
reflective substance, on a CD, 241
refresh rate, 430
    adjusting, 306, 307
    of a CRT screen, 293
    increasing, 315
registered jack (RJ), 403
Regular AT motherboard. See AT
    motherboards
release latch, for a faceplate, 20
release levers, for a fan and heat sink
    assembly, 42
remanufactured toner cartridges,
    379–380
remote terminals, for mainframes, 2
removable media, 176, 430
removable panel, for a system unit
    case, 20
removable resistors, using for
    termination, 272, 273
resolution, 294, 430
    changing for a monitor, 305
    of an inkjet printer, 366
    of a laser printer, 367
resolution options, for a system, 305
restocking fees, 130
rewrite speed, of a CD-RW drive, 246,
    430
ribbon cables
    installing on the back of a
        floppy drive, 180
    orienting, 214
    supporting floppy drives, 179
RIMM slots, 87
RIMMs, 69–71, 77–78, 430
riser boards, in proprietary systems, 97
RJ-11 connectors, 403, 430
RJ-45 connectors, 403, 430
RJ-45 port, 103, 104
RM sound file type, 344

rocker power switches, 161
roller ball, in a mouse, 14
rounded hard drive cables, 214
Row Array Strobe wire, 61
running, in a program, 29

■ S

S-video port, on a video card, 303
sampling, 341, 430
Sandra, by SiSoftware, 73
Scan Bus option. See Show Devices
    function
ScanDisk, 227–229, 430
    comparing to competing
        tools, 229
    running automatically, 234–235
scanners, 11, 12
scientific calculator, in Windows, 59
scratches, removing from a CD, 260
screen adjustment controls, for
    monitors, 13
screen flicker, 315
Screen Resolution slider, 305
screws, 154. See also thumbscrews
    retrieving, 22
    types of, 154
SCSI, 208, 268
    evolution of, 275
    flavors of, 275–279
    mixing flavors of, 279
    troubleshooting, 287
SCSI-1 standard, 275–276, 430
SCSI-2 standard, 276–277, 430
SCSI-3 standard, 278, 430
SCSI BIOS programs, functions of, 282
SCSI BIOS screen, accessing, 282, 283
SCSI cables, 269, 281
SCSI chains, 269, 430
    preventing reflection on, 272
    terminating, 272–273
    working with, 274–275
SCSI devices, 268
    installing, 279–287
    multiple copies of the same, 287
    setting SCSI IDs, 270
    testing newly installed, 287
SCSI drives, connectors used by, 208
SCSI host adapter. See host adapters
SCSI IDs, 270–272, 281
SCSI standards, flavors of, 268
SCSI Zip drive, 270, 272
SDRAM (Synchronous Dynamic
    Random Access Memory), 62, 431
    measuring the speed of, 62
    speeds of, 67
Seagate Technology, 201
SEC-style CPUs, 33, 431
second hard drive, adding, 215
secondary controller, 211

sectors, 431
    on CDs, 241
    on a floppy disk, 177
sectors per track, 202–203, 431
Select Disks dialog box, in the New
    Volume Wizard, 226
Select Volume Type dialog box, in the
    New Volume Wizard, 225
self-terminating SCSI devices, 272
self-tests, for printers, 383
serial connectors
    on a mouse, 14
    powering down before inserting
        or removing, 324
serial ports, 13, 92, 431
server cases, 150, 151, 431
servers, power supplies for, 160, 161
Set Active Partition option, on the
    FDISK screen, 217, 218, 219
Set Up or Change Your Internet
    Connection option, in Windows
    XP, 399
Settings tab, of the Windows XP
    Display Properties dialog box,
    305–306
setup information file, 135
setup program, finding on an
    installation disk, 134–135
shadow mask, 293–294, 431
Shared folder, creating, 410
Shared Properties dialog box, Sharing
    tab, 410
sharing, enabling on networked
    systems, 393
Sharing tab, of the Shared Properties
    dialog box, 410
shims, removing from expansion slots,
    132–133
short-depth monitors, 295
short-term memory, of a CPU, 18
shorting, 270
Show Details mode, running Defrag
    in, 230
Show Devices function, in the SCSI
    BIOS, 282, 283–284, 287
shunt, placing on a jumper, 91, 270
shutdown procedure, for an operating
    system, 16
signal-to-noise ratio, for an input port,
    346, 347
signature, placing on a drive, 221
SIMMs (Single Inline Memory
    Modules), 64–66, 76–77, 431
Simple volume, 222
single-edge cartridge package. See
    SEC-style CPUs
single piece design, for a system unit
    case, 20
single-sided sticks, of RAM, 75

SiSoftware Sandra SCSI scan
software, 284
sizes, of LCD monitors, 298
slave, 210, 431
sleep mode. *See* hibernate mode
Slot 1 and Slot A processors,
fans for, 48
Slot A, 34
slot covers, covering empty expansion
bays, 171, 431
slot-style CPUs, with an attached fan
and heat sink assembly, 43
slots, assessing the number available
for RAM, 75
slotted CPUs, 86
inserting, 46–47
installing the heat sink and fan
assembly, 50
orientation ridges on, 45
removing, 44
slow pixel response time, on LCD
monitors, 314
small computer systems interface.
See SCSI
SO (Small Outline) DIMMs, 68, 69
Socket 423, for Intel Pentium
4 CPUs, 86
Socket 462, for AMD Athlon XP
processors, 86
Socket A, 34
socket sizes, 86
socket type, of a CPU, 39
socketed CPUs, 86
inserting, 45–46
installing the heat sink and fan
assembly, 50
orientation corners on, 45
removing, 43
socketed processors, fans for, 48
sockets
for CPUs, 87
for different CPU packages, 34
soft power feature, of ATX
motherboards and power supplies,
162, 431
software, 1, 4. *See also* computer
programs
software protocols, for
communication, 407–408
Sony/Philips digital interface (SPDIF)
connector, 350, 351, 431
sound-capture, basics of, 341–342
sound cards, 19, 112, 431
applications supplied with, 357
characteristics of, 345–348
extra features provided by, 348
installing drivers for, 354–355
installing in Windows systems,
351–357

sound file formats, 255, 343
sound modeling, 345
sound ports, on an ATX motherboard,
92–93
sound processors, capabilities of, 345
sound programs, installing, 355–357
sound wave, characteristics of, 341
SoundBlaster Live! Platinum sound
card, breakout box, 348, 431
Sounds and Audio Devices applet,
355–356, 431
sounds, components for capturing
and outputting, 341
sounds, playing, 342, 344
Sounds tab, of the Sounds and Audio
Devices applet, 355–356
Southbridge chip, 85, 88, 89, 126
Spanned volume, 222
SPDIF connector, 350, 351, 431
speakers, 10, 11, 12, 348–351
as the source of sound
problems, 358
standards for, 349
support provided by sound
cards, 345–346
speckles
on LCD monitors, 313
on printouts, 384
speed rating, for added RAM, 75
speeds
achieving gains for CPUs, 33
advertised versus actual for
printers, 369–370
of CD-ROM drives, 243
setting for CPUs, 39–40
split P8/P9 style, of power socket, 94
SRAM (static Random Access
Memory), 57
stand-off screws, 154
Standard check, in ScanDisk, 228
standard mouse, 14, 326
standard resolutions, defined by the
video industry, 294
standardization system, for SDRAM, 67
standardized software, 4
standout screws, for installing a
motherboard, 100
standouts, mounting the motherboard
to the case, 99
Star Bus topology, 401–402, 431
Start Programs Faster option, in
Defrag, 230
startup disks. *See* bootable floppy disks
state, of hardware devices, 59
static electricity, 7
Static Random Access Memory
(SRAM), 57
/STATUS switch, in FDISK, 220

steering wheel and accelerator sets,
330–331
step-down transformer, 156
stereo sound, recording, 341
stereo speakers, 349
sticks, 431
of memory, 18
of RAM, 19, 58, 75
still and video cameras, 332
streaks and spots, on printouts, 384
streaming audio, running, 344
streaming media, 344
stripe set, 222
Striped volume, 222, 223
striping, with parity, 222–223
subwoofer, 11, 12, 345–346, 349,
350, 431
SuperDisk drives, 187, 428, 431
booting to, 188–189
cleaning, 187–188
surround sound
speaker standards, 349–351
support of, 345, 346
swap file, 72, 431
switches
for LANs, 406–407, 431
substituting for hubs, 402
Synchronous Dynamic Random
Access Memory. *See* SDRAM
System attribute, 191
system BIOS, 102, 103
system clock battery. *See* date and
time battery
system controller chip. *See*
Northbridge chip
system devices
changeable, 104–105
unchanging, 104
System Information tool, in Windows,
35, 431
System Properties dialog box, 35, 36
system resources, 72–73, 114
system setup problems, with hard
drives, 234
System Setup utility, 104, 431
accessing, 104–105
Autodetect setting, 212–213
running the Autodetect
feature, 214
supporting Zip or LS-120 drives
in the boot sequence, 188–189
system speed, providing, 32
system stability, improving by adding
RAM, 71–72
system unit, 10, 11, 12–13, 431
connections on the back of, 12–13
opening, 20–21

T

tablets, 332–333
Tandy TRS-80, 4
tape backup
    devices, 176, 431
    strategies, 191–195
tape drive technologies, 189–191
tape drives
    accessing, 193
    compressed versus
      uncompressed
      capacities of, 190
    types of, 189–191
tapes, for backup jobs, 192
Task Manager, in Windows 2000 and
    XP, 72–73
TCP/IP, 408–412
tech way, of measuring DDR SDRAM
    speed, 69
telephone jack, 13
telephone line, checking for
    problems, 412
temporary files, 232
temporary Internet files, 232
termination, for a SCSI device, 281
terminators, 272, 273, 431
test page, printing, 383
textures, 301, 431
thermal compound, 43, 431
    applying, 48, 50
thin-vaned heat sinks, 47
third-party refurbished ink
    cartridges, 380
third-party toner cartridges, 379
third-party tools, for partitioning and
    formatting, 223–224
Thorough check, in ScanDisk, 228
thrashing, by hard drives, 72
thumbscrews. *See also* screws
    for system unit cases, 20
    on a video connector, 17
timbre, 341
TOC (table of contents), on an audio
    CD, 241
toner, 367, 384, 431
toner cartridges, 368, 369, 379, 432
topology, 401, 432
touch pads, 327–328, 432
touch screens, 333, 432
touch sensitivity, of tablet pens, 333
traces, in the motherboard, 30
trackball mouse, 15
trackballs, 326–327, 336, 432
tracks, 432
    on an audio CD, 241
    on a hard drive, 202
    of sound, 341
Transmission Control Protocol/
    Internet Protocol. *See* TCP/IP

Travan tapes, 190, 432
troubleshooting
    CD media, 259–262
    hard drives, 233–235
    input devices, 335–336
    monitors, 312–315
    networks, 412–414
    SCSI, 287
    sound, 357–359
Type 1 slots, for PC Cards, 142
Type II slots, for PC Cards, 142
Type III slots, for PC Cards, 142

U

U (unit), for sizing rack-mount cases,
    151, 432
UDMA (Ultra Direct Memory Access),
    209
Ultra SCSI, 276, 432
Ultra2 SCSI, 277, 432
unit. *See* U
universal audio cables, 249, 250, 432
Universal Serial Bus. *See* USB
unlabeled RAM, 74
unplugging, a PC from its power
    source, 7
unpopulated bank, 65
unshielded twisted-pair cabling. *See*
    UTP cabling
Upgrade Device Driver Wizard, 136
upgrading, RAM, 74–76
USB (Universal Serial Bus), 138–
    140, 432
    versus FireWire, 141
    Microsoft support of, 323
    versions of, 139
USB 1.1, 139–140
USB 2.0, 139, 140
USB A connector, 140
USB B connector, 140
USB cables, 371, 372
USB connector
    installing, 324–325
    for a keyboard, 14, 322–323
    on a mouse, 14
    for a mouse, 328
USB devices, 139
USB drivers, 140
USB hubs, 139
USB plugs, 139, 140
USB ports, 12, 13, 139, 371
    on an ATX motherboard, 92, 93
    connecting modems to, 396
USB to PS/2 adapter, 91, 323
USB type A connector, 371, 432
USB type B connector, 371, 432
user's guide
    compared to the motherboard
    book, 38

for a printer, 383
UTP cabling, 402–403, 432
UTP connectors, 403

V

V standards, for modem
    technology, 395
V.90 standard, 395
V.92 standard, 395
vacuum tube, in a CRT, 293
vacuuming, of laser printers, 380
verification, of correct RAM
    installation, 78–79
VESA Local Bus (VL-Bus), 124
VGA connector, for an LCD monitor,
    298, 432
VIA Technologies, 88, 89
video, 292
video card ports, 303
video cards, 19, 292. *See also* display
    adapters; graphics adapters
    checking for the latest driver, 119
    with device driver CDs, 114
    drivers for, 304–305
    inserting into expansion slots, 22
    installing, 305
    naming, 300
    optimizing with monitors, 305
    ports on, 303
    problems with, 314
    RAM in, 299
    removing, 22
    removing screws securing, 21–22
    selecting, 299–304
video codecs, listing installed, 356
video connection, 13, 17
video drivers
    acquiring new, 309
    uninstalling, 310
    updating, 307–308
    working with, 306–310
video files, with sound built into
    them, 344
video formats, in the PC world, 344
Video Graphics Array. *See* VGA
    connector
video port, 13
video RAM, 302
video software, installing and
    configuring, 304–311
video system, 292
View tab, of the Folder Options dialog
    box, 194–195
virtual memory, 72, 432
VIS (viewable image size), 295, 298, 432
Visual Basic, 2
VL-Bus. *See* VESA Local Bus
VOC sound file type, 344
voice recognition software, 332

Voice tab, of the Sounds and Audio Devices applet, 356
volatile medium, RAM as, 58
Volpe, Hank, 412
voltage, reducing for CPUs, 33
voltage settings, for motherboards, 40–41
volume controls, for sound, 358
volume knob, on a CD-ROM drive, 243
Volume tab, of the Sounds and Audio Devices applet, 355
volumes, dynamic disks divided into, 222

W

wait state, CPU in, 61, 62
WANs (Wide Area Networks), 404
warranties, for PCs, 18
wasted viewing space, on a typical CRT, 295
watch battery, on an ATX motherboard, 89, 90
water-cooled computer, 171
watt, 157, 432
wattage, of a power supply, 157
WAV files
    compressing to MP3 format, 343
    size of, 342
    storing as compressed files, 342
WAV format, 255, 342
wavetable synthesis, 343, 432
webcams, 332
Western Digital, 201
white goo. *See* thermal compound
white paste, on the top of the CPU chip, 43
Wide Area Networks (WANs), 404
Wide SCSI, 276, 278, 432
Wide SCSI-2 standard, 269
Winamp sound player, 344
Windows
    designed to load into RAM in pieces, 73
    volume controls in, 358

Windows 9x systems, partitioning handled by FDISK, 216
Windows 98
    autoplay in, 256
    Defrag program, 229–230
    displaying a CD-ROM drive, 251
    Format dialog box, 221
    identifying the file system used by, 206–207
    installing onto a blank hard drive, 216–219
Windows 98 installation CD, making bootable, 216
Windows 98/SE, minimum- and moderate-level RAM requirements, 74
Windows 98 startup disk, creating, 184
Windows 2000
    displaying disk drive information, 207–208
    Format dialog box, 221
    minimum- and moderate-level RAM requirements, 74
    System Properties dialog box, 36
Windows calculator, 59
Windows events, adding customized sounds to, 355–356
Windows Me, minimum- and moderate-level RAM requirements, 74
Windows Media Player, 247, 342, 344
Windows NT/2000/XP systems, partitioning handled by Disk Administrator, 216
Windows operating systems, minimum- and moderate-level RAM requirements, 74
Windows Sound Recorder, configuration settings for, 342
Windows Update tool, 120, 121
Windows XP
    autoplay in, 256–257
    backup choices, 194
    burning CDs, 258–259

    burning functions built in, 257
    Disk Management and, 220
    displaying a CD-ROM drive, 251
    displaying disk drive information, 207–208
    installing a blank hard drive, 219–220
    minimum- and moderate-level RAM requirements, 74
    properties of a data CD in, 242
    System Properties dialog box, 36
wireless hub, 405
wireless keyboards, 323–324
wireless mice, 328
wireless networks, 404–405
wires, removing from motherboard connections, 98
wiring diagram, for crossover cable, 403, 404
WMA format, 255, 343
workgroup, 411
Write Signature and Upgrade Disk wizard, 221, 222
write speed, of a CD-R drive, 245, 432
writing laser, in a CD-R drive, 244, 432

X

x number, for CD-ROM drives, 243

Y

yellow ?, in the Device Manager, 138

Z

Zip drives, 11, 12, 186–187, 432
    booting to, 188–189
    cleaning, 187–188

INTERNATIONAL CONTACT INFORMATION

AUSTRALIA
McGraw-Hill Book Company Australia Pty. Ltd.
TEL +61-2-9900-1800
FAX +61-2-9878-8881
http://www.mcgraw-hill.com.au
books-it_sydney@mcgraw-hill.com

CANADA
McGraw-Hill Ryerson Ltd.
TEL +905-430-5000
FAX +905-430-5020
http://www.mcgraw-hill.ca

GREECE, MIDDLE EAST, & AFRICA
(Excluding South Africa)
McGraw-Hill Hellas
TEL +30-210-6560-990
TEL +30-210-6560-993
TEL +30-210-6560-994
FAX +30-210-6545-525

MEXICO (Also serving Latin America)
McGraw-Hill Interamericana Editores S.A. de C.V.
TEL +525-117-1583
FAX +525-117-1589
http://www.mcgraw-hill.com.mx
fernando_castellanos@mcgraw-hill.com

SINGAPORE (Serving Asia)
McGraw-Hill Book Company
TEL +65-6863-1580
FAX +65-6862-3354
http://www.mcgraw-hill.com.sg
mghasia@mcgraw-hill.com

SOUTH AFRICA
McGraw-Hill South Africa
TEL +27-11-622-7512
FAX +27-11-622-9045
robyn_swanepoel@mcgraw-hill.com

SPAIN
McGraw-Hill/Interamericana de España, S.A.U.
TEL +34-91-180-3000
FAX +34-91-372-8513
http://www.mcgraw-hill.es
professional@mcgraw-hill.es

UNITED KINGDOM, NORTHERN,
EASTERN, & CENTRAL EUROPE
McGraw-Hill Education Europe
TEL +44-1-628-502500
FAX +44-1-628-770224
http://www.mcgraw-hill.co.uk
computing_europe@mcgraw-hill.com

ALL OTHER INQUIRIES Contact:
McGraw-Hill/Osborne
TEL +1-510-420-7700
FAX +1-510-420-7703
http://www.osborne.com
omg_international@mcgraw-hill.com